FORMICA
FOREVER

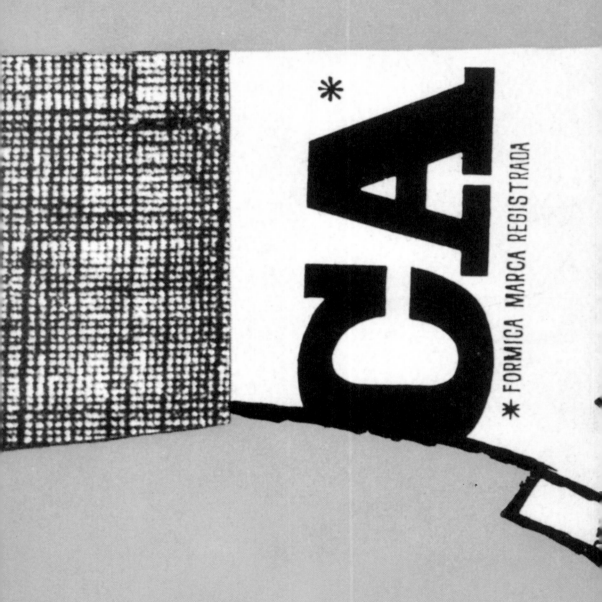

1962 Ad from *Selecciones del Reader's Digest*.

2002 (cover) Chair in Formica® Compact™
laminate, developed for interior design
showcase, Casa Decor, Madrid. DESIGNER
Ernesto de Ceano, Seville, Spain.

rendentes cualidades

BELLEZA, LIMPIEZA, LIGEREZA,

satisface plen las exigencias decorat

as en color, dimensiones

colores de F rmica

y creará s

ambiente ropio

par

s, sillas, apa

columnas,

as y en tod

cal y ho

colores,

colores,

para rea

ra a

rac

para rea

FORMICA
FOREVER

Published by
Formica Corporation
in association
with Metropolis Books

永
遠

241

นิรันดร์

241

POUR
TOUJOURS

241

241

IKUISESTI

241

PARA
SIEMPRE

241

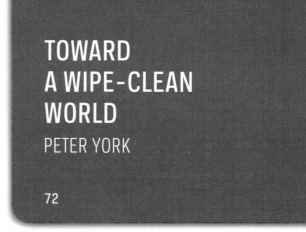
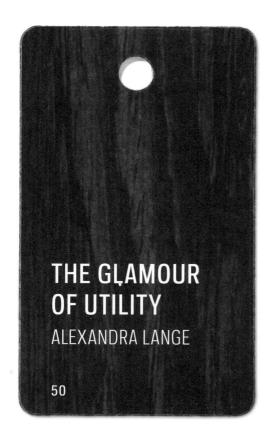
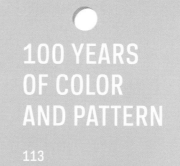

FOREWORD
MARK ADAMSON

Over the course of one century the Formica Group of Companies has seen enormous transformation, from its beginnings as a small producer of industrial components to becoming the world's largest manufacturer of high pressure laminate—a household brand name in many countries. But more than that, this century of change has shown how a pioneering surfacing material can also transform our surroundings. The Formica Group continues to evolve and meet new market demands.

It is said that the developer of the telephone, Alexander Graham Bell, predicted that one day there would be a telephone in every town in America. We may smile when we read how much he underestimated the vast reach his invention would have. The inventors of Formica® laminate, Daniel J. O'Conor and Herbert A. Faber, were able to witness the immense appeal of their versatile product. Applied in countless homes and other environments, for utilitarian and even fine arts purposes, Formica laminate appeared in kitchens and cafés, offices and schools, Radio City Music Hall and cruise liners.

This book, which celebrates Formica Group's 100th Anniversary, takes a look at the history of the business and the ways in which Formica laminate as a surfacing material has also played a part in social history. Created in a period of considerable industrial invention and evolving as a decorative laminate to fulfill dreams of modernity and freshness, design and innovation have been at the forefront of the company's development ever since.

Formica laminate is "the original," and it remains a material that offers high performance. As a business we know that nothing stands still and times can be tough, but the intrinsic value of what we offer endures. Through in-house research and development initiatives, a diverse choice of exciting and exclusive new textures has been created for our decorative laminate ranges. This goes along with continued development of pattern, decor, and color choices—in line with trend forecasting and customer feedback.

Alongside follow strategies and initiatives across all our facilities that build on being a responsible manufacturer and a "corporate citizen." We live in a time of heightened customer awareness of the look, feel, and impact of materials chosen and used in private homes, public facilities, and commercial buildings. It is this leadership that continues the momentum: today, through Formica Group operations worldwide, it is possible to absorb international trends, to reflect and respond to the tastes of customers globally. We have an exciting time ahead as the business now spans five continents. Global competitiveness is also about how the business operates, whether leveraging innovation and integration at an international level or working with individual designers to help realize their specific projects locally.

The power of the Formica brand, which is ultimately about customer experience, will underline future successes. The recognition of Formica laminate and the Formica brand during its history and in established markets is being extended and welcomed in newly industrializing countries and emerging economies. As Formica laminate establishes its place in the new cities, infrastructures, and homes of the twenty-first century, we look forward to the next one hundred years and build on all that our heritage offers.

1959 Ad from *Selecciones del Reader's Digest*.
ILLUSTRATOR Julio Cebrián.

1962 (page 6) From *American Cyanamid
Company Annual Report*. "In the home:
colorful products for modern shelter and
clothing—Formica...."

PREFACE
ABBOTT MILLER

Formica Forever presents the story of how luck and ingenuity, color and pattern, and design and manufacturing contributed to make Formica® brand laminate a truly global brand. A series of essays focus on different aspects of the story: Phil Patton shows how the dynamics of invention, manufacturing, distribution, and expansion have affected the company over its one-hundred year history; Alexandra Lange focuses on how architects and designers embraced the unique characteristics of Formica® laminate in signature projects from the 1930s to the present; and Peter York looks at the kitchens and diners of everyday life and sees the rise of a "wipe-clean world" that has influenced standards of cleanliness and hygiene everywhere.

The ubiquity of Formica laminate is underscored by passages from a range of fiction writers who have used Formica laminate to provide detail and character to a story. Like a character actor who reappears in films in different guises, Formica brand laminate is seen and known through its presence over decades of exposure. Part of this derives from its distinctive name: the Formica® trademark is in an elite group of iconic brand names of the twentieth century. The fact that the Formica trademark has become known around the world attests to its success and durability as a brand.

Not surprisingly, that name is assiduously protected as one of the company's most valuable assets. We extend special thanks to the writers and publishers who have graciously allowed us to share Formica brand laminate's recurring cameos in their work.

The middle section of the book presents a fraction of the company's archive of images and advertisements from all over the world. The company's early expansion into global markets can be seen in advertising in Spanish and French, as well as the more recent expansion in Asia. Indeed, the fact that this book is translated into Chinese, Finnish, French, Spanish, and Thai is itself a testament to the fact of Formica Group's global presence.

c. 1960 Teacher sitting on stool. Grace Jeffers Collection of Formica Materials, Archives Center, National Museum of American History, Smithsonian Institution.

PHIL PATTON

GROWING GLOBAL
A CENTURY OF
THE FORMICA® BRAND
AND BUSINESS

In its first century of existence, Formica Group has been privileged to march in parallel with changes in the wider world. Its ups and downs have reflected those of the society and culture around it. It has mirrored but also shaped, followed but also led global social and economic developments. "It seems Formica brand products have often been a proxy for larger changes," said CEO Mark Adamson as the company approached its centennial. Like a character in film or literature, Formica laminate has shown an uncanny knack for being present at historical turning points. From fairly obscure origins in mid-America, the Formica® trademark grew to become a global brand[1]—among the top ten recognized trademarks on the planet. It was born in a period of economic turmoil and technological revolution not so very different from our own era.

The simple story is that two ambitious young men, Daniel J. O'Conor and Herbert A. Faber, then working at Westinghouse Electric & Manufacturing Company in East Pittsburgh, Pennsylvania, had an idea and began to set up a business. In 1913, they established a company to produce plastic laminate items for electrical insulation. They named their product—without a great deal of study—"Formica," because it would stand in for mica, a silicate mineral with a thin, sheetlike arrangement of atoms that was used as the primary electrical insulator. Faber is credited with combining "for" and "mica," and the name of the new company was The Formica Insulation Company. The more complex story is that the two men were creating a new enterprise in the shadow of two global revolutions: the plastic revolution and the electric and electronics revolution. These technological advances would have economic, social, and cultural effects across the planet. The company was born with the creation of these two major new industries.

The financial Panic of 1907, which nearly caused the U.S. economy to collapse, resulted from the attempt of two shady characters to corner the market in copper—a great conductor of electricity. But Westinghouse, General Electric (GE), and other manufacturers also needed a substance to serve as a nonconductor of electricity for motors and other devices. The leading insulators of the time were mica, which was difficult to mine and process, and shellac, a product of insect (Lac beetle) secretions that was expensive and rare. In 1907, a breakthrough emerged. As Wall Street worried, chemist Leo Baekeland worked on a new idea.

Baekeland, as sketched out by Stephen Fenichell in his book *Plastic*,[2] was an eccentric if not quite mad scientist. His genius was evident early on at the University of Ghent, Belgium. He moved to the United States and, after selling his key invention, a photographic paper, to George Eastman of Eastman Kodak Company for $1 million in 1899, settled into Snug Rock, his house and laboratory in Yonkers north of New York City, and devoted himself to research. In 1907 he devised a way to make liquid phenol resin solid by heating it under pressure, which produced a hard, amber-colored substance. The resulting material, which he modestly called Bakelite®, was non-conductive and heat-resistant, an insulator against electricity. It could replace mica and shellac. The versatile Bakelite® synthetic plastic, which Baekeland patented in 1909, not only set off the plastics revolution, but it also abetted the electronic one. It could be used in jewelry as well as in machinery. It was billed as the material of one thousand uses, and its fame landed Baekeland on the cover of *Time* magazine in 1924.

In 1910 a Westinghouse scientist, C. E. Skinner, began exploring with Bakelite® plastic. He studied ways to dip paper in the Bakelite® resins, then bake it into insulating tubes or sheets. O'Conor was intrigued, as was his friend Faber. In 1912 O'Conor developed a process for making laminated insulators and patented it. In 1913, recognizing a business opportunity that their managers did not see, O'Conor and Faber left Westinghouse to form their own company. Each contributed $2,500, along with John G. Tomlin, a lawyer and banker from Kentucky who invested $7,500 and received a one-third stake in the new venture. They set up business in Cincinnati, Ohio, Faber's hometown.

Westinghouse had sent Faber and O'Conor off into the world with what *Fortune* magazine later called "parental blessing."[3] But before long, Westinghouse realized its mistake and launched "Micarta" as a rival. General Electric and others also entered the market. Competitors forced Baekeland to cut off supplies of Bakelite® resin to The Formica Insulation Company in an effort to strangle the infant in its crib. Faber and O'Conor scrambled to find an alternative. They came up with a product called "Redmanol," developed by the chemist L. V. Redman and produced by two brothers in Chicago, Sam and Adolph Karpen.

The first Formica company plant, a rented two-story space on Second and Main Streets, was not far from the Cincinnati stockyards. The first orders in May 1913 were to supply V-rings for electric motors to the Chalmers Motor Company. Other early customers were Ideal (later Delco) Electric, Northwest Electric, and Bell Electric Motor. After making such parts, the company produced its first sheet laminate on July 4, 1914.

World War I brought demand for insulators in radios and parts such as pulleys for aircraft controls. Aviation put a premium on light weight, and Formica brand parts could often replace metal ones for lightness and wooden ones for durability. Sales were $75,000 in 1917, $145,000 in 1918, $175,000 in 1919. A new, larger plant was needed. The company moved to Spring Grove Avenue, with offices that remained its headquarters for decades.

Initial products included timing gears for automobile engines. Made of laminate, they were lighter and quieter than metal alternatives. One early batch, however, swelled and froze in an automaker parking lot in the winter—moisture had seeped into the gears. The survival of the company was in danger, but The Formica Insulation Company's engineers identified the problem and refined the design and formula to remove water vapor. The company's role in making parts for automobiles led to the business of making parts for all sorts of new appliances.

Walton, Ky. March 17, 1913

Herbert Faber and D. J. O'Conor of Pittsburgh, Pa. desiring to start a manufactory in Cincinnati, Ohio for electrical insulating under some name to be hereafter selected and to be hereafter incorporated; and desiring to raise $7500.00 cash capital to begin said business; Now, it is agreed between said Faber and O'Conor on one side and J. G. Tomlin on the other that said Tomlin will furnish said ($7500.00) Seventy-Five hundred dollars on the following terms and conditions, namely:—Said Tomlin will take a one-third interest in said business and furnish Twenty-Five hundred ($2500.00) dollars of same and said Tomlin will lend said Faber and O'Conor Twenty-Five hundred ($2500.00) dollars each at seven percent (7%) or so much thereof as they need, each of them to endorse for the other.

Said Faber and O'Conor being experienced men in electrical work are beginning May 1st, to give their whole time and attention to this work for one hundred and fifty ($150.00) dollars per month for six months, and after that they are to have One hundred and seventy-five ($175.00) dollars per month provided the business is on basis to justify it. Said Tomlin is not to have any salary unless future wants in the way of financial or legal services make it proper; but to cover actual expenses in an advisory and consulting way, said Tomlin shall be allowed One Hundred ($100.00) dollars for first term of six months.

J. G. Tomlin
H. A. Faber
D. J. O'Conor Jr.

1913 Letter, from *Formica: Forty Years of Steady Vision*, 1953.

1910s (below) Factory and office buildings at the Spring Grove Avenue location. From *Formica: Forty Years of Steady Vision*, 1953.

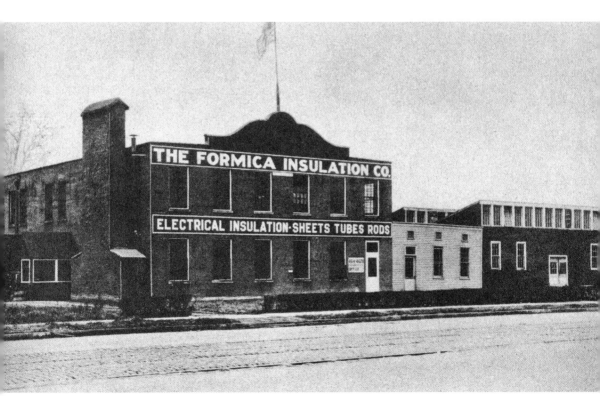

Early applications of Formica®
laminate were industrial and
in some cases used on aircraft.

During the economic boom of the 1920s, sales soared of vacuum cleaners, washing machines, refrigerators, churns, indeed anything with a motor or gears. Styled for appeal, these items were manufactured and sold based on the model of automobiles, at high, mid-, and basic levels, with advertising. Insulators, small mechanical parts, knobs, and cases for these new items meant plenty of applications for Formica brand and rival products in toasters, blenders, mixers, electric and gas stoves, refrigerators, and so on.

"Little Formica"

Beginning in 1919, legal struggles became a challenge for the new company. Five years of lawsuits over patent infringement meant The Formica Insulation Company was under constant pressure. Not until the patents covering Bakelite® synthetic plastics expired would the company be safe. It was during this period that the company acquired its reputation as a small but scrappy, fighting company. "Little Formica" it was called, by contrast to the giants it battled in court, such as General Electric and Westinghouse. These years shaped subsequent corporate culture at the Formica business. They created the idea that the little Formica company could go up against its larger rivals. The lawsuits gave the company a reputation, building up in industry the idea that helpless little Formica was being picked on. It was "Little Formica," the scrappy company, for decades afterward.

1920s: The Radio Revolution

The Formica Insulation Company benefited from an industry that also began small. In our era of computers and television, it is difficult to conceive what a revolution the radio created in the daily life of the early twentieth century. Formica laminate was a key part. "Wireless telegraph" transformed the world once it could carry more than simple Morse code and voices and music were added. To have a box in one's living room from which emerged the sounds of people halfway around the globe was something fundamentally new in human experience. The ability to transmit changed the medium from one of utilitarian communication to one of information and entertainment.

Early radios were the domain of hobbyists until the early 1920s, when amateur radio became a craze in the same way the early personal computer did in the 1970s. Thousands of radios were assembled from kits. All that was required was a crystal, some wires wound around a cardboard tube, a battery, earphones — and some sort of insulated board as a base. Soon the first ready-made radios were available for sale.

Formica laminate provided an excellent basic board for radio sets as well as other nonconducting parts. Sales of radio sets grew from 5,000 units in 1920 to more than 2.5 million in 1924. By the time listeners could follow the news of aviator Charles Lindbergh's historic transatlantic flight in 1927, some six million radio sets were in use. Sales figures for radios rose too as more elaborate sets were introduced, from $60 million in 1922 to $426 million in 1929. Faber and O'Conor's old employer, Westinghouse, was at the forefront of the new medium, cooperating with GE to sell sets with the Radio Corporation of America (RCA)® brand name and opening the first commercial broadcast station, KDKA. It began scheduled programming with the Harding-Cox presidential election returns on November 2, 1920, broadcast from a wooden shack on top of the company's factory in East Pittsburgh — the very building where Faber and O'Conor had met.

Radio unified people around the globe. In 1921 RCA's David Sarnoff conceived the idea of the first national hookup, for a heavyweight championship fight, between Jack Dempsey and Georges Carpentier. Thousands across the country listened to public radios on huge speakers in bars and dance halls. Soon radio went global. An early station was set up in Argentina in 1920, and in 1923, when Dempsey fought the young Argentinean boxer Luis Ángel Firpo, the Bull of the Pampas, radio carried the sound live from the Polo

Grounds in New York to the streets of Buenos Aires, where people crowded around huge speakers and cheered their champion. Formica laminate was often a part of it.

Most of the sets were simple boxes with knobs. The parts of a radio, tubes and windings, were attached to an insulated board—the mother board we know today from computers. The board grew into a box to hide the parts and mount the new cone speakers. The exteriors were often faced with laminate from The Formica Insulation Company in black or brown. The surface of black phenolic laminate that the Formica company provided for many early radios became visually associated with radio and later hi fi, high tech, and even computers as the no-nonsense color of electronic engineering.

The Formica Insulation Company was part of the look of that new technology. The company underwent a fundamental transition, from the maker of a functional material to the maker of a decorative, design-driven one. As a result, Formica laminate was perceived as a modern product, communicating high technology—something from the future. As design historian Jeffrey L. Meikle wrote, it "provided artificial precision."[4] In the Depression, it suggested order in economic chaos and, when deployed in streamlined forms, it suggested speed to counteract economic sluggishness. For modernists, it was one of the purest means of realizing ideas and drawings, a material as geometrically pure and fresh as glass.

Radio helped The Formica Insulation Company's sales grow from $400,000 in 1920 to $3 million in 1924. The company could afford to employ more help and in 1924 hired MIT-trained chemist Jack D. Cochrane. As head of research—his formal title was Director of Research, Decorative, and Industrial Products—he would become one of the company's secret weapons and vital to its success right up to his retirement in 1957. (He was regarded a national scientific resource in the United States and awarded the John W. Hyatt Award presented by President Truman.)

Cochrane looked into other resins. In 1927, The Formica Insulation Company introduced critical innovations. Cochrane developed a laminate that employed amino resins instead of phenol as the top layer on the base of Kraft paper. With the use of amino resins and an opaque barrier sheet to block the dark interior of the laminate, the company could add layers that bore wood grain or stone marbling. It patented a rotogravure printing process for making multilayer lithographed wood-grain surface laminate on a flat-bed press. The introduction of printed surfaces—marble or granite and abstract patterns would soon follow—gave the company its head start in decorative laminate. This also marked the beginning of the Formica company's shift from primarily industrial products to decorative ones.

1930s

In 1931, Cochrane's lab came up with the addition of a layer of metal foil to the sandwich of laminates. It made Formica laminate cigarette-resistant and thus attractive for tabletops in cafés, night clubs, and restaurants. The glamour of the material was matched by its practicality. It became sought after in soda fountains, which were springing up in drugstores and other spots. It appealed to bar owners. In the United Kingdom, one contractor specialized in arriving at pubs at closing time and replacing the bar overnight with Formica laminate so that not even a night's business was lost.

The Formica brand was much publicized when the laminate was used to cover horizontal surfaces at Radio City Music Hall in New York and desks at the Library of Congress in Washington. Yet in the mid-1930s, nowhere was it more visible than on the ocean liner RMS *Queen Mary*, with an interior constructed with Formica laminate. The *Queen Mary* competed in style as well as speed with France's *Normandie* and German and Italian rivals, writes John Maxtone-Graham in his history of ocean liners, *The Only Way to Cross*.[5] Both ships were built in Scotland by the firm of John Brown.

1920s (top) Cutting machine, located in Spring Grove plant, cut two impregnated rolls of paper simultaneously. From *Formica: Forty Years of Steady Vision*, 1953.

1927 Sales meeting, from *Formica: Forty Years of Steady Vision*, 1953.

1940 Assembly of Formica laminate decorative sheets between polished stainless plates included this manual operation. From *Formica: Forty Years of Steady Vision,* 1953.

Le Corbusier had proclaimed in 1922 that "Ocean liners are the very first step toward the realization of one perfectly controlled world to be created in a totally new spirit." The ship was a capsule of society and the economy. Every detail of life on land, writes Maxtone-Graham, was replicated at sea—and in style. For Le Corbusier, the machine for living he described as the ideal of architecture was based on the ocean liner, later replaced by his admiration for the airplane.

Speed and efficiency in transportation demanded light materials. But life in motion also required durable, easy-to-clean ones. (The success of the *Queen Mary*'s "gray pearlescent" Formica laminate lay not only in the repeated ocean crossings but also in the durability proven by the five years the ship endured as a troop carrier during World War II.) Later, ships of military navies, including the U.S. Navy, made extensive use of the material, for example in submarines such as the historic *Growler*.

The interiors of ocean liners, zeppelins, and railroad cars were the first to be covered in the materials of modernity. So were the stations, lobbies, and lounges that served them around the globe—style and technology transcended locality. This exposed Formica laminate to millions of people. Vehicles became de facto mobile sales shops for Formica brand laminate. The cabins of Zeppelins used laminate, as did many early airliners, from Pan Am Clippers flying and boats plying the Atlantic to new Douglas DC-3s. Trains with their streamlined interiors competed—a later notable example was the modern, sleek Hiawatha train. Designer Brooks Stevens used Formica laminates in the Hiawatha trains of the Chicago, Milwaukee, St. Paul, and Pacific Railroad, specifying linen finish in sleeping cars and walnut and gray-green in lounges. Formica laminate bespoke a hopeful future. Its gleaming surfaces and sleek curves evoked the world of film—Hollywood on small-town screens all over the world. It could romanticize the most mundane of spaces with a feeling of excitement and turned the quotidian into the futuristic.

The appeal of the material was demonstrated by the architect William S. Arrasmith, based in Louisville, Kentucky, who clad the interiors of dozens of bus stations in small cities and large towns across America. Even a provincial bus station could offer the sense of global modernity that streamlining and materials such as Formica laminate provided. Arrasmith's Greyhound bus terminals were built from the 1930s to the 1950s. Their exteriors had rounded concrete corners—as if cutting wind drag—as well as glass blocks and metal bands. The interiors carried out the same visual themes in dark and red Formica laminates, on wainscoting, cylindrical columns, and counters. The Formica Insulation Company ran advertising about Arrasmith's achievement in *Architectural Record*.

Around the world, other enterprises were investigating the world of laminates, among them companies whose future paths would eventually cross those of the Formica company. Many were making the same shift from utilitarian forms of laminate to decorative ones. In Sweden, for instance, the fortunes of the company Perstorp (which eventually would be acquired by the Formica companies in 2000) were unfolding in strikingly similar ways to that of the Formica company. Wilhelm Wendt founded the company in 1881, extracting chemicals from beech-wood forests on his father's farm. He sold acetic acid and alcohol and before long discovered a counterpart to Bakelite® brand plastics called Isolite® brand resins. It could also impregnate fabrics to make insulated objects and was used for radio parts. Like the Formica company, Perstorp moved to making panels that were decorative and useful, rugged and easy to clean. Perstorp Plate, as it was called, became a popular decorative material in kitchens, bathrooms, and public spaces. Just as the Formica company had a signature pattern embodying its informal, playful

quality—"Skylark"—Perstorp had its signature "VirrVarr," or "Chaos," designed by Sigvard Bernadotte in 1958. The VirrVarr pattern remained popular throughout the 1960s and 1970s and became something of a Swedish icon; it was manufactured until 1991, reintroduced by popular demand in 1998, and again globally in 2005 by then owners, the Formica companies.

In Australia, Robert M. Sykes and a partner established Laminex Pty Ltd, a firm whose early history and evolution also paralleled that of the Formica company in the United States. They set it up in 1934 to manufacture laminate primarily for functional industrial applications in automotive and electrical industries. The company's first home was a tiny tin shed in Brighton, a suburb of Melbourne.[6] Sykes' first tools were crude: instead of a press for imbuing the paper with resins, the operation used a mangle, a Dickensian, hand-operated, levered device better known for wringing out laundry. Like the Formica company, Laminex began its production with such items as timing gears for automobile engines. Around the same time, Homapal Plattenwerk GmbH in Germany, another future element of the Formica group of companies, began to move from its wood business to fiberboard and eventually laminate.

One more critical innovation remained, adding qualities that would bring worldwide success. 1937 saw the next key step in the refinement of the material: the shift to tougher melamine resins. Developed at American Cyanamid Co., Formica Corporation's future owner, by chemist Palmer Griffin, melamine resins were already proven in dishware. Jack Cochrane worked out many of the problems of saturating the surface papers and curing the laminate. The resulting material represented a breakthrough that enabled the Formica company to produce much brighter colors and lighter wood grains and patterns. This was the first step toward the blond, wood-grain Formica laminate valued by furniture manufacturers. In addition, a clear layer of melamine acted as a protective outer layer. But this refinement did not have a major impact until after World War II, according to F. Holbrook Platts,[7] a leading historian of the laminate industry. War intervened before The Formica Insulation Company could fully exploit the possibilities. After 1941, the company focused on war production, including the manufacture of bomb tubes and eighty-eight distinct parts for the top-of-the-line P-51 Mustang fighter plane.

1940s and 1950s: The Boom

The postwar building boom initiated the golden age of Formica laminates—and it happened in the kitchen. The kitchen turned into the social center of the home. No longer just a utilitarian space, it was growing larger. In many countries, household servants had found other employment after World War I, and after World War II, only very wealthy households were able to afford such help. With families cooking for themselves, the kitchen became a gathering spot and laminate was just the material needed for such lifestyles.

When furniture makers showed reluctance to apply Formica laminate to their own products, the company began to bond it to counters and tops. The dinette idea—combining a table and chairs—became the alternative to the formal dining room: the eat-in kitchen. Replacing wood, steel, or linoleum, Formica laminate countertops were found everywhere. Among the six million houses built in the United States during the last half of the 1940s, one-third, or two million, had kitchens with laminate worktops or counters, usually clad with Formica laminate. "Easy to clean" and "crayon proof" appealed to families, but nothing better expressed the buoyant optimism of this era than the Skylark pattern, designed by Brooks Stevens in 1950, with its abstract form summing up sheer possibility. Raymond Loewy, the famous industrial designer, later devised new colors for Skylark as part of his Sunrise Collection designed for The Formica Company in 1953.

The material was also found in the bathroom, thanks to new postforming techniques that allowed fabricators to bend the laminate into coved backsplash and seamless front edges. ("Post formers" were companies that bent and glued laminate onto a substrate, providing ready-made countertops that could easily be cut to size and quickly installed in kitchen or bath. They helped expand Formica laminate sales dramatically.) The company's 1953 annual report celebrates the Vanitory—a trade name combining vanity and lavatory—and notes that do-it-yourselfers were eager to buy the products, thanks to new glues.

The new boom changed the company. The original logo of The Formica Insulation Company with a swooping arch, whose initial "F" suggested the roof of an older building, was soon replaced by an "F" that looked like a bold steel girder in a modernist Mies van der Rohe building. The product mix changed. In 1940 only one-quarter of the company's earnings came from decorative laminate, the rest from industrial products. By 1950 the proportions were reversed. The company dropped the term "insulation" from its name in 1948 and changed it to The Formica Company.

With aggressive sales techniques, annual gatherings, and circuslike demonstrations at industry conventions, The Formica Company increasingly focused on the consumer. It advertised vigorously, spending about $500,000 in 1951, an amount equal to 2 percent of its sales. But when Fortune magazine visited in 1951 it also found what was still a very conservative company, manufacturing only to order—which would take four to eight weeks for fulfillment—and averse to going into debt. "Solicitousness" was the word Fortune used for the attitude toward customers. So conservatively was it managed, Fortune reported, that Formica was even building the new Evendale, Ohio, plant, nine miles from the urban Spring Grove Avenue facility, on a pay-as-you-go basis, opening in stages, 120,000

HERE'S A MODERN *Light Colored* WOOD FINISH DINETTE TOP

702 OLYMPIA BUILDING
MIAMI 32, FLORIDA

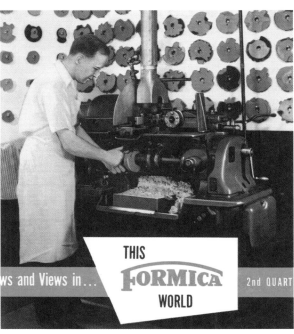

THIS FORMICA WORLD
ws and Views in... 2nd QUART

1940s Catalogue cover for Formica laminate tabletops. Grace Jeffers Collection of Formica Materials, Archives Center, National Museum of American History, Smithsonian Institution.

1949 Man working at lathe. Cover image, from *News and Views in This Formica World,* 2nd quarter. Grace Jeffers Collection of Formica Materials, Archives Center, National Museum of American History, Smithsonian Institution.

Report No 28 U.S.A.   Louisville Ky. 16-1-46

Dear Mr Garnsworthy

FORMICA INSULATION Co.
Cincinnati   Ohio.

Interviewed Mr White Mr Cochrane and Mr O'Conner

I saw these people today and after a preliminary talk Mr Cochrane showed me over all their works.

Varnish   They buy their phenolic from Bakelite Ltd, The Urea and melamine from American Cyanimid, they dissolve the dyes and mix them in the phenolic varnish by hand.   With the Ureas and melamine they use a rubber lined ball mill with flint balls (not glass as they found that the glass balls affected their curing times considerably) to mix in the pigments and a small percentage of alpha cellulose (they claim the latter helps to prevent crazing).

Impregnation   They would have at least twenty machines, the oldest machines using steam coils, the next circulating hot air steam heated and the last 8 machines infra-red. The Infra Red machines are vertical the others horizontal. They do not use reflectors, but the reflector globes which are not as efficient as our method. They roll the impregnated papers and then cut them to length on another machine The Urea and melamine impregnated papers are kept with a high moisture content until just before moulding when they are dried further in a hot air circulating oven. With all their resins they use either an alcohol water solvent or an alcohol solvent. Their impregnated ~~papers~~ materials (rolls and sheets) are stored in air conditioned rooms Phenolic materials 10 & 15% relative humidity the others 45% relative humidity   For surface sheets they recoat one side to have a 60% resin content.   Plywood The Veneers are stacked in a rectangular basket about 12 ft x 3 ft x 3 ft ~~and~~ which is lowered, end on into a steam heated vacuum tank, this cuts the cycle down to 45 minutes, where originally it used to take 48 hours. They use an alcohol water soluble phenolic resin.

Moulding The sheets are stacked between 1/8" polished stainless steel plates, the number in each daylight is dependant on the thickness take for example 1/16" sheet, ① a mild steel plate 3/32" thick, 2" larger all round than the Stainless steel sheet ② 8-10 sheets .008 paper ③ Stainless Steel Sheet polished 1 side ④ Material to be moulded by weight ⑤ Stainless Steel Sheet polished both sides (5-13) 4 + 5 are repeated until they have 6 sheets then (14) Stainless Steel Sheet polished one side (15) 8-10 sheets paper as ① (16) as ①

1946 Robert Sykes' notes written during his visit to the Formica Company in Cincinnati on January 16, 1946.

square feet at a time, until the whole 700,000-square-foot plant was done.

This attitude may have been the result of the founders remembering the Panic of 1907, or the Depression that led to the company's first downturn and loss in 1932, or the flood of 1937 that lifted the Ohio River to the second level of the factory and required desperate efforts by workers and executives. Founder Herbert Faber suffered a major heart attack soon afterward. He was never active in the business again and retired from the board in 1953. Dan O'Conor stayed on until the company was sold in 1956 and then retired to a vigorous life in Florida; he died in 1968.

The departure of the founders marked a turning point. The company was at the height of its success and self-confidence when it was purchased by one of its suppliers, the chemical conglomerate American Cyanamid, in 1956. Postwar prosperity was at its peak. The Cold War chilled much of the globe, but rock and roll and drive-in films entertained Americans spilling out of cities into the suburbs. It was not necessarily evident in those days that Formica Corporation's future would be a worldwide one. But in a remarkable foretaste of the company's global future, and understanding that the future lay in decorative laminate, Robert Sykes of Laminex paid a visit to the Spring Grove Avenue factory in Cincinnati in 1946.

During World War II, the company Sykes founded had manufactured industrial products for the war effort. In two years, annual sales grew to £75,000. His factory space now filled three tin sheds, with 15,000 square feet under cover. After the war, Sykes immediately realized that industrial uses for his material were declining. It is striking that at this juncture, he understood that his business was about to undergo the same change The Formica Company had experienced before the war, and he was willing to travel halfway around the world to learn how to adapt. Equally remarkably, it was none other than Jack Cochrane, among others, who showed Sykes around and explained everything. Astonishingly,

Sykes' notes of this visit survive. Every detail is included and every process summarized in careful, precise, tiny pencil notations, dated January 16, 1946, written on unlined paper.

Even more astonishing, perhaps, is that when Sykes visited, the company's top scientists not only did not view him as potential competition, but they welcomed him as a fellow researcher, to be greeted with warm collegiality. The men who met at the factory could not have imagined that fate would eventually bring the two companies together. Their openness was an exception. In the midst of such success, wrapped in a dream of postwar prosperity, it was easy to become isolated in Ohio.

Spring Grove Avenue could seem a long way from the rest of the world. For instance, *The Formican*, the company newsletter, recorded the story of a sander in the tube department who had traveled to Greece to visit her husband's relatives. On their farm, she missed indoor plumbing and was appalled at the pigs rooting about beside the house. She could not have been happier to be back in Ohio, she said, "You can have it, I'll take the good ol' USA." Her attitude was not a rarity.

International Expansion

The managers in Cincinnati were also more comfortable at home. But they observed the global appeal of Formica brand products and in 1946 made a key decision to license sales and manufacturing rights for much of the world—including Europe, India, Australia, New Zealand, and other parts of the British Commonwealth—to the respected British company De La Rue. It was an unusual company with a long and noble history. As recorded in *The Highest Perfection*, an official history of the company by Peter Pugh,[8] Thomas de la Rue's newspaper shop rose to prominence in the early nineteenth century. It began by printing playing cards, of all things, and did it so well that it received the royal warrant to print decks for the king. The company was chosen to print the first postage stamps in the world in 1840, bearing the image of Queen Victoria. It went on to print bank-notes for more than sixty countries around the globe as well as such official items as passports.

The company enjoyed quasi-official status in Britain, not unlike the mint in other countries. When the government shifted printing of the one-penny stamp to a De La Rue rival, King George V complained that his new printed portrait made him look like a monkey, and the *Times* of London ran an editorial of grave disapproval. The franchise was returned to De La Rue. It drew staff with back-grounds in the foreign office, diplomatic corps, and military at home in the larger world. Some of its salesmen traveled on the Orient Express® to distant lands to drum up business printing bank-notes or passports in such locations as Bulgaria and Siam. During World War II, the printing plant was destroyed by German bombers. Equipment was moved to the countryside, where De La Rue printed currency for dozens of occupied countries' governments in exile. The currency was stored in eighty-foot-deep caverns, to be pulled out as each country was liberated.

But after the war diversification was need-ed—the market for printing currency and official documents was limited. De La Rue looked to expand into the emerging consumer and high technology markets. The company began con-struction of a factory in Tyneside near Newcastle, in the northeast of England. De La Rue had ven-tured into plastics before the war, using them, among other things, for a line of pens. Seeing a link to printing, executives looked after the war to laminate panels made by Metropolitan Vick-ers, the old British Westinghouse, which made a laminate called Traffolyte (after Trafford, Penn-sylvania, site of the American factory for the prod-uct), and, after surveying the range of the world's producers in the field, to Formica Corporation and its owner American Cyanamid, with which they formed a licensing relationship to manufacture Formica® brand products. Difficult postwar con-ditions and shortages led to delay in construc-tion—the Tyneside factory did not open until

1948 and did not make money until 1952. But eventually it became profitable.[9]

A De La Rue company director reported in 1953 that the use of Formica laminate had expanded considerably: "It is now the recog-nized material for equipping a modern kitchen. At the same time, it is being increasingly used for canteens, transport services, furniture, shop fittings and a wide variety of other purposes." The company and the Formica® brand began to expand into Europe: to France in 1954, Spain in 1956—taking over from the earlier firm call-ed Ceplástica, established in 1946, which op-erated in most European countries. In 1962, De La Rue set up a Belgian branch in connec-tion with the Paris-based French one. In 1948 it had set up a branch in Australia, where Laminex was the dominant laminate maker, and in 1958 opened a plant in Thornleigh, outside Sydney. In 1959 it established a factory in Papakura, near Auckland, New Zealand. It also established a branch in India.

In 1958, executives at De La Rue and Amer-ican Cyanamid agreed to revise their agree-ment. De La Rue wanted more than a simple license to protect its future growth, and the firms formed a new arrangement, with 60 per-cent of the ownership of what was now called Formica Ltd. going to the British-based firm and 40 percent retained by American Cyanamid. But by the 1970s, even though it supplied more than half of De La Rue's sales, the company's leadership saw a diminished future for Formica brand products, the result of competition and a maturing market. "The strain was showing very clearly at Formica," recorded the official company history. "A whole host of companies have moved into laminated plastics over the world. In the 50s and 60s [it] was an entirely different ballgame." De La Rue received only 60 percent of the profits of its joint enterprise with Formica Corporation in the U.S., while it had to carry the obligation of 100 percent of borrowing for the common firm. In 1977, after two years

1954 The resin plant at Formica Company, Evendale, Ohio. Image from *Formica & Design; From the Counter Top to High Art*, by Susan Grant Lewin, 1991.

c. **1953–1954** The Formica Company's "Do it Yourself" presentation.

(page 27) Flakeboard Demonstration Kit. PHOTOGRAPHER Austin Bewsey, Cincinnati, Ohio.

(both images) Grace Jeffers Collection of Formica Materials, Archives Center, National Museum of American History, Smithsonian Institution.

of negotiations, De La Rue sold its rights back to American Cyanamid for 9.6 million pounds sterling, the equivalent of about $16.3 million contemporary U.S. dollars.

Around the Globe

Even as this deal was finalized, however, the Formica brand was growing strong around the globe. It reached every corner of the planet. Veteran laminate marketing manager Bryan Travers in New Zealand, for instance, says that the Formica brand had a worldwide reputation because it cultivated architects and designers. One of the brand's strengths was its global culture of design. As early as the 1950s, he argues, Formica Corporation had created a global recognition for design and taste that reached from Europe and the Americas to every outpost. It was tied to fashion and taste trends. "In Europe," recalls Michel Broussard, who pioneered the making of press plates for all the companies' plants around the world, "in the 1950s and sixties Formica laminate was heavily advertised on television and in other consumer media as a new aspirational 'must have' material of the modern home." The same vision that dominated the expanding market in the United Kingdom and the United States in the 1950s prevailed here. "The bold communications and awareness campaigns created at that time provide an invaluable legacy to our equity and still resound, fifty years later," says Broussard. Also important in Europe in the late 1970s were a series of new dimensional finishes such as slate, leather, wicker, and bamboo. The new textures represented an attempt to create tactile quality to match visual quality, and to differentiate from competitors.

In South America, interest in Formica brand products grew over the decades, even as the market experienced a series of complex business changes. De La Rue, which under its agreement with American Cyanamid controlled the Formica brand for South America, began sales in Brazil in the early 1960s. In the 1970s and 1980s, Formica

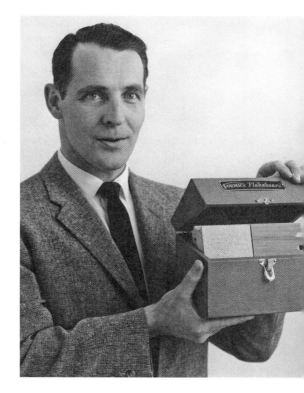

brand laminate was produced by American Cyanamid's South American subsidiaries. Today, Formica laminate is produced independently in South America under various licenses to unrelated manufacturing companies.

In the 1970s in South Africa, Formica laminate was produced under license by a company called Decorative Boards. Rights and technologies moved in a series of mergers and the company became Laminate Industries, a joint effort of American Cyanamid and PG Bison. PG Bison later acquired sole rights. Today, it is a diversified building products company in the Alrode area, near Johannesburg, manufacturing continuous or low pressure laminate (CPL) and coated boards. It made its own melamine and other resins and Formica brand high pressure laminate (HPL), exporting to other African countries until it began buying HPL directly from the Formica Group's European division in 2011 after closing its factory.

In 1965 Formica Corporation, under its British licensee De La Rue, entered the Indian market in a joint venture with the Bombay Burmah Trading Company. In 1966, the Formica company opened an Indian manufacturing facility in Pune, the industrial city with automobile and other factories, about 100 miles south of Mumbai. It was the first of its kind in India and the product was very well received. For a decade sales growth kept pace with the robust growth of the Indian economy. Then, in the late 1970s, the government of India underwent a dramatic change; controls were imposed on foreign ownership and the repatriation of capital. Profits could no longer be taken outside the country. The company left the Indian market, as did many international companies. It sold its ownership to a local industrial house, licensing the use of the Formica brand in India. Not until 2008, after the reopening of the Indian economy and shifts in policy, were the licensing rights withdrawn. The company decided to once again start its own operation in India.

Elsewhere in Asia, outside De La Rue's arrangement, it was not until the 1970s that Formica Corporation expanded into the Far East. The brand and the business quickly proved very strong. The company sold Formica laminate through agents in Hong Kong, Singapore, Malaysia, and Taiwan in the 1970s. "Architects and designers so loved the brand that the company began to invest in manufacturing facilities to support the local Asian markets," says Steve Kuo, now retired longtime president of Formica Asia. By 1980, Formica Corporation was ready for its first Asian plant, which opened in Taiwan.

New markets were opened during the 1980s and early 1990s. Formica brand laminate manufacturing plants, which had opened under De La Rue in the late 1940s and 1950s in Australia and New Zealand, expanded in the early 1980s by actually acquiring the rights to the Laminex laminate brand in those markets, producing product under both brands for a few brief years in the 1980s. This new period of interconnection between the Laminex and Formica brands, begun in the late 1940s during that visit by Sykes, would set the stage for years of back-and-forth trademark and manufacturing relationships between the two brand owners in the expanding Australia and New Zealand markets.

In 1992 Formica Corporation established a Singapore branch, Formica (Singapore) Pte Ltd., and in 1993 it expanded in Korea, as Formica Korea Corp, and in Malaysia, as House of Formica (Malaysia). Then came China itself, where Formica laminate enthralled designers as a premium material, rich in history and functionality. The company's growth would pace China's own dizzying, exponential growth. As China's economy began to expand, Formica Corporation set up Formica Shanghai in 1994 with a manufacturing joint venture with the local government.

Distribution centers were established in Beijing, Guangzhou, and Shenzhen. In 2003 followed a sales office and distribution center in Dongguan, South China, and in 2006 another distribution center in Chengdu, West China. Having outgrown the first plant, the company built a brand-new plant in 2005 and in 2006 expanded by relocating the assets of its first plant. With the acquisition in 2000 of Perstorp Surfacing Materials from Perstorp AB Sweden, Formica Corporation further expanded in Asia. With Siam Perstorp, the company gained a successful manufacturing plant and business in Thailand that supports the emerging Asian markets. The Thai factory was expanded in 2004.

1960s: The World's Fair

The symbolic moment of Formica Corporation's arrival "on top of the world" might be marked on the day the company's showcase house had opened at the World's Fair in New York in 1964. The house showed off for the whole world an ideal of living with Formica brand laminate. The bold colors and lines of Formica laminate in the 1950s echoed the swooping tail fins of Chryslers and Cadillacs. They were as upbeat as the new

1962 Showroom in Valencia, Spain.

rock and roll music and as informal as the teen slang and dance that fascinated the country. Formica Corporation, reports industry historian F. Holbrook Platts, still occupied half the U.S. market and was growing overseas. In 1962 the company held a ceremony—John Nobis, director of commercial development for Formica Corporation, announced plans for a showcase house at the World's Fair set for New York in 1964 and 1965. A photograph showed mustachioed architect Emil A. Schmidlin and interior designer Miss Ellis Leigh, who appeared in a cylindrical hat.

The seven-room, 2,600-square-foot home was a statement of the company's ideals and ambitions, laid out on a fully landscaped half-acre lot bearing the generic suburban address of "64–65 Hilltop Lane." The World's Fair house was seen amid pavilions of countries from all over the globe in the shadow of the "Unisphere," a giant multistory sculpture of the globe expressing an optimistic view of a happy planet. The

appearance only emphasized that Formica Corporation had become an international company. The name Faber had coined was now among the most recognized brands on the planet.[10]

In 1978 the U.S. Federal Trade Commission (FTC) sought to cancel the Formica trademark, charging that it had become a generic term such as thermos, aspirin, escalator, and cellophane. Under a law called the Lanham Act, the FTC could cancel a trademark if it had become "the common descriptive name of an article or substance." The FTC's power to bring such an action against a trademark created an uproar in the U.S. business community. Ultimately, the FTC's action was dropped after Congress stepped in and withdrew the funding to bring such actions. Even today, the company's lawyers tirelessly continue to patrol the integrity of the famous brand, reminding people to employ the Formica® trademark in combination with common terms and sending stern legal letters to those who do not respect

1964 Laminated painting from New York
World's Fair. Formica Group Private Collection.

1969 "A midship's view of a typical passageway. Magnolia Weave Textured finish lines the passageways, Orange Tan laminate in recessed sections. In addition the ship's plans have been reproduced by the Formica Interlaminate printing process," *The Formica Scene on the QE2*, 1970.

the company's iconic brand. "Formica is spelled with a capital F!" is a slogan they use, making the point that "Formica®" must be followed by the term "brand," "laminate," or "brand laminate."

The World's Fair house looked to the future — its kitchen offered the double ovens and double sinks comfortable kitchens would boast beginning in the 1980s. It even included the small home office in the kitchen that would arrive in the 1990s with the Internet. But there were clashing notes as well: the house showed the somewhat miscellaneous nature of Cyanamid's conglomerate catalogue and its presentation of Formica laminate. In the house were such Cyanamid products as Creslan brand acrylic fiber, Melmac® melamine dinnerware, Acrylite® decorative sheet, Skydome brand skylights, and Cyanamid's "chemical aids for the farm and garden." This awkward

mix hinted at Formica Corporation's unhappy fit inside its conglomerate.

In a very different environment and style, Formica laminate was just as critical as it had been to the *Queen Mary* when the daughter ship was designed, the *Queen Elizabeth 2*. The *QE2* began service in 1969, the year of the first moon landing and Woodstock. Some 2 million square feet of Formica laminate were used in spaces on the *QE2*. Passageways and stairways are color-coded. Pop graphics decorate modernist lounges outfitted with Bertoia chairs and Saarinen tables. The interior design team headed by Dennis Lennon worked for some three years to select the appropriate types of laminates. For first-class cabins it was a velour-textured Formica laminate. In the Jukebox, a lounge catering to teenage passengers, were bold graphics and colors, and silhouetted imagery designed by Royal College of Art students. In the coffee shop, visitors found bold stripes of poppy blue and yellow, and in washrooms and toilets, textured, weave-finished materials. The ladies' lounges were equipped with classic Formica laminate "Vanitories." The *QE2* was in effect a floating laboratory for Formica brand products of the 1960s.

But in 1969, customary means of transportation no longer held quite the same appeal. The image of Formica laminate now reflected changes in the wider culture once more: a rebellious generation sought the natural, the organic in materials. Young people perceived laminate as artificial. It was, after all, the material of their parents. The 1960s may have marked the high point of the first curve in the company's prosperity, coinciding with prosperity in recovering Europe and in the United States, the emergence of rock and roll and what historian Thomas Hines called "populuxe" in affordable home furnishings. The downturn can be pinpointed even more exactly. It was the moment in the 1969 film *The Graduate* when Dustin Hoffman's character is asked about a career in "plastics." Formica laminate came to be seen as superficial and artificial.

1969 Cover from *The Formica Scene on the QE2*, 1970.

(both images) Grace Jeffers Collection of Formica
Materials, Archives Center, National Museum of
American History, Smithsonian Institution.

1970s

The image of its products was not the only problem. Since 1956, "little Formica" had really been little. It was only a small part of a much larger and sometimes unconcerned organization, accounting for only 3 percent of Cyanamid's sales. Many observers of the industry and veterans of Formica Corporation's executive offices felt that it was starved of attention and capital. There was a sense that it was coasting on its glory and brand. The old scrappy company of the 1940s had somehow ossified into arrogance.

The Formica company had fallen, bit by bit, from half the market it enjoyed in the 1960s to aggressive competitors who undercut price and promised better service. When the company's image declined it did so slowly, but all over the globe. The deliberate, careful image of Formica Corporation—the qualities of "solicitousness" and care—turned to what one historian calls "the perception that Formica Corporation, having grown to number one, had become sluggish and arrogant, often taking weeks to deliver product."[11] By the end of the 1980s, competitors would take over market leadership of the U.S. market thanks to more aggressive sales, inventory, and delivery policies.

As is so often the case, the business story at Formica Corporation was a parable of a larger one. In the United States of the 1970s, many maturing industries were facing a shift from competing in goods to competing in services. Competitors' more aggressive sales and faster delivery, along with Formica Corporation's failure to respond, became a case study, much quoted among executives and business school students. It was included in the widely read *Competing against Time*, published in 1990.[12]

A study quoted in the book by the Boston Consulting group found that the competition took market share by getting the product to the customer faster. They could deliver almost any product in their line within ten days, as compared with twenty-five days for Formica Corporation.

Distributors were able to keep less inventory on hand—and cut prices as a result. Even in the 1950s, local distributors would stockpile some product categories because of Formica Corporation's policy of manufacturing only to order. But even with more competitors, the company's product was still good while it had lost in service. It had been "outhustled and outsmarted," in the words of one business writer. Soon, the company reduced its delivery times even for niche products to under two weeks, but the reputation stuck. One of Formica Corporation's challenges, the study suggested, was dealing with a variety of types of customers. Formica sometimes competed with and sometimes sold to fixture makers and installers, depending on the market and the country. As it grew, Formica developed close and mutually beneficial relationships with fabricators and contractors who were key customers, such as the postformers who had helped in the initial postwar boom. Many were entrepreneurs. A case in New Zealand was not unlike cases around the world. Barry and Helen O'Brien opened their business in a garage under their house in Dunedin and over four decades established seven outlets across the country, with 240 employees. At one point the counters they made and other installations accounted for 40 percent of Formica New Zealand's production. In 2007 they sold the business to Fletcher Building.

Such partners, designers, and small contractors needed a quick response and fast delivery of a color or pattern. But the company's several sets of customers each had somewhat different needs—and different competition. Lower-cost imitations lured the companies that built cabinets or office furniture (the so-called OEMs, original equipment manufacturers); they bought large quantities of Formica laminate or rival products. Those who worked on a smaller scale, designing or outfitting a café or a small cafeteria, were time-sensitive. Serving all these different needs was difficult.

Boomerang

In the 1980s, perhaps ironically and even at the same time as it faced business difficulties, Formica Corporation's products were enjoying a social and cultural revival. Materials including Formica laminate had become symbols of the baby boomer generation's childhood and their own parents, which this generation — and not just in America — wanted to reject as superficial and shallow. Yet by the 1980s, the baby boom era had circled around to again appreciate the music, film, and culture of its youth. In the normal cycles of human nature, it had reached parenthood itself. An apt symbol for this process is the boomerang. Boomerangs, with their characteristic curved, oblong shape, come flying back, a token of retro appreciation. Boomerang™ was the name given to the reissued Formica laminate pattern originally known as Skylark™ in the 1950s, reintroduced for Formica Corporation's 75th anniversary in 1988 in four new colors. A book and traveling museum exhibition called *Vital Forms* later summed up the common appeal of the materials, artifacts, and shapes of the era as organic and "free form."[13] Along with Isamu Noguchi coffee tables and Russel Wright or Eva Zeisel dishware, Formica laminate was listed as representing the same desire to echo nature, demonstrate vitality, and symbolize free thinking. The 1980s brought a new attitude toward materials. It had been gathering force for a while.

Robert Venturi, one of the leading theorists of what came to be called postmodernism, way back in 1962 had designed a coffee shop as one of his first projects that used laminate and similar materials — wanting to celebrate the mundane. He showed off the low budget rather than hiding it. He continued in this vein, helping to give rise to the high-tech look, which employed industrial materials in dining, retail, and office spaces. A new generation of architects and designers was rethinking pattern and surface.

The Italian designer and architect Ettore Sottsass led a new appreciation of laminate. In 1978 he was hired to create abstract decorative patterns for the Italian laminate firm Abet Laminati, a Formica company competitor in Europe. Sottsass was the leader of a design group called Memphis that arose in Milan around 1980. It took its name from both the Egyptian city and Elvis Presley's home in Tennessee, wanting to combine the classical with pop. The group's furniture and sculpture often used the material to supply color and pattern.

In 1983, Formica Corporation organized a traveling exhibition of pieces in ColorCore® laminate that brought together work by architects — Robert Venturi, Frank Gehry, Stanley Tigerman, James Wines of SITE, and others — to show that laminate was no longer taken as a faux material but celebrated on its own terms. In subsequent years, the exhibition traveled the world. New work by local designers was added at each stop of the global tour, emphasizing the international richness of the brand. The exhibitions served as mobile embassies of design, style, and fashion, presenting Formica laminate around the world.

Artists, designers, and architects began to use laminate more often in furniture and even sculpture. The material was no longer perceived simply as a stand-in for something else, stone or wood, but as it was in the beginning: a product valued in itself. The slogan could have been "Let Formica Be Formica!" With the arrival in 1982 of Formica Corporation's ColorCore® laminate, which maintained its hue in depth and omitted the brown line or edge of earlier products, the company's products were even more attractive. They found appeal among designers of new styles of offices. Changes in office design reflected new ideas about business. Teamwork and collaboration were emphasized. Workers were more mobile, thanks to the increasing globalization of the economy. As a consequence, offices were becoming less formal, with more common spaces, and they welcomed color.

Formica Corporation had long understood that a key component of its business was design.

The company had hired designers Brooks Stevens to devise patterns in 1951 and Raymond Loewy to create the new "Sunrise" line in 1953. The Research and Development Center at the Evendale facility, built in 1960, acquired a design studio, and in the late 1970s a Design Advisory Board was established of outside advisers. Formica's emphasis on design was part of a wider trend: firms such as Alessi in Italy, Authentics in Germany, Marimekko, Knoll, Bodum, IBM, and Sony all saw the importance of design in creating global identities for their products and their companies. Now the company stepped up its designer efforts. Following up on *Surface + Ornament*, Formica Corporation publicized the potential of its laminates and changed their public image.

1980s and 1990s: Troubled Decades as a Buyout Target

The business side of the company was less upbeat. As much as its experience had echoed lifestyles and trends, the company's problems and challenges also reflected troublesome trends in business. It had been a victim of the much maligned "conglomerate" fad that ran from the 1950s into the 1970s. When it was sold in 1956, Formica Corporation became a small part of the large $450 million American Cyanamid conglomerate. Taken for granted, it was under-supported and received inadequate investment, many veterans of the business felt. For a time, growth continued. Formica built a major new plant near Sierra in California in 1966. But by the 1980s it was clear that the road to growth lay beyond American borders. The appeal of the company and the Formica brand was global.

Conglomerates were huge corporations that combined vastly disparate enterprises in the pursuit of growth and increasing stock prices. One corporation might find itself building dynamos, selling life insurance, and baking cakes or — in one famous case — manufacturing high-tech data and telephone cables but also curing hams and bacon. Many of the conglomerates collapsed in the 1970s. But by the 1980s, there was a new trend in business. Thanks to new types of financing, including so-called speculative or junk bonds, and the possibility of realizing what was considered "locked up stockholder value," especially for companies with strong brands, the leveraged buyout became popular. Leveraged buyouts (LBOs) attracted bankers, investors, and ultimately stockholders. Ignored by a huge corporate parent during the conglomerate era, Formica Corporation suffered in different ways during the LBO period of the 1980s. The company underwent a rollercoaster of ownership changes during which investment was neglected, some industry observers believed.

In 1985 the president of Formica Corporation, Gordon D. Sterling, and Formica's management teamed up with Shearson Lehman and Donaldson, Lufkin & Jenrette in a leveraged buyout that valued the company at $200 million and carried $153 million in debt. It was a heavy burden, and to reduce it, in 1987 the company went public again, selling 5.3 million shares, one-third of the equity, for $64 million. But other investors saw more gain. Talk of a buyout swirled around the company. In 1988, Formica found itself fending off approaches from so-called raiders. First a group led by Samuel Zell, then one headed by Malcolm Glazer took positions in the stock. In 1988, chairman Sterling died suddenly. He was succeeded by CEO Vincent Langone. In 1989, in a second leveraged buyout, Formica management, Dillon Read, and Masco took the company private. But the economy was heading for recession, both in the U.S. and Europe. By 1990, the company needed $40 to $50 million annually just to meet interest payments. Worst of all, the steady cash flow on which investors had counted was weakening. The company's share of the American market had fallen from one-third to about one-quarter of the total, thanks mostly to competition from other laminate competitors.

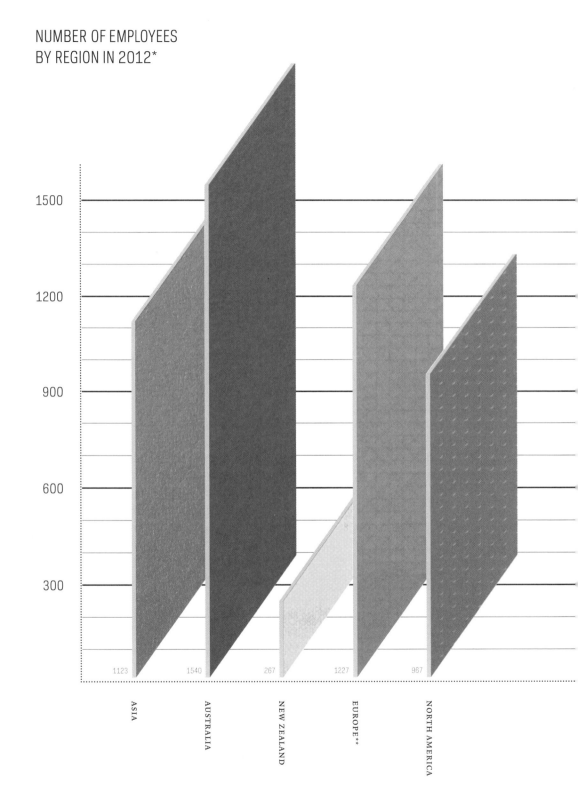

NUMBER OF EMPLOYEES
BY REGION IN 2012*

1500

1200

900

600

300

1123   1540   267   1227   967

ASIA   AUSTRALIA   NEW ZEALAND   EUROPE**   NORTH AMERICA

*Fletcher Building Laminates & Panels Division   **Includes Homapal, Germany

NUMBER OF FACTORIES
BY REGION IN 2012*

NORTH AMERICA

2

EUROPE**

6

ASIA***

4

AUSTRALIA
NEW ZEALAND

8

Formica Corporation looked for growth globally, but its perceived arrogance and reputation for poor service were a disadvantage.

In 1995, the company was bought for about $600 million by BTR Nylex, an Australian subsidiary of BTR, the British industrial conglomerate that began as British Tire and Rubber. The new owners replaced the top management, including CEO Vince Langone and CFO David Schneider, and many felt that service and sales suffered. In 1998, in a third leveraged buyout, BTR sold Formica Corporation. For $405 million, the Formica company was taken over by a venture capital group including Citicorp's CVC European Equity Partners and Donaldson, Lufkin & Jenrette. The new owners brought back Langone and Schneider and in February 1999 moved to acquire working capital to rebuild the business through the sale of $215 million of high-yield debt. The plan was to expand with strategic acquisitions. But the effort came in the teeth of a recession that unfolded beginning in 2000.

To some it seemed the company had been handed along from one group of investors to another, like a Formica laminate sample chip on a designer's sample chain. Was the Formica brand name so strong that owners felt sure it could endure any amount of handling a blue-chip brand? *Business Week* in 1999 was stern in its judgment of what the company had gone through. It called Formica Corporation "a corporate orphan looking desperately for a home." "Formica has been the neglected, even abused, stepchild of two conglomerate parents," the magazine went on. "It has endured three leveraged buyouts. It has weathered a seemingly endless array of owners and board members, not to mention a plethora of corporate strategies and restructurings."[14] During the period of decline, says Mark Adamson, "the core business fundamentals were lost. Management neglected the product, the customer and service. They also neglected research and technology, notably competitive products." They failed to see new technologies, such as rival

*Fletcher Building Laminates & Panels Division **Excludes Bilbao, which was closed in 2012. Includes purchase of India Assets from Well Pack announced in November 2012. ***A new site in Jujiang, China, currently under construction, scheduled for completion in 2013.

Corian® materials from DuPont. Later, after the buyouts, managers focused on costs and overhead to the exclusion of other factors, so that the company could be sold at a good profit. In consequence, investment and maintenance were sometimes deferred or neglected. Instead of product and service, management was focusing on its exit strategy—preparing the company for sale as soon as possible.

The Twentieth Century

As early as 1990, half of Formica Corporation's business came from outside the United States. The company's future lay with global growth, and through expansion Formica hoped to turn the tide. In 2000, the purchase of Perstorp Surface Products, a European market leader and innovator in the field, promised an opportunity to move toward global competitiveness. In 1985, the parent Perstorp had introduced a new form of laminate-based flooring, Pergo®, which became a huge success. The company decided to concentrate on this business and established Pergo Flooring as a separate division in 1998. It sold off its plastics and life sciences divisions. It also decided to sell the Perstorp Surface Products division to Formica, retaining only Chemicals and Pergo Flooring in the Group. In 2001, Pergo Flooring became a separate company and Perstorp concentrated on its raw chemicals business—in a sense a return to its origins.

The acquisition of Perstorp brought with it several high-pressure laminate factories, mainly in Europe and Brazil, but also including one factory in Thailand in the key growth area of Asia. It also brought a culture of innovation and creativity that had produced the new laminate flooring and exterior cladding. Although it would ultimately benefit the company, the Perstorp acquisition came on the eve of an economic downturn and increased the company's debts. Integrating the new acquisition proved a challenge and hopes for other acquisitions proved in vain. With the company burdened by debts of $540 million, a new

CEO, Frank Riddick, and the board in 2002 decided the company would have to seek protection in bankruptcy court. It emerged with a new plan in the spring of 2004 that brought $175 million cash investment, reduced secured debt from more than $300 million to about $127 million, and eliminated $215 million in unsecured debt.

On the other side of the globe, events were beginning to unfold that would in time dramatically affect the company's future. One of the proudest names in New Zealand business history was Fletcher Building,[15] a giant building materials and construction company with an even longer history than Formica Corporation. From a single house built in 1909 on Broad Bay near Dunedin, New Zealand, Fletcher grew to boast a global presence in construction, creating housing complexes and office towers, churches and factories, docks and pipelines, institutions and national monuments. It built New Zealand's National Museum and Wellington Railway station and in the 1930s constructed the country's social security building in just six weeks. Fletcher also developed an infrastructure to produce and deliver materials to build those structures. It maintained forests, mines, and factories, and produced paper, lumber, and cement. In Auckland the company built the Sky Tower, the tallest structure in the Southern Hemisphere, and Eden Park, which hosted the Rugby World Cup championship in 2011. Its work was seen in Canada, Hawaii, Hong Kong, and Australia. It even built the J. Paul Getty Museum in Los Angeles, designed by Richard Meier and visible to millions every day on the hill above a major freeway.

Expanding and diversifying as the conglomerate Fletcher Challenge, the company had its share of difficulties as the twentieth century ended. Reborn as Fletcher Building in 2001, the company had shed enterprises in 2000 and had begun refocusing its business in 2001, when it hired Ralph Waters as CEO. While Fletcher was best known for construction, the new chief and his board reasoned that its profitability actually came from its building materials businesses. The company decided to become a major power in building materials, in the Australasian region and globally. It aimed to be the top competitor in each market it entered. It acquired companies in the areas of roofing, insulation, steel products, concrete and plastic pipe, and other building supplies. In 2002, Fletcher bought the panel and laminate firm The Laminex Group, now Australia's leader in the field, for 759 million NZD or about $555 million USD at the time. Growing by expansion, but also alongside an expanding economy in the first years of the new millennium, Fletcher recorded dramatic earnings increases. Its 2001 revenue of 2,273 million NZD multiplied to 5,520 million NZD in 2006.

In September 2006, Fletcher chose a new CEO, Jonathan Ling—then the CEO of The Laminex Group. Ling perceived the value of the still recovering Formica Corporation, with its recent acquisition Perstorp. Fletcher would build globally and synergistically on the company's strength in the market for laminate and related products with the Formica storied brand. Ling's first decision as Fletcher's CEO was to purchase Formica Corporation, in May 2007, for about $700 million USD. The combination with the Laminex Group of companies, which by now had held the rights to use the Formica brand in Australia and New Zealand for many years, under the Fletcher umbrella would make the Formica brand the single largest player in its industry globally. The two companies had worked together, however, as far back as 1946 and Robert Sykes' visit to Cincinnati.

By the late 1940s, Laminex Pty Ltd had begun producing its first decorative panels. The first Laminex® plastic laminate sheets were basic: they were available in the standard size of 1/16th inch thick, 8 by 4 feet wide, in a limited range of a dozen or so colors and patterns, and in a gloss finish. In 1952, the Laminex company opened a new 160,000-square-foot factory in Cheltenham. This allowed the expansion of Laminex sheeting design and production. The emphasis was on ease of care, but design mattered too. During the early 1950s the color and pattern range grew. As in the U.K., Europe, or the United States, the popular colors of the 1940s, such as Coral Pink and Apple Green, were joined in the more energetic 1950s by stronger primary colors. "Patterns included wood grains, marbles, linen weaves, basket weaves and metallic threads, drawing inspiration from the South Pacific and abstracted organic designs," reports Kelly Wynne in her history of Laminex.

Indeed, Laminex® established its brand in Australia much as the Formica brand did in other countries. At first, Laminex Pty Ltd sold only to wholesalers in building and furniture industries, which in turn sold products using the laminates through department stores and other outlets. But following a worldwide pattern, the arrival of improved glues and tools sparked a do-it-yourself movement. Homeowners installed fixtures covered with laminate themselves, creating a new market in the 1950s. The company advertised in Australian *Home Beautiful* and *House and Garden* with the slogan "Laminex: Lovelier for a Lifetime," emphasizing both ruggedness and ease of cleaning. Laminex, like Formica Corporation, became known for the samples or chips that could be picked up at retail centers and taken home for matching. Some ten million chips have been distributed. In the 1980s, the company built a showcase house featuring Laminex brand products in Warrandyte in suburban Melbourne. During the 1970s, 1980s, and 1990s, Laminex Industries expanded its market reach with the addition of a series of metropolitan and regional branches, now numbering some thirty-six locations across Australia.

In the 1990s, Laminex Industries bought the Formica laminate plant and distribution operations in New Zealand, continuing to manufacture products under both brands. The Formica brand products' manufacturing plant in Australia, set up in 1948 by De La Rue, lagged behind in the market—an exception to the general rule. The

Formica laminate plant in Australia was shut down in 1998.[16] Amatek Limited acquired the rights to the Formica trademark in July 1999 when it purchased the Formica business from CSR. Amatek Limited changed its name to Laminex Group Limited and was sold by CVC to Fletcher Building in November 2002.

Australia was one of the few countries in the world where the Formica brand was not the dominant brand for laminates — Laminex's brand was the iconic brand in that part of the world. Over the decades and in the two markets of Australia and New Zealand, the two rivals passed through several stages of ownership in a complex business history. The confusion finally ended when they were happily united under the roof of Fletcher Building.

Producing Formica® Brand Laminate

So much about the Formica company had changed in one century — and very little of that was on display in the company's plants, which produce the iconic laminate. Technology, precision, and efficiency had adjusted to the times, and yet care, quality, and artistry had remained the same. A visitor to the Evendale factory in Cincinnati on the eve of the company centennial might find little change from the first days of that factory in 1950, at least on the exterior. The same plain brick walls are outside, the same exposed girders overhead, the same racks laden with huge rolls of brown Kraft paper and smaller rolls of printed and solid color paper. Yellow forklifts zip along, avoiding carefully painted green sidewalks that guide the visitor among machines.

The machinery in Ohio is pretty much the same as the machinery at a Formica laminate factory in Canada or in Thailand. The presses last a long time. These are big, rugged machines, some decades old but updated with new generations of electronics and controllers. This is not a white room full of robots, à la Silicon Valley, but more a machine shop or a commercial bakery. Making laminate is something like printing and

something like baking. "We make cakes, basically," the factory chief says. "We use heat and pressure. It takes a certain temperature to heat and cool." Like baking, it cannot be rushed.

Most of Formica laminate is paper. Its manufacture begins with many layers of paper. The base is several core layers of Kraft, a heavy version of the stuff familiar from brown paper bags. The layers are first treated with resins or "dipped and squeezed." The Kraft paper is topped with a printed or solid color decor layer. Sheets resembling old-fashioned wax paper for wrapping sandwiches also go on top of the laminate sandwich. They become transparent melamine protective and release layers. The paper layers are built in "doubles" or "pairs," two sheets set between steel plates, very thin but very heavy. Then the units are assembled in packs or books. The whole process is sometimes called "the build out."[17]

To move the plates in the factory, machines swing to grab the plates with suction cups the size of dessert plates, like those used by glaziers. But that machinery is an exception. Much of the work still requires human teamwork and physical cooperation. In the process called collating, a factory visitor might see a pair of ladies moving sheets from their rack with a quick, expert twist, an operation similar to folding towels or sheets.

The result of the buildup is a series of packs, like slabs, that go into the press. The largest press in the Ohio factory is Number 28, although the reason for the numbers is long lost. The presses suggest huge pizza ovens. There are multiple fixtures for sheets, just as in a pizza oven, and a look at the end shows a similar maze of piping. Look in one end and there is a plumber's nightmare of work, bringing hot water. At venerable Number 28, six huge gleaming silver hydraulic columns and pipes supply some 1,500 pounds per square inch, or about 105 kg/cm² at a temperature of about 284° F (140° centigrade). Racks let the "packs" slide in like pizzas on sheets. After they leave the press, the sheets, still warm like baked goods, are trimmed and

LAMINATE MANUFACTURING

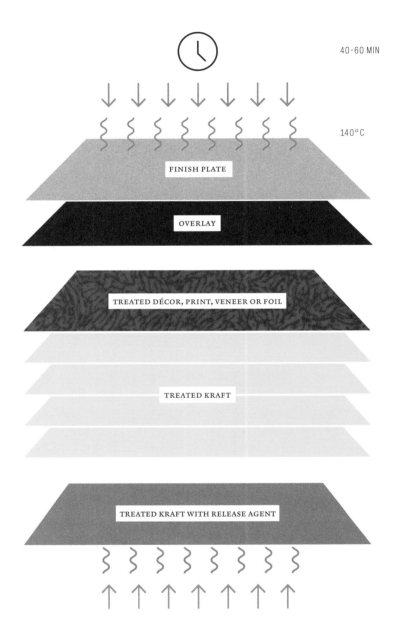

40-60 MIN

140°C

FINISH PLATE

OVERLAY

TREATED DÉCOR, PRINT, VENEER OR FOIL

TREATED KRAFT

TREATED KRAFT WITH RELEASE AGENT

their backs sanded. Then they are sliced into appropriate sizes for shipment.

Charts at every work station note quality control standards and blare the letters QCDSM, which are familiar in quality-oriented factories around the world: they stand for Quality, Cost, Delivery, Safety, and Morale. This is the working slogan of a quality-improvement system. It is all done with fewer workers than before, but much of the veteran equipment is rugged and built to purpose. As Mark Adamson states, "One of the realities of our business is that the machinery has a very long lifespan. The major components are huge chunks of metal." Sometimes these huge machines move around the world. A laminate press from Mexico was moved to North Shields in the United Kingdom after the company bought out the local Mexican firm. It remains a superb piece of machinery, now modified with modern electronics. In the gray of the factory floor, new, well-lit break rooms stand out, painted white, sealed off from the noise of the machines and set up with tables and vending machines. There, the visitor meets several long-term employees with forty-five and forty-seven years of work history with the company. Says one employee, "I am the third generation of our family to work for Formica. And that includes my grandmother."

Global Green

Other parts of the Evendale plant are radically if invisibly changed. The oil-fired and coal-fired boilers are long gone, replaced by those fired by gas, although some factories around the world still depend on the older fuels. Scraps of paper are sent back to the paper mills and other loose waste is burned to generate energy in the factory. Similar practices have become standard at Formica Group's plants around the world.

The company began to consider the environment long ago. But its global thinking took on a new meaning as concerns about global warming, energy, and sustainability shaped the view of business and consumers. In the new millennium, Formica Group began to review every aspect of its business with regard to its impact on the planet. "It all comes back to the fact that we breathe the same air and water," says CEO Adamson. "Being green is necessarily global. The technology solutions are also likely to be global because the laws of biology and physics are not different in different countries. We have been able to combine our resources at the global level. As time goes on it will be more and more an economic imperative....Our business is very energy intensive....Every day I have to worry about the price of coal and gas. There are real hard-nosed economic reasons why we want to limit lifecycle energy costs."

The company also began to test products for indoor emissions. One key area was the safety of desktop and other products used in classrooms and children's products. Key Formica brand products were submitted and became Greenguard Indoor Air Quality Certified, a standard that is now achieved in all plants producing Formica laminate around the world. Several years ago, the company began a process of Life Cycle Assessment (LCA), measuring the resources and energy consumed by its products. The process reaches from the cutting of a tree to the day the panel ends up in a landfill or is recycled. Sustainable practices are now critical to business. "Consumers want to do the right thing," says Gavin Todd, development manager of the Formica Group. "They have been conditioned to expect environmental certifications and they drive architects and designers."

The impact of the green certification program called Leadership in Energy and Environmental Design (LEED) has been important in changing the way designers and contractors plan in the United States, Asia, India, and other markets around the world. The standards are built around a set of criteria compiled in 1994 by the U.S. Green Building Council (USGBC) to encourage sustainable building. Points are awarded to

EUROPE

- **RESIDENTIAL**
  Single Family, Apartments,
  K&B Retail

- **RESIDENTIAL REMODEL**
  Single Family, Apartments,
  K&B Retail

- **COMMERCIAL**
  Healthcare, Hospitality,
  Retail, Education

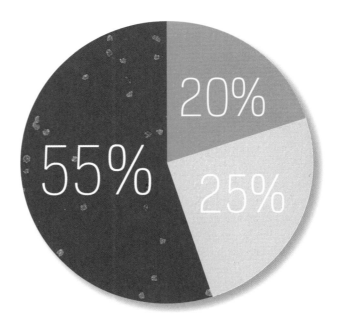

AUSTRALIA AND NEW ZEALAND

- **RESIDENTIAL**
  Single Family, Apartments,
  K&B Retail

- **RESIDENTIAL REMODEL**
  Single Family, Apartments,
  K&B Retail

- **COMMERCIAL**
  Healthcare, Hospitality,
  Retail, Education

- **EXPORT**

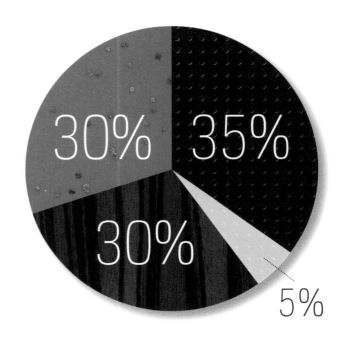

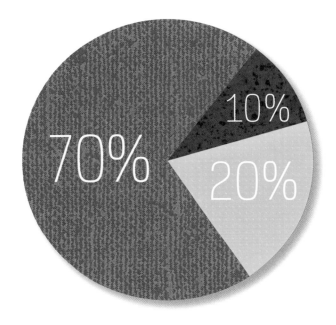

ASIA

RESIDENTIAL
Single Family, Apartments,
K&B Retail

RESIDENTIAL REMODEL
Single Family, Apartments,
K&B Retail

COMMERCIAL
Healthcare, Hospitality,
Retail, Office, Education

NORTH AMERICA

RESIDENTIAL
Single Family, Apartments,
Home Centers, K&B Retail

RESIDENTIAL REMODEL
Single Family, Apartments,
Home Centers, K&B Retail

COMMERCIAL
Healthcare, Hospitality, Retail,
Education

rank a building certified, silver, gold, or platinum. Each material and system in the building is taken into account. In the United Kingdom, sustainability is measured by the Building Research Establishment Environmental Assessment Method (BREEAM), a counterpart of LEED. Formica Group has also worked with the Carbon Trust targeting reductions in its carbon footprint and greenhouse gas emissions. In 2012, Formica Group became the first laminate manufacturer in the world to be awarded the Carbon Trust's Carbon Reduction Label. Many structures today are built to LEED and other standards of ensuring environmental sustainability.

"We are now moving slowly but purposefully on the sustainability path," Todd says. "What we do is not like making a car, where you take parts and assemble them. We bake cakes, bringing together many raw materials to formulate a chemical change to their properties. When you bake cakes, there is much more variability within the manufacturing process that requires precise controls to maintain the product's performance."

In looking at lifecycle environmental assessment, companies consider the environmental impact of products, materials, emissions, water, and energy from raw material to end of use—"cradle to grave." Formica laminates are an intermediate product. The laminate is usually employed to construct furniture or countertops. The company's LCA revealed that manufacturing consumes only about 25 percent of the total energy consumed throughout the product's full life. The remainder is used either throughout the supply chain that delivers raw materials to the plants or the downstream activities that fabricate Formica brand products into finished components. As CEO Adamson says, "Sixty percent of our product is paper." Making that paper sustainable was critical.

In three years, the company moved to using wood from sustainable forests and bearing the Forest Stewardship Council (FSC) label. This designates that forests have complied with the rigorous procedures set out in the FSC standards.

"There are only three main suppliers of Kraft paper for the worldwide laminates industry, two in the U.S. and one in Finland and we are only a small part of their business," says Todd. "It was pressure from Formica Group and our industry that helped change the FSC landscape. There is a limited amount of FSC forest and FSC pulp in the world. Now all three suppliers have been able to achieve the FSC standards….To achieve sustainability is something we have to act on as a company. It can't be done just with one geographical region such as North America or Asia. It makes far more strategic sense to have a common sustainability strategic program that will meet our global footprint." Acting globally at all levels was at the top of Formica Group's agenda as the centennial approached. During 2012, Formica Group qualified all its manufacturing facilities to the FSC Chain of Custody standard.

2010s: Reset

Mark Adamson headed Formica Europe and took over as CEO in March 2008. (Adamson had joined the Formica Group in 1998 through the Perstorp acquisition, as CFO of the European division, and in 2004 became president of Formica Europe. In October 2011, he became head of the entire Laminates and Panels division of Fletcher Building.) He arrived just in time for the global recession and the credit crunch that struck construction especially hard. He set out on what he calls a "re-set" at the Formica Group of companies. Formica Group's travails reflected the world economic crisis in extreme form. "At first it was a matter of triage," states Adamson. In the crisis of 2008, "we lost half our business," he says. Costs were cut and product lines trimmed, rationalized, and integrated. The staff was reduced. In 2009, a new European headquarters in Newcastle, United Kingdom, became the catalyst for a major organizational change, integrating the European business. "We took the customer offer down to the things people wanted AND needed," he says. Half the products, or SKUs, were reduced and palettes rationalized. The design department revised national palettes; regional collections were streamlined and coordinated. In Asia, the color range was harmonized into a single Asian collection. The European Specification Collection supplanted the formerly separate British and European collections.

New introductions did not stop. Important new products included new texture and design developments such as 180FX® laminate, which conveyed the effect of a single stone slab without repetition of pattern. Formica® Exterior Compact, the colorful UV-resistant exterior compact structural laminate first offered in Europe in 2005, was rebranded VIVIX® for all markets when it was introduced in North America in 2010, with new production in St. Jean, Quebec. Some of the possibilities for the material were highlighted in 2007, when French artist Daniel Buren used it to sheath a landmark bridge next to Frank Gehry's Guggenheim Museum in Bilbao, Spain, for the museum's tenth anniversary. Now, he says, "We want to reunify the Formica brand globally."

This does not mean a tyrannical top-down approach, he emphasizes, or a one-size-fits-all overrunning local variations. "Local people will run local businesses," he says. "There's something in between." Formica Group operates with three regional divisions. Adamson envisioned a sort of federalist approach in which the things best done at the local level remain local and others are done at the global level. As a unified global company, he noted Formica Group was in a position to enjoy huge economies of scale in materials—"And we can globally leverage innovation." Developing a global strategy and coordinating innovations would make a big difference. The company still aims to cut costs by 3 percent a year. (In 2011, it cut $40 million.)

Adamson believed that innovation entailed far more than simple research and development. Among many ideas, the key was choosing the right ones. It lay in finding what people really wanted. At one point, the company employed one

hundred people in a laboratory doing research. In the past, he says, the company had produced things people said they wanted, only to realize they did not really buy them. The business often depended on trends in design. Formica Group reaffirmed its commitment to design in 2008 with an exhibition of Formica® laminate furniture and sculpture by such architects as Michael Graves, Massimo Vignelli, Zaha Hadid, and Thomas Mayne at the Contemporary Arts Center, Cincinnati, and in 2010 with a pioneering show of sculpture using Formica laminate by Chinese architects in Beijing.

Homapal Plattenwerk

In keeping with Adamson's strategy of rationalizing the company's offerings globally and providing an organized strategy of innovation, in early 2012 Formica Group bought the rest of Homapal Plattenwerk GmbH, a German firm of which it had owned half for nearly three decades. Homapal is based in Herzberg in the Lower Saxony region of Germany. The company's entrance into the panel business came indirectly. Founded by Fritz Homann in 1876, the business built wooden tubs in which to package its primary product, margarine. In 1929, what was then called Company Homann bought a saw mill in Herzberg am Harz to supply wood for the tubs. Owner Hugo Homann focused on wood. He developed the idea for a new product, fiberboard. Realizing this vision took a long time, but by 1950, with the German postwar economic miracle, the company was flourishing. In 1955 it began to produce melamine-faced panels, and in 1958 laminate, under the trademark Homapal, derived from the owner's name. Innovation came quickly, in the form of electronics to control the presses and, in 1970, the first production of metal laminates. The company became known for these and for its line of wood veneer laminates, which were popular in Europe. Formica Corporation's relationship with Homapal grew from shared products to shared facilities to ownership. Formica had earlier partnered with Homapal in launching metallic laminates and had been its largest customer and half-owner since 1983. The popularity of metal laminates had been growing in Europe and expanding to other areas of the world, notably China.

The Markets of the Future

In China, sales of Formica laminate have been tracking the 10 to 20 percent annual growth of China's economy. China's boom was the economic story of the new millennium, and again Formica Group was at the center of the big story. In retail spaces, hotels, hospitals, and other rapidly expanding sectors, Formica's products were in demand. Its popularity in the People's Republic was a further ratification of the global power of the Formica brand. Recently in China, consumers have grown familiar with the bold logos and colors of Kentucky Fried Chicken®, KFC®, now the fastest-growing restaurant chain in China with nearly 3,700 restaurants in more than 700 cities. Formica Group has been one of the key suppliers in the expansion, working with KFC's design agencies and in-house teams on interiors, decoration, and signage.

The Qing Pu plant outside Shanghai has added presses over the years, most recently its fourth, expanding capacity by one-third. In 2007, the plant was upgraded and in 2011, the company announced its plan for a second plant in China, part of a $200 million investment in the Asian operation. For the centennial year, Formica Group is marking more than twenty years in China and celebrates with the completion of that new factory, in Jiujiang. With more than 50,000 square feet and a workforce of four hundred, the $70 million plant will double the company's capacity in China and keep it poised for the future.

In India, meanwhile, Formica Group is surveying a market likely to grow at rates similar to those enjoyed by China. It is predicted to double over the next decade. Years after leaving the Indian market, the company negotiated control of its trademark there in 2008. "Now we have the brand back," says Adamson. Formica laminate remains the preferred choice among Indian architects, contractors, and other customers. Prospects for the company in its new incarnation in India are bright thanks to GDP growth that has been registering around 8 percent annually for several years. The acquisition of India Assets from Well Pack was announced in November 2012.

Global Integration

As it enters its second century, Formica Group finds itself ahead of the larger sine curve; its recovery and persistence through hard times serve as a model for others. Perhaps its century of reflecting large economic and social shifts has given the company the cumulative experience to survive the latest crisis. As a model for a more focused and agile global company, Formica Group might serve as an example, says CEO Mark Adamson. Having paced a century of innovations, "I think we can be a proxy. I think others can learn from us." The century that began with the daring of experiment ends with the wisdom of experience. Adamson would soon have the chance to apply Formica's lessons himself to a wider canvas. In one of those twists that had marked the underdog company's colorful history, both wisdom and experience were ratified when in October 2012, after leading Formica Group's revival and transition to a new century, Mark Adamson became the CEO of parent Fletcher Building. The company would have a new leader for its new century.

Notes

1. Formica® is the registered trademark of The Diller Corporation. Reference to Formica company or business refers to Formica Group, or its predecessor companies. Formica Group is a global group of companies consisting of Formica Canada, Inc., Formica Corporation, Formica de Mexico S.A. de C.V., Formica IKI Oy, Formica Limited, Formica S.A., Formica S.A.S., Formica Taiwan Corporation, Formica (Thailand) Co., Ltd., and Formica (Asia) Ltd., among others.

Bakelite® is the registered trademark of Borden Chemical Investments, Inc. RCA® is the registered trademark of Audiovox Corporation. Isolite® is the registered trademark of Altana Electrical Insulation GmbH. Orient Express® is the registered trademark of Société Nationale des Chemins de fer Français-S.N.C.F. Melmac® is the registered trademark of Cytec Technology Corporation. Acrylite® is the registered trademark of Evonik Cyro LLC. Corian® is the registered trademark of E. I. du Pont de Nemours and Company or its affiliates. Pergo® is the registered trademark of Pergo (Europe) AB. Kentucky Fried Chicken® and KFC® are the registered trademarks of KFC Corporation.

2. Stephen Fenichell, *Plastic: The Making of a Synthetic Century* (New York, 1996).

3. "Formica Is on Top," *Fortune* (October 1951): 116.

4. Jeffrey L. Meikle, "Plastics," in *Formica & Design* (New York, 1991), 42.

5. John Maxtone-Graham, *The Only Way to Cross* (New York, 1972).

6. Unpublished history of Laminex by Kelly Wynne, Deakin University. See also Barnaby Feder, "Formica: When a Household Name Becomes an 'Also-Ran,'" *The New York Times* (August 12, 1990): 12F.

7. F. Holbrook Platts, *The History of Decorative High Pressure Laminates* (Hampton, SC, n.d. [2008]).

8. Peter Pugh, *The Highest Perfection: A History of De La Rue* (London, 2011).

9. Years later a man named Frank Hamill wrote to the company in appreciation for the jobs that he and his two brothers had found at the Tyneside factory sixty-five years earlier. The Formica laminate business was to be commended because it provided work for many thousands of workers over the years. He was one of the first laboratory assistants to join the plant, in 1947, and with the job he was able to go to school at night at Newcastle College and earn a degree in chemistry. His brothers Dylan and Harry also worked at the company, together amassing more than seventy years of service. "It is incredible that a product that is essentially technically similar to the 1947 type has survived for 60 years," he writes.

10. So powerful was the Formica name, in fact, that a downside emerged. It was often applied generically by others to competitive products and the company constantly had to patrol misuse of the trademark.

11. http://www.fundinguniverse.com/company-histories/formica-corporation-history/ (accessed July 2012); *International Directory of Company Histories*, vol. 13 (St. James Press, 1996).

12. George Stalk Jr. and Thomas M. Hout, *Competing against Time* (New York and London, 1990).

13. Brooke Kamin Rapaport and Kevin Stayton, *Vital Forms: American Art in the Atomic Age, 1940−1960* (New York, 2001).

14. Debra Sparks, "How Formica Got Burned Out by Buyouts," *Business Week* (March 22, 1999).

15. Paul Goldsmith, *Fletchers: A Centennial History of Fletcher Building* (Auckland, 2009).

16. The Formica laminate plant in Australia was in Thornleigh, a suburb of Sydney. It was closed in December 1998 following a decision to consolidate Australian and New Zealand volumes in the more modern Papakura plant, outside Auckland. The last press load at the Thornleigh plant was ceremonially scheduled to run exactly forty years to the day after the first press load.

17. Since 1964, the textured plate has been a critical element to keep Formica laminates ahead of competition and to afford design variety and innovations. The plates are etched by specialized craftsmen to produce textures that echo natural forms or geometric patterns. They are treated carefully, because a scratched plate must be ground down and repaired, demanding hours of labor.

1960 Ad. Image courtesy Regina Porter.

ALEXANDRA LANGE

THE GLAMOUR OF UTILITY
FORMICA® LAMINATE, DESIGN AND LUXURY

Gold! 1959 will be the year of the modern gold rush. Sequin gold flecks set into the pastel background colors of Formica will put gold into the surfaces of thousands of American homes and into the pockets of the fabricators and builders who use Formica Sequin.

Formica Corporation promotion, 1959

What is luxury? Is it rosewood and leather, silk and lacquer, gold leaf and silver? Or is it the freedom from the cost of installing and maintaining these fine natural materials, the off-limits living room, the war against fingerprints, the battle against tarnish? From its earliest adoption by designers in the 1930s, Formica® laminate offered its users the luxury of time: ease of upkeep, durability, practicality—and, together with synthetic contemporaries such as vinyl, nylon, and melamine, the look of traditional luxury materials at a fraction of the price.

"Sequin," introduced in 1952, presented an ideal solution to the seemingly contradictory aesthetic goals of luxury and utility by incorporating a precious metal into a product most often

seen in suburban kitchens and roadside diners, and thus adding sparkle to everyday tasks such as making lunch. This 1959 Sequin promotion introduces eight new pastel colors backing the irregular gold flecks, following fashion trends and consumer feedback that softer hues were more adaptable. Baby pink and aqua were, in their own way, as luxurious as gold: no longer were hotels and hostesses limited to dark colors that would not show wear. Celadon could be as tough as black.

Design historian Grace Jeffers has written of Formica laminate and its competitors: "Decorative plastic laminate can be seen as a marriage between modernism and the mundane, where modernist concerns for form and function are inextricably linked with popular decoration. Unlike wallpaper, which is jewelry for a wall, laminate is armor."[1] Modern architects and designers were constantly in search of new multifunctional and industrial materials that were beautiful all on their own, such as bicycle tubing or bent plywood. Formica laminate, often combined with those materials in the early twentieth century, was an ideal candidate for ongoing experiments. It has maintained its place at the forefront of technology and design for the past century by repeatedly rising to the challenges of new transportation, retail, domestic, and industrial demands, and it has morphed from a decorative surface into a structural material—one tough enough to rival Frank Gehry's Guggenheim Bilbao for architectural drama.

Decade by decade through the twentieth century, designers have deployed Formica laminate for both its aesthetic and functional qualities in spectacular environments, in architecture as well as interiors. The malleability of the surface—made of melamine, a thermosetting plastic, which can permeate almost any material—has allowed the product to keep up with trends, while its essential nature, a sandwich of resins and paper, pressed and heated, has remained largely the same. Gold-flecked wallpaper installed in 1959 has long vanished, but aqua Sequin countertops (at least at my grandmother's house) continue to do their job, with nary a burn, stain, or chip.

In the 1930s, Formica laminate moved from its original industrial applications into the studios of modern furniture designers. Initially available only in a few dark colors because chemists had yet to perfect the clear melamine resin required for a light or patterned top surface, the black version turned out to be both an excellent substitute for then-popular lacquer and a symbol of the dawning industrial age. As design historian Jeffrey L. Meikle writes in *American Plastic: A Cultural History*, "American modernists became aware of phenolic laminate as an industrial material reflecting the machine spirit they wanted to convey in custom furniture for Manhattan sophisticates. Although each designer displayed minor personal touches, their work collectively suggested an impersonal precision"; and Austrian-born art deco furniture designer Paul T. Frankl, who began experimenting with a range of plastics in the 1920s, called on his fellow designers "to create a grammar of these new materials" that already spoke "in the vernacular of the twentieth century...the language of invention, of synthesis."[2] Frankl saw, perhaps before the inventors of Formica laminate did, that their product could become more than an imitation—it would become luxurious and symbolic on its own.

One of the first extensive and influential installations of Formica laminate was at Radio City Music Hall in Manhattan, which opened in 1932 with a suite of custom furniture designed by Donald Deskey. Deskey, who had used cork, corrugated iron, and asbestos in window displays for the Franklin Simon department store on Fifth Avenue, later experimented with solid Formica laminate for private clients, even placing it on the walls of philanthropist Abby Aldrich Rockefeller's apartment. But in the lobbies and lounges at Radio City, horizontal surfaces of high-gloss black Formica laminate played a leading role, reflecting the bold murals and wallpapers Deskey commissioned from artists such as Stuart Davis, Yasuo Kuniyoshi, and Henry Billings.[3]

A side table designed for the so-called Nicotine Room has uprights of curved, tubular chrome, reminiscent of some of the contemporaneous Bauhaus experiments with cantilevered tubular-steel chairs but still reflecting art deco sensibilities. The wallpaper in that room, showing the stages of tobacco production, was designed by Deskey himself as an experiment in applying the new aluminum foil from Reynolds for decorative purposes. A decade later, the Formica company would incorporate foil into its product as well, using it as a protective layer underneath the decorative paper to make it resistant to cigarette burns. Deskey's other Radio City Formica laminate designs are combined with polished metal as well, from round tables held up by a triumvirate of shiny columns to sideboards balanced on bentwood half-circles. The reflectivity of the laminate and the metal helped Deskey's experiments with new lighting concepts, including copper and gold-leaf ceilings, linear light fixtures tucked into mirrored corners, and bowl-shaped metallic up-lights. Formica laminate allowed Deskey to incorporate the swankiness of his furniture designs for urbane

1959 "Sequin" sample book, 1959, pattern introduced 1952, Formica Corporation, Cincinnati, Ohio.

private clients into public spaces, and to highlight the theatrical qualities of new materials.

The next Formica laminate innovation widely adopted by designers was "Realwood," introduced in the late 1940s and incorporating a thin sheet of actual wood veneer. Deskey had substituted black Formica laminate for lacquer, but Realwood meant the designer and homeowner did not have to choose between the real thing and an industrial substitute. Realwood was the laminate of choice for the Terrace Plaza Hotel in Cincinnati, Ohio, one of the first modern buildings designed by the legendary American architecture firm Skidmore, Owings & Merrill and completed in 1948. The use of Formica laminate in this important hometown project was an obvious coup. The brick building included two largely windowless department stores at the base and

a slablike hotel beginning at the seventh floor.[4] At the top of the building was the circular Gourmet Restaurant, with a wall of slanted glass windows on one side of the curve and a mural by Joan Miró on the other. Downstairs, in the Skyline Restaurant, the wall decoration was by Saul Steinberg, a caricature of Cincinnati life. Above a grouping of chairs in the eighth-floor lobby hung a mobile by Alexander Calder.

The architects intended the interior design to be as forward-thinking as the architecture and the art, and a period brochure, billed as a "Sight-Seeing Tour," states that the rooms feel as if "you're standing in the living room of a lovely modern home."[5] The use of Formica laminate began at the front desk, which was impressively faced with Realwood to simulate a long row of matched veneers. The wall behind the desk was also covered

1932 Donald Deskey, Nicotine Room, Radio City Music Hall, New York, 1932; Donald Deskey Archive. Cooper-Hewitt, National Design Museum, Smithsonian Institution / Art Resource, NY; Photo: Matt Flynn © Smithsonian Institution.

1932 Donald Deskey, Grand Lounge, Radio City Music Hall, New York, 1932; Donald Deskey Archive. Cooper-Hewitt, National Design Museum, Smithsonian Institution / Art Resource, NY; Photo: Matt Flynn © Smithsonian Institution.

1950 (right) Brooks Stevens, "Skylark" pattern, introduced 1950. Ad from *The Australian Women's Weekly,* October 5, 1960.

in Realwood, with a built-in clock. In the rooms, much of the furniture was built-in, including a studio couch that rolled out into a bed with the flip of a switch, and a drop-down desk camouflaged behind a yellow laminate panel. The movable furniture, manufactured by Thonet, had bentwood arms and legs and black laminate tops. In the bathroom, the architects chose laminate in the brilliant red Linen pattern for the combination sink and vanity. Suites included a view from that vanity through a large window; a mirror was mounted on the countertop with two slender metal legs. The brochure assures the nervous smoker (or perhaps the nervous hotel owner) that all horizontal surfaces are "Beauty Bonded Formica": "On no Formica surface is there a trace of alcohol stain or cigarette burns left by the guests who have preceded you." Luxury, the brochure suggests, is having everything appear brand new.

Initially the company's consumer product line was limited to dark colors and motifs that simulated wood grain and marble. But after perfecting the use of melamine resin for a clear, decorative top surface in 1938, the company was ready to expand into the consumer market. Visually brilliant advertisements placed in magazines such as *Architectural Record, Good Housekeeping*, and *House Beautiful* showed designers and homeowners what Formica laminate could do.[6] As part of this marketing effort, the company also hired its first outside design consultant, Milwaukee-based industrial designer Brooks Stevens, a founding member of the Industrial Design Society of America and best known for his work on boats, trains, and cars. He consulted the company as it developed Realwood, and he came to believe that it was "ridiculous" to use a forest product when a photographic reproduction of wood would suffice.[7] His solution was called "Luxwood" and marketed on its introduction in 1950 as a less expensive, look-alike alternative.

Stevens was also responsible for the company's first graphic invention, the still-iconic "Skylark" pattern introduced in 1950. In *Industrial*

t!

nakers
!

rk

From left to right:
TURQUOISE SKYLARK
TUDOR WHITE SKYLARK
ROSE GREY SKYLARK
LEMON YELLOW SKYLARK
PINK SKYLARK

FORMIC

1948 Skidmore, Owings & Merrill, Lobby of the Terrace Plaza Hotel, Cincinnati, featuring "Realwood"; Ezra Stoller © Esto. All rights reserved.

1948 (right) Skytop Lounge of the Olympian Hiawatha. Designed by Brooks Stevens; Brooks Stevens Archive, Milwaukee Art Museum, Gift of the Brooks Stevens Family and the Milwaukee Institute of Art and Design.

Strength Design: How Brooks Stevens Shaped Your World, design historian and curator Glenn Adamson argues for Skylark as part of a larger modernist infatuation with the amoeba, reflected in Stevens' later iconic logo for Miller Brewing Company and Isamu Noguchi's contemporary glass-topped coffee table.[8] Skylark is the apt result of the Formica's Company's charge to bring the material out of the realm of imitation and into the currents of modern design. The Skylark design is often attributed to better-known industrial designer Raymond Loewy, who followed Stevens as a consultant. But Loewy's office merely recolored Skylark in 1954, when it was also renamed "Boomerang." If Sequin suggested luxury in the late 1950s, Skylark played with the shapes of the dawning atomic age, pointing to Formica laminate's emergent associations with new forms of high-speed travel.

Stevens, who worked for the Formica Company from 1946 to 1952, was designing a set of new trains for the Chicago, Milwaukee, St. Paul, and Pacific Railroad (a.k.a. the Milwaukee Road), known as the Olympian Hiawatha, which traveled from Chicago to the Pacific Northwest. Stevens' firm was responsible for all aspects of the train design, from the creation of a new engine with stacked headlights to an observation lounge with lozenge-shape windows on walls and domed ceiling to the interior fittings and accessories.[9] Much of the latter was done with Formica laminate. Milwaukee Road's traditional colors were harvest orange and royal maroon, the basis for a two-tone stripe on the exterior of the train (maroon above, orange below). Stevens continued the two-tone effect in the interior, substituting a subtler combination of solid gray-green and Realwood paneling in the coaches. In the women's lounge, Realwood was replaced with ivory laminate featuring French costume prints and floral prints inlaid on opposite walls.[10] In the dining car, Formica laminate took the place of wallpaper, with panels in a pale green falling-leaf pattern and matching tabletops. In a drawing room

paneled in Oak Realwood, watercolors of native waterfowl were embedded in the laminate.[11] Stevens' goal was to re-create a detailed home experience on the rails, albeit one for large numbers of families (the Olympian Hiawatha advertisements often featured families and emphasized the train's service to popular vacation spots such as Yellowstone National Park). He told the trade magazine *Plastics Newsfront*: "In the Olympian Hiawatha, bright, cheerful colors and the discreet use of woods and plastics combine to produce a homey interior in contrast to the regimented look of some transportation equipment which, in general, has had a very cold atmosphere, trimmed, as it was, with chromium moldings and bizarre lighting schemes."[12] As at the Terrace Plaza Hotel, Formica laminate allowed designers to create a homelike setting that also happened to be practically bulletproof.

Formica laminate had been used on trains (most notably on General Motors' Train of Tomorrow and the Pennsylvania Railroad's Jeffersonian), but never as extensively and in such an integrated manner. Luxury ocean liners followed suit. White laminate was installed in all the bathrooms of Cunard's *Queen Mary* when it began service in 1936, but the public rooms had actual wood paneling. Loewy, the company's designer from 1954 to 1960, used laminate for paneling, dressers, and tabletops on the refitted SS *Lurline*, which ran between San Francisco and Honolulu from 1948 to 1963. But Cunard's *Queen Elizabeth 2*, in service from 1969 to 2009, was the ocean liner that naval architect Dan Wallace and interior designer Dennis Lennon were able to treat as a total Formica laminate design project, developing a new textured and moldable laminate with the feeling of woven fabric for extensive onboard use. A special publication, "The Formica Scene of the QE2," includes a chart of the dozens of colors, patterns, and finishes used for the project.[13] Among the highlights are a textured floral blue-on-white weave in the ladies' powder rooms, a black-and-white paisley for the

1969 Britannia restaurant (right), Mural, and Theater Bar Foyer (above and upper right), from *The Formica Scene on the QE2*, 1970; INTERIOR DESIGNER Dennis Lennon. Grace Jeffers Collection of Formica Materials, Archives Center, National Museum of American History, Smithsonian Institution.

1964 Brochure introducing the
Formica World's Fair House
logo. Grace Jeffers Collection of
Formica Materials, Archives Center,
National Museum of American
History, Smithsonian Institution.

men's, hounds-tooth check in the showers and toilets, and a number of custom laminate murals for the nightclub, coffee shop, and children's room.

On the *QE2* a supergraphic theme prevails, one that references both the painted murals of the early 1960s by Barbara Stauffacher Solomon for Sea Ranch in northern California and the groovy animation of the Beatles' *Yellow Submarine* of 1968. In the Theater Bar Foyer is a wall of nautical pennants in red, blue, and gold in suede-finish Formica laminate and picking up on the red upholstery of a set of Bertoia Diamond chairs. In the Britannia restaurant, laminate seats with a postformed or rolled edge are upholstered in orange to match a set of orange laminate-trimmed niches. A black-and-white figurative mural designed by students at London's Royal College of Art was reproduced in Formica laminate and lines the long hallway between two of the casual restaurants. In the guest rooms the color is more restrained, but the new curved laminates are used for tabletops and dresser drawers, eliminating sharp edges in the small cabins. On the Hiawatha trains Stevens was going for homey, while Dennis Lennon, almost twenty years later, was pushing the limits of plastic, trying to eliminate as many joins and additional materials to make the whole ship into a low-maintenance work of art.

While Formica laminate made its way across America and the world glamorizing travel, it also had a huge effect on the American home. The question of labor was as important to the housewife and contractor as to the train operator, and Formica Corporation's advertisements in magazines appealed to the homemaker and the home renovator, suggesting that the product made keeping up appearances a breeze (one mid-century advertisement shows a young mother serving dinner in a strapless New Look dress) and improving your home just as easy. A high point for Formica Corporation was the World's Fair House at the 1964 World's Fair, held at Flushing Meadows in Queens, New York.[14] The house was designed by Emil A. Schmidlin, a New

1964–1965 Breakfast room, from "World's Fair House; Book of Home Styling Ideas." Formica Corporation, Cincinnati, Ohio, 1964.

1964–1965 Girl's Room, from "World's Fair House; Book of Home Styling Ideas." Formica Corporation, Cincinnati, Ohio, 1964.

Jersey architect who was among the first to build split-level houses in that state as well as a number of exposition homes. The house was long and low, with a hipped roof, recessed front door, and long rows of vertical windows. Neither interior nor exterior was designed to shock, because the main function was to show that the house of the present could be thoroughly rendered in Formica brand laminate.

As for the appliances Stevens, Loewy, and other industrial designers had been redesigning, the dream was of maintenance-free beauty, and the house shows a strikingly gendered world, its high-tech improvements built into the surfaces. As architectural historian Rosemarie Haag Bletter writes in *Remembering the Future*: "The boy's room of the Formica House had a desk, a great place to call his 'turf' but also an incentive to homework…in a room that's youthful and male in every detail."[15] Details included Formica wood laminate walls and furniture, a bunk bed with supports reminiscent of the *beton brut* architecture of Brasilia, and a storage cupboard faced with decorative panels in a geometric "Navajo" motif. "In the girl's room," Bletter writes, "with pink wall paneling, there were 'compact ready-made units windows [that] convert to supports for sewing machine, typewriter, small ironing board.'" The girl's cupboard featured front panels with large pink flowers, which opened to reveal mirrored shelves and a baby-pink interior. The walls were also paneled in pink Formica laminate with raspberry splines.

The kitchen was a color-coordinated command center with avocado counters, cupboards faced in birch bark "textured" green and white, and curtains and decorative doors with botanical patterns. There were double electric ovens and a built-in laundry center, a pull-out cutting board, and a breakfast room with Saarinenesque pedestal furniture and matching Melmac plates. But the real futurism occurred in a little green nook, fitted with drawers and a white phone.

DON'T J

WORL

W

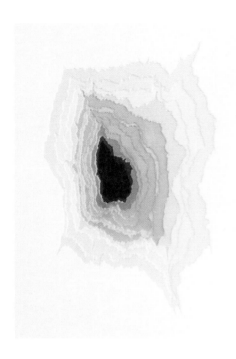

The compact office, tucked into an out-of-the-way corner of the kitchen, took up no more space than a pantry closet but controls the entire house. Here menus were planned, groceries ordered, and bills and files kept orderly. With a house-wide Miami-Carey intercom system, it was possible to answer the front door or speak to members of the family in any of the various rooms without leaving the desk.[16]

Such kitchen-office spaces are now commonplace, as are intercoms, but the house showed Formica laminate as a product that added richness to home life by making household tasks more efficient. An essay by Raymond Loewy and partner William Snaith in Formica Corporation's commemorative World's Fair book offers tricks of the trade for choosing colors. One of the Loewy firm's major contributions was updating the palette to reflect contemporary color choices, as well as adding a number of new patterns that suggested exoticism and travel (the most popular, Capri, resembles an irregular mosaic of island

tiles). At the World's Fair House, every room seems set up for crafts and games, entertaining, and family time. The work of domestic life is acknowledged, but the utility spaces are made luxurious with pattern. As the copy says, "all the work places became beautiful rooms."[17]

In the 1970s, Formica Corporation formed its Design Advisory Board (DAB), with a group of influential interior designers and architects tasked to bring Formica laminate into the present day. As Susan Grant Lewin writes in *Formica & Design: From the Counter Top to High Art*, "'Synthetic' and 'man-made' lost the promise they had held at Formica Corporation's 1964 World's Fair House, when Formica laminate seemed the ideal material to surface the world, almost universal in its appeal."[18] The DAB recommended that the company stop trying to imitate natural materials and instead celebrate its synthetic nature. The Design Concepts Collection included high gloss and matte laminates with geometric grids, diagonals, and squares, tougher and more graphic than previous patterns. They also pushed for a brand-new product, eventually named ColorCore®, which had been delayed in product development. ColorCore laminate featured solid color, eliminating the dark line around the edge of the traditional countertop. To promote ColorCore laminate among the new generation of designers, Formica Corporation embarked on collaborations with architects. The first, the 1983 exhibition *Surface + Ornament*, featured a range of projects. These included Frank Gehry's Fish Lamp, constructed of ColorCore laminate torn into "fish scales" and lit from within, revealing the material's translucency. Another one was the architecture firm SITE's *Door,* which used layers of shattered ColorCore laminate to achieve the trompe l'oeil effect of a hole blasted through a solid door. These projects suggested a new design currency and emphasized ColorCore's suitability for three-dimensional, highly colored and patterned installations. The exhibition was so successful that it traveled internationally, tracing the path of Formica Corporation's own distribution

1983 SITE (James Wines and Alison Sky), *Door*, ColorCore® laminate, porcelain door knob, brass hinges. Formica Corporation, Cincinnati, Ohio.

2012–2013 Frank Gehry, *Untitled (Los Angeles III)*, 2012 version of Fish Lamp, metal wire, Formica® ColorCore® laminate, and silicone, © Frank Gehry. Courtesy of the Artist and Gagosian Gallery. Photograph by Benjamin Lee Ritchie Handler.

1983 Lee Payne, Neapolitan, ColorCore® laminate.

2007 Daniel Buren, The Red Arches/
Arcos Rojos, Bilbao, Spain, using
Formica® Exterior grade Compact
panel, Formica Group, Europe.-
PHOTOGRAPHER Jorge Flores.

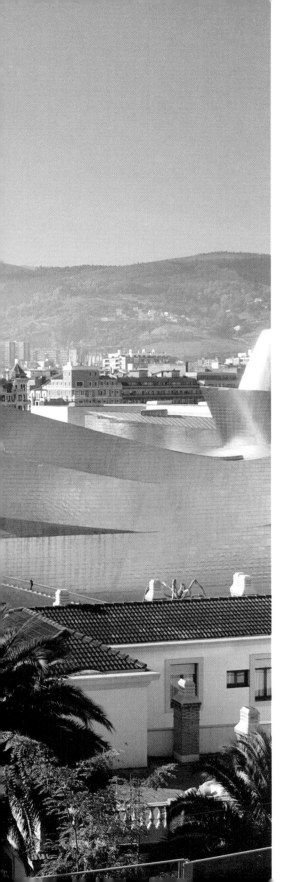

networks and adding architects and designers in every location. The show eventually included Eva Jiřičná and Rodney Kinsman in Britain, and Arata Isozaki and Shiro Kuramata in Japan before it finished its five-year tour in Singapore.[19]

The same year, the company and *Interiors* magazine commissioned a three-dimensional exhibition project featuring its new product. Industrial designer Michael McCoy used ColorCore laminate in a themed office for an aerospace industry executive. An article in *Interiors* reports on the result, "McCoy…appropriately proposes the office as machine, an aesthetic that communicates a certain imagery about the activities that take place there. The dynamism of the office as machine implies that the inhabitant is not static."[20] Eschewing the neutrality of the traditional workspace, McCoy's conference table top, fabricated of ColorCore laminate, looks like a runway. More yellow stripes mark the handles on closet doors, and a line of pivoting panels, faced in red and green high-gloss laminate and shaped like ailerons, divides the desk and seating area. Black textured carpet and black leather furniture set off the bright colors of the laminate, turning it into the graphic highlight rather than a supporting player. The Formica laminate elements might almost be prototypes for some future spacecraft, so that the office becomes a showroom for the machine as well as a low-maintenance, high-impact machine for working. The utility here is obvious: ColorCore laminate is a flexible, sculptural material, one that eliminates the traditional two-dimensional quality of high-pressure laminate. The luxury is in the project's futurism: Formica laminate has moved beyond the surface of the earth and is still aesthetically and functionally relevant to the next generation of craft.

In 1997, Formica laminate again starred in an installation that bridged art, entertainment, and hospitality. Artist Damien Hirst worked with designer Mike Rundell on the refurbishment of the Pharmacy restaurant in Notting Hill, London, outfitting it to resemble a working drug store.

White molded-plastic Jasper Morrison chairs and laminate-topped tables were set in a room lined with glass-fronted white laminate cupboards, with real medicine boxes and surgical instruments inside.[21] The bar stools were shaped like aspirin. Hirst's use of Formica laminate in this public setting recalls its ubiquity in real drug stores and pharmacies, as well as the bathrooms where we often take pills. But in choosing stark white Formica laminate, Hirst accentuated its cleanliness and toughness (what else could survive night after night of restaurant patrons), while making it glamorous through the use of neon lights. Ultimately, it was a perverse idea for a theme restaurant, and after initial notoriety, the partnership soured. When the restaurant closed in 2003, Hirst's designs, including the medicine cabinets, sold for millions at a Sotheby's auction and are now part of the Tate Modern's permanent museum collection. Hirst took Formica brand laminate from High Street to high art.

Another artist turned to Formica laminate for the Red Arches project in Bilbao, the company's longtime home in Spain. As part of the tenth anniversary celebrations for architect and Formica company's collaborator Frank Gehry's much-admired Guggenheim Bilbao, the museum commissioned from artist Daniel Buren a site-specific work for the city's La Salve Bridge.[22] Buren felt the existing steel arch distorted the relationship between the bridge and the museum, which "embraces" its span with an armlike building and a stone tower. Resurfacing the bridge in red, with a series of the artist's signature black-and-white stripes along the exposed edge, would better link the green of the bridge span, the iridescent titanium scales of the museum, and the new arch. In 2007, Buren's scheme was built and named Red Arches/Arcos Rojos. The material chosen to create the red arch was Formica Exterior grade Compact panel, selected because of its stiffness, color-fastness, and resistance to water. The red, black, and white surfaces are actually a cover placed over the bridge's existing structure; the art installation

had to leave the existing steel structure untouched. Buren had originally planned to use a synthetic, tentlike textile to create this effect, but Formica's exterior product proved to be more durable and equally spectacular.

In 2008, the Formica company launched a new collaboration with architects, asking ten with ties to Cincinnati to design a limited edition piece of furniture using ColorCore2™ laminate, Compact structural laminate, or solid surfacing materials. The results were shown at Cincinnati's Contemporary Arts Center in an exhibition called *Form: Contemporary Architects at Play*. Zaha Hadid's "Cirrus," which echoes the forms of the building, used layers of black Formica laminate to create a seating piece that combined wall, bench, and ramp. Other architects in the exhibition, which traveled internationally, included Peter Eisenman, Michael Graves, Thom Mayne of Morphosis, and Laurinda Spear of Arquitectonica. Mayne's contribution took the form of a scissoring bench in Arctic Solid Surfacing material, while Spear took a more organic approach. Her "Treeleaf" triangular bench, in lime, Spectrum Yellow, and Organic Green, suggests traditional woven furniture—or midcentury Italian designer Franco Albini's popular rattan poufs—despite its superior material strength.

Grace Jeffers wrote that wallpaper was jewelry, Formica armor, but in recent years, as contemporary architects and designers again embrace color, pattern, and ornament, Formica laminate has been used as both. At Seville's Gran Meliá Colón Hotel, guestrooms have accent walls of Damask-pattern screen-printed laminate in silver and black, while the doors feature custom prints of Spanish old master paintings (Are you staying in El Greco or Velázquez?).[23] For a boutique of the French perfume house Diptyque at the Liberty of London department store, design studio Special Projekt specified laser-cut laminate in five colors to create a three-dimensional patterned screen inspired by Diptyque's classic "Choriambe" fabric design. On the reverse was printed one of Liberty's iconic botanical patterns, with hundreds of laser-cut

2008 (below) *Typogram*, Bernard Tschumi, ColorCore 2™ laminate by Formica Group. (right) *Chair #1*, Peter Eisenman, Formica® Solid Surfacing. (bottom) *TransFormica*, Bill Pedersen, Formica® Solid Surfacing.

From *Form: Contemporary Architects at Play*. Tony Walsh Photography, courtesy Contemporary Arts Center, Cincinnati, Ohio.

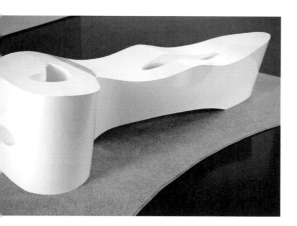

2009 (top) Boscombe Beach Huts, Bournemouth, U.K. Formica® Impress Laminate. DESIGNER Hemingway Design.

2009 Gran Meliá Colón Hotel, Seville, Spain. Formica® Bespoke Laminate. DESIGNER Agustin Diaz Giner.

2010 Diptyque/Liberty, London. Formica® Bespoke and High Pressure Laminate (HPL). DESIGNER Special Projekt.

peepholes allowing a view through the screens onto a mirrored back wall.[24] Finally, in Boscombe, Bournemouth, new "Beach Pods" use patterns created by Hemingway Design that offer an update on Skylark, with turquoise and orange backgrounds and stylized drawings of fish and seaside.[25] In the resort's main building, the changing rooms feature laminate stripes in magenta, clementine, and sea blue.

As a company, Formica Group is investing in design research, creating workshops with young designers to ask new questions about the limits of laminate. Should a surface be perforated, open, transparent, or translucent? Should a surface become the support system? Should it be made of virgin or reclaimed materials?[26] At the beginning of the twentieth century, Formica laminate took the form of a stiff, shiny, dark surface, and yet designers such as Donald Deskey found it inspirational. Over the course of the last century, new layers, dimensions, textures, and cores have been added to that pioneering product, and at every turn, designers and architects have incorporated those technological developments into interiors for new industries. There is every reason to think that the sparkle and function of Sequin can be brought into the twenty-first century, as Formica laminate adds new layers of reflectivity, transparency, and sustainability.

Notes

Formica® is the registered trademark of The Diller Corporation. ColorCore2™ is a trademark of The Diller Corporation. Reference to Formica company or business refers to Formica Group, or its predecessor companies. Formica Group is a global group of companies consisting of Formica Canada, Inc., Formica Corporation, Formica de Mexico S.A. de C.V., Formica IKI Oy, Formica Limited, Formica S.A., Formica S.A.S., Formica Taiwan Corporation, Formica (Thailand) Co., Ltd., and Formica (Asia) Ltd., among others.

1. Grace Jeffers, "Machine Made Natural: The Decorative Products of the Formica Corporation, 1947–1962," Master's thesis, Bard Graduate Center for Studies in the Decorative Arts, 1998, 3.

2. Jeffrey L. Meikle, *American Plastic: A Cultural History* (New Brunswick, NJ, 1995), 108.

3. David A. Hanks with Jennifer Toher, *Donald Deskey: Decorative Designs and Interiors* (New York, 1987), 100–108.

4. Nicholas Adams, *Skidmore, Owings & Merrill: The Experiment since 1936* (Milan, 2007), 58–63.

5. "Your Formica Sight Seeing Tour Through Cincinnati's New Terrace Plaza Hotel," Formica advertising brochure, 1948.

6. Jeffers 1998, 30.

7. Glenn Adamson, *Industrial Strength Design: How Brooks Stevens Shaped Your World* (Milwaukee Art Museum, Milwaukee, 2003), 111.

8. Adamson 2003, 112–113.

9. Adamson 2003, 18–19.

10. "Olympian Hiawatha," *Plastics Newsfront* 2 (October 1947): 4–7.

11. "How Good Can a Train Be?" *This Formica World* (Fourth Quarter 1949): 10–11, 14.

12. "Olympian Hiawatha," 7.

13. "The Formica Scene on the QE2," 1969.

14. *The World's Fair House: Book of Home Styling Ideas* (Formica Corporation, Cincinnati, 1964).

15. Rosemarie Haag Bletter, "The 'Laissez-Fair,' Good Taste, and Money Trees: Architecture at the Fair," in *Remembering the Future: The New York World's Fair from 1939 to 1964* (New York, 1989), 132.

16. The *World's Fair House*, 22.

17. The *World's Fair House*, 24.

18. Susan Grant Lewin, *Formica & Design* (New York [1988], 1991), 146.

19. Lewin 1991, 150–151.

20. Maeve Slavin, "Interiors Initiative: Hypermodern," *Interiors* (May 1983): 153–161.

21. "Pharmacy Restaurant in London," *Domus* 806 (July–August 1998): 44–50.

22. http://www.guggenheim.org/bilbao/406-homepage/355-also-of-interest, accessed July 10, 2012.

23. http://www.formica.eu/pdf/case_studies/hotel_colon.pdf, accessed July 10, 2012.

24. http://www.formica.eu/pdf/case_studies/retail_diptyque.pdf, accessed July 10, 2012.

25. http://www.formica.eu/pdf/case_studies/leisure_boscome.pdf, accessed July 10, 2012.

26. Renee Hytry Derrington, "Laminate Design Competitions," PowerPoint2011.

1954 Ad, "Formica Makes News in the Package Kitchen" for builders' trade magazines. Grace Jeffers Collection of Formica Materials, Archives Center, National Museum of American History, Smithsonian Institution.

PETER YORK

TOWARD A WIPE-CLEAN WORLD FORMICA® BRAND IN CONTEXT

What you don't see in gloriously photographed eighteenth-century re-creations such as Stanley Kubrick's 1975 film *Barry Lyndon,* with its lovely dappled candlelight, is the wildlife—the jumping fleas in the towering wigs and the other stuff. The authentic period thing you miss in the Palace of Versaille's magnificently maintained Hall of Mirrors is the smell. Contemporaries reported an odor of ammonia around the splendor, the scent of seventeenth-century aristocrats who did not have what we know as basic amenities.

It's just as well that really sharp color photography became widely available only when it did, because otherwise dirt would have been visible everywhere. You actually do see the dirt in early photographs of, say, 1890s slum children—their faces are streaked with it; and you can guess it in all those fern-cluttered, chenille-draped petit-bourgeois interiors.

Students of social change will remember that magical injunction in nineteenth-century and early twentieth-century novels and home decoration books to buy dark fabrics and surfaces that don't show the dirt. That meant chocolate, dark

red, and dark green paint, "burgundy"-colored fabrics, and early linoleum imitating dark wood. Dirt was everywhere. It came from open fires, oil lamps, outdoor smoke, from muddy boots, and from cooking from scratch and all the mess it generates. The world was without detergents, deodorants, or effective dry-cleaning. The ideology and aesthetic that marks the difference between the Old and New Worlds is the ideal of a clean world. Among a host of post–World War I innovations in surfaces and cleaners, the outstanding "miracle surface," for its combination of functionality and design potential, is Formica® laminate.[1] Think of the roll-out of popular modern design (what Thomas Hine so brilliantly called "Populuxe") from the USA to the rest of the West and then to the world, and you think of houses, diners, cinemas, and airplanes made smooth and shiny—and wildly decorated—with Formica brand surfaces.

Of course, as you moved up the class scale of late nineteenth-century Britain and America, people tried their best; an increasing army of underpaid housemaids spent hours laying fires,

1950 Formica brand label. Grace Jeffers Collection of Formica Materials, Archives Center, National Museum of American History, Smithsonian Institution.

1960s (right) Kitchen decorated with Formica laminates in patterns, wood grains, and solid colors. From *Formica & Design; From the Counter Top to High Art*, by Susan Grant Lewin, 1991.

washing clothes, and polishing floors — and scrubbing pine kitchen tables. Just like all the other traditional kitchen and scullery surfaces — floors and countertops — these wooden tables have those wonderful authentic, organic, deeply natural qualities of porosity, perviousness, and absorbency (and resolutely plain looks). They are, in other words, the exact opposite of Formica laminate with its "No Entry" message to everything from food to babies and dogs — and yet, by contrast, its extreme design versatility. The old traditional surfaces retained, absorbed, and positively clung to every kind of organic matter; they took it, and its smell, unto them and into them. Dirt, as we all know, is matter out of place — mud from unpaved roads, subtly worked into respectable ladies' hems. The past was filthy, not least because everything was so difficult to clean. There was congealed wax on floor boards; there were sticky brown patches on ceilings from oil lamps, pipes, and cigarettes. Dirt was an integral part of traditional interior decoration.

It's not surprising that the nineteenth-century fight against dirt found its strongest and longest-lasting chapter in the United States. There it took on that fascinating American combination of proselytizing and popular consumer science. It was ancient and modern. The build-up included the constant quotation of the old Hebrew proverb "Cleanliness is next to godliness," first recycled by Francis Bacon, then by the globally influential preacher John Wesley, and on to a thousand nineteenth-century American pulpits and hundreds of books telling American middle-class housewives how to live healthier, more fragrant, and altogether godlier lives. The dream was a world where everything was washable — and constantly washed.

There were substantive innovations — better toilets, branded soaps, enameled kitchen surfaces — in the second half of the nineteenth and the early twentieth century. (Primeval, labor-intensive washing machines for the rich were available by the turn of the century too.) The rhetoric

and the aesthetic of cleanliness ("sweetness and light," "sunlight and fresh air") were building, following popular science from bugs to bacteria, creating anxieties and expectations in the emerging American middle class. It was a group growing rapidly to include a host of new sectors and occupations—every sort of clerk, shop assistant, and trained artisan, people working in the new technologies of the telephone and the telegraph, an expanding world.

Most late nineteenth-century domestic surfaces, floors, walls, and furniture, remained stubbornly natural and porous well into the twentieth century. The late nineteenth century had produced varnished wallpapers for halls and kitchens, imitating tiles and mosaics. But they were relatively expensive and difficult to hang, while other wallpapers remained hugely susceptible to smudging and staining, which explained the dense popular patterns featuring dots and ornamentation, and the dark colors.

A kitchen or bathroom positively sheathed in marble, mosaic, or, more modestly, tile was the mark of the plutocratic and even established middle-class American house. Yet these traditional surfaces were costly, heavy, and difficult to install. The "sweetness and light" disciples had urged women, in books and magazines, to replace "unhygienic" wallpaper with fresh paint in light colors. But prewar paint technology—preplastics, based on natural ingredients—meant products that were not easily applied by amateurs (the great DIY explosion was postwar too, driven by new products, mass marketing, and extensive media coverage). In most instances paints were as porous and easily scuffed as wallpaper.

The real wipe-clean world that we know only came together after World War II. It needed a host of substantive innovation, a new level of communication, and real social change first. The expectations were there, the rich already had some of the tools—and certainly the available labor—but the mass "miracle" products hadn't arrived yet.

A great driver toward the eternal sunshine of a spotless world was media innovation. It allowed increasing audiences in the U.S., the U.K., and Europe to see how the other half really lived, and it allowed advertisers to demonstrate what a perfect world might look like. Color movies, growing through the 1930s, became mainstream in postwar Hollywood, showing interiors that were moving from hazy escapist dream-sequences to instructive guides. Postwar television, with its family-based soap operas and sitcoms, was a basic course in the domestic side of the American Dream. A stack of mass-audience magazines—general family titles such as *Life* or *The Saturday Evening Post*—and the growing group of home decorating magazines such as *House Beautiful* and *House and Garden*—all at their highest-ever circulations in the 1950s and 1960s—showed the Good Life and perfect houses in living color. The initial magazine assault, imperfect color but a mass of consumer advertising for "hygienic" and allegedly easy-to-use cleaning products, had started early in the twentieth century. By the 1920s, American radio, overwhelmingly commercial, unlike radio in the U.K. and Europe, was urging women to wash and clean on a constant basis. Radio drama gave the U.S. the first "soap operas" with mass audiences for housewife serials such as *Ma Perkins* and *Big Sister*, sponsored by the producers of packaged laundry soaps made by corporate giants such as the Proctor & Gamble Company (P&G) and Lever Brothers.

Postwar social change extended the Western world's middle class even further, particularly in America, as a group of better-paid unionized industrial workers reached middle-class status in the American sense of income, consumption, and expectations. The great postwar growth of suburban residential development moved millions of these people from inner-city houses and apartments in nineteenth-century developments out to a new life in a new town (architectural critics said these developers' suburbs weren't really

1957–1958 Ad from *Home Modernizing*, Edition 12.

towns at all). But a new house meant a new start; nearly 2 million were built between 1945 and 1950 in the United States alone. A round of credit-based refurnishing followed and a new round of neighborly competition with the Joneses—traditional communities and extended families had been altogether more forgiving. Postwar new suburban life focused on the nuclear family and the home, and on the housewife's role as its guardian.

Persistent advertising had told postwar women that dirt and germs lurked everywhere, on them and in their houses, and that they would be judged for their housekeeping efforts. But now help, absolute and effective help, was at hand. Lifetime exposure to media and advertising had shown what "Good" looked like. A chorus of beautiful models (often, inexplicably, in evening dresses and long evening gloves) had pointed at picture-perfect kitchens and living rooms, immaculately set dining tables, and manicured outdoor space. By then—by the mid-1950s, when practically everything seemed to be new—a deluge of miracle products meant it was all achievable.

Some miracles were real postwar wonders; others had been in development earlier. The dates that matter are those of mass-marketing, when an innovation becomes understandable, accessible, and affordable, when it has the distribution and branding momentum of a giant corporation, one that reaches everyone. In the postwar world, but especially in the first truly consumer-driven society, the United States, domestic miracles arrived on a constant basis in the 1950s. New surfaces were not only colorful and extravagantly patterned, they were sealed, glazed, plasticized. They were overwhelmingly impervious, nonporous, and resistant by right, almost by law. Taken together, they made for a world of easy maintenance.

Paint technology changed after the war, from traditional oil-based paints and "distempers" to new plastic paints; they were easier to apply and dried much faster, suiting the DIY painter. They were also overwhelmingly tougher and easier

1950s Formica twin vanity.

c. 1940 Ad, "Quit worrying! We'll put on a new [counter] top."

(both images) Grace Jeffers Collection of Formica Materials, Archives Center, National Museum of American History, Smithsonian Institution.

So you Think Your Sink is Sunk?

So your sink top's curled and rotted?

So you think a new top costs a lot?

Quit Worrying!

to clean. Plasticized flat or matte paint could be washed. So too could vinyl flooring, lighter, cheaper, and easier to lay than traditional solid linoleum and far tougher than the cheaper "painted" kind—and amazingly easy to clean. Another 1950s miracle were the new plastic sealants for real wood floors—the "sand-and-seal" easy-living recipe was a staple of young, middle-class, domestic home improvement in the 1960s. "Real" wood, generously plasticized, kept its color—often a glowing orange—for years, didn't need polishing, and could be washed just like a vinyl floor.

Furniture, televisions, and stereo sets also adopted a new glossy finish in the 1960s. Large television consoles and living-room music equipment had traditionally been surfaced in wood veneers with fragile varnishes that degraded over time. The new miracle hard polyurethane varnish was astonishingly thick, shiny, and durable, and the television set became somehow immortalized in this new amber—and, of course, extremely easy to clean; wiping it left it glowing. Polyester paints achieved a similar effect on the upright panels of some new furniture—wardrobes, kitchen doors, and drawers. Shiny as lacquer, it made new furniture look really new. And wipe-clean.

But the most durable and democratic of these new miracle surfaces was Formica®, the leading plastic laminate brand. Formica laminate was more than just a finish. It was a material in its own right, with a huge range of proprietary colors and patterns, a problem-solver for the most symbolically important surfaces in the consciously modern 1950s house, the kitchen countertops and the kitchen table, the setting of all those soap-opera family gatherings—"the heart of the home."

Formica laminate achieved a philosopher's-stone miracle among modern materials. Like textiles or paper—it was, after all, based on Kraft paper—it was capable of accommodating an extraordinary range of designs, later even including textures. It was also hard, smooth, stable, and completely, glowingly impervious. It was *the*

wipe-clean material, and it became the global symbol of the coming easy-maintenance world.

Formica laminate started just before World War I in an industrial application as a substitute for mica in electrical insulation, and then developed, slowly at first, as a sheet material with domestic and other applications. Hard, shiny, and potentially very decorative, it was used as paneling by pioneering designers fitting out important new spaces—the ocean liner RMS *Queen Mary*, Radio City Music Hall—and it was part of aspirational domestic "town of tomorrow" settings such as the 1939 World's Fair. But it took a postwar building boom to see it ensconced in a majority of new American homes.

From the mid-1950s on, as American popular design became more colorful and more audaciously patterned, and as kitchens in particular became more integrated, designed, and fashion-focused, the Formica brand too gained a larger share of the expenditures related to the home. Several Formica laminate patterns could create the fashionable two-tone look in the kitchen—one for the tabletop, another for the cabinets, and even a third—often a wood effect—for the walls. As the built-in kitchen became a universal in the United States (the United Kingdom and Europe took longer), from the mid-1950s on, decorative effects took on a larger role (the basics changed relatively little until the 1990s).

"Wipe-clean" combined a moral injunction with an aesthetic of progress. It was the world view of a generation that had survived the Depression, the inner city, and the reality of all those natural-organic-authentic materials and surfaces. Like rural peasants escaping to the modern world, they weren't remotely sentimental about what they'd left behind. DuPont, the giant chemical company that initially pioneered miracle products such as nylon, Teflon® brand polymers, and later Lycra® brand synthetic fibers, said in its corporate motto, "Better things for better living… through chemistry." Its rival Monsanto, advertising

1959 Ad from *Home Modernizing Guide*, Fall/Winter; FORMICA SURFACES Blue Color Grain 14-CW-38 and Fruitwood Picwood 19-CR-27. Cabinets by Youngstown Kitchens.

its acrylic fiber in carpets, said, "It isn't what you think, it's something better."

While the intelligentsia condemned plastics for imitating everything from marble to lacquer, for replacing the old "authentic" materials with new factory-fresh surfaces, an overwhelming majority of Americans took them into their hearts and their homes. The kitchen table, clad with Formica laminate, for instance, is a shared memory for baby-boomer Americans right across all income levels (and for their British contemporaries too). Andy Warhol famously said, "What's great about this country is that America started the tradition where the richest consumers buy essentially the same things as the poorest. You can be watching TV and see Coca-Cola, and you know that the President drinks Coke, Liz Taylor drinks Coke, and just think, you can drink Coke, too. A Coke is a Coke and no amount of money can get you a better Coke...."[2]

The Formica-laminate topped table has that same democratic universality. The 1950s urge to clad as many surfaces as possible in Formica laminate was only partly driven by the company's marketing. Any reading of the postwar zeitgeist—popular DIY magazines, for instance—suggests that consumers were thinking up new ways to replace every old surface with something new that signaled modernity (not modernism, a strict, uptight, self-denying monastic modernity, but a more demotic celebratory sort) and cleanliness. In Britain, the 1950s television DIY guru, Barry Bucknell, showed viewers how to update their houses with hardboard. Paneled internal doors and other elaborate joinery could be transformed—made clean and modern at modest cost with minimal skills—by applying hardboard panels that would offer the New Look. Flush doors and smooth, built-in wardrobes helped the owners and tenants of battered old houses to wipe away the past. Over the next decade millions of Britons moved into new homes and apartments where modernity was the norm and where light, in the form of picture windows and wrap-around

glazing of all kinds, defined the contrast from dark old houses. More natural light and more artificial light, in houses with new wiring or rewired for electricity, made for more demanding environments where everything had to be newer and cleaner. Smooth, bright, shiny surfaces that wiped clean became a global obsession. By applying them almost everywhere, postwar homeowners—born in the 1920s and 1930s—could wipe out the horrors of the recent past and mark their participation in the modern mainstream—they could "Live the Dream."

Once sheathed in Formica laminate, a surface seemed to become as clean and godly as a sanatorium, but as cheerful as a diner. The universal American diner was part of the imagery of everyday America that attracted European immigrants. The idea that ordinary Americans—the people they could become—enjoyed these standards as their right was utterly compelling. In Britain a whole new generation of pre-Starbucks independent cafés and coffee bars responded to those yearnings. They were covered in cheerful Formica laminate surfaces—the surviving ones, now part of a sort of heritage trail, are usually called the Formica Cafés—with linoleum floors and sometimes new Italian coffee machines.

Along with the hardware of this emerging wipe-clean world, with its smooth surfaces under picture windows, its expressive patterns, and its popular aesthetic consensus, came a raft of other new miracles—cleaning, wiping miracles. Proctor & Gamble's Mr. Clean® brand of household cleaners, developed in 1957 from an invention the Procter & Gamble Company acquired from a business that cleaned ships, was a dedicated miracle for tough cleaning of new hard surfaces in the Ideal Home. Mr. Clean had amazing qualities; it cut hardened grease in a really aggressive way. Unlike laundry detergents, it didn't foam and it didn't need rinsing. As claimed in early advertising, it "cut cleaning time in half." It cleaned surfaces that simply weren't washed or wiped before, walls and woodwork—now covered in

Notes on Easy Formica Care!

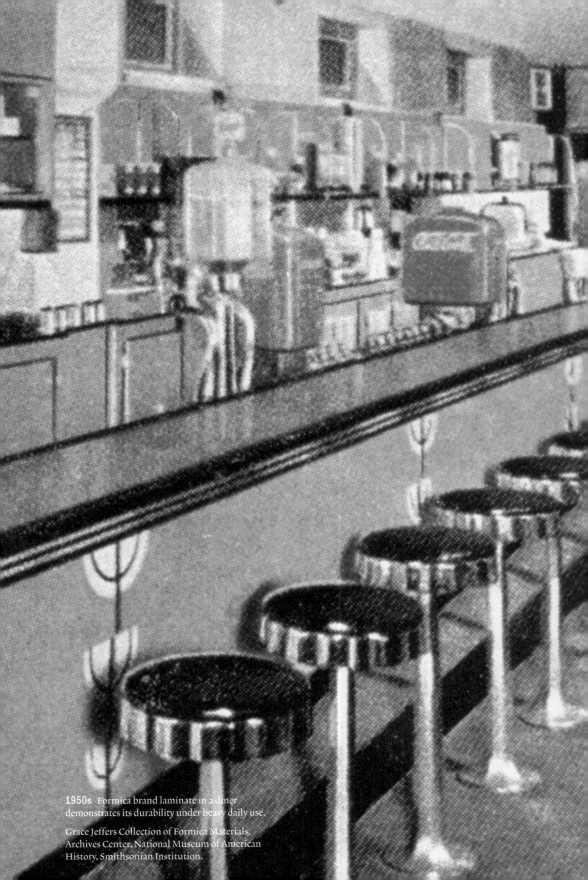

1950s Formica brand laminate in a diner
demonstrates its durability under heavy daily use.

Grace Jeffers Collection of Formica Materials,
Archives Center, National Museum of American
History, Smithsonian Institution.

vinyl-coated wallpapers and hard plastic paints, vinyl floors, and kitchen tables topped with Formica laminate. The new household cleaners made the potentially super-clean world a reality, and surfaces were washed and wiped more often and more vigorously. (Just as the 1950s mass-marketing of automatic washer-driers had meant clothes were simply washed more often.) Synthetic sponges and mops made it all much easier. The postwar pantheon of new cleaners, from synthetic detergents replacing soap powders to the new synthetic dishwashing liquids, really worked. They really eliminated the drudgery of scrubbing.

By this century, that first generation of effective synthetic cleaners had evolved into an army of cleaners dedicated to cleaning practically everything—even, ironically enough, one for natural wood. One of the most popular products for anxious young mothers was a spray surface cleaner committed to killing germs. The basic function—easy surface cleaning—is matter-of-fact now. The premium, the added value, lies in the assurance that the invisible evil in tile grouting and the junctions of countertops and wall panels will be attacked vigorously. As a popular 1970s British television advertising campaign promised, "Kills 99 percent of known germs." In just twenty years of the postwar world, from 1945 to 1965, all the prewar domestic aspirations for a new place that was light, bright, and perpetually clean, were achieved. Like all dreams that are realized, this new place then became invisible, taken for granted, commoditized.

By the 1970s, the houses of all except the very poor or most marginal were expected to be clean and well equipped, containing a built-in kitchen with all the machines, a modern color television and, later, a computer with Internet connection, all the things that billions in developing countries still don't have. The symbolic, expressive role of 1950s domestic modernity—those long-gloved hands pointing in amazement—has practically disappeared. We're all blasé about it. For baby boomers and their children, this is the natural order of things. So natural indeed, such a basic guarantee, that it's allowed another generation, living in a more complex world with different expectations, to display a widely varied range of styles in their houses. They could be—taking the chapter headings of the London-based interior photographer Andreas von Einsiedel's recent *Dream Homes—100 Inspirational Interiors*—"Classic Contemporary," "Eclectic," "Exotic," "Country," or "Opulent," with a mass of subcategories in each—Gustavian, Brit-Pop, and Bauhaus retro, for example.[3] There's also one compelling chapter illustrating a persistent trend of the last twenty years—"Cool Minimalism." Here we are again, with the sparkling, all-white interiors; the massive windows; the revived Saarinen, Jacobsen, and Eames classics; the gleaming composite floors, and the acres of wall-to-floor storage paneled in matte laminates. There are a few concessions to an ancient authenticity—a bit of bare brick, some self-consciously rough-hewn wood—but with the midcentury modernist we're back to our real roots: we're back to a wipe-clean world.

Notes

1. Formica® is the registered trademark of The Diller Corporation. Reference to Formica company or business refers to Formica Group, or its predecessor companies. Formica Group is a global group of companies consisting of Formica Canada, Inc., Formica Corporation, Formica de Mexico S.A. de C.V., Formica IKI Oy, Formica Limited, Formica S.A., Formica S.A.S., Formica Taiwan Corporation, Formica (Thailand) Co., Ltd., and Formica (Asia) Ltd., among others.

Teflon® is the registered trademark of E. I. du Pont de Nemours and Company or its affiliates. Lycra® is the registered trademark of Invista North America S.A.R.L. Coca-Cola® and Coke® are the registered trademarks of The Coca-Cola Company. Mr. Clean® is the registered trademark of The Proctor & Gamble Company.

2. Andy Warhol, *The Philosophy of Andy Warhol* (New York, 1975).

3. Andreas von Einsiedel and Johanna Thornycroft, *Dream Homes—100 Inspirational Interiors* (London, 2005).

1950s A model home kitchen of the late 1950s featuring Formica laminate. From *Formica & Design; From the Counter Top to High Art*, by Susan Grant Lewin (1991).

Back cover image from *The Art of the Versatile: A Survey of Formica Limited*.

1913
CHRONOLOGY
2013

1876

Fritz Homann in Germany founds a business that will eventually be Homapal Plattenwerk. It builds wooden tubs to package its primary product, margarine.

1881

Wilhelm Wendt in Sweden founds Perstorp, extracting chemicals from beech-wood forest.

1913

February 1 Daniel J. O'Conor, while working at Westinghouse Electric & Manufacturing Company (Westinghouse) in Pittsburgh, Pennsylvania, files a patent application for a process to make laminated insulators. The patent is not issued until November 12, 1918, a cause of litigation years later.

March 17 Herbert A. Faber and O'Conor leave Westinghouse and, with banker John G. Tomlin, join partnership as "Formica Products Company"; they coin the name "Formica" as they plan to produce commutator V-rings with laminate, replacing mica.

May 2 First rented plant opens on Second and Main Streets in Cincinnati, Ohio. First orders to supply V-rings for electric motors to the Chalmers Motor Company. The founders are the only employees, using only hand presses to turn commutator rings, small tubes, and small sheets.

September 1 Company has eighteen employees.

October 15 Incorporated as "The Formica Insulation Company"; board of directors remains intact until 1935.

1914

July 4 Company produces first large sheet laminates to be cut into commutator rings.

New plant rented at Spring Grove Avenue and Alabama Streets, Cincinnati. Press manufacturers Boomer and Boschert supply a press for a small down payment.

1917

The Formica Insulation Company makes first contacts with infant radio industry, develops communications components for the U.S. Navy and Signal Corps.

Sales at $75,000 include aircraft pulleys.

1918

Sales at $145,000.

1919

June 1 Westinghouse sues The Formica Insulation Company for patent infringement, but the case is eventually dismissed.

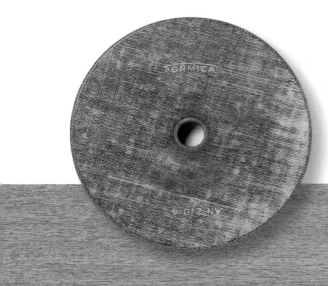

1919

Sales at $175,000.

Company pursues sales of laminated gears.

Negotiates purchase of future plant property at Spring Grove Avenue and Winton Road, Cincinnati.

1920

1920

Sales of basic board for radio sets grow from 5,000 units in 1920 to 2.5 million in 1924.

1921

Sales at $360,000. The company is so busy that it takes two months to move into new Winton Place plant.

Period of home manufacture of radios, assembled from kits, with exteriors of exclusively made Formica® laminate polished sheets in black or brown.

1922

Formica® registers federally for the first time as a trademark.

1923

Company becomes self-sufficient financially, installs new presses and treating machines, builds new two-story concrete facility.

New product developed, automotive timing gears.

Sales reach $1,900,000.

1924

MIT-trained Jack D. Cochrane is hired as Director of Research, Decorative, and Industrial Products. He is vital to the company's success as an innovator until his retirement in 1957.

Sales reach $3,000,000, helped by the popularity of radio.

1927

Company creates first decorative laminate using amino resins and an opaque barrier sheet to block the dark interior.

Patents rotogravure printing process for making multilayer lithographed wood-grain laminate on a flat-bed press.

Inventions signify beginning of shift from industrial products to decorative ones.

1929

Homapal, then called Company Homann, buys a saw mill in Herzberg am Harz, Germany.

1930

1931

Jack Cochrane invents cigarette-proof laminate by adding a layer of metal foil, opening up the material for tabletops in popular soda fountains, cafés, night clubs, and restaurants.

1932

One of the first extensive and influential installations of decorative Formica® laminate is at Radio City Music Hall in Manhattan. In the 1930s, speed and efficiency in transportation call for light, durable, easy-to-clean materials. The interiors of ocean liners, zeppelins, and railroad cars are covered in Formica® laminate, as are the stations, lobbies, and lounges around the globe that serve them.

The Formica Insulation Company produces 6,000 timing gears a day at the peak for Maxwell, Haynes, Graham-Paige, McFarlane, Auburn, Buick, Nash, Studebaker, Chevrolet, Pontiac, and Willys-Overland.

The Depression leads to the company's first downturn and loss in 1932.

1934

In Australia, Robert M. Sykes and a partner establish Laminex Pty Ltd to manufacture laminate primarily for functional industrial applications in automotive and electrical industries.

1936

Formica® laminate is installed in all the bathrooms of Cunard's ocean liner RMS *Queen Mary* when it begins service.

1937

The Ohio River floods the Cincinnati plant, with water rising to the second level of the factory and requiring desperate efforts by workers and executives.

1940

Renewed June 6, 1942 to The Formica Insulation Company, Cincinnati, Ohio.

RENEWED

JUN 6 - 1942

UNITED STATES PATENT OFFICE.

THE FORMICA INSULATION COMPANY, OF CINCINNATI, OHIO.

TRADE-MARK FOR ELECTRIC INSULATING COMPOUND.

ACT OF FEBRUARY 20, 1905.

155,689. Registered June 6, 1922.

Application filed October 15, 1921. Serial No. 154,140.

STATEMENT.

To all whom it may concern:

Be it known that THE FORMICA INSULA-
TION COMPANY, a corporation organized and
existing under and by virtue of the laws of
the State of Ohio, located in the city of Cincinnati, county of Hamilton, State of Ohio,
and doing business at 4614-28 Spring Grove
Avenue, Cincinnati, Ohio, has adopted and
used the trade-mark shown in the accom-
panying drawing, for an electric insulating
compound, in Class 21, Electrical apparatus,
machines, and supplies.

The trademark has been continuously used

in the business of said corporation since on
or about the first day of July, 1914.

The trademark is applied or affixed to the
goods by placing thereon, or upon the receptacles or containers in which the goods
are shipped, a label, name-plate, ticket or
tag, on which the trademark appears, or by
stenciling, molding or otherwise impressing
the trademark upon the goods themselves or
upon the receptacles containing the same.

THE FORMICA INSULATION COMPANY,

By D. J. O'CONOR,

Vice President.

FORMICA

DECLARATION.

State of Ohio, county of Hamilton, ss.

D. J. O'CONOR, being duly sworn, deposes
and says that he is the vice president of the
corporation, the applicant named in the fore-
going statement; that he believes the fore-
going statement is true; that he believes
said corporation is the owner of the trademark sought to be registered; that no other
person, firm, corporation, or association, to
the best of his knowledge and belief, has the
right to use the said trademark in the United
States, either in the identical form or in any
such near resemblance thereto as might be
calculated to deceive; that said trademark

is used by said corporation in commerce
among the several States of the United
States; that the description and drawing
presented truly represent the trademark
sought to be registered, and that the speci-
mens (or facsimiles) show the trademark as
actually used upon the goods.

D. J. O'CONOR.

Subscribed and sworn to before me this
5th day of October, 1921.

[L.S.] JOHN S. HARST,

Notary Public.

Republished, under the Act of 1946, May 4, 1948, by
The Formica Insulation Co., Cincinnati, Ohio.

1941

After the beginning of World War II, The Formica Insulation Company focuses on war production, the manufacture of bomb tubes, and eighty-eight distinct parts for the P-51 Mustang fighter plane.

1946

Robert Sykes pays a visit to the company's Spring Grove Avenue factory in Cincinnati to meet with Jack Cochrane.

The Formica Insulation Company's managers in Cincinnati observe the global appeal of Formica® brand products and make a key decision to license sales and manufacturing rights for much of the world—including Europe, India, Australia, New Zealand, and other parts of the British Commonwealth—to the respected British company De La Rue.

1948

In 1940 only one-quarter of the company's earnings comes from decorative laminate, the rest from industrial products. By 1950 the proportions are reversed. The company drops the term "insulation" from its name and changes it to The Formica Company.

"Realwood" is the Formica® laminate product of choice for the Terrace Plaza Hotel in Cincinnati, Ohio, one of the first modern build-ings designed by the legendary American architecture firm Skidmore, Owings & Merrill and completed in 1948. The use of Formica® laminate in this important hometown project is an obvious coup.

1948

Under De La Rue, the Tyneside Factory in Newcastle, Great Britain, is opened. They license rights to use the Formica® brand.

De La Rue sets up a branch in Australia, where Laminex is the dominant laminate maker.

1949

By the late 1940s, the Laminex Company had begun producing its first decorative panels.

1950

1950

Industrial designer Brooks Stevens designs the company's first graphic invention, the still iconic "Skylark" pattern. The company hires Stevens to design patterns.

June 28 Ground is broken for new plant in Evendale, Ohio; built in three phases and completed in 1953.

1951

During the postwar building boom, the Formica company increasingly focuses on the consumer. It advertises vigorously, spending about $500,000 that year, an amount equal to 2 percent of its sales.

1952

"Sequin" is introduced, an iconic laminate design.

1952

De La Rue reports that the use of Formica® laminate has expanded considerably internationally as the recognized material for equipping a modern kitchen.

Laminex opens a new 160,000-square-foot factory in Cheltenham, Australia. This allows the expansion of Laminex sheeting design and production. The emphasis is on ease of care, but design matters too.

1953

Founder Herbert A. Faber retires from the board because of health issues.

New postforming techniques allow fabricators to bend the laminate into covered back-splash and seamless front edges; ready-made countertops are easily installed.

Annual report highlights the Vanitory with postformed edges.

The company hires Raymond Loewy to create the new "Sunrise" line in 1953.

1954

Loewy's office recolors Skylark, renamed "Boomerang."

De La Rue expands into France.

1955

Homapal begins to produce melamine-faced panels.

1956

Founders sell The Formica Company to a chemical conglomerate, American Cyanamid. Formica Corporation becomes a small part of the large $450 million American Cyanamid.

Founder Daniel J. O'Conor retires when the company is sold.

1958

April 5 Submarine USS *Growler* is launched with extensive use of Formica® brand laminate. She is decommissioned, restored, and reopened on May 21, 2009, during New York City's Intrepid Museum "Fleet Week 2009" celebration.

Prince Sigvard Bernadotte designs the Swedish classic pattern "VirrVarr" for Perstorp.

De La Rue opens a plant in Thornleigh, outside Sydney.

Executives at De La Rue and American Cyanamid agree to revise their agreement. De La Rue wants more than a simple license to protect its future growth, and the firms form a new arrangement, with 60 percent of the ownership of what is now called Formica International Limited going to the British-based firm and 40 percent retained by American Cyanamid.

Laminex becomes a wholly owned subsidiary of ACI; Sykes remains managing director.

Homapal begins to produce laminate under the trademark Homapal, after the owner's name.

1959

De La Rue establishes a factory in Papakura, near Auckland, New Zealand, to sell Formica brand laminate.

1960

1960

The Research and Development Center at the Evendale facility, built in 1960, acquires a design studio.

1962

De La Rue sets up a Belgian branch in connection with the Paris-based French one.

August 2 De La Rue and American Cyanamid acquire 51 percent of licensee Ceplástica and constitute Formica Española, S.A.

Robert Venturi—one of the leading theorists of what comes to be called postmodernism—wanting to celebrate the mundane, designs a coffee shop as one of his first projects using laminate and similar materials.

1964

Formica Corporation's World's Fair House is shown at the 1964 World's Fair, held at Flushing Meadows in Queens, New York. The house is designed by Emil A. Schmidlin, a New Jersey architect who is among the first to build split-level houses in that state as well as a number of exposition homes.

1965

Formica Corporation, under its British licensee De La Rue, enters the Indian market in a joint venture with the Bombay Burmah Trading Company.

1966

The first of its kind in India, Formica Corporation opens a manufacturing facility in Pune, the

industrial city with automobile and other factories, about 100 miles south of Mumbai.

Growth in the U.S. continues and the company builds a major new plant near Sierra in California.

1969

Cunard's *Queen Elizabeth 2*, in service from 1969 to 2009, is the ocean liner that naval architect Dan Wallace and interior designer Dennis Lennon are able to treat as a total Formica® laminate design project, developing a new textured and moldable laminate with the feeling of woven fabric for extensive onboard use.

Formica Corporation's emphasis on design is part of a wider trend: companies such as Alessi in Italy, Authentics in Germany, Marimekko, Knoll, Bodum, IBM, and Sony all see the importance of design in creating global identities for their products and their companies.

1970

In the 1970s, Formica® brand laminate is produced under license in South Africa by a company called Decorative Boards. Rights and technologies move in a series of mergers and the company becomes Laminate Industries, a joint effort of American Cyanamid and PG Bison. PG Bison later acquires rights to the Formica® brand in certain African countries.

Homapal begins the first production of metal laminates and becomes known for these and for its line of wood veneer laminates.

In the 1970s, the company sells Formica® laminate through agents in Hong Kong, Singapore, Malaysia, and Taiwan.

During the decade, Formica Corporation is only a small part of a much larger and sometimes unconcerned organization, accounting for only 3 percent of American Cyanamid's sales.

In the late 1970s, Formica Corporation forms its Design Advisory Board (DAB) with a group of influential interior designers and architects tasked with bringing Formica® brand laminate out of the 1960s and into the present day.

1977

After two years of negotiations, De La Rue sells 60 percent of its rights back to American Cyanamid for 9.6 million pounds sterling, the equivalent of about $16.3 million USD.

1978

The U.S. Federal Trade Commission (FTC) seeks to cancel the Formica® federal trademark registration under Section 14 of the

Lanham Act, charging that it has become a generic name for decorative laminate. The FTC's power to bring such an action against a trademark creates an uproar in the U.S. business community, which views the FTC's action as an attempt to eradicate the function of trademarks in the economy. The FTC's action prompts the introduction and passage of several pieces of federal legislation aimed at limiting the FTC's authority under the Lanham Act. Ultimately, the FTC's action is dropped.

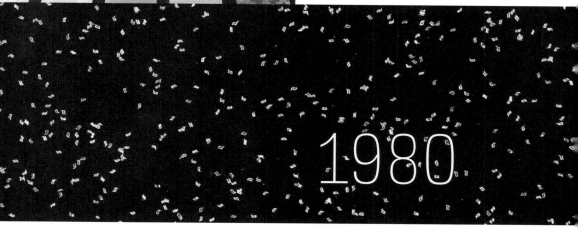

1980

1980

Formica Corporation opens its first Asian plant in Taiwan.

Laminex Industries are formed within ACI embracing both AV Wehl and Laminex.

1981

February 5 Current Formica Corporation operating entity is first incorporated as Wildon Industries Inc. 2000X is a new product category, a solid surfacing material.

1982

ColorCore® laminate is introduced, an innovative surfacing material that maintains its hue in depth and omits the brown line or edge of earlier products, making the company's products even more attractive.

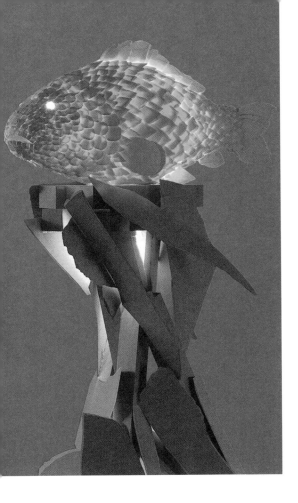

CSR Formica acquires the New Zealand assets of Laminex Industries, a division of Alex Harvey.

Formica Corporation organizes a traveling exhibition of pieces in ColorCore® laminate that brings together work by architects—Robert Venturi, Frank Gehry, Stanley Tigerman, James Wines of SITE, Massimo Vignelli and others—to show that laminate is no longer taken as a faux material but celebrated on its own terms.

1983

The exhibition *Surface + Ornament* features a range of projects, including Frank Gehry's Fish Lamp, constructed of ColorCore® laminate chipped and torn into "fish scales" and lit from within, revealing the material's translucency.

Formica Corporation had earlier partnered with Homapal in launching metallic laminates and is its largest customer and half-owner from 1983.

1985

May 1 Vincent Langone is named Vice President and COO, appointed President and CEO in 1988. In 1985 the president of Formica Corporation, Gordon D. Sterling, and Formica's management team up with Shearson Lehman and Donaldson, Lufkin & Jenrette in a leveraged buyout that values the company at $200 million and carries $153 million in debt.

1987

Formica Corporation debt is a heavy burden. To reduce it, the company goes public, selling 5.3 million shares, one-third of the equity, for $64 million or $12 per share.

1988

Formica Plastics Pty Ltd (Australian subsidiary of the Formica Corporation USA) changes its name to Formica Australia Pty Ltd.

Formica Corporation celebrates its 75th anniversary with the reintroduction of Skylark, renamed Boomerang, and the book *Formica & Design, From the Counter Top to High Art* by Susan Grant Lewin.

75 YEARS

FORMICA
BRAND

1913–1988

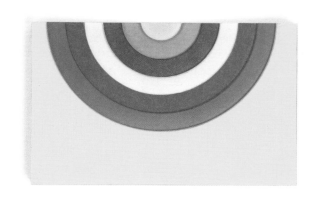

1988

Formica Corporation finds itself fending off approaches from so-called raiders. First a group led by Samuel Zell, then one headed by Malcolm Glazer take positions in the stock. Chairman Sterling dies suddenly and is succeeded by CEO Vincent Langone.

1989

Formica Corporation is taken private by management, Dillon Read, and Masco.

1990

1990

As early as 1990, half of Formica Corporation's business comes from outside the United States. The company's future lies in global growth, and through expansion the Formica company hopes to turn the tide.

Introduces International Collection of Metal Laminates.

1991

Formica® Formations® is launched and introduces a series of organic designs such as Bayou Oxide, Almond Dust, and Graphite Graphix.

1992

Formica Corporation establishes a Singapore branch, Formica (Singapore) Pte Ltd.

1993

Expanded in Korea as Formica Korea Corp. and in Malaysia as House of Formica.

1994

As China's economy begins to expand, Formica Corporation sets up Formica Shanghai with a manufacturing joint venture, followed by full ownership.

1995

January Formica Corporation is acquired for about $600 million by BTR Nylex Ltd. ("BTR"), an Australian subsidiary of BTR plc, the British industrial conglomerate that began as British Tire and Rubber.

1997

Formica Flooring brand, manufactured in Seattle, Washington, is introduced at a public relations event held at the World Trade Center in New York City.

1998

May 1 In a third leveraged buyout, BTR sells Formica Corporation. For $405 million, the Formica company is taken over by a venture capital group including Citicorp's CVC European Equity Partners and Donaldson, Lufkin & Jenrette (DLJ). The new owners bring back Langone as CEO and Schneider as CFO and in February 1999 move to acquire working capital to rebuild the business through the sale of $215 million of high-yield debt.

Releases Laurinda Spear Collection, collaboration with renowned architect.

ACI Ltd (parent of Laminex) taken over by BTR Nylex.

1999

On July 22, Amatek, parent company of Laminex Industries, acquires the Formica operations in Australia and New Zealand from CSR Timber products.

2000

March 1 Formica Corporation acquires Perstorp Surface Materials, a leading international producer of laminates, printed papers, and foils. The purchase promises an opportunity to move toward global competitiveness.

Formica Corporation expands in Asia. With the addition of Siam Perstorp from Perstorp Division of Surface Materials aquisition, the company gains a successful manufacturing plant and business in Thailand that supports the emerging Asian markets.

2002

With the company burdened by debts of $540 million, a new CEO, Frank Riddick, and the board decide the company will have to seek protection in bankruptcy court. It emerges with a new plan in the spring of 2004 that brings $175 million cash investment, reduces secured debt from more than $300 million to about $127 million, and eliminates $215 million in unsecured debt.

The Laminex Group operates as a separate division within the Amatek group of companies, acquired from BTR Nylex Limited in 1999. Fletcher Building Ltd buys the panel and laminate firm, now Australia's leader in the field, for $759 million (Australian) or about $555 million USD.

2003

Sells Unidur division of PSM, printed paper and foil business.

Quillan HPL plant in south of France is shut down.

Introduces "Etchings" in North America, begins decorated finish strategy for margin growth.

The Laminex Group New Zealand launches combining Formica NZ, Fletcher Wood Panels, Scott Panels, and Hardwood.

Sales office and distribution center open in Dongguan, South China.

2004

June 10 Wildon Industries Inc. changes its name to Formica Corporation for the U.S.-based entity.

June 10 Emerges from bankruptcy with Cerberus, Oaktree, and others investing $175 million cash equity.

Sells Formica Flooring plant in Seattle and exits business.

Lenders provide $199 million in exit debt financing.

The Laminex Group merges Formex® and Formica® brands under one powerful brand: Formica®—World's Favorite Laminate.

Formica Thailand plant expands to meet growing demand in South East Asia with an additional press.

2005

Formica Corporation reintroduces the classics Boomerang and VirrVarr in Asia, Europe, and North America, simultaneously.

Having outgrown the first plant, the company opens a second, new and improved facility in Qingpu, China, HPL facility; expands in 2006 by relocating the assets of its first plant.

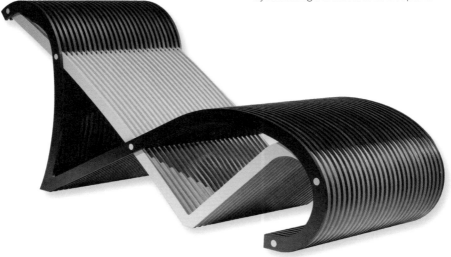

The company offers a unique product to the growing market for architectural exterior cladding. Called Formica® Exterior Compact in Europe, the colorful UV-resistant compact structural laminate is rebranded VIVIX® for all markets when it is introduced in North America.

Formica® brand is licensed to Kronotex USA for use on flooring products.

2006

September Fletcher Building chooses a new CEO, Jonathan Ling, then CEO of Laminex. Ling perceives the value of the still recovering Formica Corporation, with its recent acquisition Perstorp. Fletcher will build globally and synergistically on the company's strength in the market for laminate and related products with the company's storied Formica® brand. Ling's first decision as Fletcher's CEO is to purchase the Formica Group of companies in July 2007, for about $700 million. The combination with Laminex® brand under the Fletcher umbrella will make the Formica® brand the single largest player in its industry globally. The two companies had worked together, however, as far back as 1946 and Robert Sykes' visit to Cincinnati, Ohio.

Distribution center opened in Chengdu, West China.

2007

July 1 Fletcher Building Ltd. acquires Formica Group divisions of Asia, Europe, and North America from private equity firms Cerberus Capital Management LP and Oaktree Capital Management LLC for $700 million.

Barry and Helen O'Brien, a postforming company in Dunedin, New Zealand, sell their business to Fletcher Building.

French artist Daniel Buren uses exterior compact structural laminate to surface the bridge next to the Guggenheim Museum in Bilbao, Spain.

2008

After the reopening of the Indian economy and shifts in policy, the Formica® brand license is renewed. The company decides to once again start its own operation in India.

Sierra California Plant shut down.

In March, Mark Adamson, head of Formica Europe, takes over as CEO.

Formica Group reaffirms its commitment to design with an exhibition of Formica® laminate furniture and sculpture by such architects as Michael Graves, Massimo Vignelli, Zaha Hadid, and Thomas Mayne at the Contemporary Arts Center, Cincinnati.

2009

A new European headquarters in Newcastle, Great Britain, opens and becomes the catalyst for a major organizational change, integrating the European business.

A reset project is begun. Half the products are reduced and palettes rationalized. The design department devises international palettes; regional collections are streamlined and coordinated. In Asia, the color range is harmonized into a single Asian collection.

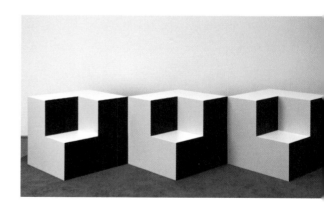

Important new products include new texture and design developments, for example 180FX® laminate, which conveys the effect of a single stone slab such as granite without repetition of pattern.

With Siam Perstorp the company gains a successful manufacturing plant and business in Thailand that supports the emerging Asian markets.

The acquisition of Perstorp strengthens presence in the U.K. Finished countertops under the Axiom brand reach revenues of $50 million.

2010

2010

Pioneering show of sculpture using Formica® products by Chinese architects in Beijing.

2011

October Mark Adamson takes over as head of the entire Laminates and Panels division of Fletcher Building.

All plants become standardized to Greenguard Indoor Air Quality Certified, a standard that is now achieved in all plants producing Formica® laminate around the world.

2012

Formica Group is the first laminate manufacturer in the world to be awarded the Carbon Trust's Carbon Reduction Label. Many structures today are built to LEED and other standards of ensuring environmental sustainability. Key to this achievement, starting in 2010, the company begins a process of Life Cycle Assessment (LCA), measuring the resources and energy consumed by its products.

Formica Group buys remainder, 50 percent ownership, of Homapal Plattenwerk GmbH.

Company announces its plan for a second plant in China, part of a $200 million investment in the Asian operation. For the centennial year, Formica Group is marking more than twenty years in China and celebrates with the ground-breaking of the new factory in Jiujiang.

In July, Bilbao plant is shut down and manufacturing transferred to Valencia plant in eastern Spain.

In October, Mark Adamson becomes CEO of Fletcher Building.

In November, Fletcher Building announces purchase by its India affiliate, Formica Laminates (India) Private Limited, of the Well Pack decorative laminate business assets, including land, buildings, and machinery, with plans to expand operations.

FOREVER®

2013

The Formica® brand celebrates its 100th
Anniversary.

Chronology Captions

Formica®, the Formica® Anvil
logo are registered trademarks of
The Diller Corporation.

1910

(page 89, right, top) H.A. Faber,
Chairman of the Board and co-founder,
and D.J. O'Conor, President and
co-founder of The Formica Company.
From *Formica: Forty Years of Steady
Vision*, 1953.

(page 89, right, bottom) 1910s,
The third and fourth floors of this
building in Cincinnati were the
first factory of The Formica Company.
From *Formica: Forty Years of Steady
Vision*, 1953.

CHIP Lipstick Red Linen, 41-C-30
(1960s).

(page 90) 1910s, In the early days, gear
blanks were band-sawed from
Formica sheet stock. From *Formica:
Forty Years of Steady Vision*, 1953.

(page 90) Signatures of H.A. Faber,
Chairman of the Board and co-founder
of The Formica Company, and D.J.
O'Conor, President and co-founder of
The Formica Company. From *Formica:
Forty Years of Steady Vision*, 1953.

(page 91) 1910s, Cable pulley. Early
applications of Formica laminate
were industrial and in some cases
used on aircraft.

1920

CHIP Platinum Mahogany Picwood,
65-WP-90 (pre-1953).

(page 91) 1920s, Formica logo.

(page 91) Tube rolling. From *Formica:
Forty Years of Steady Vision*, 1953.

(page 92) 1920s, With more and more
production and office space being
needed, Formica kept adding to the
Spring Grove Avenue plant. From
Formica: Forty Years of Steady Vision, 1953.

(page 92) 1925, In 1925 the "Build-up"
department looked like this. Here
Formica sheet materials were placed
between polished copper plates. From
Formica: Forty Years of Steady Vision, 1953.

1930

CHIP Spectrum Blue, 851-58 (1981).

(page 92) Identification tape for
cigarette-resistant Formica laminate
introduced in 1931.

(page 93) 1930s, Formica logo.

(page 93, middle) Formica Laboratory. Grace Jeffers Collection of Formica Materials, Archives Center, National Museum of American History, Smithsonian Institution.

(page 93, lower right) Main reading room in Library of Congress Annex at Washington, D.C. Desk in background entirely made of Formica, as is the shelving behind the desk and the dark panels on the walls. All table tops Realwood Formica. Pierson & Wilson, Architects. From *Formica: A Modern Plastic* publication.

(page 93, lower left) 1930s, Formica laminate objects. Early applications of Formica laminate were mostly industrial. From *Formica & Design; From the Counter Top to High Art*, 1991, by Susan Grant Lewin.

1940

CHIP Fiesta Blue matt 2767, B.S. 7-084 (1960s).

(page 94, top) Group of US Army officers watching a woman make pulleys. Grace Jeffers Collection of Formica Materials, Archives Center, National Museum of American History, Smithsonian Institution.

(page 94, bottom) 1942, June 6, Formica trademark renewed.

(page 95) 1940s, Formica logo.

1950

CHIP Charcoal Skylark, 88-L-4 (pre-1953).

(page 95) c. 1953-1954, Men and women in western costume square dancing on stage during the Formica Ad Rodeo. Grace Jeffers Collection of Formica Materials, Archives Center, National Museum of American History, Smithsonian Institution.

(page 96) 1950s, Formica logo.

(page 96) 1959, Black Sequin, 3-SE-9.

(page 96) From *New Decorator Ideas for Kitchen, Bath, Every Room: by Formica.*

(page 97) 1955, From *Monsanto Chemical Company Annual Report.*

(page 97) c. 1950, F. C. Walter home. Grace Jeffers Collection of Formica Materials, Archives Center, National Museum of American History, Smithsonian Institution.

1960

CHIP Pluie D'or 3, Brillant Série A (1959).

(page 98) Back cover from *The Formica Scene on the QE2*, 1970.

(page 98) Queen Elizabeth II.

(page 99) 1960s, Formica logo.

(page 99, top) 1964-1965, "The compact office tucked into an out-of-the-way corner of the kitchen, takes no more space than a pantry closet but controls the entire house...." (left) From *The World's Fair House; American Contemporary Styling at its Best.*

(page 99) 1966, Launch of new Mahogany line. PHOTOGRAPHER Leopoldo Pomés. MODEL Romy.

1970

CHIP Yellow color grain, 18-CW-16 (late 1950s).

(page 100) 1970s, Formica logo.

(page 100) 1970, Promotion for woodgrain laminates with woman perched on stool. Grace Jeffers Collection of Formica Materials, Archives Center, National Museum of American History, Smithsonian Institution.

(page 101) Model pretending to water flowers growing from Formica. Grace Jeffers Collection of Formica Materials, Archives Center, National Museum of American History, Smithsonian Institution.

1980

CHIP Black Silversnow, 57-J-9 (1950s).

(page 101) 1984-1985, Folding table and chair made of Formica ColorCore® laminate and metal. DESIGNER Eva Jircna.

(page 102) 1983, Frank O. Gehry, Ryba. The translucent quality of shredded ColorCore® was discovered by the architect in a series of "fish" and "snake" lamps. From *Formica & Design; From the Counter Top to High Art*, 1991, by Susan Grant Lewin.

(page 102) 1988, Formica logo, 75th Anniversary.

(page 103) Collage made of bright ColorCore® laminate.

1990

CHIP Burnt Strand 6307-58 (2009).

(page 103) 1998, Red Aerial Fields, 7477-58, The Laurinda Spear Collection.

(page 104) 1990s to present, Formica logo designed by Michael Bierut.

2000

(page 104) 2006, Classroom, featured in *Trends*.

CHIP Natural Cane 6930-NT (2005).

(page 105, top) 2008, Dave Pallas, Formica Group VP Operations, visits Hsinfeng plant.

(page 105) 2005, Formica laminate and plywood used to create sculpture. Featured in *Trends*. DESIGNER Lage Pergon.

(page 106, top) 2008, Laminate Hat, London Fashion Week. DESIGNERS Basso and Brooke and Stephen Jones.

(page 106) 2008, *Sunergy*, Buzz Yudell, ColorThru Compact by Formica. PHOTOGRAPHER Gregg Goldman.

(page 107) 2008, *CuboSeat*, Massimo Vignelli, ColorCore2™ by Formica. Tony Walsh Photography, courtesy Contemporary Arts Center.

(page 108) 2008, *J Chair*, Michael Graves, Veneer by Formica. ColorCore2™ by Formica. PHOTOGRAPHER Gregg Goldman.

2010

CHIP Scarlet 845(-64) (1970).

(page 108) Un_Natural exhibition, *Object Manipulation*, Qingyun Ma.

(page 109, top) Un_Natural exhibition, *Book Pillar*, Yi Ding.

(page 109) 2009, Zhenzhou KFC, China. Published in Annual Review: "Formica at KFC China: Formica is bringing brand to the surface."

(page 109) Sept. 15, 2005, Qingpu factory grand opening ceremony.

(page 110) 2013 Anniversary, Formica logo, designed by Michael Bierut.

(page 110) Anniversary Collection of Formica brand laminate designed by Abbott Miller made into custom Eames tables manufactured by Herman Miller. PHOTOGRAPHER Jay Zuckerkorn.

Our famous name starts with a capital "F" and ends with an "®"

The Formica Group is the world's leading manufacturer of decorative laminate surfacing materials. The Formica® brand name is recognized around the globe as representing our commitment to quality, dependability, integrity, and innovation. We've covered millions of surfaces and have been a mainstay in homes, roadside diners, and just about every other kind of interior. Our brand name often graces the pages of novels, newspapers, and magazines.

The following pages contain literary excerpts that—although not compliant with our trademark usage requirements*—illustrate the global historical impact of Formica® brand products.

*Formica Group does not sanction misuse of its trademark and engages in an active campaign to ensure the correct use of the Formica® trademark. When using our trademark and referring to our products, please use our famous trademark as an "adjective" followed by the common name of the product. For example, reference Formica® brand laminate, Formica® decorative laminate, or Formica® laminate. In print, capitalize either the entire trademark or the first letter and, in at least the first mention of our name, add the federal trademark registration symbol.

c. 1960 From Formica "Go for the IN look" publication. Grace Jeffers Collection of Formica Materials, Archives Center, National Museum of American History, Smithsonian Institution.

100 YEARS
OF COLOR
AND PATTERN

1969

1960s

1960s

1981

2000

YELLOW

1969

1981

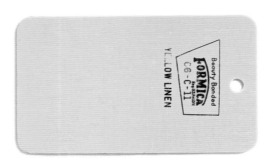

1950s Yellow Linen, C6-C-11.

1931 Identification tape for
cigarette-resistant Formica® laminate.

1951 "Looking for Beauty in a Dinette?" Ad, *American Home*. Grace Jeffers Collection of Formica Materials, Archives Center, National Museum of American History, Smithsonian Institution.

THE LASER AGE

Justin Tussing

She turned to look at me head on. "Thomas, do you have a girlfriend?"

"Currently I have exactly zero girlfriends." I felt like I was leaking information.

The longer we sat there, the greater the odds that I would be left without secrets or hope.

Back behind the counter, the woman poured popping corn into a hopper.

"I don't think I'm going to college," I said, though I hadn't given the matter any thought before.

The woman I'd been sitting with disappeared and a more familiar person took her place. "What do you think you're going to do?" she asked, and then, almost as an afterthought, she added, "You know you would probably be able to get in somewhere."

I said, "I think I'd prefer to learn in a more realistic environment."

"Sure," she said, but something in her tone suggested that she didn't quite agree with me.

"Or maybe I'll travel."

Miss Lowe drew shapes on the Formica tabletop with her fingertip. "Do you ever get lonely, Thomas?"

It was obvious that she didn't know the first thing about me. My bedroom and my parents' room shared a wall — only the dehumidifier in Mary's closet disguised our night sounds. Pawpaw's military background meant that he didn't think twice about visiting me in the bathroom. How, in that house, could a person feel lonely? "Why?" I asked. "Do you?"

2005 Architectural door surfaced with 6900 Neon Yellow Formica® brand laminate in MicroDot finish.

1960s (left) Jasmine Yellow Matt, B.S. 4-055.

los tableros que decoran

...AL CUARTO DE BAÑO,
...ÓN DE LOS NIÑOS A LA COCINA,
...ORCIONA A LOS MUEBLES Y
...SUPERFICIES COLOREADAS,

FORMICA APORTA UNA SOLUCIÓN A
TODOS LOS PROBLEMAS DEL REVESTIMIENTO,
AJUSTÁNDOSE A TODAS LAS VARIANTES
DE LA INSPIRACIÓN DECORATIVA.

2005 Formica® Exterior Compact on private
housing. ARCHITECT Eduardo Aurtenechea.
PHOTOGRAPHER Jorge Flores.

1956 (left) Ad, from *Seleccións del Reader's
Digest*. "Formica®, The boards that decorate."

2006 "Out" Prototype garden chair. MATERIAL K3142 Midas Formica® Exterior Compact. DESIGNER Mikael Åstrand, Stockholm.

2010 Kitchen presented at the SICI furniture show, Madrid. MATERIAL Formica® Compact on countertop and shelves. Vertical fronts with Chrome Yellow F1485. Worktop in 3467 Blue Storm 180fx® Compact. ARCHITECT Héctor Ruiz Velázquez. PHOTOGRAPHER Pedro Martínez (Fotoarquitectura).

1953 (following spread, top) Children's play room, from *This Formica World*, 4th Quarter. Grace Jeffers Collection of Formica Materials, Archives Center, National Museum of American History, Smithsonian Institution.

(following spread, bottom) From *This is Evendale: A tour through Formica's Evendale plant* brochure.

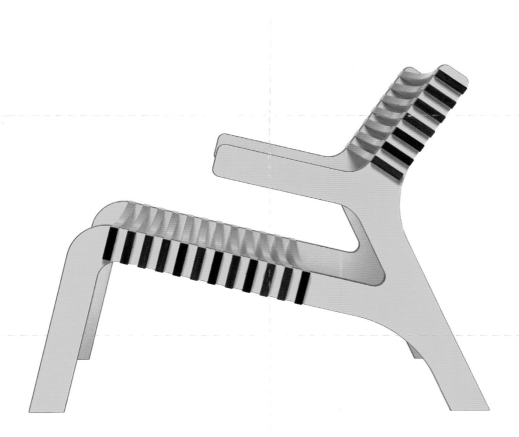

This mark certifies

RUB OFF WITH LOTS OF BAR SOAP ON A

genuine **FORMICA**®
Laminated Plastic

MP CLOTH

REPLACEMENT OR REFUND OF MONEY
★
Guaranteed by
Good Housekeeping
IF NOT AS ADVERTISED THEREIN

2003 Authentix Quilted Collection,
Quilted Brass, No. 5165-15.

1950s (right) Yellow Color Grain,
18-CW-16.

SUNDOWNERS

Monica Ali

The Potts girl walked into the cafe preceded by her reputations so that everyone was obliged to stare. Even Stanton, who had been in Mamarrosa for less than a month, looked her over once more than was strictly necessary. Vasco, stuffed behind the grand Formica counter, served her with pineapple Sumol and unsmiling vigilance. The girl sat on the edge of the pool table, swinging her legs and examining her navel stud. Her hair fell forward, revealing an ugly brown hearing aid, and Stanton averted his eyes.

Conversation spluttered and died, then was just as suddenly resurrected. The old men stood at the bar caressing their Macieiras and coughing up memories. In their black felt fedoras and black waistcoats, red handkerchiefs tied at the neck, they looked to Stanton like postcards from the past, as picturesque as the crooked Portuguese streets, the whitewashed houses, the doors and windows framed gaily in blue and yellow.

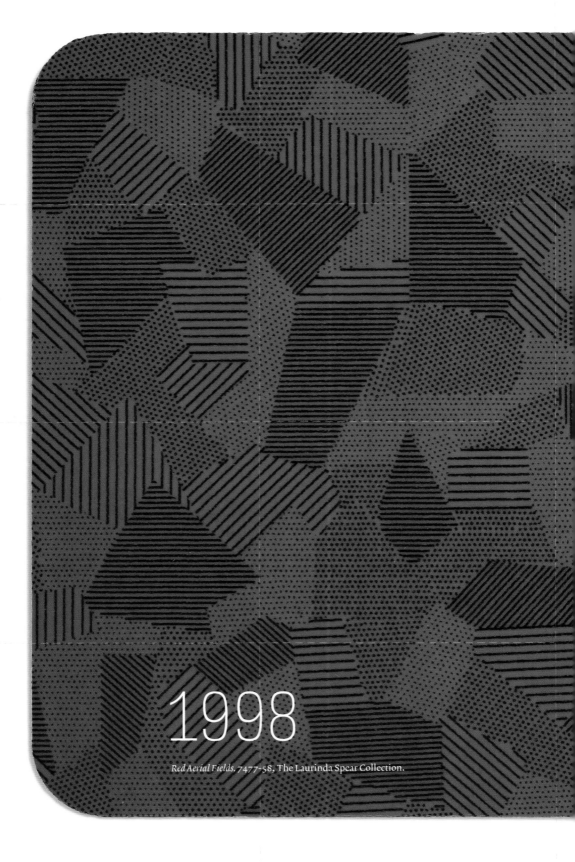

1998

Red Aerial Fields, 7477-58, The Laurinda Spear Collection.

RED

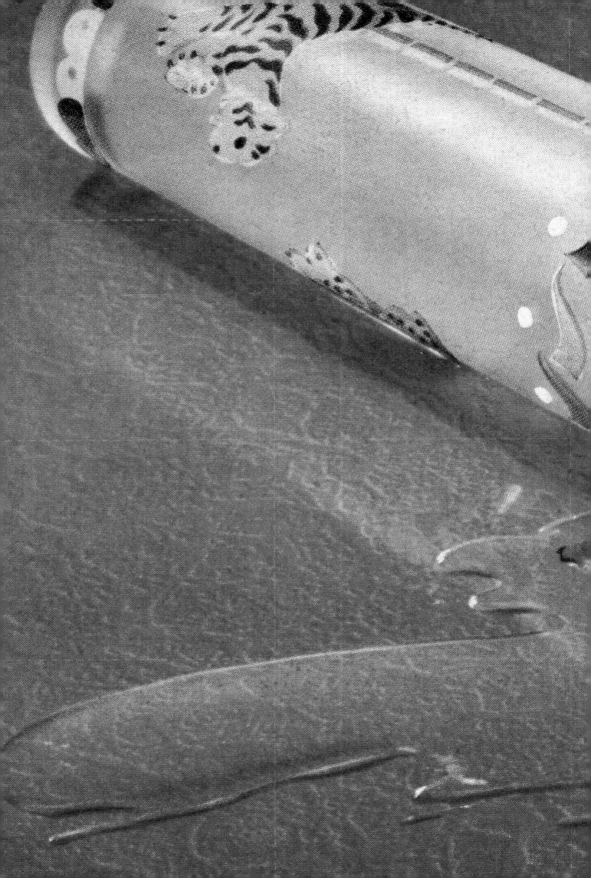

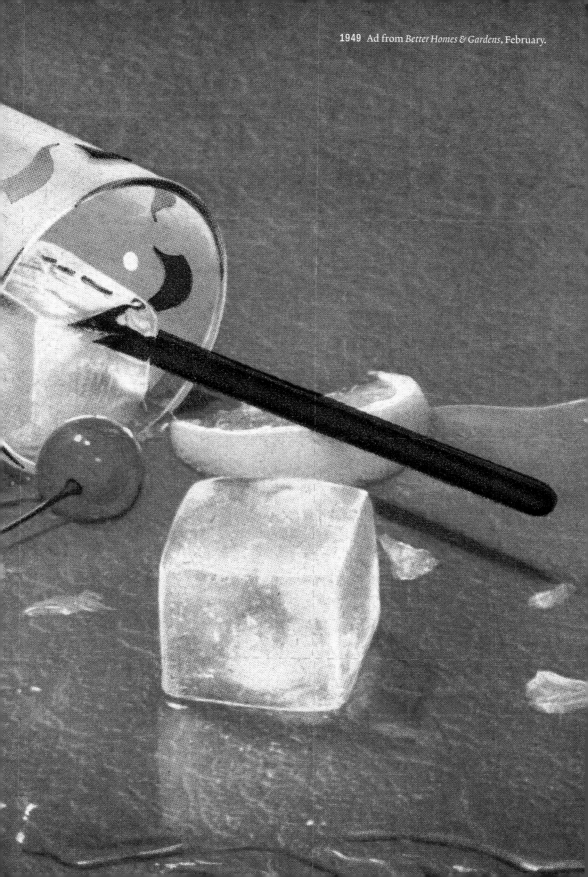

1954 Ad, "Formica® is...here...there."
1960s (right) Post Office Red 2779, B.S. o-006.

DEAD GUY'S STUFF

Sharon Fiffer

Jane hadn't seen the table before. It had been covered with junk mail and newspapers and smeared glasses and plates. It still was, for the most part, but both she and Tim saw now that it was a gorgeous red formica table flecked with gold. It looked like it was in fine shape, perhaps protected by its layer of grime and debris. It would clean up beautifully. And there were four matching chairs, the seat cushions that were visible, plump and unripped. They were still oohing and aahing about the fifties kitchen set when they heard a gravelly voice behind them.

"This is all about a dead guy's stuff, isn't it?"

"Detective Munson, what a pleasure!" Tim held out his hand, and when Munson reluctantly put his out, Tim grasped it with both of his. For a minute, Jane was afraid he was going to go too far and kiss it, he made such a scene.

"I've been trying to tell Janie that she's crazy with her worries that there's a murderer loose in Kankakee. And even if there was, we wouldn't have to worry with you on the case."

Was Jane crazy, or did Tim bat his eyelashes at the dumbfounded detective? She knew Tim hated homophobes and tried to bait them whenever he could, but this was the most outrageous performance she had ever seen him give.

2007 *Horisont* (horizon), Featured at the Milano fair "That's Design." Image from *Trends 2*, 2007. DESIGNER Jörgen Backman. MATERIAL Formica® laminate, K1238 Carnaval HPL. PHOTOGRAPHER Juuso Paloniemi.

2005 Kitchen. MATERIAL Formica® laminate 6902-SP Grenadine and 2042 Brass-toned Aluminum.

1949 Ad, "So you're going to buy a Dinette Set...."
House Beautiful, November. Ad by Perry-Brown, Inc.
Grace Jeffers Collection of Formica Materials, Archives
Center, National Museum of American History,
Smithsonian Institution.

THE ROBBER BRIDE

Margaret Atwood

Charis is already there, sitting in the corner at a red for-mica table with gold sprinkles baked into it and aluminum legs and trim, which is either authentic fifties or else a reproduction. She's got them a bottle of white wine already and a bottle of Evian water. She sees them and smiles, and airy kisses go around the table.

Today Charis is wearing a sagging mauve cotton jersey dress, with a fuzzy grey cardigan over top and an orange-and-aqua scarf with a design of meadow flowers draped around her neck. Her long straight hair is grey-blonde and parted in the middle; she has her reading glasses stuck up on top of her head. Her peach lipstick could be her real lips. She resembles a slightly faded advertisement for herbal shampoo—healthful, but verging on the antique. What Ophelia would have looked like if she'd lived, or the Virgin Mary when middle-aged—earnest and distracted, and with an inner light. It's the inner light that gets her in trouble.

2003 Hospital of Fuenlabrada, Madrid. ARCHITECTS
Andrés Perea & Luis González. Formica® Laminate
F7845 Spectrum Red. PHOTOGRAPHER Jorge Flores.

1965 (left) Softglow, Scarlet Red 2, Glossy C.P.

2008 Showroom, Bilbao, Spain. Bench: Spectrum Red F7845, *Boulevard*, Hiroshi Tsunoda. Parasol: Alpino K1040, *Ensombra* by Odosdesign. Flooring: Fog Grey F7961. Window sills: ColorCore® Polar White CC2255, MicroDot. Wall paneling: Formica® Laminate custom design. Kitchen furniture: Crystal White F3091. Countertop: Cosmopolitan Concrete F5214, Riverwash. Cabinet: Smoky Brown Pear F5488, Naturelle. INTERIOR DESIGNER Mireia Masdeu. PHOTOGRAPHER Jorge Flores.

2013 (left) Red Ellipse 1913, Anniversary Collection of Formica brand laminate designed by Abbott Miller.

HELL-HEAVEN

Jhumpa Lahiri

Central Square is the first place I can recall living, and in my memories of our apartment, in a dark-brown shingled house on Ashburton Place, Pranab Kaku is always there. According to the story he liked to recall often, my mother invited him to accompany us back to our apartment that very afternoon, and prepared tea for the two of them; then, after learning that he had not had a proper Bengali meal in more than three months, she served him the leftover curried mackerel and rice that we had eaten for dinner the night before. He remained into the evening, for a second dinner, after my father got home, and after he showed up for dinner almost every night, occupying the fourth chair at our square Formica kitchen table, and becoming a part of our family in practice as well as in name.

He was from a wealthy family in Calcutta and had never had to do so much as pour himself a glass of water before moving to America, to study engineering at M.I.T. Life as a graduate student in Boston was a cruel shock, and in his first month he lost nearly twenty pounds. He had arrived in January, in the middle of a snowstorm, and at the end of a week he had packed his bags and gone to Logan, prepared to abandon the opportunity he worked toward all his life, only to change his mind at the last minute. He was living on Trowbridge Street in the home of a divorced woman with two young children who were always screaming and crying. He rented a room in the attic and was permitted to use the kitchen only at specified times of the day, and instructed always to wipe down the stove with Windex and a sponge. My parents agreed that it was a terrible situation, and if they'd had a bedroom to spare they would have offered it to him. Instead, they welcomed him to our meals, and opened up our apartment to him at any time, and soon it was there he went between classes and on his days off, always leaving behind some vestige of himself: a nearly finished pack of cigarettes, a newspaper, a piece of mail he had not bothered to open, a sweater he had taken off and forgotten in the course of his stay.

1965 Cover, *Idea/Fact Book: for Architects and Designers.*
Grace Jeffers Collection of Formica Materials,
Archives Center, National Museum of American
History, Smithsonian Institution.

1960s (left) Poppy matt 2751, B.S. 0-005.

2004 Author Jacinto Moros, Spain. F2-001. Formica® Laminate AR Plus Premium Gloss bonded on Maple/Birch Plywood.

2004 (right) Artwork in Formica® laminate, Furniture Show in Valencia, Spain. GRAPHIC DESIGNER Boke Bazan.

BLUE

1960s

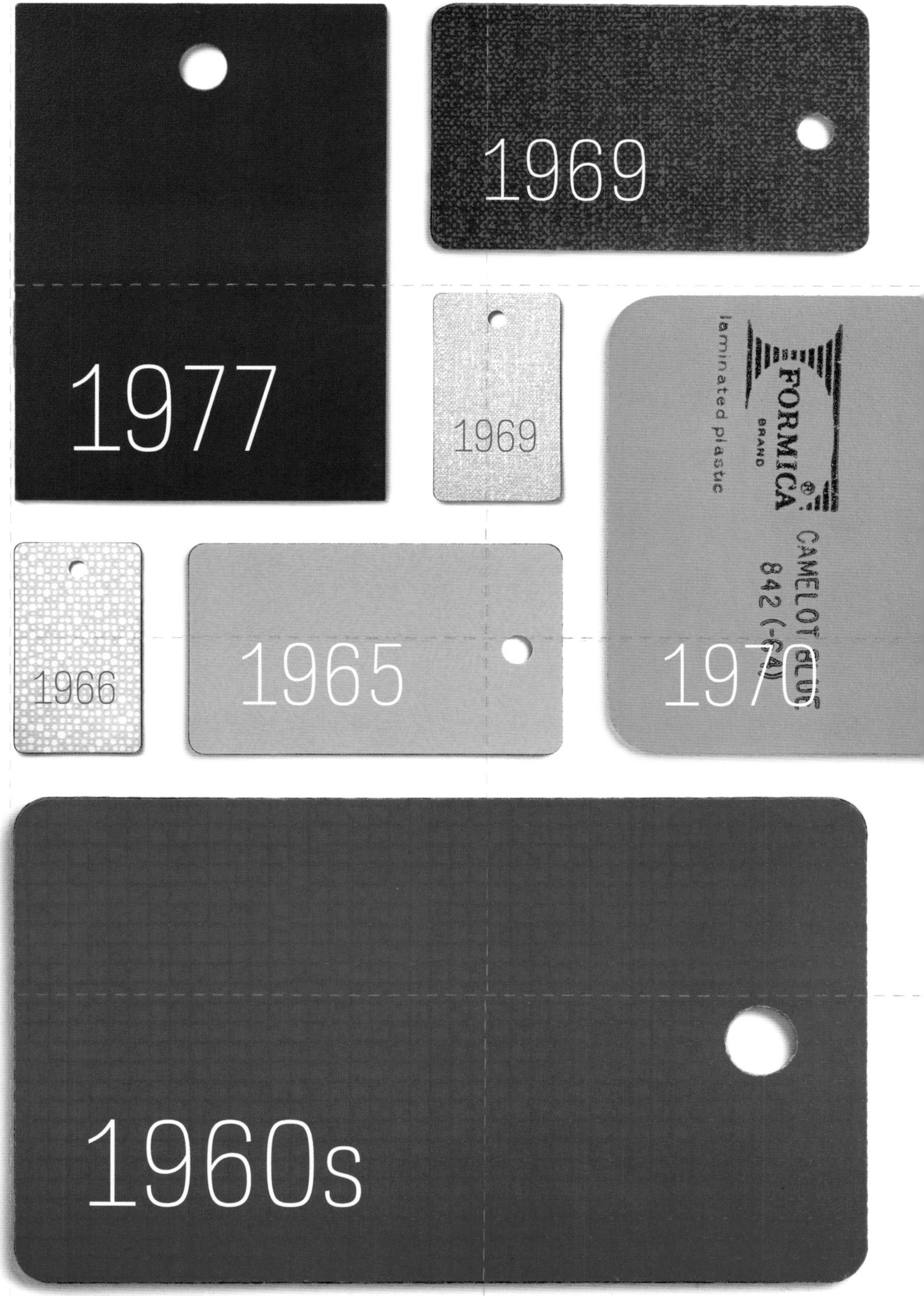

1969

1977

1969

laminated plastic

FORMICA

BRAND

CAMELOT BLUE

842 (-2A)

1966

1965

1970

1960s

1980 From cover of *Fabricator*, January issue.

bathrooms can

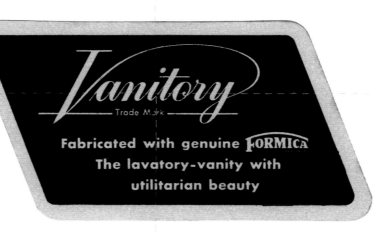

1949 Formica® Vanitory label.

2011 Kitchen, Sant Martí de Empuriès, Costa Brava, Spain. MATERIAL Formica® Laminate, Marine Blue F7914 AR Plus® premium gloss finish. ARCHITECT Elena Hachuel, Habitan Arquitectos. PHOTOGRAPHER Nuria Vila.

2005 Vanity table, presented at Milan Furniture Fair. MATERIAL Formica® laminate custom artwork. DESIGNER Hiroshi Tsunoda, Tokyo, Japan.

2009-2010 (left) Centro de Enseñanza Secundaria. Ondarroa. Vizcaya, Spain. MATERIAL Vivix® architectural panel. ARCHITECT Dueñas. PHOTOGRAPHER Jorge Flores.

1965 Turquoise Softglow 21672.

e moderne sans Formica...*

1959 Formica Ad.
1953´ (right) Aqua 921.
(*before 1953.)

Beauty Bonded

FORMICA

Reg. U.S. Pat. Off.

921

AQUA

THIS FINE LIFE

Eva Marie Everson

"I'm glad you like tuna salad," I said to Missy at lunch that day as she waddled toward the kitchen table. "It's about all I know how to prepare for lunch."

Missy eased herself down into a chair at the kitchen table. She laughed lightly and said, "You still haven't mastered the art of cooking." Then she tapped the top of the new Formica table Mama and I had picked out and said, "I'm thinking of having our kitchen remodeled with Formica. Did I tell you that? One thing about buying an old house; there's plenty to do to keep you busy."

1960s

1960s

1960s

2010

1960s

1994

1960s •

1960s

BROWN

1965 Ad from *Cocina y hogar.* "For you to feel, Formica creates the new Natural finish."

(right) From "Modern Formica Interiors" brochure. Grace Jeffers Collection of Formica Materials, Archives Center, National Museum of American History, Smithsonian Institution.

2005 Kitchen. MATERIAL Formica®
Stone Natural Quartz Surfacing
Black Andes and vertical surface with
Formica® Laminate 9011-NT Zebrano.

2006 Cathedral Cherry, Formica®
Veneer Premium Wood Surfacing.

1958 (right) Formica ad. "He fell
down.... Formica resists everything."

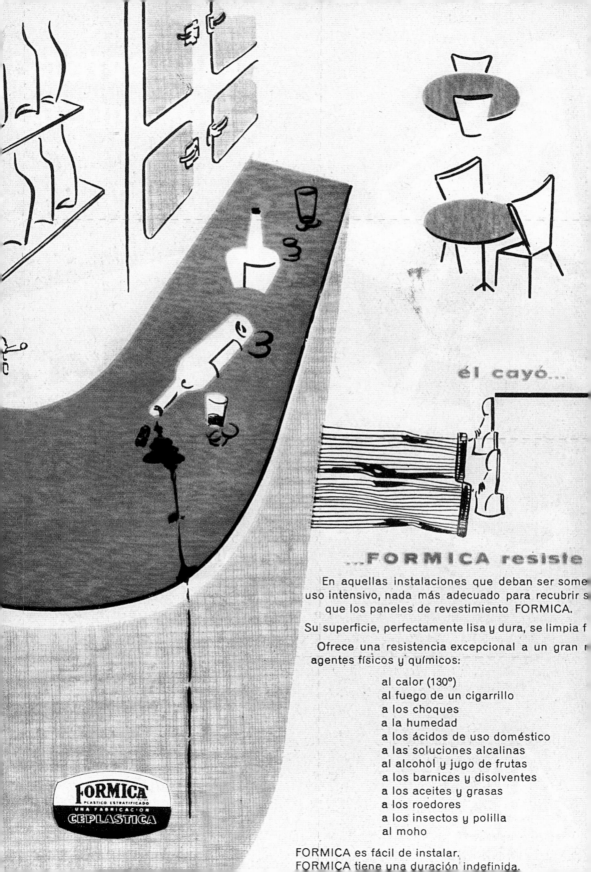

él cayó...

...FORMICA resiste

En aquellas instalaciones que deban ser some
uso intensivo, nada más adecuado para recubrir s
que los paneles de revestimiento FORMICA.

Su superficie, perfectamente lisa y dura, se limpia f

Ofrece una resistencia excepcional a un gran
agentes físicos y químicos:

al calor (130º)
al fuego de un cigarrillo
a los choques
a la humedad
a los ácidos de uso doméstico
a las soluciones alcalinas
al alcohol y jugo de frutas
a los barnices y disolventes
a los aceites y grasas
a los roedores
a los insectos y polilla
al moho

FORMICA es fácil de instalar.
FORMICA tiene una duración indefinida.

1953* Natural Maple Picwood, 80-GP-92. (*before 1953)

1953 Ad, "Reserved for a Man," from *American Builder*. Grace Jeffers Collection of Formica Materials, Archives Center, National Museum of American History, Smithsonian Institution.

1953 (right) Autumn Walnut, 20-FC-25.

LOVE AIN'T NOTHING BUT
SEX MISSPELLED

Harlan Ellison

The thick-armed counterman, leaning across the formica counter-top, furrowed his brow and said, very carefully, so there was no chance for misinterpretation, "Sorry fellah, we can't serve you."

2006 Pear 4485, Formica® Veneer Premium Wood Surfacing.

2005 (right) Walls: Formica Ligna®, Armagnac 4415. Countertop: Formica Stone, Natural Quartz Surfacing, Blue Crystalle 9044. Counter Face: Formica DecoMetal, Brushed Black Aluminum, 4254.

Beauty Bonded

FORMICA
Reg. U.S. Pat. Off.
886

SPACKLED AND SPOOKED

Jennie Bentley

COCOA

This long, low ranch was as different as could be from Aunt Inga's cottage, the last— the only— house we'd worked on together, but I could already see the finished product in my head. And there would be no pink walls or daisies. What there would be were gleaming hardwood floors instead of stained, tan carpets, walls painted in bright but neutral colors— cocoa, gray, taupe— and some to-die-for retro accessories. Something to really set the tone and the mood without turning potential buyers off. The kitchen would have to be gutted and modernized. Formica counters would be nice. Formica was huge in the '60s, and these days, the new solid surface Formica is fabulous. And maybe we could put in some of those sleek, Scandinavian cabinets Derek had in his loft, along with some ultramodern stainless steel appliances.

2011 Apartment, Barcelona, Spain.
MATERIAL DecoMetal® Metal Laminates
by Formica Group. Copper veil M5392.
ARCHITECTS YLAB. PHOTOGRAPHER Ciro
Frank Schiappa.

1953* (left) Cocoa 886. (*before 1953)

This is a Photo Reproduction of the
New FORMICA® "Tawny Walnut"

Even the finest printing can never hope to do justice to the beauty and depth of pattern of the two new flat cut walnuts recently added to the Formica Sunrise Color Line. Turn the page to see the other side of this sheet for procedure to secure actual samples.

Beauty Bonded
FORMICA®
Laminated Plastic
Pays in Performance

REPLACEMENT OR REFUND OF MONEY
Guaranteed by
Good Housekeeping
IF NOT AS ADVERTISED THEREIN

Photo reproduction of the Formica® "Tawny Walnut" pattern. Grace Jeffers Collection of Formica Materials, Archives Center, National Museum of American History, Smithsonian Institution.

2010 (right) Petrified Wood 3474, 180fx® laminate.

Formica Group archives.

1981

1965

SPROUT GREEN
Beauty Bonded
FORMICA
Reg.U.S.Pat.Off.
907

1953*

Beauty Bonded
FORMICA
Reg.U.S.Pat.Off.
914

SPRUCE

1953*

1981

1981

GREEN

1969

1981

1953*

(*before 1953)

1969 The Chart room on the bridge of the QE2. White Parchment for the ceiling. Magnolia Weave for the wall. From *The Formica Scene on the QE2*, 1970; INTERIOR DESIGNER, Dennis Lennon. Grace Jeffers Collection of Formica Materials, Archives Center, National Museum of American History, Smithsonian Institution.

1953 (right) Sprout Green 907. (*before 1953)

THUNDERBALL

Ian Fleming

They followed him down and along a passage to the mess hall, a well-lighted dining room finished in cream with pastel pink and green panels. They took their places at the head of one of the Formica-top tables away from the other officers and men, who looked curiously at the two civilians. The captain waved a hand at the walls of the room. "Bit of a change from the old battleship grey. You'd be surprised how many eggheads are involved in the design of these ships. Have to be, if you want to keep your crew happy when the ship's submerged for a month or more at a time."

2006 Tables for the MetroNova restaurant square in Stockholm shopping center. Image from *Trends 2, 2007*. MATERIAL Formica Impress. TABLE MANUFACTURER Ragnar Inredningar.

1957 (right) Ad from *Destino*. "Defend your furniture with a guaranteed brand."

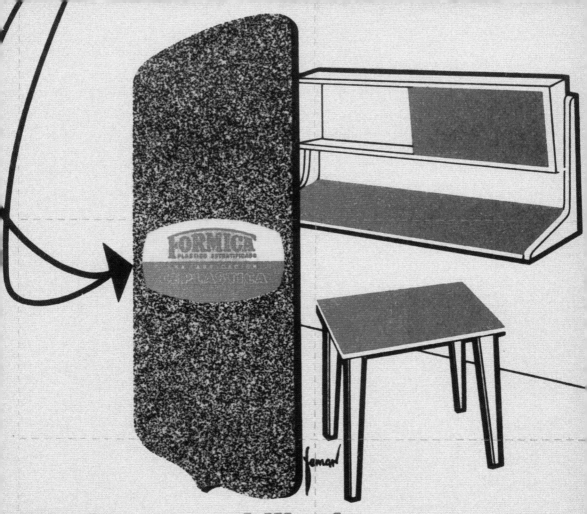

efienda su mobiliario
on la garantía
e una marca

Desde el salón al cuarto de baño,
de la habitación de los niños a la cocina
FORMICA proporciona a los muebles y
paredes, bellas superficies coloreadas,
que con sus múltiples dibujos
se prestan a todas las variantes
de la inspiración decorativa.

FORMICA aporta una soluc
los problemas del revestim

2009 Centro de Enseñanza Secundaria, Vizcaya, Spain. MATERIAL Vivix® architectural panels. ARCHITECT Dueñas. PHOTOGRAPHER Jorge Flores.

2009 (left) Civic center Mesoiro, A Coruña, Galicia, Spain. MATERIAL Vivix® architectural panels, F6901 Vibrant Green, F7967 Hunter Green, F3007 Pale Olive. ARCHITECT Naos Arquitectura. PHOTOGRAPHER Santos-Díez.

COOKING FOR HARRY

Kay-Marie James

"Every night, I walk in the door and there he stands, complaining about my furniture. Go on home, I tell him, but he says he's lonely, he's confused, he's going to hang with me until he figures out the next step. Maybe, says he, I can help you with some renovations. Baby, says I, no offense, but I don't care to love in a place that looks like the inside of a microwave. So what does he do? Pulls up my nice green Formica counter and puts in a slab of some butt-ugly rock. Expensive butt-ugly rock."

Malva spun back to Amber, who was smiling in spite of herself, her gaze gone soft with affection.

"You children need to make nice before you tear this whole neighborhood to pieces! Your daddy's cookbooks, my nice Formica. Don't you think this has gone far enough?"

1968 Ad from *Triunfo*. "A new world of Formica®."

1960s (left) Bottle Green 2787, B.S. 6-073.

1968 Ad, promoting the application of Formica®
laminate to bathroom furniture, Spain.

Beauty Bonded
FORMICA
Reg. U.S. Pat. Off.
851

PINK

1953*

Des. Pat. 157, 633

1953*

Beauty Bonded
FORMICA
Reg. U.S. Pat. Off.
79-L-40

PINK SKYLARK

1953

©DESIGN COPYRIGHTED

1965

1981

(*before 1953)

PINK

1971

FORMICA ®
BRAND

laminated plastic

PANTHER
PINK
850-(64

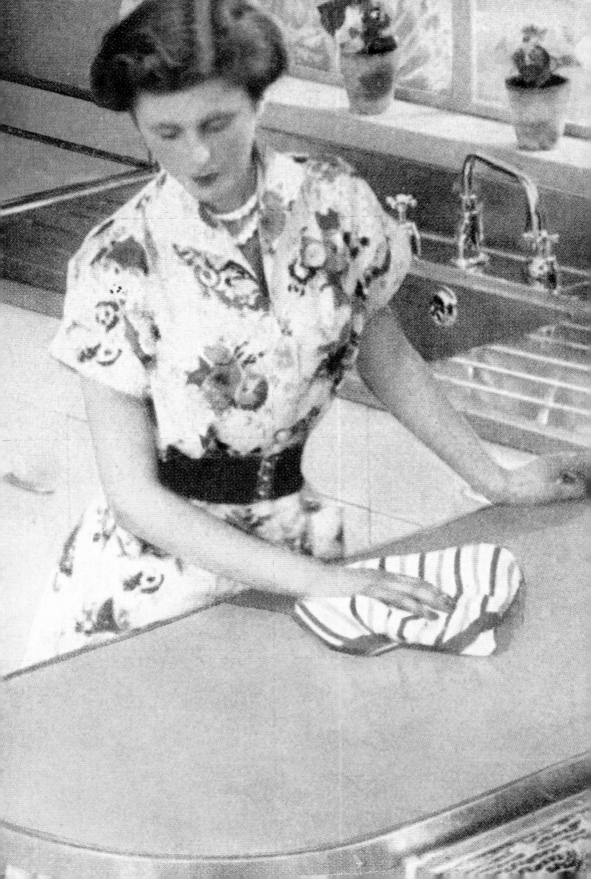

1983 Lee Payne, *Neapolitan*. Coffee table of ColorCore® laminate from exhibition *Site*. Image from *Contemporary Landscape; From the Horizon of Postmodern Design*, 1985.

1954 (left) Ad, "Clean at a Wipe!"

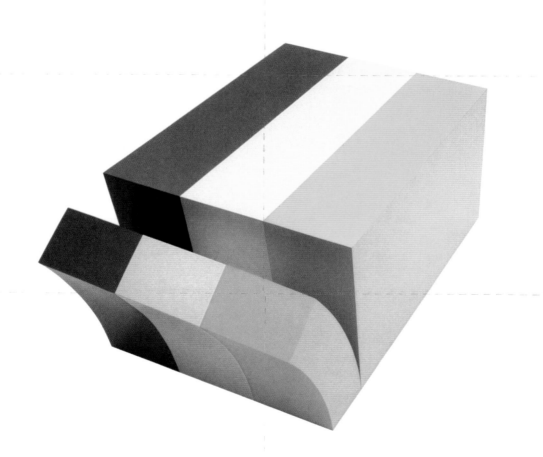

1955 "Put Your Bathrooms to Work!" Ad from *This Formica World, Volume 7*. (Second quarter). Bathroom built by J.G. Lehman and Assoc., Cincinnati, Ohio. Formica® laminate fabricated by Muellers Cabinet Shop.

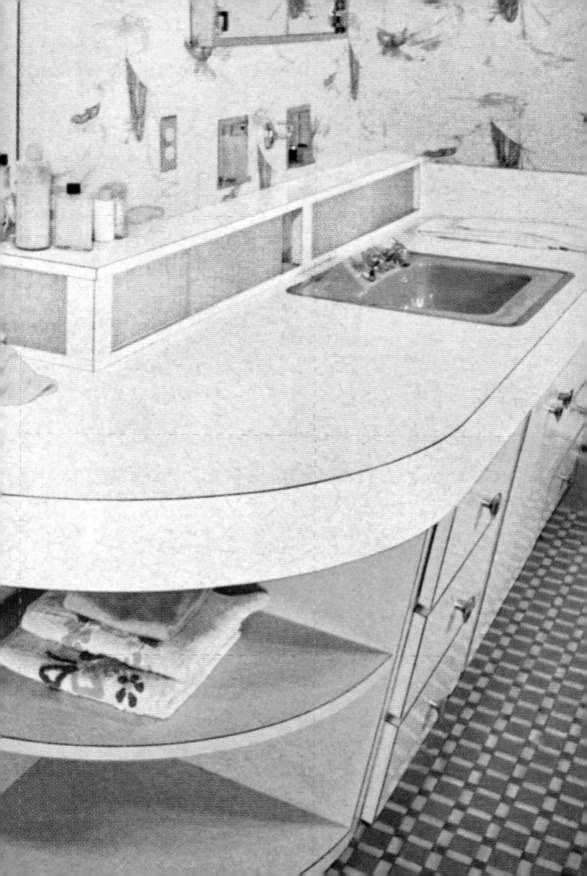

1953 Ad from *House and Garden*, July 1953. "You don't need a door on a Formica kitchen." "With the use of lovely Formica® laminate colors and beautiful wood grains there is every reason to plan an open kitchen that is part of the dining room–living room."

1959

1966

1960s

Beauty Bonded
FORMICA
Reg. U.S.Pat.Off.
949

WHITE

1953

WHITE

1960s

1960

1960s

(*before 1953)

2009 Reception desk and meeting tables, Modesco Insurance Offices, Belgium. MATERIAL AR Plus High Gloss in White.

2010 (left) Counter, Polar White ColorCore® laminate, Juzgados de Villaviciosa, Asturias, Spain. ARCHITECT Jovino Martínez Sierra. PHOTOGRAPHER Marcos Morilla.

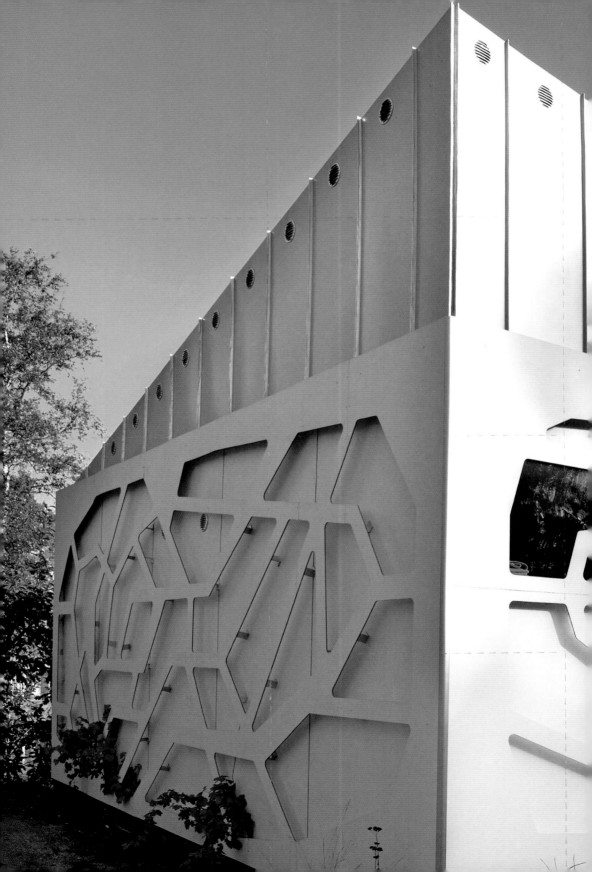

2006 Summer cottage outside Copenhagen.
MATERIAL Formica® Exterior Compact 6mm
thick. Colourway K1040 Alpino. ARCHITECT Mads
Lützen, Los arkitekter, Copenhagen, Denmark.
PHOTOGRAPHER Peter Jörgensen.

2008 Thomas Mayne, Morphosis, *Untitled*, Formica® Solid Surfacing, color Arctic (102), wood, steel. Rendering. From *Form: Contemporary Architects at Play*. Courtesy Contemporary Arts Center, Cincinnati, Ohio.

2009 (right) World of Wearable Arts Competition entry *Behind Closed Doors*. Snowdrift Formica® laminate, designed by Kathryn Preston & Angie Robinson of Christchurch, New Zealand.

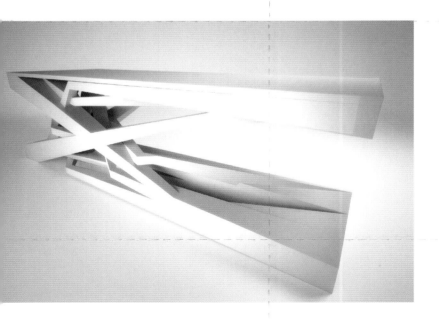

"C" IS FOR CORPSE

Sue Grafton

The room was large, with deep-set windows looking onto the rear of the property. The wall-to-wall carpeting was white, a dense cut-pile so recently vacuumed that I could see Bobby's footprints in places. His double bed seemed diminutive in a room that was probably thirty feet square, with a large dressing room opening off to the left and what was apparently a bathroom beyond that. A television set rested in an antique pine blanket-chest at the foot of the bed. On the wall to my right was a long built-in desk with a white Formica surface. An IBM Selectric II and the keyboard, monitor, and printer for a home computer were lined up along its length. The bookshelves were white Formica too, filled almost exclusively with medical texts. There was a sitting area in the far corner: two over-stuffed chairs and an ottoman covered in a plaid fabric of rust, white, and slate blue. The coffee table, reading lamp, books and magazines stacked nearby suggested that this was where Bobby spent his leisure time.

He went to an intercom on the wall and pressed a button. "Callie, we're starving up here. Could you send us a tray? There are two of us and we'll need some white wine, too."

2010 Doors, Heidenstamskolan.
By Metod Arkitekter. MATERIAL
Formica® Impress, colors F2296 Sno
White and F2297 Terril.

1960s (left) Polar White, Plain
Color, 40395.

1969 FURNITURE, SPACE DESIGN
Klaus Wagner. PHOTOGRAPHER
Leopoldo Pomés.

2005 (right) Kitchen, 949 SP White
laminate, Sculpted Finish.

CROSSINGS

Chuang Hua

Unless he was in bed or in the kitchen or not at home, he was to be found usually seated in either armchair reading, meditating or dozing, surrounded by neat piles of magazines, newspapers and financial reports. Sometimes he would go into the small study next to his bedroom if he had letters to write or figures to calculate on an electric adding machine which rested on the white formica desk ledge. Built into one wall, it had drawers on either side in which he kept documents and papers such as certificates of medical studies completed in China, Germany and America, assorted travel documents, and official papers, military decrees in Chinese, yellowed postcard mementoes of a week in Torquay with Mr. and Mrs. Stiff, watches purchased in Geneva, camera, old sturdy Parker fountain pens, stamps and paper clips, a rubber doll from the Folies Bergère, a thank-you note in a thin box of handkerchiefs presented to him by a woman whose handbag he had found in the subway and returned, his Zeiss microscope in the square black box, surgical instruments hurriedly picked from the glass-doored cabinets of his clinic and packed into his physician's bag in the dark, leaving the rest to the Japanese who took the city in the morning, a commemorative medal from the World's Fair of 1939, collected on the occasion of his first visit alone to America, children's school bills, letters from those who entered and left his life, people from whom he received and to whom he gave he could not part with.

2011 Stools. MATERIAL Formica® Laminate, Crystal White F3091 on plywood. DESIGNER Juan Pablo Quintero, Mediodesign, Barcelona, Spain. PHOTOGRAPHER Lucía Carretero.

1960 (left) Tidewood Matt, 7650.

Beauty Bonded

FORMICA
Reg. U.S. Pat. Off.
872

PUMPKIN

1953*

1960s

1970

ORANGE

1981

1993

FORMICA®
BRAND

laminated plastic

BITTERSWEET
871

-64 SUEDE

1963

1955 Cover from *This Formica World, Volume 7.* (Fourth quarter).

2005 Cabinet door. MATERIAL Formica® Laminate AR Plus® premium gloss finish, Levante Orange K3210. PHOTOGRAPHER Aitor Ortiz.

2007 (right) Cosmetic counter. MATERIAL 7223-MC New White and 909-90 Black. ColorCore2™ laminate.

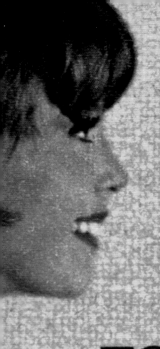
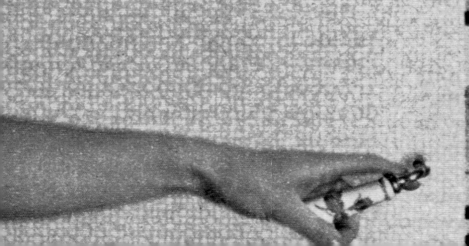
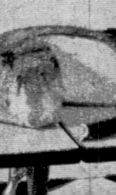

FORMICA*

un vrai soleil !

1993 Fiesta, 2013-58.

2006 Waterschap Hollandse Delta 1, MATERIAL Rattan Cane F3699 NAT and Natural Cane F6930 NAT architectural doors. ARCHITECT EGM Architecten/ Evert van Reijswoud.

2002 (right) Washroom, Mercedes Benz plant, Vitoria, Spain. MATERIAL Formica® Compact, Clementine F2962, Matte 58. PHOTOGRAPHER Jorge Flores.

2008 Miribilla Fitness Club changing room lockers and benches. Bilbao, Spain. MATERIAL Formica® Laminate, AR Plus Gloss finish, Clementine F2962. ARCHITECT Aitor Martínez de Zuazo & Igor Zorrakin. PHOTOGRAPHER Jaizki Fontaneda.

1953* (right) Pumpkin 872. (*before 1953).

PIGEON FEATHERS
AND OTHER STORIES

John Updike

Griffin squealed in ecstasy and cried, "Oh, Kruppman! Kruppman, how you do go on!" and jabbed Virginia in the arm so hard an English Oval jumped from her hand and hobbled across the Formica table. William gazed over their heads in pain.

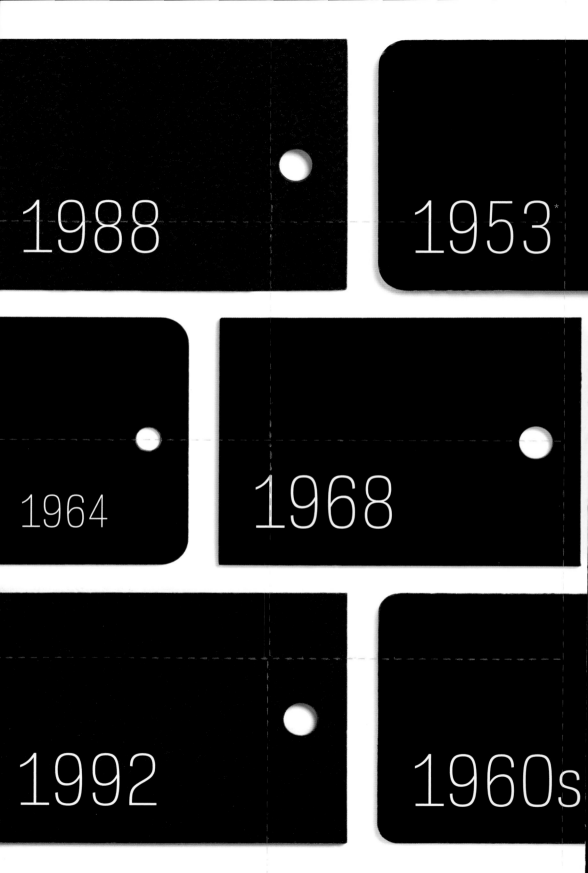

1988

1953*

1964

1968

1992

1960s

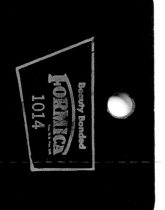

Beauty Bonded
FORMICA
1014

1953*

BLACK

1960s

1959

(*before 1953)

2011 Sports Center La Pobla de Vallbona, Valencia, Spain. Exterior façade with Vivix® architectural panels K1040 Alpino and K3735 Krypton. ARCHITECT Emilio Conejero. PHOTOGRAPHER Carlos Gutiérrez.

2009 (left) Linewood surface finish mimics wire brushed or sandblasted soft woods. Formica® Unilin Collection. PHOTOGRAPHER Eva Hoernisch.

2004 (below) Formica® laminate ensemble modeled on the catwalk at the launch event, Madame Tussaud's museum, London. DESIGNER Lyn Randall.

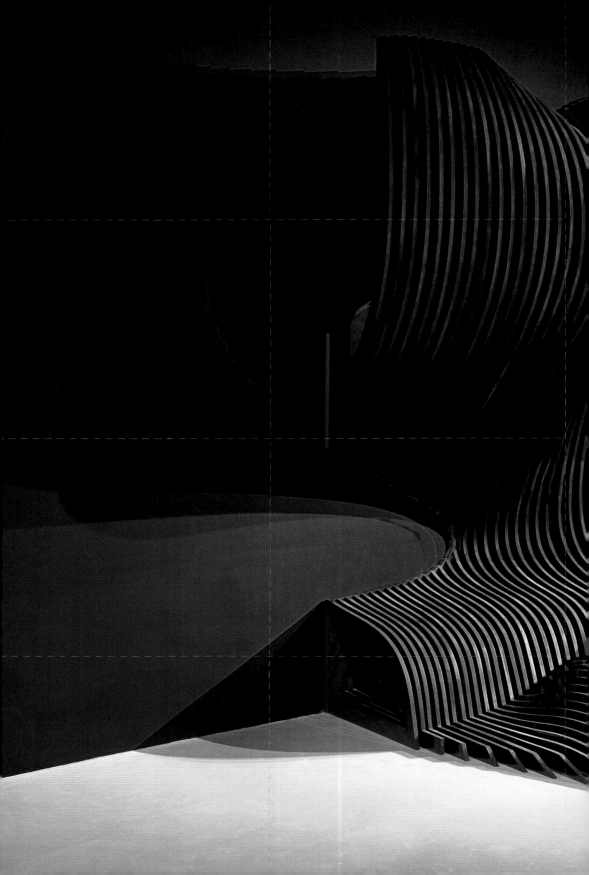

2004 Formica® Stone Natural Quartz Surfacing, 9047 Black Andes.

1960s (right) Diamond Black Matt 2253, B.S. 9-103.

COUPLES

John Updike

Why don't you take the afternoon off and walk me through the Common over to Newbury Street and look at pictures? You understand pictures. What's this new gimmick of making things look like comic strips?

She put her hand palm up on the tabletop; it was moist, a creased pink saucer of moisture on the silver-flecked formica. When he put his hand in hers, the gesture, amid the clatter and breeze of the cafeteria, felt hugely inflated: two immense white hands, like the mock-up of a beefburger, advertising love.

1973 (previous page) Ad image from campaign "Conozca del todo a Formica" (Get to know all of Formica).

ตลอดกาล

永远

永遠

IKUISESTI

PARA SIEMPRE

POUR TOUJOURS

Au cours d'un siècle, le groupe de sociétés Formica a vu une énorme transformation, depuis ses débuts en tant que petit producteur de composants industriels jusqu'à devenir le plus grand fabricant au monde de stratifié haute pression—un nom de marque reconnu dans de nombreux pays. Mais plus que cela, ce siècle de changement a démontré comment un matériau de revêtement pionnier peut aussi transformer notre environnement. Formica Group continue d'évoluer et de répondre aux nouvelles exigences du marché.

Il est dit que le créateur du téléphone, Alexander Graham Bell, a prédit qu'un jour il y aurait un téléphone dans chaque ville des États-Unis. On peut sourire en constatant combien il avait sous-estimé la vaste portée de son invention. Les inventeurs du stratifié Formica®, Daniel J. O'Conor et Herbert A. Faßber, ont pu assister à l'immense attrait de leur produit polyvalent. Appliqué dans de nombreux foyers et d'autres environnements, à des fins utilitaires et même dans les beaux-arts, le stratifié Formica est apparu dans les cuisines et les cafés, les bureaux et les écoles, au Radio City Music Hall et sur les paquebots de croisière.

Ce livre, qui célèbre le 100ème anniversaire de Formica Group, présente l'histoire de l'entreprise et la façon dont le stratifié Formica, en tant que matériau de revêtement, a joué un rôle dans l'histoire de notre société. Créé durant une période d'invention industrielle considérable puis se transformant en stratifié décoratif permettant ainsi de réaliser les rêves de modernité et de fraîcheur, le design et l'innovation ont été au premier plan du développement de l'entreprise.

En el transcurso de un siglo, el grupo de empresas Formica ha experimentado una enorme transformación, desde sus comienzos como pequeño productor de componentes industriales hasta convertirse en el fabricante más grande del mundo de laminado de alta presión; una marca de renombre en varios países. Pero además de eso, este siglo de cambio ha demostrado cómo un material pionero de revestimiento también puede transformar nuestros alrededores. El Grupo Formica continúa evolucionando y cumple con las nuevas demandas del mercado.

Se dice que el inventor del teléfono, Alexander Graham Bell, predijo que un día iba a haber un teléfono en cada pueblo de los Estados Unidos. Quizá sonreímos al leer cuánto él mismo subestimó el inmenso alcance que su invento tendría. Los inventores del laminado Formica®, Daniel J. O'Conor y Herbert A. Faber, fueron capaces de presenciar el inmenso atractivo de su producto versátil. Aplicado en incontables hogares y en otros ambientes, con fines utilitarios e incluso en las bellas artes, el laminado Formica se utilizó en cocinas, cafés, oficinas y escuelas, en el Radio City Music Hall y en cruceros.

Este libro, que celebra el primer centenario del Grupo Formica, presenta la historia de la empresa y las formas en que el laminado Formica, como material de revestimiento, ha influido también en la historia social. Creado durante un período de considerable invención industrial, su evolución como laminado decorativo hizo realidad los sueños de modernidad y originalidad; en ese sentido, el diseño y la innovación han estado, desde entonces, al frente del desarrollo de la empresa.

Yhden vuosisadan aikana Formica Group on kokenut valtavia muutoksia. Se aloitti toimintansa pienenä teollisuuskomponenttien valmistajana ja kasvoi maailman suurimmaksi korkeapainelaminaatin tuottajaksi – monessa maassa sen nimi tunnetaan jokaisessa kodissa. Eikä siinä kaikki. Tämä muutosten vuosisata on osoittanut, kuinka uraauurtava pintamateriaali voi täysin muuntaa ympäristömme. Formica Group jatkaa kehitystään ja tyydyttää markkinoiden uudet tarpeet.

Puhelimen keksijän Alexander Graham Bellin sanotaan ennustaneen, että jonakin päivänä jokaisessa amerikkalaisessa kylässä olisi puhelin. Tänään hänen keksintönsä saavuttaman valtavan levinneisyyden aliarviointi saattaa hymyilyttää. Formica®-laminaatin keksijät Daniel J. O'Conor ja Herbert A. Faber näkivät itse monipuolisen tuotteensa suunnattoman menestyksen. Formica-laminaattia käytettiin lukuisissa kodeissa ja muissa ympäristöissä käytännöllisiin ja jopa taiteellisiin tarkoituksiin: Formicaa nähtiin keittiöissä ja kahviloissa, toimistoissa ja kouluissa, Radio City Music Hallissa ja loistoristeilijöillä.

Tämä kirja, jolla juhlistetaan Formica Groupin satavuotispäivää, tarkastelee yrityksen historiaa ja eri rooleja, joita Formica-laminaatti on esittänyt yhteiskuntahistoriassa. Tuote luotiin huomattavien teollisten keksintöjen aikana, ja siitä kehitetty koristelaminaatti vastasi ajan nykyaikaisuuden ja tuoreuden vaatimuksia. Aina siitä saakka yhtiön kehitystyössä on painotettu muotoilua ja innovaatiota.

Formica-laminaatti on "alkuperäinen" ja edelleenkin korkealuokkainen materiaali. Liikeyrityksenä tiedämme,

在過去的一個世紀裡，富美家公司集團 (Formica Group of Companies) 經歷了巨大的變革，從最初工業部件的小製造商，成為世界上規模最大的高壓美耐板製造商——其家用品牌在許多國家家喻戶曉。但更重要的是，這個世紀的變化表明，一種開拓性的貼面材料如何改變了我們周圍的環境。富美家集團在不斷發展，滿足新的市場需求。

據說電話的發明者亞歷山大·格雷厄姆·貝爾 (Alexander Graham Bell) 預測有一天美國每個城鎮都會有一部電話。當我們讀到他如此低估了自己的發明的普及範圍時，我們會一笑置之。富美家公司的美耐板發明者丹尼爾 J. 奧康納 (Daniel J.O'Conor) 和赫伯特 A. 費伯 (Herbert A. Faber) 有力地見證了用途廣泛的產品具有巨大的吸引力。富美家的美耐板應用在無數的家庭和不同的環境中，既實用又達到藝術目的，出現在廚房、咖啡廳、辦公室、學校、無線電城音樂廳和遊輪上。

本書為紀念富美家集團成立一百週年而作，縱觀了該行業的歷史以及富美家美耐板作為一種貼面材料如何在社會歷史中的作用。美耐板創始於工業發明創造盛行的時代，逐漸演變成一種裝飾性貼面，去完成現代性和新鮮感的夢想，該產品的設計和創新從那時起就處於公司發展的前沿。

富美家貼面是「原創產品」，現在仍然是一種高性能材料。作為企業，我們知道，沒有什麼是靜止不動的，有時可能會很難，但我們提供的內在價值

在过去的一个世纪里，富美家公司集团 (Formica Group of Companíes) 经历了巨大的变化，从最初工业部件的小制造商，成为世界上规模最大的高压耐火板制造商——其家用品牌在许多国家都家喻户晓。但更重要的是，这个世纪的变化表明，一种开拓性的贴面材料如何改变了我们周围的环境。富美家集团在不断发展，满足新的市场需求。

据说电话的发明者亚历山大·格雷厄姆·贝尔 (Alexander Graham Bell) 预测有一天美国每个城镇都会有一部电话。当我们读到他如此低估了自己的发明的普及范围时，我们会置之一笑。富美家公司耐火板的发明者丹尼尔 J. 奥康纳 (Daniel J.O'Conor) 和赫伯特 A. 费伯 (Herbert A. Faber) 有力地见证了用途广泛的产品具有巨大的吸引力。富美家的耐火板应用在无数的家庭和不同的环境中，既实用又有艺术性，应用在厨房、咖啡厅、办公室、学校、无线电城音乐厅和游轮上。

本书为纪念富美家集团成立一百周年而作，纵观了该行业的历史以及富美家耐火板作为一种贴面材料如何在社会历史中起作用。耐火板创始于工业发明创造盛行的时代，逐渐演变成一种装饰性贴面，去完成现代性和新鲜感的梦想，该产品的设计和创新从那时起就处于公司发展的前沿。

富美家贴面是 "原创产品"，现在仍是一种高性能材料。作为企业，我们知道，没有什么是静止不动的，有时可能会很难，但我们提供的内在价值

ตลอดช่วงหนึ่งศตวรรษที่ผ่านมา ได้มีการเปลี่ยนแปลงอย่างมากมายกับกลุ่มบริษัทฟอร์ไมก้า จากจุดเริ่มต้นในฐานะผู้ผลิตชิ้นส่วนอุตสาหกรรมรายเล็กจนกลายมาเป็นผู้ผลิตแผ่นลามิเนทแรงอัดสูงรายใหญ่ที่สุดของโลกที่ชื่อกลายเป็นชื่อเรียกแทนวัสดุปิดผิวลามิเนทในหลายประเทศ แต่ยิ่งไปกว่านั้นศตวรรษแห่งการเปลี่ยนแปลงนี้ได้แสดงให้เห็นว่าวัสดุปิดผิวที่บุกเบิกตลาดสามารถเปลี่ยนแปลงสิ่งต่างๆ รอบตัวของเราได้อย่างไรบ้าง กลุ่มบริษัทฟอร์ไมก้า ยังคงพัฒนาและตอบสนองความต้องการใหม่ๆ ของตลาดต่อไป

ทั้งนี้ มีการกล่าวว่าว่า อเล็กซานเดอร์ เกรแฮม เบลล์ ผู้คิดค้นโทรศัพท์ ได้คาดการณ์ไว้ว่าวันหนึ่งทุกเมืองในอเมริกาจะมีโทรศัพท์หนึ่งเครื่อง เราอาจยิ้มเมื่อเราอ่านและเห็นว่าเขาได้ประเมินสิ่งประดิษฐ์ของเขาซึ่งได้เข้าถึงผู้คนในวงกว้างไว้ต่ำเกินไปเพียงได เดเนียล เจ โอ โคเนอร์และเฮอร์บิร์ต เอเฟเบอร์ ผู้ประดิษฐ์แผ่นลามิเนทฟอร์ไมก้าได้มีโอกาสเห็นว่าผลิตภัณฑ์อเนกประสงค์ของพวกเขาน่าดึงดูดใจอย่างมากจากการที่ผลิตภัณฑ์ถูกนำไปใช้ในบ้านและในและสถานที่ต่างๆ จำนวนนับไม่ถ้วน ทั้งเพื่อวัตถุประสงค์ในด้านประโยชน์ใช้สอยและแม้กระทั่งในด้านวิจิตรศิลป์ แผ่นลามิเนทฟอร์ไมก้าปรากฏอยู่ในห้องครัวร้านกาแฟ สำนักงาน โรงเรียน หอแสดงดนตรีเรดิโอซิติ และบนเรือสำราญ

หนังสือเล่มนี้ พิมพ์ขึ้นเพื่อฉลองการครบรอบ 100 ปีของกลุ่มบริษัทฟอร์ไมก้าบอกถึงประวัติของธุรกิจนี้และแนวทางที่ผลิตภัณฑ์ลามิเนทมีส่วนในประวัติศาสตร์ในฐานะวัสดุปิดผิว เนื่องจากผลิตภัณฑ์นี้ผลิตขึ้นในช่วงที่มีการประดิษฐ์คิดค้นเชิงอุตสาหกรรมเป็นอย่างมากและค่อยๆ พัฒนาเป็นลามิเนทตกแต่งเพื่อเติมเต็มความฝัน ของความทันสมัยและความสดใหม่การออกแบบและนวัตกรรมของผลิตภัณฑ์นี้

Le stratifié Formica est « l'original » et il demeure un matériau de haute performance. En tant qu'entreprise, nous savons que le temps ne s'arrête jamais et qu'il peut y avoir des moments difficiles, mais la valeur intrinsèque de ce que nous offrons perdure. Grâce à des initiatives de recherche et de développement internes, un choix varié de textures intéressantes et exclusives a été créé pour nos gammes de stratifiés décoratifs. Ceci va de pair avec le développement continu de motifs, décors et couleurs ; le tout en suivant l'évolution des tendances et les commentaires des clients.

Outre les stratégies et initiatives à travers toutes nos installations, nous voulons être un fabricant responsable et une « entreprise citoyenne ». Nous vivons à une époque de prise de conscience accrue de la clientèle au sujet de l'apparence, de la perception et de l'impact des matériaux choisis et utilisés dans les maisons, les établissements publics et les immeubles commerciaux. C'est ce leadership qui poursuit cette lancée. Aujourd'hui, à travers les activités de Formica Group dans le monde entier, il est possible d'absorber les tendances internationales, de réfléchir et de répondre aux goûts des clients partout au monde. L'avenir est rempli de possibilités excitantes, puisque l'entreprise s'étend désormais sur cinq continents. La concurrence mondiale joue également sur la façon dont fonctionne l'entreprise, que ce soit en matière d'innovation ou d'intégration au niveau international, ou par l'intervention des designers individuels qui contribuent à réaliser des projets spécifiques au niveau local.

La puissance de la marque Formica se base en fin de compte sur l'expérience de la clientèle et contribue aux succès futurs. La reconnaissance du stratifié Formica et de la marque Formica au cours de notre histoire et sur les marchés établis se prolongent par l'accueil dans les pays nouvellement industrialisés et les économies émergentes. Alors que le stratifié Formica trouve sa place dans de nouvelles villes, infrastructures et des maisons du vingt-et-unième siècle, nous attendons avec impatience les cent prochaines années et nous nous appuyons sur tout ce que notre héritage peut nous offrir.

El laminado Formica es "el original" y continúa siendo un material que ofrece un gran resultado. Como empresa, sabemos que nada se detiene y que puede haber tiempos difíciles, pero el valor intrínseco de lo que ofrecemos perdura. Por medio de iniciativas internas de investigación y desarrollo, se creó una opción diferente de texturas nuevas, apasionantes y exclusivas para nuestras líneas de laminado decorativo. Esto acompaña el desarrollo continuo de alternativas de diseño, decoración y color, a la par de las proyecciones de diseño y las opiniones de los clientes.

A esto se le suman las estrategias y las iniciativas en todas nuestras instalaciones, que aportan para que seamos un fabricante y "ciudadano corporativo" responsable. Vivimos en tiempos de una elevada conciencia del cliente con respecto a la apariencia, la textura y el impacto de los materiales que se eligen y utilizan en hogares particulares, instalaciones públicas y edificios comerciales. Es este liderazgo lo que mantiene el impulso: hoy en día, a través de las operaciones del Grupo Formica alrededor del mundo, es posible asimilar las tendencias internacionales para reflejar y satisfacer los gustos de los clientes a nivel global. Prevemos un futuro apasionante, ya que la empresa está presente en cinco continentes. La competitividad global también se refiere a cómo funciona la empresa, ya sea generando innovación e integración a nivel internacional o ayudando a los diseñadores individuales a realizar sus proyectos específicos a nivel local.

El poder de la marca Formica, que a fin de cuentas se trata de la experiencia del cliente, será importante para el éxito futuro. El reconocimiento del laminado Formica y de la marca Formica durante su historia y en mercados consolidados se está extendiendo y es bienvenido en países recientemente industrializados y en economías emergentes. A medida que el laminado Formica establece su lugar en nuevas ciudades, infraestructuras y hogares del siglo XXI, esperamos con entusiasmo los próximos cien años y construimos sobre todo lo que ofrece nuestro legado.

que mikään ei pysy paikallaan ja ajat voivat olla kovia, mutta tarjoamiemme tuotteiden todellinen arvo kestää. Olemme luoneet omien tutkimus- ja kehitysaloitteiden kautta monipuolisen valikoiman jännittäviä ja ainutlaatuisia uusia pintatekstuureja koristelaminaateillemme. Trendiennusteiden ja asiakaspalautteen pohjalta jatkamme samanaikaisestieri kuosien, tyylien ja värivalikoimien kehittämistä.

Kaikissa toimipaikoissamme sovelletaan strategioita ja aloitteita, jotka perustuvat luotettavan valmistajan ja "yrityskansalaisen" maineellemme. Elämme aikaa, jona asiakkaat ovat erittäin tietoisia materiaalien ulkonäöstä, tunnusta ja vaikutuksesta, käytettiinpä niitä sitten yksityisissä asunnoissa, julkisissa tiloissa tai kaupallisissa rakennuksissa. Johtajuus pitää meidät kärjessä: Formica Groupin maailmanlaajuinen toiminta mahdollistaa sen, että voimme omaksua kansainväliset trendit ja heijastaa globaalien asiakkaiden makuja. Toimintamme laajennuttua viidelle mantereelle meillä on jännittävät ajat edessä. Globaalissa kilpailukyvyssä on myös tärkeää miten yritys toimii, pystyykö se käyttämään innovaatiota ja integraatiota tehokkaasti hyväkseen kansainvälisellä tasolla tai työskentelemään yksittäisten designerien kanssa ja toteuttamaan heidän erityiset projektinsa paikallisella tasolla.

Formica-brändin ytimessä on aina asiakaskokemus, ja sen vahvuus korostuu tulevaisuuden menestyksessä. Formica-laminaatin ja Formicabrändin vuosien varrella vakiintuneilla markkinoilla saama tunnustus jatkuu ja laajenee uusiin teollisuusmaihin ja kehittyviin talouksiin. Formica-laminaatin vahvistaessa paikkansa uusissa kaupungeissa, infrastruktuureissa ja 21. vuosisadan kodeissa voimme katsoa luottavaisesti seuraaviin sataan vuoteen ja rakentaa perinteellemme.

是永恆的。透過內部研究和開發活動，已經為我們的裝飾性美耐板領域創造了令人興奮和獨特的新紋理的多樣選擇。與此同時還伴隨有花樣、裝潢和色彩選擇的持續發展——與發展趨勢預測和客戶反饋同步。

還有我們所有設施的策略和計劃都建立在成為負責任的製造商和「企業公民」的基礎上。我們生活在一個顧客對材料外觀、感覺和影響的認知度極高的時代，私人住宅、公共設施和商業建築都選擇和使用這些材料。正是這種領先力量保持了這一發展勢頭：今天，透過富美家集團遍及世界各地的業務，吸收國際流行趨勢、反映和迎合全球顧客的欣賞水平才成為可能。我們的業務跨越五大洲，激動人心的時刻還在等待著我們。全球競爭力也關係到企業的運作方式，是否充分利用國際水準的創新和整合能力或與獨立設計師合作，幫助在本地實現他們自己的具體項目。

富美家品牌的魅力最終是為了提高客戶的體驗，也是未來成功的立足點。富美家美耐板和富美家品牌在歷史上和成熟市場中的認可也擴大到發展中國家和新興經濟體，並受到歡迎。隨著富美家美耐板在新的城市、基礎設施和二十一世紀的家庭確立其地位，我們期待著下一個百年，並續寫我們所傳承的輝煌歷史。

是永恒的。通过内部研究和开发活动，已经为我们的装饰耐火板领域创造了令人兴奋和独特的新纹理的多样选择。与此同时还伴随有花样、装潢和色彩选择的持续发展——与发展趋势预测和客户反馈同步。

还有，我们所有设施的策略和计划都建立在成为负责任的制造商和"企业公民"的基础上。我们生活在一个顾客对材料外观、感觉和影响的认知度极高的时代，私人住宅、公共设施和商业建筑都选择和使用这些材料。正是这种领先力量保持了这一发展势头：今天，通过富美家集团遍及世界各地的业务，吸收国际流行趋势、反映和迎合全球顾客的欣赏水平成为可能。我们的业务跨越五大洲，激动人心的时刻还在等待着我们。全球竞争力也关系到企业的运作方式，是否充分利用国际水平的创新和整合能力或与独立设计师合作，帮助在本地实现他们自己的具体项目。

富美家品牌的魅力最终是为了提高客户的体验，也是未来成功的立足点。富美家耐火板和富美家品牌在历史上和成熟市场中的认可也扩大到发展中国家和新兴经济体，并受到赞誉。随着富美家耐火板在新的城市、基础设施和二十一世纪的家庭确立其地位，我们期待着下一个百年，并续写我们传承的辉煌历史。

ได้เป็นแกนนำในการพัฒนาของบริษัทนับแต่นั้นเป็นต้นมา

แผ่นลามิเนทฟอร์ไมก้า คือ "ต้นฉบับ" และยังคงเป็นวัสดุที่มีประสิทธิภาพสูง ในฐานะธุรกิจหนึ่ง เราทราบดีว่าไม่มีสิ่งใดหยุดนิ่งอยู่กับที่และบางครั้งอาจมีปัญหา แต่คุณค่าที่แท้จริงของสิ่งที่เราเสนอจะยังคงอยู่ ดังนั้นบริษัทจึงได้สร้างสรรค์ทางเลือกที่หลากหลายของผิวสัมผัสใหม่ที่น่าตื่นเต้นและพิเศษสุดสำหรับลามิเนท ตกแต่งของเราผ่านทางความคิดริเริ่มด้านการวิจัยและพัฒนาในบริษัท ซึ่งเกิดขึ้นควบคู่ไปกับการพัฒนาลวดลาย และสีของผลิตภัณฑ์ที่มีให้เลือกอย่างต่อเนื่อง โดยสอดคล้องกับการคาดการณ์ถึงแนวโน้มและผลตอบรับจากลูกค้า

นอกจากนั้น บริษัทยังดำเนินการตามกลยุทธ์และความคิดริเริ่มต่าง ๆ ในโรงงานของบริษัททุกแห่งโดยยึดถือแนวคิดของการเป็นผู้ผลิตที่มีความรับผิดชอบและ "บรรษัทพลเมือง" เป็นพื้นฐาน เราอยู่ในช่วงเวลาที่ลูกค้ามีความตระหนักเพิ่มมากขึ้นเกี่ยวกับรูปลักษณ์ ความรู้สึก และผลกระทบของวัสดุที่เลือกใช้ในบ้าน สถานที่สาธารณะและอาคารพาณิชย์ ความเป็นผู้นำนี้คือพลังผลักดันของบริษัท ทุกวันนี้เครือข่ายของกลุ่มบริษัทฟอร์ไมก้าทั่วโลกสามารถซึมซับแนวโน้มความนิยมสากล เพื่อสะท้อนและตอบสนองรสนิยมของลูกค้าในระดับโลกเรามีช่วงเวลาที่น่าตื่นเต้นรอเราอยู่ข้างหน้าเนื่องจากขณะนี้ธุรกิจของเราขยายไปถึงห้าทวีป การแข่งขันระดับโลกยังรวมถึงวิธีการดำเนินธุรกิจไม่ว่าจะเป็นการใช้ประโยชน์จากนวัตกรรมและการบูรณาการในระดับนานาชาติหรือการทำงานกับนักออกแบบตัวต่อตัวเพื่อช่วยให้โครงการระดับท้องถิ่นเป็นไปได้

พลังของตราสินค้า ฟอร์ไมก้า ซึ่งท้ายที่สุดคือประสบการณ์ของลูกค้าจะเป็นตัวบ่งชี้ความสำเร็จในอนาคต การจดจำได้ถึงผลิตภัณฑ์ลามิเนทและตราสินค้าฟอร์ไมก้าทั้งในอดีตและในปัจจุบันที่กำลังแผ่ขยายและได้รับการต้อนรับจากประเทศอุตสาหกรรมใหม่และระบบเศรษฐกิจเกิดใหม่ ในขณะที่ฟอร์ไมก้า ได้รับการยอมรับในเมืองในโครงสร้างพื้นฐานและบ้านใหม่ของศตวรรษที่ 21 เรามองอนาคตไปอีกหนึ่งร้อยปีข้างหน้าและพัฒนาต่อยอดไปจากความยิ่งใหญ่ของฟอร์ไมก้าที่เราได้รับมา

KASVUA MAAILMANLAAJUISESTI: VUOSISATA FORMICA® TAVARAMERKKIÄ JA LIIKETOIMINTAA

CRECIMIENTO A NIVEL MUNDIAL: UN SIGLO DE LA MARCA Y LA EMPRESA FORMICA®

CROISSANCE AU NIVEAU MONDIAL: UN SIÈCLE DE MARQUE ET D'ACTIVITÉ FORMICA®

การเติบโตขึ้นอย่างต่อเนื่องในโลก:
แบรนด์และการขยายธุรกิจของฟอร์ไมก้าที่มีอายุครบหนึ่งร้อยปีในโลกาภิวัตน์

在全球不断增长:
富美家 (FORMICA®) 品牌和业务发展一百年

在全球不斷增長:
富美家 (FORMICA®) 品牌和業務發展一百年

PHIL PATTON

Au cours de son premier siècle d'existence, Formica Group a eu le privilège d'accompagner les changements dans le reste du monde. Ses hauts et ses bas ont reflété ceux de la société et de la culture environnante. Il a reflété mais aussi façonné, suivi et entraîné les développements mondiaux sociaux et économiques. « Il semble que les produits de la marque Formica ont souvent été pionniers de changements plus importants, » a déclaré le PDG Mark Adamson à l'approche du centenaire de l'entreprise. Comme un personnage de film ou de roman, le stratifié Formica a montré un talent particulier pour se trouver là où le canon tonne, lors des changements historiques. De ses débuts obscurs au milieu des États-Unis, la marque Formica® a grandi pour devenir une marque mondiale, parmi les dix premières marques reconnues de la planète. Elle est née dans une période de crise économique et de révolution technologique, finalement pas si différente de notre propre époque.

C'est l'histoire simple de deux jeunes hommes ambitieux : Daniel J. O'Conor et Herbert A. Faber, qui travaillaient alors chez Westinghouse Electric Corporation (« Westinghouse ») à East Pittsburgh, Pennsylvanie. En 1913, ils ont constitué une société pour produire des articles en plastique stratifié à des fins d'isolation électrique. Ils ont nommé leur produit, sans beaucoup d'étude, « Formica », parce que celui-ci remplaçait mica, un minéral silicaté qui présentait une organisation de feuille d'atomes utilisée comme isolant électrique primaire. C'est Faber qui aurait trouvé le nom associant « for » et « mica ». Le nom de la nouvelle entreprise était The Formica Insulation Company. Si le nom est simple, l'histoire est plus complexe. Les deux hommes ont créé une nouvelle entreprise à l'ombre des deux révolutions globales : la révolution des matières plastiques ainsi que la révolution de l'électricité et de l'électronique. Ces avancées technologiques allaient avoir des effets économiques, sociaux et culturels dans le monde entier. L'entreprise est née avec ces deux nouvelles industries majeures.

PHIL PATTON

En su primer siglo de existencia, el Grupo Formica ha tenido el privilegio de discurrir en paralelo con los cambios en el mundo entero. Sus altibajos han reflejado aquellos de la sociedad y de la cultura a su alrededor. Ha reflejado pero también ha dado forma, ha seguido pero también ha liderado acontecimientos sociales y económicos a nivel mundial. "Parece que los productos de la marca Formica han sido, a menudo, un representante de mayores cambios", señaló el director ejecutivo Mark Adamson al acercarse la empresa a su centenario. Como el personaje de una película u obra literaria, el laminado Formica ha mostrado una increíble habilidad para estar presente en momentos cruciales de la historia. Desde sus orígenes muy poco conocidos en la región central de los Estados Unidos, la marca comercial Formica® creció hasta convertirse en una marca mundial, situándose entre las diez marcas comerciales más reconocidas del planeta. Esta nació en un período de agitación económica y revolución tecnológica no muy diferente de nuestra propia era.

La sencilla historia es que dos jóvenes ambiciosos, Daniel J. O'Conor y Herbert A. Faber, que entonces trabajaban en Westinghouse Electric Corporation ("Westinghouse"), en East Pittsburgh, Pensilvania, tuvieron una idea y crearon una empresa. En 1913, establecieron una compañía para producir artículos de laminado plástico para aislamiento eléctrico. Denominaron a su producto —sin un exhaustivo estudio— "Formica", porque funcionaría como un sustituto de la mica (en inglés: "for mica"), un mineral silicato con una disposición delgada y laminada de átomos que se utilizaba principalmente como el aislante eléctrico. A Faber se le atribuye haber combinado los términos en inglés "for" y "mica", y el nombre de la nueva empresa fue The Formica Insulation Company. La historia más compleja es que estos dos hombres estaban creando una nueva empresa a la sombra de dos revoluciones mundiales: la revolución del plástico y la revolución eléctrica y de componentes electrónicos.

PHIL PATTON

Olemassa olonsa ensimmäisenä vuosisatana Formica Groupilla on ollut erikoisetuna marssia maailman yleisten muutosten rinnalla. Sen nousut ja laskut ovat kuvastaneet sitä ympäröivää yhteiskuntaa ja kulttuuria. Se on kuvastanut, mutta myös muokannut, ja seurannut, mutta myös johtanut globaalia yhteiskunnallista ja taloudellista kehitystä. "Formica-merkkisistä tuotteista näyttää usein tulleen suurempien muutosten edustajia", sanoi CEO Mark Adamson, yhtiön lähestyessä satavuotispäiväänsä. Filmin tai kirjallisuuden henkilön tavoin Formica-laminaatti on osoittanut hämmästyttävää taipumusta olla läsnä historian käännekohdissa. Melko tuntemattomista oloista Amerikan keskiosista lähtenyt Formica® tavaramerkki kasvoi globaaliksi merkiksi — kymmenen parhaiten tunnetun tavaramerkin joukkoon maailmassa. Se syntyi taloudellisen kuohunnan ja teknologisen vallankumouksen kautena, ei kovinkaan erilaisen kuin oma aikakautemme.

Yksinkertainen tarina on se, että kaksi kunnianhimoista nuorta miestä, Daniel J. O'Conor ja Herbert A. Faber, ollessaan Westinghouse Electric Corporationin ("Westinghouse") palveluksessa East Pittsburghissa, Pennsylvaniassa, saivat idean ja alkoivat puuhata liikeyritystä. Vuonna 1913 he perustivat yrityksen, joka valmisti muovilaminaatista sähköä eristäviä tarvikkeita. He antoivat tuotteelleen nimeksi — ilman suurempaa tutkimista — "Formica," koska se viittaisi kiilteeseen (mica), silikaattimineraaliin, jolla on ohut levymäinen atomien järjestely, ja jota käytettiin ensisijaisena sähkön eristimenä. Faberin ansioksi katsotaan sanojen "for" ja "mica" yhdistäminen ja uuden yhtiön nimeksi tuli The Formica Insulation Company. Monimutkaisempi tarina on se, että kaksi miestä olivat luomassa uutta yritystä kahden maailmanlaajuisen vallankumouksen varjossa: muovin vallankumous ja sähkön ja elektroniikan vallankumous. Näillä teknisillä edistysaskeleilla tuli olemaan taloudellisia, yhteiskunnallisia ja kulttuurillisia vaikutuksia maailman laajuisesti. Yhtiö syntyi näitä kahta tärkeää uutta teollisuutta luotaessa.

菲爾·巴頓

在其存在的第一個世紀裡，富美家集團（Formica Group）有幸與更廣闊世界中的變化並駕齊驅。它的跌宕起伏反映了週圍的社會和文化。它反射了但也改變了，遵從但也領導了全球性社會和經濟的發展。首席執行官馬克·亞當森（Mark Adamson）在公司接近百年華誕時說：「看來，富美家品牌的產品往往是更大變化的代言人。」像電影或文學作品中的人物一樣，富美家美耐板總是站在歷史的轉折關頭，顯示出不可思議的靈犀。雖然它在美國中部的發跡相當不起眼，富美家商標已成長為一個全球性品牌——在這個星球上躋身前十名最著名商標的行列。它誕生在一個經濟動盪和技術革命的時期，與我們的時代沒有多大的不同。

這個故事很簡單：兩個胸懷大志的年輕男子，丹尼爾·奧康納（Daniel J. O'Conor）和赫伯特·費伯（Herbert A. Faber），當時在賓夕法尼亞州東匹茲堡市美國西屋電氣公司（Westinghouse Electric Corporation/簡稱「西屋」）就職，他們有一個想法，並開始創立自己的事業。1913 年，他們成立了一家為製造電氣絕緣塑膠美耐板的公司。他們把自己的產品命名為——未經大量的研究——「富美家」（Formica），因為它代表雲母，一種矽酸鹽礦物，原子呈薄薄的片狀，主要用於電氣絕緣體。費伯被認為是把「for」和「mica」組合在一起的人，新公司的名稱是富美家絕緣公司（Formica Insulation Company）。更複雜的故事是，這兩名男人在兩個全球性革命：塑膠革命和電器電子革命——的陰影裡創建了一個新企業。這些技術的進步將影響整個地球的經濟、社會和文化。該公司伴隨著這兩大新產業的創造而誕生。

1907 年的金融恐慌幾乎導致美國經濟的崩潰，其原因是兩個聲譽不佳的人物企圖壟斷銅市場——銅是一種極好的導電體。但是，西屋公司、通用電氣公司（General Electric/簡稱 GE）

菲尔·巴顿

在其存在的第一个世纪里，富美家集团（Formica Group）有幸与更广阔世界中的变化并驾齐驱。它的跌宕起伏反映了周围的社会和文化。它反射了但改变了遵从但领导了全球性社会和经济的发展。首席执行官马克·亚当森（Mark Adamson）在公司接近百年华诞时说："看来，富美家品牌的产品往往是更大变化的代言人。"像电影或文学作品中的人物一样，富美家®装饰耐火板总是站在历史的转折关头，显示出不可思议的灵犀。虽然它在美国中部的发迹相当不起眼，富美家商标已成长为一个全球性品牌——在这个星球上跻身前十名最著名商标的行列。它诞生在一个经济动荡和技术革命的时期，与我们的时代没有多大的不同。

这个简单的故事就是，两个胸怀大志的年轻男子，丹尼尔·奥康纳（Daniel J. O'Conor）和赫伯特·费伯（Herbert A. Faber），当时在宾夕法尼亚州东匹兹堡市美国西屋电气公司（Westinghouse Electric Corporation/简称 "西屋"）就职，他们有一个想法，并开始创立自己的事业。1913 年，他们成立了一家为制造电气绝缘塑料耐火板的公司。他们把自己的产品命名为——未经大量的研究——"富美家"（Formica），因为它代表云母，一种硅酸盐矿物，原子呈薄薄的片状，主要用于电气绝缘体。费伯被认为是把 "for" 和 "mica" 组合在一起的人，新公司的名称是富美家绝缘公司（Formica Insulation Company）。更复杂的故事是，这两名男人在两个全球性革命：塑料革命和电器电子革命——的阴影里创建了一个新企业。这些技术的进步将影响整个地球的经济、社会和文化。该公司伴随着这两大新产业的创造而诞生。

1907 年的金融恐慌几乎导致美国经济的崩溃，其原因是两个声誉不佳的人物企图垄断铜市场——铜是一种极好的导电体。但是，西屋公司、通用电

ฟิล แพตตัน

ในศตวรรษแรก ฟอร์ไมก้า มีโอกาสพิเศษในการได้เดินทางพร้อมกับการเปลี่ยนแปลงต่าง ๆ ของโลก สถานการณ์ที่ดีและไม่ดีได้สะท้อนออกมาในสังคมและวัฒนธรรมโดยรอบ ซึ่งเป็นการสะท้อนและสร้าง รวมถึงการนำไปสู่การพัฒนาสังคมและเศรษฐกิจทั่วโลก มาร์ค อดัมสัน ประธานเจ้าหน้าที่บริหารได้กล่าวเมื่อบริษัทใกล้ก้าวเข้าสู่ 100 ปีว่า "ดูเหมือนว่าผลิตภัณฑ์ฟอร์ไมก้ามักจะเป็นตัวแทนในการเปลี่ยนแปลงที่ยิ่งใหญ่" ฟอร์ไมก้าเปรียบเสมือนตัวละครในภาพยนตร์หรือบทกวี ผลิตภัณฑ์ลามิเนทฟอร์ไมก้าได้แสดงพรสวรรค์ลึกลับในการเข้าไปมีส่วนร่วมในจุดหักเหสำคัญต่าง ๆ ในประวัติศาสตร์จากถิ่นกำเนิดเล็ก ๆ ในอเมริกากลาง ตราสินค้าฟอร์ไมก้า Formica® ได้เติบโตจนเป็นตราสินค้าที่เป็นที่รู้จักกันทั่วโลก – เป็นตราสินค้าหนึ่งในสิบที่เป็นที่รู้จักมากที่สุดในโลก ฟอร์ไมก้าก่อกำเนิดในช่วงเศรษฐกิจพลิกผันและการปฏิวัติทางด้านเทคโนโลยี ซึ่งก็ไม่แตกต่างจากยุคของบริษัทเอง

เรื่องราวเรียบง่าย ก็คือ ชายหนุ่มผู้มีความทะเยอทะยานสองคน คือ เดเนียล เจ โอคอเนอร์ และ เฮอร์เบิร์ต เอ เฟเบอร์ ซึ่งขณะนั้นได้ทำงานอยู่ที่ บริษัท เวสติงเฮาส์ อิเลคทริค คอร์ปอเรชั่น ("เวสติงเฮาส์") ณ กรุงพิตต์สเบิร์กตะวันออก มลรัฐเพนซิลเวเนีย มีความคิดและเริ่มก่อตั้งธุรกิจ ในปี ค.ศ. 1913 พวกเขาได้ก่อตั้งบริษัทเพื่อผลิตผลิตภัณฑ์ที่ทำจากพลาสติกลามิเนทสำหรับใช้เป็นฉนวนไฟฟ้า พวกเขาตั้งชื่อผลิตภัณฑ์ – โดยไม่ได้ทำการศึกษามากมาย - ว่า "ฟอร์ไมก้า" เนื่องจากผลิตภัณฑ์นี้จะถูกนำมาใช้แทนไมก้า (mica) ซึ่งเป็นแร่ซิลิเกตที่มีการจัดเรียงตัวของอะตอมที่บางและเป็นแผ่นซึ่งเดิมใช้เป็นฉนวนไฟฟ้า เฟเบอร์เป็นผู้ที่ผสมคำว่า "for (แทน)" และ "mica (ไมก้า)" เข้าด้วยกัน และชื่อบริษัทใหม่ดังกล่าวก็คือ เดอะ ฟอร์ไมก้า อินซูเลชั่น คอมพานี เรื่องที่ซับซ้อนกว่านั้นก็คือ ชายสองคนกำลังก่อให้เกิดองค์กรใหม่ภายใต้การปฏิวัติระดับโลกถึงสองอย่างคือ การปฏิวัติพลาสติกและการปฏิวัติไฟฟ้าและอิเลคทรอนิกส์ ความก้าวหน้าในเทคโนโลยีเหล่านี้จะมีผลต่อเศรษฐกิจ สังคม และวัฒนธรรมทั่วโลก บริษัทเกิดขึ้นพร้อมกับการสร้างอุตสาหกรรมใหม่สองแขนงนี้

ปัญหาด้านการเงินในปี ค.ศ. 1907 ซึ่งเกือบทำให้เศรษฐกิจของสหรัฐอเมริกาล่มสลาย เกิดจากความพยายามของบุคคลสองคนที่จะผูกขาดตลาดทองแดงซึ่งเป็นตัวนำไฟฟ้าชั้นยอด แต่ เวสติงเฮาส์ เจนเนอรัล

La panique financière de 1907, qui a failli provoquer l'effondrement de l'économie américaine, avait pour origine la tentative de deux personnages louches d'accaparer le marché du cuivre, un grand conducteur d'électricité. Mais Westinghouse, General Electric (GE) et d'autres fabricants avaient également besoin d'une substance qui ne conduisait pas l'électricité pour les moteurs et autres appareils. Les isolants de premier ordre de l'époque étaient le mica, difficile à extraire et à transformer, et la gomme-laque, issue des sécrétions d'insecte, qui était rare et coûteuse. 1907 correspond à une véritable percée. Pendant que Wall Street s'inquiétait, le chimiste Leo Baekeland travaillait sur une nouvelle idée.

Baekeland, comme décrit par Stephen Fenichell dans son livre *Plastic*, était un excentrique, voire un savant fou. Son génie était manifeste dès ses débuts à l'Université de Gand en Belgique. Il a déménagé aux États-Unis et après avoir vendu son invention clé, un papier photographique, à George Eastman de la société Eastman Kodak pour un million de dollars de l'époque en 1899, s'est installé à Snug Rock, avec sa maison et son laboratoire à Yonkers, au nord de New York, et s'est consacré à la recherche. En 1907, il a trouvé un moyen de rendre solide la résine phéno-

Estos avances tecnológicos tendrían efectos económicos, sociales y culturales en todo el planeta. La empresa nació con la creación de estas dos nuevas industrias principales.

El pánico financiero de 1907, que casi provocó el colapso de la economía de EE. UU., surgió del intento de dos personajes sospechosos de arrinconar al mercado del cobre, un gran conductor de la electricidad. Sin embargo, Westinghouse, General Electric (GE) y otros fabricantes también necesitaban una sustancia que funcionara como un aislante de electricidad para motores y otros dispositivos. Los aislantes líderes de la época eran la mica, que era difícil de extraer y procesar, y la goma laca, un producto derivado de las secreciones de un insecto (cochinilla de la laca) que era costoso y poco común. En 1907, se produjo un gran descubrimiento. Mientras Wall Street estaba en apuros, el químico Leo Baekeland trabajaba en una nueva idea.

Baekeland, como lo esbozó Stephen Fenichell en su libro *Plastic* fue un excéntrico, por no decir un científico bastante loco. Su genialidad era evidente ya en la Universidad de Gante, Bélgica. Se mudó a los Estados Unidos y, tras vender su invento clave, un papel fotográfico, a George Eastman de Eastman Kodak Company por 1 millón de dólares estadounidenses en 1899, se estableció en Snug Rock, su casa y laboratorio en Yonkers, al norte de la ciudad de Nueva York, y se dedicó a la investigación. En 1907, ideó una manera de convertir la resina de fenol líquida a estado sólido calentándolo bajo presión, lo que produjo una sustancia dura, de color ámbar. El material resultante, que modestamente denominó Bakelite®, era no conductivo y resistente al calor, un aislante contra la electricidad. Podía reemplazar a la mica y a la goma laca. El plástico sintético y versátil Bakelite®, que Baekeland patentó en 1909, no solo desencadenó la revolución del plástico, sino que también fomentó la revolución electrónica. Se podía utilizar tanto en joyas como en máquinas. Se anunciaba como el material de los mil usos, y su fama colocó a Baekeland en la portada de la revista *Time* en 1924.

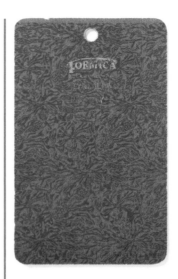

Rahamarkkinoiden paniikki v. 1907, joka melkein aiheutti USA:n talouden romahduksen, oli seuraus kahden hämäräperäisen tyypin yrityksestä vallata kuparin, erinomaisen sähköä johtavan aineen markkinat. Westinghouse, General Electric (GE), ja muut valmistajat tarvitsivat kuitenkin myös sähköä johtamatonta ainetta moottoreita ja muita laitteita varten. Ensisijaisina eristeinä oli tuolloin kiille, jota oli vaikea louhia ja käsitellä, sekä sellakka, hyönteisen (Lac kuoriaisen) eritteestä tehty tuote, joka oli kallista ja harvinaista. Vuonna 1907 tapahtui ratkaiseva edistysaskel. Wall Street oli huolissaan, mutta Leo Baekeland työskenteli uuden idean parissa.

Kuten Stephen Fenichell luonnosteli kirjassaan *Plastic*, Baekeland oli eksentrinen, ellei suorastaan hullu tiedemies. Hänen neroutensa ilmeni varhain Ghentin yliopistossa, Belgiassa. Hän muutti Yhdysvaltoihin ja myytyään avainkeksintönsä, valokuvapaperin, Eastman Kodak Companyn George Eastmanille miljoonalla dollarilla v. 1899, hän asettui Snug Rockiin, taloonsa ja laboratorioonsa Yonkersissa, New York Cityn pohjoispuolella ja omistautui tutkimukselle. Vuonna 1907 hän keksi keinon tehdä nestemäisen fenyylihartsin kiinteäksi, kuumentamalla sitä paineen alaisena, joka sai aikaan kovan meripihkanvärisen aineen. Tuloksena saatu materiaali, jolle hän vaatimattomasti antoi nimeksi Bakelite®, oli sähköä johtamaton ja lämpöä kestävä, eli sähköinen eriste.

和其他製造商也需要一種物質作為非導電體，用於電機和其他設備。當時的主要絕緣體是雲母，但卻難以開採和加工，另外一種昆蟲（紫膠蟲）分泌物蟲膠即昂貴又稀有。1907 年，出現了突破。由於華爾街的擔心，化學家里奧·貝克蘭（Leo Bakeland）研究了一個新的方法。

如斯蒂芬·芬內舍爾（Stephen Fenichell）在他的《塑膠》（Plastic）一書中所說，貝克蘭是一位怪異但還不致瘋狂的科學家。他的天賦早在比利時根特大學就讀時就顯露出來。他移居到美國之後，1899 年把他的關鍵發明照相紙以 100 萬美元的價錢賣給了柯達公司（Eastman Kodak Company）的喬治·伊士曼柯達（George Eastman）。然後他在 Snug Rock 落戶，他的房子和實驗室建在紐約市以北的揚克斯區，並潛心研究。1907 年，他發明了一種方法，通過壓力加熱的方法使液體酚醛樹脂凝固，產生一種堅硬的、琥珀色的物質。他謙虛地將所得到的材料稱為酚醛塑膠（Bakelite®），這種物質具有非導電性和耐熱性，對電力絕緣，可以代替雲母和蟲膠。貝克蘭 1909 年為多功能酚醛（Bakelite®）合成塑膠申請了專利，不僅掀起了塑膠革命，同時還促進了電子革命。它既可用於珠寶也可用於機械，被宣傳為有千種用途的材料，其名聲讓貝克蘭在 1924 年登上《時代》（Time）雜誌的封面。

1910 年，西屋公司的一位科學家 C.E. 斯金納（C.E. Skinner）開始探索酚醛樹脂塑膠。他研究了把紙浸入酚醛塑膠，再將其烘烤成絕緣管和薄片。奧康納很感興趣，他的朋友費伯（Faber）也很感興趣。1912 年，奧康納開發了一種用於製造層疊絕緣體的程序，並申請了專利。1913 年，奧康納和費伯看到了一個他們的經理沒有看到的商機，他們離開了西屋，成立了自己的公司。每人出資 2,500 美元，再加上一個來自肯塔基州的律師

气公司（General Electric/简称 GE）和其他制造商也需要一种物质作为非导电体，用于电机和其他设备。当时的主要绝缘体是云母，但却难以开采和加工，另外一种昆虫（紫胶虫）分泌物虫胶即昂贵又稀有。1907 年，出现了突破。由于华尔街的担心，化学家里奥·贝克兰（Leo Bakeland）研究了一个新的方法。

如斯蒂芬·芬内舍尔（Stephen Fenichell）在他的《塑料》（Plastic）一书中所说，贝克兰是一位怪异但还不致疯狂的科学家。他的天赋早在比利时根特大学就读时就显露出来。他移居到美国之后，1899 年把他的关键发明照相纸以 100 万美元的价钱卖给了柯达公司（Eastman Kodak Company）的乔治·伊士曼柯达（George Eastman）。然后他在 Snug Rock 落户，他的房子和实验室建在纽约市以北的扬克斯区，并潜心研究。1907 年，他发明了一种方法，通过压力加热的方法使液体酚醛树脂凝固，产生一种坚硬的、琥珀色的物质。他谦虚地将所得到的材料称为酚醛塑料（Bakelite®），这种物质具有非导电性和耐热性，对电力绝缘，可以代替云母和虫胶。贝克兰 1909 年为多功能酚醛（Bakelite®）合成塑料申请了专利，不仅掀起了塑料革命，同时还促进了电子革命。它既可用于珠宝也可用于机械，被宣传为有千种用途的材料，其名声让贝克兰在 1924 年登上《时代》（Time）杂志的封面。

1910 年，西屋公司的一位科学家斯金纳（C.E. Skinner）开始探索酚醛树脂塑料。他研究了把纸浸入酚醛塑料，再将其烘烤成绝缘管和薄片。奥康纳很感兴趣，他的朋友费伯（Faber）也很感兴趣。1912 年，奥康纳开发了一种用于制造层叠绝缘体的程序，并申请了专利。1913 年，奥康纳和费伯看到了一个他们的经理没有看到的商机，他们离开了西屋，成立了自己的公司。每人出资 2,500 美元，再加上一个来自肯塔基州的律师兼银行家汤姆林

อิเลคทริค (จีอี) และผู้ผลิตรายอื่น ๆ ก็ต้องใช้สารเพื่อเป็นฉนวนไฟฟ้าสำหรับมอเตอร์และอุปกรณ์อื่น ๆ ฉนวนที่ดีที่สุดในขณะนั้นคือไมก้า ซึ่งหายากและการแปรรูปทำได้ยากและชะแล็ก (shellac) ซึ่งเป็นผลิตภัณฑ์หลังจากแมลง (ด้วงครั่ง – Lac beetle) ซึ่งมีราคาแพงและหายาก ในปี ค.ศ. 1907 ได้มีการเปลี่ยนแปลงครั้งยิ่งใหญ่ ตามที่วอลสตรีทกังวล นักเคมีชื่อ ลีโอ เบคแลนด์ ได้มีความคิดสร้างสรรค์ใหม่

ตามที่สตีเฟน เฟนิเชลล์ เขียนไว้ในหนังสือของเขาที่ชื่อว่า พลาสติก (Plastic) เบคแลนด์เป็นนักวิทยาศาสตร์ที่ค่อนข้างประหลาดหรือออกไปทางเพี้ยน ความเป็นอัจฉริยะของเขาได้แสดงออกมาตอนที่เขาศึกษาอยู่ที่มหาวิทยาลัยเกนต์ ประเทศเบลเยียม เขาย้ายมาอยู่ที่สหรัฐอเมริกาและหลังจากที่ได้ขายสิ่งประดิษฐ์สำคัญ คือ กระดาษอัดรูป ให้แก่จอร์จ อีสต์แมน แห่งบริษัท อีสต์แมน โกดักคอมพานี ในราคา 1 ล้านดอลลาร์สหรัฐในปี ค.ศ. 1899 เขาเข้าไปอยู่ในบ้านสนัก ร็อคซึ่งเป็นบ้านและห้องทดลองของเขาในเมืองยองเคอร์ส อยู่ทางตอนเหนือของนิวยอร์กซิตี้และทุ่มเทให้กับการค้นคว้า ในปี ค.ศ. 1907 เขาได้ค้นพบวิธีที่ทำให้สารฟีนอลเรซินเหลวให้แข็งตัวโดยการทำให้ร้อนด้วยความดัน ซึ่งทำให้เกิดสารสีเหลืองอำพันลักษณะแข็ง เขาตั้งชื่อสารที่เกิดขึ้นมาใหม่นั้นว่า แบคคาไลท์ ซึ่งไม่ใช่ตัวนำไฟฟ้า แต่ทนต่อความร้อนและเป็นฉนวนป้องกันไฟฟ้า สารดังกล่าวสามารถใช้แทนไมก้าและชะแล็กได้ พลาสติกสังเคราะห์แบคคาไลท์ ซึ่งมีคุณสมบัติที่เป็นประโยชน์หลากหลาย เบคแลนด์จึงได้ทำการจดสิทธิบัตรในปี ค.ศ. 1909 ไม่เพียงแต่เป็นการปฏิวัติพลาสติก แต่ยังเป็นการกระตุ้นการเกิดการปฏิวัติอิเล็กทรอนิกส์ด้วย สารดังกล่าวสามารถใช้ในเครื่องประดับและเครื่องจักรด้วย ซึ่งได้รับการขนานนามว่าเป็นวัสดุที่ใช้งานได้กับทุกอย่าง และชื่อเสียงของสารดังกล่าวทำให้เบคแลนด์ได้ขึ้นปกนิตยสารไทม์ในปี ค.ศ. 1924

ในปี ค.ศ. 1910 นักวิทยาศาสตร์ของบริษัท เวสติงเฮาส์ ชื่อว่า ซี. อี. สกินเนอร์เริ่มทำการทดลองกับพลาสติกแบคคาไลท์ เขาศึกษาวิธีการจุ่มกระดาษในเรซินแบคคาไลท์ และอบให้เป็นหลอดหรือแผ่นฉนวนกันไฟฟ้า ซึ่งโอคอเนอร์และเฟเบอร์ให้ความสนใจมาก ในปี ค.ศ. 1912 โอคอเนอร์ได้พัฒนากระบวนการทำฉนวนไฟฟ้าลามิเนตและทำการจดสิทธิบัตร ในปี ค.ศ. 1913 โอคอเนอร์และเฟเบอร์รู้ว่ามีโอกาสทางธุรกิจที่ผู้จัดการของตนมองไม่เห็น จึงได้ลาออกจากบริษัทเวสติงเฮาส์เพื่อตั้งบริษัทของพวกเขาเอง พวกเขาลงเงินคนละ

lique liquide en la chauffant sous pression, ce qui produisait un matériau dur, de teinte ambre. Il appela modestement le produit obtenu la Bakelite®, un isolant électrique non conducteur et résistant à la chaleur. Ce produit pouvait remplacer le mica et la gomme-laque. La matière plastique synthétique polyvalente Bakelite®, brevetée par Baekeland en 1909, a non seulement déclenché la révolution des matières plastiques, mais elle a aussi encouragé celle de l'électronique. Le matériau pouvait être utilisé dans les bijoux aussi bien que dans les machines. Il fut présenté comme un matériau universel et sa renommée fut telle que Baekeland s'est retrouvé en couverture du magazine *Time* en 1924.

En 1910, un chercheur de Westinghouse, C. E. Skinner, a commencé à explorer les possibilités du plastique Bakelite®. Il a étudié les moyens de plonger le papier dans les résines Bakelite®, puis l'a fait cuire dans des feuilles ou des tubes isolants. O'Conor était intrigué, tout comme son ami Faber. En 1912, O'Conor a mis au point un procédé de fabrication d'isolants stratifiés et l'a fait breveter. En 1913, identifiant une opportunité commerciale que leurs dirigeants n'avait pas vue, O'Conor et Faber quittent Westinghouse pour constituer leur propre société. Chaque associé a contribué 2500 $, avec J. G. Tomlin, un avocat et banquier du Kentucky qui a investi 7500 $ et a reçu un tiers des actions. Ils ont implanté l'entreprise à Cincinnati, dans l'Ohio, la ville natale de Faber.

Westinghouse avait envoyé Faber et O'Conor à travers le monde avec ce que le magazine *Fortune* a appelé plus tard « la bénédiction des parents. » Mais Westinghouse a réalisé son erreur et a lancé « Micarta », un produit concurrent. General Electric et d'autres sont également entrés sur le marché. Les concurrents ont contraint Baekeland de couper les approvisionnements en résine Bakelite® à la Formica Insulation Company pour étrangler le bébé dans son berceau. Faber et O'Conor ont dû trouver une alternative. Ils ont trouvé un produit appelé « Redmanol », développé par le chimiste L. V. Redman et produit par deux frères à Chicago, Sam et Adolph Karpen.

En 1910, un científico de Westinghouse, C. E. Skinner, comenzó a experimentar con el plástico Bakelite®. Analizó maneras de sumergir papel en las resinas Bakelite® para luego cocerlo al horno en tubos o láminas aislantes. O'Conor estaba intrigado, al igual que su amigo Faber. En 1912, O'Conor desarrolló un proceso para elaborar aislantes laminados y lo patentó. En 1913, al reconocer una oportunidad comercial que sus gerentes no vieron, O'Conor y Faber dejaron Westinghouse para formar su propia empresa. Cada uno contribuyó con $2,500, junto con J. G. Tomlin, un abogado y banquero de Kentucky que invirtió $7,500 y recibió una participación de un tercio en la nueva empresa. Crearon la empresa en Cincinnati, Ohio, la ciudad natal de Faber.

Westinghouse les dio a Faber y a O'Conor lo que la revista *Fortune* denominó después "la bendición de los padres" para que pudieran seguir su propio camino. Sin embargo, muy pronto, Westinghouse se dio cuenta de su error y lanzó "Micarta" como rival. General Electric y otros también ingresaron en el mercado. Los competidores obligaron a Baekeland a cortar los suministros de la resina Bakelite® a The Formica Insulation Company en un esfuerzo por ahogar a la criatura recién nacida. Faber y O'Conor lucharon por encontrar una alternativa. Presentaron un producto denominado "Redmanol", desarrollado por el químico L. V. Redman y producido por dos hermanos en Chicago, Sam y Adolph Karpen.

La primera planta de la empresa Formica, un espacio alquilado de dos pisos en las calles Main y Second, no estaba lejos de los corrales de ganado de Cincinnati. Los primeros pedidos en mayo de 1913 fueron para suministrar anillos en V para motores eléctricos a Chalmers Motor Company. Entre los primeros clientes figuraban Ideal (posteriormente, Delco) Electric, Northwest Electric y Bell Electric Motor. Tras fabricar dichas piezas, la empresa produjo su primer laminado el 4 de julio de 1914.

La Primera Guerra Mundial demandó aislantes para radios y piezas, como poleas, para controles de aeronaves. La aviación hizo hincapié en el peso ligero, y las piezas de la marca Formica, a menudo, podían reemplazar a las de metal por la ligereza y a

Sillä voitiin korvata kiille ja sellakka. Monikäyttöinen Bakelite® synteettinen muovi, jonka Baekeland patentoi v. 1909, käynnisti sekä muovin vallankumouksen, että auttoi elektroniikan mullistusta. Sitä voitiin käyttää sekä koruissa että koneissa. Sitä kehuttiin tuhannen käytön materiaaliksi, ja sen maine vei Baekelandin *Time*-aikakauslehden kanteen v. 1924.

Vuonna 1910 Westinghousen tiedemies C. E. Skinner ryhtyi kokeilemaan Bakelite® muovia. Hän tutki tapoja kastaa paperia Bakelite® hartseihin ja sen jälkeen paahtaa se eristäviksi putkiksi tai levyiksi. O'Conor oli kiinnostunut, kuten myös hänen ystävänsä Faber. Vuonna 1912 O'Conor kehitti laminoitujen eristimien valmistusprosessin ja patentoi sen. Vuonna 1913, oivaltaessaan liiketoimintatilaisuuden, joka oli jäänyt johtajilta näkemättä, O'Conor ja Faber lähtivät Westinghouselta ja perustivat oman yrityksen. Kumpikin sijoitti 2500 dollaria ja J. G. Tomlin, lakimies ja pankkiiri Kentuckysta, sijoitti 7500 dollaria ja sai kolmanneksen uuden yrityksen omistuksesta. He aloittivat liiketoiminnan Cincinnatissa, Ohiossa, Faberin kotikaupungissa.

Westinghouse oli lähettänyt Faberin ja O'Conorin maailmalle, kuten *Fortune*-aikakauslehti myöhemmin kuvasi "vanhempien siunauksella". Ennen pitkää Westinghouse kuitenkin havaitsi erehdyksensä ja lanseerasi kilpailijaksi "Micarta" -tuotteen. Myös General Electric ja muut lähtivät markkinoille. Kilpailijat pakottivat Baekelandin lopettamaan Bakelite® hartsin toimitukset The Formica Insulation Companylle, yrittäen kuristaa pikkulapsen kehtoonsa. Faber ja O'Conor alkoivat kiireesti etsiä vaihtoehtoa. He keksivät "Redmanol" nimisen tuotteen, jonka kehitti kemisti L. V. Redman ja jota valmistivat kaksi veljeä Chicagossa, Sam ja Adolph Karpen.

Ensimmäinen Formica-yhtiön tehdas, kaksikerroksinen vuokratila Second ja Main Street katujen kulmassa, ei ollut kaukana Cincinnatin karjapihoilta. Ensimmäisinä tilauksina toukokuussa 1913 oli toimittaa V-renkaita sähkömoottoreita varten Chalmers Motor Companylle. Toisia asiakkaita alkuaikoina olivat Ideal (myöhemmin Delco) Electric, Northwest Electric ja Bell Electric Motor.

和銀行家湯姆林（J.G. Tomlin）投資了7,500 美元，得到新合資企業三分之一的股權。他們在費伯的故鄉俄亥俄州辛辛那提市建立了自己的事業。

西屋電氣公司放手費伯和奧康納走向世界，後來被《財富》（Fortune）雜誌稱為帶著「父母的祝福」。但沒過多久，西屋電氣公司發現了自己的錯誤，就成立了「Micarta」作為競爭對手。通用電氣和其他公司也進入了這個市場。競爭對手迫使貝克蘭切斷了對富美家絕緣公司（Formica Insulation Company）的酚醛樹脂供應。企圖將嬰兒扼殺在搖籃裡。費伯和奧康納急忙尋找替代品。他們想出了一個替代產品，叫做「Redmanol」，由化學家雷德曼（L.V. Redman）開發，由芝

（J.G. Tomlin）投资了 7,500 美元，得到新合资企业三分之一的股权。他们在费伯的故乡俄亥俄州辛辛那提市建立了自己的事业。

西屋电气公司放手费伯和奥康纳走向世界，后来被《财富》（Fortune）杂志称为带着"父母的祝福"。但没过多久，西屋电气公司发现了自己的错误，就成立了"Micarta"作为竞争对手。通用电气和其他公司也进入了这个市场。竞争对手迫使贝克兰切断了对富美家绝缘公司（Formica Insulation Company）的酚醛树脂供应。企图将婴儿扼杀在摇篮里。费伯和奥康纳急忙寻找替代品。他们想出了一个替代产品，叫做"Redmanol"，由化学家雷德曼（L.V. Redman）开发，由芝加哥的两兄弟山姆

2,500 ดอลลาร์สหรัฐ ร่วมกับ ทนายความและนายธนาคารจากมลรัฐเคนทักกี ชื่อว่า เจจี ทอมลิน ลงเงินจำนวน 7,500 ดอลลาร์สหรัฐ และได้รับหุ้นหนึ่งในสามในการลงทุนใหม่นี้ พวกเขาก่อตั้งธุรกิจขึ้นในเมืองซินซินนาติ มลรัฐโอไฮโอ ซึ่งเป็นบ้านเกิดของเฟเบอร์

บริษัท เวสติงเฮาส์ ได้ส่งเฟเบอร์และโอคอเนอร์ออกไปเผชิญกับโลกภายนอก ซึ่งนิตยสารฟอร์จูน เรียกว่า "พรจากผู้ให้กำเนิด" แต่จากนั้นไม่นาน บริษัท เวสติงเฮาส์ได้ตระหนักถึงความผิดพลาดของตัวเองและได้ทำการเปิดตัว "Micarta" เพื่อเป็นคู่แข่งบริษัท เจนเนอรัล อิเลคทริค และบริษัทอื่นๆ ก็นำผลิตภัณฑ์ชนิดเดียวกันเข้าสู่ตลาดเช่นกัน คู่แข่งได้กดดันให้เบคแลนด์ตัดการจำหน่ายเรซินแบคคาไลท์ให้กับบริษัท เดอะ ฟอร์มิก้า อินโซลูชั่น คอมพานี เพื่อทำให้หมดหนทางเฟเบอร์และโอคอเนอร์พยายามที่จะหาทางเลือกอื่น และได้คิดค้นผลิตภัณฑ์ใหม่ชื่อว่า "Redmanol" ซึ่งพัฒนาขึ้นโดยนักเคมีชื่อว่า แอล วี เรดแมน และผลิตโดยสองพี่น้องในเมืองชิคาโก ชื่อว่าแซมและอะดอล์ฟ คาร์เพ็น

โรงงานแห่งแรกของบริษัทฟอร์มิก้าเป็นพื้นที่เช่าสองชั้นบนถนนเมนที่สองและถนนเมนสตรีท และไม่ไกลจากลานปศุสัตว์ของเมืองซินซินนาติ คำสั่งซื้อแรกในเดือนพฤษภาคมปี ค.ศ. 1913 คือการผลิตซีลยาง (V-ring) สำหรับมอเตอร์ไฟฟ้าให้กับบริษัทชาวเมอร์สมอเตอร์ ลูกค้าแรกๆ รายอื่น ได้แก่ บริษัทไอดีลอิเลคทริค (ภายหลังเปลี่ยนชื่อเป็น เดลโค) บริษัท นอทเวส อิเลคทริค และ บริษัท เบลอิเลคทริค มอเตอร์ ภายหลังจากที่ผลิตชิ้นส่วนดังกล่าว บริษัทได้ผลิตแผ่นลามิเนทเป็นครั้งแรกเมื่อวันที่ 4 กรกฎาคม ค.ศ. 1914

สงครามโลกครั้งที่ 1 ได้ทำให้มีความต้องการฉนวนกันไฟฟ้าสำหรับวิทยุและชิ้นส่วนเพิ่ม เช่น รอกสำหรับการควบคุมอากาศยาน ธุรกิจการบินมักใช้อุปกรณ์ที่มีน้ำหนักเบา และชิ้นส่วนยี่ห้อฟอร์มิก้า มักถูกใช้แทนชิ้นส่วนโลหะเนื่องจากมีน้ำหนักเบาและถูกใช้แทนชิ้นส่วนที่เป็นไม้ เนื่องจากมีความทนทาน ยอดขายในปี ค.ศ. 1917 อยู่ที่ 75,000 ดอลลาร์สหรัฐ ในปี ค.ศ. 1918 อยู่ที่ 145,000 ดอลลาร์สหรัฐ และในปี ค.ศ. 1919 อยู่ที่ 175,000 ดอลลาร์สหรัฐ บริษัทต้องการโรงงานใหม่ที่ใหญ่ขึ้น จึงย้ายไปที่ถนนสปริง โกรฟ อเวนิว และตั้งสำนักงานซึ่งใช้เป็นสำนักงานใหญ่ของบริษัทมานานหลายทศวรรษ

ผลิตภัณฑ์ตัวแรกๆ ประกอบด้วยเฟืองเพลาสำหรับเครื่องยนต์ซึ่งเบากว่าและเงียบกว่าชนิดโลหะ เพราะทำจากลามิเนท

La première usine de la société Formica, deux étages en location au coin de Second Streets and Main, n'était pas loin des parcs bestiaux de Cincinnati. Les premières commandes en mai 1913 consistaient à fournir des bagues en V pour les moteurs électriques à la Société Chalmers Motor. D'autres premiers clients étaient Ideal Electric (plus tard Delco), Northwest Electric et Bell Electric Motor. Après ces premières commandes, la société a produit sa première feuille stratifiée le 4 juillet 1914.

Pendant la première guerre mondiale, une demande se manifeste pour des isolateurs dans les radios et les pièces tels que les poulies des commandes d'avion. L'aviation mettait l'accent sur la légèreté et les pièces en Formica pouvaient souvent remplacer celles en métal pour la légèreté et celles en bois pour la durabilité. Les ventes s'élevaient à 75 000 $ en 1917, 145 000 $ en 1918 et 175 000 $ en 1919. Un agrandissement de l'usine s'avérait nécessaire. La société déménagea sur Spring Grove Avenue, avec des bureaux qui sont restés son siège pendant des décennies.

Les produits initiaux incluaient des pignons de distribution pour les moteurs des automobiles. Réalisés en stratifié, ils étaient plus légers et plus silencieux que les pignons métalliques. Un lot initial, cependant, a gonflé et s'est figé dans un parking de constructeur automobile en hiver, l'humidité s'étant infiltrée dans les engrenages. La survie de l'entreprise était en danger, mais les ingénieurs de la Formica Insulation Company identifièrent le problème et modifièrent la conception ainsi que la formule pour rejeter la vapeur d'eau. Après la production de pièces pour l'automobile, l'entreprise a réalisé des pièces pour toutes sortes de nouveaux appareils.

Pendant le boom économique des années 1920, les ventes d'aspirateurs, de machines à laver, de réfrigérateurs, de barattes, et de tous les appareils avec moteur ou engrenage ont fortement augmenté. Ces appareils séduisants étaient fabriqués et vendus sur le modèle de l'automobile (gamme haute, moyenne et basse), à grand renfort de publicité. Les isolants, les petites pièces mécaniques, les boutons et les boîtiers des nouveaux

las de madera por la durabilidad. Las ventas fueron de $75,000 en 1917, de $145,000 en 1918 y de $175,000 en 1919. Se necesitaba una nueva planta más grande. La empresa se mudó a Spring Grove Avenue, con oficinas que permanecieron como sede durante décadas.

Los productos iniciales incluían engranajes de distribución para motores de automóviles. Fabricados en laminado, eran más ligeros y más silenciosos que las alternativas de metal. Uno de los primeros lotes, sin embargo, se hinchó y congeló en el estacionamiento de un fabricante de automóviles en el invierno —se había filtrado humedad en los engranajes. La supervivencia de la empresa estaba en peligro; no obstante, los ingenieros de The Formica Insulation Company identificaron el problema y refinaron el diseño y la fórmula para eliminar el vapor de agua. El papel de la empresa en la fabricación de piezas para automóviles la llevó a fabricar piezas para toda clase de nuevos electrodomésticos.

Durante el auge económico en la década de los veinte, las ventas se dispararon con aspiradoras, lavadoras, refrigeradores, centrífugas; de hecho, cualquier artefacto con motor o engranajes. Con diseños atractivos, estos artículos se fabricaban y vendían según el modelo de los automóviles, en los niveles alto, medio o básico, con publicidad. Los aislantes, las piezas mecánicas pequeñas, las perillas y las carcasas para estos nuevos artículos representaban abundantes aplicaciones para la marca Formica y los productos rivales en tostadoras, licuadoras, batidoras, estufas eléctricas y de gas, refrigeradores y demás.

"Little Formica"

A principios de 1919, las luchas legales se convirtieron en un reto para la nueva empresa. Cinco años de juicios por violación de patente significaba que The Formica Insulation Company estaba bajo una presión constante. La empresa no estaría a salvo hasta que no se vencieran las patentes que cubrían los plásticos sintéticos Bakelite®. Fue durante dicho período cuando la empresa adquirió su reputación como una empresa pequeña pero aguerrida y luchadora. Se la llamaba "Little Formica" (Pequeña Formica), en comparación

Tällaisia osia tehtyään yhtiö valmisti ensimmäisen laminaattilevynsä 4. heinäkuuta 1914.

Ensimmäinen maailmansota aiheutti kysyntää radioiden eristimille ja sellaisille osille kuin väkipyörät lentokoneiden ohjaimissa. Ilmailussa oli tärkeää keveys, ja Formica-merkkisillä osilla voitiin usein korvata metalliset osat keveytensä, ja puiset kestävyytensä takia. Liikevaihto oli 75 000 dollaria v. 1917, 145 000 dollaria v. 1918 ja 175 000 dollaria v. 1919. Tarvittiin uusi suurempi tehdas. Yhtiö muutti Spring Grove Avenuen varrelle toimistoineen, jotka pysyivät sen pääkonttorina vuosikymmenien ajan.

Ensimmäisiin tuotteisiin sisältyivät ajoitushammaspyörät auton moottoriin. Laminaatista tehtyinä ne olivat kevyempiä ja äänettömämpiä kuin metalliset vastineet. Eräs varhaisista toimituseristä kuitenkin paisui ja jäätyi autojen valmistajan parkkipaikalle talvella — hammaspyöriin oli päässyt kosteutta. Yhtiön henkiinjääminen oli vaarassa, mutta The Formica Insulation Companyn insinöörit tunnistivat ongelman ja paransivat rakenteen ja koostumuksen vesihöyryn poistamiseksi. Yhtiön rooli auton osien valmistajana johti kaikenlaisten uusien sähkölaitteiden osien valmistustoimintaan.

Taloudellisen nousukauden aikana 1920-luvulla myytiin huimasti pölynimureja, pesukoneita, jääkaappeja, kirnuja, tosiaankin kaikkea sellaista, joissa oli moottori tai hammaspyöriä. Viehätysvoimaa ajatellen tyyliteltyinä nämä nimikkeet valmistettiin ja myytiin automallien tapaan, korkean, keskiluokan ja perustasojen perusteella mainosten mukaisesti. Eristimet, pienet mekaaniset osat, nupit ja kotelot näitä uusia nimikkeitä varten merkitsivät runsaasti sovelluksia Formica tavaramerkille ja kilpaileville tuotteille leivänpaahtimissa, tehosekoittimissa, sähkö- ja kaasuliesissä, jääkaapeissa ja niin edelleen.

"Pikkuinen Formica"

Vuodesta 1919 lähtien lakiasiat tulivat haasteellisiksi uudelle yhtiölle. Viiden vuoden ajan oikeusjutut patenttiloukkauksista aiheuttivat sen, että Formica Insulation Company oli jatkuvan paineen alaisena. Vasta sitten kun synteettisen Bakelite®-muovin patentit vanhenevat, olisi yhtiö turvassa.

加哥的兩兄弟山姆和阿道夫·卡彭 (Sam and Adolph Karpen) 製造。

富美家公司的第一家工廠坐落在第二街和主街交界的一座租來的兩層樓上,不遠處便是辛辛那提牲畜飼養場。1913 年 5 月的第一筆訂單是為查默斯汽車公司 (Chalmers Motor Company) 的電動馬達製作 V 型環。其他早期的客戶有理想電氣公司 (Ideal Electric) (後來更名為德科電氣公司 (Delco Electric))、西北電氣公司 (Northwest Electric) 和貝爾電機公司 (Bell Electric Motor)。在製作了這些部件後,該公司於 1914 年 7 月 4 日生產出第一片美耐板。

第一次世界大戰帶來了對收音機絕緣子以及飛機控制部件 (如皮帶輪) 的需求。航空飛行注重重量輕,富美家品牌的部件往往可以因重量輕取代金屬,因經久耐用取代木製部件。1917 年的銷售額為 7.5 萬美元,1918 年為 14.5 萬美元。1919 年為 17.5 萬美元。一家新的、更大的工廠刻不容緩。公司遷移到春天樹叢大道,這裡的辦公室幾十年來一直是公司的總部。

最初的產品包括汽車發動機定時齒輪。它們由美耐板製成,比金屬的替代品更輕、噪音更小。但早期的一批貨物冬天在一家汽車製造廠的停車場被膨漲和上凍——皆因濕氣滲透到齒輪內所致。公司生存危在旦夕,但富美家絕緣公司的工程師們找出了原因,完善了設計和配方,去除了水蒸氣。公司在為汽車製造零件方面的作用帶來了為各種新家電製造零件的業務。

二十世紀二十年代的經濟繁榮時期,真空吸塵器、洗衣機、冰箱、攪拌器的銷量猛增,只要用電機或齒輪的任何東西都是這樣。這些部件的製造風格為了吸引人,都是按汽車型號製造出售,在高、中、基本檔次用廣告以推廣。絕緣子、小型機械零件、旋鈕和裝這些新部件的盒子意味著富美家的品牌和競爭對手的產品可

和阿道夫·卡彭 (Sam and Adolph Karpen) 制造。

富美家公司的第一家工厂坐落在第二街和主街交界的一座租来的两层楼上,不远处便是辛辛那提牲畜饲养场。1913 年 5 月的第一笔订单是为查默斯汽车公司 (Chalmers Motor Company) 的电动马达制作 V 型环。其他早期的客户有理想电气公司 (Ideal Electric) (后来更名为德科电气公司 (Delco Electric))、西北电气公司 (Northwest Electric) 和贝尔电机公司 (Bell Electric Motor)。在制作了这些部件后,该公司于 1914 年 7 月 4 日生产出第一片耐火板。

第一次世界大战带来了对收音机绝缘子以及飞机控制部件 (如皮带轮) 的需求。航空飞行注重重量轻,富美家品牌的部件往往可以因重量轻取代金属,因经久耐用取代木制部件。1917 年的销售额为 7.5 万美元,1918 年为 14.5万美元。1919 年为 17.5 万美元。建设一家新的、更大的工厂刻不容缓。公司迁移到春天树丛大道,这里的办公室几十年来一直是公司的总部。

最初的产品包括汽车发动机定时齿轮。它们由耐火板制成,比金属的替代品更轻、噪音更小。但早期的一批货物冬天在一家汽车制造厂的停车场被膨涨和上冻——皆因湿气渗透入齿轮内所致。公司生存危在旦夕,但富美家绝缘公司的工程师们找出了原因,完善了设计和配方,去除了水蒸气。公司在为汽车制造零件方面的作用带来了为各种新家电制造零件的业务。

二十世纪二十年代的经济繁荣时期,真空吸尘器、洗衣机、冰箱、搅拌器的销量猛增,只要用电机或齿轮的任何东西都是这样。这些部件的制造风格为了吸引人,都是按汽车型号制造出售,在高、中、基本档次用广告以推广。绝缘子、小型机械零件、旋钮和装这些新部件的盒子意味着富美家的品牌和竞争对手的产品可

อย่างไรก็ตาม ผลิตภัณฑ์รุ่นแรกๆ บวมและกลายเป็นน้ำแข็งในลานจอดรถของผู้ผลิตเครื่องยนต์ตอนฤดูหนาว เนื่องจากความชื้นซึมเข้าไปในเฟือง ความอยู่รอดของบริษัทตกอยู่ในอันตราย แต่วิศวกรของ เดอะ ฟอร์ไมก้า คอมพานี ได้ทำการแก้ปัญหา ปรับแบบ และสูตรการผลิตเพื่อกำจัดไอน้ำ บทบาทของบริษัทในการทำผลิตชิ้นส่วนรถยนต์นำไปสู่ธุรกิจผลิตชิ้นส่วนสำหรับอุปกรณ์ใหม่ๆ หลายชนิด

ในยุคที่เศรษฐกิจเจริญรุ่งเรืองในช่วงทศวรรษที่ 1920 ยอดขายเพิ่มสูงขึ้นจากเครื่องดูดฝุ่น เครื่องซักผ้า ตู้เย็น เครื่องปั่นและแทบทุกอย่างที่มีมอเตอร์หรือเฟือง และเนื่องจากการกำหนดรูปแบบให้น่าดึงดูดใจวัสดุดังกล่าวได้มีการผลิตและขายตามรุ่นของรถยนต์ในระดับสูง กลาง และพื้นฐานโดยการโฆษณา ฉนวน ชิ้นส่วนเครื่องจักรกลขนาดเล็ก ลูกบิด และภาชนะใส่ผลิตภัณฑ์ใหม่นี้ หมายความว่า มีการใช้ผลิตภัณฑ์ยี่ห้อฟอร์ไมก้าและคู่แข่งมากมายในเครื่องปั่น เครื่องปั่น เครื่องผสม เตาไฟฟ้า และเตาแก๊สตู้เย็น ฯลฯ

"ลิตเติล ฟอร์ไมก้า"

ในช่วงต้นในปี ค.ศ. 1919 ปัญหาทางกฎหมายกลายเป็นสิ่งที่ท้าทายสำหรับบริษัทใหม่ การดำเนินคดีเกี่ยวกับการละเมิดสิทธิบัตรเป็นเวลาห้าปีทำให้ เดอะ ฟอร์ไมก้า อินซูเลชั่น คอมพานีอยู่ภายใต้ความกดดันอย่างต่อเนื่อง บริษัทจะไม่ปลอดภัยจนกว่าสิทธิบัตรของพลาสติกสังเคราะห์เบคาไลต์จะหมดอายุ ในช่วงเวลาดังกล่าว บริษัทฟอร์ไมก้ามีชื่อเสียงในฐานะบริษัทขนาดเล็กที่ต่อสู้อย่างไม่ลดละ บริษัทถูกเรียกว่า "ลิตเติ้ล ฟอร์ไมก้า" ซึ่งตรงข้ามกับบริษัทยักษ์ใหญ่ซึ่งบริษัทต่อสู้ด้วยในศาล เช่น บริษัท เจนเนอรัล อิเลคทริค และ บริษัทเวสติงเฮาว์ ช่วงระยะเวลาดังกล่าวก่อให้เกิดวัฒนธรรมทางธุรกิจของบริษัทฟอร์ไมก้า โดยมีความคิดว่าบริษัทเล็กๆ และบริษัทฟอร์ไมก้าสามารถต่อสู้กับคู่แข่งที่ใหญ่กว่าได้ คดีความทำให้บริษัทมีชื่อเสียง และก่อให้เกิดความคิดในอุตสาหกรรมว่า ลิตเติล ฟอร์ไมก้า กำลังถูกกลั่นแกล้ง บริษัทได้รับการขนานนามว่าบริษัท "ลิตเติล ฟอร์ไมก้า" ในหลายทศวรรษหลังจากนั้น

ช่วงทศวรรษที่ 1920
การปฏิวัติของวงการวิทยุ

เดอะ ฟอร์ไมก้า อินซูเลชั่น คอมพานีได้รับประโยชน์จากอุตสาหกรรมที่เริ่มต้นจากขนาดเล็กๆ เช่นกัน ในยุคของคอมพิวเตอร์และโทรทัศน์เป็นการยากที่จะเข้าใจว่า วิทยุ

appareils constituaient une foule d'applications pour la marque Formica et les produits concurrents dans les grille-pain, les mélangeurs, les malaxeurs, les cuisinières électriques et à gaz, les réfrigérateurs, etc.

La Petite Formica

À partir de 1919, les luttes juridiques sont devenues un défi pour la nouvelle entreprise. Cinq années de procès en contrefaçon de brevet montrent que la Formica Insulation Company subissait une pression constante. Ceci dura jusqu'à la fin des brevets couvrant les plastiques synthétiques Bakelite®. C'est pendant cette période que la société a acquis sa réputation d'entreprise petite, certes, mais combattante. L'entreprise acquit le surnom de « Little Formica » (la petite Formica), par contraste avec les géants qui s'affrontaient au tribunal, tels que General Electric et Westinghouse. Ces années ont façonné la culture de l'entreprise Formica. Elles ont développé l'idée que la société Formica ne pouvait lutter contre des concurrents plus importants. Les poursuites ont donné à l'entreprise une réputation : la petite Formica impuissante était harcelée. C'était « Little Formica », la société combattante, pour des décennies à venir.

1920 : La révolution de la radio

La Formica Insulation Company a bénéficié d'un secteur qui a aussi commencé modestement. Dans notre ère d'ordinateurs et de télévisions, il est difficile de concevoir la révolution créée par la radio dans la vie quotidienne du début du vingtième siècle. Le stratifié Formica est un élément essentiel. La « télégraphie sans fil » a transformé le monde en pouvant transporter davantage que le code simple Morse, la voix et la musique se sont ainsi ajoutées. Avoir une boîte dans son salon d'où sortent les voix des gens à travers le monde représentait quelque chose de fondamentalement nouveau dans l'expérience humaine. La possibilité de transmission a fait passer le cercle utilitaire de communication en un mode de communication d'informations et de divertissement.

Les premières radios étaient le domaine des amateurs jusqu'au début des années 1920, lorsque la radio ama-

con los gigantes con los que batallaba en los tribunales, como General Electric y·Westinghouse. Estos años dieron forma a una cultura empresarial subsiguiente en el negocio de Formica. Crearon la idea de que la pequeña empresa Formica podía enfrentarse a sus rivales más grandes. Los juicios le dieron a la empresa una reputación, lo que generó en la industria la idea de que estaban acosando a la indefensa y pequeña Formica. "Little Formica" fue la aguerrida empresa, durante varias décadas.

La Década De Los Veinte: La Revolución De La Radio

The Formica Insulation Company se benefició de una industria que también comenzó siendo pequeña. En nuestra era de computadoras y televisores, es difícil concebir qué revolución creó la radio en la vida diaria de principios del siglo XX. El laminado Formica fue clave. El "telégrafo inalámbrico" transformó al mundo una vez que pudo transmitir más que el simple código morse y se agregaron voces y música. Tener una caja en la propia sala de la que surgían los sonidos de personas al otro lado del mundo era algo absolutamente nuevo en la experiencia humana. La capacidad de transmitir cambió el medio de la comunicación utilitaria a la de información y entretenimiento.

Los primeros radios pertenecían a aficionados hasta principios de la década de los veinte, cuando un radio no profesional se convirtió en un furor similar al causado por la primera computadora personal en la década de los setenta. Se ensamblaban miles de radios a partir de kits. Todo lo que se requería era un cristal de cuarzo, algunos alambres enrollados en un tubo de cartón, una batería, auriculares y alguna clase de tablero aislante como base. Pronto, los primeros radios estaban disponibles para la venta.

El laminado Formica resultaba ser un tablero básico excelente para los aparatos de radio, como así también para otros componentes no conductores. Las ventas de radios crecieron de 5,000 unidades en 1920 a más de 2.5 millones en 1924. Para la época en la que los oyentes podían seguir las noticias del histórico vuelo transatlántico del aviador Charles Lindbergh en 1927, existían unos seis millones de aparatos de radio. Las cifras de las ventas de

Juuri näinä aikoina yhtiö sai pienen, mutta sinnikkään, hanttiin panevan yhtiön maineen. Sitä kutsuttiin nimellä "Pikkuinen Formica", verrattuna jättiläisiin, kuten General Electric ja Westinghouse, joita vastaan se kamppaili oikeudessa. Nämä vuodet muokkasivat sitä seuranneen yrityskulttuurin Formican liiketoiminnassa. Siitä lähti idea, että Pikkuinen Formica yhtiö pystyi olemaan napit vastakkain suurempien kilpailijoidensa kanssa. Oikeusjutut antoivat yhtiölle maineen, joka perustui käsitykseen, että avutonta Pikkuista Formicaa härnättiin. Siitä tuli vuosikymmeniksi "Pikkuinen Formica", sinnikäs yhtiö.

1920-Luku: Radion vallankumous

Formica Insulation Company hyötyi toisesta teollisuudesta, joka samoin lähti pienestä alkuun. Tietokoneiden ja television aikakautena on vaikea kuvitella minkä vallankumouksen radio sai aikaan jokapäiväisessä elämässä 1900-luvun alkupuolella. Formica laminaatti oli avainosana. "Langaton lennätin" muutti maailman, kun pystyttiin kuljettamaan muutakin kuin yksinkertaista sähkötystä, ja lisättiin puhe ja musiikki. Asettaa olohuoneeseen laatikko, josta tulee ihmisten ääniä maapallon toiselta puolelta, oli pohjimmiltaan jotain aivan uutta ihmisen kokemuksi. Kyky lähettää muutti viestintävälineen hyödyllisestä yhteydenpidosta tiedon ja viihteen välineeksi.

Alkuaikojen radiot olivat harrastelijoiden alaa 1920-luvun alkupuolelle saakka, kun radioamatööritoiminnasta tuli villitys samaan tapaan kuin alkuaikojen henkilökohtaisesta tietokoneesta 1970-luvulla. Tuhansia radioita koottiin rakennussarjoista. Tarvittiin vain kide, joitakin pahviputken ympärille käämittyjä johtimia, paristo, kuulokkeet — ja jonkinlainen eristävä levy alustaksi. Pian tulivat myyntiin ensimmäiset valmiiksi tehdyt radiot.

Formica-laminaatti tarjosi erinomaisen aluslevyn radiovastaanottimille sekä muille sähköä johtamattomille osille. Radiovastaanottimien myynti kasvoi 5000 kappaleesta v. 1920 yli 2,5 miljoonaan v. 1924. Siihen mennessä kun kuuntelijat pystyivät seuraamaan uutisia lentäjä Charles Lindberghin historiallisesta Atlantin yli lennosta

以應用在烤麵包機、攪拌機、電爐和燃氣爐、冰箱等產品上。

「小富美家」

從 1919 年開始，法律上的鬥爭成為新公司面臨的一個挑戰。五年的專利侵權訴訟意味著富美家絕緣公司一直承受著重壓。直到涵蓋酚醛合成塑膠的專利到期，該公司才感到安全。正是在此期間，公司贏得了小而鬥志旺盛的美名。它被稱為「小富美家」，以區別它在法庭上對陣的巨頭公司，如通用電氣公司和西屋公司。這些年塑造了後來富美家在商場上的企業文化。它們創造了小富美家公司可以對陣大競爭對手的概念。這些訴訟給公司贏得了名聲，在行業裡形成一種看法，即無助的小富美家被欺負了。這就使「小富美家」在今後幾十年裡一直爭強好勝。

二十世紀二十年代：無線電革命

富美家絕緣公司受益於一個小規模創始的行業。在我們電腦和電視時代，很難想像無線電給二十世紀早期的日常生活帶來了多麼大的一場革命。富美家美耐板是一個重要組成部分。「無線電報」一旦可以攜帶更多的不僅是簡單的莫爾斯電碼，加上聲音和音樂，就會改變世界。放在起居室裡的一個盒子，裡面傳出地球另一邊的人的聲音，這在人類的經歷中是全新的東西。傳輸能力從一個功利性的溝通媒介改變成資訊和娛樂媒介。

早期的收音機是業餘愛好者的天地，直到二十世紀二十年代，業餘無線電成了一股熱潮，就像個人電腦在二十世紀七十年代一樣。成千上萬的收音機用配件組裝。所需的只是一個晶體、一些捲繞紙板管的導線、一節電池、一副耳機——和某種形式的絕緣板作為底板。不久，第一個現成的收音機上市。

富美家美耐板為收音機和其他非導體零件提供了一個很好的底板。無

以应用在烤面包机、搅拌机、电炉和燃气炉、冰箱等产品上。

"小富美家"

从 1919 年开始，法律上的斗争成为新公司面临的一个挑战。五年的专利侵权诉讼意味着富美家绝缘公司一直承受着重压。直到涵盖酚醛合成塑料的专利到期，该公司才感到安全。正是在此期间，公司赢得了小而斗志旺盛的美名。它被称为"小富美家"，以区别它在法庭上对阵的巨头公司，如通用电气公司和西屋公司。这些年塑造了后来富美家在商场上的企业文化。它们创造了小富美家公司可以对阵大竞争对手的概念。这些诉讼给公司赢得了名声，在行业里形成一种看法，即无助的小富美家被欺负了。这就使"小富美家"在今后几十年里一直争强好胜。

二十世纪二十年代：无线电革命

富美家绝缘公司受益于一个小规模创始的行业。在我们计算机和电视时代，很难想象无线电给二十世纪早期的日常生活带来了多么大的一场革命。富美家®装饰耐火板是一个重要组成部分。"无线电报"一旦可以携带更多的不仅是简单的莫尔斯电码，加上声音和音乐，就会改变世界。放在起居室里的一个盒子，里面传出地球另一边的人的声音，这在人类的经历中是全新的东西。传输能力从一个功利性的沟通媒介改变成信息和娱乐媒介。

早期的收音机是业余爱好者的天地，直到二十世纪二十年代，业余无线电成了一股热潮，就像个人计算机在二十世纪七十年代一样。成千上万的收音机用配件组装。所需的只是一个晶体、一些卷绕纸板管的导线、一节电池、一副耳机——和某种形式的绝缘板作为底板。不久，第一个现成的收音机上市。

富美家®装饰耐火板为收音机和其他非导体零件提供了一个很好的底板。

ได้ปฏิวัติสิ่งใดในช่วงต้นศตวรรษที่ยังสืบบ้างแผ่นลามิเนทฟอร์ไมก้ามีส่วนสำคัญมาก "วิทยุโทรเลข" เปลี่ยนโลกเมื่อมันสามารถส่งสารได้มากกว่ารหัสมอร์สและสามารถเพิ่มเสียงและเพลงเข้าไป การที่เรามีกล่องๆ หนึ่งในห้องนั่งเล่นที่ส่งเสียงจากคนที่อยู่ไกลกว่าครึ่งโลกย่อมเป็นประสบการณ์ใหม่สำหรับมนุษย์ ความสามารถในการส่งผ่านข้อมูล เปลี่ยนแปลงสื่อจากการสื่อสารเป็นข้อมูลและความบันเทิง

ในช่วงแรก วิทยุถูกใช้โดยผู้เล่นวิทยุเป็นงานอดิเรกจนกระทั่งช่วงต้นศตวรรษที่ 1920 ซึ่งเป็นช่วงวิทยุสมัครเล่นได้รับความนิยมอย่างบ้าคลั่ง เช่นเดียวกับคอมพิวเตอร์ส่วนบุคคลในช่วงศตวรรษที่ 1970 มีการประกอบวิทยุจากชุดอุปกรณ์เป็นพันๆ เครื่อง สิ่งที่ต้องใช้มีเพียงคริสตัล สายไฟพันหลอด กระดาษแข็ง ถ่านหูฟัง และแผ่นฉนวนสำหรับใช้เป็นฐาน ในไม่ช้าวิทยุที่ประกอบเสร็จสมบูรณ์มีให้มีขายในตลาด

แผ่นลามิเนทฟอร์ไมก้าใช้เป็นบอร์ดชั้นเยี่ยมสำหรับชุดวิทยุและชิ้นส่วนที่ไม่ใช่ฉนวนไฟฟ้าส่วนอื่นๆ ยอดขายชุดวิทยุเพิ่มจาก 5,000 หน่วยในปี ค.ศ. 1920 ไปสู่ยอดขายที่มากกว่า 2.5 ล้านหน่วยในปี ค.ศ. 1924 ในเวลาที่ผู้ฟังสามารถติดตามข่าวเที่ยวบินประวัติศาสตร์ข้ามมหาสมุทรแอตแลนติกของนักบินชื่อ ชาร์ลส์ ลินด์เบิร์กได้ในปี ค.ศ. 1927 มีการใช้ชุดวิทยุถึง 6 ล้านเครื่อง ยอดขายวิทยุเพิ่มขึ้นอีกจาก 60 ล้านดอลลาร์สหรัฐในปี ค.ศ. 1922 เป็น 426 ล้านดอลลาร์สหรัฐในปี ค.ศ. 1929 เมื่อมีการจำหน่ายชุดที่มีความซับซ้อนยิ่งขึ้น บริษัทเวสติงเฮาส์ ซึ่งเป็นนายจ้างเก่าของเฟเบอร์และโอคอเนอร์ อยู่แถวหน้าในการสื่อสารรูปแบบใหม่นี้ โดยร่วมมือกับบริษัท จีอีเพื่อขายสินค้าภายใต้ยี่ห้อเรดิโอ คอร์ปอเรชันออฟ อเมริกา (RCA)® และทำการเปิดตัวสถานีกระจายเสียงเชิงพาณิชย์แห่งแรก คือเคดีเคเอ โดยเริ่มจัดตารางการถ่ายทอดด้วย

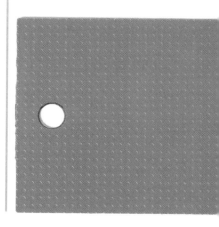

257

teur est devenue un véritable engouement, de la même manière que l'ordinateur personnel au début des années
1970. Des milliers de radios ont été
assemblées à partir de kits. Tout ce qu'il
fallait, c'était un cristal, des fils enrou-
lés autour d'un tube en carton, une
batterie, des écouteurs et une sorte de
panneau isolé à la base. Bientôt, les
premières radios manufacturées
étaient disponibles à la vente.

Le stratifié Formica constituait un
excellent panneau de base pour les
postes de radio et d'autres pièces non
conductrices. Les ventes de postes de
radio sont passées de 5000 unités en
1920 à plus de 2,5 millions d'unités
en 1924. Au moment où les auditeurs
pouvaient suivre les nouvelles de
l'aviateur Charles Lindbergh lors du
vol transatlantique historique de
1927, quelques six millions de postes
de radio étaient en cours d'utilisation.
Les ventes de radios se sont encore
accélérées avec l'apparition de radios
plus évoluées. Elles sont passées de
60 millions de dollars en 1922 à 426
millions de dollars en 1929. L'ancien
employeur de Faber et O'Conor, Westinghouse, était à l'avant-garde du
développement de ce nouveau média,
en collaboration avec GE pour la vente
d'ensembles avec la marque Radio
Corporation of America (RCA)® et
l'ouverture du premier émetteur de
radiodiffusion commercial, KDKA. La
programmation a commencé avec les
retransmissions de l'élection prési-
dentielle Harding-Cox le 2 novembre

radios también se elevaron a medida
que se presentaban aparatos más
elaborados, de $60 millones en 1922
a $426 millones en 1929. El antiguo
empleador de Faber y O'Conor, Westinghouse, estaba a la vanguardia del
nuevo medio de comunicación, al coo-
perar con GE para vender aparatos con
la marca Radio Corporation of America
(RCA)® y al abrir la primera estación
emisora comercial, KDKA. Comenzó la
programación regular con los resultados de la elección presidencial entre
Harding y Cox el 2 de noviembre de
1920, transmitida desde una cabina
de madera en la parte superior de la
fábrica de la empresa en East Pittsburgh —el mismo edificio en el que
Faber y O'Conor se conocieron.

La radio unificó a las personas alrededor del mundo. En 1921, David Sarnoff de RCA concibió la idea de la primera transmisión en cadena nacional
para una pelea por el campeonato de
peso pesado entre Jack Dempsey y
Georges Carpentier. Miles de personas
en todo el país escuchaban las radios
públicas en enormes altavoces en
bares y salones de baile. Pronto, la
radio se volvió mundial. Una de las
primeras estaciones se instaló en Argentina en 1920 y en 1923, cuando
Dempsey peleó con el joven boxeador
argentino Luis Ángel Firpo, el Toro
Salvaje de las Pampas, la radio transmitió el sonido en vivo desde el Polo
Grounds en Nueva York hasta las calles
de Buenos Aires, donde las personas
se abarrotaban alrededor de enormes

v. 1927, käytössä oli kuutisen miljoonaa
radiovastaanotinta. Monimutkaisem-
pien vastaanottimien tullessa markkinoille, myös radioiden myyntiluvut
kohosivat 60 miljoonasta dollarista v.
1922, 426 miljoonaan dollariin v.
1929. Faber ja O'Conorin entinen työn-
antaja Westinghouse olivat uuden tie-
dotusvälineen eturivissä, yhteistyössä
GE:n kanssa myymässä vastaanottimia
Radio Corporation of America (RCA)®
-tavaramerkillä ja avaamassa ensimmäistä kaupallista yleisradioasemaa
KDKA. Se aloitti säännölliset ohjelmat
Harding-Cox presidentinvaalin tuloksil-
la 2. marraskuuta 1920, lähettäen pui-
sesta vajasta yhtiön tehtaan katolla
East Pittsburghissa — aivan saman
rakennuksen päältä, jossa Faber ja
O'Conor olivat tavanneet.

Radio yhdisti ihmisiä ympäri maailmaa. Vuonna 1921 RCA:n David
Sarnoff keksi idean ensimmäisestä
kansallisesta verkkoyhteydestä Jack
Dempseyn ja Georges Carpentierin
välistä raskaan sarjan mestaruusotte-
lua varten. Tuhansittain ihmisiä maan
laajuisesti kuunteli julkisia radioita
valtavan suurista kaiuttimista baareis-
sa ja tanssisaleissa. Radiosta tuli pian
globaali. Varhainen asema otettiin
käyttöön Argentiinassa v. 1920 ja v.
1923, kun Dempsey otteli nuoren ar-
gentiinalaisen nyrkkeilijän Luis Ángel
Firpon, pampan härän, kanssa ja radio
toi suorana lähetyksenä äänen Polo
Groundsilta New Yorkissa Buenos Ai-
resin kaduille, jossa ihmisjoukot ke-
rääntyivät valtavan suurten kaiuttimien
ympärille huutamaan eläköötä mesta-
rilleen. Formica oli siinä usein mukana.

Useimmat vastaanottimet olivat
yksinkertaisia laatikoita, joissa oli
nuppeja sivulla. Radion osat, putket
ja käämit, kiinnitettiin eristettyyn le-
vyyn — nykypäivän tietokoneista
tuttuun emolevyyn. Levy kasvoi laati-
koksi osien piilottamiseksi ja uusien
kartiokaiuttimien kiinnittämiseksi.
Ulkosivut päällystettiin usein Formica
Insulation Companyn mustalla tai rus-
kealla laminaatilla. Pinta mustassa
fenolilaminaatissa, jota Formica-yhtiö
toimitti moniin alkuvuosien radioihin,
tuli visuaalisesti liittymään radioon ja
myöhemmin hi-fi ja hi-tech-laitteisiin
ja jopa tietokoneisiin, elektroniikan
suunnittelun hillittynä värinä.

Formica Insulation Company oli
osana tämän uuden teknologian ulko-

線電收音機的銷售量從 1920 年的 5,000 台增長到 1924 年超過 250 萬台。到了聽眾可以跟蹤飛行員查爾斯·林德伯格 (Charles Lindbergh) 1927 年歷史性的跨越大西洋飛行的新聞時,已有約 600 萬台無線電收音機在使用中。收音機的銷售額隨著更高級的機型的出現也在增長,從 1922 年的 6,000 萬美元到 1929 年的 4.26 億美元。費伯和奧康納的老雇主西屋公司走在這個新媒體的前列,與通用電氣公司合作,銷售美國無線電公司 (Radio Corporation of America/簡稱 RCA®) 的品牌,並開啟了第一個商業廣播電臺 KDKA。該電臺從 1920 年 11 月 2 日哈丁 (Harding) 與考克斯 (Cox) 總統選舉開始籌劃節目,從該公司在東匹茲堡工廠頂樓的一間木棚裡廣播——這裡正是費伯和奧康納首次見面的地方。

廣播統一了世界各地的人們。1921 年,RCA 公司的大衛·薩諾夫 (David Sarnoff) 突發奇想,全國聯播傑克·登普西 (Jack Dempsey) 對喬治·卡彭鐵爾 (Georges Carpentier) 的重量級冠軍爭奪賽。全國各地成千上萬的公眾從酒吧和舞廳的巨大揚聲器裡收聽公眾廣播。不久無線電走向全球。1920 年,早期的一個電臺在阿根廷成立,

无线电收音机的销售量从 1920 年的 5,000 台增长到 1924 年超过 250 万台。到了听众可以跟踪飞行员查斯·林德伯格 (Charles Lindbergh) 1927 年历史性的跨越大西洋飞行的新闻时,已有约 600 万台无线电收音机在使用中。收音机的销售额随着更高级的机型的出现也在增长,从 1922 年的 6,000 万美元到 1929 年的 4.26 亿美元。费伯和奥康纳的老雇主西屋公司走在这个新媒体的前列,与通用电气公司合作,销售美国无线电公司 (Radio Corporation of America/简称 RCA®) 的品牌,并开启了第一个商业广播电台 KDKA。该电台从 1920 年 11 月 2 日哈丁 (Harding) 与考克斯 (Cox) 总统选举开始筹划节目,从该公司在东匹兹堡工厂顶楼的一间木棚里广播——这里正是费伯和奥康纳首次见面的地方。

广播统一了世界各地的人们。1921 年,RCA 公司的大卫·萨诺夫 (David Sarnoff) 突发奇想,全国联播杰克·登普西 (Jack Dempsey) 对乔治·卡彭铁尔 (Georges Carpentier) 的重量级冠军争夺赛。全国各地成千上万的公众从酒吧和舞厅的巨大扬声器里收听公众广播。不久无线电走向全球。1920 年,早期的一个电台在阿根廷成立,1923 年登普西迎战年轻的阿根廷拳击手号称潘帕斯的公牛的路易斯·安赫尔·福尔珀 (Luis Ángel Firpo),电台转播了实况,从纽约马球场到布宜诺斯艾利斯街头,人们把大扬声器围得水泄不通,为他们的冠军呐喊助威。富美家往往是其中的一部分。

大多数的收音机是带旋钮的简单盒子。收音机的部件、管子和线圈都连接在一块绝缘板上——就像我们今天所知道的计算机主板。主板变成一个盒子,藏起了零件,并装有一个新的喇叭形扬声器。外观往往贴上黑色或棕色的富美家绝缘公司的耐火板。富美家公司为许多早期收音机提供的黑色酚醛耐火板在视觉上与收音机联系在一起,后来又与高保真 (Hi-Fi)、高科技、

การเลือกตั้งประธานาธิบดีระหว่าง ฮาร์ดิง คอกซ์ ในวันที่ 2 พฤศจิกายน ค.ศ. 1920 โดยกระจายเสียงจากเพิงไม้ด้านบนอาคารโรงงานของบริษัทในภาคตะวันออกของเมืองพิตส์เบิร์ก – เป็นตึกที่ เฟเบอร์และโอคอนเนอร์ได้พบกันครั้งแรก

วิทยุทำให้คนทั่วโลกเป็นหนึ่งเดียวกัน ในปี ค.ศ. 1921 เดวิด ซาร์นอฟฟ์ แห่งอาร์ซีเอ ได้มีความคิดริเริ่มศึกชิงแชมป์ประกับประเทศ ประเภทเฮวี่เวท ระหว่างแจ็ค เด็มพ์ซ และจอร์จ คาร์เพนเตอร์ คนหลายพันคนทั่วประเทศได้ฟังวิทยุสาธารณะจากเครื่องกระจายเสียงขนาดใหญ่ในบาร์และสถานที่เต้นรำ ในไม่ช้าวิทยุก็เป็นที่รู้จักกันทั่วโลก – สถานีแห่งแรกๆ ได้ตั้งขึ้นที่ประเทศอาร์เจนตินาในปี ค.ศ. 1920 และต่อมาในปี ค.ศ. 1923 เมื่อเด็มพ์ซี ขึ้นชกกับนักมวยหนุ่มชาวอาร์เจนตินาชื่อว่า Luis Ángel Firpo กระจายเสียงสดจากโปโลกราวด์ส ในครนิวยอร์กมายังสถานที่ต่างๆ ในเมืองบัวโนสไอเรส ซึ่งมีผู้คนมากมายล้อมรอบเครื่องกระจายเสียงขนาดใหญ่และให้กำลังใจแชมป์ของพวกเขา ฟอร์ไมก้าก็เป็นส่วนหนึ่งของเหตุการณ์เหล่านั้น

ชุดอุปกรณ์ส่วนใหญ่เป็นกล่องและลูกบิดแบบง่ายๆ ชิ้นส่วนของวิทยุ หลอด และลวดถูกติดไว้บนบอร์ดวงจรไฟฟ้า หรือแผงวงจรหลักที่เรารู้จักกันจากคอมพิวเตอร์ บอร์ดถูกเปลี่ยนเป็นกล่องเพื่อซ่อนชิ้นส่วนและลำโพงรูปโคนแบบใหม่ ภายนอกมักจะเคลือบด้วยลามิเนทจากฟอร์ไมก้าสีดำหรือสีน้ำตาล พื้นผิวบนที่เป็นลามิเนทฟีโนลิคสีดำ ซึ่งบริษัทฟอร์ไมก้าผลิตสำหรับวิทยุในยุคแรกๆ จนกลายเป็นสิ่งที่เห็นอยู่คู่กับวิทยุ และต่อมาเป็นไฮไฟ ไฮเทค และแม้แต่คอมพิวเตอร์ด้วย ใช้สีเขียวๆ ซึ่งเหมาะสมกับงานวิศวกรรมไฟฟ้า

เดอะ ฟอร์ไมก้า อินซูเลชัน คอมพานีเป็นส่วนหนึ่งของเทคโนโลยีใหม่ บริษัทผ่านการปรับเปลี่ยนโครงสร้างพื้นฐานของบริษัทจากผู้ผลิตวัสดุที่เน้นด้านประโยชน์ใช้งานจนเป็นผู้ผลิตวัสดุที่ขับเคลื่อนด้วยการดีไซน์ ทำให้แผ่นลามิเนทฟอร์ไมก้าถูกมองว่าเป็นผลิตภัณฑ์ที่ทันสมัย ซึ่งสื่อถึงเทคโนโลยีชั้นสูงเป็นวัสดุที่มาจากอนาคต เจฟฟรี เมคเคิล นักประวัติศาสตร์ด้านการออกแบบได้เคยเขียนไว้ว่า วัสดุนี้ "ให้ความเที่ยงตรงอย่างที่ไม่มีอยู่ในธรรมชาติ" ในช่วงยุคเศรษฐกิจตกต่ำ วัสดุนี้ให้ความมีระเบียบแก่เศรษฐกิจที่กำลังวุ่นวายและเมื่อใช้ในการปรับปรุงรูปแบบการจัดการ วัสดุนี้ให้ความเร็วสำหรับการรับมือกับการชะลอตัวของเศรษฐกิจ สำหรับนักคิดสมัยใหม่ วัสดุนี้เป็นหนึ่งในบรรดาหนทางที่ชัดเจนที่สุดที่จะทำให้ความคิดและแบบร่างต่างๆ เป็นจริง

1920, à partir d'une cabane en bois placée au-dessus de l'usine de l'entreprise à East Pittsburgh, précisément le bâtiment dans lequel Faber et O'Conor s'étaient rencontrés.

La radio a réuni les gens autour du monde. En 1921, David Sarnoff de RCA a conçu l'idée du premier branchement national, pour un combat de championnat des poids lourds, entre Jack Dempsey et Georges Carpentier. Des milliers de gens à travers le pays ont écouté les radios publiques sur des grands haut-parleurs dans les bars et les salles de danse. Peu après, la radio devenait mondiale. Une première station a été installée en Argentine en 1920 et en 1923, lorsque Dempsey a combattu le jeune boxeur argentin Luis Ángel Firpo, le Taureau de la Pampa, la radio a réalisé une retransmission en direct depuis la salle Polo Grounds de New York jusque dans les rues de Buenos Aires, où les gens se pressaient autour des haut-parleurs énormes et encourageaient leur champion. Formica était souvent de la partie.

La plupart des radios étaient de simples boîtes avec des boutons. Les pièces de la radio, les tubes et les bobinages, étaient fixés à une carte isolée, la carte maîtresse que nous connaissons aujourd'hui dans les ordinateurs. La carte est devenue une boîte dissimulant les pièces et de nouveaux cônes de haut-parleur y étaient montés. L'extérieur était souvent revêtu du stratifié noir ou marron de la Formica Insulation Company. La surface de stratifié phénolique noir que la société Formica a fourni pour de nombreuses radios des débuts est devenue visuellement associée avec la radio et plus tard avec la haute fidélité, les hautes technologies et même les ordinateurs comme la teinte naturelle de l'ingénierie électronique.

La Formica Insulation Company faisait partie de la nouvelle technologie. La société a subi une transition fondamentale, de fabricant d'un matériau fonctionnel à fabricant d'un matériau décoratif créé par les designers. En conséquence, le stratifié Formica a été perçu comme un produit moderne, communiquant la haute technologie, quelque chose provenant de l'avenir. Comme l'historien du design Jeffrey Meikle l'a écrit, « il a fourni une précision artificielle. » Pendant la grande

altavoces y alentaban a su campeón. Formica solía formar parte de eso.

La mayoría de los aparatos eran simples cajas con perillas. Las piezas de un radio, tubos y bobinados, se fijaban a un tablero aislante —la placa madre que conocemos actualmente de las computadoras. El tablero se convirtió en una caja para esconder piezas y montar los nuevos altavoces de cono. Los exteriores solían estar revestidos con laminado de The Formica Insulation Company en color negro o marrón. La superficie de laminado fenólico color negro que la empresa Formica suministró para muchos de los primeros radios se comenzó a asociar visualmente con la radio y, posteriormente, con la tecnología de alta fidelidad e, incluso, con las computadoras como el color clásico de la ingeniería electrónica.

The Formica Insulation Company formaba parte de la apariencia de esa nueva tecnología. La empresa experimentó una transición fundamental, de ser fabricante de un material funcional a fabricante de un material decorativo y orientado hacia el diseño. Como resultado, el laminado Formica se percibía como un producto moderno, que transmitía alta tecnología —un aspecto del futuro. Como escribió el historiador de diseño Jeffrey Meikle: "brindaba precisión artificial" . Durante la Depresión, sugirió orden en un caos económico y, cuando se destacó en formas estilizadas, sugirió velocidad para contrarrestar el estancamiento económico. Para los modernistas, era uno de los medios más puros de hacer realidad ideas y dibujos, un material tan geométricamente puro y fresco como el vidrio.

La radio ayudó a que crecieran las ventas de The Formica Insulation Company de $400,000 en 1920 a $3 millones en 1924. La empresa podía permitirse emplear más personas para ayudar y, en 1924, contrató al químico formado en el MIT (Instituto Tecnológico de Massachusetts) Jack D. Cochrane. Como jefe de investigación, su cargo formal era el de Director de Productos de investigación, decorativos e industriales. Se convertiría en una de las armas secretas de la empresa y en un componente vital para su éxito hasta que se jubiló en 1957. (Se le consideraba un recurso científico nacional en los Estados Unidos, y recibió el premio John W. Hyatt de manos del Presidente Truman).

asussa. Yhtiö kävi läpi perustavan muutoksen toiminnallisten materiaalien valmistajasta koristeellisen, suunnitteluun perustuvan materiaalin tuottajaksi. Seurauksena oli, että Formica-laminaattia pidettiin nykyaikaisena tuotteena, joka kertoo korkeasta teknologiasta — jostakin tulevasta. Suunnittelualan historioitsija Jeffrey Meikle kirjoitti: "se sai aikaan keinotekoisen täsmällisyyden". Suurina pulavuosina se ehdotti järjestystä taloudellisessa kaaoksessa ja virtaviivaisessa muodossa sovellettuna se ehdotti nopeutta taloudellisen verkkaisuuden vastavaikutukseksi. Modernisteille se oli yksi puhtaimmista keinoista toteuttaa ideoita ja piirustuksia, materiaali, joka oli geometrisesti puhdas ja tuore kuin lasi.

Radio auttoi Formica Insulation Companyn myynnin kasvua 400 000 dollarista v. 1920, 3 miljoonaan dollariin v. 1924. Yhtiöllä oli varaa työllistää enemmän väkeä ja v. 1924 otettiin palvelukseen MIT-koulutettu kemisti D. Cochrane. Tutkimuksen vetäjänä — hänen virallinen tittelinsä oli koristeellisten ja teollisten tuotteiden tutkimuspäällikkö — hänestä tuli yksi yhtiön salaisista aseista ja elintärkeä menestykselle, aivan hänen eläkkeelle siirtymiseensä asti v. 1957. (Häntä pidettiin kansallisena tieteellisenä voimavarana Yhdysvalloissa ja hänelle myön-

1923 年登普西迎戰年輕的阿根廷拳擊手號稱潘帕斯的公牛的路易斯·安赫爾·福爾珀 (Luis Ángel Firpo)，電臺轉播了實況，從紐約馬球場到布宜諾斯艾利斯街頭，人們把大揚聲器圍得水洩不通，為他們的冠軍吶喊助威。富美家往往是其中的一部分。

大多數的收音機是帶旋鈕的簡單盒子。收音機的部件、管子和線圈都連接在一塊絕緣板上——就像我們今天所知道的電腦主板。主板變成一個盒子，藏起了零件，並裝一個新的喇叭形揚聲器。外觀往往貼上黑色或棕色的富美家絕緣公司的美耐板。富美家公司為許多早期收音機提供的黑色酚醛美耐板在視覺上與收音機聯繫在一起，後來又與高保真 (Hi-Fi)、高科技、甚至電腦聯繫在一起，成了電子工程名正言順的色彩。

富美家絕緣公司成了那項新技術外觀的一部分。該公司經歷了一段根本性的轉變，從製造功能性材料到製造追求裝飾和設計的材料。因此，富美家美耐板被視為一種現代化的產品，傳輸高科技——來自未來的東西。正如設計史學家傑弗里·米克爾 (Jeffrey Meikle) 所說，它「提供了人工的精確度」。在經濟大蕭條期間，它暗示了經濟混亂中的秩序，在以精簡的形式部署時，則暗示了速度，以抗衡經濟的不景氣。對於現代主義者，它是實現理想和構圖的一個最純淨的方式，在幾何學上如玻璃一樣純淨和清新的材料。

廣播幫助富美家絕緣公司的銷售量從 1920 年的 40 萬美元增長到 1924 年的 300 萬美元。該公司有能力雇用更多的幫手，於 1924 年聘請了麻省理工學院 (MIT) 訓練有素的化學家傑克·科克倫 (Jack D. Cochrane)。作為研究部的領導——他的正式頭銜是研究、裝飾和工業產品主任——他將成為該公司的秘密武器之一，直到他在 1957 年退休，他對該公司的成功都至關重要。(他在美國被

甚至计算机联系在一起，成了电子工程名正言顺的色彩。

富美家绝缘公司成了那项新技术外观的一部分。该公司经历了一段根本性的转变，从制造功能性材料到制造追求装饰和设计的材料。因此，富美家®装饰耐火板被视为一种现代化的产品，传输高科技——来自未来的东西。正如设计史学家杰弗里·米克尔 (Jeffrey Meikle) 所说，它"提供了人工的精确度"。在经济大萧条期间，它暗示了经济混乱中的秩序，在以精简的形式部署时，则暗示了速度，以抗衡经济的不景气。对于现代主义者，它是实现理想和构图的一个最纯净的方式，在几何学上如玻璃一样纯净和清新的材料。

广播帮助富美家绝缘公司的销售量从 1920 年的 40 万美元增长到 1924 年的 300 万美元。该公司有能力雇用更多的帮手，于 1924 年聘请了麻省理工学院 (MIT) 训练有素的化学家杰克·科克伦 (Jack D. Cochrane)。作为研究部的领导——他的正式头衔是研究、装饰和工业产品主任——他将成为该公司的秘密武器之一，直到他在 1957 年退休，他对该公司的成功都至关重要。(他在美国被认为是国家科学资源，并获得杜鲁门总统颁发的约翰·海厄特奖 (John W Hyatt Award))。

科克伦 (Cochrane) 研究了其他树脂。1927 年，富美家绝缘公司推出了关键创新。科克伦开发了一种采用氨基树脂的耐火板，作为牛皮纸的最上层，代替苯酚。因为使用氨基树脂和不透明阻挡片，遮挡耐火板阴暗的内部，公司可能添加带木纹或大理石花纹的层板。公司为在一台平面压力机上制作多层平版印刷木纹表面耐火板的凹版印刷工艺申请了专利。印刷面板的引入——大理石或花岗岩和抽象图案将很快推出——让公司在装饰性耐火板方面捷足先登。这也标志着富美家公司从主要工业产品向装饰产品的转变。

วัสดุนี้เป็นวัสดุที่มีความเป็นรูปทรงเรขาคณิตแท้ๆ และสดใสดั่งแก้ว

วิทยุช่วยให้ยอดขายของฟอร์ไมก้า เพิ่มขึ้นจาก 400,000 ดอลลาร์สหรัฐในปี ค.ศ. 1920 เป็น 3 ล้านดอลลาร์สหรัฐในปี ค.ศ. 1924 บริษัทมีกำลังจ้างพนักงานเพิ่ม และในปี ค.ศ. 1924 ได้จ้าง แจ็ค ดี ค็อกเครน ซึ่งเป็นนักเคมีจากมหาวิทยาลัย เอ็มไอที มารับตำแหน่งผู้อำนวยการฝ่ายค้นคว้าวิจัยผลิตภัณฑ์อุตสาหกรรมและตกแต่งในฐานะที่เป็นหัวหน้าแผนกค้นคว้าวิจัย เขาจึงกลายเป็นอาวุธลับของบริษัทและมีส่วนสำคัญในความสำเร็จของบริษัทจนกระทั่งเขาเกษียณอายุไปในปี ค.ศ. 1957 (เขาถือได้ว่าเป็นผู้เชี่ยวชาญด้านวิทยาศาสตร์ระดับชาติในสหรัฐอเมริกาและได้รับรางวัล John W. Hyatt ซึ่งมอบให้โดยประธานาธิบดีทรูแมน)

ค็อกเครนทำการศึกษาเรซินชนิดอื่นๆ ในปี ค.ศ. 1927 ซึ่งทำให้ฟอร์ไมก้าได้ก่อกำเนิดสิ่งประดิษฐ์ที่สำคัญ ค็อกเครนได้พัฒนาลามิเนทที่ใช้อะมิโนเรซินแทนฟีนอลเรซินอาบผิวด้านบนของกระดาษคราฟต์ โดยการใช้อะมิโนเรซินและแผ่นกั้นทึบแสงเพื่อกันความเข้มของกระดาษคราฟต์ บริษัทจึงสามารถเพิ่มลายไม้หรือลายหินอ่อนได้ บริษัทได้จดสิทธิบัตรกระบวนการพิมพ์ภาพโดยใช้แม่พิมพ์ที่อุ้มหมึกซึมเข้าไปในกระดาษเพื่อผลิตผิวหน้าลายไม้ บนพื้นผิวลามิเนทโดยการอัดบนแผ่นเพลทแบบผิวหน้าเรียบ การเปิดตัวลามิเนทแบบพิมพ์ลาย เช่น ลายหินอ่อน ลายหินแกรนิต และลายศิลปะอะมามา ทำให้บริษัทเริ่มการทำลามิเนทเพื่อการตกแต่ง เหตุการณ์นี้จึงเป็นจุดเริ่มต้นของบริษัทฟอร์ไมก้าในการเปลี่ยนจากผลิตภัณฑ์อุตสาหกรรมขั้นต้นมาเป็นผลิตภัณฑ์เพื่อการตกแต่ง

ช่วงทศวรรษที่ 1930

ในปี ค.ศ. 1931 ห้องทดลองของค็อกเครนได้เพิ่มแผ่นฟอยล์โลหะเข้าไปเป็นอีกชั้นหนึ่งในลามิเนท ซึ่งจะทำให้แผ่นลามิเนทฟอร์ไมก้าทนทานต่อการไหม้จากบุหรี่ ดังนั้นจึงนิยมใช้สำหรับหน้าโต๊ะในร้านกาแฟ ไนท์คลับ และร้านอาหาร ผลิตภัณฑ์มีความหรูหราและในขณะเดียวกันสามารถใช้งานได้ดี ได้รับความนิยมในการใช้กับที่ขายเซ้าน์อัคคมที่นิยมเปิดกันมากในร้านขายยาและสถานที่อื่นๆ และได้รับความนิยมในหมู่เจ้าของบาร์ ในสหราชอาณาจักรมีผู้รับเหมารายหนึ่งที่เชี่ยวชาญในการเข้าไปปรับปรุงตกแต่งผับในช่วงหลังปิดร้าน เพื่อเปลี่ยนบาร์โดยใช้แผ่นลามิเนทฟอร์ไมก้าตกแต่งเพียงภายในข้ามคืน ทำให้ธุรกิจไม่สูญเสียรายได้แม้แต่คืนเดียว

大多數的收音機是帶旋鈕的簡單盒子。收音機的部件、管子和線圈都連接在一塊絕緣板上——就像我們今天所知道的電腦主板。主板變成一個盒子，藏起了零件，並裝一個新的喇叭形揚聲器。外觀往往貼上黑色或棕色的富美家絕緣公司的美耐板。富美家公司為許多早期收音機提供的黑色酚醛美耐板在視覺上與收音機聯繫在一起，後來又與高保真 (Hi-Fi)、高科技、甚至電腦聯繫在一起，成了電子工程名正言順的色彩。

富美家絕緣公司成了那項新技術外觀的一部分。該公司經歷了一段根本性的轉變，從製造功能性材料到製造追求裝飾和設計的材料。因此，富美家美耐板被視為一種現代化的產品，傳輸高科技——來自未來的東西。正如設計史學家傑弗里·米克爾 (Jeffrey Meikle) 所說，它「提供了人工的精確度」。在經濟大蕭條期間，它暗示了經濟混亂中的秩序，在以精簡的形式部署時，則暗示了速度，以抗衡經濟的不景氣。對於現代主義者，它是實現理想和構圖的一個最純淨的方式，在幾何學上如玻璃一樣純淨和清新的材料。

廣播幫助富美家絕緣公司的銷售量從 1920 年的 40 萬美元增長到 1924 年的 300 萬美元。該公司有能力雇用更多的幫手，於 1924 年聘請了麻省理工學院 (MIT) 訓練有素的化學家傑克·科克倫 (Jack D. Cochrane)。作為研究部的領導——他的正式頭銜是研究、裝飾和工業產品主任——他將成為該公司的秘密武器之一，直到他在 1957 年退休，他對該公司的成功都至關重要。(他在美國被

dépression, il a fait preuve d'ordre dans le chaos économique et en se déployant dans des formes simplifiées, il a suggéré des formes aérodynamiques pour s'opposer à la morosité économique. Pour les modernistes, il a été l'un des moyens les plus purs de réaliser des idées et des dessins, avec un matériau aussi géométriquement pur et frais que le verre.

L'avènement de la radio a permis à la Formica Insulation Company de faire passer ses ventes de 400 000 dollars en 1920 à 3 millions de dollars en 1924. La société pouvait engager davantage de personnes et en 1924 elle a employé le chimiste formé au MIT Jack D. Cochrane. En tant que chef de la recherche, son titre officiel était celui de directeur de la recherche, des produits décoratifs et industriels, il est devenu l'une des armes secrètes de l'entreprise et a largement contribué au succès de l'entreprise jusqu'à sa retraite en 1957. (Jack D. Cochrane a été considéré comme une ressource scientifique nationale aux États-Unis et a reçu le prix John W. Hyatt décerné par le président Truman.)

Il a examiné d'autres résines. En 1927, la société Formica introduit d'importantes innovations. Cochrane a développé un stratifié employant des résines aminées au lieu de phénol comme couche supérieure sur base de papier Kraft. Avec l'utilisation de résines aminées et une feuille barrière opaque pour bloquer l'intérieur sombre du stratifié, la société pouvait ajouter des couches imitant le bois ou la pierre marbrée. La société a breveté un procédé d'impression en héliogravure pour produire du stratifié multicouche lithographié imitant le bois, sur une presse à plat. Le lancement de surfaces imprimées imitant le marbre, le granit ou présentant des motifs abstraits s'est rapidement développé, donnant à l'entreprise son avance en matière de stratifié décoratif. C'était aussi le début du passage de la société Formica des produits industriels primaires à des produits décoratifs.

1930

En 1931, le laboratoire de Cochrane a proposé d'ajouter une feuille d'aluminium au sandwich des stratifiés. Il a réalisé un stratifié résistant aux cigarettes et donc adapté aux tables des

Cochrane analizó otras resinas. En 1927, The Formica Insulation Company introdujo innovaciones críticas. Cochrane desarrolló un laminado que empleaba resinas amínicas en vez de fenol como la capa superior en la base del papel Kraft. Con la utilización de resinas amínicas y una hoja de barrera opaca para bloquear el interior oscuro del laminado, la empresa podía agregar capas que contenían vetas de madera o marmoleados de piedra. Patentó un proceso de impresión en rotograbado para hacer laminado de superficie en veta de madera litografiada de múltiples capas en una prensa planocilíndrica (de lecho plano). La introducción de las superficies impresas —pronto aparecerían el mármol o el granito y los diseños abstractos— dio a la empresa su notable ventaja en el laminado decorativo. Esto también marcó el comienzo del cambio de la empresa Formica de productos primordialmente industriales a productos decorativos.

La década de los treinta

En 1931, el laboratorio de Cochrane presentó el agregado de una capa de hoja metálica al panel intercalado de laminados. Esto hizo al laminado Formica resistente al cigarrillo y, por lo tanto, atractivo para superficies de mesas en cafés, clubes nocturnos y restaurantes. El esplendor del material igualaba a su practicidad. Se comenzó a usar para fuentes de soda, que surgían en tiendas y en otros lugares. Era atractivo para los propietarios de bares. En el Reino Unido, un contratista se especializó en llegar a cantinas a la hora de cierre y reemplazar la barra por una de laminado Formica de la noche a la mañana, a fin de que no se suspendiera ni un negocio nocturno. La marca Formica fue muy publicitada cuando el laminado se utilizó para cubrir las superficies horizontales en el Radio City Music Hall en Nueva York y de los escritorios en la Biblioteca del Congreso en Washington. No obstante, a mediados de la década de los treinta, no había otro lugar en el que fuera más visible que en el transatlántico HMS *Queen Mary*, con un interior construido con laminado Formica. El *Queen Mary* competía en estilo y en velocidad con el *Normandie* de Francia y con rivales alemanes e italianos, escribe John Maxtone-Graham en su historia de los

nettiin John W. Hyatt -palkinto, jonka ojensi presidentti Truman).

Cochrane tutki muitakin hartseja. Vuonna 1927 Formica Insulation Company toi markkinoille kriittisen tärkeitä innovaatioita. Cochrane kehitti laminaatin, jossa fenolin sijasta käytettiin aminohartseja ylimpänä kerroksena voimapaperialustan päällä. Käyttämällä aminohartseja ja himmeää suojalevyä laminaatin tumman sisäosan peittämiseksi, yhtiö pystyi lisäämään kerroksia, joissa näkyy puun syitä tai kivinen marmorikuvio. Se patentoi rotogravuuripainamisen prosessin monikerroksisen litografialla suoritetun puusyisen pintalaminaatin valmistamista varten vaakakerrospuristimella. Painettujen pintojen käyttöönotto — marmori tai graniitti ja abstraktit kuviot tulisivat pian perässä — antoi yhtiölle hyvän lähtöaseman koristeellisille laminaateille. Tästä myös alkoi Formica-yhtiön siirtyminen pääasiassa teollisista koristeellisiin tuotteisiin.

1930-luku

Vuonna 1931 Cochranen laboratorio keksi lisätä metallikalvon laminaattikerroksiin. Näin Formica-laminaatista tuli savukkeenkestävä ja siten haluttu pöydän pintoihin kahvibaareissa, yökerhoissa ja ravintoloissa. Materiaalin lumoukseen yhdistyi sen käytännöllisyys. Siitä tuli haluttua tavaraa jäätelöbaareihin, joita alkoi ilmestyä kemikaalikauppoihin ja muihin paikkoihin. Baarien omistajat pitivät siitä. Yhdistyneessä kuningaskunnassa eräs urakoitsija erikoistui saapumaan pubeihin sulkemisaikana ja vaihtamaan baaritiskin yön aikana Formica-laminaattiin siten, ettei menetetty edes yhden illan liiketoimintaa.

Formica-tavaramerkki sai runsaasti julkisuutta, kun laminaatti tuli käyttöön vaakasuorien pintojen päällysteenä Radio City Music Hall -salissa New Yorkissa ja Library of Congress -kirjaston pöydissä Washingtonissa. 1930-luvun puolivälissä se ei kuitenkaan ollut missään muualla paremmin esillä, kuin matkustajalaivassa HMS *Queen Mary*, jossa sisustus tehtiin Formica-laminaatilla. *Queen Mary* kilpaili sekä tyylissä että nopeudessa Ranskan *Normandien* sekä saksalaisten ja italialaisten kilpailijoiden kanssa, kirjoittaa John Maxtone-Graham valtamerialuksia koskevassa historiassaan *The Only Way to*

認為是國家科學資源,並獲得杜魯門總統頒發的約翰·海厄特獎(John W Hyatt Award))。

科克倫(Cochrane)研究了其他樹脂。1927年,富美家絕緣公司推出了關鍵創新。科克倫開發了一種採用氨基樹脂的美耐板,作為牛皮紙的最上層,代替苯酚。因為使用氨基樹脂和不透明阻擋片,遮擋美耐板陰暗的內部,公司可能添加帶木紋或大理石花紋的層板。公司為在一臺平面壓力機上製作多層平版印刷木紋表面美耐板的凹版印刷工藝申請了專利。印刷面板的引入——大理石或花崗岩和抽象圖案將很快推出——讓公司在裝飾性美耐板方面捷足先登。這也標誌著富美家公司從主要工業產品向裝飾產品的轉變。

二十世紀三十年代

1931年,科克倫的實驗室發明了在美耐板的夾心添加另一層金屬箔的方法。這讓富美家美耐板耐香煙燒燙,因而在咖啡館、夜總會和餐廳的桌面用材上都具有吸引力。其材料的魅力與其實用性相媲美,從而受到蘇打水噴泉的追捧,在藥店等地點紛紛湧現。該產品吸引了酒吧雇主。在英國,一位承包商專門承包在閉市時到達酒吧並在一夜之間將酒吧更換為富美家美耐板的項目,不讓店主損失一個晚上的生意。

富美家品牌得到廣泛的宣傳,這正是美耐板被用在紐約無線電城音樂廳的各個平面和華盛頓美國國會圖書館的桌面時期。然而,二十世紀三十年代中期,表現得最為明顯的卻是HMS女王瑪麗號(Queen Mary)海輪,富美家美耐板建造了全部內部構造。約翰·麥克斯通-格雷厄姆(John Maxtone-Graham)在他的遠洋巨輪史《越洋唯一的路》(The Only Way to Cross)中寫道,女王瑪麗號與法國的諾曼底號(Normandie)以及德國和意大利的對手在風格和速度上相較量。

二十世紀三十年代

1931年,科克倫的实验室发明了在耐火板的夹心添加另一层金属箔的方法。这让富美家耐火板耐香烟烧烫,因而在咖啡馆、夜总会和餐厅的桌面用材上都具有吸引力。其材料的魅力与其实用性相媲美,从而受到苏打水喷泉的追捧,在药店等地点纷纷涌现。该产品吸引了酒吧雇主。在英国,一位承包商专门承包在闭市时到达酒吧并在一夜之间将酒吧更换为富美家®装饰耐火板的项目,不让店主损失一个晚上的生意。

富美家品牌得到广泛的宣传,这正是耐火板被用在纽约无线电城音乐厅的各个表面和华盛顿美国国会图书馆的桌面时期。然而,二十世纪三十年代中期,表现得最为明显的却是HMS女王玛丽(Queen Mary)海轮,富美家®装饰耐火板建造了全部内部构造。约翰·麦克斯通-格雷厄姆(John Maxtone-Graham)在他的远洋巨轮史《越洋唯一的路》(The Only Way to Cross)中写道,女王玛丽号与法国的诺曼底号(Normandie)以及德国和意大利的对手在风格和速度上相较量。两艘船都是由苏格兰的约翰·布朗公司(John Brown)建造。

勒·柯布西耶(Le Corbusier)在1922年宣布"远洋巨轮是以一种全新的精神实现一个完全控制的世界的第一步。"船是社会和经济的缩影。麦克斯通-格雷厄姆写道,陆地上每一个生活细节都在海里被复制——只是更具风格。对勒·柯布西耶来说,他所描述为建筑理想的生活机器就是基于远洋轮船,后来被他对飞机的仰慕取代。

运输的速度和效率要求轻质材料。但是,运动中的生命也需要耐用、易于清洁。(女王玛丽号上"灰色珠光"富美家®装饰耐火板的成功不仅在于屡次越洋,而且在于五年里该船像二战期间的一辆运兵车一样被证明经久耐用。)后来,海军的船舶(包括美国海军)广泛地使用了这种材料,例如用在潜艇上,像历史悠久的"咆哮者号"(Growler)。

ยี่ห้อฟอร์ไมก้าเป็นที่รู้จักแพร่หลายมากขึ้นเมื่อมีการนำลามิเนททามาปิดพื้นผิวในแนวตั้งที่ Radio City Music Hall ในนครนิวยอร์ก และโต๊ะที่ห้องทอสมุดสภาในกรุงวอชิงตัน ในช่วงกลางทศวรรษที่ 1930 แผ่นลามิเนทฟอร์ไมก้าเห็นได้ชัดเจนบนเรือเดินสมุทร เฮสเอ็มเอส ควีนแมรี่ โดยมีการตกแต่งภายในด้วยแผ่น ลามิเนทฟอร์ไมก้า จอห์น แมกซ์โทน-แกรห์ม ได้เขียนไว้ในหนังสือประวัติศาสตร์เรือเดินสมุทรของเขาชื่อ The Only Way to Cross ว่า เรือเดินสมุทร ควีนแมรี่ ได้แข่งขันกับเรือ นอร์มังดี ของประเทศฝรั่งเศส ทั้งด้านการออกแบบและด้านความเร็ว รวมถึงคู่แข่งจากประเทศเยอรมนีและอิตาลี เรือทั้งสองลำสร้างขึ้นที่สกอตแลนด์โดยบริษัทของจอห์น บราวน์

เลอ คอร์บูซีเออร์ ได้ประกาศไว้ในปีค.ศ. 1922 ว่า "เรือเดินสมุทรเป็นก้าวแรกที่จะทำให้รู้ว่า โลกถูกควบคุมได้ทั่วทั้งหมดเพื่อสร้างสรรค์จิตวิญญาณใหม่ได้อย่างสมบูรณ์" เรือเป็นศูนย์รวมของสังคมและเศรษฐกิจ แมกซ์โทน-แกรห์มเขียนไว้ว่า ทุกๆรายละเอียดของชีวิตบนภาคพื้นดินจะถูกจำลองแบบในท้องทะเลอย่างมีสไตล์สำหรับ เลอ คอร์บูซีเออร์ แล้ว เขาอธิบายว่า "เครื่องจักรที่ใช้ในการดำรงชีพ" เป็นอุดมคติของสถาปัตยกรรมที่มีพื้นฐานมาจากเรือเดินสมุทร ซึ่งต่อมาถูกแทนที่ด้วยเครื่องบินได้อย่างน่าชื่นชม

ความเร็วและประสิทธิภาพในการเดินทางทำให้ต้องการวัสดุที่เบา แต่ความเคลื่อนไหวก็ต้องการความคงทนและการทำความสะอาดง่ายด้วย (ความสำเร็จของแผ่นลามิเนทฟอร์ไมก้า "สีเทามุก" บนเรือ ควีนแมรี่ ไม่เพียงแต่มีความคงทนในการเดินสมุทรหลายครั้ง แต่ยังมีความทนทานเพื่อให้เป็นเรือโดยสารกองกำลังทหารเป็นเวลาถึงห้าปีในช่วงสงครามโลกครั้งที่ 2) ต่อมาเรือของทหารเรือ รวมถึงกองทัพเรือยูเนียนสหรัฐอเมริกา ได้ใช้วัสดุดังกล่าวในจำนวนมาก เช่น ในเรือดำน้ำ อย่างเรือประวัติศาสตร์ชื่อ โกรเลอร์

ภายในของเรือเดินสมุทร เรือบิน เซพพีลิน และรถรางเป็นยานพาหนะแรกๆ ที่ใช้วัสดุที่มีความทันสมัย รวมถึงสถานี ลือบบี้ และเลาน์จต่างๆ ทั่วโลก ซึ่งตกแต่งแบบมีสไตล์และใช้เทคโนโลยีสูงตามยุคเมืองนั้น สิ่งนี้ทำให้แผ่นลามิเนทฟอร์ไมก้าเป็นที่รู้จักของคนนับล้าน ยานพาหนะกลายเป็นร้านขายลามิเนทยี่ห้อฟอร์ไมก้าเคลื่อนที่โดยปริยายห้องคนขับของเรือบินเซพพีลินใช้ลามิเนทสายการบินช่วงแรกเริ่มอย่างสายการบิน แพนแอม และเรือข้ามมหาสมุทรแอตแลนติก ไปจนถึงเครื่องบิน ดักลาส ดีซี-3 รุ่นใหม่ก็

cafés, des discothèques et des restaurants. Aux charmes du matériau s'ajoutaient les aspects pratiques. Il devint recherché pour les fontaines de soda qui surgissaient dans les pharmacies et à d'autres emplacements. Il séduisait les propriétaires de bar. Au Royaume-Uni, un entrepreneur se spécialisait en arrivant à la fermeture des bars et en remplaçant les comptoirs durant la nuit avec du stratifié Formica de sorte qu'aucune fermeture ne soit nécessaire.

La marque Formica a fait couler beaucoup d'encre lorsque le stratifié a été utilisé pour recouvrir les surfaces horizontales du Radio City Music Hall de New York et des bureaux de la bibliothèque du Congrès à Washington. Pourtant, au milieu des années 1930, il n'était nulle part plus visible que sur le paquebot HMS *Queen Mary*, avec un intérieur construit en stratifié Formica. Le *Queen Mary* concurrençait l'élégance et la vitesse du *Normandie* français et de ses rivaux allemands et italiens, écrit John Maxtone-Graham dans son histoire des paquebots, *The Only Way to Cross*. Les deux navires ont été construits en Écosse par John Brown.

Le Corbusier avait proclamé en 1922 que « les paquebots sont la première étape vers la réalisation d'un monde parfaitement contrôlé pour être créé dans un esprit totalement nouveau. » La capsule était un concentré de la société et de l'économie. Chaque détail de la vie sur terre, écrit Maxtone-Graham, a été reproduit en mer avec élégance. Pour Le Corbusier, la machine à habiter qu'il a décrite comme l'idéal de l'architecture est basée sur le paquebot, remplacé plus tard par son admiration pour l'avion.

La rapidité et l'efficacité dans le transport exigeaient des matériaux légers. Mais la vie en mouvement exigeait également des matériaux durables et faciles à entretenir. (Le succès du stratifié Formica gris perlé du *Queen Mary* ne résidait pas seulement dans les traversées océaniques multiples mais aussi dans la longévité prouvée par les cinq années du navire en tant que transporteur de troupes pendant la seconde guerre mondiale.) Plus tard, les bâtiments de navires militaires, y compris l'U.S. Navy, ont fait un large usage du matériau, comme dans le cas des sous-marins *Growler* et autres.

transatlánticos, *The Only Way to Cross*. Ambos barcos fueron construidos en Escocia por la firma John Brown.

Le Corbusier había proclamado en 1922 que "los transatlánticos eran el primer paso hacia la realización de un mundo perfectamente controlado que sería creado en un espíritu totalmente nuevo". El barco era una cápsula de la sociedad y de la economía. Cada detalle de la vida en la tierra, escribe Maxtone-Graham, se repetía en el mar, y en el estilo. Para Le Corbusier, la máquina para vivir que describía como el ideal de la arquitectura se basaba en el transatlántico; posteriormente, la reemplazaría por su admiración por el avión.

La velocidad y la eficiencia en el transporte demandaban materiales ligeros. Pero la vida en movimiento también requería materiales duraderos y fáciles de limpiar. (El éxito del laminado Formica "gris perlado" del *Queen Mary* residía no solo en los repetidos cruces oceánicos, sino también en la durabilidad comprobada en los cinco años que el barco soportó como transporte de tropas durante la Segunda Guerra Mundial). Posteriormente, los barcos de las marinas de guerra, incluida la Marina de EE.UU., utilizaron asiduamente el material; por ejemplo, en submarinos, como el histórico *Growler*.

Los interiores de los transatlánticos, zepelines y vagones ferroviarios fueron los primeros en estar cubiertos de los materiales modernos. De la misma forma lo estaban las estaciones, los vestíbulos y los salones en los que prestaban su servicio alrededor del

Cross (ainoa tapa ylittää valtameri). Molemmat laivat rakensi Skotlannissa John Brownin yritys.

Le Corbusier oli julistanut v. 1922, että "Valtamerialukset ovat aivan ensimmäinen askel kohti yhden täydellisesti hallitun maailman toteuttamista, joka luodaan täysin uudessa hengessä". Laiva oli tiivistelmä yhteiskunnasta ja taloudesta. Elämän jokainen yksityiskohta maissa oli kopioitu laivaan — ja tyylikkäästi, kirjoittaa Maxtone-Graham. Corbusierin mielestä hänen kuvaamansa kone elämistä varten arkkitehtuuriltaan ihanteellisena, perustui valtamerialukseen, jonka myöhemmin korvasi hänen ihailemansa lentokone.

Kuljetuksen nopeus ja tehokkuus vaativat kevyitä materiaaleja. Liikkuva elämä vaati kuitenkin niiden olevan myös kestäviä ja helposti puhdistettavia. (*Queen Mary*-aluksen "harmaan helmenhohtoisen" Formica-laminaatin menestys ei johtunut yksinomaan toistuvista valtameren ylityksistä, vaan myös osoitetusta kestävyydestä viiden vuoden palveluksesta, jonka se läpäisi joukkojen kuljetuslaivana toisen maailmansodan aikana). Myöhemmin laivastojen alukset, USA:n laivasto mukaan lukien, käyttivät laajasti materiaalia esimerkiksi sukellusveneissä, kuten historiallinen *Growler*.

Valtamerialusten, zeppeliinien ja rautatievaunujen sisustukset olivat ensimmäiset, jotka päällystettiin nykyajan materiaaleilla. Sellaisia olivat myös niitä ympäri maailmaa palvelevat asemat, aulat ja salongit — tyyliä ja teknologiaa, jotka ylittivät paikallisuuden. Tämä toi Formica-laminaatin miljoonien ihmisten tietoisuuteen. Kulkuvälineistä tuli tosiasiassa Formica-merkkisen laminaatin liikkuvia myyntipisteitä. Zeppeliinien hyteissä käytettiin laminaattia, samoin monissa alkuajan lentokoneissa, Atlantin poikki liikennöivistä Pan Am Clippereistä ja laivoista alkaen aina uusiin Douglas DC-3 -koneisiin saakka. Virtaviivaisesti sisustetut junat kilpailivat — myöhempänä huomattavana esimerkkinä oli nykyaikainen, sulavalinjainen Hiawatha-juna. Suunnittelija Brooks Stevens käytti Formica-laminaatteja Hiawatha-junissa Chicagon, Milwaukeen, St. Paulin ja Pacific Railroad -reiteillä, valiten pellavatyylisen viimeistelyn makuuvaunuihin ja pähkinäpuun ja

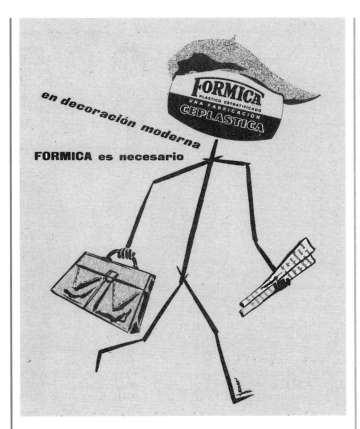

en decoración moderna

FORMICA es necesario

兩艘船都是由蘇格蘭的約翰‧布朗公司 (John Brown) 建造。

勒‧柯布西耶 (Le Corbusier) 在 1922 年宣佈「遠洋巨輪是以一種全新的精神實現一個完全控制的世界的第一步。」船是社會和經濟的縮影。麥克斯通-格雷厄姆寫道，陸地上每一個生活細節都在海裡被覆製——只是更具風格。對勒‧柯布西耶來說，他所描述為建築理想的生活機器就是基於遠洋輪船，後來被他對飛機的仰慕取代。

運輸的速度和效率要求輕質材料。但是，運動中的生命也需要耐用、易於清潔。（女王瑪麗號上「灰色珠光」富美家美耐板的成功不僅在於屢次越洋，而且在於五年裡該船像二戰期間的一艘運兵車一樣被證明經久耐用。）後來，海軍的船舶（包括美國海軍）廣泛地使用了這種材料，例如

远洋客轮、飞艇和火车车厢的内部装饰首先用现代化材料覆盖。因此，在全球各地为它们服务的车站、大厅和休息室也一样——风格和技术超越了地域。这使数百万的人看到富美家的耐火板。车辆成为富美家品牌耐火板事实上的活动推销店。飞艇的驾驶舱使用了耐火板，许多早期的客机也用了耐火板，从泛美飞机飞行和来往大西洋的船只到新的道格拉斯 DC-3。火车流线型的内部也加入了竞争——后来的一个鲜明的例子是现代化的流线型西亚瓦塔 (Hiawatha) 火车。设计师布鲁克斯‧史蒂文斯 (Brooks Stevens) 把富美家®装饰耐火板用在西亚瓦塔来往于芝加哥、密尔沃基、圣保罗和太平洋铁路上的列车里，特别指定在卧铺车厢使用亚麻布贴面，在休息室里用核桃色和灰绿色。富美家®装饰耐火板预示着一个充满希望的未来。它那闪闪发光的表面和流线形

ใช้ลามิเนท รถไฟที่มีการตกแต่งภายในใหม่ ตัวอย่างสำคัญ ได้แก่ รถไฟเฮียวาธาที่ทันสมัย นักออกแบบที่ชื่อบรูคส์ สตีเวนส์ ใช้แผ่นลามิเนทฟอร์ไมก้าในรถไฟ เฮียวาธาของชิคาโก้ มิลวอกี้ เซ็นต์พอล และบริษัทเดินรถไฟ แปซิฟิค เรลโร้ด โดยใช้ลามิเนทผิวลินินในตู้นอนและใช้ลามิเนทลายไม้วอลนัทและสีเขียวเทาในห้องเล้าจ์ แผ่นลามิเนทฟอร์ไมก้าเป็นตัวแทนของอนาคตที่มีความหวัง พื้นผิวที่เปล่งประกายและรูปทรงโค้งโฉบเฉี่ยวสี่อถึงโลกแห่งภาพยนตร์ หรือฮอลลีวูดบนหน้าจอขนาดเล็กทั่วทุกมุมโลก สามารถสร้างความเข้าวนจิใจแม้กับพื้นที่ที่ธรรมดาที่สุดโดยให้ความรู้สึกตื่นเต้นและเปลี่ยนความซ้ำซากจำเจให้เป็นความล้ำสมัย

ความสวยงามของวัสดุนี้ถูกแสดงโดยสถาปนิกชื่อ วิลเลียม เอส อาร์รสมิท ซึ่งทำงานอยู่เมืองหลุยส์วิลล์ มลรัฐเคนทักกี้ ผู้ออกแบบตกแต่งภายในให้กับสถานีรถโดยสารหลายแห่งในเมืองเล็กและเมืองใหญ่ทั่วสหรัฐอเมริกา แม้แต่สถานีรถในต่างจังหวัดก็สามารถแสดงถึงความทันสมัยในโลกได้จากการใช้วัสดุอย่างแผ่นลามิเนทฟอร์ไมก้า สถานีรถบัสเกรฮาวด์ ที่อาร์รสมิทออกแบบสร้างขึ้นในช่วงทศวรรษที่ 1930 ถึงทศวรรษที่ 1950 ภายนอกมีมุมโค้งทำด้วยคอนกรีตราวกับว่าสามารถตัดลมปะทะได้ รวมทั้งอิฐบล็อกแก้วและแถบโลหะ การตกแต่งภายในใช้รูปแบบเดียวกับภายนอก โดยใช้แผ่นลามิเนทฟอร์ไมก้าสีเข้มและสีแดงปิดบนเสาไม้และเคาน์เตอร์ ฟอร์ไมก้า ได้ลงโฆษณาผลงานที่ประสบความสำเร็จของอาร์รสมิทลงในนิตยสาร Architectural Record

องค์กรอื่นๆ ทั่วโลกกำลังตรวจสอบโลกของลามิเนท ซึ่งในบรรดาบริษัทเหล่านี้มีเส้นทางในอนาคตที่จะสามารถไปได้ไกลกว่าบริษัทฟอร์ไมก้า หลายบริษัทพยายามที่จะเปลี่ยนแปลงลามิเนทในรูปแบบการใช้ประโยชน์ไปเป็นรูปแบบการตกแต่ง ตัวอย่างเช่น ในประเทศสวีเดน ความมั่งคั่งของบริษัทเพอร์สตอร์ป (ซึ่งในที่สุด บริษัทในกลุ่มฟอร์ไมก้าก็ได้ซื้อกิจการไปในปี ค.ศ. 2000) พยายามดำเนินการคล้ายวิธีการของบริษัทฟอร์ไมก้ามาก วิลเฮล์ม เว็นท์ ก่อตั้งบริษัทขึ้นเมื่อปี ค.ศ. 1881 เว็นท์สกัดสารเคมีจากไม้บีชจากป่าในฟาร์มของพ่อของเขา เขาขายกรดอะซิติกและแอลกอฮอล์ และไม่นานก็ค้นพบสิ่งที่คล้ายกับเรซินเบคไลต์ ซึ่งก็คือเรซินยี่ห้อ Isolite® วัสดุนี้สามารถซึมผ่านเนื้อผ้าเพื่อทำเป็นรูปฉนวนวงใบได้และใช้เป็นชิ้นส่วนของวิทยุ เช่นเดียวกับบริษัทฟอร์ไมก้าเพอร์สตอร์ป เปลี่ยนไปทำวัสดุบุฝาผนังที่ใช้ตกแต่งและเป็นประโยชน์ มีความทนทาน

L'intérieur des paquebots, des dirigeables et des voitures de chemin de fer fut le premier à être traité avec les matériaux modernes. C'était également le cas des gares, des halls d'entrée et des salons à travers le monde : l'élégance y était associée à la technologie. Ceci exposait le stratifié Formica à la vue de millions de personnes. Les véhicules devenaient tout simplement la salle d'exposition de la marque de stratifié Formica. Les cabines des dirigeables utilisaient le stratifié, de même que de nombreux avions de ligne comme dans le cas des avions Pan Am Clipper et des bateaux qui sillonnaient l'Atlantique, jusqu'aux nouveaux Douglas DC-3. Les trains en étaient également équipés, comme dans le cas remarquable de l'élégant train Hiawatha. Le designer Brooks Stevens a utilisé le stratifié Formica dans les trains Hiawatha de Chicago, Milwaukee, St. Paul & Pacific Railroad, en utilisant une finition lin pour les voitures avec couchette, le noyer et le gris-vert pour les salons. Le stratifié Formica annonçait un avenir plein d'espoir. Ses surfaces brillantes et ses courbes lisses évoquées dans le monde du cinéma hollywoodien se reflétaient sur tous les écrans du monde. Il pouvait idéaliser le plus banal des espaces avec un sentiment d'excitation et transformer le quotidien en futurisme.

L'apprêt du matériau a été démontré par l'architecte William S. Arrasmith, basé à Louisville, dans le Kentucky, qui a revêtu l'intérieur de dizaines de stations de bus dans les petites et grandes localités à travers les États-Unis. Même une station de bus provinciale pouvait offrir une modernité mondiale et la rationalité apportée par les matériaux tels que le stratifié Formica. Les terminaux Arrasmith de bus Greyhound ont été construits entre les années 1930 et 1950. Les façades de béton présentaient des angles arrondis, comme érodés par le vent, des blocs de verre et des bandes métalliques. Les intérieurs présentaient les mêmes effets visuels dans l'obscurité et le stratifié rouge Formica, les lambris, les colonnes cylindriques et les comptoirs. La Formica Insulation Company a fait de la publicité au sujet des réalisations Arrasmith dans la revue *Architectural Record*.

mundo —el estilo y la tecnología trascendían localidades. Esto expuso al laminado Formica a millones de personas. Los vehículos se convirtieron, de hecho, en tiendas de ventas móviles para el laminado de la marca Formica. Las cabinas de los zepelines utilizaban laminado, como lo hacían muchas de las primeras aerolíneas, desde los Clippers de Pan Am que volaban y los botes que navegaban por el Atlántico hasta los nuevos Douglas DC-3. Los trenes con sus interiores estilizados competían —un notable ejemplo posterior fue el moderno y lustroso tren Hiawatha. El diseñador Brooks Stevens utilizó los laminados Formica en los trenes Hiawatha del Ferrocarril de Chicago, Milwaukee, St. Paul y el Pacífico, y especificaba un acabado tipo lino en los vagones cama y tonos nogal y gris verdoso en los salones. El laminado Formica revelaba un futuro prometedor. Sus superficies relucientes y curvas elegantes evocaban el mundo de las películas —Hollywood en las pantallas de ciudades pequeñas en todo el mundo. Podía hacer romántico el más mundano de los espacios con una sensación de entusiasmo y transformaba lo cotidiano en futurista.

El atractivo del material lo demostró el arquitecto William S. Arrasmith, en Louisville, Kentucky, que revistió los interiores de una gran cantidad de estaciones de autobús en ciudades pequeñas y en ciudades grandes en todo los Estados Unidos. Incluso una estación de autobús provincial podía ofrecer el sentido de modernidad global que brindaban las formas estilizadas y los materiales, como el del laminado Formica. Las terminales de autobús de Greyhound de Arrasmith se construyeron entre las décadas de los treinta y de los cincuenta. Sus exteriores tenían esquinas redondeadas, como si se cortara la resistencia al viento, así como también bloques de vidrio y bandas metálicas. Los interiores incorporaban los mismos temas visuales en laminados Formica oscuros y rojos, en revestimiento de madera, columnas cilíndricas y mostradores. The Formica Insulation Company publicitaba el logro de Arrasmith en *Architectural Record*.

Alrededor del mundo, otras empresas investigaban el mundo de los laminados; entre ellas, las empresas cuyos caminos futuros se cruzarían, con el

harmaanvihreän salonkeihin. Formica-laminaatti enteili toiveikasta tulevaisuutta. Sen hohtavat pinnat ja sulavalinjaiset kaaret saivat aikaan elokuvien maailman — Hollywoodia pikkukaupunkien valkokankaille kaikkialla maailmassa. Se pystyi romantisoimaan mitä arkipäiväisimmät tilat jännittävän tuntuisiksi ja tekemään jokapäiväisestä futuristisen.

Materiaalin viehätyksen osoitti arkkitehti William S. Arrasmith, Louisvillesta, Kentuckysta, joka päällysti kymmenien linja-autoasemien sisätilat pienissä ja suurissa kaupungeissa ympäri Amerikkaa. Myös maaseudun linja-autoasema pystyi tarjoamaan globaalin nykyaikaisuuden vaikutelman, jonka virtaviivaisuus ja Formica-laminaatin kaltaiset materiaalit saivat aikaan. Arrasmithin Greyhound linja-autoasemia rakennettiin 1930-luvulta 1950-luvulle saakka. Niiden ulkosivuilla oli pyöristetyt betoniset nurkat — ikään kuin tuulen vaimentamiseksi — sekä lasilohkoja ja metallikaistaleita. Sisustukset noudattivat samoja visuaalisia teemoja tummissa ja punaisissa Formica-laminaateissa, paneloinnissa, sylinterimäisissä pilareissa ja palvelutiskeissä. Formica Insulation Company esitti mainoksia Arrasmithin saavutuksista *Architectural Record* -lehdessä.

Eri puolilla maailmaa muut yritykset tutkivat laminaattien maailmaa, niiden joukossa yhtiöt, joiden tulevaisuuden reitit liittyisivät aikanaan Formica-yhtiöön. Monet olivat samalla tavoin siirtymässä laminaatin käytännöllisistä sen koristeellisiin muotoihin. Esimerkiksi Ruotsissa Perstorp-yhtiön menestys (jonka Formica-yhtiöt lopulta tulisivat hankkimaan yhtiökauppana v. 2000) käsitti hätkähdyttävän samanlaisia vaiheita kuin Formica-yhtiössä. Wilhelm Wendt perusti yrityksen v. 1881, uutteen kemikaaleja pyökkimetsistä isänsä maatilalla. Hän myi etikkahappoa ja alkoholia ja löysi ennen pitkää vastineet Bakelite® merkkiselle muoville, jota nimitetään Isolite® merkkisiksi hartseiksi. Sillä voitiin myös kyllästää kankaita eristävien kohteiden valmistamiseksi ja sitä käytettiin radion osiin. Formica-yhtiön tavoin, Perstorp ryhtyi valmistamaan paneeleja, jotka olivat koristeellisia ja hyödyllisistä, ja helppoja puhdistaa. Perstorp Plate -levystä, joksi sitä kutsuttiin, tuli suosittu koristeellinen materiaali keittiöissä, kylpy-

用在潛艇上，像歷史悠久的「咆哮者號」（Growler）。

遠洋客輪、飛艇和火車車廂的內部裝飾首先用現代化材料覆蓋。因此，在全球各地為它們服務的車站、大廳和休息室也一樣——風格和技術超越了地域。這使數百萬的人看到富美家的美耐板。車輛成為富美家品牌美耐板事實上的活動推銷店。飛艇的駕駛艙使用了美耐板，許多早期的客機也用了美耐板，從泛美飛機飛行和來往大西洋的船隻到新的道格拉斯 DC-3。火車流線型的內部也加入了競爭——後來的一個鮮明的例子是現代化的流線型西亞瓦塔（Hiawatha）火車。設計師布魯克斯·史蒂文斯（Brooks Stevens）把富美家美耐板用在西亞瓦塔來往於芝加哥、密爾沃基、聖保羅和太平洋鐵路上的列車裡，特別指定在臥鋪車廂使用亞麻布貼面，在休息室用核桃色和灰綠色。富美家美耐板預示著一個充滿希望的未來。它那閃閃發光的表面和流線形的曲線引起了電影世界的好奇——好萊塢在世界各地小城鎮的螢幕上。它可以把最平凡的空間浪漫化，帶來興奮感，把司空見慣變為未來主義。

這種材料的魅力被建築師威廉·阿拉史密斯（William S. Arrasmith）所證明，他以肯塔基州路易斯維爾為基地，為幾十個美國各地的小城市和大城鎮的巴士站做內部裝修。即使是地方汽車站也可以帶有富美家美耐板可以提供的流線型和材料的全球現代感。阿拉史密斯（Arrasmith）的灰狗巴士總站建造於二十世紀三十年代到五十年代。車站外表有圓形的混凝土牆角——仿佛要減少風的阻力——和玻璃磚和金屬圍帶。內飾在護牆板、圓柱和桌檯上延伸了黑紅色美耐板的相同視覺主題。富美家絕緣公司在《建築實錄》（Architectural Record）中為阿拉史密斯的成就作了廣告。

在世界各地，其他企業也在對美耐板領域進行研究，其中有些公司的未

的曲線引起了電影世界的好奇——好萊塢在世界各地小城鎮的屏幕上。它可以把最平凡的空間浪漫化，帶來興奮感，把司空見慣變為未來主義。

这种材料的魅力被建筑师威廉·阿拉史密斯（William S. Arrasmith）所证明，他以肯塔基州路易斯维尔为基地，为几十个美国各地的小城市和大城镇的巴士站做内部装修。即使是地方汽车站也可以带有富美家®装饰耐火板可以提供的流线型和材料的全球现代感。阿拉史密斯（Arrasmith）的灰狗巴士总站建造于二十世纪三十年代到五十年代。车站外表有圆形的混凝土墙角——仿佛要减少风的阻力——和玻璃砖和金属围带。内饰在护墙板、圆柱和桌台上延伸了黑红色耐火板的相同视觉主题。富美家绝缘公司在《建筑实录》（Architectural Record）中为阿拉史密斯的成就作了广告。

在世界各地，其他企业也在对耐火板领域进行研究，其中有些公司的未来发展方向最终将与富美家公司的未来相交。许多公司同样作出转变，从耐火

และทำความสะอาดง่าย วัสดุดังกล่าวเรียกว่าแผ่นเพอร์สตอร์ป และกลายเป็นวัสดุตกแต่งห้องครัว ห้องน้ำ และสถานที่สาธารณะที่เป็นที่นิยม เหมือนที่บริษัทฟอร์ไมก้ามีลายที่เป็นเอกลักษณ์ "Skylark" ซึ่งแสดงถึงความขี้เล่นเพอร์สตอร์ป ก็มี "VirrVarr" หรือ "Chaos" ที่เป็นเอกลักษณ์ซึ่งออกแบบโดยซิการ์ดเบอร์นาดอตต์ ใน ค.ศ. 1958 ลาย VirrVarr เป็นที่นิยมตลอดช่วงทศวรรษที่ 1960 และ 1970 และกลายเป็นสัญลักษณ์ของชาวสวีเดน มีการผลิตจนถึงปี ค.ศ. 1991 และนำออกจำหน่ายอีกครั้งเนื่องจากได้รับความนิยมในปี ค.ศ. 1998 และอีกครั้งทั่วโลกในปี ค.ศ. 2005 ครั้งนี้โดยกลุ่มบริษัทฟอร์ไมก้า ซึ่งกลายเป็นเจ้าของในขณะนั้น

ในประเทศออสเตรเลีย โรเบิร์ต เอ็มไซท์ส และคู่ค้าได้ก่อตั้งบริษัท ลามิเนกซ์ พีทีวาย แอลทีดี ซึ่งเป็นบริษัทที่มีประวัติศาสตร์และวิวัฒนาการในช่วงแรกคล้ายคลึงกับของบริษัทฟอร์ไมก้าในสหรัฐอเมริกา พวกเขาก่อตั้งบริษัทขึ้นใน ปี ค.ศ. 1934 เพื่อผลิตลามิเนทเพื่อใช้ในงานอุตสาหกรรมยานยนต์และไฟฟ้าเป็นหลัก ที่แรกของบริษัทเป็นเพิงสังกะสีเล็ก ๆ ในเมืองไบรตัน ซึ่งตั้งอยู่แถบชานเมืองของเมลเบิร์น เครื่องมือเริ่มแรกของไซท์สเป็นเครื่องมือธรรมดา แทนที่จะใช้แทนกระดาษอัดเรซิน เขาใช้การรีดโดยเครื่อง Dickensian ที่ใช้มือโยกเหมือนการบิดผ้า

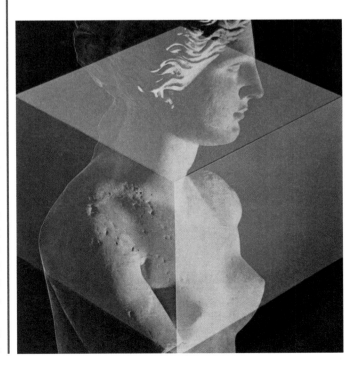

267

Partout dans le monde, d'autres entreprises se sont intéressées au monde du stratifié, parmi lesquelles des entreprises dont les chemins finiraient par croiser ceux de la société Formica. Beaucoup de ces entreprises passaient également des formes utilitaires aux formes décoratives pour le stratifié. En Suède, par exemple, la société Perstorp (qui finira par être rachetée par Formica en 2000) évoluait de manière très similaire à la société Formica. Wilhelm Wendt a fondé l'entreprise en 1881, en extrayant des produits chimiques provenant des forêts de hêtre de la ferme de son père. Il a vendu de l'acide acétique et de l'alcool et peu après a découvert un concurrent du plastique Bakelite® appelé résine de marque Isolite®. Il pouvait également imprégner les tissus pour en faire des objets isolés et a été utilisé dans des pièces pour la radio. Comme la société Formica, Perstorp a évolué vers la fabrication de panneaux décoratifs et utiles, robustes et faciles à entretenir. Perstorp Plate est devenu un matériau décoratif apprécié dans les cuisines, les salles de bain et les espaces publics. À l'image de la société Formica qui avait sa marque Skylark, Perstorp avait quant à elle « VirrVarr » et « Chaos », conçus par Sigaard Bernadotte en 1958. Le modèle VirrVarr est resté populaire tout au long des années 1960 et 1970 et est devenu une icône suédoise. VirrVarr a été fabriqué jusqu'en 1991 puis relancé par la demande en 1998 et à nouveau en 2005 par les nouveaux propriétaires, les sociétés Formica.

En Australie, Robert M. Sykes et un partenaire établi Laminex Pty Ltd avaient également eu une évolution parallèle à celle de Formica aux États-Unis. Une société fut créée en 1934 pour la fabrication de stratifiés fonctionnels, principalement pour les applications industrielles dans l'automobile et l'électricité. Le premier siège de l'entreprise était une toute petite cabane à Brighton, dans la banlieue de Melbourne. Les premiers outils Sykes étaient rudimentaires : au lieu d'une presse pour imprégner le papier de résine, c'est une simple calandre manuelle Dickens qui était utilisée, surtout connue pour l'essorage pendant la lessive. Comme la société Formica, Laminex a commencé sa

tiempo, con los de la empresa Formica. Muchas estaban haciendo el mismo cambio de formas utilitarias de laminado a formas decorativas. En Suecia, por ejemplo, las fortunas de la empresa Perstorp (que, finalmente, serían adquiridas por las empresas Formica en el año 2000) se desarrollaban en formas sorprendentemente similares a las de la empresa Formica. Wilhelm Wendt fundó la empresa en 1881, extrayendo sustancias químicas de los bosques de madera de haya en la granja de su padre. Vendió ácido acético y alcohol, y, en poco tiempo, descubrió un homólogo de los plásticos de la marca Bakelite® que recibió el nombre de resinas de la marca Isolite®. También podía impregnar telas para fabricar objetos aislantes y se utilizaba para piezas de radio. Al igual que la empresa Formica, Perstorp comenzó a fabricar paneles que eran decorativos y útiles, resistentes y fáciles de limpiar. La placa Perstorp, como se denominó, se convirtió en un material decorativo popular en cocinas, baños y espacios públicos. Tal como la empresa Formica tenía un diseño exclusivo que reflejaba su calidad práctica e informal, Skylark, también Perstorp tenía sus diseños exclusivos "VirrVarr" o "Chaos", diseñados por Sigaard Bernadotte en 1958. El diseño VirrVarr fue popular durante las décadas de los sesenta y de los setenta, y se convirtió en una especie de icono sueco; se fabricó hasta 1991, luego se reintrodujo por la demanda existente en 1998 y, una vez más, globalmente en 2005, por sus entonces propietarios, las empresas Formica.

En Australia, Robert M. Sykes y un socio establecieron Laminex Pty Ltd, una firma cuyos comienzos y evolución también eran semejantes a los de la empresa Formica en los Estados Unidos. La crearon en 1934 para fabricar laminado, primordialmente, para aplicaciones industriales funcionales en las industrias automotriz y eléctrica. La primera casa de la empresa fue un pequeño cobertizo de zinc en Brighton, un suburbio de Melbourne. Las primeras herramientas de Sykes eran básicas: en vez de una prensa para impregnar el papel con resinas, la operación utilizaba rodillos exprimidores, un dispositivo dickensiano manual con una manivela muy conocido para exprimir la ropa. Al igual que la empresa

huoneissa ja julkisissa tiloissa. Formica-yhtiön tavoin, jolla oli tunnusmerkin kaltainen kuvio ilmentämässä sen vapaamuotoista leikkisää laatua — Skylark — samoin myös Perstorpilla oli tunnusomainen "VirrVarr" eli "kaaos", jonka Sigaard Bernadotte suunnitteli v. 1958. VirrVarr-kuvio pysyi suosiossa koko 1960- ja 1970-lukujen ajan ja siitä tuli eräänlainen ruotsalainen ikoni; sitä valmistettiin vuoteen 1991 saakka ja tuotiin sitten uudelleen markkinoille yleisön vaatimuksesta v. 1998 ja vielä globaalisti v. 2005 silloisten omistajien, Formica-yhtiöiden toimesta.

Australiassa Robert M. Sykes ja eräs kumppani perustivat Laminex Pty Ltd -yhtiön, jonka alkuaikojen historia ja kehitys olivat samoin rinnastettavissa Formica-yhtiöön Yhdysvalloissa. He ryhtyivät v. 1934 valmistamaan laminaattia pääasiallisesti toiminnallisiin sovelluksiin auto- ja sähköteollisuuksissa. Yhtiön ensimmäinen koti oli pikkuinen peltivaja Brightonissa, Melbournen esikaupungissa. Sykesin ensimmäiset työkalut olivat alkukantaisia: sen sijaan, että puristin kyllästäisi paperin hartseilla, operaatio käytti mankelia, Dickensin aikaista käsikäyttöistä, vivulla toimivaa vehjettä, joka tunnetaan paremmin pyykin puristamisesta. Formica-yhtiön tavoin Laminex aloitti valmistuksensa nimikkeillä kuten ajoitushammaspyörät autojen moottoreissa. Samoihin aikoihin Homapal Plattenwerk GmbH Saksassa, toinen Formica Group -yhtiöiden tuleva osa, alkoi siirtyä puun liiketoiminnastaan kuituleyvyyn ja lopulta laminaattiin.

Jäljellä oli vielä eräs toinen kriittinen innovaatio, laatuominaisuuksien lisäys, joka toisi maailmanlaajuista menestystä. Vuonna 1937 nähtiin seuraava avainvaihe materiaalin parantelussa: siirryttiin lujempiin melamiini-hartseihin. Kemistin, Palmer Griffinin kehittämät melamiinihartsit American Cyanamid Co. -yhtiössä, josta aikanaan tuli Formica Corporationin omistaja, oli jo osoitettu hyviksi astioissa. Jack Cochrane ratkaisi monet pintapaperien kyllästämiseen ja laminaatin kovettamiseen liittyvistä ongelmista. Tuloksena saatu materiaali edusti ratkaisevaa edistysaskelta, jonka ansiosta Formica-yhtiö pystyi tuottamaan paljon kirkkaampia värejä ja vaaleampia puun syitä ja kuvioita. Tämä oli ensimmäinen

来發展方向最終將與富美家公司的未來相交。許多公司同樣作出轉變，從美耐板的實用型轉變為裝飾型。例如，瑞典柏斯托公司(Perstorp)(最終被富美家公司於2000年收購)的命運與富美家公司以驚人相似的方式發展。威爾海姆·溫特(Wilhelm Wendt)於1881年成立該公司，在他父親的農場上從櫸木森林提取化學品。他賣過醋酸和酒精，不久發現了一種與酚醛品牌塑膠相同的東西，稱為矽藻石(Isolite®)品牌樹脂。這種樹脂也可以浸入織物，製造絕緣體，並用於無線電零件。和富美家公司一樣，帕斯托轉而製造有裝飾和實用性的鑲板，這種鑲板堅固耐用，易於清潔，被稱為「柏斯托的板材」，成了用在廚房、浴室和公共場所的一種流行裝飾材料。正如富美家公司有一個代表性的圖案「雲雀」體現其非正式、娛樂性的性質一樣，柏斯托也有其標誌性的「Virr-Varr」或「混沌」圖案，由斯嘉得·貝納多特(Sigaard Bernadotte)於1958年設計。在整個二十世紀六十年代和七十年代，VirrVarr圖案一直很受歡迎，成為瑞典人的偶像；直到1991年以前一直在製造，然後1998年因普遍要求而重新推出，於2005年又在全球範圍內由當時的業主富美家公司推出。

在澳洲，羅伯特·賽克斯(Robert M. Sykes)和合作夥伴成立了Laminex私人有限公司(Laminex Pty Ltd.)，其早期的歷史和演變也和美國的富美家公司非常相似。他們於1934年成立該公司主要為了製造美耐板，在汽車和電子行業用於工業用途。該公司的第一個地址是在墨爾本郊區布萊頓的一個小錫棚裡。賽克斯的第一套工具很原始：不是用壓力機將樹脂壓入紙張，而是操作一臺裝有手工操作拉桿裝置的狄更斯式碾壓機，往常是用來撐出衣服中的水。和富美家公司一樣，Laminex開始也是生產汽車發動機定時齒輪等零件。大約在與德國Homa-

板的实用型转变为装饰型。例如，瑞典柏斯托公司(Perstorp)(最终被富美家公司于2000年收购)的命运与富美家公司以惊人相似的方式发展。威尔海姆·温特(Wilhelm Wendt)于1881年成立该公司，在他父亲的农场上从榉木森林提取化学品。他卖过醋酸和酒精，不久发现了一种与酚醛品牌塑料相同的东西，称为硅藻石(Isolite®)品牌树脂。这种树脂也可以浸入织物，制造绝缘体，并用于无线电零件。和富美家公司一样，帕斯托转而制造有装饰和实用性的镶板，这种镶板坚固耐用，易于清洁，被称为"柏斯托的板材"，成了用在厨房、浴室和公共场所的一种流行装饰材料。正如富美家公司有一个代表性的图案"云雀"体现其非正式、娱乐性的性质一样，柏斯托也有其标志性的"VirrVarr"或"混沌"图案，由斯嘉得·贝纳多特(Sigaard Bernadotte)于1958年设计。在整个二十世纪六十年代和七十年代，VirrVarr图案一直很受欢迎，成为瑞典人的偶像；直到1991年以前一直在制造，然后1998年因普遍要求而重新推出，于2005年又在全球范围内由当时的业主富美家公司推出。

在澳大利亚，罗伯特·赛克斯(Robert M. Sykes)和合作伙伴成立了Laminex私人有限公司(Laminex Pty Ltd.)，其早期的历史和演变也和美国的富美家公司非常相似。他们于1934年成立该公司主要为了制造耐火板，在汽车和电子行业用于工业用途。该公司的第一个地址是在墨尔本郊区布莱顿的一个小锡棚里。赛克斯的第一套工具很原始：不是用压力机将树脂压入纸张，而是操作一台装有手工操作拉杆装置的狄更斯时代的压力机，往常是用来拧出衣服中的水。和富美家公司一样，Laminex开始也是生产汽车发动机定时齿轮等零件。大约在与德国Homapal Plattenwerk GmbH相同的时间内，富美家公司集团的另一个未来元素开始从木材业务转向纤维板，最终成为耐火板。

บริษัทลามิเนกซ์เริ่มการผลิตชิ้นส่วนต่าง ๆ เช่น เฟืองเพลาสำหรับเครื่องยนต์เช่นเดียวกับบริษัทฟอร์ไมก้า ในช่วงเวลาเดียวกันบริษัทโฮมาพอล เพลตเทนเวิร์ค จีเอ็มบีเอช ในประเทศเยอรมนี ซึ่งในอนาคตจะกลายเป็นส่วนหนึ่งของกลุ่มบริษัทฟอร์ไมก้าเริ่มหันเหจากธุรกิจไม้ไปเป็นแผ่นไฟเบอร์บอร์ด และในที่สุดก็ทำการผลิตแผ่นลามิเนท

หนึ่งในนวัตกรรมที่สำคัญยังคงอยู่และเพิ่มคุณค่าที่จะทำให้ประสบความสำเร็จทั่วโลก ในปี ค.ศ. 1937 บริษัทเห็นก้าวที่สำคัญถัดไปในการพัฒนาวัสดุ นั่นคือ การเปลี่ยนไปใช้เรซินเมลามีนที่มีความแข็งแกร่งขึ้น เมลามีนที่ผลิตขึ้นโดย พาล์มเมอร์ กริฟฟิน จากบริษัท อเมริกันไซอานามิด ซึ่งต่อมาเป็นเจ้าของบริษัทฟอร์ไมก้า คอร์ปอเรชัน ได้นำไปใช้กับผลิตภัณฑ์จานชาม แจ๊ค ค็อกเครนได้แก้ไขปัญหาการอาบกระดาษและผลลัพธ์ที่ได้คือวัสดุชนิดใหม่ที่ทำให้บริษัทฟอร์ไมก้าสามารถผลิตผลิตภัณฑ์ที่มีสีสันสดใสขึ้นและลายไม้และลวดลายที่อ่อนลงสิ่งนี้เป็นก้าวแรกที่นำไปสู่แผ่นลามิเนทฟอร์ไมก้า ลายไม้สีอ่อนที่ผู้ผลิตเฟอร์นิเจอร์นิยมมาก นอกจากนี้ ชั้นเมลามีนใสยังช่วยเป็นตัวป้องกันพื้นผิวนอกอีกด้วย แต่การเปลี่ยนแปลงนี้ไม่ได้มีผลมากมายจนกระทั่งหลังสงครามโลกครั้งที่ 2 ตามที่นักประวัติศาสตร์อุตสาหกรรมลามิเนทชั้นนำชื่อ เอฟ ฮอลบรูค แพลตต์ลส ได้เขียนไว้ สงครามเกิดขึ้นก่อนที่บริษัทฟอร์ไมก้า จะหาช่องทางได้อย่างเต็มที่ ภายหลังปี ค.ศ. 1941 บริษัทเน้นการผลิตผลิตภัณฑ์เพื่อใช้ในสงคราม รวมถึงการผลิตหลอดระเบิดและชิ้นส่วนจำนวน 88 ชิ้นที่แตกต่างกันของเครื่องบินรบแนวหน้า P-51 Mustang

ช่วงทศวรรษที่ 1940 และ 1950 – ช่วงเจริญรุ่งเรือง

หลังสงครามมีการก่อสร้างอาคารมากมายทำให้ยุคทองของแผ่นลามิเนทฟอร์ไมก้าเริ่มต้นขึ้น โดยเกิดขึ้นในห้องครัว ครัวกลายเป็นศูนย์กลางของบ้าน ไม่ใช่แค่เพียงพื้นที่ใช้สอยแต่เริ่มมีขนาดใหญ่ขึ้น ในหลายประเทศคนรับใช้ในบ้านไปหางานอื่นทำหลังสิ้นสุดสงครามโลกครั้งที่ 1 และหลังสงครามโลกครั้งที่ 2 มีเพียงบ้านคนรวยเท่านั้นที่จะสามารถจ้างคนรับใช้ได้ ครอบครัวทำอาหารรับประทานกันเอง ห้องครัวจึงกลายเป็นศูนย์รวม และแผ่นลามิเนทก็เป็นวัสดุที่เหมาะสมที่สุดสำหรับวิถีชีวิตแบบนี้

เมื่อผู้ผลิตเฟอร์นิเจอร์ลังเลที่จะใช้แผ่นลามิเนทฟอร์ไมก้ากับผลิตภัณฑ์ของตนบริษัทที่เริ่มติดตั้งแผ่น ลามิเนทกับเคาน์เตอร์

production avec des éléments tels que les pignons de distribution pour les moteurs de voiture. Vers la même époque, Homapal Plattenwerk GmbH en Allemagne, un autre futur membre de Formica Group, a commencé à passer de la menuiserie aux panneaux de fibres et finalement au stratifié.

Une innovation plus essentielle a ajouté des qualités qui allaient conduire au succès mondial. En 1937, un raffinement important du matériau est apparu : le passage à des résines de mélamine plus résistantes. Développées à l'American Cyanamid Co., futur propriétaire de la Formica Corporation, par le chimiste Palmer Griffin, des résines de mélamine avaient déjà été utilisées pour la vaisselle. Jack Cochrane a travaillé sur de nombreux problèmes de saturation du papier de surface et sur le durcissement du stratifié. Le matériau obtenu a représenté une percée qui a permis à la société Formica de produire des teintes beaucoup plus vives et des imitations bois et motifs avec davantage de légèreté. Ce fut le premier pas vers le stratifié Formica imitation de bois blond apprécié par les fabricants de meubles. En outre, une couche transparente de mélamine procurait une couche de protection extérieure. Mais cette amélioration n'a eu d'impact majeur qu'après la seconde guerre mondiale selon F. Holbrook Platts, un historien de premier plan de l'industrie du stratifié. La guerre est intervenue avant que la société Formica n'exploite complètement les possibilités. Après 1941, la société s'est concentrée sur la production de guerre, y compris la fabrication de tubes pour les bombes et de 88 pièces pour l'avion de chasse haut de gamme Mustang P-51.

1940 et 1950 : le boom

Le boom de la construction après-guerre a lancé l'âge d'or du stratifié Formica qui s'est imposé dans la cuisine. La cuisine devenait la plaque tournante de la maison. Ce n'était plus seulement un espace utilitaire et elle s'agrandissait. Dans de nombreux pays, les domestiques avaient trouvé un autre emploi après la première guerre mondiale, et après la seconde guerre mondiale, seuls les ménages les plus aisés pouvaient se permettre une telle aide. Avec les familles cuisi-

Formica, Laminex comenzó su producción con artículos tales como engranajes de distribución para motores de automóviles. Durante la misma época, Homapal Plattenwerk GmbH en Alemania, otro integrante futuro del grupo de empresas Formica, comenzó a cambiar y pasó de su negocio de la madera al de madera comprimida y, finalmente, al de laminado.

Quedaba una innovación más crítica, que agregó cualidades que alcanzarían el éxito mundial. En 1937, se observó el próximo paso clave en el refinamiento del material: el cambio a resinas de melamina más resistentes. Desarrolladas en American Cyanamid Co., el futuro propietario de Formica Corporation, por el químico Palmer Griffin, las resinas de melamina ya se habían probado en vajillas. Jack Cochrane resolvió muchos de los problemas relacionados con la saturación de los papeles de superficie y con el curado del laminado. El material resultante representaba un gran descubrimiento que permitió a la empresa Formica producir colores mucho más brillantes y vetas de madera y diseños más claros. Este fue el primer paso hacia el laminado Formica en veta de madera claro valorado por los fabricantes de muebles. Además, una capa clara de melamina actuaba como una capa protectora externa. Pero este refinamiento no tuvo un impacto importante hasta después de la Segunda Guerra Mundial, según F. Holbrook Platts, un historiador líder de la industria del laminado. La guerra irrumpió antes de que The Formica Insulation Company pudiera explotar totalmente las posibilidades. Después de 1941, la empresa se concentró en la producción bélica, que incluía la fabricación de tubos para bombas y ochenta y ocho piezas distintas para el avión de combate de tecnología de punta P-51 Mustang.

Las décadas de los cuarenta y de los cincuenta: el auge

El auge de la construcción durante la posguerra inició la época dorada de los laminados Formica —y ocurrió en la cocina. La cocina se convirtió en el centro social del hogar. Ya no era solo un espacio utilitario, se hacía más grande. En varios países, el personal doméstico había encontrado otro empleo después de la Primera Gue-

vaihe kohti vaaleaa, huonekalujen valmistajien arvostamaa puusyistä Formica-laminaattia. Läpinäkyvä melamiinikerros toimi lisäksi suojaavana ulompana kerroksena. Tällä hienoudella ei kuitenkaan ollut kovin suurta vaikutusta ennen kuin vasta toisen maailmansodan jälkeen, huomauttaa F. Holbrook Platts, johtava historioitsija laminaattiteollisuudessa. Sota tuli väliin, ennen kuin The Formica Insulation Company pystyi täysin käyttämään mahdollisuuksia hyväksi. Vuoden 1941 jälkeen yhtiö keskittyi sotateollisuuteen, mukaan lukien pommiputkien valmistus ja 88 erillistä osaa huippuluokan P-51 Mustang -hävittäjään.

1940- ja 1950-luvut: Nousukausi

Sodan jälkeinen rakennusbuumi pani alkuun Formica-laminaattien kultakauden — ja se tapahtui keittiössä. Keittiöstä tuli kodin seurustelupaikka. Se ei ollut enää vain hyötytila, siitä alkoi tulla suurempi. Monissa maissa kotiapulaiset olivat löytäneet muita töitä ensimmäisen maailmansodan jälkeen, ja toisen maailmansodan päätyttyä vain hyvin harvoissa talouksissa oli varaa tällaiseen apuun. Perheiden valmistaessa omat ruokansa, keittiöstä tuli kokoontumispaikka ja laminaatti oli juuri sellainen materiaali, jota tarvittiin tällaisiin elämäntyyleihin.

Kun huonekalujen valmistajat vaikuttivat haluttomilta lisäämään Formica-laminaattia omiin tuotteisiinsa, yhtiö alkoi liimata sitä kaappien ja pöytien pintoihin. Ruokailuopen ideasta — yhdistää pöydän ja tuolit — tuli vaihtoehto muodolliselle ruokailuhuoneelle: syötiin keittiössä. Puun, teräksen tai linoleumin korvaavia Formica-laminaattisia keittiön pöytälevyjä oli kaikkialla. Kuudesta miljoonasta talosta, jotka rakennettiin Yhdysvalloissa 1940-luvun toisen puolikkaan aikana, kolmanneksessa, eli kahdessa miljoonassa oli keittiössä laminaattiset tiskipöydät tai kaappien pinnat, tavallisesti Formica-laminaatilla päällystettyinä. "Helppo puhdistaa" ja "väriliidun kestävä" miellytti perheitä, mutta mikään muu ei paremmin ilmaise tämän aikakauden iloista optimismia kuin Brooks Stevensin v. 1950 suunnittelema Skylark-kuvio, jonka abstrakti muoto kuvasti selviä mahdollisuuksia. Raymond Loewy, kuuluisa teollinen suunnittelija,

pal Plattenwerk GmbH 相同的時間內，富美家公司集團的另一個未來元素開始從木材業務轉向纖維板，最終成為美耐板。

還有更重要的一項創新沒有解決，即提高品質，這將在全球帶來成功。1937 年出現了完善材料方面的下一個關鍵的步驟：轉移到更堅硬的三聚氰胺樹脂。三聚氰胺樹脂在美國氰胺公司 (American Cyanamid Co.) (也是富美家公司未來的主人) 由化學家帕爾默·格里芬 (Palmer Griffin) 開發，已經在餐具上得到證明。傑克·科克倫 (Jack Cochrane) 解決了表面紙飽和與美耐板固化的許多問題。由此產生的材料代表一項突破，使富美公司能生產出更亮麗的色彩、更輕的木紋和圖案。這是向傢俱製造商們青睞的金髮色、木紋富美家美耐板邁進的第一步。此外，透明的三聚氰胺層可以作為保護外層。但據美耐板行業一位主要歷史學家霍爾布魯克·普萊茨 (F. Holbrook Platts) 說，這一改進並沒有產生重大影響。富美家絕緣公司還未來得及充分探討其可能性，戰爭就爆發了。1941 年後，公司專注於為戰爭生產，包括製造炸彈管和為 P-51 野馬戰鬥機製作 88 個不同的頂級部件。

还有更重要的一项创新没有解决，即提高质量，这将在全球带来成功。1937 年出现了完善材料方面的下一个关键的步骤：转移到更坚硬的三聚氰胺树脂。三聚氰胺树脂在美国氰胺公司 (American Cyanamid Co.) (也是富美家公司未来的主人) 由化学家帕尔默·格里芬 (Palmer Griffin) 开发，已经在餐具上得到证明。杰克·科克伦 (Jack Cochrane) 解决了表面纸饱和与耐火板固化的许多问题。由此产生的材料代表一项突破，使富美公司能生产出更亮丽的色彩、更轻的木纹和图案。这是向家具制造商们青睐的金发色、木纹富美家®装饰耐火板迈进的第一步。此外，透明的三聚氰胺层可以作为保护外层。但据耐火板行业一位主要历史学家霍尔布鲁克·普莱茨 (F. Holbrook Platts) 说，这一改进并没有产生重大影响。富美家绝缘公司还未来得及充分探讨其可能性，战争就爆发了。1941 年后，公司专注于为战争生产，包括制造炸弹管和为 P-51 野马战斗机制作 88 个不同的顶级部件。

二十世纪四十年代和五十年代：繁荣时代

战后的建设热潮开启了富美家®装饰耐火板的黄金时代——它发生在厨房里。厨房变成家庭的社交中心。厨房不再只是一个实用的空间，它的功能在不断增大。在许多国家，家庭佣人在一次世界大战后发现了其他的职业，第二次世界大战后，只有非常富有的家庭能够负担得起这样的家庭帮手。因为家庭要自己烹饪，厨房成了聚会场所，而耐火板正是这种生活方式所需要的材料。

当家具制造商表示不愿把富美家®装饰耐火板用在自己的产品上时，公司开始把它固定在台面和桌面上。小餐室的想法——把桌子和椅子相结合——成了正式餐厅的替代物：有餐桌的厨房。富美家®装饰耐火板的台面替代了木材、钢材和油毡板，随处可见。二十世纪四十年代在美国建造的 600 万套

และผิวหน้าโต๊ะ แนวความคิดของห้องรับประทานอาหารเล็กๆ ซึ่งมีโต๊ะกับเก้าอี้ เป็นทางเลือกใหม่แทนห้องรับประทานอาหารแบบเป็นทางการ นั่นก็คือ การทานอาหารในครัว แผ่นลามิเนทฟอร์ไมก้าถูกนำมาใช้กับพื้นผิวบนเคาน์เตอร์ทุกแห่งหน แทนไม้ โลหะ หรือเสื่อน้ำมัน ในบ้านจำนวนกว่า 6 ล้านหลังที่สร้างขึ้นในสหรัฐอเมริกาในช่วงครึ่งหลังของทศวรรษที่ 1940 บ้านจำนวนหนึ่งในสามหรือสองล้านหลังมีครัวที่ผิวหน้าโต๊ะหรือเคาน์เตอร์เป็นลามิเนท ซึ่งส่วนใหญ่ใช้แผ่นลามิเนทฟอร์ไมก้า การที่มีคุณสมบัติ "ทำความสะอาดง่าย" และ "ใช้ดินสอสีเทียนเขียนได้" ทำให้บรรดาครอบครัวต่างๆ สนใจ แต่ก็ไม่มีอะไรที่แสดงความสดใสของยุคนี้ได้ดีกว่าลาย Skylark ซึ่งออกแบบโดยบรูคส์ สตีเวนส์ เมื่อปี ค.ศ. 1951 ด้วยลวดลายศิลปะ ต่อมาเรย์มอนด์ โลวีย์ นักออกแบบผลิตภัณฑ์อุตสาหกรรมที่มีชื่อเสียง ได้คิดสร้มให้กับลาย Skylark ในผลิตภัณฑ์คอลเลคชั่น Sunrise

วัสดุดังกล่าวยังใช้ในห้องน้ำด้วย โดยมีเทคนิคใหม่ที่สามารถทำให้ลามิเนทโค้งงอลงบนไม้รูปทรง backsplash และขอบด้านหน้าที่ไร้รอยต่อ ("ผู้ผลิตลามิเนทแบบดัดโค้ง" คือ บริษัทที่ทำการดัดและติดลามิเนทบนวัสดุต้นแบบ ซึ่งทำให้เป็นผิวหน้าโต๊ะสำเร็จรูปและติดตั้งในห้องครัวหรือห้องน้ำโดยไม่เสียเวลา ช่วยเพิ่มยอดขายให้แผ่นลามิเนทฟอร์ไมก้าอย่างรวดเร็ว) ในปี ค.ศ. 1953 รายงานประจำปีของบริษัทได้ฉลอง Vanitory ซึ่งเป็นชื่อทางการค้าที่รวมเอาโต๊ะเครื่องแป้งและห้องน้ำไว้ด้วยกัน เหมาะสำหรับผู้ที่ชอบประกอบของด้วยตนเองมีความกระตือรือร้นที่จะซื้อผลิตภัณฑ์ ทั้งนี้ต้องยกความดีความชอบให้แก่การชนิดใหม่

ความเจริญรุ่งเรืองเรื่องใหม่นี้ได้เปลี่ยนแปลงบริษัท โลโก้เดิมของฟอร์ไมก้า ที่มีโครงรูปโค้งตัวอักษร "F" เป็นตัวแรก ซึ่งเป็นสัญลักษณ์ของอาคารหลังเก่า และถูกแทนที่ด้วยอักษร "F" ที่มีลักษณะเหมือนคานเหล็กหนาในอาคารของ Mies van der Rohe ซึ่งเป็นนักคิดสมัยนิยม ส่วนผสมของผลิตภัณฑ์ที่ได้เปลี่ยนแปลงไป ในปี ค.ศ. 1940 รายได้ของบริษัทเพียงหนึ่งในสี่มาจากแผ่นลามิเนทเพื่อการตกแต่ง ที่เหลือมาจากผลิตภัณฑ์อุตสาหกรรม แต่พอถึงปี ค.ศ. 1950 สัดส่วนรายได้ได้สลับกัน บริษัทตัดคำว่า "insulation" ออกจากชื่อของบริษัทในปี ค.ศ. 1948 และเปลี่ยนชื่อบริษัทเป็น The Formica Company

ด้วยเทคนิคการขายเชิงรุก การชุมนุมประจำปี และการสาธิตที่น่าตื่นตาตื่นใจคล้าย

nant elles-mêmes, la cuisine devenait un lieu de rassemblement et le stratifié était le matériau idéal pour un tel mode de vie.

Lorsque les fabricants de meubles se sont montrés réticents à utiliser le stratifié Formica pour leurs produits, la société a associé son produit aux plans de travail et aux éléments supérieurs. L'idée de la dînette, combinant une table et des chaises, devenait une alternative à la salle à manger classique : la cuisine où l'on mange. Remplaçant le bois, l'acier ou le linoléum, les dessus de table en stratifié Formica se sont répandus partout. Parmi les six millions de maisons construites aux États-Unis pendant la dernière moitié des années 1940, un tiers, soit deux millions, possédaient des cuisines avec plan de travail ou comptoir en stratifié, généralement de Formica. Les thèmes de la facilité d'entretien et de la résistance au crayon de cire plaisaient aux familles, mais rien n'a mieux exprimé l'optimisme dynamique de cette époque que le modèle Skylark, conçu par Brooks Stevens en 1950, avec sa forme abstraite si évidente. Raymond Loewy, le célèbre designer industriel, a mis au point ultérieurement de nouvelles teintes pour Skylark dans le cadre de sa collection Sunrise conçue pour la société Formica en 1953.

Le matériau s'est également répandu dans les salles de bain, grâce à de nouvelles techniques qui permettent aux fabricants de postformage de plier le stratifié et de l'utiliser comme dosseret concave et bord avant sans joints. (Les postformeurs étaient des entreprises qui pliaient et collaient le stratifié sur un substrat, fournissant des plans de travail tout faits qui pouvaient être facilement découpés au format nécessaire et rapidement installés dans la cuisine ou la salle de bain. Ceci a considérablement contribué au développement des ventes du stratifié Formica.) Le rapport annuel de 1953 de la société a célébré Vanitory — une marque combinant « vanity » et « lavatory » — et note que le bricoleur était désireux d'acheter les produits grâce à l'apparition de nouvelles colles.

Le nouvel essor commercial a transformé l'entreprise. Le logo original de la société Formica Insulation était un arc dont le « F » suggérait le toit d'un ancien bâtiment. Il fut remplacé rapi-

rra Mundial, y después de la Segunda Guerra Mundial, solo las familias muy acaudaladas podían permitirse tal ayuda. Como las familias cocinaban sus propios alimentos, la cocina se convirtió en un punto de reunión, y el laminado era justamente el material necesario para tales estilos de vida.

Cuando los fabricantes de muebles se mostraron poco dispuestos a aplicar el laminado Formica a sus propios productos, la empresa comenzó a integrarlo a mostradores y encimeras. La idea del comedor pequeño, que combina una mesa y sillas, se convirtió en la alternativa al comedor formal: la cocina-comedor. Al reemplazar la madera, el acero o el linóleo, las cubiertas prefabricadas de laminado Formica se encontraban en todos lados. Entre los seis millones de casas construidas en los Estados Unidos durante la segunda mitad de la década de los cuarenta, un tercio, dos millones, tenían cocinas con encimeras o mostradores laminados, generalmente revestidos con el laminado Formica. Las características "fácil de limpiar" y "resistente a los crayones" atraían a las familias, pero nada expresaba mejor el optimismo boyante de esa época que el diseño Skylark, creación de Brooks Stevens en 1950, con su forma abstracta que resumía la mera posibilidad. Raymond Loewy, el famoso diseñador industrial, posteriormente ideó nuevos colores para Skylark como parte de su colección Sunrise diseñada para The Formica Company en 1953.

El material también se encontraba en el baño, gracias a las nuevas técnicas de postformado que permitían a los fabricantes doblar el laminado en protectores contra salpicaduras cóncavos y perfiles frontales uniformes. (Los "postformadores" eran empresas que doblaban y pegaban el laminado en un sustrato, lo que permitía lograr cubiertas prefabricadas que podían cortarse fácilmente a medida e instalarse rápidamente en la cocina o en el baño. Esto ayudó a aumentar las ventas del laminado Formica de manera considerable). El informe anual de 1953 de la empresa celebra el Vanitory — un nombre comercial que combina los términos en inglés "vanity" (tocador) y "lavatory" (lavamanos) — y destaca que los amantes del "hágalo usted mismo" estaban más deseosos de comprar los productos, gracias a los nuevos pegamentos.

keksi myöhemmin uusia värejä Skylarkia varten, osana hänen The Formica Companylle v. 1953 suunnittelemaansa Sunrise-kokoelmaa.

Materiaali löytyi myös kylpyhuoneesta uuden jälkimuoustekniikan ansiosta, joka antoi valmistajien taivuttaa laminaatin koveraksi takalistaksi ja saumattomiksi etureunoiksi. ("Jälkimuovaajat" olivat yrityksiä, jotka taivuttivat ja liimasivat laminaatin alustan päälle, toimittaen valmiiksi tehtyjä pöytälevyjä, joita oli helppo sahata oikean kokoisiksi ja asentaa nopeasti keittiöön tai kylpyhuoneeseen. Ne auttoivat dramaattisesti Formica-laminaatin myynnin laajentumista). Yhtiön 1953 vuosikertomus juhlii Vanitorya — kauppanimi, joka yhdistää kampauspöydän ja lavuaarin — ja huomauttaa, että tee-se-itse asiakkaat olivat innokkaita ostamaan tuotteita uusien liimojen ansiosta.

Uusi nousukausi muutti yhtiön. Formica Insulation Companyn alkuperäinen logo pyyhkäisevine kaarineen, jossa alkukirjain "F" muistutti vanhan rakennuksen kattoa, korvattiin "F"-kirjaimella, joka oli kuin jykevä teräspalkki modernisti Mies van der Rohen rakennuksessa. Tuotevalikoima muuttui. Vuonna 1940 vain neljännes yhtiön liikevoitosta tuli koristelaminaatista, loput teollisuustuotteista. Vuoteen 1950 mennessä suhteet olivat päinvastaiset. Vuonna 1948 yhtiö pudotti nimestään termin "eristys" ja muutti nimekseen The Formica Company.

Aggressiivisilla myyntitekniikoilla, vuosittaisilla kokoontumistilaisuuksilla ja sirkustyylisillä esittelyillä alan konferensseissa The Formica Company keskittyi yhä enemmän kuluttajaan. Se mainosti vahvasti, käyttäen noin 500 000 dollaria v. 1951, määrän, joka vastaa 2 prosenttia sen myynnistä. Mutta kun aikakauslehti *Fortune* vieraili v. 1951 se myös näki edelleen hyvin varovaisen yhtiön, joka valmisti vain tilauksesta — mikä kestäisi neljästä kahdeksaan viikkoa toimittaa — ja oli haluton joutumaan velkaan. "Huolestuneisuus" oli sana, jota *Fortune* käytti asenteesta asiakkaita kohtaan. Niin varovaisesti sitä johdettiin, kuten *Fortune* raportoi, että Formica jopa rakensi uutta Evendalen tehdasta yhdeksän mailin päähän esikaupungin Spring Grove Avenuen laitoksesta kustannuserä kerrallaan -periaatteella,

二十世紀四十年代和五十年代：繁榮時代

戰後的建設熱潮開啟了富美家美耐板的黃金時代——它發生在廚房裡。廚房變成家庭的社交中心。廚房不再只是一個實用的空間，它的功能在不斷增大。在許多國家，家庭傭人在一次世界大戰後發現了其他的職業，第二次世界大戰後，只有非常富有的家庭能夠負擔得起這樣的家庭幫手。因為家庭要自己烹飪，廚房成了聚會場所，而美耐板正是這種生活方式所需要的材料。

當傢俱製造商表示不願把富美家美耐板用在自己的產品上時，公司開始把它固定在檯面和桌面上。小餐室的想法——把桌子和椅子相結合——成了正式餐廳的替代物：有餐桌的廚房。富美家美耐板的檯面替代了木材、鋼材和油氈板，隨處可見。二十世紀四十年代在美國建造的 600 萬套房子中，有三分之一（或 200 萬套）有帶美耐板檯面的廚房，通常用的是富美家美耐板。「易清潔」和「不染蠟筆」對家庭很有吸引力，但更能表現這個時代的蓬勃樂觀精神的莫過於雲雀圖案了，這是布魯克斯·史蒂文斯於 1950 年設計的，它的抽象的形式總結了純粹的可能性。著名工業設計師雷蒙德·洛伊 (Raymond Loewy) 後來為雲雀設計了新的顏色，作為他為富美家公司在 1953 年設計的日出收藏設計的一部分。

這種材料也用在浴室裡，由於新的後成型技術，使製造商將美耐板彎曲成拱形擋板和無縫前緣……「後成型公司」是把美耐板彎曲和膠合成層壓基板的公司，它們提供的現成檯面很容易被切割成需要的尺寸，並迅速安裝在廚房或浴室內。這些產品極大地幫助擴大了富美家美耐板的銷售。公司 1953 年度報告讚揚了 Vanitory——把盥洗檯和洗手間結合在一起的商標名稱——並指出，由於新膠

房子中，有三分之一（或 200 万套）有带耐火板台面的厨房，通常用的是富美家®装饰耐火板。"易清洁"和"不染蜡笔"对家庭很有吸引力，但更能表现这个时代的蓬勃乐观精神的莫过于云雀图案了，这是布鲁克斯·史蒂文斯于 1950 年设计的，它的抽象的形式总结了纯粹的可能性。著名工业设计师雷蒙德·洛伊 (Raymond Loewy) 后来为云雀设计了新的颜色，作为他为富美家公司在 1953 年设计的日出收藏设计的一部分。

这种材料也用在浴室里，由于新的后成型技术，使制造商将耐火板弯曲成拱形挡板和无缝前缘……"后成型公司"是把耐火板弯曲和胶合成层压基板的公司，它们提供的现成台面很容易被切割成需要的尺寸，并迅速安装在厨房或浴室内。这些产品极大地帮助扩大了富美家®装饰耐火板的销售。公司 1953 年年度报告赞扬了 Vanitory——把盥洗台和洗手间结合在一起的商标名称——并指出，由于新胶水的发明，自己动手的人迫切希望买这些产品。

新的热潮改变了公司。富美家绝缘公司原先的标志是一个俯冲拱，其开头字头 "F" 代表老建筑的屋顶，很快就被看似现代派密斯·凡德罗 (Mies van der Rohe) 建筑里醒目的钢梁的 "F" 所取代。产品结构起了变化。

กับได้ดูแลครสัตว์ตามการประชุมอุตสาหกรรมต่างๆ บริษัท The Formica Company มุ่งเน้นที่ผู้บริโภคมากขึ้น และทุ่มกับการโฆษณาอย่างมหาศาลโดยใช้งบประมาณประมาณ 500,000 ดอลลาร์สหรัฐในปี ค.ศ. 1951 ซึ่งคิดเป็นจำนวนเท่ากับร้อยละ 2 ของยอดขายของบริษัท แต่เมื่อนิตยสาร Fortune มาเยี่ยมชมบริษัทในปี ค.ศ. 1951 ยังพบบริษัทที่ค่อนข้างอนุรักษ์นิยมมาก การผลิตเป็นไปตามคำสั่งเท่านั้น ซึ่งจะใช้เวลาสี่ถึงแปดสัปดาห์จึงจะผลิตเสร็จ และไม่ชอบการก่อหนี้ "การกระทำด้วยความเต็มใจ" เป็นคำที่นิตยสาร Fortune ใช้สำหรับทัศนคติที่บริษัทมีต่อลูกค้า อีกทั้ง นิตยสาร Fortune ได้รายงานว่า บริษัทฟอร์ไมก้ามีการบริหารจัดการแบบอนุรักษ์นิยม และยังกำลังสร้างโรงงานใหม่ที่มีชื่อว่า Evendale ห่างจากโรงงานในเมืองที่ Spring Grove Avenue เก้าไมล์ โดยใช้ระบบดำเนินการไปจ่ายค่าใช้จ่ายไป และเปิดโรงงานทีละส่วน ครั้งละ 120,000 ตารางฟุต จนครบพื้นที่โรงงานทั้งหมดขนาด 700,000 ตารางฟุต

ทัศนคติแบบนี้อาจเป็นผลมาจากการที่ผู้ก่อตั้งจัดการเหตุการณ์ความหวันวิตกในปี ค.ศ. 1907 หรือยุคเศรษฐกิจตกต่ำที่นำไปสู่การชะลอตัวในครั้งแรกและการขาดทุนในปี ค.ศ. 1932 ของบริษัท หรือเหตุการณ์น้ำท่วมในปี ค.ศ. 1937 ที่ระดับน้ำของแม่น้ำโอไฮโอสูงขึ้นถึงขั้นสองของตัวโรงงาน คนงานและเจ้าหน้าที่ฝ่ายบริหารต้องใช้ความพยายามอย่างเอาเป็นเอาตายกับเหตุการณ์ครั้งนี้ จนกระทั่งเฮอร์เบิร์ต เฟเบอร์ ผู้ก่อตั้ง มีอาการหัวใจวายครั้งสำคัญ หลังจากนั้น เขาไม่เคยออกหน้าในธุรกิจอีก และเกษียณอายุจากคณะกรรมการของบริษัทในปี ค.ศ. 1953 แดนโอคอเนอร์ ยังอยู่ต่อไปจนกระทั่งบริษัทถูกขาย

dement par un « F » qui ressemblait à une poutre d'acier d'un bâtiment de l'architecte d'avant-garde Mies van der Rohe. Le produit avait changé. En 1940, seul un quart des revenus de l'entreprise provenaient du stratifié décoratif et le reste provenait des produits industriels. En 1950, les proportions étaient inversées. L'entreprise a abandonné le terme « Insulation » de son nom en 1948. La société s'appelait désormais la Formica Company.

Grâce à des techniques de vente agressives, des rassemblements annuels, des démonstrations barnumesques et des congrès industriels, la société *Formica* s'est davantage concentrée sur le client. En 1951, la société a dépensé près de 500 000 $ en publicité, un montant égal à deux pour cent de ses ventes. Mais lorsque les journalistes du magazine *Fortune* ont visité l'entreprise en 1951, ils ont également constaté que c'était une entreprise très conservatrice, fabriquant uniquement sur commande, qui avait besoin de quatre à huit semaines pour la fabrication et était opposée à l'endettement. Fortune a utilisé le mot « sollicitude » pour caractériser l'attitude de l'entreprise vis-à-vis des clients. L'entreprise était gérée d'une manière si conservatrice que Formica avait même construit la nouvelle usine Evendale à 15 km environ de l'établissement urbain de Spring Grove Avenue, en payant au fur et à mesure, en ouvrant par étapes, par 36 000 mètres carrés à la fois, jusqu'à ce que

El nuevo auge cambió a la empresa. El logo original de The Formica Insulation Company con un arco hacia abajo, cuya inicial "F" sugería el techo de una construcción antigua, pronto se reemplazó por una "F" que parecía una audaz viga de acero en un edificio modernista de Mies van der Rohe. La gama de productos cambió. En 1940, solo un cuarto de las ganancias de la empresa provenían del laminado decorativo, el resto, de productos industriales. En 1950, las proporciones se revirtieron. La empresa descartó el término "insulation" (aislamiento) de su nombre en 1948 y cambió su nombre a The Formica Company.

Con técnicas de venta agresivas, reuniones anuales y demostraciones cuasi circenses en convenciones industriales, The Formica Company se centraba cada vez más en el consumidor. Publicitaba enérgicamente, gastando alrededor de $500,000 en 1951, monto que equivalía al 2 % de sus ventas. Pero cuando la revista *Fortune* visitó la empresa en 1951, también encontró que la empresa aún era muy conservadora, ya que fabricaba solo a pedido —los pedidos se despachaban en un plazo de cuatro a ocho semanas— y que era reacia a endeudarse. "Solicitousness" ("Solícita") fue la palabra que utilizó *Fortune* para describir la actitud hacia los clientes. Estaba administrada de manera tan conservadora, informó *Fortune*, que Formica hasta estaba construyendo la nueva planta de Evendale, a catorce kilómetros de las instalaciones urbanas de Spring Grove Avenue, con el sistema de pago según se recibe, abriendo por etapas, 11,148 metros cuadrados cada vez, hasta que la planta completa de 65,032 metros cuadrados estuvo lista.

Esta actitud quizá se debió a que los fundadores recordaban aquel pánico financiero de 1907 o la Depresión que condujo a la primera recesión económica y pérdida de la empresa en 1932, o la inundación de 1937 que elevó el río Ohio hasta el segundo nivel de la fábrica y requirió esfuerzos desesperados de los trabajadores y de los ejecutivos. El fundador Herbert Faber sufrió un grave ataque al corazón poco después. Nunca más volvió a desempeñar un rol activo en la empresa y se retiró de la junta en 1953. Dan O'Conor permaneció hasta que la empresa fue vendida en 1956 y,

avaamalla sen vaiheittain, 11 000 neliömetriä kerrallaan, kunnes koko 65 000 neliön tehdas oli valmis.

Tämä asenne saattoi johtua siitä, että perustajat muistivat tuon paniikin vuodelta 1907, tai suuret pulavuodet, jotka johtivat yhtiön ensimmäiseen laskusuuntaan ja tappioon v. 1932, tai vuoden 1937 tulvan, joka kohotti Ohiojoen tehtaan toisen kerroksen tasalle ja vaati epätoivoiset ponnistukset työntekijöiltä ja johtajilta. Perustaja Herbert Faber sai vakavan sydänkohtauksen pian sen jälkeen. Hän ei enää koskaan ollut aktiivinen liiketoiminnassa ja erosi johtokunnasta v. 1953. Dan O'Conor jäi mukaan, kunnes yhtiö myytiin v. 1956 ja lähti sitten viettämään elinvoimaisia eläkepäiviä Floridassa. Hän kuoli v. 1968.

Perustajien lähtö merkitsi käännekohtaa. Yhtiö oli menestyksensä ja itsevarmuutensa huipulla, kun sen osti yksi sen toimittajista, kemian monialayritys American Cyanamid, v. 1956. Sodan jälkeinen hyvinvointi oli huipussaan. Kylmä sota jäähdytti suuren osan maailmasta, mutta rock and roll ja sisään ajettavat elokuvateatterit viihdyttivät amerikkalaisia, jotka tulvivat pois kaupungeista lähialueille. Noina aikoina ei ollut välttämättä ilmeistä, että Formica Corporationin tulevaisuudesta tulisi maailmanlaajuinen. Mutta merkittävänä esimakuna yhtiön globaalista tulevaisuudesta ja ymmärtäen, että tulevaisuus liittyy koristeelliseen laminaattiin, Laminexin Robert Sykes teki vierailun Spring Grove Avenuen tehtaaseen Cincinnatissa v. 1946.

Sykesin perustama yhtiö oli toisen maailmansodan aikana valmistanut teollisuustuotteita sodankäyntiä varten. Kahdessa vuodessa vuosittainen myynti kasvoi 75 000 Englannin puntaan. Hänen tehdastilansa täytti kolme peltivajaa, joissa katon alla oli 1400 neliömetriä. Sodan jälkeen Sykes tajusi välittömästi, että hänen materiaalinsa teollinen käyttö oli vähenemässä. On silmäänpistävää että hän tässä vaiheessa tajusi, että hänen liiketoimintansa oli muuttumassa samalla tavoin kuin mitä The Formica-yhtiö oli kokenut ennen sotaa ja hän oli valmis matkustamaan maapallon toiselle puolelle ottamaan oppia miten oli sopeuduttava. Yhtä huomattavaa oli se, että kukapa muu kuin Jack Cochrane, mui-

水的發明，自己動手的人迫切希望買這些產品。

新的熱潮改變了公司。富美家絕緣公司原先的標誌是一個俯衝拱，其開頭字頭「F」代表老建築的屋頂，很快就被看似現代派密斯·凡德羅 (Mies van der Rohe) 建築裡醒目的鋼樑的「F」所取代。產品結構起了變化。1940 年，公司盈利只有四分之一來自裝飾性美耐板，其餘來自工業產品。1950 年，這個比例則相反。1948 年，公司把「絕緣」從名字中去掉，更名為富美家公司。

積極的銷售技巧、年度聚會和行業大會上的馬戲團式的展示讓富美家公司越來越多地專注於消費者。它大打廣告，在 1951 年花費約 50 萬美元做廣告，相當於其銷售額的 2%。但是，1951 年當《財富》雜誌造訪時，發現這仍然是一個非常保守的公司，只按訂單製造——需要四到八週時間交貨——不願意負擔債務。「關心」是《財富》用來描寫對客戶態度的字眼。《財富》報道說，管理是如此保守，富美家甚至要在離市區的春天樹叢大道設施九英里之外建立新的埃汶代爾廠，用隨建隨付的辦法，階段性開工，每 12 萬平方英尺為一段，直到整個 70 萬平方英尺的工廠完工。

這種態度可能是創辦人記住了 1907 年的大恐慌的結果，或者是導致該公司第一次經濟衰退和損失的 1932 年大蕭條，或是 1937 年的洪水，將俄亥俄河水升高到工廠的第二層，需要工人和管理人員的拼命努力。不久之後創辦人赫伯特·費伯患了嚴重的心臟病。他此後再沒有積極參與業務活動，1953 年從董事會退休。丹·奧康納繼續留任，直到該公司於 1956 年出售，然後退休，在美國佛羅里達州過了充滿活力的生活，於 1968 年去世。

創始人的謝世標誌著一個轉折點。公司正當成功和自信心的鼎盛時期，就被自己的供應商之一美國氰胺

1940 年，公司盈利只有四分之一来自装饰性耐火板，其余来自工业产品。1950 年，这个比例则相反。1948 年，公司把"绝缘"从名字中去掉，更名为富美家公司。

积极的销售技巧、年度聚会和行业大会上的马戏团式的展示让富美家公司越来越多地专注于消费者。它大打广告，在 1951 年花费约 50 万美元做广告，相当于其销售额的 2%。但是，1951 年当《财富》杂志造访时，发现这仍然是一个非常保守的公司，只按订单制造——需要四到八周时间交货——不愿意负担债务。"关心"是《财富》用来描写对客户态度的字眼。《财富》报道说，管理是如此保守，富美家甚至要在离市区的春天树丛大道设施九英里之外建立新的埃汶代尔厂，用随建随付的办法，阶段性开工，每 12 万平方英尺为一段，直到整个 70 万平方英尺的工厂完工。

这种态度可能是创办人记住了 1907 年的大恐慌的结果，或者是导致该公司第一次经济衰退和损失的 1932 年大萧条，或是 1937 年的洪水，将俄亥俄河水升高到工厂的第二层，需要工人和管理人员的拼命努力。不久之后创办人赫伯特·费伯得了严重的心脏病。他此后再没有积极参与业务活动，1953 年从董事会退休。丹·奥康纳继续留任，直到该公司于 1956 年出售，然后退休，在美国佛罗里达州度过了充满活力的生活，于 1968 年去世。

创始人的谢世标志着一个转折点。公司正当成功和自信心的鼎盛时期，就被自己的供应商之一美国氰胺公司 (American Cyanamid) 的化工企业集团于 1956 年购买。战后繁荣已达顶峰。冷战让全球陷入冰冷，但摇滚乐和汽车电影院让美国人娱乐无穷，从城市出走到郊区。在那些日子里，还看不出富美家公司的未来将具有世界性。但是，作为该公司全球未来的预示，理解未来就在于装饰性耐火板，Laminex 的罗伯特·赛克斯 (Robert Sykes)

ไปในปี ค.ศ. 1956 และเกษียณอายุออกไปใช้ชีวิตที่สดใสในฟลอริดา แล้วเสียชีวิตลงในปี ค.ศ. 1968

การจากไปของผู้ก่อตั้งถือเป็นจุดผันเปลี่ยนของบริษัท บริษัทอยู่ในจุดที่สูงที่สุดของความสำเร็จและความเชื่อมั่นในตนเองเมื่อบริษัทถูกผู้จัดหาสินค้ารายหนึ่งของบริษัทซื้อไปในปี ค.ศ. 1956 ซึ่งก็คือ กลุ่มบริษัทสารเคมีอเมริกัน ไซอานามิด ความเจริญรุ่งเรืองหลังสงครามถึงจุดสูงสุด สงครามเย็นทำให้เกือบทุกส่วนของโลกหวาดกลัว แต่ภาพยนตร์ร็อคแอนด์โรลและไดรฟ์อินให้ความบันเทิงแก่ชาวอเมริกัน ซึ่งส่งผลให้ผู้คนออกจากเมืองไปสู่ย่านชานเมือง ในช่วงเวลานั้นไม่ปรากฏหลักฐานที่ชัดเจนใด ๆ ว่า อนาคตของ บริษัทฟอร์ไมก้า คอร์ปอเรชั่น จะไปไกลทั่วโลก แต่ในการคาดการณ์ล่วงหน้าถึงอนาคตทั่วโลกของบริษัทและการเข้าใจว่า อนาคตของบริษัทอยู่ที่ผลิตภัณฑ์ลามิเนทเพื่อการตกแต่ง โรเบิร์ตไซก์ส จาก บริษัทลามิเนกซ์ จึงไปเยี่ยมชมโรงงาน Spring Grove Avenue ที่ซินซินนาติในปี ค.ศ. 1946

ในช่วงสงครามโลกครั้งที่ 2 บริษัทที่ไซก์สก่อตั้งขึ้นได้ผลิตสินค้าอุตสาหกรรมสำหรับใช้ในการสงคราม ภายในระยะเวลาสองปี ยอดขายต่อปีเติบโตขึ้นไปถึง 75,000 ปอนด์ พื้นที่โรงงานของเขาตอนนี้เต็มไปด้วยเชิงสังกะสีสามหลัง มีพื้นที่ในร่ม 15,000 ตารางฟุตหลังสงคราม ไซก์สตระหนักทันทีว่า การใช้งานวัสดุของเขาในทางอุตสาหกรรมกำลังลดลง แต่เป็นเรื่องที่น่าทึ่งว่า ในช่วงหัวเลี้ยวหัวต่อเช่นนี้ เขากลับเข้าใจว่า ธุรกิจของเขากำลังจะผ่านการเปลี่ยนแปลงแบบเดียวกับที่บริษัทฟอร์ไมก้า เคยประสบมาก่อนสงคราม และเขาก็เต็มใจที่จะเดินทางไปยังอีกครึ่งหนึ่งของโลกเพื่อเรียนรู้วิธีที่จะปรับตัว ที่ง่ายๆไม่แน่นัก จะเป็นใครไม่ได้เลย หากไม่ใช่แจ็ค ค็อกเครน ที่เป็นคนพาไซก์ส เยี่ยมชมปรอบๆ และอธิบายทุกสิ่งทุกอย่าง เป็นเรื่องที่น่าประหลาดใจมากว่าที่บันทึกการไปเยี่ยมชมครั้งนั้นของไซก์สยังเหลือรอดอยู่ได้ โดยในบันทึกได้มีการรวบรวมไว้ทุกรายละเอียดและสรุปทุกกระบวนการอย่างดีและกระชับ บนกระดาษไม่มีเส้นบรรทัด มีการทำหมายเหตุตัวเล็กด้วยดินสอ ลงวันที่ 16 มกราคม ค.ศ. 1946

เรื่องที่น่าประหลาดใจว่านั้น อาจเกิดขึ้นตอนที่ไซก์สไปเยี่ยมชมโรงงาน นักวิทยาศาสตร์ชั้นนำของบริษัทไม่ได้มองไซก์สว่าเป็นคนที่จะมาเป็นคู่แข่งในอนาคต แต่กลับให้การต้อนรับเขาในฐานะเพื่อนนักวิจัย และท้าทายแบบกัลยาณมิตรที่อบอุ่น พวกเขาที่ได้พบกันในโรงงานคงไม่ได้คิดว่าโชคชะตะจะนำทั้งสองบริษัทมารวมกันในท้ายที่สุด การเปิด

l'usine complète de 200 000 mètres carrés soit construite.

Cette attitude pouvait refléter le souvenir qu'avait les fondateurs de la panique de 1907, ou de la dépression qui a conduit à la première perte de l'entreprise en 1932, ou encore de l'inondation de 1937 qui a fait monter la rivière Ohio jusqu'au deuxième étage de l'usine et nécessité des efforts désespérés de la part des travailleurs et des cadres. Le fondateur Herbert Faber avait subi une crise cardiaque majeure peu après cet événement. Il était peu enclin aux nouveautés et a quitté le conseil en 1953. Dan O'Conor est resté jusqu'à ce que la société soit vendue en 1956, puis s'est retiré de la vie active en Floride. Il est décédé en 1968.

Le départ des fondateurs a marqué un tournant. La société était en plein succès et en pleine confiance lors-qu'elle fut achetée par un de ses fournisseurs, le conglomérat chimique American Cyanamid, en 1956. La pros-périté d'après-guerre était à son apogée. La guerre froide refroidissait beaucoup le monde, mais le rock and roll et les cinémas drive-in amusaient les Américains qui quittaient les villes pour les banlieues. Il n'était alors pas évident que la société Formica de-viendrait un acteur au niveau mondial. Cependant, dans une vision remarquable de l'avenir de l'entreprise et en comprenant que l'avenir se trou-vait dans le stratifié décoratif, Robert Sykes de Laminex avait visité l'usine de Spring Grove Avenue à Cincinnati, en 1946.

Au cours de la seconde guerre mondiale, les entreprises fondées par Sykes avaient fabriqué des produits industriels pour l'effort de guerre. En deux ans, les ventes ont atteint 75 000 livres. Son espace de fabrication occupait maintenant trois hangars métalliques de 4500 mètres carrés. Après-guerre, Sykes s'est immédiatement rendu compte que les usages industriels de son matériel étaient en baisse. Il est frappant de constater qu'à ce stade, il comprit que son entreprise était sur le point de subir le même changement qu'avait connu la société Formica avant la guerre, et il était disposé à voyager à l'autre bout du monde pour apprendre à s'adapter. C'est Jack Cochrane lui-même, parmi d'autres, qui a tout montré et tout expliqué à

luego, se retiró a una vida lozana en Florida; murió en 1968.

La partida de los fundadores marcó un momento crucial. La empresa estaba en la cima de su éxito y autoconfianza cuando fue adquirida por uno de sus proveedores, el conglomerado químico American Cyanamid, en 1956. La prosperidad de la posguerra estaba en su apogeo. La Guerra Fría coartó a gran parte del mundo, pero el *rock and roll* y los autocines entretenían a los estadounidenses que se trasladaban de las ciudades a los suburbios. No parecía evidente en aquellos días que Formica Corporation tendría futuro a nivel mundial. Pero en un notable presentimiento del futuro global de la empresa y al entender que el futuro residía en el laminado decorativo, Robert Sykes, de Laminex, realizó una visita a la fábrica de Spring Grove Avenue, en Cincinnati, en 1946.

Durante la Segunda Guerra Mundial, la empresa que fundó Sykes había fabricado productos industriales para fines bélicos. En dos años, las ventas anuales crecieron a £75,000. El espacio de su fábrica ahora llenaba tres cobertizos de zinc con 1,394 metros cuadrados cubiertos. Después de la guerra, Sykes inmediatamente se dio cuenta de que los usos industriales para su material estaban disminuyendo. Es impresionante que en ese momento entendiera que su empresa estaba cerca de experimentar el mismo cambio que The Formica Company había experimentado antes de la guerra, y estaba dispuesto a viajar por medio mundo para aprender cómo adaptarse. Igual de notable es el hecho de que no fue otro que Jack Cochrane, entre otros, quien enseñó y explicó todo a Sykes. Asombrosamente, se conservan las notas de Sykes de esa visita. Se incluyó cada detalle y se resumió cada proceso en anotaciones cuidadosas, precisas y en letra diminuta, fechadas el 16 de enero de 1946, y escritas a lápiz en papel sin líneas.

Aún más asombroso, quizá, es que cuando Sykes hizo su visita, los científicos principales de la empresa no solo no lo vieron como un potencial competidor, sino que le dieron la bienvenida como a un colega investigador, al que se le debía saludar con cálido compañerismo. Los hombres que se encontraron en la fábrica no podían

den ohella, esitteli Sykesille paikkoja ja selitti kaiken. On hämmästyttävää, että Sykesin muistiinpanot tästä käynnistä ovat tallella. Jokainen yksityiskohta on mukana ja jokainen prosessi kuvattu huolellisilla, täsmällisillä pienillä lyijykynän merkinnöillä, päivättynä 16. tammikuuta 1946, viivattomalle paperille kirjoitettuna.

On ehkä vieläkin hämmästyttävämpää, että Sykesin vieraillessa yhtiön huipputiedemiehet eivät katsoneet häntä mahdolliseksi kilpailijaksi vaan toivottivat tervetulleeksi tutkijakollegana ja tervehtivät häntä lämpimästi ammattiveljenä. Tehtaalla tavanneet miehet eivät olisi voineet kuvitella, että kohtalo lopulta toisi nämä kaksi yritystä yhteen. Heidän avoimuutensa oli poikkeus. Tällaisen menestyksen keskellä, sodan jälkeisen hyvinvoinnin unelman vallassa, jäätiin helposti eristetyiksi Ohiossa.

Spring Grove Avenue saattoi tuntua kovin kaukaiselta muusta maailmasta. Esimerkiksi *The Formican*, yhtiön tiedotuslehti, kertoi jutun eräästä putkiosaston hiojasta, joka oli matkustanut Kreikkaan miehensä sukulaisia katsomaan. Heidän maatilallaan hän kaipasi sisävessaa ja kauhistui sitä, että siat tonkivat talon vieressä. Hän ei olisi voinut olla onnellisempi päästessään takaisin

公司 (American Cyanamid) 的化工企業集團於 1956 年購買。戰後繁榮到達頂峰。冷戰讓全球陷入冰冷，但搖滾樂和汽車電影院讓美國人娛樂無窮，從城市出走到郊區。在那些日子裡，還看不出富美家公司的未來將具有世界性。但是，作為該公司全球未來的預示，理解未來就在於裝飾性美耐板，Laminex 的羅伯特．賽克斯 (Robert Sykes) 在 1964 年拜訪了辛辛那提春天樹叢大道上的工廠。

第二次世界大戰期間，賽克斯創立的公司已經為戰爭製造了工業產品。在兩年時間裡，年銷售額增長到 75,000 英鎊。現在他的工廠佔據了三個錫棚，共有 15,000 平方英尺。戰爭結束後，賽克斯立刻意識到對他的材料的工業用途在下降。值得注意的是，在這個關口，他明白他的生意即將發生富美家公司在戰前已經經歷過的同樣變化，他願意繞地球半週，學習如何適應。同樣明顯的是，在眾人中，正是傑克·科克倫帶賽克斯遊覽，並解釋一切。令人驚訝的是，賽克斯這次訪問的筆記留了下來。每一個細節都包括在內，每一個程序都用仔細、精確和微小的鉛筆符號總結了下來，日期為 1946 年 1 月 16 日，記錄在不帶行的紙上。

也許更令人驚訝的是，當賽克斯造訪時，公司的頂尖科學家不僅沒有把他看成潛在的對手，而且把他當做同僚研究員來歡迎，並以溫暖的同事關係相待。在工廠見到的人誰也無法想像命運最終會將這兩家公司合併在一起。其開放性是個例外。在這樣的成功之中，置身於戰後繁榮的夢想，很容易在俄亥俄州被孤立。

春天樹叢大道似乎與世界的其他地方相隔甚遠。例如，公司的小報《富美家人》(The Formican) 記錄了鋼管部一名磨砂工的故事，她曾前往希臘看望她的丈夫的親屬。在他們的農場，她想念室內的水暖，對豬在房子週圍亂拱感到震驚。她回到俄亥俄州

在 1964 年拜訪了辛辛那提春天樹叢大道上的工廠。

第二次世界大战期间，赛克斯创立的公司已经为战争制造了工业产品。在两年时间里，年销售额增长到 75,000 英镑。现在他的工厂占据了三个锡棚，共有 15,000 平方英尺。战争结束后，赛克斯立刻意识到对他的材料的工业用途在下降。值得注意的是，在这个关口，他明白他的生意即将发生富美家公司在战前已经经历过的同样变化，他愿意绕地球半周，学习如何适应。同样明显的是，在众人中，正是杰克·科克伦带赛克斯游览，并解释一切。令人惊讶的是，赛克斯这次访问的笔记留了下来。每一个细节都包括在内，每一个程序都用仔细、精确和微小的铅笔符号总结了下来，日期为 1946 年 1 月 16 日，记录在不带行的纸上。

也许更令人惊讶的是，当赛克斯造访时，公司的顶尖科学家不仅没有把他看成潜在的对手，而且把他当做同僚研究员来欢迎，并以温暖的同事关系相待。在工厂见到的人谁也无法想象命运最终会将这两家公司合并在一起。其开放性是个例外。在这样的成功之中，置身于战后繁荣的梦想，很容易在俄亥俄州被孤立。

กว้างของพวกเขาเป็นสิ่งที่พบได้ไม่บ่อยนัก ท่ามกลางความสำเร็จดังกล่าวที่ห้อมล้อมไปด้วยความฝันที่จะเจริญรุ่งเรืองหลังสงคราม การที่จะถูกทิ้งให้โดดเดี่ยวในมลรัฐโอไฮโอนั้นถือเป็นเรื่องง่าย

Spring Grove Avenue อาจดูเหมือนห่างไกลจากส่วนที่เหลือของโลก ตัวอย่างเช่น ในจดหมายข่าวของบริษัทที่ชื่อ The Formican ได้บันทึกเรื่องราวของผู้ขัดทรายในฝ่ายหลอดซึ่งได้เดินทางไปยังประเทศกรีซเพื่อไปเยี่ยมญาติของสามีของเธอ ที่ฟาร์มของพวกเขาเธอคิดถึงระบบประปาในตัวอาคารและตกใจเมื่อเห็นหมูใช้จมูกขุดหารากไม้ข้างบ้าน เธอมีความสุขมากที่ได้กลับมาที่มลรัฐโอไฮโอ เธอกล่าวว่า "คุณมีทุกสิ่ง ฉันจะขึมขับสิ่งดีๆ ทุกอย่างของประเทศสหรัฐอเมริกา" ทัศนคติของเธอก็ไม่แตกต่างจากคนอื่นๆ

การขยายตัวออกไปนอกประเทศ

เหล่าผู้จัดการในชินชินนาติผู้รู้สึกสะดวกสบายมากขึ้นเมื่ออยู่ที่บ้าน แต่พวกเขาก็เห็นความน่าดึงดูดใจของผลิตภัณฑ์ยี่ห้อฟอร์ไมก้าในระดับโลก และในปี ค.ศ. 1946 ได้ตัดสินใจที่สำคัญที่ให้สิทธิ์การจัดพิมพ์สำหรับไฟล์สำหรับบนัดารัย์ บริษัทได้รับเลือกให้จัดพิมพ์สำหรับ ได้รับเลือกให้จัดพิมพ์สำหรับไฟล์สำหรับบนัดารัย์ บริษัทได้รับเลือกให้จัดพิมพ์สแตมป์เป็นครั้งแรกในโลกในปี ค.ศ. 1840 ที่มีพระบรมฉายาลักษณ์ของสมเด็จพระราชินีวิกตอเรียพิมพ์อยู่ แล้วยังได้รับโอกาสให้พิมพ์ธนบัตรสำหรับกว่าหกสิบประเทศทั่วโลก รวมทั้งเอกสารทางการต่างๆ เช่น หนังสือเดินทาง

บริษัท เดอ ลา รู จึงมีสถานะกึ่งทางการในสหราชอาณาจักร ซึ่งไม่แตกต่างจากบริษัทใหญ่ในประเทศอื่นๆ เมื่อรัฐบาลเปลี่ยนไปให้คู่แข่งของบริษัท เดอ ลา รู จัดพิมพ์แสตมป์เพนนี กษัตริย์จอร์ทที่ 5 ทรงตรัสว่า ภาพพิมพ์ใหม่ของพระองค์ทำให้พระองค์ทรงดูคล้ายลิง และนิตยสาร ไทม์ ของลอนดอนตีพิมพ์บทความเรื่องความไม่พอใจจากหลุมฝังศพสิทธิ์จึงกลับมาอยู่ที่บริษัท เดอ ลา รู อีกครั้ง

Sykes. Étonnamment, les notes de visite de Sykes ont survécu. Chaque détail s'y trouve et chaque processus est résumé dans des annotations minutieuses au crayon, datées du 16 janvier 1946, sur papier non ligné (fig. 1).

Peut-être encore plus étonnant : lors de la visite de Sykes, les principaux chercheurs de l'entreprise l'ont non seulement vu comme un concurrent potentiel, mais l'ont également chaleureusement accueilli comme l'un des leurs. Les hommes qui se sont rencontrés à l'usine ne pouvaient imaginer que le destin finirait par rapprocher les deux entreprises. Leur ouverture a été une exception. Au milieu d'un tel succès, enveloppé dans un rêve de prospérité d'après-guerre, il était facile de s'isoler dans l'Ohio.

Spring Grove Avenue pouvait sembler très loin du reste du monde. Par exemple, *The Formican*, le bulletin de l'entreprise, a partagé l'histoire d'une ouvrière dans le département des tubes, qui était rentrée en Grèce pour visiter les parents de son mari. Dans leur ferme, elle regrettait l'eau courante et la vue des cochons farfouillant aux abords de la maison la consternait. Elle fut enchantée de retrouver l'Ohio et a déclaré qu'elle était très heureuse de rentrer aux États-Unis. Son attitude n'était pas rare.

Expansion internationale

Les gestionnaires de Cincinnati étaient également plus à l'aise chez eux. Mais ils ont constaté l'attrait mondial des produits de la marque Formica et ont décidé en 1946 de vendre des licences et des droits de fabrication pour une grande partie du monde, y compris l'Europe, l'Inde, l'Australie, la Nouvelle-Zélande et d'autres parties du Commonwealth britannique, à la respectable société britannique De La Rue. Il s'agissait d'une entreprise inhabituelle avec une longue et noble histoire. Comme mentionné dans *The Highest Perfection*, une histoire officielle de l'entreprise par Peter Pugh, l'imprimeur de journal Thomas de la Rue avait accédé à la notoriété au début du XIXe siècle. Il avait commencé par imprimer des cartes à jouer parmi d'autres choses, et avait si bien travaillé qu'il avait reçu le mandat royal d'impression pour la cour du roi. La société a été choisie pour imprimer les

imaginar que el destino finalmente reuniría a las dos empresas. Su franqueza fue una excepción. En el medio de tal éxito, envuelto en un sueño de prosperidad de posguerra, era fácil quedarse aislado en Ohio.

La Spring Grove Avenue podía parecer un largo camino desde el resto del mundo. Por ejemplo, *The Formican*, el boletín informativo de la empresa, registraba la historia de una señora que trabajaba como lijadora del departamento de tubos que había viajado a Grecia para visitar a los parientes de su esposo. En la granja de estos, no existían instalaciones sanitarias interiores y se horrorizó al ver cerdos hocicando detrás de la casa. No podía sentirse más feliz cuando regresó a Ohio y señaló: "Usted puede quedárselo, yo prefiero lo bueno de Estados Unidos". Su actitud no era una rareza.

Expansión internacional

Los gerentes en Cincinnati también estaban más cómodos en casa. Pero observaron el atractivo global de los productos de la marca Formica y, en 1946, tomaron una decisión clave para autorizar los derechos de ventas y fabricación para gran parte del mundo, como Europa, India, Australia, Nueva Zelanda y otras partes de la Mancomunidad Británica, hasta la respetada empresa británica De La Rue. Era una empresa inusual con una larga y noble historia. Como se registra en *The Highest Perfection*, una historia oficial de la empresa por Peter Pugh, la tienda de periódicos de Thomas de la Rue adquirió importancia a principios del siglo XIX. Sorprendentemente, comenzó con la impresión de naipes, y lo hizo tan bien que recibió la garantía real para imprimir mazos de naipes para el rey. La empresa fue elegida para imprimir los primeros sellos postales del mundo en 1840, que llevaban la imagen de la Reina Victoria. Continuó imprimiendo papel moneda para más de sesenta países alrededor del mundo, así como también documentos oficiales, como pasaportes.

La empresa disfrutó de un estado cuasioficial en Gran Bretaña, semejante al de la casa de la moneda en otros países. Cuando el gobierno cambió la impresión del sello de un penique otorgándosela a un rival de De La Rue, el Rey Jorge V se quejó de que su nuevo retrato impreso lo hacía ver como un

Ohioon, ja sanoi, "Pitäkööt sen, minulle sopii vanha hyvä USA". Hänen asenteensa ei ollut harvinainen.

Kansainvälinen laajentuminen

Myös johtajat Cincinnatissa pysyivät mieluimmin kotona. He havaitsivat kuitenkin Formica-merkkisten tuotteiden globaalin vetovoiman ja v. 1946 tekivät avainpäätöksen antaa lisenssin myynti- ja valmistusoikeuksille suuressa osassa maailmaa — mukaan lukien Eurooppa, Intia, Australia, Uusi-Seelanti ja muita Brittiläisen kansainyhteisön osia — arvostetulle englantilaiselle De La Rue -yhtiölle. Se oli epätavallinen yhtiö, jolla oli pitkä ja ylevä historia. Kuten julkaisussa *The Highest Perfection*, yhtiön virallisessa historiassa, kerrotaan, kirjoittajana Peter Pugh, Thomas de la Ruen sanomalehtipaino nousi huomattavaan asemaan 1800-luvun alkuaikoina. Se muuten aloitti painamalla pelikortteja ja teki sitä niin hyvin, että sai kuninkaallisen valtakirjan painaa korttipakkoja kuninkaalle. Yritys valittiin painamaan ensimmäiset postimerkit maailmassa v. 1840, aiheena kuningatar Victoria. Se siirtyi painamaan setelirahoja yli 60 maalle ympäri maailmaa sekä virallisia nimikkeitä kuten passeja.

Yhtiö nautti puolivirallisesta asemasta Isossa-Britanniassa, samaan tapaan kuin rahapajat muissa maissa. Kun valtionhallinto antoi yhden pennyn postimerkin painettavaksi De La Ruen kilpailijalle, kuningas Yrjö V valitti, että hänen uusi painettu muotokuvansa teki hänestä apinan näköisen ja *Times* of London julkaisi pääkirjoituksessaan jyrkän paheksumisen. Toimisopimus palautettiin De La Ruelle. Se otti palvelukseen työväkeä, jolla oli kokemusta ulkoministeriössä, diplomaattikunnassa ja sotilasasioissa sekä kotona että laajemmin maailmassa. Jotkut sen myyntimiehistä matkustivat Orient Express® -junassa kaukaisiin maihin rummuttamaan kokoon setelien tai passien painatustyötä sellaisista paikoista kuin Bulgaria ja Siam. Saksalaiset pommikoneet tuhosivat painolaitoksen toisen maailmansodan aikana. Laitteisto siirrettiin maaseudulle, missä De La Rue painoi rahaa kymmenien miehitettyjen maiden pakolaishallituksille. Valuuttaa säily-

感到再高興不過了，她說：「你可以去過那種生活，我還是要美好的老美國。」她的態度並不罕見。

國際擴展

在辛辛那提的經理們也感到在家裡更舒適。但他們觀察到富美家品牌產品在全球的吸引力，並在 1946 年做了一項重要的決定，許可在世界上大部分地區頒發銷售和生產權特許，包括歐洲、印度、澳洲、紐西蘭和英聯邦其他地區——授予受人尊敬的英國公司德拉魯 (De La Rue)。這是一個非同尋常的公司，有著漫長而高貴的歷史。根據彼得·普格 (Peter Pugh) 撰寫的該公司官方歷史《最高的完美》(The Highest Perfection) 記載，托馬斯·德拉魯 (Thomas De La Rue) 的報亭在十九世紀初聲名鵲起。最初是印刷撲克牌，印得如此之好，以致它得到皇室的認證，專為國王印製撲克牌。1840 年，該公司被選中印製世界上第一版郵票，郵票上印有維多利亞女王的頭像。後來它繼續為世界各地 60 多個國家和地區印製鈔票，以及護照之類的官方證件。

該公司在英國享有半官方的地位，而不是像其他國家的製幣廠。當政府把一便士郵票的印製轉交給德拉魯的競爭對手時，英王喬治五世抱怨說，他的新印刷的肖像讓他看上去像一隻猴子，倫敦《泰晤士報》(Times) 發表了一篇大為不滿的評論。這個專營權又落回到德拉魯的手中。該公司吸引了國內更大範圍的來自駐外機構、外交官隊伍和軍方的工作人員。其銷售人員乘坐「東方快車」(Orient Express®) 前往遙遠的國度，在保加利亞和暹羅等地招徠印刷鈔票或護照的生意。第二次世界大戰期間，印刷廠被德國轟炸機摧毀。設備被轉移到鄉下，德拉魯在這裡為數十個被佔領國家的流亡政府印刷貨幣。貨幣被存放在 80 英尺深的洞穴裡，等每個國家被解放後提出來使用。

春天樹叢大道似乎与世界的其他地方相隔甚远。例如，公司的小报《富美家人》(The Formican) 记录了钢管部一名磨砂工的故事，她曾前往希腊看望她的丈夫的亲属。在他们的农场，她想念室内的水暖，对猪在房子周围乱拱感到震惊。她回到俄亥俄州感到再高兴不过了，她说："你可以去过那样的生活，我还是要美好的老美国。"她的态度并不罕见。

国际扩展

在辛辛那提的经理们也感到在家里更舒适。但他们观察到富美家品牌产品在全球的吸引力，并在 1946 年做了一项重要的决定，许可在世界上大部分地区颁发销售和生产权特许，包括欧洲、印度、澳大利亚、新西兰和英联邦其他地区——授予受人尊敬的英国公司德拉鲁 (De La Rue)。这是一个非同寻常的公司，有着漫长而高贵的历史。根据彼得·普格 (Peter Pugh) 撰写的该公司官方历史《最高的完美》(The Highest Perfection) 记载，托马斯·德拉鲁 (Thomas De La Rue) 的报亭在十九世纪初声名鹊起。最初是印刷扑克牌，印得如此之好，以致它得到皇室的认证，专为国王印制扑克牌。1840 年，该公司被选中印制世界上第一版邮票，邮票上印有维多利亚女王的头像。后来它继续为世界各地 60 多个国家和地区印制钞票，以及护照之类的官方证件。

该公司在英国享有半官方的地位，而不是像其他国家的制币厂。当政府把一便士邮票的印制转交给德拉鲁的竞争对手时，英王乔治五世抱怨说，他的新印刷的肖像让他看上去像一只猴子，伦敦《泰晤士报》(Times) 发表了一篇大为不满的评论。这个专营权又落回到德拉鲁的手中。该公司吸引了国内更大范围的来自驻外机构、外交官队伍和军方的工作人员。其销售人员乘坐"东方快车"(Orient Express®) 前往遥远的国度，在保加利亚和暹罗等地招徕印刷钞票或护照的生意。第二次世界大战期

บริษัทดึงตัวพนักงานที่มีภูมิหลังมาจากสำนักงานต่างประเทศ คณะทูตานุทูต และการทหารในประเทศต่างๆ ของคนทั่วโลก พนักงานขายบางส่วนเดินทางโดยรถไฟโอเรียน เอ็กซ์เพรส เพื่อไปยังดินแดนที่ห่างไกลเพื่อไปโฆษณาธุรกิจการพิมพ์ธนบัตรหรือหนังสือเดินทาง เช่น บัลแกเรีย และสยาม ในช่วงสงครามโลกครั้งที่ 2 โรงพิมพ์ถูกทำลายโดยระเบิดของเยอรมัน อุปกรณ์ถูกเคลื่อนย้ายไปชนบท ซึ่งเป็นที่ที่บริษัท เดอ ลา รู พิมพ์สกุลเงินสำหรับรัฐบาลพลัดถิ่นของประเทศที่ถูกยึดครองหลายสิบประเทศ สกุลเงินดังกล่าวถูกจัดเก็บไว้ในถ้ำลึกแปดฟุต ซึ่งจะถูกดึงออกมาเมื่อแต่ละประเทศเป็นไท

หลังจากสงครามสิ้นสุดลง ความหลากหลายเป็นสิ่งที่จำเป็น ตลาดสำหรับการพิมพ์สกุลเงินและเอกสารทางการก็จำกัด บริษัท เดอ ลา รู มองหาลู่ทางที่จะขยายไปยังตลาดผู้บริโภคเกิดใหม่และตลาดเทคโนโลยีสูง บริษัทเริ่มก่อสร้างโรงงานที่เมืองไทน์ไซด์ ใกล้กับเมืองนิวแคสเซิลทางตะวันออกเฉียงเหนือของประเทศอังกฤษ ก่อนเกิดสงครามบริษัท เดอ ลา รู เคยลงทุนในธุรกิจพลาสติกมาก่อน สำหรับสายผลิตภัณฑ์กลุ่มปากกาจากการเห็นความเชื่อมโยงกับการพิมพ์ หลังสงคราม เจ้าหน้าที่บริหารจึงเล็งไปที่วัสดุบุผาผนังที่ทำจากลามิเนทที่ทำโดยบริษัท Metropolitan Vickers ที่เดิมเป็นบริษัท British Westinghouse ซึ่งทำลามิเนทที่เรียกว่า Traffolyte (ตามชื่อเมือง Trafford ในมลรัฐเพนซิลเวเนีย ที่ตั้งของโรงงานผลิตผลิตภัณฑ์ในสหรัฐอเมริกา) หลังจากที่ได้สำรวจผู้ผลิตในสาขาทั่วโลก ก็พบบริษัท ฟอร์ไมก้า คอร์ปอเรชั่น และบริษัท อเมริกัน ไซอานามิด เจ้าของบริษัท และทำสัญญาให้สิทธิ์ผลิตผลิตภัณฑ์ยี่ห้อฟอร์ไมก้า สภาพที่ยุ่งวุ่นวายหลังสงครามและความขาดแคลนส่งผลให้การก่อสร้างล่าช้าออกไป—โรงงานที่เมืองไทน์ไซด์ไม่ได้เปิดจนกระทั่งปี ค.ศ. 1948 และไม่มีรายได้จนกระทั่งปี ค.ศ. 1952 แต่ท้ายที่สุดประสบความสำเร็จ

ผู้อำนวยการของบริษัท เดอ ลา รู คนหนึ่งได้รายงานในปี ค.ศ. 1953 ว่า การใช้แผ่นลามิเนทฟอร์ไมก้าได้ขยายออกไปมาก "ตอนนี้แผ่นลามิเนทของเราเป็นวัสดุที่ได้รับการยอมรับสำหรับการติดตั้งในห้องครัวที่ทันสมัยในเวลาเดียวกัน ก็ถูกนำมาใช้อย่างมากในโรงอาหาร การบริการขนส่ง เฟอร์นิเจอร์ การตกแต่งร้าน และเพื่อวัตถุประสงค์อื่นๆ อีกมากมาย" บริษัทและยี่ห้อ ฟอร์ไมก้า เริ่มขยายไปสู่ทวีปยุโรป โดยไปประเทศฝรั่งเศสในปี ค.ศ. 1954 ประเทศสเปนในปี ค.ศ. 1956—โดยเข้าไปซื้อกิจการของบริษัทก่อนหน้า

premiers timbres-poste dans le monde en 1840, à l'effigie de la reine Victoria. Elle a ensuite imprimé des billets pour plus de soixante pays à travers le monde ainsi que des articles tels que des passeports officiels.

La société a bénéficié d'un statut quasi officiel en Grande-Bretagne, un peu comme les ateliers de fabrication de la monnaie dans d'autres pays. Lorsque le gouvernement a commandé l'impression du timbre d'un penny à un concurrent de De La Rue, le roi George V s'est plaint de ce que son nouveau portrait imprimé le faisait ressembler à un singe, et le *Times* de Londres a publié un éditorial emprunt de désapprobation. La commande est retournée à De La Rue. Elle a engagé du personnel ayant une formation dans l'administration étrangère, le corps diplomatique et l'armée à l'aise partout dans le monde. Certains de ses vendeurs empruntaient l'Orient Express® vers de lointaines contrées pour développer des affaires afin d'imprimer les billets de banque ou les passeports de Bulgarie ou du Siam, par exemple. Pendant la seconde guerre mondiale, l'imprimerie a été détruite par les bombardements allemands. L'imprimerie a déménagé à la campagne, où De La Rue a imprimé des billets de banque pour des dizaines de gouvernements de pays occupés en exil. Les billets de banque étaient stockés dans de profondes cavernes, dont ils devaient être retirés lorsque chacun des pays serait libéré.

Mais après la guerre, une diversification était nécessaire étant donné que le marché de l'impression des billets de banque et des documents officiels était limité. De La Rue a cherché à se développer sur les nouveaux marchés et la haute technologie. La société a lancé la construction d'une usine à Tyneside, près de Newcastle, dans le nord-est de l'Angleterre. De La Rue s'était aventurée dans les matières plastiques avant la guerre en les utilisant notamment pour une ligne de stylos. Étant donné le lien avec les activités d'imprimerie, les cadres ont étudié après-guerre les panneaux stratifiés réalisés par Metropolitan Vickers, l'ancien British Westinghouse, qui fabriquait un stratifié appelé Traffolyte (d'après le site Trafford de Pennsylvanie, l'usine américaine pour le produit)

mono y el *Times* de Londres publicó una editorial con un matiz de severa desaprobación. La franquicia volvió a De La Rue. Atrajo a personal con antecedentes en la cancillería, los cuerpos diplomáticos y el ejército del país diseminado en el mundo. Algunos de sus vendedores viajaban en el Orient Express® hasta tierras lejanas para aumentar los negocios imprimiendo papel moneda o pasaportes en lugares tales como Bulgaria y Siam. Durante la Segunda Guerra Mundial, la planta de impresión fue destruida por bombarderos alemanes. Los equipos se trasladaron al campo, donde De La Rue imprimía moneda para una gran cantidad de gobiernos de países ocupados en el exilio. La moneda se almacenaba en cavernas de 24 metros de profundidad, para ser retirada a medida que se liberaba cada país.

Pero, después de la guerra, se necesitaba diversificación —el mercado de la impresión de moneda y documentos oficiales era limitado. De La Rue buscó expandirse hacia los mercados de consumo y alta tecnología emergentes. La empresa comenzó la construcción de una fábrica en Tyneside, cerca de Newcastle, en el noreste de Inglaterra. De La Rue se había aventurado con los plásticos antes de la guerra, utilizándolos, entre otras funciones, para una línea de lapiceros. Al vislumbrar un enlace con la impresión, después de la guerra, los ejecutivos se centraron en laminar paneles fabricados por Metropolitan Vickers, la anterior British Westinghouse, que fabricaba un laminado denominado Traffolyte (por Trafford, Pensilvania, sitio de la fábrica estadounidense para el producto) y, tras evaluar el alcance de los productores del área en el mundo, se decidieron por Formica Corporation y su propietario American Cyanamid, con la que formaron una relación de licencia para fabricar los productos de la marca Formica®. Las difíciles condiciones y carencias de la posguerra demoraron la construcción —la fábrica de Tyneside no abrió hasta 1948 y no hizo dinero hasta 1952. Pero, finalmente, rindió sus frutos.

Un director de la empresa De La Rue informó en 1953 que la utilización del laminado Formica se había expandido considerablemente: "Es ahora el material reconocido para equipar una

tettiin 24 m syvissä luolissa ulos vedettäväksi sitä mukaa kun kukin maa vapautettaisiin.

Sodan jälkeen tarvittiin kuitenkin monipuolistumista — valuutan ja virallisten asiakirjojen painomarkkinat olivat rajoitettuja. De La Rue tutki laajentamista kuluttajien ja korkean teknologian yleistyville markkinoille. Yhtiö alkoi rakentaa tehdasta Tynesidessä, Newcastlen lähellä, Englannin koillisosassa. De La Rue oli ennen sotaa uskaltautunut muoveihin, käyttäen niitä muun ohella kynien tuotelinjaan. Nähdessään yhteyden painotyöhön, johtajat harkitsivat sodan jälkeen laminaattipaneeleja, joita teki Metropolitan Vickers, vanha British Westinghouse, joka teki Traffolyte-nimistä laminaattia (tuotteen amerikkalaisen tehtaan sijaintipaikan Trafford, Pennsylvaniamukaan) ja arvioituaan maailman tuottajien valikoiman alalla, harkitsivat Formica Corporationia ja sen omistajaa American Cyanamid, jonka kanssa he muodostivat lisenssisuhteen Formica® tavaramerkin tuotteiden valmistamiseksi. Vaikeat sodanjälkeiset olosuhteet ja puutteet johtivat viivytyksiin rakentamisessa — Tyneside tehdas avattiin vasta v. 1948 eikä se tuottanut voittoa ennen kuin v. 1952. Mutta lopulta se kannatti.

Eräs De La Rue yhtiön johtaja raportoi v. 1953 että Formica-laminaatin käyttö oli lisääntynyt huomattavasti: "Se tunnetaan nyt materiaalina nykyaikaisen keittiön varustamiseen. Samaan aikaan sitä aletaan käyttää lisääntyvästi ruokaloissa, kuljetuspalveluissa, huonekaluissa, työpajakalusteissa ja moniin muihin tarkoituksiin". Yhtiö ja Formica® tavaramerkki alkoivat laajentua Eurooppaan: Ranskaan v. 1954, Espanjaan v. 1956 — ottaen haltuunsa v. 1946 perustetun aikaisemman Ceplastica nimisen yrityksen, joka toimi useimmissa Euroopan maissa. Vuonna 1962 De La Rue perusti Belgian sivuliikkeen Pariisissa olevan ranskalaisen yksikön yhteyteen. Vuonna 1948 se oli perustanut sivuliikkeen Australiaan, jossa Laminex oli johtava laminaattien valmistaja, ja avasi v. 1958 tehtaan Thornleighiin, Sydneyn ulkopuolella. Vuonna 1959 se perusti tehtaan Papakuraan Aucklandin lähelle Uuteen-Seelantiin. Se perusti sivuliikkeen myös Intiaan.

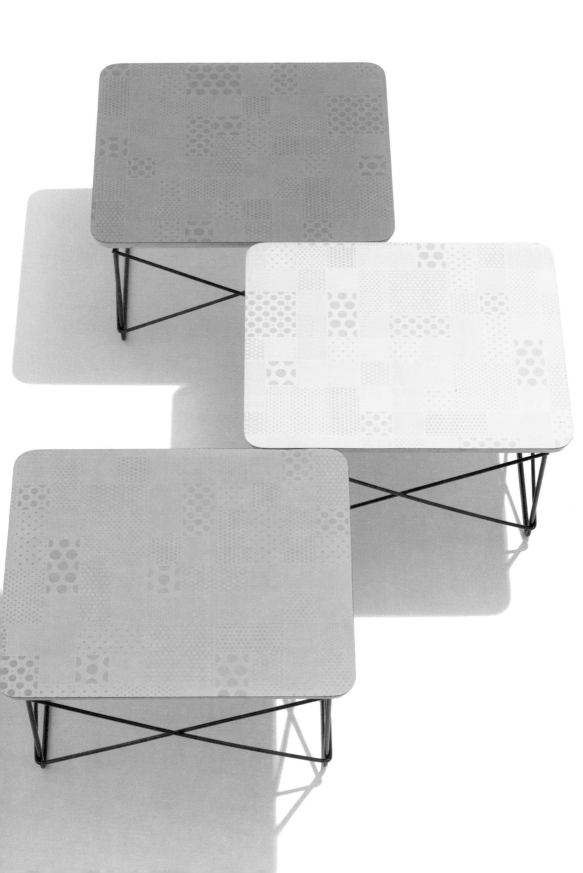

et, après avoir examiné l'éventail des produits mondiaux dans le domaine, ils se sont adressés à la société Formica et à son propriétaire American Cyanamid, avec qui ils avaient constitué une relation de licence pour fabriquer les produits sous la marque Formica®. Les difficiles conditions d'après-guerre et les pénuries ont conduit à un retard dans la construction de l'usine Tyneside qui n'a pu ouvrir avant 1948 et n'a pas dégagé de bénéfices avant 1952. Mais finalement, le succès est arrivé.

Un dirigeant de l'entreprise De La Rue a constaté en 1953 que l'usage du stratifié Formica s'était considérablement développé. « C'est à présent le matériau reconnu pour l'équipement de la cuisine moderne. Simultanément, il est de plus en plus utilisé pour les cantines, les services de transport, le mobilier, les agencements de magasins et une grande variété d'autres applications. » L'entreprise et la marque Formica® commençaient à s'étendre en Europe, en France en 1954, en Espagne en 1956, prenant la relève de l'entreprise antérieure appelée Ceplastica, établie en 1946, qui était présente dans la plupart des pays européens. En 1962, De La Rue mettait en place une filiale belge en connexion avec la première entreprise française basée à Paris. En 1948, elle avait une succursale en Australie où Laminex était le fabricant principal de stratifié et a ouvert en 1958 une usine à Thornleigh, à l'extérieur de Sydney. En 1959, il a établi une usine à Papakura, près d'Auckland, en Nouvelle-Zélande. Il a également établi une succursale en Inde.

En 1958, les dirigeants de De La Rue et American Cyanamid ont révisé leur accord. De La Rue voulait davantage qu'une simple licence pour protéger sa future croissance, et les entreprises ont signé un nouvel accord, avec 60 pour cent de la propriété de ce qui est appelé maintenant Formica Ltd. pour la firme basée en Angleterre et 40 pour cent pour American Cyanamid. Mais dans les années 1970, même si elle a fourni plus de la moitié des ventes de De La Rue, le leadership de l'entreprise a connu une baisse de la vente des produits Formica, étant donné la concurrence sur un marché à maturité. Comme il est relaté dans

cocina moderna. Al mismo tiempo, está siendo cada vez más utilizado para comedores, servicios de transporte, muebles, aditamentos de tiendas y para una variedad de otros fines". La empresa y la marca Formica® comenzaron a expandirse en Europa: a Francia en 1954 y a España en 1956, sustituyendo a la firma anterior denominada Ceplastica, establecida en 1946, que funcionaba en la mayoría de los países europeos. En 1962, De La Rue estableció una sucursal belga en relación con la francesa con sede en París. En 1948, había establecido una sucursal en Australia, donde Laminex era el fabricante de laminados dominante y, en 1958, abrió una planta en Thornleigh, en las afueras de Sídney. En 1959, estableció una fábrica en Papakura, cerca de Auckland, Nueva Zelanda. También estableció una sucursal en la India.

En 1958, los ejecutivos de De La Rue y American Cyanamid aceptaron revisar su acuerdo. De La Rue deseaba más que una simple licencia para proteger su crecimiento futuro, y las firmas celebraron un nuevo arreglo, con el 60 % de la propiedad de lo que en ese momento se denominaba Formica Ltd. para la firma con sede británica y el 40 % para American Cyanamid. Pero en la década de los setenta, aunque proporcionaba más de la mitad de las ventas de De La Rue, el liderazgo de la empresa vio un futuro deficiente para los productos de la marca Formica, el resultado de la competencia y un mercado que maduraba. "La tensión era evidente en Formica", registraba la historia oficial de la empresa. "Una gran cantidad de empresas se habían trasladado a los plásticos laminados alrededor del mundo. En las décadas de los cincuenta y de los sesenta, el panorama había cambiado totalmente". De La Rue recibía solo el 60 % de las ganancias de su empresa conjunta con Formica Corporation en EE. UU., mientras tenía que cumplir con la obligación del 100 % del préstamo de la firma común. En 1977, tras dos años de negociaciones, De La Rue vendió sus derechos nuevamente a American Cyanamid por 9.6 millones de libras esterlinas, el equivalente de, aproximadamente, 16.3 millones de dólares estadounidenses contemporáneos.

Alrededor del mundo

Aun cuando este negocio había finalizado, la marca Formica crecía de ma-

Vuonna 1958 De La Ruen ja American Cyanamidin johdot sopivat sopimuksensa muuttamisesta. De La Rue halusi enemmän kuin pelkän lisenssin tulevaisuuden kasvunsa suojaksi ja yritykset tekivät uuden järjestelyn, jossa 60 prosenttia yhtiön omistuksesta, jonka nimi oli nyt Formica Ltd., meni englantilaiselle yritykselle ja 40 prosenttia piti American Cyanamid. 1970-lukuun mennessä, huolimatta siitä, että se toimitti yli puolet De La Ruen myynnistä, yhtiön johto näki heikkenevän tulevaisuuden Formica-merkkisille tuotteille, seurauksena kilpailusta ja vakiintuvista markkinoista. "Rasitus oli hyvin selvästi havaittavissa Formican piirissä", sanottiin yhtiön historiikissa. "Kokonainen liuta yrityksiä on lähtenyt mukaan laminoituun muoviin ympäri maailmaa. 50- ja 60-luvuilla [se] oli ihan eri juttu". De La Rue sai vain 60 prosenttia tuotoista yhteisyrityksestään Formica Corporationin kanssa USA:ssa, vaikka sen oli otettava vastuulleen 100 prosenttia lainoista yhteistä yritystä varten. Kaksi vuotta neuvoteltuaan De La Rue myi v. 1977 oikeutensa takaisin American Cyanamidille 9,6 miljoonalla sterlingpunnalla, joka vastaa noin 16,3 miljoonaa sen aikaista USA:n dollaria.

Ympäri maailmaa

Tätä kauppaa valmisteltaessakin Formican tavaramerkki kasvoi voimakkaasti ympäri maailmaa. Se saavutti maapallon jokaisen kolkan. Kokenut laminaattien markkinointipäällikkö Bryan Travers Uudessa-Seelannissa sanoo esimerkiksi, että Formica-tavaramerkillä oli maailmanlaajuinen maine koska se kultivoi arkkitehteja ja suunnittelijoita. Yksi tavaramerkin vahvuuksista oli sen suunnittelun globaali kulttuuri. Hänen mukaansa Formica Corporation oli jo 1950-luvulla saanut globaalin tunnustuksen suunnittelusta ja mausta, joka ulottui Europasta ja Amerikoista joka kolkkaan. Sillä oli yhteys muotiin ja makusuuntauksiin. Michel Broussard, joka oli uranuurtaja painolevyjen valmistajana kaikkia yhtiön tehtaita varten eri puolilla maailmaa, muistelee, että "Euroopassa 1950- ja 1960-luvuilla Formica-laminaattia mainostettiin voimakkaasti televisiossa ja muissa kuluttajamedioissa uutena tavoiteltuna nykyaikaisen kodin 'pitää olla' -materiaalina". Sama

但是，在戰爭結束後，多樣化成為必要——印刷貨幣和官方文件的市場很有限。德拉魯希望擴展到新興的消費者和高科技市場。該公司開始在英格蘭東北部紐卡斯爾附近的泰恩賽德建造一家工廠。德拉魯戰前曾涉足塑膠，用它們製作過鋼筆系列的東西。因為看到和印刷之間的聯繫，高級管理人員在戰後希望使用由大都會維克斯公司(Metropolitan Vickers)製作的美耐板，這是個老牌的英國西屋電氣公司，製造一種美耐板，叫做 Traffolyte (根據美國生產此種產品的賓夕法尼亞州的特拉福德命名)。在調查全球範圍內該領域的製造商之後，找到了富美家公司及其母公司美國氰胺公司，並同它們結成特許頒發的關係，製造富美家品牌的產品。戰後形勢的艱難和短缺導致建築延誤——泰恩賽德工廠直到 1948 年才開工，到 1952 年才開始盈利。但最終得到了回報。

德拉魯公司 1953 年的一份董事報告說，富美家美耐板的使用範圍大大擴大了：「這是現在裝備現代化的廚房的必備材料。同時，美耐板正在被越來越多地用於食堂、運輸服務、傢俱、商店設施和其他各種各樣的用途。」本公司與富美家品牌開始向歐洲擴展：1954 年發展到法國，1956 年發展到西班牙——從成立於 1964 年以前的一家在大多數歐洲國家經營的名為 Ceplastica 的公司接手。1962 年，德拉魯成立了與巴黎的法國分公司有關的比利時分公司。1948 年，在澳洲成立了分公司，那裡 Laminex 是佔主導地位的美耐板製造商，並於 1958 年在悉尼郊區松雷開設了一家工廠。1959 年，在紐西蘭奧克蘭附近的帕帕庫拉建立了一家工廠。另外還在印度設立了分公司。

1958 年，德拉魯和美國氰胺公司的高管們同意修改協議。德拉魯希望不只有一個簡單的許可證，以保護其未來的增長，公司達成一項新的安排，現名為富美家有限公司的 60% 的

间，印刷厂被德国轰炸机摧毁。设备被转移到乡下，德拉鲁在这里为数十个被占领国家的流亡政府印刷货币。货币被存放在 80 英尺深的洞穴里，等每个国家被解放后提出来使用。

但是，在战争结束后，多样化成为必要——印刷货币和官方文件的市场很有限。德拉鲁希望扩展到新兴的消费者和高科技市场。该公司开始在英格兰东北部纽卡斯尔附近的泰恩赛德建造一家工厂。德拉鲁战前曾涉足塑料，用它们制作过钢笔系列的东西。因为看到和印刷之间的联系，高级管理人员在战后希望使用由大都会维克斯公司(Metropolitan Vickers)制作的耐火板，这是个老牌的英国西屋电气公司，制造一种耐火板，叫做 Traffolyte (根据美国生产此种产品的宾夕法尼亚州的特拉福德命名)。在调查全球范围内该领域的制造商之后，找到了富美家公司及其母公司美国氰胺公司，并同它们结成特许颁发的关系，制造富美家品牌的产品。战后形势的艰难和短缺导致建筑延误——泰恩赛德工厂直到 1948 年才开工，到 1952 年才开始盈利。但最终得到了回报。

德拉鲁公司 1953 年的一份董事报告说，富美家®装饰耐火板的使用范围大大扩大了："这是现在装备现代化的厨房的必备材料。同时，耐火板正在被越来越多地用于食堂、运输服务、家具、商店设施和其他各种各样的用途。"本公司与富美家品牌开始向欧洲扩展：1954 年发展到法国，1956 年发展到西班牙——从成立于 1964 年以前的一家在大多数欧洲国家经营的名为 Ceplastica 的公司接手。1962 年，德拉鲁成立了与巴黎的法国分公司有关的比利时分公司。1948 年，在澳大利亚成立了分公司，那里 Lamine 是占主导地位的耐火板制造商，并于 1958 年在悉尼郊区松雷开设了一家工厂。1959 年，在新西兰奥克兰附近的帕帕库拉建立了一家工厂。另外还在印度设立了分公司。

นั้น ซึ่งมีชื่อว่า Ceplastica ที่ก่อตั้งขึ้นเมื่อปี ค.ศ. 1946 และประกอบการอยู่ในประเทศส่วนใหญ่ในทวีปยุโรป ต่อมาในปี ค.ศ. 1962 บริษัท เดอ ลา รู ตั้งสาขาขึ้นในประเทศเบลเยียมเพื่อเชื่อมโยงกับสาขาในประเทศฝรั่งเศสที่ตั้งอยู่ในกรุงปารีส ในปี ค.ศ. 1948 บริษัทตั้งสาขาในประเทศออสเตรเลีย ซึ่งเป็นที่ที่บริษัทลามิเนกซ์เป็นผู้ผลิตแผ่นลามิเนทรายหลักอยู่ และในปี ค.ศ. 1958 ได้เปิดโรงงานที่เมืองทอร์นเลห์ นอกเมืองซิดนีย์ ในปี ค.ศ. 1959 บริษัทได้โรงงานที่เมืองพาพาคูรา ใกล้เมืองอ็อคแลนด์ ประเทศนิวซีแลนด์ และยังตั้งสาขาในประเทศอินเดียอีกด้วย

ในปี ค.ศ. 1958 เหล่าเจ้าหน้าที่บริหารของบริษัท เดอ ลา รู และบริษัท อเมริกัน ไซอานามิด ตกลงที่จะแก้ไขข้อตกลงที่ทำระหว่างกัน บริษัท เดอ ลา รู ต้องการมากกว่าเพียงการให้สิทธิ์ เพื่อปกป้องการเจริญเติบโตในอนาคตของบริษัท ทั้งสองบริษัทได้ทำข้อตกลงใหม่ขึ้นมา โดยให้บริษัทอังกฤษชื่อกรรมสิทธิ์ในหุ้นร้อยละ 60 ของบริษัทชื่อ Formica Ltd. และร้อยละ 40 ถือโดยบริษัทอเมริกัน ไซอานามิด พอมาถึงช่วงทศวรรษที่ 1970 แม้ว่าบริษัทจะจัดส่งผลิตภัณฑ์มูลค่ามากกว่าครึ่งหนึ่งของยอดขายของ บริษัท เดอ ลา รู แต่ผู้บริหารของบริษัทมองเห็นแนวโน้มในอนาคตที่แฝงของผลิตภัณฑ์ที่ห้อฟอร์ไมก้า ซึ่งเป็นผลของการแข่งขันและตลาดที่เติบโตเต็มที่สำหรับผลิตภัณฑ์นี้ ประวัติศาสตร์ของบริษัทได้บันทึกไว้ว่า "ความตึงเครียดปรากฏขึ้นอย่างชัดเจนที่บริษัทฟอร์ไมก้า" "บริษัทหลายบริษัทมากได้เปลี่ยนมาผลิตพลาสติกลามิเนททั่วโลก ซึ่งเป็นสถานการณ์ที่แตกต่างจากในช่วงทศวรรษที่ 50 และ 60 อย่างสิ้นเชิง" บริษัท เดอ ลา รู ได้รับกำไรเพียงร้อยละ 60 ของกำไรที่บริษัทร่วมทุนกัน บริษัท ฟอร์ไมก้า คอร์ปอเรชั่น ในสหรัฐอเมริกาได้รับ ในขณะที่บริษัทมีภาระจากเงินกู้ร้อยละ 100 ที่ได้ให้บริษัทกู้ ในปี ค.ศ. 1977 สองปีหลังจากการเจรจาต่อรองบริษัท เดอ ลา รู ขายสิทธิ์กลับไปให้บริษัทอเมริกัน ไซอานามิด เป็นจำนวนเงิน 9.6 ล้านปอนด์สเตอร์ลิง ซึ่งเทียบเท่ากับจำนวนเงินประมาณ 16.3 ล้านดอลลาร์สหรัฐในปัจจุบัน

เหตุการณ์รอบโลก

อย่างไรก็ตาม ในขณะที่ข้อตกลงดังกล่าวมาถึงจุดยุติ ยี่ห้อฟอร์ไมก้ากำลังเติบโตอย่างแข็งแกร่งทั่วโลก และเข้าถึงทุกมุมของโลกเห็นได้จากใบรอัน เทรเวอร์ส ผู้จัดการฝ่ายการตลาดผลิตภัณฑ์ลามิเนทที่มีประสบการณ์ในประเทศนิวซีแลนด์ กล่าวไว้ว่า ยี่ห้อฟอร์ไมก้าที่มีชื่อเสียงไปทั่วโลกเพราะบริษัทลงทุนกับสถาปนิกและนักออกแบบ

l'histoire officielle de l'entreprise, « La tension montait très clairement chez Formica. De nombreuses entreprises se sont lancées dans les plastiques stratifiés dans le monde. Dans les années 50 et 60, le jeu devenait complètement différent. » De La Rue a reçu seulement 60 pour cent des profits de sa collaboration avec la Formica Corporation des États-Unis tout en supportant l'obligation de 100 pour cent de l'emprunt pour la société commune. En 1977, après deux ans de négociations, De La Rue a revendu ses droits à American Cyanamid pour 9,6 millions de livres sterling, soit l'équivalent d'environ 16,3 millions de dollars américains de l'époque.

Autour du globe

Alors même que cette transaction était finalisée, la marque Formica était de plus en plus présente dans le monde entier. Elle allait atteindre les confins de la planète. Vétéran dans la gestion du marketing des stratifiés, Bryan Travers (Nouvelle-Zélande) a par exemple déclaré que la marque Formica avait une réputation mondiale grâce aux architectes et aux designers qu'elle côtoyait. L'un des points forts de la marque était sa culture globale du design. Dès les années 1950, soutient-il, Formica Corporation a obtenu une reconnaissance mondiale pour le design et le goût qui ont été reconnus dans toute l'Europe et les Amériques. Ceci était lié à l'évolution de la mode et du goût. Comme le rappelle Michel Broussard, un pionnier de la fabrication des plaques de presse pour toutes les entreprises dans le monde, « En Europe dans les années 1950 et 1960, le stratifié Formica a été largement diffusé à la télévision et dans les médias grand public comme le matériau absolu de la maison moderne. » La même vision qui a dominé le marché en pleine expansion au Royaume-Uni et aux États-Unis dans les années 1950 a prévalu ici. « Les fortes campagnes de sensibilisation lancées à l'époque ont créé un héritage inestimable et résonnent encore cinquante ans plus tard », explique Broussard. Une nouvelle série de finitions telles que l'ardoise, le cuir, l'osier et le bambou ont joué un rôle important à la fin des années 1970 en Europe. Les

nera sólida alrededor del mundo. Llegó a todos los rincones del planeta. El experimentado gerente de *marketing* Bryan Travers, en Nueva Zelanda, dice, por ejemplo, que la marca Formica tenía una reputación mundial porque cultivaba a arquitectos y diseñadores. Una de las fortalezas de la marca fue su cultura de diseño global. A principios de la década de los cincuenta, sostiene, Formica Corporation había creado un reconocimiento global por diseño y buen gusto que abarcaba de Europa y América hasta cualquier lugar remoto. Estaba ligada a las tendencias de moda y buen gusto. "En Europa", recuerda Michel Broussard, que fue pionero en fabricar placas prensadas para todas las plantas de empresas alrededor del mundo, "en la década de los cincuenta y de los sesenta, el laminado Formica se publicitaba masivamente en la televisión y en otros medios de comunicación para el consumo como un material 'imprescindible' que queda muy bien en la casa moderna". La misma visión que dominaba el mercado en expansión en el Reino Unido y los Estados Unidos en la década de los cincuenta prevalecía aquí. "Las comunicaciones audaces y las campañas de concienciación creadas en esa época dejaron un legado invaluable a nuestro patrimonio y todavía resuenan, cincuenta años después", expresa Broussard. También eran importantes en Europa, a fines de la década de los setenta, una serie de nuevos acabados dimensionales, como pizarra, cuero, mimbre y bambú. Las nuevas texturas representaban un intento de crear una calidad táctil para igualar la calidad visual y para diferenciarse de la competencia.

En América del Sur, el interés en los productos de la marca Formica creció con las décadas, incluso cuando el mercado experimentaba una serie de cambios comerciales complejos. De La Rue, que en virtud del acuerdo con American Cyanamid controlaba la marca Formica en América del Sur, comenzó a vender en Brasil a principios de la década de los sesenta. En las décadas de los setenta y de los ochenta, la producción del laminado de la marca Formica estaba a cargo de las subsidiarias de American Cyanamid en América del Sur. Actualmente, el laminado Formica se produce independientemente en América del Sur

kaukonäköisyys, joka hallitsi laajentuvia markkinoita Yhdistyneessä kuningaskunnassa ja Yhdysvalloissa 1950-luvulla, pääsi voitolle täällä. "Näihin aikoihin luodut rohkea yhteydenpito ja tietoisuuskampanjat antoivat korvaamattoman perinnön omaisuudellemme ja ne kaikuvat edelleen, viisikymmentä vuotta myöhemmin," sanoo Broussard. 1970-luvun loppupuolella Euroopassa olivat tärkeitä myös sarja uusia ulotteisia pintoja, kuten laattakivi, nahka, pajunvitsa ja bambu. Uudet tekstuurit edustivat pyrkimystä luoda käsinkosketeltavaa laatua, joka vastaisi näkyvää laatua ja erottuisi kilpailijoista.

Etelä-Amerikassa mielenkiinto kasvoi Formica-merkkisiä tuotteita kohtaan vuosikymmenien kuluessa, vaikka markkinoilla tapahtuikin sarja monimutkaisia liiketoiminnan muutoksia. American Cyanamidin kanssa tehdyn sopimuksen mukaisesti De La Rue kontrolloi Formica-tavaramerkkiä Etelä-Amerikassa ja alkoi myynnin Brasiliassa 1960-luvun alkupuolella. American Cyanamidin etelä-amerikkalaiset tytäryhtiöt tuottivat Formica-merkkistä laminaattia 1970- ja 1980-luvulla. Formica-laminaattia valmistetaan tällä hetkellä itsenäisesti Etelä-Amerikassa erilaisilla yhteen kuulumattomille teollisuusyhtiöille annetuilla lisensseillä.

Etelä-Afrikassa Formica-laminaattia valmisti 1970-luvulla lisenssillä yhtiö nimeltään Decorative Boards. Oikeudet ja teknologiat siirtyivät fuusioiden sarjassa ja yhtiöstä tuli Laminate Industries, American Cyanamidin ja PG Bisonin yhteisyritys. PG Bison hankki myöhemmin yksinomaiset oikeudet. Nykyisin se on moninainen rakennustuotteiden yritys Alroden alueella, Johannesburgin lähellä, valmistaen yhtäjaksoista eli matalapaineista laminaattia (CPL) sekä pinnoitettuja levyjä. Se valmisti oman melamiininsa ja muita hartseja ja Formica-merkkistä korkeapainelaminaattia (HPL), vieden niitä muihin Afrikan maihin, kunnes alkoi ostaa HPL:ää suoraan Formica Groupin Euroopan jaostolta v. 2011 jälkeen, suljettuaan oman HPL-tehtaansa.

Vuonna 1965 Formica Corporation, englantilaisen lisenssinhaltijansa De La Ruen kautta, lähti Intian markkinoille yhteisyrityksenä Bombay Burmah Trading Companyn kanssa. Vuonna

所有權歸總部在英國的公司所有，40% 由美國氰胺公司保留。但到了二十世紀七十年代，雖然這項安排提供了德拉魯的銷售量的一半以上，公司的領導層看到了富美家品牌產品未來的衰退，這是競爭和市場成熟的結果。公司官方歷史中記載「壓力在富美家表現得非常清楚。一大批公司在世界各地已經進入層壓塑膠的領域。在上世紀五十年代和六十年代，這是完全不同的狀況。」德拉魯從在美國與富美公司合資企業只收到 60% 的利潤，卻為共同企業承擔了 100% 的借貸。1977 年，經過兩年的談判，德拉魯把所有權以 960 萬英鎊的價格售回給美國氰胺公司，約合 1,630 萬美元。

全球縱覽

然而，就在這筆交易已成定局之時，富美家品牌的發展壯大遍布世界各地。它遍及這個星球的每一個角落。例如，紐西蘭退伍軍人美耐板市場行銷經理布賴恩·特拉沃斯（Bryan Travers）說，富美家品牌享有世界聲譽，因為它培養了建築師和設計師。品牌的優勢之一是其設計的全球文化。他說，早在二十世紀五十年代，富美家公司已建立了全球認可的設計和品味，從歐洲和美洲到每一個行銷點。它與時尚和品味的趨勢相連。米歇爾·布魯薩爾（Michael Broussard）回憶說：「在歐洲，二十世紀五十年代，富美家美耐板在電視和其他消費者媒體上大做廣告，說是現代家居新的理想‘必備’材料。」布魯薩爾曾為世界各地的工廠率先製作美耐板模板。在英國和美國不斷擴大的市場佔主導的同樣願景在這裡也很盛行。布魯薩爾說：「當時製造的大膽溝通和宣傳活動為我們的權益提供了寶貴的遺產，五十年後仍有影響。」在二十世紀七十年代的歐洲同樣重要的是一系列新的空間板材，如石板、皮革、柳條和竹子。新的紋理代表了一種創造與

1958 年，德拉魯和美国氰胺公司的高管们同意修改协议。德拉鲁希望不只有一个简单的许可证，以保护其未来的增长，公司达成一项新的安排，现名为富美家有限公司的 60% 的所有权归总部在英国的公司所有，40% 由美国氰胺公司保留。但到了二十世纪七十年代，虽然这项安排提供了德拉鲁的销售量的一半以上，公司的领导层看到了富美家品牌产品未来的衰退，这是竞争和市场成熟的结果。公司官方历史中记载"压力在富美家表现得非常清楚。一大批公司在世界各地已经进入层压塑料的领域。在上世纪五十年代和六十年代，这是完全不同的状况。"德拉鲁从在美国与富美家公司合资企业只收到 60% 的利润，却为共同企业承担了 100% 的借贷。1977 年，经过两年的谈判，德拉鲁把所有权以 960 万英镑的价格售回给美国氰胺公司，约合 1,630 万美元。

全球纵览

然而，就在这笔交易已成定局之时，富美家品牌的发展壮大遍布世界各地。它遍及这个星球的每一个角落。例如，新西兰退伍军人耐火板市场营销经理布赖恩·特拉沃斯（Bryan Travers）说，富美家品牌享有世界声誉，因为它培养了建筑师和设计师。品牌的优势之一是其设计的全球文化。他说，早在二十世纪五十年代，富美家公司已建立了全球认可的设计和品味，从欧洲和美洲到每一个营销点。它与时尚和品味的趋势相连。米歇尔·布鲁萨尔（Michael Broussard）回忆说："在欧洲，二十世纪五十年代，富美家®装饰耐火板在电视和其他消费者媒体上大做广告，说是现代家居新的理想'必备'材料。"布鲁萨尔曾为世界各地的工厂率先制作耐火板模板。在英国和美国不断扩大的市场占主导的同样愿景在这里也很盛行。布鲁萨尔说："当时制造的大胆沟通和宣传活动为我们的权益提供了宝贵的遗产，五十年后仍有影响。"在二十世

จุดแข็งของยี่ห้อนี้อันหนึ่งคือ วัฒนธรรมการออกแบบที่บริษัทมีในทั่วโลก ย้อนกลับไปตั้งแต่ในช่วงทศวรรษที่ 1950 เทรเวอร์สระบุว่าบริษัท ฟอร์ไมก้า คอร์ปอเรชั่น ได้สร้างการยอมรับไปทั่วโลกในเรื่องการออกแบบและรสนิยมที่ได้รับจากในทวีปยุโรป ทวีปอเมริกาไปจนถึงดินแดนห่างไกลทุกแห่ง ซึ่งเป็นไปตามกระแสความนิยมและรสนิยม ไมเคิล บรูสซาร์ด ซึ่งเป็นผู้บุกเบิกการทำลวดลายอัดสำหรับโรงงานของบริษัททุกแห่งรอบโลก หวนระลึกว่า "ในยุโรป ในช่วงทศวรรษที่ 1950 และ 1960 แผ่นลามิเนทฟอร์ไมก้ามีการโฆษณาอย่างหนักในโทรทัศน์และในสื่อผู้บริโภคอื่นๆ ว่าเป็นวัสดุที่ 'ต้องมีให้ได้' ในบ้านสมัยใหม่" วิสัยทัศน์เดียวกันกับที่ครองตลาดที่ขยายตัวในสหราชอาณาจักรและสหรัฐอเมริกาในช่วงทศวรรษที่ 1950 เป็นจริงที่นี่ "การสื่อสารอย่างหนักและแคมเปญเพื่อให้ผลิตภัณฑ์เป็นที่รู้จักที่ทำกันในเวลานั้นให้มรดกอันล้ำค่าเพื่อเป็นทุนของเราและยังคงก้องกังวานอยู่อีกห้าสิบปีต่อมา" สิ่งที่มีความสำคัญเช่นกันในยุโรปในช่วงปลายทศวรรษที่ 1970 คือ ลามิเนทผิวสัมผัสมิติใหม่ที่หลากหลาย เช่น ผิวหินชนวน ผิวหนัง ผิวไม้หวาย และผิวไม้ไผ่ ผิวสัมผัสใหม่แสดงถึงความพยายามที่จะสร้างคุณภาพผิวสัมผัสเพื่อให้ตรงกับคุณภาพที่มองเห็น และเพื่อสร้างความแตกต่างจากคู่แข่ง

ในอเมริกาใต้มีความสนใจในผลิตภัณฑ์ยี่ห้อฟอร์ไมก้าเติบโตในช่วงหลายทศวรรษที่ผ่านมา แม้ในขณะที่ตลาดจะประสบกับการเปลี่ยนแปลงทางธุรกิจที่ซับซ้อน บริษัทเดอ ลา รู ซึ่งอยู่ภายใต้ข้อตกลงกับ บริษัทอเมริกัน ไซอานามิด ควบคุมยี่ห้อฟอร์ไมก้าในอเมริกาใต้ เริ่มจำหน่ายผลิตภัณฑ์ในประเทศบราซิลในช่วงต้นทศวรรษที่ 1960 ในช่วงทศวรรษที่ 1970 และ 1980 แผ่นลามิเนทฟอร์ไมก้าผลิตขึ้นโดยบริษัทลูกในอเมริกาใต้ของบริษัท อเมริกัน ไซอานามิด ทุกวันนี้แผ่นลามิเนทฟอร์ไมก้าผลิตโดยอิสระในอเมริกาใต้ภายใต้สัญญาให้สิทธิต่างๆ ที่ให้แก่บริษัทผู้ผลิตที่ไม่เกี่ยวข้องกัน

ในช่วงทศวรรษที่ 1970 ในแอฟริกาใต้แผ่นลามิเนทฟอร์ไมก้าผลิตขึ้นภายใต้การให้สิทธิแก่บริษัทหนึ่ง ที่มีชื่อว่า Decorative Boards สิทธิและเทคโนโลยีต่างๆ เปลี่ยนแปลงไปตามการรวมบริษัท และต่อมาบริษัทกลายเป็น Laminate Industries ที่ตั้งขึ้นโดยบริษัท อเมริกัน ไซอานามิด และบริษัทพีจี บีซัน ต่อมาบริษัท พีจี บีซัน ได้รับสิทธิแต่เพียงผู้เดียว ปัจจุบัน บริษัทนี้เป็นบริษัทผลิตผลิตภัณฑ์สำหรับการก่อสร้างที่มีความหลากหลายในบริเวณเมืองอัลโรด ใกล้กับ

FORMICA
garantiza
la calidad de un
tablero plástico

nouvelles textures représentaient une tentative de création d'une qualité tactile correspondant à la qualité visuelle et de différenciation par rapport aux concurrents.

En Amérique du Sud, l'intérêt pour les produits Formica a grandi au fil des décennies, alors même que le marché a connu des évolutions complexes. De La Rue, qui en vertu de son entente avec American Cyanamid contrôlait la marque Formica en Amérique du Sud, a commencé à vendre au Brésil dans les années 1960. Dans les années 1970 et 1980, le stratifié Formica a été produit par les filiales sud-américaines d'American Cyanamid. Aujourd'hui, le stratifié Formica est produit indépendamment en Amérique du Sud sous différentes licences par des entreprises indépendantes.

Dans les années 1970 en Afrique du Sud, le stratifié Formica a été produit sous licence par une entreprise

bajo diversas licencias con empresas fabricantes no relacionadas entre sí.

En la década de los setenta en Sudáfrica, el laminado Formica era producido bajo licencia por una empresa denominada Decorative Boards. Los derechos y las tecnologías se traspasaban mediante una serie de fusiones, y la empresa se convirtió en Laminate Industries, un esfuerzo conjunto de American Cyanamid y PG Bison. Posteriormente, PG Bison adquirió los derechos absolutos. Actualmente, es una empresa de productos de construcción diversificados en el área de Alrode, cerca de Johannesburgo, que fabrica laminados de proceso continuo (*continuous process laminate*, CPL) o de baja presión y tableros revestidos. Fabricaba su propia melamina, además de otras resinas, y el laminado de alta presión (*high pressure laminate*, HPL) de la marca Formica, que exportaba a otros países africanos hasta que

1966 Formica avasi Intian tehdaslaitoksen Punessa, teollisuuskaupungissa, jossa oli auto- ja muita tehtaita, noin 160 km Mumbaista etelään. Se oli lajissaan ensimmäinen Intiassa ja tuote sai hyvän vastaanoton. Vuosikymmenien ajan myynnin kasvu pysyi samalla tasolla Intian vankan talouskasvun kanssa. Sitten 1970-luvun loppupuolella Intian hallinto kävi läpi dramaattisen muutoksen; ulkomaiselle omistukselle ja pääoman kotiin palauttamiselle asetettiin rajoituksia. Tuottoja ei voitu enää viedä maan ulkopuolelle. Yhtiö jätti Intian markkinat, kuten monet kansainväliset yhtiöt. Se myi omistuksen paikalliselle teollisuuslaitokselle, antaen lisenssin käyttää Formica-tavaramerkkiä Intiassa. Lisenssioikeudet otettiin takaisin vasta v. 2008, sen jälkeen kun Intian talous jälleen avautui ja politiikassa tapahtui muutoksia. Yhtiö päätti käynnistää uudelleen oman toimintansa Intiassa.

Muualla Aasiassa, De La Ruen järjestelyn ulkopuolella, Formica Corporation laajeni Kaukoitään vasta 1970-luvulla. Tavaramerkki ja liiketoiminta osoittautuivat pian hyvin vahvoiksi. Yhtiö myi Formica-laminaattia edustajien kautta Hong Kongissa, Singaporessa, Malesiassa ja Taiwanissa 1970-luvulla. "Arkkitehdit ja suunnittelijat olivat niin ihastuneita tavaramerkkiin, että yhtiö alkoi sijoittaa tuotantotiloihin paikallisia Aasian markkinoita tukemaan", sanoo Steve Kuo, Formica Asia -yhtiön nykyisin eläkkeellä oleva pitkäaikainen toimitusjohtaja. Vuoteen 1980 mennessä Formica Corporation oli valmiina ensimmäistä Aasian tehdasta varten, joka avattiin Taiwanissa.

Uusia markkinoita avautui 1980-uvulla ja 1990-luvun alkuvuosina. Formica-merkkisen laminaatin tuotantolaitokset, jotka oli avattu De La Ruen aikana 1940-luvun loppupuolella ja 1950-luvulla Australiassa ja Uudessa-Seelannissa, laajenivat 1980-luvun alussa itse asiassa hankkimalla oikeudet Laminex-laminaatin tavaramerkkiin kyseisillä markkinoilla, valmistaen tuotetta kummankin merkkinä muutaman lyhyen vuoden ajan 1980-luvulla. Tämä uusi keskinäisten yhteyksien aikakausi Laminex- ja Formica-tavaramerkkien välillä, joka alkoi 1940-luvun loppupuolella Sykesin kyseisen vierailun aikana, valmisti tietä vuosikausia

視覺品質相匹配的觸覺品質，以區別於競爭對手。

在南美洲，對富美家品牌產品的興趣幾十年來都在增長，即使是在市場經歷了一系列複雜的業務變化之時亦如此。德拉魯根據其與美國氰胺公司的協議控制了富美家南美洲品牌，在二十世紀六十年代初開始在巴西銷售。在二十世紀七十年代和八十年代，富美家品牌美耐板是由美國氰胺公司南美子公司生產。今天，富美家美耐板是由南美無關聯的製造商根據不同的許可證製造。

在二十世紀七十年代的南非，富美家美耐板是根據許可證由一家名為裝飾板公司(Decorative Boards)的公司生產。股權和和技術在一系列的兼並中轉來轉去，公司變為美耐板工業——美國氰胺公司和 PG 野牛公司(PG Bison)的合資企業。PG 野牛後來獲得獨家權利。今天，它是約翰內斯堡附近的 Alrode 區一家多元化併建築產品公司，生產連續或低壓美耐板(CPL)和塗層板。它製造自己使用的三聚氰胺及其他樹脂和富美家品牌高壓美耐板(HPL)，向非洲國家出口，直到2011年關閉自己的 HPL 工廠後，開始從富美家集團的歐洲分部直接購買 HPL。

1965 年，富美家公司在英國執照持有人德拉魯的領導下，與孟買伯馬貿易公司(Bombay Burmah Trading Company)組成合資企業，進軍印度市場。1966 年，富美家在工業城市浦那開設了一家印度製造廠，浦那是孟買以南約 100 公里處的一個有汽車和其他工廠的工業城市。這是印度的第一個此類工廠，產品很受歡迎。十年來，銷售增長與印度經濟的強勁增長保持一致的步伐。然後，在二十世紀七十年代後期，印度政府經歷了戲劇性的變化，強行控制外國所有權，進行資金返還。利潤不可能再被帶到國外。該公司像其他許多公司一樣離開了印度市場。它向當地一家工業公

紀七十年代的歐洲同樣重要的是一系列新的空間板材，如石板、皮革、柳條和竹子。新的紋理代表了一種創造與視覺品質相匹配的觸覺品質，以區別于競爭對手。

在南美洲，对富美家品牌产品的兴趣几十年来都在增长，即使是在市场经历了一系列复杂的业务变化之时亦如此。德拉鲁根据其与美国氰胺公司的协议控制了富美家南美洲品牌，在二十世纪六十年代初开始在巴西销售。在二十世纪七十年代和八十年代，富美家品牌耐火板是由美国氰胺公司南美子公司生产。今天，富美家®装饰耐火板是由南美无关联的制造商根据不同的许可证制造。

在二十世纪七十年代的南非，富美家®装饰耐火板是根据许可证由一家名为装饰板公司(Decorative Boards)的公司生产。股权和和技术在一系列的兼并中转来转去，公司变为耐火板工业——美国氰胺公司和 PG 野牛公司(PG Bison)的合资企业。PG 野牛后来获得独家权利。今天，它是约翰内斯堡附近的 Alrode 区一家多元化的建筑产品公司，生产连续或低压耐火板(CPL)和涂层板。它制造自己使用的三聚氰胺及其他树脂和富美家品牌高压耐火板(HPL)，向非洲国家出

กรุงโยฮันเนสเบิร์ก และผลิตลามิเนตต่อเนื่องหรือแรงดันต่ำ (CPL) และแผ่นบอร์ดเคลือบบริษัทผลิตเมลามีนและเรซินชนิดต่างๆ ของบริษัทเอง และผลิตแผ่นลามิเนตแรงอัดดันสูงยี่ห้อฟอร์ไมก้า และส่งออกไปยังประเทศอื่นๆ ในทวีปแอฟริกาจนกระทั่งบริษัทเริ่มซื้อแผ่นลามิเนตแรงอัดดันสูง โดยตรงจากกลุ่มบริษัทฟอร์ไมก้าในยุโรปในปี ค.ศ. 2011 หลังจากปิดโรงงานลามิเนตแรงอัดดันสูงไป

ในปี ค.ศ. 1965 บริษัท ฟอร์ไมก้าคอร์ปอเรชั่น ภายใต้บริษัท เดอ ลา รู ผู้รับสิทธิ์ในสหรัฐอาณาจักร เข้าสู่ตลาดประเทศอินเดียโดยการร่วมทุนกับบริษัท บอมเบย์เบอร์มาห์ เทรดดิ้ง ในปี ค.ศ. 1966 บริษัทฟอร์ไมก้าเปิดโรงงานผลิตในประเทศอินเดียที่เมืองปูเน ซึ่งเป็นเมืองอุตสาหกรรมที่มีโรงงานผลิตรถยนต์และโรงงานอื่น อยู่ห่างจากเมืองมุมไบไปทางทิศใต้ประมาณ 100 ไมล์ โรงงานแห่งนี้เป็นโรงงานผลิตผลิตภัณฑ์ชนิดนี้แห่งแรกในประเทศอินเดีย และผลิตภัณฑ์ได้รับการตอบรับที่มาก ภายในหนึ่งทศวรรษยอดขายเติบโตไปตามการเติบโตที่แข็งแกร่งของเศรษฐกิจประเทศอินเดีย ต่อมาในช่วงปลายทศวรรษที่ 1970 รัฐบาลอินเดียต้องเผชิญกับการเปลี่ยนแปลงอย่างมาก มีการกำหนดมาตรการควบคุมกรรมสิทธิ์ของชาวต่างชาติและการส่งเงินลงทุนกลับประเทศ บริษัทส่งกำไรออกนอกประเทศไม่ได้ บริษัทจึงออกจากตลาดอินเดียเช่นเดียวกับบริษัทต่างชาติจำนวนมาก บริษัทขายกรรมสิทธิ์ให้แก่บริษัทอุตสาหกรรมในท้องถิ่น โดยให้สิทธิ์ใช้ยี่ห้อฟอร์ไมก้าในประเทศอินเดีย หลังจากประเทศอินเดียเปิดเศรษฐกิจอีกครั้งและมีการเปลี่ยนแปลงนโยบายในปี ค.ศ. 2008 บริษัทจึงเพิกถอนการให้สิทธิ์ และตัดสินใจกลับมาประกอบการเองในประเทศอินเดียอีกครั้ง

บริษัท ฟอร์ไมก้า คอร์ปอเรชั่น ไม่ได้ขายไปยังประเทศอื่นใดในเอเชียที่อยู่นอกเหนือข้อตกลงกับบริษัท เดอ ลา รู จนกระทั่งช่วงทศวรรษที่ 1970 ซึ่งเป็นช่วงที่บริษัทขยายไปยังตะวันออกไกล ยี่ห้อและธุรกิจได้พิสูจน์ตนเองให้เห็นว่ามีความแข็งแรงมากอย่างรวดเร็ว บริษัทจำหน่ายแผ่นลามิเนตฟอร์ไมก้าผ่านตัวแทนในฮ่องกง สิงคโปร์มาเลเซีย และไต้หวันในช่วงทศวรรษที่ 1970 สตีฟ กัว ผู้ดำรงตำแหน่งประธานบริษัทฟอร์ไมก้าเอเชียเป็นเวลานาน ซึ่งปัจจุบันได้เกษียณอายุแล้ว กล่าวว่า "สถาปนิกและนักออกแบบชื่นชอบยี่ห้อมากจนบริษัทต้องเริ่มลงทุนในโรงงานผลิตเพื่อรองรับตลาดในเอเชีย" พอถึงปี ค.ศ. 1980 บริษัท ฟอร์ไมก้าคอร์ปอเรชั่น ก็พร้อมเปิดโรงงานแห่งแรกในเอเชีย ที่ได้ไต้หวัน

appelée Decorative Boards. Les licences et les technologies ont été déplacées dans diverses acquisitions d'entreprise et l'entreprise est devenue Laminate Industries, une association entre American Cyanamid et PG Bison. PG Bison a ensuite acquis les droits exclusifs. Aujourd'hui, il s'agit d'une entreprise diversifiée de produits de construction dans la zone d'Alrode, près de Johannesbourg, qui produit du stratifié continu ou basse pression (CPL) et des panneaux enduits. Elle a réalisé sa propre mélamine et d'autres résines ainsi que le stratifié de marque Formica (HPL), l'exportation vers d'autres pays africains et a commencé à acheter du HPL directement à partir de la division européenne de Formica Group en 2011, après la fermeture de son usine HPL.

En 1965, Formica Corporation, en vertu de la licence accordée à son partenaire britannique De La Rue, est entré sur le marché indien dans le cadre d'un accord avec la Société Bombay Burmah Trading. En 1966, Formica a ouvert une usine de fabrication indienne à Pune, la ville industrielle comprenant des usines automobiles et autres, à environ 150 km au sud de Mumbai. Il a été le premier de son genre en Inde et le produit a été très bien accueilli. Pendant une décennie, les ventes ont augmenté au même rythme que l'ensemble de l'économie indienne en croissance rapide. Puis, à la fin des années 1970, le gouvernement de l'Inde a changé radicalement et des contrôles ont limité les propriétés étrangères et le rapatriement des capitaux. Les bénéfices ne pouvaient plus quitter le pays. L'entreprise a quitté le marché indien, à l'instar de nombreuses entreprises internationales. Elle a vendu sa participation à une entreprise industrielle locale, ainsi que les licences d'utilisation de la marque Formica en Inde. Ce n'est qu'en 2008, après la réouverture de l'économie indienne et les changements politiques, que les droits de licence ont été retirés. La société a décidé de relancer son activité en Inde.

Ailleurs en Asie, en dehors du contrat De La Rue, il a fallu attendre les années 1970 pour que Formica Corporation s'étende à l'Extrême-Orient. La marque et l'entreprise se sont dévelop-

comenzó a comprar HPL directamente de la división europea del Grupo Formica en 2011 tras el cierre de su fábrica de HPL.

En 1965, Formica Corporation, mediante su licenciatario británico De La Rue, ingresó en el mercado de la India en una empresa conjunta con Bombay Burmah Trading Company. En 1966, Formica abrió instalaciones de fabricación en la India, en Pune, la ciudad industrial con fábricas automotrices y de otro tipo, ubicada unos 160 kilómetros al sur de Bombay. Fue la primera de este tipo en la India, y el producto fue muy bien recibido. Durante una década, el crecimiento de las ventas se mantuvo al ritmo del crecimiento sólido de la economía de la India. Posteriormente, a fines de la década de los setenta, el Gobierno de la India experimentó un cambio significativo; se impusieron controles sobre la propiedad extranjera y la repatriación del capital. Las ganancias ya no podían llevarse fuera del país. La empresa dejó el mercado de la India, como lo hicieron muchas empresas internacionales. Vendió su propiedad a una casa industrial local, otorgando la licencia para utilizar la marca Formica en la India. No fue hasta 2008, tras la reapertura de la economía de la India y cambios en las políticas, que se retiraron los derechos de licencia. La empresa decidió, una vez más, comenzar su propia operación en la India.

En otros lugares de Asia, fuera del arreglo de De La Rue, no fue hasta la década de los setenta que Formica Corporation se expandió al Lejano Oriente. La marca y la empresa se consolidaron rápidamente. La empresa vendía el laminado Formica a través de agentes en Hong Kong, Singapur, Malasia y Taiwán en la década de los setenta. "A los arquitectos y diseñadores les agradaba tanto la marca que la empresa comenzó a invertir en las instalaciones de fabricación para atender los mercados asiáticos locales", indica Steve Kuo, presidente durante mucho tiempo de Formica Asia, ya jubilado. En 1980, Formica Corporation estaba preparada para su primera planta en Asia, que abrió en Taiwán.

Se abrieron nuevos mercados durante la década de los ochenta y principios de la década de los noventa. Las plantas de fabricación del laminado marca For-

kestäville edestakaisille tavaramerkki- ja valmistussuhteille näiden kahden tavaramerkin omistajien kesken, laajenevilla Australian ja Uuden-Seelannin markkinoilla.

Vuonna 1992 Formica Corporation perusti Singaporen sivuliikkeen Formica (Singapore) Pte Ltd., ja v. 1993 se laajensi Koreaan nimellä Formica Korea Corp ja Malesiaan nimellä House of Formica (Malaysia). Sitten tuli varsinainen Kiina, jossa Formica-laminaatti lumosi suunnittelijat huippumateriaalina, rikkaana historiasta ja funktionaalisuudesta. Yhtiön kasvu tuli pysyttelemään Kiinan huimaavan räjähdysmäisen kasvun tasolla. Kiinan talouden alkaessa laajentua, Formica Corporation perusti Formica Shanghai -yrityksen v. 1994, valmistusta harjoittavana yhteisyrityksenä paikallishallinnon kanssa.

Jakelupisteitä perustettiin Pekingiin, Guangzhouhun ja Shenzheniin. Vuonna 2003 tulivat perässä myyntitoimisto ja jakelukeskus Dongguaniin, Etelä-Kiinaan ja v. 2006 toinen jakelukeskus Chengduun, Länsi-Kiinaan. Tultuaan liian suureksi ensimmäiseen tehtaaseen, yhtiö rakensi upouuden tehtaan v. 2005 ja laajensi v. 2006 siirtämällä pois ensimmäisen tehtaan voimavarat. Hankkimalla v. 2000 Perstorp Division of Surface Materials -jaoston, Perstorp AB Sweden -yhtiöltä, Formica Corporation laajensi edelleen Aasiassa. Siam Perstorpin välityksellä yhtiö sai menestyvän tehtaan ja Thaimaan liiketoiminnan, joka tukee nousevia Aasian markkinoita. Thaimaalainen tehdas laajennettiin v. 2004.

1960-luku: Maailmanmessut

Symboliseksi hetkeksi, jolloin Formica Corporation saapui "maailman huipulle" voitaisiin katsoa päivää, jolloin yhtiön näyttelytalo avattiin maailmanmessuilla New Yorkissa v. 1964. Talo ylpeili koko maailmalle ihanteellisesta elämäntyylistä Formica-merkkisillä laminaateilla. Formica-laminaatin rohkeat värit ja linjat 1950-luvulla toivat mieleen Chryslerien ja Cadillacien vauhdikkaat takasiivekkeet. Ne olivat täynnä luottamusta kuin uusi rock and roll musiikki, ja yhtä vapaamuotoisia kuin teini-ikäisten slangi ja maata hurmaa-

司出售了其所有權，給予在印度使用富美家品牌的許可證。直到 2008 年，印度經濟重新開放，政策起了變化，許可證才被收回。該公司決定再次開始在印度自己營銷。

在亞洲其他地區不在德拉魯的安排之內，直到二十世紀七十年代，富美家公司才將業務擴展至遠東。品牌與業務很快被證明非常強勁。二十世紀七十年代，公司透過香港、新加坡、馬來亞和泰國的代理商銷售富美家美耐板。現已退休的富美家亞洲區資深總裁史蒂夫·郭 (Steve Kuo) 說：「建築師和設計師如此喜愛這個品牌，以至於該公司開始在製造設施上投資，以支援亞洲本地市場。」到 1980 年，富美家公司已準備好在亞洲開設首家工廠，後來在臺灣開設。

二十世紀八十年代和九十年代，新的市場被打開。德拉魯在二十世紀四十年代後期和五十年代在澳洲和紐西蘭開設的富美家品牌美耐板製造工廠，在二十世紀八十年代初得到擴大，其途徑是收購了 Laminex 層壓品牌在這些市場中的經營權，在八十年代的短短幾年內使用兩個品牌製造產品。該 Laminex 和富美家品牌聯手的新時期開始於二十世紀四十年代塞克斯訪之時，為這兩種品牌的持有人在澳洲和紐西蘭市場商標和製造關係上多年的來往做好準備。

1992 年，富美家公司成立了新加坡分公司富美 (新加坡) 私人有限公司 (Formica (Singapore) Pte Ltd.)，並於 1993 年擴大到韓國，名為富美家韓國公司 (Formica Korea Corp)，在馬來西亞成立了富美家 (馬來西亞) 之家 (House of Formica (Malaysia))。然後是中國，富美家美耐板讓設計師們著迷，它既是一種優質材料，又有豐富的歷史和功能。該公司的增長步伐將會與中國人自己的令人目不暇接、呈指數的增長相媲美。隨著中國經濟開始擴張，富美家公司 1994 年成立了上海富美公

口，直到 2011 年关闭自己的 HPL 工厂后，开始从富美家集团的欧洲分部直接购买 HPL。

1965 年，富美家公司在英国执照持有人德拉鲁的领导下，与孟买伯马贸易公司 (Bombay Burmah Trading Company) 组成合资企业，进军印度市场。1966 年，富美家在工业城市浦那开设了一家印度制造厂，浦那是孟买以南约 100 公里处的一个有汽车和其他工厂的工业城市。这是印度的第一个此类工厂，产品很受欢迎。十年来，销售增长与印度经济的强劲增长保持一致的步伐。然后，在二十世纪七十年代后期，印度政府经历了戏剧性的变化，强行控制外国所有权，进行资金返还。利润不可能再被带到国外。该公司像其他许多公司一样离开了印度市场。它向当地一家工业公司出售了其所有权，给予在印度使用富美家品牌的许可证。直到 2008 年，印度经济重新开放，政策起了变化，许可证才被收回。该公司决定再次开始在印度自己经营。

在亚洲其他地区不在德拉鲁的安排之内，直到二十世纪七十年代，富美家公司才将业务扩展至远东。品牌与业务很快被证明非常强劲。二十世纪七十年代，公司通过香港、新加坡、马来亚和泰国的代理商销售富美家®装饰耐火板。现已退休的富美家亚洲区资深总裁史蒂夫·郭 (Steve Kuo) 说："建筑师和设计师如此喜爱这个品牌，以至于该公司开始在制造设施上投资，以支持亚洲本地市场。"到 1980 年，富美家公司已准备好在亚洲开设首家工厂，后来在台湾开设。

二十世纪八十年代和九十年代，新的市场被打开。德拉鲁在二十世纪四十年代后期和五十年代在澳大利亚和新西兰开设的富美家品牌耐火板制造厂，在二十世纪八十年代初得到扩大，其途径是收购了 Laminex 耐火板品牌在这些市场中的经营权，在八十年代的短短几年内使用两个品牌制造产品。该 Laminex 和富美家品牌联手的新时

ตลาดใหม่ๆ เริ่มเปิดในช่วงทศวรรษที่ 1980 และช่วงต้นทศวรรษที่ 1990 โรงงานผลิตลามินเนตที่ห้อฟอร์ไมก้า ซึ่งเคยเปิดดำเนินการภายใต้บริษัท เดอ ลา รู ในช่วงปลายทศวรรษที่ 1940 และทศวรรษที่ 1950 ในประเทศออสเตรเลียและนิวซีแลนด์ ขยายออกไปในช่วงต้นทศวรรษที่ 1980 โดยได้รับสิทธิ์ผลิตแผ่นลามิเนตที่ห้อลามิเนกซ์ ในตลาดเหล่านั้น และทำการผลิตผลิตภัณฑ์ภายใต้ทั้งสองยี่ห้อเป็นระยะเวลาสั้นๆ ในช่วงทศวรรษที่ 1980 เป็นอีกครั้งหนึ่งที่ยี่ห้อลามิเนกซ์และฟอร์ไมก้าเชื่อมโยงกัน ครั้งแรกในช่วงปลายทศวรรษที่ 1940 ที่ไฮก์สมาเยี่ยม ถือเป็นการเตรียมพร้อมไว้สำหรับปีแห่งความสัมพันธ์แบบกลับไปกลับมาของเครื่องหมายการค้าและการผลิตระหว่างเจ้าของยี่ห้อสินค้าทั้งสองในตลาดออสเตรเลียและนิวซีแลนด์ที่กำลังขยายตัว

ในปี ค.ศ. 1992 บริษัท ฟอร์ไมก้าคอร์ปอเรชั่น ได้จัดตั้งสาขาที่ประเทศสิงคโปร์ ซึ่งก็คือ Formica (Singapore) Pte Ltd. และในปี ค.ศ. 1993 บริษัทได้ขยายไปยังเกาหลีภายใต้ชื่อว่า Formica Korea Corp และในมาเลเซียภายใต้ชื่อว่า House of Formica (Malaysia) แล้วจึงมาที่จีน ซึ่งเป็นที่ที่แผ่นลามิเนทฟอร์ไมก้าทำให้นักออกแบบติดใจ ในฐานะวัสดุระดับพรีเมียม ซึ่งมีประวัติศาสตร์และการนำมาใช้ประโยชน์มากมาย การเจริญเติบโตของบริษัทก้าวไปตามการเจริญเติบโตอย่างก้าวกระโดดของจีนเอง และเนื่องจากเศรษฐกิจของจีนเริ่มขยายตัว บริษัท ฟอร์ไมก้าคอร์ปอเรชั่น จึงจัดตั้งบริษัทร่วมทุนผลิตสินค้าชื่อ Formica Shanghai ในปี ค.ศ. 1994 โดยร่วมทุนกับรัฐบาลในท้องถิ่น

ศูนย์กระจายสินค้าถูกตั้งขึ้นในกรุงปักกิ่ง กว่างโจว และเฉินเจิ้น ในปี ค.ศ. 2003 มีการตั้งสำนักงานขายและศูนย์กระจายสินค้าในเมืองตงกวน ภาคใต้ของจีน และในปี ค.ศ. 2006 ศูนย์กระจายสินค้าอีกแห่งหนึ่งในเมืองเฉิงตู ภาคตะวันตกของจีน จากการเจริญเติบโตอย่างรวดเร็วจนเกินกำลังโรงงานแห่งแรก บริษัทสร้างโรงงานแห่งใหม่ขึ้นในปี ค.ศ. 2005 และในปี ค.ศ. 2006 ขยายตัวโดยการโยกย้ายทรัพย์สินของโรงงานแห่งแรกของบริษัท บริษัท ฟอร์ไมก้า คอร์ปอเรชั่น ขยายกิจการในเอเชียต่อไปด้วยการซื้อกิจการ เพอร์สตอร์ป เซอร์เฟส แมททีเรียลส์ จากบริษัท เพอร์สตอร์ป เอ บี ของประเทศสวีเดนในปี ค.ศ. 2000 บริษัทตั้ง สยาม เพอร์สตอร์ป ซึ่งเป็นโรงงานผลิตและธุรกิจที่ประสบความสำเร็จในประเทศไทย ที่ช่วยรองรับตลาดเอเชียที่เกิดใหม่ มีการขยายโรงงานในประเทศไทยเมื่อปี ค.ศ. 2004

pées rapidement. L'entreprise a vendu le stratifié Formica par l'intermédiaire d'agents à Hong Kong, Singapour, en Malaisie et à Taiwan dans les années 1970. « Les architectes et les designers ont tellement aimé la marque que l'entreprise a commencé à investir dans des usines pour soutenir les marchés asiatiques locaux, » déclare Steve Kuo, longtemps président de Formica Asia, à présent retraité. En 1980, la société Formica était prête pour sa première usine asiatique qui s'est ouverte à Taiwan.

De nouveaux marchés ont été ouverts au cours des années 1980 et au début des années 1990. Les usines de stratifié de la marque Formica qui avaient ouvert sous l'ère De La Rue à la fin des années 1940 et dans les années 1950 en Australie et en Nouvelle-Zélande, se sont développées au début des années 1980 en achetant les droits du stratifié Laminex sur ces marchés, produisant le produit sous les deux marques pendant quelques années de la décennie 1980. Cette nouvelle période d'interconnexion entre les marques Laminex et Formica a commencé à la fin des années 1940 lors de la visite de Sykes, et a marqué les relations commerciales et industrielles entre les deux propriétaires de marque sur les marchés en développement d'Australie et de Nouvelle-Zélande.

En 1992, Formica Corporation a établi une succursale à Singapour : Formica (Singapore) Pte Ltd., et en 1993, elle a créé en Corée, Formica Korea Corp et en Malaisie, House of Formica (Malaisie). Puis vint le tour de la Chine, où les designers du stratifié Formica ont été fascinés par ce matériau haut de gamme, riche d'histoire et de fonctionnalité. La croissance de la société suivra la croissance vertigineuse et exponentielle de la Chine. Alors que l'économie chinoise a commencé à se développer, Formica Corporation a mis en place Formica Shanghai en 1994, avec une entreprise de fabrication conjointe avec le gouvernement local.

Les centres de distribution ont été établis à Pékin, Guangzhou et Shenzhen. En 2003, ont été mis en place un bureau de vente et un centre de distribution à Dongguan, en Chine du Sud, et en 2006, un autre centre de distribution à Chengdu, en Chine de l'Ouest.

mica, que se habían abierto mediante De La Rue a fines de las décadas de los cuarenta y de los cincuenta en Australia y Nueva Zelanda, se expandieron a principios de la década de los ochenta al adquirir, de hecho, los derechos de la marca del laminado Laminex en aquellos mercados, que fabricaban productos bajo ambas marcas durante unos pocos años en la década de los ochenta. En 1992, Formica Corporation estableció una sucursal en Singapur, Formica (Singapore) Pte Ltd. y, en 1993, se expandió a Corea, como Formica Korea Corp, y a Malasia, como House of Formica (Malaysia). Posteriormente llegó a la misma China, donde el laminado Formica cautivó a los diseñadores como un material de primera calidad, rico en historia y funcionalidad. El crecimiento de la empresa marcaría el ritmo del crecimiento exponencial y vertiginoso de China. Como la economía de China comenzó a expandirse, Formica Corporation estableció Formica Shanghai en 1994 con una empresa conjunta de fabricación con el gobierno local.

Los centros de distribución se establecieron en Beijing, Guangzhou y Shenzhen. En 2003, se crearon una oficina de ventas y un centro de distribución en Dongguan, China del Sur y, en 2006 se creó otro centro de distribución en Chengdu, China Occidental. Cuando el tamaño de la primera planta resultó insuficiente, la empresa construyó una planta nueva en 2005 y, en 2006 se expandió al reubicar los activos de su primera planta. Con la adquisición en 2000 de la División de Perstorp Surface Materials, de Perstorp AB de Suecia, Formica Corporation se expandió aún más en Asia. Con Siam Perstorp, la empresa adquirió una planta de fabricación exitosa y una empresa en Tailandia que atiende a los mercados asiáticos emergentes. La fábrica tailandesa se expandió en 2004.

La década de los sesenta: la Feria mundial

El momento simbólico de la llegada "a la cima del mundo" de Formica Corporation se podría marcar el día en que se abrió la casa de exhibición de la empresa en la Feria mundial en Nueva York, en 1964. La casa mostró ante todo el mundo un ideal de vida con el laminado marca Formica. Los colores y líneas audaces del laminado Formica en la

va tanssi. Teollisuusalan historioitsija F. Holbrook Platts toteaa, että Formica Corporationin hallussa oli edelleen puolet USA:n markkinoista ja se laajeni ulkomailla. Vuonna 1962 yhtiö järjesti seremonian — John Nobis, Formica Corporationin kaupallisen kehityksen johtaja ilmoitti suunnitelmasta esitellä talo New Yorkissa vuosina 1964 ja 1965 pidettävillä maailmanmessuilla. Valokuvassa näkyivät viiksekäs arkkitehti Emil A. Schmidlin ja sisustussuunnittelija Miss Ellis Leigh, jotka esiintyivät silinterit päässä.

Seitsemän huoneen, 240 neliömetrin koti oli ilmaisu yhtiön ihanteista ja pyrkimyksistä, sijoitettuna täysin maisemoidulle 0,2 hehtaarin tontille, jonka geneeriseksi osoitteeksi oli annettu "64–65 Hilltop Lane". Maailmanmessujen talo oli esillä eri maiden paviljonkien joukossa kaikkialla maailmassa "Unispheren" varjossa, joka oli jättiläinen monikerroksinen veistos maapallosta, antaen optimistisen kuvan tyytyväisestä planeetasta. Vaikutelma tähdensi sitä, että Formica Corporationista oli tullut kansainvälinen yhtiö. Faberin keksimästä nimestä tuli nyt yksi tunnetuimmista tavaramerkeistä maailmassa.

Vuonna 1978 USA:n kauppakomissio (FTC) yritti peruuttaa Formica-tavaramerkin, väittäen, että siitä oli tullut yleisnimi, kuten thermos, aspirin, escalator ja cellophane. Lanham Act -nimisen lain nojalla FTC pystyi peruuttamaan tavaramerkin, jos siitä oli tullut "yleinen kuvaava nimitys esineestä tai aineesta". FTC:n valta tällaisen toimenpiteen suorittamiseksi tavaramerkkiä vastaan nostatti metelin USA:n liike-elämän piirissä. Lopulta FTC:n toimenpide mitätöintiin, kun kongressi puuttui asiaan ja peruutti määrärahat tällaisiin toimenpiteisiin. Tänä päivänäkin yhtiön lakimiehet partioivat uupumatta kuuluisan tavaramerkin koskemattomuutta, muistutaen ihmisiä käyttämään Formica-tavaramerkkiä tavallisten termien kanssa ja lähettävät tylyjä lainmukaisia kirjeitä niille, jotka eivät kunnioita yhtiön ikonista tavaramerkkiä. "Formica kirjoitetaan isolla F-kirjaimella!" on heidän käyttämänsä iskulause, korostaen sitä, että sanan "Formica" perässä pitää olla termi "tavaramerkki", "laminaatti" tai "merkkinen laminaatti".

司 (Formica Shanghai)，與當地政府合資生產。

在北京、廣州、深圳等地相繼建立了經銷中心。後來在 2003 年又先後在中國南部東莞市設立了銷售辦事處和分銷中心，並於 2006 年在中國西部成都市另建了一個經銷中心。由於成長之快超出了第一家工廠的能力，公司在 2005 年和 2006 年建立了一家全新的工廠，搬遷了第一家工廠的資產，擴大了廠房。2000 年從瑞典柏仕德 AB 公司 (Perstorp AB Sweden) 手中收購了其表面材料部之後，富美家公司進一步在亞洲擴大。在收購了暹羅柏仕德公司 (Siam Perstorp) 之後，該公司獲得了一家成功的製造廠和其在泰國支持新興亞洲市場的生意。2004 年，泰國的工廠得到擴建。

二十世紀六十年代：
世界博覽會

富美家公司抵達「世界之巔」的象徵時刻可能是該公司在 1964 年紐約舉行的世界博覽會的展室開幕的日子。這個展室向整個世界展示了用富美家品牌美耐板建造的理想家居。富美家二十世紀五十年代的大膽的色彩和線

期开始于二十世纪四十年代塞克斯造访之时，为这两种品牌的持有人在澳大利亚和新西兰市场商标和制造关系上多年的来往做好准备。

1992 年，富美家公司成立了新加坡分公司富美 (新加坡) 私人有限公司 (Formica (Singapore) Pte Ltd.)，并于 1993 年扩大到韩国，名为富美家韩国公司 (Formica Korea Corp)，在马来西亚成立了富美家（马来西亚）之家 (House of Formica (Malaysia))。然后是中国，富美家®装饰耐火板让设计师们着迷，它既是一种优质材料，又有丰富的历史和功能。该公司的增长步伐将会与中国人自己的令人目不暇接、呈指数的增长相媲美。随着中国经济开始扩张，富美家公司 1994 年成立了上海富美家公司 (Formica Shanghai)，与当地政府合资生产。

在北京、广州、深圳等地相继建立了经销中心。后来在 2003 年又先后在中国南部东莞市设立了销售办事处和分销中心，并于 2006 年在中国西部成都市另建了一个经销中心。由于成长之快超出了第一家工厂的能力，公司在 2005 年和 2006 年建立了一家全新的工厂，搬迁了第一家工厂的资产，扩大了厂房。2000 年从瑞典柏仕德

ทศวรรษที่ 1960
งานแสดงโลก (World's Fair)

ช่วงเวลาที่สำคัญของการมาถึง "จุดสูงที่สุดในโลก" ของ บริษัท ฟอร์ไมก้า คอร์ปอเรชั่น อาจเป็นวันที่บริษัทเปิดการจัดการแสดงที่ World's Fair ณ กรุงนิวยอร์กในปี ค.ศ. 1964 งานดังกล่าวแสดงให้ทั้งโลกเห็นถึงการพักอาศัยในอุดมคติด้วยแผ่นลามิเนทฟอร์ไมก้า สีสันและลายเส้นที่เด่นชัดของแผ่นลามิเนทฟอร์ไมก้าในช่วงทศวรรษที่ 1950 สะท้อนเส้นสายบั้นท้ายรถไครสเลอร์ และรถคาดิลแลค ซึ่งแสดงความสนุกสนานรื่นเริงเหมือนกับจังหวะเพลงร็อคแอนด์โรลใหม่ และเป็นกันเองเหมือนกับศัพท์แสลงของวัยรุ่นและการเต้นรำที่ดึงดูดทั้งประเทศ ตามการรายงานของเอฟ ฮอลบรูค แพลตต์ส นักประวัติศาสตร์อุตสาหกรรม บริษัท ฟอร์ไมก้า คอร์ปอเรชั่น ยังคงครองครึ่งหนึ่งของตลาดสหรัฐอเมริกา และกำลังเติบโตในต่างประเทศ ในปี ค.ศ. 1962 บริษัทจัดพิธีขึ้นครั้งหนึ่งจอห์น โนบิส ผู้อำนวยการฝ่ายการพัฒนาเชิงพาณิชย์ของ บริษัท ฟอร์ไมก้า คอร์ปอเรชั่น ประกาศแผนการจัดการแสดงที่ World's Fair ที่จะมีขึ้นที่กรุงนิวยอร์กในปี ค.ศ. 1964 และ ค.ศ. 1965 มีภาพถ่ายของเอมิล เอชมิดลิน สถาปนิกที่มีหนวดโค้งและเอลลิสเลฆ์ นักออกแบบตกแต่งภายใน สวมหมวกทรงกระบอก

บ้านขนาดเจ็ดห้องนอน พื้นที่ 2,600 ตารางฟุต บนพื้นที่ขนาดครึ่งเอเคอร์ที่รายล้อมไปด้วยภูมิทัศน์ และมีที่อยู่แถบชานเมืองทั่วไป เช่น "64-65 Hilltop Lane" เป็นอุดมคติและความทะเยอทะยานของบริษัท บ้านในงาน World's Fair จะเห็นตั้งอยู่ท่ามกลางงานแสดงของประเทศต่างๆ จากทั่วทุกมุมโลกในร่มเงาของ "Unisphere" ประติมากรรมลูกโลกหลายชั้นขนาดใหญ่ยักษ์ที่แสดงถึงมุมมองในแง่บวกเกี่ยวกับดาวเคราะห์ที่มีความสุข ซึ่งการแสดงนี้เน้นย้ำว่า บริษัท ฟอร์ไมก้า คอร์ปอเรชั่น ได้กลายเป็นบริษัทระหว่างประเทศ ชื่อที่เฟเบอร์ได้สร้างขึ้นตอนนี้ติดหนึบในยี่ห้อที่ได้รับการยอมรับมากที่สุดในโลกแล้ว

ในปี ค.ศ. 1978 คณะกรรมาธิการการค้าแห่งรัฐบาลกลางสหรัฐอเมริกา หรือ เอฟ ที ซี พยายามหาหนทางที่จะยกเลิกเครื่องหมายการค้าฟอร์ไมก้า โดยอ้างว่า เครื่องหมายการค้านี้ได้กลายเป็นคำสามัญแล้ว เช่นเดียวกับ คำว่า เทอร์มอส (thermos) แอสไพริน (aspirin) เอสคาเลเตอร์ (escalator) และเซลโลเฟน (cellophane) ภายใต้กฎหมายที่เรียกว่า พระราชบัญญัติแลนแฮม เอฟ ที ซี สามารถยกเลิกเครื่องหมายการค้าได้ ถ้าเครื่องหมายการค้านั้นได้กลายเป็น "ชื่อที่ใช้

La première usine étant devenue trop étroite, une usine flambant neuve a vu le jour en 2005 et en 2006, le personnel a été déplacé de sa première usine. Avec l'acquisition en 2000 de la division de Perstorp Division of Surface Materials, de Perstorp AB en Suède, la société Formica s'est encore développée en Asie. Avec Siam Perstorp, la société a obtenu une usine de production et des activités en Thaïlande pour les marchés asiatiques émergents. L'usine thaïlandaise a été agrandie en 2004.

Années 60 : l'Exposition universelle

Le moment symbolique de l'apogée de la société Formica pourrait bien être le jour où l'entreprise a présenté une maison à l'Exposition universelle de New York en 1964. La maison a dévoilé au monde entier un idéal de vie de stratifié Formica. Les teintes vives et les lignes du stratifié Formica dans les années 1950 avaient fait écho aux ailerons Chrysler et Cadillac. C'était aussi optimiste que la nouvelle musique rock and roll et aussi informel que l'argot des adolescents et la danse qui avaient fasciné le pays. Formica Corporation, rapporte l'historien de l'industrie F. Platts Holbrook, a toujours occupé la moitié du marché américain et a été de plus en plus présente à l'étranger. En 1962, la société a organisé une cérémonie au cours de laquelle John Nobis, directeur du développement commercial de Formica Corporation, a annoncé des plans pour une maison d'exposition à l'Exposition universelle de New York en 1964 et 1965. Une photographie montre l'architecte moustachu Emil A. Schmidlin et la designer d'intérieur Miss Ellis Leigh, coiffée d'un haut de forme.

L'habitation de sept pièces et 790 mètres carrés était une déclaration des idéaux et des ambitions de la société, aménagée sur un terrain entièrement paysagé de deux mille mètres carrés dont l'adresse générique est : 64–65 Hilltop Lane. La maison de l'Exposition universelle figurait parmi les pavillons de divers pays du monde, à l'ombre de la sculpture « Unisphere », une sculpture géante de plusieurs étages du globe exprimant la vision optimiste d'une planète heureuse. Le simple

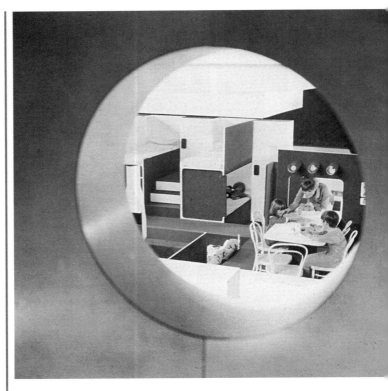

década de los cincuenta reproducían las pronunciadas aletas de cola de los modelos Chrysler y Cadillac. Eran tan alegres como la nueva música, el *rock and roll*, y tan informales como el lenguaje de los adolescentes y el baile que fascinaban al país. Formica Corporation, informa el historiador de la industria F. Holbrook Platts, todavía dominaba la mitad del mercado estadounidense y crecía en el extranjero. En 1962, la empresa realizó una ceremonia —John Nobis, director de desarrollo comercial para Formica Corporation, anunció planes para una casa de exhibición en la Feria mundial en Nueva York en 1964 y 1965. Una fotografía mostraba al arquitecto Emil A. Schmidlin con bigote, y a la diseñadora de interiores Ellis Leigh, que tenía puesto un sombrero cilíndrico.

La vivienda de 242 metros cuadrados con siete habitaciones era una expresión de los ideales y las ambiciones de la empresa, diseñada en un lote de 2,023 metros cuadrados paisajísticamente tratada en su totalidad y que llevaba la dirección suburbana genérica de "64-65 Hilltop Lane". La Feria

Maailmanmessujen talo tähtäsi tulevaisuuteen — sen keittiö tarjosi kaksi uunia ja kaksi pesuallasta, joista käyttömukavat keittiöt tulisivat ylpeilemään 1980-luvulta alkaen. Se sisälsi keittiössä jopa pienen toimistotilan, joka saapuisi 1990-luvulla Internetin myötä. Oli kuitenkin myös ristiriitaisia yksityiskohtia: talo paljasti Cyanamidin monialayrityksen luettelolla ja sen Formica-laminaattien esittelyllä olevan jonkin verran sekalainen luonne. Talossa olivat sellaiset Cyanamidin tuotteet kuin Creslan-merkkinen akryylikuitu, Melmac® melamiiniastiat, Acrylite® koristelevy, Skydome-merkkiset valaisimet ja Cyanamidin "kemialliset hyödykkeet maatilaa ja puutarhaa varten". Tämä hankala yhdistelmä antoi vihjeen Formica Corporationin epäonnistuneesta sopivuudesta tähän monialayritykseen.

Hyvin erilaisessa ympäristössä ja tyylissä Formica-laminaatti oli aivan yhtä kriittinen kuin se oli ollut *Queen Maryn* tapauksessa tytäralusta *Queen Elizabeth 2* suunniteltaessa. *QE2* tuli liikenteeseen v. 1969, samana vuonna kuin tapahtui ensimmäinen kuuhun

條呼應了克萊斯勒和凱迪拉克的俯衝尾翼。它們像新時代的搖滾樂一樣樂觀向上，像舉國為之風靡的青少年俚語和舞蹈一樣無拘無束。行業歷史學家霍爾布魯克·普萊茨（F.Holbrook Platts）報道說，富美家公司仍佔據一半的美國市場，並不斷在海外增長。1962 年，公司舉行了一個儀式——富美家公司商業發展總監約翰·諾比斯（John Norbis）宣佈，計劃在 1964 年和 1965 年的紐約世界博覽會上展示一所展房。一幅照片顯示了留著鬍子的建築師埃米爾·史密德林（Emil A. Schmidlin）和室內設計師埃利斯·利（Ellis Leigh）女士，她戴了一頂圓柱形的帽子。

這個有七間屋子面積為 2,600 平方英尺的住宅是該公司的理想和抱負的表現，坐落在帶有美觀景觀的半公頃土地上，用了一個通用地址「山頂巷 64-65 號」。世博會之家躋身於全球各國的展廳中，隱藏在「巨型地球儀」的暗影裡，這個地球儀是一個多層樓高的地球雕塑，表達了一種快樂星球的樂觀態度。這種外觀著重強調了富美家公司已成為國際化的公司。費伯創造的這個名字現在已經成為這個星球上最知名的品牌。

1978 年，美國聯邦貿易委員會（U.S. Federal Trade Commission/簡稱 FTC）試圖取消富美家這個商標，指稱它已變成一個通用術語，如熱水瓶、阿司匹林、自動扶梯和玻璃紙。根據一項名稱為《蘭哈姆法》（Lanham Act）的法律，如果一個商標已成為「常見的物品或物質的描述名稱」，美國聯邦貿易委員會就可以取消該商標。聯邦貿易委員會對一個商標採取法律行為的權力，在美國商界引起一片譁然。最終，美國國會出面干預和撤消了起訴的資金，美國聯邦貿易委員會的法律程序被取消。即使到了今天，公司的律師仍繼續不知疲倦地維護著該著名品牌的完整性，提醒人們用富美家商標時要加上普通名詞，向

AB 公司（Perstorp AB Sweden）手中收購了其表面材料部之後，富美家公司進一步在亞洲擴大。在收購了暹羅柏仕德公司（Siam Perstorp）之後，該公司獲得了一家成功的製造廠和其在泰國支持新興亞洲市場的生意。2004 年，泰國的工廠得到擴建。

二十世紀六十年代：世界博覽會

富美家公司抵達 "世界之巔" 的象徵時刻可能是該公司在 1964 年紐約舉行的世界博覽會的展室開幕的日子。這個展室向整個世界展示了用富美家品牌耐火板建造的理想居家。富美家二十世紀五十年代的大膽的色彩和線條呼應了克萊斯勒和凱迪拉克的俯衝尾翼。它們像新時代的搖滾樂一樣樂觀向上，像舉國為之風靡的青少年俚語和舞蹈一樣無拘無束。行業歷史學家霍爾布魯克·普萊茨（F.Holbrook Platts）報道說，富美家公司仍占據一半的美國市場，并不斷在海外增長。1962 年，公司舉行了一個儀式——富美家公司商業發展總監約翰·諾比斯（John Norbis）宣布，計划在 1964 年和 1965 年的紐約世界博覽會上展示一所展房。一幅照片顯示了留著胡子的建築師埃米爾·史密德林（Emil A. Schmidlin）和室內設計師埃利斯·利（Ellis Leigh）女士，她戴了一頂圓柱形的帽子。

這個有七間屋子面積為 2,600 平方英尺的住宅是該公司的理想和抱負的表現，坐落在帶有美觀景觀的半公頃土地上，用了一個通用地址 "山頂巷 64-65 號"。世博會之家躋身于全球各國的展廳中，隱藏在 "巨型地球儀" 的暗影里，這個地球儀是一個多層樓高的地球雕塑，表達了一種快樂星球的樂觀態度。這種外觀更強調了富美家公司已成為國際化的公司。費伯創造的這個名字現在已經成為這個星球上最知名的品牌。

1978 年，美國聯邦貿易委員會（U.S. Federal Trade Commission/簡

เรียกวัตถุหรือสารเป็นการทั่วไป" อำนาจของ เอฟ ที ซี ในการดำเนินการกับเครื่องหมาย การค้าดังกล่าวสร้างความโกลาหลในกลุ่ม ธุรกิจของสหรัฐอเมริกา ในท้ายที่สุด การ ดำเนินการของ เอฟ ที ซี ก็ตกไปหลังจากที่ รัฐสภาของสหรัฐอเมริกาเข้ามามีส่วนร่วมด้วย และถอดถอนเงินทุนสำหรับการดำเนินการดัง กล่าว ทุกวันนี้ ทนายความของบริษัทยังคง ต้องตรวจความสมบูรณ์ของยี่ห้อที่มีชื่อเสียง นี้อย่างไม่รู้จักเหน็ดเหนื่อย โดยคอยเตือนให้ คนใช้เครื่องหมายการค้าฟอร์ไมก้า ร่วมกับคำ สามัญ และส่งจดหมายทางกฎหมายที่เข้มงวด ไปยังผู้ที่ไม่เคารพต่อตราสินค้าที่เป็นเสมือน สัญลักษณ์ของบริษัท "คำว่า ฟอร์ไมก้า ต้อง สะกดด้วย F ตัวพิมพ์ใหญ่!" เป็นสโลแกนที่ พวกเขาใช้ โดยอธิบายว่า "ฟอร์ไมก้า" ต้อง ใช้พร้อมกับคำว่า "ยี่ห้อ" "ลามิเนท" หรือ "ลามิเนทยี่ห้อ"

งานแสดง World's Fair มองไปยังอนาคต ห้องครัวมีเตาอบและอ่างล้างจานคู่ ห้องครัว ที่สะดวกสบายจะเริ่มเป็นที่ยอมรับในช่วง ทศวรรษที่ 1980 ยังมีการเอาห้องทำงาน ขนาดเล็กไปไว้ในห้องครัว ที่มาพร้อมกับการ ใช้อินเทอร์เน็ต ในช่วงทศวรรษที่ 1990 แต่ อย่างไรก็ตาม ก็มีบันทึกที่ขัดแย้งด้วยเช่นกัน อาทิ บ้านแสดงลักษณะเบ็ดเตล็ดบางส่วน จากแค็ตตาล็อกของกลุ่มบริษัท ไชอานามิด และแสดงแผ่นลามิเนทฟอร์ไมก้า ในบ้าน มีผลิตภัณฑ์ของ ไชอานามิด เช่น เส้นใย อะคริลิกยี่ห้อ Creslan เครื่องจานชามเมลามีน Melmac® แผ่นตกแต่ง Acrylite® ช่องแสง บนหลังคายี่ห้อ Skydome และ "สารเคมีเพื่อ ใช้ในฟาร์มและสวน" ของ ไชอานามิด การ ผสมปนเปที่ดูขัดขูดขัดตานี้ สื่อถึงการที่ บริษัท

293

fait de participer à cette manifestation a montré que Formica était devenue une entreprise internationale. Le nom que Faber avait inventé était désormais une des marques les plus connues de la planète.

En 1978, la U.S. Federal Trade Commission (FTC) a cherché à supprimer la marque Formica, parce qu'elle était devenue un terme générique tel que thermos, aspirine, escalator et cellophane. En vertu de la loi Lanham, la FTC peut annuler une marque si elle est devenue le nom descriptif d'un article ou d'une substance. Le pouvoir de la FTC d'intenter une telle action contre une marque provoqua un tollé dans les milieux d'affaires américains. En fin de compte, l'action de la FTC a été abandonnée après que le Congrès soit intervenu et ait retiré le financement de tels recours. Même aujourd'hui, les avocats de la société continuent à patrouiller sans relâche au sujet de l'intégrité de la marque, rappelant aux gens d'utiliser la marque Formica en combinaison avec des termes communs et en envoyant des avertissements légaux stricts à ceux qui ne respectent pas la marque emblématique de la société. « Formica est orthographié avec un F majuscule ! » est un slogan utilisé, faisant valoir que « Formica » doit être précédé des mots « marque », « laminé » ou « stratifié de la marque. »

La maison de l'Exposition universelle était tournée vers l'avenir. Sa cuisine était composée de doubles fours et de doubles éviers confortables pour les années 1980. Elle prévoyait même le petit bureau dans la cuisine qui arriverait dans les années 1990 avec l'Internet. Mais tout n'était pas parfait : la maison a montré le caractère quelque peu hétéroclite du catalogue du conglomérat Cyanamid et de sa présentation du stratifié Formica. La maison incluait les produits Cyanamid tels que la marque de fibre acrylique Creslan, la vaisselle en mélamine Melmac®, la feuille décorative Acrylite®, les lucarnes de marque Skydome et Cyanamid, « les produits chimiques pour la ferme et le jardin. » Ce mélange maladroit fait allusion au positionnement malheureux de Formica à l'intérieur du conglomérat.

Dans un environnement et un style très différents, le stratifié Formica était

mundial de la vivienda se veía entre pabellones de países de todo el mundo a la sombra de "Unisphere", una escultura gigante del mundo con múltiples pisos que expresaba una visión optimista de un planeta feliz. La apariencia solo enfatizaba que Formica Corporation se había convertido en una empresa internacional. El nombre que Faber había acuñado estaba ahora entre las marcas más reconocidas del planeta.

En 1978, la Comisión de Comercio Federal de EE. UU. (*U.S. Federal Trade Commission*, FTC) buscó cancelar la marca comercial Formica, indicando que se había convertido en un término genérico, como termo, aspirina, escalera mecánica y celofán. Según una ley denominada la Ley Lanham, la FTC podía cancelar una marca comercial si se había convertido en "el nombre descriptivo común de un artículo o de una sustancia". El poder de la FTC para tomar tal medida en contra de una marca comercial creó un escándalo en la comunidad comercial de EE. UU. Finalmente, se descartó la medida de la FTC después de que el Congreso interviniera y retirara los fondos para tomar tales medidas. Incluso en la actualidad, los abogados de la empresa continúan vigilando incansablemente la integridad de la famosa marca, recordando a las personas emplear la marca comercial Formica en combinación con términos comunes y enviando severas cartas legales a aquellos que no respetan la marca icónica de la empresa. "¡Formica se escribe con F mayúscula!" es un eslogan que se utiliza, que resalta que a "Formica" se le debe anteponer el término "marca", "laminado" o "laminado de la marca".

La Feria mundial de la vivienda miraba al futuro, su cocina ofrecía los hornos dobles, y las cómodas cocinas con fregaderos dobles que se harían populares a principios de la década de los ochenta. Hasta incluía un pequeño espacio de oficina en la cocina, algo que llegaría en la década de los noventa con Internet. Pero también había puntos débiles: la casa mostraba la naturaleza algo miscelánea del catálogo del conglomerado de Cyanamid y su presentación del laminado Formica. En la casa, se encontraban productos de Cyanamid tales como la fibra acrílica de la marca Creslan, la vajilla de melamina Melmac®, la lámina decora-

lento ja Woodstock. Noin 185 000 neliömetriä Formica-laminaattia käytettiin *QE2*-aluksen sisätiloissa. Käytävät ja portaikot ovat värikoodattuja. Pop-grafiikka koristi modernistisia oleskelutiloja, sisusteinaan Bertoian tuolit ja Saarisen pöydät. Dennis Lennonin johtama sisustussuunnitteluryhmä työskenteli kolmisen vuotta sopivan tyyppisten laminaattien valitsemiseksi. Ensimmäisen luokan hyteissä se oli veluuripintaista Formica-laminaattia. Jukeboxissa, teini-ikäisiä matkustajia palvelevassa oleskelutilassa oli rohkea grafiikka ja värit, ja Royal College of Art -oppilaitoksen opiskelijoiden suunnittelemat siluettikuvat. Kahvibaarista vierailijat löysivät rohkeita unikonsinisiä ja keltaisia juovia ja pesuhuoneissa ja vessoissa pintakäsiteltyjä, kudotun näköisiä materiaaleja. Naistenhuoneissa oli varusteina klassiset Formica-laminaattiset "Vanitory"-lavuaarit. *QE2* oli itse asiassa kelluva laboratorio Formica-merkkisille 1960-luvun tuotteille.

Vuonna 1969 tavanomaisilla kulkuvälineillä ei kuitenkaan ollut enää aivan samaa vetovoimaa. Formica-laminaatin vaikutelma heijasti jälleen kerran laajemmassa kulttuurissa tapahtuneita muutoksia: kapinallinen sukupolvi etsi materiaaleista luonnollista ja orgaanista. Nuorempi väki piti laminaattia keinotekoisena. Sehän oli ollut heidän vanhempiensa materiaalia. Ehkäpä 1960-luvulle on osunut yhtiön ensimmäisen kukoistuksen käyrän kohokohta, sattuen samaan aikaan kuin hyvinvointi toipuvassa Euroopassa ja Yhdysvalloissa, rock and rollin esiintulo ja se mitä historioitsija Thomas Hines kutsuu nimellä "populuxe" kohtuuhintaisista kodin sisusteista. Alas kääntyminen on paikannettavissa sitäkin tarkemmin. Hetki oli vuoden 1969 elokuvassa *The Graduate*, kun Dustin Hoffmanin roolilta kysytään urasta "muovin parissa". Formica-laminaattia alettiin pitää pinnallisena ja keinotekoisena.

1970-luku

Tuotteiden imago ei ollut ainoa ongelma. Vuodesta 1956 "pikkuinen Formica" oli todellakin ollut pieni. Se oli vain pieni osa paljon suuremmasta ja toisinaan välinpitämättömästä organisaatiosta, edustaen kolmea prosenttia Cyanamidin liikevaihdosta. Monet

那些不尊重公司的標誌性品牌的人發出嚴厲的法律信函。「富美家是用‘F’大寫字母拼寫的！」是他們使用的一個口號，提醒「富美家」，必須在後邊加上「品牌」、「美耐板」或「品牌美耐板」。

世界博覽會之家展望未來——廚房配備雙眼爐灶和雙洗菜池，這都是舒適的廚房在二十世紀八十年代初所引以自詡的。它甚至還包括了廚房裡的一個小型家庭辦公室，到二十世紀九十年代隨著網際網路的出現應運而生。但也有相互矛盾的音符：這座房子表現了氰胺企業集團目錄的某種零散的個性和富美家美耐板。在這所房子裡展覽了氰胺產品，如 Creslan 品牌腈編織維、Melmac® 品牌三聚氰胺餐具、Acrylite® 品牌的裝飾板、Skydome 品牌的天窗、氰胺的「用於農場和花園的化學助劑」。這種不自然的混雜暗示著，富美家公司在企業集團內部的不愉快的地位。

如果處於一個非常不同的環境和風格中，富美家美耐板會像對瑪麗女王號一樣重要，即使是在其女兒船伊麗莎白女王二號 (Queen Elizabeth 2) 設計之時。伊麗莎白女王二號從 1969 年開始服役，正值首次登月和伍德斯托克 (Woodstock) 音樂節的那一年。約 200 萬平方英尺的富美家美耐板用在伊麗莎白二號的船上。通道和樓梯都有顏色編碼。流行圖案裝點著現代主義的休息廳，配有伯托埃式的椅子和沙里寧式的桌子。由丹尼斯‧列儂 (Dennis Lennon) 帶領的室內設計團隊工作了三年多時間，挑選了合適的美耐板。頭等艙用的是絲絨質地的富美家美耐板。在自動點唱機上和為迎合少年乘客的休息室裡，使用了大膽的圖形和顏色，以及英國皇家藝術學院的學生們設計的剪影圖像。在咖啡廳，遊客們會發現罌粟藍和黃色的大膽條紋，而洗手間和衛生間用的是帶紋理、編織面的材料。女士休息室配有經典的富美家美耐板

称 FTC) 试图取消富美家这个商标，指称它变成一个通用术语，如热水瓶、阿司匹林、自动扶梯和玻璃纸。根据一项名称为《兰哈姆法》(Lanham Act) 的法律，如果一个商标已成为"常见的物品或物质的描述名称"，美国联邦贸易委员会就可以取消该商标。联邦贸易委员会对一个商标采取法律行为的权力，在美国商界引起一片哗然。最终，美国国会出面干预和撤消了起诉的资金，美国联邦贸易委员会的法律程序被取消。即使到了今天，公司的律师仍继续不知疲倦地维护着该著名品牌的完整性，提醒人们用富美家商标时要加上普通名词，向那些不尊重公司的标志性品牌的人发出严厉的法律信函。"富美家是用‘F’大写字母拼写的！"是他们使用的一个口号，提醒"富美家"，必须在后边加上"品牌"、"耐火板"或"品牌耐火板"。

世界博览会之家展望未来——厨房配备双眼炉灶和双洗菜池，这都是舒适的厨房在二十世纪八十年代初所引以自诩的。它甚至还包括了厨房里的一个小型家庭办公室，到二十世纪九十年代随着互联网的出现应运而生。但也有相互矛盾的音符：这座房子表现了氰胺企业集团目录的某种零散的个性和富美家®装饰耐火板。在这所房子里展览了氰胺产品，如 Creslan 品牌腈纶纤维、Melmac® 品牌三聚氰胺餐具、Acrylite® 品牌的装饰板、Skydome 品牌的天窗、氰胺的"用于农场和花园的化学助剂"。这种不自然的混杂暗示着，富美家公司在企业集团内部的不愉快的地位。

如果处于一个非常不同的环境和风格中，富美家®装饰耐火板会像对玛丽女王号一样重要，即使是在其女儿船伊丽莎白女王二号 (Queen Elizabeth 2) 设计之时。伊丽莎白女王二号从 1969 年开始服役，正值首次登月和伍德斯托克 (Woodstock) 音乐节的那一年。约 200 万平方英尺的富美家®装

ฟอร์ไมก้า คอร์ปอเรชัน ร่วมเป็นส่วนหนึ่งของกลุ่มบริษัทอย่างไม่มีความสุขนัก

ในสภาพแวดล้อมและรูปแบบที่แตกต่างกันมาก แผ่นลามิเนทฟอร์ไมก้ามีความสำคัญเท่ากับที่เคยมีต่อเรือ *ควีนแมรี* เมื่อมีการออกแบบเรือลูก คือ เรือ *ควีน อลิซาเบธที่ 2* เรือ *คิวอี 2* เริ่มให้บริการในปี ค.ศ. 1969 ซึ่งเป็นปีของการเหยียบดวงจันทร์เป็นครั้งแรก และ Woodstock มีการใช้แผ่นลามิเนทฟอร์ไมก้าประมาณ 2 ล้านตารางฟุตบนเรือ *คิวอี 2* ทางเดินและบันไดใช้คนละสี ที่เลาจน์ตกแต่งด้วยป๊อปกราฟิกทันสมัยและมีการติดตั้งด้วยเก้าอี้ Bertoia และโต๊ะ Saarinen ทีมงานออกแบบตกแต่งภายในนำทีมโดยเดนนิส เลนนอน ใช้เวลาสามปีในการเลือกแผ่นลามิเนทประเภทที่เหมาะสม สำหรับห้องโดยสารชั้นหนึ่ง ใช้แผ่นลามิเนทฟอร์ไมก้าที่มีผิวสัมผัสแบบกำมะหยี่ ในห้องตู้เพลง เลาจน์ที่ให้บริการอาหารและเครื่องดื่มแก่ผู้โดยสารวัยหนุ่มสาว ใช้กราฟิกและสีที่โดดเด่นชัดเจนและภาพเงาทึบที่ออกแบบโดยนักเรียนจาก Royal College of Art ในร้านกาแฟ ผู้ที่เข้าร้านจะพบแถบสีฟ้าและเหลืองโดดเด่นสะดุดตา และในห้องอาบน้ำและห้องน้ำใช้วัสดุปิดผิวที่มีผิวสัมผัสแบบสาน เลาจน์ของสุภาพสตรีติดตั้งแผ่นลามิเนทฟอร์ไมก้าคลาสสิกรุ่น "Vanitories" เรือ *คิวอี 2* จึงเป็นเสมือนห้องปฏิบัติการลอยน้ำสำหรับผลิตภัณฑ์ยี่ห้อฟอร์ไมก้าแห่งทศวรรษที่ 1960

พอมาถึงปี ค.ศ. 1969 การเดินทางแบบเดิมไม่ค่อยน่าตื่นตาตื่นใจเหมือนเช่นก่อนอีกต่อไป ปัจจุบัน ภาพลักษณ์ของแผ่นลามิเนทฟอร์ไมก้าสะท้อนถึงการเปลี่ยนแปลงวัฒนธรรมที่กว้างขึ้นอีกครั้งหนึ่ง ซึ่งก็คือ คนรุ่นที่ต่อต้านและมองหาวัสดุธรรมชาติหรือได้มาจากสิ่งมีชีวิต คนหนุ่มสาวคิดว่าแผ่นลามิเนทเป็นวัสดุเทียม และว่าจะอย่างไรแผ่นลามิเนทก็เป็นวัสดุของรุ่นพ่อรุ่นแม่ ทศวรรษที่ 1960 อาจถือเป็นจุดสูงสุดของเส้นโค้งแรกในความเจริญรุ่งเรืองของบริษัท ซึ่งประจวบกับความเจริญรุ่งเรืองในทวีปยุโรปที่กำลังฟื้นตัวและในสหรัฐอเมริกาการปรากฏขึ้นของแฮร์รือฮอแอนด์โรลและสิ่งที่โทมัส ไฮน์ส นักประวัติศาสตร์ เรียกว่า "การแห่ตามกระแส (populuxe)" ในการตกแต่งบ้านราคาไม่แพง กระแสขาลงสามารถถูกชี้ชัดมากยิ่งขึ้น นี่เป็นช่วงเวลาในภาพยนตร์ *The Graduate* ในปี ค.ศ. 1969 เมื่อตัวละครของ ดัสติน ฮอฟฟ์แมน กำลังสอบถามเกี่ยวกับอาชีพในอุตสาหกรรม "พลาสติก" แผ่นลามิเนทฟอร์ไมก้าถูกมองว่าไม่สำคัญและเป็นของเทียม

295

tout aussi important qu'il l'avait été pour le *Queen Mary* lorsque le navire avait donné lieu à un nouveau-né, le *Queen Elizabeth 2*. Le *QE2* a commencé son service en 1969, l'année du premier alunissage et de Woodstock. Quelque 600 000 mètres carrés de stratifié Formica ont été utilisés dans des espaces du QE2. Les passages et les escaliers sont codés par teinte. Des graphismes pop décorent les salons modernes équipés de chaises Bertoia et de tables Saarinen. L'équipe de design intérieur dirigée par Dennis Lennon a travaillé pendant près de trois ans pour sélectionner les stratifiés adéquats. Pour les cabines de première classe, il s'agissait d'un stratifié Formica texturé velours. Dans la salle de restaurant Jukebox, destinée aux passagers adolescents, des graphismes et des teintes audacieux ainsi que des silhouettes conçues par les élèves du Royal College of Art étaient utilisés. Dans le café, les visiteurs découvraient des rayures audacieuses de pavot bleu et jaune et dans les toilettes, des matériaux avec texture tissée. Les salons des dames étaient équipés du stratifié classique Formica Vanitories. Le *QE2* était en fait un laboratoire flottant pour les produits de la marque Formica dans les années 1960.

Mais en 1969, les moyens habituels de transport ne possédaient plus tout à fait le même pouvoir. L'image du stratifié Formica a désormais reflété les changements dans la culture au sens large, une fois encore : une génération rebelle recherchait le naturel et le bio dans les matériaux. Les jeunes percevaient le stratifié comme de nature artificielle. Il était finalement le matériau de leurs parents. Les années 1960 ont peut-être marqué le point culminant de la première courbe descendante de prospérité de l'entreprise, qui coïncide avec la prospérité de la notion de récupération en Europe et aux États-Unis, avec l'émergence du rock and roll et de ce que l'historien Thomas Hines a appelé le « populuxe » dans l'ameublement à prix abordable. Le ralentissement peut être mis en évidence de manière encore plus précise. C'est le moment de la projection du film *Le Lauréat (The Graduate)* en 1969 où Dustin Hoffman est interviewé au sujet d'une carrière dans les matières plastiques. Le stra-

tiva Acrylite®, los tragaluces de la marca Skydome y los "agentes químicos para el huerto y el jardín" de Cyanamid. Esta inconveniente mezcla dejó entrever la a veces complicada interrelación entre Formica Corporation y el resto de empresas del mismo *holding*.

En un ambiente y un estilo muy diferentes, el laminado Formica era tan válido como lo había sido para el *Queen Mary* cuando se diseñó su barco heredero, el *Queen Elizabeth 2* (QE2). El *QE2* comenzó a prestar servicio en 1969, el año del primer alunizaje y de Woodstock. Se utilizaron cerca de 185,807 metros cuadrados de laminado Formica en espacios del *QE2*. Los pasillos y las escaleras están codificados por color. Los gráficos populares decoran salones modernistas acondicionados con sillas Bertoia y mesas Saarinen. El equipo de diseño de interiores, encabezado por Dennis Lennon, trabajó unos tres años para seleccionar los tipos de laminado adecuados. Para los camarotes de primera clase, se utilizó un laminado Formica texturizado tipo terciopelo. En la rocola, un salón de entretenimiento para los pasajeros adolescentes, había gráficos y colores audaces e imágenes destacadas diseñadas por los estudiantes del Royal College of Art. En el café, los visitantes encontraban franjas audaces de amapolas azules y amarillas, y en los baños y sanitarios, materiales texturizados con acabados trenzados. Los salones para damas estaban equipados con el clásico laminado Formica "Vanitories". El *QE2* era, en efecto, un laboratorio flotante para los productos de la marca Formica de la década de los sesenta.

Pero en 1969, los medios de transporte habituales ya no ofrecían precisamente el mismo atractivo. La imagen del laminado Formica reflejaba ahora cambios en la cultura más amplia una vez más: una generación rebelde buscaba lo natural, lo orgánico en los materiales. Los jóvenes percibían el laminado como artificial. Después de todo, era el material de sus padres. La década de los sesenta quizá haya marcado el punto culminante de la primera curva en la prosperidad de la empresa, que coincidía con la prosperidad de la recuperación de Europa y de los Estados Unidos, el surgimiento del *rock and roll* y lo que el historiador Thomas Hines denominó "populuxe" en el mobiliario

alan tarkkailijat ja Formica Corporationin johtoportaan toimistohuoneiden veteraanit olivat sitä mieltä, että se kärsi huomion ja pääoman nälästä. Oli sellainen vaikutelma, että se ajoi vapaalla maineensa ja tavaramerkkinsä varassa. Vanha sinnikäs 1940-luvun yhtiö oli jostakin syystä luutunut ylimielisyyteen.

Formica-yhtiö oli tippunut vähän kerrallaan puolesta markkinoita, jotka sillä oli 1960-luvulla, aggressiivisten kilpailijoiden takia, jotka myivät halvemmalla ja lupasivat paremman palvelun. Yhtiön yrityskuvan huonontuessa se tapahtui hitaasti, mutta koko maailmassa. Tarkoituksellinen, huolellinen kuva Formica Corporationista — "huolestuneisuuden" ja varovaisuuden ominaisuudet — muuttui erään historioitsijan mukaan "käsitykseksi, että Formica Corporationista oli ykkössijalle noustuaan tullut verkkainen ja ylimielinen, usein käyttäen viikkoja tuotteen toimittamiseen". 1980-luvun loppuun mennessä kilpailijat ottivat haltuun johtoaseman USA:n markkinoilla aggressiivisemman myynti-, varasto- ja toimituskäytäntöjen ansiosta.

Kutein kovin usein tapahtuu, Formica Corporationin tapauksessa liiketoiminnan tarina oli vertauskuva suuremmasta. Yhdysvalloissa 1970-luvulla monet pitemmälle kehittyneet alat joutuivat siirtymään kilpailusta hyödykkeissä kilpailemiseen palveluissa. Kilpailijoiden aggressiivisempi myynti ja nopeampi toimitus, sekä Formica Corporationin kykenemättömyys reagoida tulivat tapaustutkimusten aiheeksi, johon on paljon viitattu johtajien ja kauppaoppilaitosten opiskelijoiden piirissä. Se mainittiin laajasti luetussa kirjassa *Competing against Time*, joka julkaistiin v. 1990.

Kirjassa siteerattu bostonilaisen konsulttiryhmän tekemä tutkimus totesi, että kilpailija vei markkinaosuutta saadessaan tuotteen nopeamman asiakkaalle. He pystyivät toimittamaan lähes minkä tahansa tuotteen linjastaan kymmenessä päivässä Formica Corporationin 25 päivän sijasta. Jälleenmyyjät pystyivät pitämään pienempää varastoa käsillä — ja siten myydä halvemmalla. Jo 1950-luvulla paikalliset jälleenmyyjät pitivät varastossa joitakin tuotekategorioita sen takia, että Formica Corporationin käytäntönä oli valmistaa vain tilauksesta.

「盥洗盆架」。女王伊麗莎白二號實際上是二十世紀六十年代富美家品牌產品的一個水上實驗室。

但在 1969 年，慣常的交通工具已不再有昔日的魅力。富美家美耐板現在的形象再一次反映了更廣泛的文化：叛逆的一代人尋求材料中的自然和有機。年輕人覺得美耐板太過虛假。這畢竟是他們的父輩用的材料。二十世紀六十年代或許標誌著公司繁榮的第一條曲線的最高點，恰逢正在復甦的歐洲和美國的繁榮，搖滾樂的出現和歷史學家托馬斯・海因斯 (Thomas Hines) 所稱的廉價家居用品的「大眾性奢侈」。這個下滑的趨勢還可以更準確地定在某一點，這就是 1969 年的電影《畢業生》(The Graduate) 中，達斯汀・霍夫曼 (Dustin

飾耐火板用在伊丽莎白二号的船上。通道和楼梯都有颜色编码。流行图案装点着现代主义的休息厅，配有伯托埃式的椅子和沙里宁式的桌子。由丹尼斯・列侬 (Dennis Lennon) 带领的室内设计团队工作了三年多时间，挑选了合适的耐火板。头等舱用的是丝绒质地的富美家®装饰耐火板。在自动点唱机上和为迎合少年乘客的休息室里，使用了大胆的图形和颜色，以及英国皇家艺术学院的学生们设计的剪影图像。在咖啡厅，游客们会发现罂粟蓝和黄色的大胆条纹，而洗手间和卫生间用的是带纹理、编织面的材料。女士休息室配有经典的富美家®装饰耐火板"盥洗盆架"。女王伊丽莎白二号实际上是二十世纪六十年代富美家品牌产品的一个水上实验室。

ทศวรรษที่ 1970

ปัญหาภาพลักษณ์ของผลิตภัณฑ์ไม่ได้เป็นเพียงปัญหาเดียวของบริษัท ตั้งแต่ปี ค.ศ. 1956 "ลิตเติล ฟอร์ไมก้า" มีขนาดเล็กจริง ๆ บริษัทเป็นเพียงแค่ส่วนเล็ก ๆ ของบริษัทที่มีขนาดใหญ่กว่าและไม่ให้ความสนใจ ยอดขายผลิตภัณฑ์ฟอร์ไมก้าคิดเป็นเพียงร้อยละ 3 ของยอดขายของบริษัท ใช่อานามิตนักสังเกตการหลายคนของอุตสาหกรรมและผู้มีประสบการณ์ของสำนักบริหารงานของ บริษัท ฟอร์ไมก้า คอร์ปอเรชั่น รู้สึกว่าบริษัทไม่ได้รับการเหลียวแลและเงินทุน มีความรู้สึกกันว่า บริษัททายาทบารมีความรุ่งโรจน์และห้อที่มีอยู่โดยเดิมไม่ทำอะไร บริษัทเก่าที่ดำเนินงานอย่างกระท่อนกระแท่นในช่วงทศวรรษที่ 1940 ได้เปลี่ยนเป็นความเฉื่อยหนึ่งแทน

บริษัทฟอร์ไมก้าค่อย ๆ ร่วมลงทีละนิดจากครึ่งหนึ่งของตลาดที่บริษัทได้รับในช่วงทศวรรษที่ 1960 ตกเป็นของคู่แข่งขันรุกที่ตัดราคาและให้บริการที่ดีกว่า เมื่อภาพลักษณ์ของบริษัทแย่ลง ก็แย่ลงอย่างช้า ๆ แต่แย่ลงทุกหนทุกแห่งทั่วโลก ภาพลักษณ์ที่คิดมาอย่างรอบคอบและระมัดระวังของบริษัท ฟอร์ไมก้า คอร์ปอเรชั่น คุณภาพของ "การกระทำด้วยความเต็มใจ" และการเอาใจใส่ เปลี่ยนเป็นสิ่งที่นักประวัติศาสตร์รายหนึ่งเรียกว่า "ความเข้าใจว่า บริษัท ฟอร์ไมก้า คอร์ปอเรชั่น เจริญเติบโตจนเป็นอันดับหนึ่งกลายเป็นเพียงความเฉื่อยชาและหยิ่งโส มักใช้เวลาหลายสัปดาห์กว่าจะจัดส่งผลิตภัณฑ์" ภายในช่วงปลายทศวรรษที่ 1980 คู่แข่งได้ชิงตำแหน่งผู้นำในตลาดสหรัฐอเมริกาไป เพราะมีนโยบายการขาย การคลังสินค้า และการจัดส่งในเชิงรุกกว่า

เรื่องราวเกี่ยวกับธุรกิจของ บริษัท ฟอร์ไมก้า คอร์ปอเรชั่น ถือเป็นคติสอนใจจากบริษัทที่ใหญ่กว่า ซึ่งมักเกิดกรณีเช่นนี้ขึ้น ในสหรัฐอเมริกาในช่วงทศวรรษที่ 1970 อุตสาหกรรมที่เติบโตเต็มที่มากมายกำลังเผชิญกับการเปลี่ยนแปลงจากการแข่งขันกันด้วยผลิตภัณฑ์ไปเป็นการแข่งขันกันด้วยบริการ การขายที่มีลักษณะในเชิงรุกมากกว่าและการจัดส่งที่รวดเร็วกว่าของคู่แข่ง พร้อมกับความล้มเหลวในการตอบสนองของ บริษัท ฟอร์ไมก้า คอร์ปอเรชั่น กลายเป็นกรณีศึกษาและเป็นที่กล่าวถึงกันมากในกลุ่มเจ้าหน้าที่บริหารและนักเรียนโรงเรียนธุรกิจ และมีการกล่าวถึงในหนังสือที่มีการอ่านกันในวงกว้างชื่อ *Competing against Time* ดีพิมพ์ในปี ค.ศ. 1990

การศึกษาที่มีการกล่าวถึงในหนังสือจัดทำโดยกลุ่ม Boston Consulting พบว่า วิลสันอาร์ต การได้ส่วนแบ่งตลาดโดย

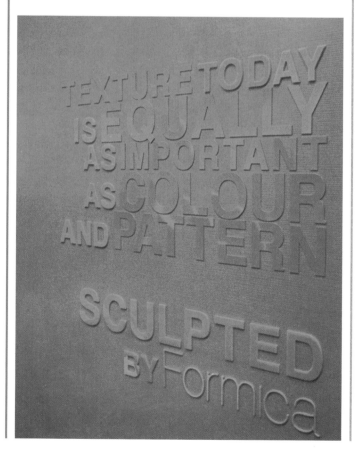

tifié Formica en vint à être considéré comme superficiel et artificiel.

1970

L'image des produits n'était pas le seul problème. Depuis 1956, le « petit Formica » était vraiment devenu petit. Il n'était qu'une petite partie d'une organisation plus vaste et parfois indifférente. Il ne représentait que trois pour cent des ventes de Cyanamid. De nombreux observateurs de l'industrie et des anciens des bureaux exécutifs de la société Formica ont estimé qu'il manquait d'attention et de capital. La société vivait sur sa gloire et sa marque. L'ancienne société agressive des années 1940 était en quelque sorte figée dans l'arrogance.

La société Formica était passée peu à peu de la moitié du marché en 1960 à la portion congrue suite à l'agressivité de concurrents qui misaient sur le prix et un meilleur service. Le déclin de l'image de l'entreprise a été lent mais généralisé dans le monde entier. Les qualités de soin et de sollicitude de la société Formica ont évolué vers ce que l'historien appelle la perception de ce que Formica Corporation, une fois devenue numéro un, était devenue molle et arrogante, prenant souvent des semaines pour livrer un produit. À la fin des années 1980, les concurrents ont progressivement dominé le marché des États-Unis grâce à des ventes plus agressives, une politique de stocks et de livraison rapide.

Comme c'est souvent le cas, l'histoire des affaires chez Formica a suivi une courbe classique. Aux États-Unis dans les années 1970, de nombreuses industries mûres ont été confrontées à un changement dans la concurrence des biens et des services. Les ventes de concurrents plus agressifs et une livraison plus rapide, avec l'incapacité de la société Formica à y répondre, sont devenues une étude de cas, souvent citée parmi les cadres et les étudiants des écoles de commerce. Le cas est notamment cité dans une publication largement diffusée, intitulée *Competing against Time*, publiée en 1990.

Selon une étude citée dans le livre par le Boston Consulting Group, il a été constaté que la concurrence a pris des parts de marché en fournissant rapidement le produit au client. Ils pou-

doméstico asequible. La recesión se puede identificar de manera aún más exacta. Fue el momento en la película de 1969 *El graduado* cuando se le pregunta al personaje de Dustin Hoffman sobre una carrera en "plástico". Se comenzó a ver al laminado Formica como superficial y artificial.

La década de los setenta

La imagen de sus productos no era el único problema. Desde 1956, "Little Formica" había sido realmente pequeña. Era solo una pequeña parte de una organización mucho más grande y, algunas veces, despreocupada, que representaba solo el 3 % de las ventas de Cyanamid. Muchos observadores de la industria y las personas experimentadas de las oficinas ejecutivas de Formica Corporation sentían que carecía de atención y capital. Había una sensación de que navegaba en su gloria y marca. La antigua empresa aguerrida de la década de los cuarenta, de alguna forma, se había anquilosado en la arrogancia.

La empresa Formica había caído, gradualmente, de la mitad del mercado del que disfrutaba en la década de los sesenta a las manos de agresivos competidores que rebajaban el precio y prometían un mejor servicio. Cuando declinó la imagen de la empresa, lo hizo muy despacio, pero en todo el mundo. La imagen deliberada y atenta de Formica Corporation —las cualidades de "solícita" y cuidadosa— se volvieron lo que un historiador denomina "la percepción de que Formica Corporation, al haberse convertido en la número uno, se había vuelto perezosa y arrogante, a menudo tomándose semanas para entregar un producto". A finales de la década de los ochenta, los competidores asumirían el liderazgo del mercado de los EE. UU., gracias a las ventas, un inventario y políticas de entrega más agresivas.

Como sucede a menudo, la historia comercial en Formica Corporation era una alegoría de algo más grande. En los Estados Unidos de la década de los setenta, muchas industrias que maduraban estaban haciendo frente a un cambio sustancial al pasar de competir en bienes a competir en servicios. Las ventas más agresivas y la entrega más rápida por parte de los competidores, junto con la falta de respuesta de Formica Corporation, se convirtieron en un

Vaikka kilpailijoita olikin enemmän, yhtiön tuote oli siitä huolimatta hyvää, vaikka se olikin menettänyt palvelun osalta. Erään liikealan kirjoittajan sanojen mukaan se oli "jäänyt toiseksi tyrkyttämisessä ja oveluudessa". Pian yhtiö lyhensi toimitusaikansa jopa erikoisalansa tuotteille alle kahteen viikkoon, mutta maine jäi ennalleen. Tutkimuksen mukaan yksi Formica Corporationin haasteista oli kaupanteko monien eri tyyppisten asiakkaiden kanssa. Joskus Formica kilpaili kalusteiden valmistajien ja asentajien kanssa ja toisinaan myi heille, markkinoista ja maasta riippuen. Kasvaessaan Formica kehitti läheisiä ja molempia hyödyttäviä suhteita valmistajiin ja urakoitsijoihin, jotka olivat avainasiakkaita, kuten jälkimuovaajat, jotka olivat auttaneet alkuun sodan jälkeistä nousukautta. Monet olivat yksityisyrittäjiä. Uuden-Seelannin tapaus ei eronnut tapauksista ympäri maailmaa. Barry ja Helen O'Brien avasivat yrityksensä kotinsa alla olevassa autotallissa Dunedinissä ja perustivat neljän vuosikymmenen kuluessa seitsemän jakelupistettä maan laajuisesti, joissa oli 240 työntekijää. Yhteen aikaan heidän valmistamansa keittiökalusteet ja muut asennukset käsittivät 40 prosenttia Formican Uuden-Seelannin tuotannosta. Vuonna 2007 he myivät liiketoimintansa Fletcher Building -yhtiölle.

Tällaiset liikekumppanit, suunnittelijat ja pienet urakoitsijat tarvitsivat pikaisen reaktion ja nopean toimituksen jollekin värille tai kuviolle. Yhtiön useilla asiakasryhmillä oli kuitenkin jokaisella jonkin verran erilaiset tarpeet — ja erilaiset kilpailijat. Alempihintaiset jäljitelmät houkuttelivat kaapistojen tai toimistohuonekalujen valmistajia (niin sanottuja OEM:iä, alkuperäisiä tuotteen valmistajia); he ostivat suuria määriä Formica-laminaattia tai kilpailevia tuotteita. Pienemmällä mittakaavalla toimivat, kahviloita tai pieniä ruokaloita suunnittelevat tai kalustavat yrittäjät olivat tarkkoja ajasta. Kaikkien näiden erilaisten tarpeiden palveleminen oli vaikeaa.

Bumerangi

1980-luvulla, kenties ironisesti ja jopa samaan aikaan kuin sillä oli vaikeuksia liiketoiminnassa, Formica Corporationin tuotteet pääsivät nauttimaan sosi-

Hoffman) 扮演的角色被問及「塑膠」職業生涯的那一時刻。富美家美耐板被視作膚淺和虛假。

二十世紀七十年代

產品的形象不是唯一的問題。自 1956 年以來，「小富美家」真得沒長大。它只是一個更大的、有時漠不關心的組織的一小部分，只佔氰胺公司銷售量的 3%。許多行業觀察家和富美家公司行政辦公室的資深人員認為，它急需關注和資本。從某種意義上說，它在吃自己的榮耀和品牌的老本。二十世紀四十年代那個曾經幹勁十足的公司不知有何故僵化到如此傲慢自大的地步。

富美家公司已經衰落，一點一點從六十年代佔據一半的市場，輸給了出價低、承諾更好服務的咄咄逼人的競爭對手。當公司的形象下落時，是慢慢下落的，而且是在全球。富美家公司謹慎和小心的形象——那種「熱心」和關注的素質——變成了一位歷史學家所說的「那種感覺，即富美家公司，由於成長為頂尖公司，已變得遲緩與傲慢，經常需要幾個星期才能交付產品」。到八十年代末，競爭對手由於更積極的促銷、庫存和交貨政策獲得了美國市場的領先地位。

如往常一樣，富美家公司的創業故事是一個更大故事的寓言。二十世紀七十年代的美國，許多成熟的行業正面臨著一個從商品競爭到服務競爭的轉變。競爭對手更積極地銷售和更快地交付，再加上富美家公司沒有反應，成為了一個典型的案例，被高官們和商學院的學生多次引用。它被列入 1990 年出版的廣泛閱讀的《與時間競爭》(Competing against Time) 一書。

書中引述了波士頓諮詢集團做的一項研究，這項研究發現，競爭是通過把產品更快地交付客戶而佔領市場。他們可以在 10 天內交付幾乎

但在 1969 年，慣常的交通工具已不再有昔日的魅力。富美家®裝飾耐火板現在的形象再一次反映了更广泛的文化：叛逆的一代人寻求材料中的自然和有机。年轻人觉得耐火板太过虚假。这毕竟是他们的父辈用的材料。二十世纪六十年代或许标志着公司繁荣的第一条曲线的最高点，恰逢正在复苏的欧洲和美国的繁荣，摇滚乐的出现和历史学家托马斯·海因斯 (Thomas Hines) 所称的廉价家居用品的 "大众性奢侈"。这个下滑的趋势还可以更准确地定在某一点，这就是 1969 年的电影《毕业生》(The Graduate) 中，达斯汀·霍夫曼 (Dustin Hoffman) 扮演的角色被问及 "塑料" 职业生涯的那一时刻。富美家®装饰耐火板被视作肤浅和虚假。

二十世纪七十年代

产品的形象不是唯一的问题。自 1956 年以来，"小富美家" 真得没长大。它只是一个更大的、有时漠不关心的组织的一小部分，只占氰胺公司销售量的 3%。许多行业观察家和富美家公司行政办公室的资深人员认为，它急需关注和资本。从某种意义上说，它在吃自己的荣耀和品牌的老本。二十世纪四十年代那个曾经干劲十足的公司不知何故僵化到如此傲慢自大的地步。

富美家公司已经衰落，一点一点从六十年代占据一半的市场，输给了出价低、承诺更好服务的咄咄逼人的竞争对手。当公司的形象下落时，是慢慢下落的，而且是全球性的。富美家公司谨慎和小心的形象——那种 "热心" 和关注的素质——变成了一位历史学家所说的 "那种感觉，即富美家公司，由于成长为顶尖公司，已变得迟缓与傲慢，经常需要几个星期才能交付产品"。到八十年代末，竞争对手由于更积极的促销、库存和交货政策获得了美国市场的领先地位。

如往常一样，富美家公司的创业故事是一个更大故事的寓言。二十世纪七

การจัดส่งผลิตภัณฑ์ให้ลูกค้าให้รวดเร็วกว่าวิลสันอาร์ด สามารถจัดส่งผลิตภัณฑ์เกือบทุกประเภทในสายผลิตภัณฑ์ได้ภายในระยะเวลาสิบวัน เมื่อเทียบกับระยะเวลายี่สิบห้าวันสำหรับ บริษัท ฟอร์ไมก้า คอร์ปอเรชั่น ผู้กระจายสินค้าสามารถเก็บสินค้าในคลังไว้ในจำนวนที่น้อยลง ส่งออกตัดราคาลงได้ แม้แต่ในช่วงทศวรรษที่ 1950 ผู้กระจายสินค้าในท้องถิ่นจะกักตุนผลิตภัณฑ์บางประเภทไว้เนื่องจากนโยบายของ บริษัท ฟอร์ไมก้า คอร์ปอเรชั่น ที่จะมีการผลิตตามคำสั่งซื้อเท่านั้น แม้ว่าจะมีคู่แข่งจำนวนมากขึ้น แต่ผลิตภัณฑ์ของบริษัทก็ยังคงเป็นผลิตภัณฑ์ที่ดีอยู่ เสียแต่เรื่องบริการเท่านั้น ตามคำพูดของนักเขียนบทความธุรกิจหนึ่งกล่าวว่า นี่เป็น "การเร่งเร้าและการชิงไหวชิงพริบกัน" ในไม่ช้า บริษัทก็ลดระยะเวลาในการจัดส่งลง แม้กระทั่งสำหรับผลิตภัณฑ์เฉพาะกลุ่มให้ต่ำกว่าสองสัปดาห์ แต่ชื่อเสียงในทางติดลบกระจายไปแล้ว

ความท้าทายอย่างหนึ่งของ บริษัท ฟอร์ไมก้า คอร์ปอเรชั่น ที่การศึกษาชี้แนะไว้ก็คือ การรับมือกับลูกค้าประเภทต่างๆ บางครั้งบริษัทฟอร์ไมก้าก็แข่งขันกันและบางครั้งก็ขายให้ผู้ผลิตอุปกรณ์ยึดติดและผู้ติดตั้งโดยขึ้นอยู่กับตลาดและประเทศ เมื่อบริษัทเติบโตขึ้น ได้พัฒนาความสัมพันธ์อย่างใกล้ชิดและได้ประโยชน์ร่วมกันกับผู้ผลิตและผู้รับเหมาซึ่งเป็นลูกค้าหลัก เช่น ผู้ตัดติวลามิเนท ซึ่งให้ความช่วยเหลือในช่วงเริ่มต้นความเจริญรุ่งเรืองหลังสงคราม โดยหลายคนเป็นผู้ประกอบการ กรณีหนึ่งในประเทศนิวซีแลนด์ไม่เหมือนกับกรณีอื่นๆ ทั่วโลก แบรีและเฮเลน โอไบรเอน เริ่มธุรกิจในโรงรถใต้บ้านของเขาในเมืองดูนดิน และตลอดสี่ทศวรรษที่ผ่านมาได้จัดตั้งร้านค้าทั่วประเทศขึ้นเจ็ดสาขา มีพนักงาน 240 คน เมื่อถึงจุดหนึ่งเคาน์เตอร์ที่พวกเขาทำและเครื่องมือติดตั้งอื่นๆ คิดเป็นร้อยละ 40 ของการผลิตของบริษัทฟอร์ไมก้าในประเทศนิวซีแลนด์ ในปี ค.ศ. 2007 พวกเขาขายธุรกิจให้กับ บริษัทเฟลตเชอร์ บิลดิ้ง

คู่ค้า นักออกแบบ และผู้รับเหมารายเล็กดังกล่าวต้องการการบริการและการจัดส่งลามินทสีพื้นหรือลวดลายที่รวดเร็ว แต่ลูกค้าหลายกลุ่มของบริษัทมีความต้องการที่แตกต่างกัน และมีการแข่งขันที่แตกต่างกัน ผลิตภัณฑ์เลียนแบบที่มีต้นทุนต่ำกว่าเป็นสิ่งข่อยั่วยวนบริษัทที่สร้างตู้หรือเฟอร์นิเจอร์สำนักงาน (ซึ่งเรียกว่า OEM หรือผลิตอุปกรณ์ดั้งเดิม) พวกเขาซื้อผลิตภัณฑ์ลามิเนทฟอร์ไมก้าหรือผลิตภัณฑ์ของคู่แข่งในปริมาณมาก ส่วนผู้ที่มีขนาดของธุรกิจขนาดเล็กลงมา อาทิ

vaient offrir presque n'importe quel produit de leur catalogue dans les dix jours, contre 25 jours pour le Formica. Les distributeurs avaient besoin d'un stock moins important et réduisaient les prix en conséquence. Même dans les années 1950, les distributeurs locaux devaient stocker certaines catégories de produits en raison de la politique de Formica Corporation de fabrication uniquement sur commande. Mais même avec plus de concurrents, les produits de la société étaient encore bons même s'ils avaient perdu en fonctionnalité. La société avait été dépassée par plus malin. Ensuite, la société a réduit ses délais de livraison, même des produits de niche, à moins de deux semaines, mais la réputation était faite. Il a été constaté que Formica Corporation avait affaire à des clients très variés. Formica était parfois en concurrence avec des fabricants et installateurs mais leur vendait aussi des produits, en fonction des marchés et des pays. En grandissant, Formica développait des relations étroites et stables avec les fabricants et les entre-

estudio de caso, muy citado entre ejecutivos y estudiantes de escuelas de negocios. Se incluyó en el ampliamente leído *Competing against Time*, publicado en 1990.

Un estudio citado en el libro del grupo Boston Consulting determinó que la competencia adquirió una participación en el mercado al llevar el producto más rápidamente al cliente. Podían entregar casi cualquier producto de su línea dentro de diez días, comparado con los veinticinco días de Formica Corporation. Los distribuidores podían mantener menos inventario a mano, y, como resultado, rebajar los precios. Incluso en la década de los cincuenta, los distribuidores locales acumularían algunas categorías de productos debido a la política de fabricación solo a pedido de Formica Corporation. Pero incluso con más competidores, el producto de la empresa era todavía bueno, aunque había perdido en el servicio. Había sido "demasiado presionada y aventajada" según las palabras de un escritor de negocios. Pronto, la empresa redujo sus tiempos

aalisesta ja kulttuurillisesta elpymisestä. Materiaaleista, Formica-laminaatti mukaan lukien, oli tullut vauvabuumin sukupolven lapsuuden ajan ja heidän omien vanhempiensa symboleja, jotka tämä sukupolvi — eikä vain Amerikassa — halusi hylätä pintapuolisena. Kuitenkin 1980-lukuun mennessä vauvabuumin aikakausi oli käsillä, arvostaakseen jälleen nuoruutensa musiikkia, elokuvia ja kulttuuria. Ihmisluonteen normaalivaiheissa se oli itse saavuttanut vanhempana olon asteen. Osuva symboli tälle prosessille on bumerangi. Bumerangit, joilla on niille ominainen kaareva, pitkulainen muoto, palaavat lentäen takaisin, tunnustuksena menneen ajan arvostuksesta. Boomerang ™ oli nimi, joka annettiin Formican laminaattikuviolle, joka alun perin tunnetaan nimellä Skylark™ 1950-luvulla, ja joka tuotiin uudelleen markkinoille Formica Corporationin 75-vuotispäivänä v. 1988 neljänä uutena värinä. Kirja ja liikkuva museonäyttely nimeltään *Vital Forms* (elintärkeät muodot) esittivät myöhemmin yhteenvedon aikakauden materiaalien,

任何他們生產的產品，而相比之下，富美家公司需要 25 天。經銷商們能夠保持較低的庫存——因此可以降價。即使是在二十世紀五十年代，當地經銷商會儲存某些類型的產品，因為富美家公司的政策是只按訂單製作。但即使競爭者增加，公司的產品還是很不錯的，雖然它在服務上輸給了別人。用一位商業作家的話說，它已「不如別人拼命，也不如別人聰明」。不久，公司將其特定產品的交貨時間減少為兩週，但名聲已不可改變。該項研究指出，富美家公司面臨的挑戰之一是處理不同類型的客戶。根據國家和市場的不同，富美家有時與像傢俱製造商和安裝商競爭，有時又向他們銷售產品。隨著富美家的成長，它與製造商和承包商結成了密切和互利的關係，這些人都是幫助戰後最初繁榮的後期製造商的重點客戶。他們中間許多人是企業家。紐西蘭的一個案例與世界各地的情況沒有什麼不同。巴里和海倫·奧布萊恩 (Barry & Helen O'Brien) 在達尼丁自家房子的底層車庫開始了他們的業務，在過去四十年來建立了遍佈全國的七個網點，聘用了 240 名員工。有一段時間，他們製作的檯面和其他安裝材料佔富美家紐西蘭生產的 40%。2007 年，他們把生意賣給了弗萊徹建築公司 (Fletcher Building)。

這種合作夥伴、設計師和小型承包商需要快速反應和對某種顏色和圖案的快速交貨。但公司的幾種客戶分別都有不同的需求——競爭也不同。成本較低的仿製品吸引了櫥櫃或辦公室傢俱公司 (所謂的原設備製造商／簡稱 OEM)，他們買了大量的富美家美耐板或競爭對手的產品。那些較小規模的製造商，設計或裝備咖啡廳或小食堂的人，對時間較敏感。迎合所有這些不同的需求是很困難的。

十年代的美国，许多成熟的行业正面临着一个从商品竞争到服务竞争的转变。竞争对手更积极地销售和更快地交付，再加上富美家公司没有反应，成为了一个典型的案例，被高官们和商学院的学生多次引用。它被列入 1990 年出版的广泛阅读的《与时间竞争》(Competing against Time) 一书。

书中引述了波士顿咨询集团做的一项研究，这项研究发现，竞争是通过把产品更快地交付客户而占领市场的。他们可以在 10 天内交付几乎任何他们生产的产品，而相比之下，富美家公司需要 25 天。经销商们能够保持较低的库存——因此可以降价。即使是在二十世纪五十年代，当地经销商会储存某些类型的产品，因为富美家公司的政策是只按订单制作。但即使竞争者增加，公司的产品还是很不错的，虽然它在服务上输给了别人。用一位商业作家的话说，它 "不如别人拼命，也不如别人聪明"。不久，公司将其特定产品的交货时间减少为两周，但名声已不可改变。该项研究指出，富美家公司面临的挑战之一是处理不同类型的客户。根据国家和市场的不同，富美家有时与家具制造商和安装商竞争，有时又向他们销售产品。随着富美家的成长，它与制造商和承包商结成了密切和互利的关系，这些人都是帮助战后最初繁荣的后期制造商的重点客户。他们中间许多人是企业家。新西兰的一个案例与世界各地的情况没有什么不同。巴里和海伦·奥布莱恩 (Barry & Helen O'Brien) 在达尼丁自家房子的底层车库开始了他们的业务，在过去四十年来建立了遍布全国的七个网点，聘用了 240 名员工。有一段时间，他们制作的台面和其他安装材料占富美家新西兰生产的 40%。2007 年，他们把生意卖给了弗莱彻建筑公司 (Fletcher Building)。

这种合作伙伴、设计师和小型承包商需要快速反应和对某种颜色和图案的快速交货。但公司的几种客户分别都

ผู้ที่ออกแบบหรือตกแต่งร้านกาแฟหรือร้านอาหารขนาดเล็กนั้น เวลาเป็นเรื่องสำคัญ การตอบสนองความต้องการที่แตกต่างกันทั้งหมดนี้จึงเป็นเรื่องที่ยาก

บูมเมอแรง

ในช่วงทศวรรษที่ 1980 แม้จะเป็นช่วงเวลาที่บริษัท ฟอร์ไมก้า คอร์ปอเรชั่น เผชิญปัญหาทางธุรกิจ แต่ผลิตภัณฑ์ของบริษัทกลับได้รับความนิยม ทั้งในเชิงสังคมและวัฒนธรรม วัสดุต่าง ๆ ซึ่งรวมทั้งแผ่นลามิเนทฟอร์ไมก้าซึ่งได้กลายเป็นสัญลักษณ์แทนยุคสมัยของคนที่เกิดในช่วงหลังสงครามโลกครั้งที่ 2 หรือที่เรียกว่า คนยุคเบบี้บูม และพ่อแม่ของคนยุคนี้ ซึ่งคนในยุคนี้ ไม่เฉพาะแต่ในสหรัฐอเมริกาเท่านั้น ต้องการจะปฏิเสธเนื่องจากเห็นว่าแสดงความฉาบฉวยไม่ลึกซึ้ง อย่างไรก็ดีในช่วงทศวรรษที่ 1980 ความชื่นชอบในดนตรี ภาพยนตร์ และวัฒนธรรมเมื่อครั้งวัยเยาว์ของยุคเบบี้บูมได้วนกลับมาอีกครั้ง เหมือนวงจรตามธรรมชาติของมนุษย์ที่เติบโตจนพร้อมเป็นพ่อแม่คน สัญลักษณ์ที่เหมาะสมของกระบวนการนี้คือบูมเมอแรง บูมเมอแรงซึ่งมีลักษณะเป็นสี่เหลี่ยมผืนผ้าโมเดิร์นหักโค้งตรงกลางและบินกลับมาได้จึงกลายเป็นสัญลักษณ์ของการย้อนกลับมาอีกชื่นชอบของย้อนยุค บริษัทใช้บูมเมอแรง เป็นชื่อลวดลายแผ่นลามิเนทฟอร์ไมก้า ซึ่งเดิมเคยเป็นที่รู้จักในช่วงทศวรรษที่ 1950 ภายใต้ชื่อ สายลาร์ค ที่นำกลับมาเปิดตัวใหม่อีกครั้งในโอกาสครบรอบ 75 ปีของ บริษัท ฟอร์ไมก้า คอร์ปอเรชั่น ในปี ค.ศ. 1988 โดยมีสีใหม่ให้เลือกสี่สี หนังสือและนิทรรศการพิพิธภัณฑ์สัญจรชื่อว่า ไวทัล ฟอมส์ ได้ให้คำสรุปลักษณะของวัสดุ สิ่งประดิษฐ์ และรูปทรงที่ของยุคนี้ในภายหลังว่ามีความเป็น ธรรมชาติและ "รูปทรงอิสระ" มีการกล่าวถึงแผ่นลามิเนทฟอร์ไมก้า ว่าเป็นตัวแทนของความต้องการที่จะสะท้อนธรรมชาติ แสดงความมีชีวิตชีวา และเป็นสัญลักษณ์แห่งความคิดที่เป็นอิสระ เช่นเดียวกับ โต๊ะกาแฟของนายอีซามุ โนงูจิ และเครื่องจานชามของนายรัชเซล ไรท์ หรือ อีวา ซีเซล ช่วงทศวรรษที่ 1980 เป็นช่วงที่เกิดทัศนคติใหม่เกี่ยวกับวัสดุต่าง ๆ ซึ่งก่อตัวมาระยะหนึ่งแล้ว

ย้อนเวลากลับไปเมื่อปี ค.ศ. 1962 โรเบิร์ตเวนทูรี นักทฤษฎีแนวคิดที่ต่อมาเรียกกันว่าแนวคิดยุคหลังสมัยใหม่ขึ้นนำผู้หนึ่ง ได้ออกแบบร้านกาแฟเป็นส่วนหนึ่งในโครงการแรก ๆ ของเขา โดยใช้แผ่นลามิเนทและวัสดุที่คล้ายกัน เพื่อที่จะยกย่องความธรรมดานายเวนทูรีกล่าวว่าใช้งบประมาณน้อยแทนที่จะปกปิดเอาไว้ แนวความคิดของนายเวนทูรี

preneurs qui étaient ses principaux clients, comme les postformeurs qui avaient contribué à la flambée initiale d'après-guerre. Beaucoup étaient des entrepreneurs. C'était le cas en Nouvelle-Zélande mais également ailleurs dans le monde. Barry et Helen O'Brien ont ouvert leur entreprise dans un garage sous leur maison, à Dunedin et quarante ans plus tard, ont établi sept points de vente à travers le pays, avec 240 employés. À un moment donné, les plans de travail qu'ils ont réalisés et d'autres installations représentaient quarante pour cent de la production Formica de la Nouvelle-Zé-lande. En 2007, ils ont vendu l'entreprise à Fletcher Building.

Ces partenaires, designers et petits entrepreneurs avaient besoin d'une réponse et d'une livraison rapides d'une teinte ou d'un motif. Mais les divers groupes de clients avaient chacun des besoins différents et la concurrence était diversifiée. Des imitations moins coûteuses ont séduit des entreprises qui construisaient des armoires ou du mobilier de bureau (des équipementiers comme les fabricants d'équipement d'origine). Ils ont acheté de grandes quantités de stratifié Formica ou des produits concurrents. Ceux qui travaillaient à petite échelle, en dessinant ou en installant un café ou une petite cafétéria, étaient sensibles au délai de livraison. Servir ces clients différents était difficile.

Boomerang

Dans les années 1980, de manière presque ironique, au moment même où Formica Corporation rencontrait des difficultés commerciales, ses produits connaissaient un renouveau social et culturel. Des matériaux comme le stratifié Formica étaient devenus des symboles de l'enfance de la génération des baby boomers et de leurs parents, rejetés par cette génération, et pas seulement en Amérique, car superficiels et peu profonds. Pourtant, dans les années 1980, la génération du baby-boom s'est remise à apprécier la musique, le cinéma et la culture de sa jeunesse. Dans les cycles normaux de la nature humaine, ils avaient atteint la parentalité. Un bon symbole de ce processus est le boomerang. Les boomerangs, avec leur caractéristique courbe, de forme oblongue, sont réap-

de entrega, incluso para los productos específicos, a menos de dos semanas, pero la reputación quedó. Uno de los retos de Formica Corporation, sugería el estudio, era tratar con una variedad de tipos de clientes. Formica algunas veces competía con fabricantes e instaladores de estructuras fijas y, en otras oportunidades les vendía a estos, según el mercado y el país. A medida que crecía, Formica entabló relaciones estrechas y mutuamente beneficiosas con los fabricantes y contratistas que eran clientes clave, como los postformadores que habían ayudado en el auge inicial de la posguerra. Muchos eran empresarios. Un caso en Nueva Zelanda era semejante a otros casos alrededor del mundo. Barry y Helen O'Brien abrieron su negocio en un garaje debajo de su casa en Dunedin y, durante cuatro décadas, establecieron siete puntos de venta en todo el país, con 240 empleados. En un determinado momento, los mostradores que fabricaban y otras instalaciones representaban el 40 % de la producción de Formica en Nueva Zelanda. En 2007, vendieron la empresa a Fletcher Building.

Como socios, diseñadores y contratistas pequeños necesitaban una rápida respuesta y la pronta entrega de un color o diseño. Pero cada uno de los diversos tipos de clientes de la empresa tenía alguna necesidad diferente, y una competencia diferente. Las imitaciones de bajo costo tentaban a las empresas que construían gabinetes o muebles de oficina (los llamados "fabricantes de equipos originales" [*original equipment manufacturer*, OEM]); compraban grandes cantidades de laminado Formica o productos rivales. Aquellos que trabajaban en una escala menor, diseñando o acondicionando un café o una cafetería pequeña lo hacían con urgencia. Atender todas estas diferentes necesidades era difícil.

Boomerang

En la década de los ochenta, irónicamente , en un momento en que se enfrentaban dificultades comerciales, los productos de Formica Corporation disfrutaban de un resurgimiento social y cultural. Los materiales, incluido el laminado Formica, se habían convertido en símbolos de la infancia de la generación de personas nacidas inmediatamente después de la posguerra y de sus propios padres; materiales que dicha genera-

artefaktien ja muotojen yleisestä vetovoimasta orgaanisena ja "vapaamuotoisena". Yhdessä Isamu Noguchin kahvipöytien ja Russel Wrightin tai Eva Zeiselin astioiden kanssa Formica-laminaatti oli listalla, edustaen samaa halua kuvastaa luontoa, osoittaa elinvoimaa ja symboloida vapaata ajattelutapaa. 1980-luku toi uuden asenteen materiaaleja kohtaan. Se oli ollut kerännyt voimaa jo jonkin aikaa.

Robert Venturi, yksi johtavista teoreetikoista alalla, jota alettiin kutsua jälkimodernismiksi, oli aikoinaan v. 1962 suunnitellut kahvibaarin yhtenä hänen ensimmäisistä laminaatteja ja vastaavia materiaaleja käyttävistä projekteistaan — haluten ylistää arkipäiväisyyttä. Hän oli ylpeä pienistä kustannuksistaan eikä salannut niitä. Hän jatkoi tähän tyyliin, auttaen high-tech -vaikutelman luomisessa, jossa käytetään teollisuuden materiaaleja ruokailu-, myymälä- ja toimistotiloissa. Uusi arkkitehtien ja suunnittelijoiden sukupolvi harkitsi uudelleen kuvioita ja pintoja.

Italialainen suunnittelija ja arkkitehti Ettore Sottsass johti uutta laminaatin arvostusta. Vuonna 1978 hänet palkattiin luomaan abstrakteja koristekuvioita italialaiselle laminaattiyritykselle Abet Laminatille, Formica-yhtiön kilpailijalle Euroopassa. Sottsass veti Memphis-nimistä suunnitteluryhmää, joka vaikutti Milanossa vuoden 1980 paikkeilla. Nimi otettiin sekä egyptiläisestä kaupungista että Elvis Presleyn kodista Tennesseessä, millä

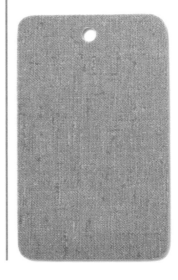

回飛鏢

二十世紀八十年代，也許具有諷刺意味的是，即使在富美家公司面臨商業困難的同時，它的產品卻經歷了社會和文化的復興。使用富美家美耐板的材料已成為嬰兒潮一代人的童年和自己的父母的象徵，而這一代人——不只是在美國——因這產品流於表面和膚淺而拒絕使用。然而，二十世紀八十年代，嬰兒潮時代繞了一個大圈，又回到欣賞他們年輕世代的音樂、電影和文化。作為人類本性的正常週期，他們自己已經為人父母了。這個過程的一個貼切的象徵就是回飛鏢（boomerang）。回飛鏢特有的彎曲、橢圓形狀，出去又飛回來，是復古欣賞的象徵。回飛鏢（Boomerang™）是為重新發佈的富美家美耐板圖案起的名字，最初在二十世紀五十年代被稱為雲雀（Skylark™），1998 年在富美家公司七十五週年紀念日重新以新的色彩發行。一本名字叫做《重要形式》（Vital Forms）的書和巡迴博物館展覽後來總結了那個時代的材料、工藝和形狀，說它們是有機和「自由的形式」。同野口勇（Isamu Noguchi）設計的咖啡桌和羅素·賴特（Russel Wright）或艾娃·齊塞爾（Eva Zeisel）的餐具一樣，富美家美耐板被列為代表同樣的回應自然、表現出活力和象徵自由思想的願望。二十世紀八十年代對材料有了一種新的看法。它積聚力量已經有了一段時間。

後來被稱為後現代主義的主要理論家之一羅伯特·文丘里（Robert Venturi）早在 1962 年就設計了一個咖啡廳，作為他用美耐板和類似材料的第一個項目——希望慶祝世俗觀念。他炫耀了低預算，而不是把它隱藏起來。他繼續在這方面努力，把工業材料用在餐飲、零售和辦公場所，幫助創造了高科技的外觀。新一代的建築師和設計師在重新思考圖案和表面。

有不同的需求——競爭也不同。成本較低的仿製品吸引了櫥櫃或辦公室家具公司（所謂的原設備制造商/簡稱 OEM），他們買了大量的富美家®裝飾耐火板或競爭對手的產品。那些較小規模的製造商，設計或裝備咖啡廳或小食堂的人，對時間較為敏感。迎合所有這些不同的需求是很困難的。

回飞镖

二十世纪八十年代，也许具有讽刺意味的是，即使在富美家公司面临商业困难的同时，它的产品却经历了社会和文化的复兴。使用富美家®装饰耐火板的材料已成为婴儿潮一代人的童年和自己的父母的象征，而这一代人——不只是在美国——因这种产品流于表面和肤浅而拒绝使用。然而，二十世纪八十年代，婴儿潮时代绕了一个大圈，又回到欣赏他们年轻世代的音乐、电影和文化。作为人类本性的正常周期，他们自己已经为人父母了。这个过程的一个贴切的象征就是回飞镖（boomerang）。回飞镖特有的弯曲、椭圆形状，出去又飞回来，是复古欣赏的象征。回飞镖（Boomerang™）是为重新发布的富美家®装饰耐火板图案起的名字，最初在二十世纪五十年代被称为云雀（Skylark™），1998 年在富美家公司七十五周年纪念日重新以新的色彩发行。一本名字叫做《重要形式》（Vital Forms）的书和巡回博物馆展览后来总结了那个时代的材料、工艺和形状，说它们是有机和"自由的形式"。同野口勇（Isamu Noguchi）设计的咖啡桌和罗素·赖特（Russel Wright）或艾娃·齐塞尔（Eva Zeisel）的餐具一样，富美家®装饰耐火板被列为代表同样的回应自然、表现出活力和象征自由思想的愿望。二十世纪八十年代对材料有了一种新的看法。它积聚力量已经有了一段时间。

后来被称为后现代主义的主要理论家之一罗伯特·文丘里（Robert Venturi）早在 1962 年就设计了一个咖啡厅，

นี้ ช่วยยกระดับความนิยมให้การออกแบบที่ดูเหมือนมีการใช้เทคโนโลยีชั้นสูง ที่ใช้วัสดุอุตสาหกรรมในห้องรับประทานอาหาร ร้านค้าปลีก และพื้นที่สำนักงาน สถาปนิกและนักออกแบบรุ่นใหม่สมัยนั้นเริ่มคิดถึงลวดลายและพื้นผิวในมุมมองใหม่

แผ่นลามิเนทได้รับความชื่นชอบอีกครั้งเมื่อนายเอตตอร์ ซอตต์แซสส์ นักออกแบบและสถาปนิกชาวอิตาลีได้รับการว่าจ้างให้ออกแบบลวดลายตกแต่งแบบ แอ็บสแตรกให้กับบริษัทลามิเนทอิตาเลียนชื่อ เอเบต ลามินาติ ที่เป็นคู่แข่งของบริษัทฟอร์ไมก้าในทวีปยุโรป ในปี ค.ศ. 1978 นายซอตต์แซสส์นั้นเป็นหัวหน้ากลุ่มนักออกแบบ ที่เรียกตัวเองว่า เมมฟิส ซึ่งก่อตัวขึ้นที่เมืองมิลานราวปี ค.ศ. 1980 ชื่อกลุ่มนี้มาจากทั้งชื่อเมืองในประเทศอียิปต์และชื่อเมืองบ้านเกิดของเอลวิส เพรสลีย์ ในมลรัฐเทนเนสซี เพื่อเป็นการรวมเอาความคลาสสิกกับป๊อปเข้าด้วยกัน เฟอร์นิเจอร์และประติมากรรมที่กลุ่มนี้ออกแบบมักจะใช้ลามิเนทเพื่อให้ได้ผลงานที่มีสีสันและลวดลาย

ในปี ค.ศ. 1983 ฟอร์ไมก้า คอร์ปอเรชั่น จัดนิทรรการสัญจรแสดงผลงานลามิเนทคัลเลอร์คอร์ ซึ่งเป็นผลงานออกแบบของสถาปนิกโรเบิร์ต เวนทูรี แฟรงก์ เกหรี สแตนลีย์ ไทเกอร์แมน นายเจมส์ ไวเนส แห่งบริษัทออกแบบชื่อ ไซต์ และสถาปนิกอื่น ๆ นิทรรการดังกล่าวแสดงให้เห็นว่า แผ่นลามิเนทไม่ได้ถูกมองเป็นเพียงวัสดุเทียมอีกต่อไปแล้ว แต่เป็นวัสดุที่ได้รับความนิยมโดยตัวของมันเองและจัดแสดงผลิตภัณฑ์ไปทั่วโลกในปีต่อมา ในแต่ละครั้งจะมีผลงานออกแบบใหม่ของนักออกแบบในพื้นที่เข้าร่วมแสดงด้วย เป็นการเน้นว่า ตราผลิตภัณฑ์ฟอร์ไมก้าเต็มไปด้วยการออกแบบในระดับสากล บริษัทใช้นิทรรการนี้เป็นสื่อเคลื่อนที่สำหรับเผยแพร่งานออกแบบ สไตล์ และแฟชั่น ของผลิตภัณฑ์ลามิเนทฟอร์ไมก้าไปทั่วโลก

ศิลปิน นักออกแบบ และสถาปนิกเริ่มที่จะใช้แผ่นลามิเนทในการผลิตเฟอร์นิเจอร์และแม้กระทั่งในงานประติมากรรมกันมากขึ้น วัสดุลามิเนทได้กลายเป็นผลิตภัณฑ์ที่มีคุณค่าในตัวเอง และไม่ถูกมองว่าเป็นวัสดุที่ใช้แทนสิ่งอื่น เช่น หินหรือไม้ อีกต่อไป คำโฆษณาในตอนนั้นอาจเป็น "ให้ ฟอร์ไมก้าเป็น ฟอร์ไมก้า!" ในปี ค.ศ. 1982 ที่บริษัทฟอร์ไมก้า คอร์ปอเรชั่น ออกผลิตภัณฑ์ลามิเนทคัลเลอร์คอร์ ที่มีสีเดียวกันทั้งแผ่นรวมทั้งด้านข้างที่ไม่มีเส้นหรือขอบน้ำตาลปรากฏอย่างในผลิตภัณฑ์รุ่นก่อน ๆ ทำให้ผลิตภัณฑ์ของบริษัทน่าสนใจยิ่งขึ้น โดยเฉพาะในหมู่นักออกแบบสำนักงานสมัยใหม่ การออกแบบ

parus, en signe de reconnaissance rétro. Boomerang™ est le nom donné au motif de stratifié Formica réédité qui s'appelait à l'origine Skylark™, dans les années 1950. Ce produit a été relancé pour le 75ème anniversaire de Formica en 1988 en quatre nouvelles teintes. Un livre et une exposition itinérante du musée appelée plus tard *Vital Forms* ont repris l'aspect des matériaux, des objets et des formes de l'époque comme étant biologique et « libre ». Outre les tables de café d'Isamu Noguchi et le stratifié de vaisselle Formica de Russel Wright ou Eva, le stratifié représentait le même désir de faire écho à la nature, de démontrer la vitalité et de symboliser la libre pensée. Il a montré la faiblesse du budget plutôt que de la cacher, il a continué dans cette veine, contribuant ainsi à donner un aspect haute technologie en employant des matériaux industriels dans les espaces de restauration, du commerce de détail et des bureaux. Une nouvelle génération d'architectes et de designers a repensé les motifs et les surfaces.

Le dessinateur et architecte italien Ettore Sottsass a relancé l'intérêt pour le stratifié. En 1978, il a été embauché pour créer des motifs décoratifs abstraits pour la firme italienne de stratifié Abet Laminati, un concurrent de Formica en Europe. Sottsass était le chef d'un groupe de design appelé Memphis qui a surgi à Milan vers 1980. Il tire son nom de la ville égyptienne ainsi que la ville où se trouve la maison d'Elvis Presley dans le Tennessee, dans un souci de combinaison du classique et de la pop. Le mobilier et les sculptures du groupe utilisaient souvent le matériau pour donner la couleur et le motif.

En 1983, Formica a organisé une exposition itinérante de pièces en stratifié ColorCore® qui a réuni les œuvres d'architectes tels que Robert Venturi, Frank Gehry, Stanley Tigerman, James Wines de SITE et autres, pour montrer

ción, y no solo en los Estados Unidos, deseaba rechazar por ser superficial y trivial. Sin embargo, en la década de los ochenta, la era del *baby boom* había girado en torno a apreciar nuevamente la música, las películas y la cultura de su juventud. En los ciclos normales de la naturaleza humana, había alcanzado la misma paternidad. Un símbolo atinado para este proceso es el búmeran (en inglés: "boomerang"). Los bumeranes, con su forma característica curvada y alargada, volvían volando al punto de partida, una señal de apreciación de lo retro. Boomerang™ fue el nombre que se le dio al diseño de laminado Formica reestrenado, originalmente conocido como Skylark™ en la década de los cincuenta, reintroducido para el 75° aniversario de Formica Corporation en 1988 en cuatro nuevos colores. Posteriormente, un libro y una exhibición de museo itinerante denominada *Vital Forms* resumieron el atractivo común de los materiales, los artefactos y las formas de la era como orgánicos y "de formas libres". Junto con las mesas de centro de Isamu Noguchi y la vajilla de Russel Wright o Eva Zeisel, se mencionaba al laminado Formica como representante del mismo deseo de reproducir la naturaleza, demostrar vitalidad y simbolizar el libre pensamiento. La década de los ochenta devino en una nueva actitud hacia los materiales. Había estado reuniendo fuerzas durante algún tiempo.

Robert Venturi, uno de los teóricos líderes en lo que se denominaría posmodernismo, allá en 1962, había diseñado un café como uno de sus primeros proyectos que utilizaba laminado y materiales similares, deseando celebrar lo mundano. Expuso el bajo presupuesto en vez de esconderlo. Continuó en esa línea, ayudando a elevar la apariencia de alta tecnología, que empleaba materiales industriales en espacios de comedores, comercios minoristas y oficinas. Una nueva generación de arquitectos y diseñadores estaba repensando el diseño y la superficie.

El diseñador y arquitecto italiano Ettore Sottsass condujo a una apreciación del laminado. En 1978, fue contratado para crear diseños decorativos abstractos para la firma italiana de laminados Abet Laminati, una empresa competencia de Formica en Europa. Sottsass era el líder de un grupo de diseño denominado Memphis que sur-

haluttiin yhdistää klassinen ja popkulttuuri. Ryhmän huonekaluissa ja veistoksissa käytettiin usein materiaaleja värin ja kuvion aikaansaamiseksi.

Vuonna 1983 Formica Corporation järjesti siirtyvän näyttelyn ColorCore® laminaatilla tehtyjä teoksia, joka keräsi yhteen arkkitehtien töitä — Robert Venturi, Frank Gehry, Stanley Tigerman, SITE:n James Wines, ja muiden — osoittaakseen, että laminaattia ei enää pidetä faux-materiaalina vaan sitä juhlitaan sen omilla ehdoilla. Tulevina vuosina näyttely kiersi maailmalla. Uusia paikallisten suunnittelijoiden töitä lisättiin maailmankiertueen jokaisessa pysähdyspaikassa, korostaen tavaramerkin kansainvälistä rikkautta. Näyttelyt palvelivat liikkuvina lähetystöinä suunnittelulle, tyylille ja muodille, esitellen Formica-laminaattia eri puolilla maailmaa.

Taiteilijat, suunnittelijat ja arkkitehdit alkoivat käyttää laminaattia useammin huonekaluihin ja jopa veistoksiin. Materiaalia ei enää pidetty vain jonkin muun, kuten kiven tai puun korvikkeena, vaan kuten se oli alkujaan: tuotteena, jota arvostettiin itsessään. Iskulauseena olisi voinut olla "Antakaa Formican olla Formica!". Kun markkinoille tuli v. 1982 Formica Corporationin ColorCore® laminaatti, joka säilytti sävyt syvällä ja jätti pois ruskean viivan eli aikaisempien tuotteiden reunan, yhtiön tuotteet olivat entistä halutumpia. Ne miellyttivät uusien toimistotyylien suunnittelijoita. Toimiston suunnittelussa tapahtuneet muutokset kuvastavat uusia ideoita liiketoiminnassa. Ryhmätyötä ja yhteistoimintaa tähdennettiin. Työntekijöistä tuli liikkuvampia talouselämän lisääntyvän globalisoitumisen ansiosta. Tämän seurauksena toimistoista tuli vähemmän muodollisia, niissä oli enemmän yhteistä tilaa ja väri oli niissä tervetullutta.

Formica Corporation oli kauan sitten ymmärtänyt, että avainosana sen liiketoiminnassa oli suunnittelu. Yhtiö oli palkannut suunnittelutoimistot Brooks Stevensin keksimään kuvioita v. 1951 ja Raymond Loewyn luomaan uuden "Sunrise" tuotelinjan v. 1953. Vuonna 1960 rakennettu tutkimus- ja kehityskeskus Evendalen toimitiloissa hankki suunnittelustudion, ja v. 1969 muodostettiin ulkopuolisista neuvonantajista suunnittelussa avustava

意大利設計師和建築師索特薩斯 (Ettore Sottsass) 率先重新認識了美耐板。1978 年，他受聘於意大利美耐板公司 Abet Laminati，這是富美家公司在歐洲的競爭對手，為其創造抽象的裝飾圖案。索特薩斯是一個 1980 年成立於米蘭的名叫孟菲斯 (Memphis) 的設計團體的領導者。它的名字取自埃及城市和貓王在田納西州的家，希望把古典與流行結合起來。這個團體的傢俱和雕塑經常利用材料來提供顏色和圖案。

1983 年，富美家公司組織了一場用「彩虹芯」(ColorCore) 美耐板製造的傢俱巡迴展，彙集了由建築師羅伯特·文丘里、弗蘭克·蓋里、斯坦利·泰格曼 (Stanley Tigerman)、詹姆斯·萬 (James Wine) 的作品，以表明美耐板已不再被視為一種虛假的材料，其自身就值得讚美。在隨後的幾年中，該展覽走遍世界。當地設計師在全球巡演的每一站都添新作，強調了品牌的國際豐富性。該展覽為設計、風格和時尚起到了巡迴使館的作用，向世界推薦富美家美耐板。

藝術家、設計師和建築師開始更頻繁地使用美耐板製作傢俱，甚至雕塑。這種材料不再被簡單地作為其他東西 (如石頭或木頭) 的替代品，而是和最初時一樣：是本身就有價值的產品。口號本應該是「讓富美家擔起富美家的名聲！」隨著 1982 年富美家公司彩虹芯美耐板的問世，這種材料保持了色調的深度，並拋棄了早期產品的棕色線條或邊緣，公司的產品更具吸引力。在新辦公室風格的設計師中產生了吸引力。辦公室設計的變化反映業務的新思路。團隊精神和協作得到加強。由於經濟的日益全球化，工人流動性更大。因此，辦公室變得不那麼正式，有更多的公共空間，更需要顏色。

富美家公司早已領悟到，其業務的一個關鍵組成部分是設計。該公司 1951 年聘請了設計師布魯克斯·

作為他用耐火板和類似材料的第一個項目——希望慶祝世俗觀念。他炫耀了低預算，而不是把它隱藏起來。他繼續在這方面努力，把工業材料用在餐飲、零售和辦公場所，幫助創造了高科技的外觀。新一代的建築師和設計師在重新思考圖案和表面。

意大利設計師和建築師索特薩斯 (Ettore Sottsass) 率先重新认识了耐火板。1978 年，他受聘于意大利耐火板公司 Abet Laminati，这是富美家公司在欧洲的竞争对手，为其创造抽象的装饰图案。索特萨斯是一个 1980 年成立于米兰的名叫孟菲斯 (Memphis) 的设计团体的领导者。它的名字取自埃及城市和猫王在田纳西州的家，希望把古典与流行结合起来。这个

สำนักงานสมัยใหม่แสดงให้เห็นถึงความคิดใหม่ ๆ เกี่ยวกับธุรกิจ มีการเน้นการทำงานร่วมกันเป็นทีม พนักงานมีความคล่องตัวขึ้นสืบเนื่องมาจากที่เศรษฐกิจเชื่อมโยงกันทั่วโลก ด้วยเหตุนี้ สำนักงานไม่จำเป็นต้องดูเป็นทางการมากนัก มีพื้นที่ส่วนกลางมากขึ้น และใช้สีสันได้มากขึ้น

บริษัท ฟอร์ไมก้า คอร์ปอเรชั่น เข้าใจมานานแล้วว่า ปัจจัยสำคัญของธุรกิจของบริษัทคือ การออกแบบ บริษัทได้ว่าจ้างนายบรูคส์สตีเวนส์ ให้ออกแบบลวดลายให้บริษัทในปี ค.ศ. 1951 และจ้างนายเรย์มอนด์ โลวีย์ ให้ออกแบบลาย "ซันไรซ์" ใหม่ให้ในปี ค.ศ. 1953 ศูนย์วิจัยและพัฒนาของโรงงานที่อีเวนเดล ซึ่งสร้างขึ้นเมื่อปี ค.ศ. 1960 ซื้อสตูดิโอออกแบบ และในปี ค.ศ. 1969 มีการตั้งคณะกรรมการที่ปรึกษาการออกแบบขึ้นประกอบด้วยที่ปรึกษาซึ่งเป็นบุคคลภายนอกการที่บริษัท ฟอร์ไมก้า ให้ความสำคัญต่อการออกแบบนั้น เป็นแนวคิดที่แพร่หลาย

que le stratifié n'était plus un matériau factice mais qu'il existait par lui-même. Dans les années suivantes, l'exposition a parcouru le monde. De nouveaux travaux par des designers locaux ont été ajoutés à chaque arrêt de la tournée mondiale, soulignant la richesse internationale de la marque. Les expositions se sont faites les ambassadrices du design, du style et de la mode, en présentant le stratifié Formica à travers le monde.

Les artistes, les designers et les architectes ont commencé à utiliser plus souvent le stratifié dans les meubles et même la sculpture. Le matériau n'était plus perçu simplement comme remplaçant quelque chose d'autre, la pierre ou le bois, mais au contraire comme le début d'un produit ayant une valeur véritable. Le slogan aurait pu être : laissez le Formica être Formica ! Avec l'arrivée en 1982 du stratifié Formica Color-Core®, qui conservait sa teinte en profondeur sans la ligne ou le bord marron des produits antérieurs, les produits Formica étaient devenus plus attrayants. Ils rencontraient l'intérêt des designers pour des nouveaux styles de bureaux. Les changements dans la conception des bureaux reflétaient de nouvelles idées sur les entreprises. Le travail d'équipe et la collaboration étaient mis en valeur. Les travailleurs étaient plus mobiles, grâce à la mondialisation croissante de l'économie. En conséquence, les bureaux ont été de moins en moins formels, avec des espaces plus communautaires et sont devenus plus colorés.

Formica Corporation a compris depuis longtemps qu'un élément clé de son activité était le design. L'entreprise avait embauché des designers tels que Brooks Stevens pour concevoir les motifs en 1951 et Raymond Loewy pour créer la nouvelle ligne « Sunrise » en 1953. Le Centre de recherche et de développement à Evendale, construit en 1960, a acquis un studio de design et en 1969, le Design Advisory Board a été établi en utilisant des conseillers extérieurs. L'accent mis par Formica sur le design faisait partie d'une tendance plus générale : les entreprises telles qu'Alessi en Italie, Authentics en Allemagne, Marimekko, Knoll, Bodum, IBM et Sony ont toutes compris l'importance du design pour les identités globales de leurs produits et de leurs en-

gió en Milán cerca de 1980. Tomó su nombre tanto de la ciudad egipcia como de la casa de Elvis Presley en Tennessee, deseando combinar lo clásico con lo popular. Los muebles y las esculturas del grupo solían utilizar el material para ofrecer color y diseño.

En 1983, Formica Corporation organizó una exhibición itinerante de piezas en el laminado ColorCore® que unió el trabajo de los arquitectos Ro-bert Venturi, Frank Gehry, Stanley Tigerman, James Wines de SITE y otros, para mostrar que el laminado ya no se consideraba un material de imitación, sino que resaltaba por sí mismo. En años subsiguientes, la exhibición viajó por el mundo. Se agregaron nuevos trabajos de diseñadores locales en cada evento, para enfatizar la riqueza internacional de la marca. Las exhibiciones sirvieron como embajadas móviles de diseño, estilo y moda, presentando al laminado Formica en todo el mundo.

Los artistas, los diseñadores y los arquitectos comenzaron a utilizar el laminado más a menudo en muebles y hasta en esculturas. Ya no se percibía al material simplemente como un sustituto de algo más, piedra o madera, sino como era en el comienzo: un producto valioso en sí mismo. El eslogan pudo haber sido "¡Dejen que Formica sea Formica!". Con la llegada en 1982 del laminado Color-Core® de Formica Corporation, que mantuvo su matiz en la profundidad y omitió la línea o borde marrón de los primeros productos, los laminados de la empresa se hicieron aún más atractivos. Los diseñadores de nuevos estilos de oficinas descubrieron su encanto. Los cambios en el diseño de oficina reflejaron nuevas ideas sobre los negocios. Se enfatizó el trabajo en equipo y la colaboración. Los trabajadores tenían más movilidad, gracias a la creciente globalización de la economía. Como consecuencia, las oficinas se hacían menos formales, con más espacios comunes, y se dio la bienvenida al color.

Formica Corporation ya había entendido que un componente clave de su empresa era el diseño. La empresa había contratado a los diseñadores Brooks Stevens para idear diseños en 1951 y a Raymond Loewy para crear la nueva línea "Sunrise" en 1953. El Centro de Investigación y Desarrollo en las instalaciones de Evendale, construido en 1960, adquirió un estudio de diseño y,

lautakunta. Formican painotus suunnitteluun oli osa laajempaa suuntausta: yritykset, kuten Alessi Italiassa, Authentics Saksassa, Marimekko, Knoll, Bodum, IBM ja Sony, näkivät kaikki suunnittelun tärkeyden globaalien identiteettien luomisessa heidän tuotteilleen ja yrityksilleen. Yhtiö tehosti nyt ponnistuksiaan suunnittelussa. Noudattamalla johdonmukaisesti pintoja ja koristeita, Formica teki tunnetuksi laminaattiensa mahdollisuuksia ja muutti niiden antamaa kuvaa julkisuudessa.

1980- ja 1990-luku: Hankalat vuosikymmenet yrityskaupan kohteena

Yhtiön liiketoiminnan puolella oltiin vähemmän optimistisia. Vaikka sen kokemus olikin ennakoinut elämäntyylejä ja suuntauksia, yhtiön ongelmat ja haasteet kuvastivat myös huolta aiheuttavia suuntauksia liiketoiminnassa. Se oli joutunut paljon parjatun "monialayritysten" muotihulluuden uhriksi, joka vallitsi 1950-luvulta 1970-luvulle. Kun se myytiin v. 1956, Formica Corporation tuli pieneksi osaksi suuresta 450 miljoonan dollarin American Cyanamid -monialayrityksestä. Katsottuna itsestään selväksi, se ei monien liiketoiminnan veteraanien mielestä saanut riittävää tukea eikä riittäviä investointeja. Kasvu jatkui jonkin aikaa. Formica rakensi suurehkon uuden tehtaan Sierran lähelle Kaliforniaan v. 1966. 1980-lukuun mennessä oli kuitenkin selvää, että tie kasvuun kulkee Amerikan rajojen ulkopuolelle. Yhtiön ja Formica tavaramerkin vetovoima oli maailman laajuisia.

Monialayritykset olivat valtavan suuria yhtiöitä, jotka sulkivat sisäänsä toisiinsa varsin sopimattomia yrityksiä pyrkimyksenään kasvu ja osakkeiden hintojen nousu. Yksi yhtiö voisi todeta valmistavansa dynamoja, myyvänsä henkivakuutuksia ja leipovansa kakkuja tai — eräässä kuuluisassa tapauksessa — valmistavansa high-tech data- ja puhelinkaapeleita, mutta myös savustavansa kinkkua ja pekonia. Monialayhtymistä monet romahtivat 1970-luvulla. Uudet tuulet puhalsivat kuitenkin 1980-lukuun mennessä liiketoiminnassa. Uuden tyyppisen rahoituksen ansiosta, mukaan lukien niin sanotut spekulatiiviset eli roska-arvopaperit, sekä

史蒂文斯設計圖案，1953 年聘請了雷蒙德·洛伊創造了新的「日出」系列產品。位於埃汶代爾設施的研究與開發中心創建於 1960 年，收購了一家設計工作室，並在 1969 年成立了由外部顧問組成的設計諮詢委員會。富美家對設計的注重是一個更廣泛的趨勢：像意大利的阿萊西公司(Alessi)、德國 Authentics 公司、瑪麗馬克公司(Marimekko)、諾爾公司(Knoll)、波頓公司(Bodum)、國際商業機器公司(IBM) 和索尼公司的設計室都看到了設計的重要性，能為它們的產品和它們的公司在全球創建個性。現在，公司加大了設計力度。繼表面材料和裝飾之後，富美家公佈了其美耐板的潛力，並改變了在公眾中的形象。

二十世紀八十年代和九十年代：作為被收購目標困擾幾十年

公司的業務方面並不太樂觀。就像其經歷反映了生活方式和發展趨勢一樣，公司的問題和挑戰也反映了業務方面令人煩惱的趨勢。從二十世紀五十年代到七十年代它一直備受「企業集團」時風的損害。1965 年被賣出後，富美家公司成了資產達 4.5 億美元的美國氰胺公司企業集團的一小部分。許多業界元老認為，它理所當然地得不到足夠的支援，也沒有收到足夠的投資。一時間裡，增長在繼續。1966 年，富美家加利福尼亞州塞拉附近建造了一家新工廠。但到了二十世紀八十年代，很明顯，成長之路要超出美國國界。公司與富美家品牌的吸引力是全球性的。

企業集團是聯合大不相同的各種企業追求經濟增長和增加股價的龐大公司。一家公司可能會發現自己製造發電機、銷售壽險和烘烤蛋糕——或在一個著名的例子中——製造高科技資料和電話線，但也醃製火腿和

团体的家具和雕塑经常利用材料来提供颜色和图案。

1983 年，富美家公司组织了一场用"彩虹芯"(ColorCore)耐火板制造的家具巡回展，汇集了由建筑师罗伯特·文丘里、弗兰克·盖里、斯坦利·泰格曼 (Stanley Tigerman)，詹姆斯·万 (James Wine)的作品，以表明耐火板已不再被视为一种虚假的材料，其自身就值得赞美。在随后的几年中，该展览走遍世界。当地设计师在全球巡演的每一站都添新作，强调了品牌的国际丰富性。该展览为设计、风格和时尚起到了巡回使馆的作用，向世界推荐富美家®装饰耐火板。

艺术家、设计师和建筑师开始更频繁地使用耐火板制作家具，甚至雕塑。这种材料不再被简单地作为其他东西(如石头或木头)的替代品，而是和最初时一样：是本身就有价值的产品。口号本应该是"让富美家担起富美家的名声！"随着 1982 年富美家公司彩虹芯耐火板的问世，这种材料保持了色调的深度，并抛弃了早期产品的棕色线条或边缘，公司的产品更具吸引力。在新办公室风格的设计师中产生了吸引力。办公室设计的变化反映业务的新思路。团队精神和协作得到加强。由于经济的日益全球化，工人流动性更大。因此，办公室变得不那么正式，有更多的公共空间，更需要颜色。

富美家公司早已领悟到，其业务的一个关键组成部分是设计。该公司 1951 年聘请了设计师布鲁克斯·史蒂文斯设计图案，1953 年聘请了雷蒙德·洛伊创造了新的"日出"系列产品。位于埃汶代尔设施的研究与开发中心创建于 1960 年，收购了一家设计工作室，并在 1969 年成立了由外部顾问组成的设计咨询委员会。富美家对设计的注重是一个更广泛的趋势：像意大利的阿莱西公司(Alessi)、德国 Authentics 公司、玛丽马克公司(Marimekko)、诺尔公司(Knoll)、波顿公司(Bodum)、国际商业机器公司(IBM)和索尼公司的设计室都

บริษัทต่างๆ ไม่ว่าจะเป็น บริษัท อเลสซี ในประเทศอิตาลี บริษัท ออเทนติกส์ ในประเทศเยอรมนี บริษัท มารีเมกโก บริษัท นอลล์ บริษัท โบดุม บริษัท ไอบีเอ็ม และ บริษัท โซนี ล้วนแล้วแต่ให้ความสำคัญกับการออกแบบและการสร้างเอกลักษณ์ให้กับผลิตภัณฑ์และบริษัทเป็นที่รู้จักระดับโลก บริษัท ฟอร์ไมก้าจึงให้ความสำคัญกับการออกแบบเพิ่มมากยิ่งขึ้น นอกจากการพัฒนาผลิตภัณฑ์ในด้านพื้นผิวและสีสันลวดลาย บริษัทยังทำการโฆษณาศักยภาพของผลิตภัณฑ์ลามิเนตของบริษัทและเปลี่ยนภาพลักษณ์ผลิตภัณฑ์ลามิเนตที่ปรากฏต่อสาธารณชน

ช่วงทศวรรษที่ 1980 และ 1990 บริษัทประสบปัญหาตกเป็นเป้าของการขายหุ้น

ด้านธุรกิจของบริษัทไม่เจริญรุ่งเรืองดังเช่นด้านผลิตภัณฑ์ของบริษัท ปัญหาของบริษัทที่สะท้อนแนวโน้มปัญหาธุรกิจมากพอๆ กับที่ประสบการณ์ของบริษัทสะท้อนอยู่ในวิถีชีวิตและความนิยม บริษัทตกเป็นเหยื่อของกระแสการดำเนินธุรกิจแบบ "กลุ่มบริษัท" ที่ใช้ในช่วงตั้งแต่ทศวรรษที่ 1950 ถึงทศวรรษที่ 1970 เมื่อบริษัทถูกขายไปในปี 1956 บริษัท ฟอร์ไมก้า คอร์ปอเรชั่น กลายเป็นส่วนเล็กๆ ของกลุ่มบริษัท อเมริกัน ไซนามิด ขนาดใหญ่ที่มีมูลค่า 450 ล้านดอลลาร์สหรัฐ ผู้ที่มีประสบการณ์มายาวนานในธุรกิจเห็นว่าไม่มีคนเห็นคุณค่าของบริษัท จึงไม่มีการสนับสนุนและเงินลงทุนที่เพียงพอ บริษัทเจริญเติบโตได้ระยะหนึ่ง ในปี ค.ศ. 1966 บริษัท ฟอร์ไมก้าสร้างโรงงานแห่งใหม่ที่สำคัญแห่งหนึ่งอยู่ใกล้กับเขตเซียร์รา มลรัฐแคลิฟอร์เนีย อย่างไรก็ดี ภายในช่วงทศวรรษที่ 1980 เห็นได้ชัด

treprises. À ce moment, l'entreprise a développé ses efforts créateurs. Après la surface et l'ornementation, Formica a fait connaître le potentiel de ses stratifiés et a modifié son image publique.

1980 et 1990 : Décennies troublées en tant que cible de rachat

Le côté commercial de la société était moins encourageant. Autant son expérience s'était faite l'écho des modes de vie et des tendances, autant les problèmes de la société et les défis reflétaient également les tendances problématiques des affaires. Formica avait été victime du système de conglomérat à la mode entre les années 1950 et 1970. Lorsque la société a été vendue en 1956, Formica est devenue une petite partie d'un grand conglomérat de 450 millions de dollars : American Cyanamid. Considéré comme acquis, il était trop peu capitalisé et manquait des investissements nécessaires ; de nombreux vétérans de l'entreprise l'avaient perçu. Pendant un certain temps, la croissance s'est poursuivie. Formica a construit une grande usine près de Sierra en Californie en 1966. Mais dans les années 1980, il est devenu clair que le chemin de la croissance traversait les frontières américaines. La société et sa marque Formica sont devenues mondiales.

Les conglomérats étaient d'énormes sociétés qui combinaient des entreprises disparates dans la poursuite de la croissance et de l'augmentation des cours de l'action boursière. Une société pouvait très bien construire des dynamos, vendre des assurances-vie et cuire des gâteaux ou, dans un célèbre cas, fabriquer des câbles pour la transmission des données et le téléphone tout en cuisant des jambons. Beaucoup de conglomérats se sont effondrés dans les années 1970. Mais dans les années 1980, il y avait une nouvelle tendance dans les affaires. Grâce à de nouveaux types de financement, y compris les « junk bonds » et la possibilité de réaliser ce qui a été considéré comme « locked up stockholder value », spécialement pour les entreprises possédant des marques réputées, les achats à effet de levier sont devenus populaires. Les achats à effet de levier (LBO) ont attiré les

en 1969, se estableció una Junta Asesora de Diseño compuesta por asesores externos. El énfasis de Formica en el diseño formaba parte de una tendencia más amplia: las firmas como Alessi en Italia, Authentics en Alemania, Marimekko, Knoll, Bodum, IBM y Sony, vieron la importancia del diseño para crear identidades globales para sus productos y sus empresas. La empresa ya avanzaba en sus esfuerzos de diseño. Al continuar con la superficie y el adorno, Formica publicitó el potencial de sus laminados y cambió su imagen pública.

Las décadas de los ochenta y de los noventa: décadas problemáticas

El lado comercial de la empresa era menos alentador. De la misma manera que su experiencia había reproducido estilos de vida y tendencias, los problemas y los retos de la empresa también reflejaron tendencias problemáticas en los negocios. Había sido víctima de la tan difamada moda del *holding* que pasó de la década de los cincuenta a la de los setenta. Cuando se vendió en 1956, Formica Corporation se convirtió en una pequeña parte del gran *holding* American Cyanamid de $450 millones. De hecho, tenía poco apoyo y no recibía una inversión adecuada, sentían muchos veteranos de la empresa. Durante un tiempo, el crecimiento continuó. En 1966, Formica construyó una nueva planta importante cerca de Sierra, en California. Pero, en la década de los ochenta, era evidente que el camino al crecimiento residía más allá de las fronteras estadounidenses. El atractivo de la empresa y la marca Formica eran globales.

Los *holdings* eran enormes corporaciones que agrupaban empresas dispares en su empeño por lograr crecimiento y aumentar los precios de la acciones. Una empresa podía encontrarse construyendo dínamos, vendiendo seguros de vida y horneando tortas o, en un caso famoso, fabricando cables de telefonía y datos de alta tecnología, pero también curando jamones y tocino. Muchos de los *holdings* colapsaron en la década de los setenta. Pero, en la década de los ochenta, había una nueva tendencia comercial. Gracias a los nuevos tipos de financiación, incluidos los llamados bonos especulativos o bonos basura, y la posibilidad de ma-

mahdollisuus saavuttaa, mitä katsottiin "lukkoon lyödyksi omistaja-arvoksi", varsinkin yhtiöiden tapauksissa joilla oli vahvat tavaramerkit, lainarahoituksella tehty yritysosto tuli suosituksi. Lainarahoituksella tehdyt yritysostot (LBO:t) vetivät puoleensa pankkiireja, sijoittajia ja viime kädessä osakkeenomistajia. Valtavan emoyrityksen jättäessä sen huomiotta monialayhtymien aikakaudella, Formica Corporation kärsi eri tavoin 1980-luvun LBO-jakson aikana. Yhtiö joutui vuoristoradan kaltaisten omistajavaihdosten kohteeksi, joiden aikana investoinnit lyötiin laimin, kuten jotkut teollisuutta seuraavat tarkkailijat uskoivat.

Vuonna 1985 Formica Corporationin toimitusjohtaja Gordon D. Sterling ja Formican hallinto aloitti hankkeen Shearson Lehman and Donaldson, Lufkin & Jenrette -ryhmän kanssa lainarahoituksella tehtyä yritysostoa varten, joka laski yhtiön arvoksi 200 miljoonaa dollaria ja jolla oli velkaa 153 miljoonaa dollaria. Se oli raskas taakka ja sen keventämiseksi yhtiöstä tuli v. 1987 jälleen julkinen, myydessään 5,3 miljoonaa osaketta, eli kolmanneksen omaisuudesta 64 miljoonalla dollarilla. Muut sijoittajat uskoivat kuitenkin suurempaan liikevoittoon. Yhtiön piirissä kierteli puheita yrityksen myymisestä. Vuonna 1988 Formica totesi torjuvansa niin sanottujen rosvojen lähentelyjä. Ensin Samuel Zellin johtama ryhmä, sitten toinen, jota johti Malcolm Glazer, hankki osakkeita. Vuonna 1988 pääjohtaja Sterling kuoli yllättäen. Hänen seuraajakseen tuli CEO Vincent L. Langone. Vuonna 1989, toisessa lainarahoituksella tehdyssä yritysostossa Formican hallinto, Dillon Lue ja Masco tekivät yrityksestä yksityisen. Talous oli kuitenkin taantumassa sekä USA:ssa että Euroopassa. Vuoteen 1990 mennessä yritys tarvitsi 40 -50 miljoonaa dollaria vuodessa yksinomaan korkojen maksuun. Mikä pahinta, tasainen kassavirta, johon sijoittajat olivat luottaneet, oli heikkenemässä. Yhtiön osuus Amerikan markkinoilla oli pudonnut kolmanneksesta noin neljännekseen kokonaismäärästä, lähinnä Wilsonart® laminaattien takia. Formica Corporation tavoitteli kasvua globaalisti, mutta sen havaittavissa oleva pöyhkeys ja huonon palvelun maine olivat haittapuolena.

熏肉。許多企業集團在二十世紀七十年代都倒閉了。但到了二十世紀八十年代，業務又有了新的發展趨勢。由於新類型的融資，包括所謂的投機或垃圾債券，並有可能實現被認為是「被鎖定的股東價值」，尤其對強勢品牌的公司來說，杠杆收購頗為流行。杠杆收購（LBO）吸引了銀行家，投資者，最終是股東。在企業集團年代裡被一個龐大的母公司所忽略的富美家公司，在二十世紀八十年代杠杆收購的年代卻慘遭另一種厄運。一些行業觀察家認為，在此期間，該公司經歷了過山車式的股權變更，投資被忽視。

1985 年，富美家公司總裁戈登·斯德林（Gordon D. Sterling）和富美家管理層在杠杆收購中與希爾森·雷曼（Shearson Lehman）、Donaldson, Lufkin & Jenrette 合作，公司被估值兩億美元，並負擔 1.53 億美元的債務。這是一個沉重的負擔，為減少這個負擔，公司在 1987 年重新上市，出售 530 萬美元的股票，合公司三分之一的股權，售價為 6,400 萬美元。但其他投資者得到的收益更多。關於收購的消息在公司傳得紛紛揚揚。1988 年，富美家發現自己要抵擋所謂搶掠者的進攻。首先，是由塞繆爾·澤

看到了設計的重要性，能為它们的产品和它们的公司在全球创建个性。现在，公司加大了设计力度。继表面材料和装饰之后，富美家公布了其耐火板的潜力，并改变了在公众中的形象。

二十世纪八十年代和九十年代：作为被收购目标困扰几十年

公司的业务方面并不太乐观。就像其经历反映了生活方式和发展趋势一样，公司的问题和挑战也反映了业务方面令人烦恼的趋势。从二十世纪五十年代到七十年代它一直备受"企业集团"时风的损害。1965 年被卖出后，富美家公司成了资产达 4.5 亿美元的美国氰胺公司企业集团的一小部分。许多业界元老认为，它理所当然地得不到足够的支持，也没有收到足够的投资。一时间里，增长在继续。1966 年，富美家加利福尼亚州塞拉附近建造了一家新工厂。但到了二十世纪八十年代，很明显，成长之路要超出美国国界。公司与富美家品牌的吸引力是全球性的。

企业集团是联合大不相同的各种企业追求经济增长和增加股价的庞大公司。一家公司可能会发现自己制造发电机、销售寿险和烘烤蛋糕——或在一个著名的例子中——制造高科技数据和电话线，但也腌制火腿和熏肉。许多企业集团在二十世纪七十年代都倒闭了。但到了二十世纪八十年代，业务又有了新的发展趋势。由于新类型的融资，包括所谓的投机或垃圾债券，并有可能实现被认为是"被锁定的股东价值"，尤其对强势品牌的公司来说，杠杆收购颇为流行。杠杆收购（LBO）吸引了银行家，投资者，最终是股东。在企业集团年代里被一个庞大的母公司所忽略的富美家公司，在二十世纪八十年代杠杆收购的年代却惨遭另一种厄运。一些行业观察家认为，在此期

ว่าความเติบโตของบริษัทจะต้องมาจากการดำเนินธุรกิจนอกสหรัฐอเมริกา บริษัทและตราฟอร์ไมก้า มีความความสนใจที่จะก้าวสู่ระดับโลก

การดำเนินธุรกิจแบบกลุ่มบริษัทเป็นการใช้บริษัทขนาดใหญ่รวมเอาธุรกิจที่แตกต่างกันอย่างมากเข้าด้วยกันเพื่อแสวงหาการเจริญเติบโตทางธุรกิจและเพื่อเพิ่มมูลค่าหุ้นของบริษัท บริษัทหนึ่งอาจดำเนินธุรกิจสร้างเครื่องผลิตกระแสไฟฟ้า ขายประกันชีวิต และอบขนมเค้ก หรือตัวอย่างกรณีที่มีชื่อเสียงกรณีหนึ่ง คือ ผลิตสายโทรศัพท์ข้อมูลเทคโนโลยีสูงและ ในขณะเดียวกันก็บ่มแฮมและเบคอนไปด้วย กลุ่มบริษัทที่ดำเนินธุรกิจเช่นนี้จำนวนมากล้มในช่วงทศวรรษที่ 1970 แต่ในช่วงทศวรรษที่ 1980 เกิดแนวทางการดำเนินธุรกิจใหม่ ทั้งนี้ จากการเกิดวิธีจัดหาเงินทุนประเภทใหม่ ซึ่งรวมถึงที่เรียกกันว่า ตราสารหนี้ระดับเก็งกำไร และวิธีแก้ปัญหา "มูลค่าหุ้นของผู้ถือหุ้นที่ต้องขายตามที่กำหนด" โดยเฉพาะกับบริษัทที่มีตราสินค้าหรือผลิตภัณฑ์ที่มีชื่อเสียง การกู้เงินมาซื้อกิจการ (LBO) เริ่มเป็นที่นิยม บรรดานายธนาคารนักลงทุน และผู้ถือหุ้นเอง ให้ความสนใจกันมาก การที่บริษัทแม่ยักษ์ใหญ่เลยไม่สนใจในยุคธุรกิจแบบกลุ่มบริษัท บริษัท ฟอร์ไมก้า คอร์ปอเรชั่น ได้รับผลกระทบรูปแบบต่าง ๆ ในยุคของการกู้เงินมาซื้อกิจการ ในช่วงทศวรรษที่ 1980 ผู้สังเกตการณ์ในวงการบางรายเชื่อว่า บริษัทฟอร์ไมก้าต้องผ่านการเปลี่ยนแปลงผู้ถือหุ้นแบบน่าเวียนหัวตลอดช่วงที่มีแต่คนสนใจจะลงทุน

ในปี ค.ศ. 1985 นายกอร์ดอน ดี สเตอร์ลิง ประธานบริษัท ฟอร์ไมก้า คอร์ปอเรชั่น และผู้บริหารของ บริษัท ฟอร์ไมก้า ได้ร่วมมือกับบริษัท เชียร์สัน ลห์แมน และ บริษัท โดนัลด์สัน ลูฟคิน แอนด์ เจนเรตต์ ทำการซื้อกิจการของบริษัทแบบกู้เงินมาซื้อกิจการ เป็นมูลค่า 200 ล้านดอลลาร์สหรัฐ โดยมีหนี้สินจำนวน 153 ล้านดอลลาร์สหรัฐ ถือเป็นภาระอันหนักหน่วงสำหรับบริษัท ทำให้บริษัทต้องนำหุ้นจำนวน 5.3 ล้านหุ้นซึ่งคิดเป็นหนึ่งในสามของจำนวนหุ้นทั้งหมดของบริษัท ออกขายต่อประชาชนอีกครั้งในปี ค.ศ. 1987 ในมูลค่า 64 ล้านดอลลาร์สหรัฐ แต่นักลงทุนรายอื่น ๆ มองเห็นรายได้มากว่านั้น ข่าวการซื้อกิจการแพร่ไปทั่วบริษัท ในปี ค.ศ. 1988 บริษัท ฟอร์ไมก้า ต้องคอยปกป้องตนเองจากการถูกบุคคลภายนอกเข้าครอบกิจการ กลุ่มแรกนำโดยนายซามูเอล เซลส์ จากนั้นเป็นกลุ่มที่นำโดยนายมัลคอล์ม เกลเซอร์ เข้าซื้อหุ้นของบริษัท ในปี ค.ศ. 1988 ประธานสเตอร์ลิงถึงแก่กรรมอย่างกะทันหัน นายวินเซนต์ แอล

banquiers, les investisseurs et finalement les actionnaires. Ignorée par une maison mère géante pendant l'ère du conglomérat, Formica Corporation a souffert de différentes façons pendant la période LBO des années 1980. La société a subi de nombreux changements de propriété au cours desquels l'investissement a été négligé, selon certains observateurs de l'industrie.

En 1985, le président de la société Formica, Gordon D. Sterling, et l'équipe de direction dirigée par Shearson Lehman et Donaldson, Lufkin & Jenrette ont effectué un LBO qui valorisait la société à 200 millions de dollars, société qui avait 153 millions de dollars de dette. C'était un lourd fardeau et pour la réduire en 1987, la société est devenue publique encore une fois avec la vente de 5 300 000 parts, soit un tiers du capital, pour 64 millions de dollars. Mais d'autres investisseurs voyaient plus loin. Les rumeurs de rachat tourbillonnaient autour de l'entreprise. En 1988, Formica a repoussé les approches de raiders. Un groupe dirigé par Samuel Zell, puis un autre dirigé par Malcolm Glazer, ont pris des positions dans les actions. En 1988, le président Sterling est décédé subitement. Il a été remplacé par le PDG Vincent L. Langone. En 1989, dans un second achat à effet de levier, la direction de Formica, Dillon Read et Masco, a rendu l'entreprise privée. Mais l'économie allait vers une récession, à la fois aux États-Unis et en Europe. En 1990, la société a eu besoin de 40 à 50 millions de dollars annuellement simplement pour payer les intérêts. Pire encore : le flux de trésorerie stable sur lequel les investisseurs avaient compté, s'affaiblissait. L'action de la société sur le marché américain était tombée d'un tiers à un quart du total, principalement suite à la concurrence des stratifiés Wilsonart®. La société Formica a recherché une croissance au niveau mondial, mais son arrogance perçue et sa réputation d'un service médiocre représentaient un inconvénient.

En 1995, la société a été achetée pour environ 600 millions de dollars par BTR Nylex, une filiale australienne de BTR, le conglomérat industriel britannique qui s'appelait initialement British Tire and Rubber. Les nouveaux propriétaires ont remplacé la haute direction, y compris le PDG Vince Lan-

terializar lo que se consideraba un "valor restringido del accionista", especialmente para empresas con marcas fuertes, la compra apalancada se volvió popular. Las compras apalancadas (*leveraged buyout*, LBO) atraían a los banqueros, inversionistas y, por último, a los accionistas. Ignorada por un enorme padre corporativo durante la era de los *holdings*, Formica Corporation sufrió de diferentes formas durante el período de LBO de la década de los ochenta. La empresa experimentó una montaña rusa de cambios de propiedad durante los que se descuidó la inversión, de acuerdo con algunos observadores de la industria.

En 1985, el presidente de Formica Corporation, Gordon D. Sterling, y la gerencia de Formica trabajaron en colaboración con Shearson Lehman y Donaldson, Lufkin & Jenrette en una compra apalancada que tasó a la empresa en $200 millones y acumuló una deuda por $153 millones. Fue una pesada carga, y para reducirla, en 1987 la empresa comenzó a cotizar en bolsa, vendiendo 5.3 millones de acciones, un tercio del patrimonio, de $64 millones. Pero otros inversionistas vieron mayores ganancias. Corría el rumor de una compra total de la empresa. En 1988, Formica se encontraba esquivando a los llamados especuladores. Primero, un grupo dirigido por Samuel Zell y, luego, otro encabezado por Malcolm Glazer participaron en las acciones. En 1988, fallece inesperadamente el presidente Sterling. Le sucedió el director ejecutivo Vincent L. Langone. En 1989, en una segunda compra apalancada, la gerencia de Formica, Dillon Read y Masco hicieron que la empresa dejara de cotizar en bolsa. Pero la economía se dirigía a una recesión, tanto en los EE. UU. como en Europa. En 1990, la empresa necesitaba entre $40 y $50 millones anualmente solo para cumplir con los pagos de intereses. Y lo peor de todo, el flujo de efectivo estable con el que contaban los inversionistas se debilitaba. Las acciones de la empresa del mercado estadounidense habían caído de un tercio a, aproximadamente, un cuarto del total, debido, en gran medida, a la competencia de los laminados Wilsonart®. Formica Corporation buscaba un crecimiento global, pero su aparente arrogancia y reputación de servicio deficiente eran una desventaja.

Vuonna 1995 yhtiön osti noin 600 miljoonalla dollarilla BTR Nylexin, BTR:n australialaisen tytäryhtiön. BTR oli englantilainen teollisuuden monialayritys, joka aloitti nimellä British Tire and Rubber. Uudet omistajat vaihtoivat ylimmän johdon, mukaan lukien CEO Vince Langone ja CFO David Schneider, ja monet olivat sitä mieltä, että palvelu ja myynti kärsivät. Vuonna 1998 BTR myi Formica Corporationin kolmannessa lainarahoituksella tehdyssä yritysostossa. Riskipääomaryhmä otti haltuunsa Formica-yhtiön 405 miljoonalla dollarilla, mukaan lukien Citicorp CVC European Equity Partners ja Donaldson, Lufkin, Jenrette. Uudet omistajat kutsuivat takaisin Langonen ja Schneiderin ja helmikuussa 1999 ryhtyivät hankkimaan käyttöpääomaa liiketoiminnan uudelleen rakentamiseksi myymällä 215 miljoonaa dollaria korkeatuottoista velkaa. Suunnitelmana oli laajentua strategisilla yrityskaupoilla. Ponnistelut kuitenkin jäivät vuonna 2000 alkaneen laskusuhdanteen hampaisiin.

Joistakin näytti siltä, kuin yhtiötä olisi ojennettu yhdeltä sijoittajien ryhmältä toiselle, aivan kuin Formica-laminaatin näytepalaa suunnittelijan näytteiden ketjussa. Oliko Formica-tavaramerkki niin vahva, että omistajat uskoivat sen kestävän minkä tahansa määrän blue-chip -tavaramerkkien käsittelyä? *Business Week* julkaisi v. 1999 tylyn arvostelun siitä, mitä yhtiö oli joutunut kokemaan. Se kutsui Formica Corporationia "orpoyritykseksi, joka epätoivoisesti etsii kotia". Lehti jatkoi: "Formica on ollut vanhempiensa, kahden monialayhtymän laiminlyöty, jopa huonosti kohdeltu lapsipuoli". "Se on kestänyt kolme lainarahoituksella tehtyä yritysostoa. Se on selviytynyt näennäisen loputtomien omistajien ja johtokuntien jäsenten jaloista, ylettömästä yrityksen strategioiden ja uudelleenorganisointien määrästä puhumattakaan". Laskukauden aikana, kuten Mark Adamson mainitsee, "liiketoiminnan ytimen perusteet kadotettiin. Hallinto löi laimin tuotteen, asiakkaat ja palvelun. He myös löivät laimin tutkimuksen ja teknologian, varsinkin kilpailevat tuotteet". Heiltä jäivät huomaamatta uudet teknologiat, kuten kilpailevat Corian® materiaalit DuPont-yhtiöstä. Myöhemmin yrityskauppo-

爾 (Samuel Zell) 領頭的小組，然後是由馬爾科姆·格雷澤倉 (Malcolm Glazer) 為首的小組增加了持倉。1988 年，董事長斯德林突然去世。他的繼任者為文森特·朗格尼 (Vincent L. Langone) 首席執行官。1989 年，在第二次杠杆收購中，富美家高管狄龍·里德 (Dillon Read) 和馬斯科 (Masco) 把公司私有化。但無論是在美國和歐洲，經濟正在走向衰退。到 1990 年，公司每年需要 4,000 萬美元到 5,000 萬美元才僅夠支付利息。最糟糕的是，投資者指望的穩定現金流在變少。公司在美國的市場所佔比重已經從總數的三分之一下降到約四分之一，主要是由於來自威盛 (Wilsonart®) 美耐板的競爭。富美家公司在尋找全球增長，但其公認的傲慢和服務差的名聲是一個不利因素。

1995 年，公司以六億美元被 BTR Nylex 公司收購，BTR Nylex 是英國工業企業集團 BTR 在澳洲的子公司，BTR 初創時為英國輪胎和橡膠公司 (British Tire and Rubber)。新業主更換了高層管理人員，包括首席執行官文斯·朗格尼和首席財務官大衛·施奈德 (David Schneider)，許多人認為，服務和銷售受到損害。1998 年，在第三次杠杆收購中，BTR 出售了富美家公司。富美家公司以 4.05 億美元的價格被一家風險投資集團接管，其中包括花旗公司 (Citicorp) CVC 歐洲股票合作夥伴和 Donaldson, Lufkin & Jenrette。新業主重新啟用了朗格尼和施耐德，並在 1999 年 2 月提出透過出售 2.15 億美元高收益債券，籌集營運資金，以重建業務。該項計劃是為了透過收購戰略擴大生產。但這種努力是在 2000 年開始的經濟衰退的關口。

對有些人來說，似乎公司在從一批投資者轉到另一批投資者手中，就像設計師的樣本鏈上的一個富美家美耐板樣片。難道富美家品牌名聲如此

間，該公司經歷了過山車式的股權變更，投資被忽視。

1985 年，富美家公司總裁戈登·斯德林 (Gordon D. Sterling) 和富美家管理層在杠杆收購中與希爾森·雷曼 (Shearson Lehman)、Donaldson, Lufkin & Jenrette 合作，公司被估值兩億美元，並負擔 1.53 億美元的債務。這是一個沉重的負擔，為減少這個負擔，公司在 1987 年重新上市，出售 530 萬美元的股票，合公司三分之一的股權，售價為 6,400 萬美元。但其他投資者得到的收益更多。關於收購的消息在公司傳得紛紛揚揚。1988 年，富美家發現自己要抵擋所謂搶掠者的進攻。首先，是由塞繆爾·澤爾 (Samuel Zell) 領頭的小組，然後是由馬爾科姆·格雷澤倉 (Malcolm Glazer) 為首的小組增加了持倉。1988 年，董事長斯德林突然去世。他的繼任者為文森特·朗格尼 (Vincent L. Langone) 首席執行官。1989 年，在第二次杠杆收購中，富美家高管狄龍·里德 (Dillon Read) 和馬斯科 (Masco) 把公司私有化。但無論是在美國和歐洲，經濟正在走向衰退。到 1990 年，公司每年需要 4,000 萬美元到 5,000 萬美元才僅夠支付利息。最糟糕的是，投資者指望的穩定現金流在變少。公司在美國的市場所佔比重已經從總數的三分之一下降到約四分之一，主要是由於來自威盛 (Wilsonart®) 耐火板的競爭。富美家公司在尋找全球增長，但其公認的傲慢和服務差的名聲是一個不利因素。

1995 年，公司以六億美元被 BTR Nylex 公司收購，BTR Nylex 是英國工業企業集團 BTR 在澳大利亞的子公司，BTR 初創時為英國輪胎和橡膠公司 (British Tire and Rubber)。新業主更換了高層管理人員，包括首席執行官文斯·朗格尼和首席財務官大衛·施奈德 (David Schneider)，許多人認為，服務和銷售受到損害。1998 年，在第三次杠杆收購中，BTR 出售了富美家公司。富美家公司以 4.05 億美元的價格被一

แลงกอน เข้ารับตำแหน่งประธานเจ้าหน้าที่บริหารแทนในปี ค.ศ. 1989 มีการซื้อกิจการแบบกู้เงินมาซื้อกิจการ ครั้งที่สอง ฝ่ายบริหารของบริษัท ฟอร์ไมก้า ดิลลอน รีด และ มาสโค แปลงบริษัทกลับเป็นบริษัทเอกชน ขณะนั้นเป็นช่วงที่กำลังเข้าสู่ภาวะเศรษฐกิจตกต่ำทั้งในสหรัฐอเมริกาและทวีปยุโรป ปี ค.ศ. 1990 บริษัทต้องการเงินจำนวน 40 ถึง 50 ล้านดอลลาร์สหรัฐต่อปีสำหรับชำระดอกเบี้ยเพียงอย่างเดียวเท่านั้น สิ่งที่แย่ที่สุดคือ กระแสเงินสดหมุนเวียนที่นักลงทุนคาดหวังกลับแย่ลง ส่วนแบ่งตลาดในสหรัฐอเมริกาของบริษัทร่วงลงจากหนึ่งในสามเหลือประมาณหนึ่งในสี่ ซึ่งเป็นผลมาจากการแข่งขันของผลิตภัณฑ์ลามิเนทวิลสันอาร์ต บริษัท ฟอร์ไมก้าคอร์ปอเรชัน ได้มองหาช่องทางที่จะเติบโตในระดับโลก แต่การถูกมองว่าเป็นบริษัทที่เย่อหยิ่งและมีชื่อเสียงในด้านบริการที่ไม่ดีเป็นจุดอ่อนของบริษัท

ในปี ค.ศ. 1995 บริษัทถูกบริษัท บีทีอาร์ ไนเลกซ์ ซึ่งเป็นบริษัทลูกในประเทศออสเตรเลียของบริษัท บีทีอาร์ ซึ่งเป็นกลุ่มบริษัทอุตสาหกรรมของสหราชอาณาจักรที่เริ่มทำธุรกิจโดยใช้ชื่อ บริษัท บริติช ไทร์ แอนด์ รับเบอร์ ซื้อไปในราคาประมาณ 600 ล้านดอลลาร์สหรัฐ ผู้ถือหุ้นใหม่ทำการเปลี่ยนผู้บริหารระดับสูง ซึ่งรวมถึง นายวินซ์ แลงกอนประธานเจ้าหน้าที่บริหาร และนายเดวิดชไนเดอร์ ประธานเจ้าหน้าที่บริหารฝ่ายการเงินด้วย หลายคนรู้สึกว่าการบริการและการขายได้รับผลกระทบจากการเปลี่ยนแปลงดังกล่าว ต่อมาในปี ค.ศ. 1998 บริษัท บีทีอาร์ ขาย บริษัทฟอร์ไมก้า คอร์ปอเรชัน ในการซื้อกิจการแบบกู้เงินมาซื้อกิจการครั้งที่สาม บริษัท ฟอร์ไมก้าคอร์ปอเรชัน ถูกกลุ่มบริษัทร่วมทุน ซึ่งรวมถึงบริษัท ซีวีซี ยูโรเปียน อีควิตี้ พาร์ทเนอร์สของบริษัท ซิตี้คอร์ป และ บริษัท โดนัลด์สันลุฟคิน แอนด์ เจนเรตต์ ซื้อกิจการไปในราคา 405 ล้านดอลลาร์สหรัฐ ผู้ถือหุ้นใหม่จ้างนายแลงกอนและนายชไนเดอร์กลับเข้ามา และดำเนินการจัดหาเงินทุนหมุนเวียนเพื่อสร้างธุรกิจใหม่โดยขายตราสารหนี้ระดับต่ำ ในเดือนกุมภาพันธ์ ค.ศ. 1999 มูลค่า 215 ล้านดอลลาร์สหรัฐ ในขณะนั้นบริษัทมีแผนขยายธุรกิจโดยการเข้าซื้อกิจการ แต่แผนดังกล่าวต้องถูกกระทบด้วยผลของภาวะเศรษฐกิจตกต่ำที่เริ่มต้นในปี ค.ศ. 2000

สำหรับบางคน ดูเหมือนว่า บริษัทถูกส่งต่อจากนักลงทุนกลุ่มหนึ่งไปยังอีกกลุ่มหนึ่งเหมือนเป็นชิปตัวอย่างลามิเนทฟอร์ไมก้าบนห่วงตัวอย่างของนักออกแบบ หรือผู้ถือหุ้นมั่นใจว่าตราฟอร์ไมก้ามีชื่อเสียงมากพอที่จะทำเช่นนั้นได้ ในปี ค.ศ. 1999 นิตยสาร

gone et le directeur financier David Schneider, et beaucoup pensaient que le service et les ventes allaient en pâtir. En 1998, lors d'un troisième achat à effet de levier, BTR a vendu Formica Corporation. Pour 405 millions de dollars, la société Formica a été reprise par un groupe de capital-risque, y compris les partenaires de Citicorp CVC European Equity et Donaldson, Lufkin, Jenrette. Les nouveaux propriétaires ont rappelé Langone et Schneider et en février 1999, ont acquis le fonds de roulement pour reconstruire l'entreprise grâce à la vente de 215 millions de dollars d'obligations à rendement élevé. Le plan consistait en une extension par des acquisitions stratégiques. Mais malheureusement, la récession se profilait à partir de 2000.

Pour certains, il semblait que la société avait été ballottée d'un groupe d'investisseurs à l'autre, comme un échantillon de stratifié Formica sur une chaîne de prototype de designer. La marque Formica était-elle à ce point si puissante que les propriétaires pensaient pouvoir soutenir n'importe quelle manipulation ? En 1999, *Business Week* était sévère dans son jugement en déclarant que la société avait fait son temps. Le magazine désigna Formica Corporation comme « un orphelin d'entreprise désespérément à la recherche d'une maison. Formica a été la belle-fille négligée, même abusée d'un conglomérat à deux parents, » prétendait encore le magazine. « La société a subi trois opérations de LBO. Elle a résisté à une série apparemment sans fin de propriétaires et de membres de conseil d'administration, sans parler d'une multitude de stratégies et restructurations d'entreprise. » Au cours de la période de déclin, a déclaré Mark Adamson, « les buts fondamentaux de l'entreprise de base ont été perdus. La direction a négligé le produit, le client et le service. Ils ont également négligé la recherche et la technologie, et ont notamment manqué de produits compétitifs. » Ils n'ont pas pris en compte les nouvelles technologies, comme les matériaux concurrents en Corian® de DuPont. Plus tard, après les rachats, les gestionnaires se sont concentrés sur les coûts et les frais généraux, à l'exclusion d'autres facteurs, pour que l'entreprise puisse être vendue à bon prix. En consé-

En 1995, la empresa fue comprada por, aproximadamente, $600 millones por BTR Nylex, una subsidiaria australiana de BTR, el *holding* industrial británico que comenzó como British Tire and Rubber. Los nuevos propietarios reemplazaron a la gerencia principal, incluidos el director ejecutivo Vince Langone y el director de finanzas David Schneider, y muchos sintieron que el servicio y las ventas se vieron afectados. En 1998, en una tercera compra apalancada, BTR vendió Formica Corporation. Por $405 millones, la empresa Formica fue absorbida por un grupo de capital de riesgo, entre los que se encontraban CVC European Equity Partners de Citicorp y Donaldson, Lufkin & Jenrette. Los nuevos propietarios incorporaron nuevamente a Langone y a Schneider, y, en febrero de 1999, adquirieron capital circulante para reconstruir la empresa mediante la venta de $215 millones de deuda de alto rendimiento. El plan era expandirse con adquisiciones estratégicas. Pero el esfuerzo se llevó a cabo en medio de las dificultades de una recisión que comenzó a principios del 2000.

Para algunos, parecía que la empresa había pasado de un grupo de inversionistas a otro, como de una pieza de muestra de laminado Formica a una cadena de muestra de diseñador. ¿Era la marca Formica tan fuerte que los propietarios confiaron en que podía soportar un sinnúmero de manejos de una marca de primer nivel? *Business Week*, en 1999, fue severa en su juicio de lo que había atravesado la empresa. Denominó a Formica Corporation "una empresa huérfana, desesperadamente en busca de un hogar". "Formica ha sido una hijastra descuidada,

jen jälkeen johtajat keskittyivät kuluihin ja yleiskustannuksiin, muut tekijät pois sulkien, siten, että yhtiö voitaisiin myydä hyvällä voitolla. Tämän seurauksena sijoitukset ja ylläpito toisinaan lykättiin tuonnemmaksi tai lyötiin laimin. Tuotteiden ja palvelun sijasta johto keskittyi omaan poistumisstrategiaansa — yhtiön valmisteluun myytäväksi mahdollisimman pian.

Kahdeskymmenes vuosisata

Jo vuonna 1990 puolet Formica Corporationin liiketoiminnasta tuli Yhdysvaltojen ulkopuolelta. Yhtiön tulevaisuus nojasi globaaliin kasvuun, ja laajennuksen kautta Formica toivoi muuttavansa suuntauksen. Perstorp Surface Materials -yhtiön, Euroopan markkinajohtajan ja alansa uudistajan osto v. 2000, tarjosi tilaisuuden siirtyä globaalin kilpailukyvyn suuntaan. Vuonna 1985 emoyhtiö Perstorp oli tuonut myyntiin uuden laminaattipohjaisen Pergo® lattiamuodon, josta tuli valtava menestys. Yhtiö päätti keskittyä tähän liiketoimintaan ja perusti Pergo Flooring -yrityksen erilliseksi jaostoksi v. 1998. Se myi pois muovin ja biotieteiden jaostonsa. Se päätti myös myydä Perstorp Surface Materials -jaoston Formicalle, pitäen vain Chemicals ja Pergo Flooring -jaostot ryhmässä. Vuonna 2001 Pergo Flooringista tuli erillinen yhtiö ja Perstorp keskittyi kemiallisten raakaaineiden liiketoimintaan — palaten tavallaan lähtöpisteeseensä.

Perstorpin osto toi tullessaan useita korkeapainelaminaattien tehtaita, pääosin Euroopassa ja Brasiliassa, mutta sisälsi myös yhden tehtaan

強大，業者認為肯定能經得起像對藍籌品牌的大量折騰嗎？1999 年，《商業週刊》(Business Week) 對該公司的經歷做出了嚴峻的裁判。它稱富美家公司是「正拼命找家的孤兒」。這家雜誌還說：「富美家一直被兩個企業集團母公司忽視 (甚至虐待) 的繼子女」。「它已經歷了三次槓桿收購。它經受住了看似無盡的一系列業主和董事會成員更換，更不用說大量的企業戰略和重組。」在衰落期，馬克·亞當森說：「核心業務的基本面被丟失。管理層忽略了產品、客戶和服務。他們也忽視了研究和技術，特別是有競爭力的產品。」他們沒有看到新的技術，如對手杜邦公司生產的可麗耐 (Corian®) 材料。後來，在收購後，管理人員集中解決成本和管理費用問題，而放棄了其他因素，為的是讓公司可以賣一個好價錢。結果，投資和維護有時會被推遲或乾脆不做。管理層的重點放在了其脫身策略，而不是產品和服務——讓公司準備好售出，越快越好。

二十世紀

早在 1990 年，富美家公司的一半業務來自美國以外地區。該公司的未來在於全球的增長，透過擴展，富美家希望能逆轉狂瀾。2000 年，購買柏斯托面材產品公司 (Perstorp Sur-face Products)，證明是邁向全球競爭的一次機會，帕斯托是歐洲市場和創新領域的領導者。1985 年，帕斯托的母公司推出了一種新形層壓地板柏麗地板 (Pergo®)，取得了巨大成功。公司決定專注於此項業務，並在 1998 年把柏麗地板建成一個獨立的分支。它變賣了其塑膠和生命科學部門。它還決定向富美家出售柏斯托面材產品，只保留了化學品和柏麗地板。2001 年，柏麗地板成為一個獨立的公司，柏斯托集中在化工原料業務上——一定意義上回歸到它的起源。

家风险投资集团接管，其中包括花旗公司 (Citicorp) CVC 欧洲股票合作伙伴和 Donaldson, Lufkin & Jenrette。新业主重新启用了朗格尼和施耐德，并在 1999 年 2 月提出通过出售 2.15 亿美元高收益债券，筹集营运资金，以重建业务。该项计划是为了通过收购战略扩大生产。但这种努力是在 2000 年开始的经济衰退的关口。

对有些人来说，似乎公司在从一批投资者转向另一批投资者手中，就像设计师的样本链上的一个富美家®装饰耐火板样品片。难道富美家品牌名声如此强大，业者认为肯定能经得起像对蓝筹品牌的大量折腾吗？1999 年，《商业周刊》(Business Week) 对该公司的经历做出了严峻的裁判。它称富美家公司是"正拼命找家的孤儿"。这家杂志还说："富美家一直被两个企业集团母公司忽视 (甚至虐待) 的继子女"。"它已经历了三次杠杆收购。它经受住了看似无尽的一系列业主和董事会成员更换，更不用说大量的企业战略和重组。"在衰落期，马克·亚当森说："核心业务的基本面被丢失。管理层忽略了产品、客户和服务。他们也忽视了研究和技术，特别是有竞争力的产品。"他们没有看到新的技术，如对手杜邦公司生产的可丽耐 (Corian®) 材料。后来，在收购后，管理人员集中解决成本和管理费用问题，而放弃了其他因素，为的是让公司可以卖一个好价钱。结果，投资和维护有时会被推迟或干脆不做。管理层的重点放在了其脱身策略，而不是产品和服务——让公司准备好售出，越快越好。

二十世纪

早在 1990 年，富美家公司的一半业务来自美国以外地区。该公司的未来在于全球的增长，通过扩展，富美家希望能逆转狂澜。2000 年，购买柏斯托面材产品公司 (Perstorp Surface Prod-ucts)，证明是迈向全球竞争的一次机会，帕斯托是欧洲市场和创新领域的

บิสซิเนสวีค ชี้ว่าการซื้อกิจการต่างๆ เหมือนบริษัท ฟอร์ไมก้า คอร์ปอเรชั่น เป็น "บริษัทกำพร้าพยายามอย่างมากที่จะหาบ้านอยู่" และ "ฟอร์ไมก้าเป็นลูกเลี้ยงที่ถูกละเลย และถูกทำร้าย ของบริษัทแม่ยักษ์ใหญ่สองบริษัท" นิตยสารดังกล่าวระบุด้วยว่า "บริษัทต้องผ่านการซื้อกิจการด้วยเงินกู้ถึงสามครั้ง และเปลี่ยนเจ้าของและคณะกรรมการหลายครั้ง ยังไม่รวมถึงการเปลี่ยนกลยุทธ์ขององค์กรและการปรับองค์กรครั้งแล้วครั้งเล่า" นายมาร์ค อดัมสัน กล่าวในช่วงที่ธุรกิจตกต่ำว่า "องค์ประกอบสำคัญของธุรกิจหลักได้หายไปแล้ว ฝ่ายบริหารไม่สนใจผลิตภัณฑ์ ลูกค้า และการบริการและไม่สนใจงานค้นคว้าและเทคโนโลยี โดยเฉพาะผลิตภัณฑ์ที่สามารถใช้ทดแทนได้" ฝ่ายบริหารมองไม่เห็นเทคโนโลยีใหม่ๆ เช่น คอเรียน ผลิตภัณฑ์ที่สามารถใช้ทดแทนของบริษัท ดูปองต์ ต่อมาหลังจากการซื้อกิจการทั้งหลาย ผู้จัดการต่างๆเน้นหนักในการควบคุมต้นทุนและค่าใช้จ่าย โดยไม่ค่อยสนใจปัจจัยอื่นๆ เพียงเพื่อบริษัทจะได้ขายได้ในราคาที่ให้กำไรดี ผลที่เกิดขึ้นก็คือ การลงทุนและการบำรุงรักษาบางครั้งถูกเลื่อนออกไปหรือถูกละเลย ฝ่ายบริหารมุ่งเน้นไปที่กลยุทธ์ในการหาทางออก นั่นคือ การเตรียมบริษัทเพื่อขายกิจการโดยเร็วที่สุด แทนที่จะเน้นผลิตภัณฑ์และบริการ

ศตวรรษที่ 20

เริ่มตั้งแต่ปี ค.ศ. 1990 ธุรกิจครึ่งหนึ่งของบริษัท ฟอร์ไมก้า คอร์ปอเรชั่น มาจากนอกสหรัฐอเมริกา อนาคตของบริษัทขึ้นอยู่กับการเติบโตในระดับโลก และบริษัท ฟอร์ไมก้าคาดหวังว่าจะสามารถพลิกสถานการณ์กลับมาได้โดยการขยายกิจการ ในปี ค.ศ. 2000 บริษัทฟอร์ไมก้าซื้อกิจการผลิตภัณฑ์พื้นผิวเพอร์สตอร์ป ซึ่งเป็นผู้นำในตลาดยุโรปและเป็นผู้นำนวัตกรรมในสาขานี้ นับเป็นโอกาสในการก้าวเข้าสู่การแข่งขันระดับโลก ในปี ค.ศ. 1985 บริษัทแม่เพอร์สตอร์ป ได้เปิดตัววัสดุพื้นลามิเนตรูปแบบใหม่ ภายใต้เครื่องหมายการค้าจดทะเบียน เพอร์โก ซึ่งประสบความสำเร็จมาก บริษัทตัดสินใจที่จะมุ่งความสนใจไปที่ธุรกิจนี้และจัดตั้งแผนกวัสดุพื้นเพอร์โก แยกออกมาต่างหากในปี ค.ศ. 1998 และขายแผนกพลาสติกและวิทยาศาสตร์สิ่งมีชีวิตออกไป นอกจากนี้ บริษัทตัดสินใจขายแผนกผลิตภัณฑ์พื้นผิวเพอร์สตอร์ป ให้แก่ บริษัท ฟอร์ไมก้า โดยเก็บเฉพาะกิจการส่วนสารเคมีและแผนกวัสดุพื้นเพอร์โกเอาไว้ในกลุ่ม ในปี ค.ศ. 2001 กิจการส่วนวัสดุพื้นเพอร์โกแยกออกไปเป็นบริษัทต่าง

quence, l'investissement et l'entretien ont été parfois différés ou négligés. Au lieu de produits et de services, la gestion se concentrait sur sa stratégie de sortie-préparation de l'entreprise pour la vente aussi tôt que possible.

Le vingtième siècle

Dès 1990, la moitié du chiffre d'affaires de Formica Corporation provenait de l'extérieur des États-Unis. L'avenir de l'entreprise participait à la croissance mondiale et grâce à cette expansion, Formica espérait renverser la vapeur. En 2000, l'achat de Perstorp Surface Materials, leader du marché européen et innovateur dans le domaine, a offert l'occasion de progresser en matière de compétitivité mondiale. En 1985, la société mère Perstorp avait introduit une nouvelle forme de stratifié à base de revêtement de sol, Pergo®, qui s'est révélé être un énorme succès. La société a décidé de se concentrer sur cette activité et Pergo Flooring a été établi comme division distincte en 1998. Les divisions des plastiques et sciences de la vie ont été vendues. Il a également été décidé de vendre la division Perstorp Surface Materials à Formica, retenant uniquement Chemicals et Pergo Flooring dans le groupe. En 2001, Pergo Flooring est devenu une société séparée et Perstorp s'est concentré sur son activité en produits chimiques bruts, en quelque sorte un retour aux sources.

L'acquisition de Perstorp a apporté avec elle plusieurs usines de stratifié haute pression, principalement en Europe et au Brésil, mais aussi une usine en Thaïlande dans les secteurs clés de croissance en Asie. Elle a également apporté une culture de l'innovation et de la créativité qui avait produit le nouveau revêtement de sol stratifié et le revêtement extérieur. Bien qu'elle finirait par profiter à l'entreprise, l'acquisition de Perstorp est intervenue à la veille d'un ralentissement économique et pendant une période d'augmentation des dettes de l'entreprise. L'intégration de la nouvelle acquisition s'est révélée être un véritable défi et les espoirs d'autres acquisitions se sont avérés vains. Avec une société criblée de dettes (540 millions de dollars), un nouveau PDG, Frank Riddick, et le conseil d'administration ont décidé en 2002 que la société allait demander

víctima de los *holdings*", continuaba la revista. "Ha soportado tres compras apalancadas. Ha superado lo que parece una infinita diversidad de propietarios y miembros de la junta, sin mencionar una plétora de estrategias corporativas y reestructuraciones". Durante el período de descenso, expresa Mark Adamson, "se perdieron los principios comerciales fundamentales. La gerencia descuidó el producto, el cliente y el servicio. También descuidaron la investigación y la tecnología, especialmente los productos competitivos". No vieron las nuevas tecnologías, como los materiales rivales Corian® de DuPont. Posteriormente, después de las compras totales, los gerentes se concentraron en los costos y en los gastos generales de estructura excluyendo otros factores, de modo que la empresa pudiera venderse para obtener una buena ganancia. En consecuencia, algunas veces, se diferían o des-cuidaban la inversión y el mantenimiento. En vez de concentrarse en el producto y en el ser-

Thaimaassa Aasian kasvun avainalueella. Se toi myös innovaation ja luovuuden kulttuurin, joka oli tuottanut uusia laminaattilattioita ja ulkosivun pinnoituksia. Vaikka Perstorpin ostaminen tulisikin aikanaan hyödyttämään yhtiötä, se osui taloudellisen laskusuunnan aattopäiviin ja lisäsi yhtiön velkoja. Uuden yrityshankinnan yhdistäminen osoittautui haasteeksi ja toiveet muista yrityskaupoista osoittautuivat turhiksi. Yhtiön velkataakan ollessa 540 miljoonaa dollaria, uusi CEO Frank Riddick ja johtokunta päättivät v. 2002, että yhtiön on haettava suojaa konkurssituomioistuimesta. Se nousi jaloilleen uuden suunnitelman kanssa keväällä 2004 joka toi 175 miljoonaa dollaria käteissijoituksia, vähensi takeelliset velat yli 300 miljoonasta dollarista noin 127 miljoonaan dollariin ja eliminoi 215 miljoonaa dollaria takeetonta velkaa.

Maapallon toisella puolella asiat alkoivat kehittyä siten, että ne tulisivat

FORMICA

LA MARCA QUE GARANTIZA LA CALIDAD DE UN TABLERO PLASTICO

收購柏斯托帶來了一些高壓美耐板工廠，主要分佈在歐洲和巴西，但也包括亞洲主要增長區域的一家泰國工廠。這同時也帶來了曾創造了新的強化木地板和外牆覆蓋的一種創新和創造力文化。雖然這將最終使公司受益，但收購柏斯托是在經濟衰退前夕，增加了公司的債務。融合新的收購證明是一項挑戰，其他收購的希望最後也是枉然。公司現在負債5.4億美元，新首席執行官弗蘭克·里迪克 (Frank Riddick) 和董事會在2002年決定，公司將在破產法庭尋求保護。2004年春天，公司走出破產，重新設定了一個方案，增加了1.75億美元的現金投資，把抵押債務從3億多美元減少到1.27億美元，銷除了2.15億美元的無抵押債務。

在地球的另一邊，形勢正開始變化，最終將極大地影響公司的未來。紐西蘭商業歷史中最值得驕傲的名稱之一是弗萊徹建築 (Fletcher Building)，這是一家巨大的建築材料和建築公司，比富美家公司的歷史更長。從紐西蘭的達尼丁附近百老灣 (Broad Bay) 的一所建於1909年的房子起步，弗萊徹成長為擁有一個全球規模的建築公司，建造住宅區、辦公大樓、教堂、工廠、碼頭和管道、機構和國家紀念碑。它建造了紐西蘭國家博物館和惠靈頓火車站，並在二十世紀三十年代僅用了短短六個星期時間就建造了該國的社會保障大樓。弗萊徹也開發了基礎設施，生產和提供建築這些設施的材料。它管理著森林、礦山、工廠，生產紙張、木材和水泥。在奧克蘭，公司修建了南半球最高的建築——天空塔 (Sky Tower) 以及曾在2011年舉行過橄欖球世界盃冠軍賽的伊甸園公園 (Eden Park)。公司的作品可以在加拿大、夏威夷、香港和澳洲見到。公司甚至建造了洛杉磯保羅·蓋蒂博物館 (J.Paul Getty Museum)，由理查德·邁耶 (Richard Meier) 設計，在主

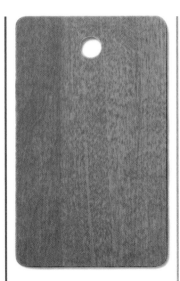

領導者。1985年，帕斯托的母公司推出了一種新形層壓地板柏麗地板 (Pergo®)，取得了巨大成功。公司決定專注於此項業務，並在1998年把柏麗地板建成一個獨立的分支。它變賣了其塑料和生命科學部門。它還決定向富美家出售柏斯托面材產品，只保留了化學品和柏麗地板。2001年，柏麗地板成為一個獨立的公司，柏斯托集中在化工原料業務上——在一定意義上回歸到它的起源。

收購柏斯托帶來了一些高壓耐火板工廠，主要分佈在歐洲和巴西，但也包括亞洲主要增長區域的一家泰國工廠。這同時也帶來了曾創造了新的強化木地板和外牆覆蓋的一種創新和創造力文化。雖然這將最終使公司受益，但收購柏斯托是在經濟衰退前夕，增加了公司的債務。融合新的收購證明是一項挑戰，其他收購的希望最後也是枉然。公司現在負債5.4億美元，新首席執行官弗蘭克·里迪克 (Frank Riddick) 和董事會在2002年決定，公司將在破產法庭尋求保護。2004年春天，公司走出破產，重新設定了一個方案，增加了1.75億美元的現金投資，把抵押債務從3億多美元減少到1.27億美元，銷除了2.15億美元的無抵押債務。

หาก โดยบริษัท เพอร์สตอร์ป มุ่งเน้นธุรกิจเคมีภัณฑ์ดิบ กล่าวคือ กลับไปทำธุรกิจดั้งเดิม

การซื้อกิจการ เพอร์สตอร์ป ทำให้บริษัทฟอร์ไมก้า ได้โรงงานผลิตแผ่นลามิเนตแรงอัดดันสูงหลายแห่ง ส่วนใหญ่ตั้งอยู่ในทวีปยุโรปและประเทศบราซิล แต่มีโรงงานหนึ่งตั้งอยู่ในประเทศไทย ซึ่งเป็นที่ตั้งสำคัญในการขยายธุรกิจในภูมิภาคเอเชีย นอกจากนั้นยังทำให้บริษัทได้รับวัฒนธรรม นวัตกรรมและความคิดสร้างสรรค์ที่ทำให้เกิดวัสดุพื้นลามิเนตและวัสดุหุ้มภายนอกชนิดใหม่ แม้ว่าในท้ายที่สุดแล้ว การซื้อกิจการ เพอร์สตอร์ปจะเป็นประโยชน์กับบริษัท แต่การซื้อกิจการครั้งนี้เกิดขึ้นไม่นานก่อนภาวะเศรษฐกิจตกต่ำและเป็นการเพิ่มหนี้สินให้กับบริษัท การรวมกิจการที่ซื้อมามีความยุ่งยาก และความหวังที่มีต่อการซื้อกิจการอื่นก็ไม่ได้ประโยชน์ จากการที่บริษัทมีภาระหนี้สิน 540 ล้านดอลลาร์สหรัฐ นายแฟรงค์ ริดดิค ประธานเจ้าหน้าที่บริหารคนใหม่และคณะกรรมการบริษัทในปี ค.ศ. 2002 ตัดสินใจให้บริษัทขอความคุ้มครองต่อศาลล้มละลาย บริษัทกลับเข้าดำเนินธุรกิจภายใต้แผนใหม่ในฤดูใบไม้ผลิในปี ค.ศ. 2004 โดยมีการนำเงินสดมาลงทุน 175 ล้านดอลลาร์สหรัฐ มีการลดหนี้ที่มีหลักประกันลงจากกว่า 300 ล้านดอลลาร์สหรัฐเหลือประมาณ 127 ล้านดอลลาร์สหรัฐ และปลดหนี้ที่ไม่มีหลักประกันจำนวน 215 ล้านดอลลาร์สหรัฐ

ในอีกด้านหนึ่งของโลก เหตุการณ์ต่าง ๆ เริ่มเกิดขึ้น ซึ่งในเวลาต่อมาจะส่งผลต่ออนาคตของบริษัทเป็นอย่างมาก ชื่อหนึ่งที่ได้สร้างความภาคภูมิใจที่สุดในประวัติศาสตร์ธุรกิจของประเทศนิวซีแลนด์คือ เฟลทเชอร์ บิวดิ้งซึ่งเป็นชื่อบริษัทวัสดุก่อสร้างและบริษัทก่อสร้างยักษ์ใหญ่ที่มีประวัติศาสตร์ยาวนานกว่า บริษัท ฟอร์ไมก้า คอร์ปอเรชั่น เสียอีกเฟลทเชอร์ บิวดิ้งเริ่มต้นจากการสร้างบ้านเดี่ยวในปี ค.ศ. 1909 ที่บรอดเบย์ ใกล้เมืองดูนดินประเทศนิวซีแลนด์ บริษัทเฟลทเชอร์ เติบโตจนมีชื่อเสียงระดับโลกในด้านการก่อสร้างโครงการที่อยู่อาศัยและอาคารสำนักงานโบสถ์และโรงงาน ท่าเทียบเรือและระบบท่อส่ง อนุสาวรีย์ให้กับองค์กรและประเทศต่าง ๆ บริษัทเฟลทเชอร์ เป็นบริษัทที่สร้างพิพิธภัณฑสถานแห่งชาตินิวซีแลนด์และสถานีรถไฟเวลลิงตัน และในช่วงทศวรรษที่ 1930ได้สร้างอาคารประกันสังคมของประเทศในเวลาเพียงหกสัปดาห์ บริษัทเฟลทเชอร์ ยังได้พัฒนาโครงสร้างพื้นฐานสำหรับผลิตและส่งวัสดุต่าง ๆ เพื่อการก่อสร้างโครงสร้างดังกล่าวด้วย บริษัทเฟลทเชอร์ รักษาป่าไม้เหมืองแร่ และโรงงาน และผลิตกระดาษ ไม้ซุง

315

la protection au tribunal des faillites. La société a élaboré un nouveau plan au printemps de l'année 2004 avec 175 millions de dollars d'investissement en espèces, a réduit la dette garantie de plus de 300 millions de dollars à environ 127 millions de dollars, et a éliminé 215 millions de dollars de dettes non garanties.

De l'autre côté du globe, certains événements ont largement influencé l'avenir de l'entreprise. Un des plus beaux noms de l'histoire de la Nouvelle-Zélande était l'entreprise Fletcher Building, une entreprise géante de matériaux de construction et de construction avec une histoire encore plus longue que celle de Formica Corporation. À partir d'une maison individuelle construite en 1909 sur Broad Bay près de Dunedin, Nouvelle-Zélande, Fletcher s'est développée jusqu'à prétendre à une présence mondiale dans la construction, la création de complexes d'habitation et de tours de bureaux, d'églises et d'usines, de docks et de pipelines, d'institutions et de monuments nationaux. Elle a construit le musée national de Nouvelle-Zélande et la gare de chemin de fer Wellington. Elle a construit dans les années 1930 le bâtiment de la sécurité sociale du pays en seulement six semaines. Fletcher a également développé une infrastructure pour produire et livrer des matériaux pour la construction de ces structures. Il a maintenu des forêts, des mines et des usines, et produit du papier, du bois et du ciment. À Auckland, la société a construit la Sky Tower, la plus haute structure de l'hémisphère sud, et Eden Park qui a accueilli le championnat du monde de rugby en 2011. Son travail a été vu au Canada, à Hawaï, à Hong Kong et en Australie. Elle a même construit le musée J. Paul Getty de Los Angeles, conçu par Richard Meier et visible par des millions de personnes chaque jour sur la colline surmontant un des principaux axes autoroutiers.

En se développant et en se diversifiant comme le conglomérat Fletcher Challenge, la société a rencontré sa part de difficultés à la fin du vingtième siècle. Renommée Fletcher Building en 2001, la société a revendu des filiales en 2000 et a commencé à reconcentrer ses activités en 2001, en embauchant Ralph Waters comme PDG. Bien que

vicio, la gerencia se concentraba en la estrategia de salida —preparar a la empresa para la venta lo más pronto posible.

El siglo XX

Ya en 1990, la mitad del negocio de Formica Corporation se generaba fuera de los Estados Unidos. El futuro de la empresa residía en el crecimiento global, y, mediante la expansión, Formica esperaba revertir la situación. En 2000, la compra de Perstorp Surfacing Materials, una empresa líder e innovadora del mercado europeo en el sector, prometía una oportunidad para avanzar hacia la competitividad global. En 1985, la empresa matriz Perstorp había introducido una nueva forma de pisos a base de laminado, Pergo®, que se convirtió en un éxito enorme. La empresa decidió concentrarse en este negocio y estableció Pergo Flooring como una división separada en 1998. Vendió sus divisiones de plásticos y ciencias biológicas. También decidió vender la división Perstorp Surfacing Materials a Formica, reteniendo solo las divisiones Chemicals y Pergo Flooring en el Grupo. En 2001, Pergo Flooring se convirtió en una empresa separada y Perstorp se concentró en su negocio de productos químicos —en cierto modo, volvió a sus orígenes.

La adquisición de Perstorp aportó varias fábricas de laminado de alta presión, principalmente en Europa y Brasil, pero también incluía una fábrica en Tailandia, en el área de crecimiento clave de Asia. Además, aportó una cultura de innovación y de creatividad que había producido los nuevos pisos de laminado y revestimiento para exteriores. Si bien, a fin de cuentas, beneficiaría a la empresa, la adquisición de Perstorp llegó en vísperas de una recesión económica e incrementó las deudas de la empresa. Integrar la nueva adquisición fue un reto, y las esperanzas de otras adquisiciones fueron en vano. Con la empresa sobrecargada de deudas por $540 millones, un nuevo director ejecutivo, Frank Riddick, y la junta decidieron, en 2002, que la empresa tendría que buscar protección en el tribunal de bancarrotas. Surgió con un nuevo plan en la primavera de 2004 que demandó una inversión en efectivo de $175 millones, redujo la deuda garantizada de más de $300 millones a, aproximadamente, $127 millones y eliminó $215 millones en deuda no garantizada.

aikanaan vaikuttamaan dramaattisesti yhtiön tulevaisuuteen. Yksi ylpeimmistä nimistä Uuden-Seelannin liiketoimintahistoriassa oli Fletcher Building, jättimäinen rakennusmateriaali- ja rakennusyhtiö, jolla oli vieläkin pitempi historia kuin Formica Corporationilla. Aloittaen yhdestä v. 1909 rakennetusta talosta Broad Bayssä Dunedinin lähellä, Uudessa-Seelannissa, Fletcher kasvoi ylpeilemään globaalista läsnäolostaan rakentamisessa, luoden asuntokomplekseja ja toimistotorneja, kirkkoja ja tehtaita, telakoita ja putkijohtoja, laitoksia ja kansallisia muistomerkkejä. Se rakensi Uuden-Seelannin kansallismuseon ja Wellingtonin rautatieaseman ja 1930-luvulla maan sosiaaliviraston rakennuksen vain kuudessa viikossa. Fletcher kehitti myös perusrakenteen materiaalien tuottamiseksi ja toimittamiseksi kyseisten rakenteiden rakentamista varten. Se piti yllä metsiä, kaivoksia ja tehtaita ja valmisti paperia, puutavaraa ja sementtiä. Aucklandissa yhtiö rakensi Sky Tower -tornin, eteläisen pallonpuoliskon korkeimman rakennuksen sekä Eden Park -stadionin, joka isännöi Rugbyn World Cup mestaruuskilpailut v. 2011. Sen töitä nähtiin Kanadassa, Havaijilla, Hong Kongissa ja Australiassa. Se jopa rakensi Richard Meierin suunnitteleman J. Paul Getty museon Los Angelesissa, joka on päivittäin miljoonien ihmisten nähtävissä mäen päällä suuren moottoritien yläpuolella.

Laajentuen ja monipuolistuen Fletcher Challenge -monialayrityksenä yhtiöllä oli omat vaikeutensa, kun 1900-luku päättyi. Uudesti syntyneenä nimellä Fletcher Building v. 2001, yhtiö oli poistanut yrityksiä v. 2000 ja alkanut keskittyä uudelleen omaan liiketoimintaansa v. 2001, ottaessaan palvelukseen CEO:ksi Ralph Watersin. Vaikka Fletcher olikin parhaiten tunnettu rakentamisesta, uusi johtaja ja hänen johtokuntansa olivat sitä mieltä, että sen kannattavuus itse asiassa tuli sen rakennusmateriaalien liiketoiminnasta. Yhtiö päätti tulla tärkeäksi voimatekijäksi rakennusmateriaalien alalla Australaasiassa ja maailmanlaajuisesti. Tavoitteena oli johtavan kilpailijan asema kaikilla markkinoilla, joihin se osallistui. Se hankki yrityksiä sellaisilta aloilta kuin kattaminen, eristys, terästuotteet, betoni ja muoviputket ja muut

要高速公路旁的山上每天接受數百萬人的觀賞。

弗萊徹挑戰（Fletcher Challenge）企業集團在擴張和多元化的過程中，在二十世紀結束時遇到一些困難。2001 年脫胎換骨成為弗萊徹建築公司，該公司在 2000 年曾關閉了許多公司，2001 年已開始重新調整其業務，當時公司聘請了拉爾夫·沃特斯（Ralph Waters）擔任總裁。雖然弗萊徹以建築著稱，新的主帥和董事會認為，盈利其實是來自建材業務。該公司決定在澳大拉西亞地區和全球範圍內成為建材領域的一個主要力量。它的目的是在所進入的每一個市場成為頭號競爭對手。公司收購了屋頂、保溫、鋼製品、混凝土、塑膠管道和其他建築材料供應領域的公司。2002 年，弗萊徹以 7.59 億新元（折合當時 5.55 億美元）的價格收購了面板和美耐板公司 Laminex 集團，這是澳洲該領域的頭號公司。透過擴大成長，而且伴隨著新世紀第一年經濟的擴張，弗萊徹獲得顯著的利潤增長。從 2001 年 2.273 百萬新元的收入成倍增長到 2006 年的 5.520 百萬新元。

2006 年 9 月，弗萊徹選擇了一位新首席執行官喬納森·林（Jonathan Ling），時任 Laminex 集團首席執行官。林識到，最近剛收購了柏斯托，富美家公司的價值仍然在恢復之中。弗萊徹將會用富美家的傳奇品牌在美耐板市場和相應產品方面，在該公司的實力基礎上建立其全球性和協同性。林作為弗萊徹首席執行官的第一項決定是在 2007 年 5 月以約七億美元的價格購買富美家公司。把 Laminex 集團的公司集合到弗萊徹旗下，將使富美家品牌成為本行業在全球最大的唯一廠商。到目前為止 Laminex 集團公司已經多年擁有在澳洲和紐西蘭使用富美家品牌的權力。但是，這兩家公司早在 1946 年羅伯特·賽克斯訪問辛辛那提時就開始合作。

在地球的另一邊，形勢正開始變化，最終將極大地影響公司的未來。新西蘭商業歷史中最值得驕傲的名稱之一是弗萊徹建築（Fletcher Building），這是一家巨大的建築材料和建築公司，比富美家公司的歷史更長。從新西蘭的達尼丁附近百老灣（Broad Bay）的一所建於 1909 年的房子起步，弗萊徹成長為擁有一個全球規模的建築公司，建造住宅區、辦公大樓、教堂、工廠、碼頭和管道、機構和國家紀念碑。它建造了新西蘭國家博物館和惠靈頓火車站，并在二十世紀三十年代仅用了短短六個星期時間就建造了該國的社會保障大樓。弗萊徹也开发了基礎設施，生產和提供建築這些設施的材料。它管理着森林、礦山、工廠，生產紙張、木材和水泥。在奧克蘭，公司修建了南半球最高的建築——天空塔（Sky Tower）以及曾在 2011 年舉行過橄欖球世界杯冠軍賽的伊甸園公園（Eden Park）。公司的作品可以在加拿大、夏威夷、香港和澳大利亞見到。公司甚至建造了洛杉矶保罗·盖蒂博物館（J.Paul Getty Museum），由理查德·迈耶（Richard Meier）設計，在主要高速公路旁的山上每天接受數百万人的观赏。

弗萊徹挑戰（Fletcher Challenge）企業集團在扩张和多元化的过程中，在二十世紀結束時遇到一些困難。2001 年脫胎換骨成為弗萊徹建築公司，該公司在 2000 年曾关闭了许多公司，2001 年已開始重新調整其業務，當時公司聘請了拉爾夫·沃特斯（Ralph Waters）担任總裁。雖然弗萊徹以建築著稱，新的主帥和董事會会认为，盈利其实是来自建材業務。該公司決定在澳大拉西亞地区和全球范围内成為建材領域的一個主要力量。它的目的是在所進入的每一個市場成為头号競爭對手。公司收購了屋頂、保溫、鋼製品、混凝土、塑料管道和其他建築材料供應領域的公司。2002 年，弗萊徹以 7.59 億新元（折合當時 5.55 億美元）的价格收購了面板和耐

และซีเมนต์ บริษัทเฟลทเชอร์ สร้างตึกสกายทาวเวอร์ ที่เมืองโอ๊คแลนด์ ซึ่งเป็นสิ่งก่อสร้างที่สูงที่สุดในซีกโลกใต้ และสวนอีเดน ปาร์ค ซึ่งเป็นสถานที่จัดการแข่งขันรักบี้ เวิลด์ คัพ ในปี ค.ศ. 2011 ผลงานของบริษัทปรากฏในประเทศแคนาดา มลรัฐฮาวาย ฮ่องกง และประเทศออสเตรเลีย นอกจากนี้ บริษัทเฟลทเชอร์ ยังสร้างพิพิธภัณฑ์เจ พอล เก็ตตี้ ที่เมืองลอสแอนเจลิส ซึ่งออกแบบโดยนายริชาร์ด ไมเออร์ ที่คนหลายล้านคนสามารถมองเห็นได้ต่อวัน เพราะพิพิธภัณฑ์ดังกล่าวตั้งอยู่บนเขาเหนือทางด่วนเส้นสำคัญ

จากการขยายกิจการและการสร้างความหลากหลายทางธุรกิจอันเป็นส่วนหนึ่งของกลุ่มบริษัท เฟลทเชอร์ชาเลนจ์ บริษัทเฟลทเชอร์เองเคยประสบปัญหาในช่วงปลายศตวรรษที่ยี่สิบ ก่อนที่จะกลับมาประกอบการในชื่อเฟลทเชอร์ บิวดิ้งในปี ค.ศ. 2001 นั้นบริษัทต้องลดองค์กรลงในปี ค.ศ. 2000 และเมื่อได้ว่าจ้างนายราลฟ์ วอเตอร์ส เป็นประธานเจ้าหน้าที่บริหาร บริษัทเริ่มมุ่งเน้นทำธุรกิจของบริษัทในปี ค.ศ. 2001 ในขณะที่บริษัทเฟลทเชอร์เป็นที่รู้จักมากที่สุดในเรื่องการก่อสร้าง แต่ประธานเจ้าหน้าที่บริหารคนใหม่และคณะกรรมการภายใต้การบริหารโดยประธานคนนี้ธิบายว่า กำไรของบริษัทแท้จริงแล้วมาจากธุรกิจวัสดุก่อสร้าง บริษัทเฟลทเชอร์ตั้งเป้าว่าจะเป็นบริษัทยักษ์ใหญ่ด้านวัสดุก่อสร้างในภูมิภาคออสตราเลเซียและในโลก และจะเป็นคู่แข่งสำคัญในตลาดทุกตลาดที่บริษัทเข้าไปดำเนินธุรกิจ บริษัทเฟลทเชอร์ซื้อกิจการบริษัททำหลังคาฉนวน ผลิตภัณฑ์เหล็ก คอนกรีต และท่อพลาสติก และวัสดุก่อสร้างอื่นๆ ในปี ค.ศ. 2002 บริษัทเฟลทเชอร์ซื้อบริษัทลามิเนทชื่อ เดอะลามิเนกซ์ กรุ๊ป ซึ่งปัจจุบันเป็นผู้นำวัสดุลามิเนทในประเทศออสเตรเลีย โดยซื้อมาในราคา 759 ล้านดอลลาร์นิวซีแลนด์ หรือประมาณ 555 ล้านดอลลาร์สหรัฐในเวลานั้น บริษัทเฟลทเชอร์เติบโตโดยการขยายกิจการ พร้อมกับการขยายตัวทางเศรษฐกิจในช่วงแรกของสหัสวรรษใหม่ บริษัทมีรายได้เพิ่มขึ้นอย่างมาก รายได้ในปี ค.ศ. 2001 มีจำนวน 2,273 ล้านดอลลาร์นิวซีแลนด์ เพิ่มทวีคูณเป็น 5,520 ล้านดอลลาร์นิวซีแลนด์ในปี ค.ศ. 2006

ในเดือนกันยายน ค.ศ. 2006 บริษัทเฟลทเชอร์เลือกตั้งประธานเจ้าหน้าที่บริหารคนใหม่ เป็น โจนาทาน หลิง ซึ่งขณะนั้นดำรงตำแหน่งประธานเจ้าหน้าที่บริหารของกลุ่มบริษัทลามิเนกซ์ลามิเนกซ์ หลิงเล็งเห็นคุณค่าของ บริษัท ฟอร์ไมก้า คอร์ปอเรชั่น ที่ยังอยู่ในช่วงฟื้นตัวจากการเพิ่งซื้อกิจการของ

317

Fletcher était surtout connue pour la construction, le nouveau chef et son conseil d'administration ont estimé que la rentabilité provenait en fait des matériaux de construction. La société a décidé de devenir une grande puissance dans les matériaux de construction, dans la région de l'Australasie et dans le monde. Elle visait à devenir leader dans chaque marché. Elle a acquis des entreprises dans les domaines de la toiture, l'isolation, les produits d'acier, les tuyaux de béton et de plastique, et d'autres matériaux de construction. En 2002, Fletcher a acheté la société de panneau et de stratifié Laminex Group, actuellement leader sur le marché australien, pour 759 millions de NZD, soit environ 555 millions de dollars américains de l'époque. Croissant par expansion mais également en bénéficiant d'une économie en pleine expansion dans les premières années du nouveau millénaire, Fletcher a enregistré des hausses de bénéfices spectaculaires. Ses résultats 2001 s'élevant à 2273 millions NZD ont atteints 5520 millions de NZD en 2006.

En septembre 2006, Fletcher a choisi un nouveau PDG, Jonathan Ling, alors PDG du groupe Laminex. Ling a perçu la valeur de la société Formica toujours en redressement avec sa récente acquisition de Perstorp. Fletcher se baserait mondialement et en synergie sur la force de l'entreprise sur le marché des stratifiés et produits connexes avec la marque Formica. La première décision de Ling en tant que PDG de Fletcher a été d'acheter Formica Corporation, en mai 2007, pour environ 700 millions USD. L'alliance avec le groupe d'entreprises Laminex qui avait le droit d'utiliser la marque Formica en Australie et en Nouvelle-Zélande depuis de nombreuses années, sous l'égide de Fletcher, consisterait à faire de la marque Formica le leader de son secteur au niveau mondial. Les deux sociétés avaient déjà cependant collaboré depuis 1946 et la visite de Robert Sykes à Cincinnati.

À la fin des années 1940, Laminex Pty Ltd a commencé à produire ses premiers panneaux décoratifs. Les premières feuilles de stratifié plastique Laminex® étaient simples : elles étaient disponibles dans une taille standard de 1,6 mm d'épaisseur, 2,44 x 1,22 m, dans une gamme limitée d'une dizaine

En la otra parte del mundo, se comenzaban a desarrollar eventos que, con el tiempo, afectarían de manera considerable el futuro de la empresa. Uno de los nombres más soberbios en la historia comercial de Nueva Zelanda era Fletcher Building una gigante empresa constructora y de materiales para la construcción con una historia aún más extensa que la de Formica Corporation. De una simple casa construida en 1909 en Broad Bay, cerca de Dunedin, Nueva Zelanda, Fletcher creció para hacer gala de una presencia global en la construcción, creando complejos de viviendas y torres de oficinas, iglesias y fábricas, muelles y tuberías, instituciones y monumentos nacionales. Construyó el Museo Nacional de Nueva Zelanda y la estación de ferrocarril de Wellington, y, en la década de los treinta, construyó el edificio de seguridad social del país en solo seis semanas. Fletcher también desarrolló una infraestructura para producir y entregar materiales para construir esas estructuras. Mantenía bosques, minas y fábricas, y producía papel, madera y cemento. En Auckland, la empresa construyó la torre Sky Tower, la estructura más alta en el hemisferio sur, y el estadio Eden Park, que fue el anfitrión de la Copa Mundial de Rugby en 2011. Su trabajo fue visto en Canadá, Hawái, Hong Kong y Australia. Incluso construyó el Museo J. Paul Getty en Los Ángeles, diseñado por Richard Meier, que millones de personas pueden ver a diario en la ruta de la colina ubicada sobre una autopista principal.

Al expandirse y diversificarse como el *holding* Fletcher Challenge, la empresa tuvo su cuota de dificultades a medida que terminaba el siglo XX. Al renacer como Fletcher Building en 2001, la empresa se había despojado de firmas en 2000 y había comenzado a concentrarse nuevamente en su negocio en 2001, cuando contrató a Ralph Waters como director ejecutivo. Aunque Fletcher era mejor conocida por la construcción, el nuevo director y su junta concluyeron que su rentabilidad realmente provenía de sus negocios de materiales para la construcción. La empresa decidió convertirse en una potencia principal en materiales para la construcción, en la región de Asia meridional y a nivel mundial. Aspiraba a ser la competidora principal en cada mercado en el que ingresara. Adquirió empresas en las

rakennustarvikkeet. Vuonna 2002 Fletcher osti paneeli- ja laminaattiyrityksen The Laminex Group, nykyisin Australian johtaja alalla, 759 miljoonalla Uuden-Seelannin dollarilla, eli silloisella noin 555 miljoonalla USA:n dollarilla. Laajennuksen ansiosta kasvaen, mutta myös uuden vuosituhannen alkuvuosina tapahtuneen taloudellisen nousun mukana, Fletcher kirjasi liikevoiton dramaattisen kasvun. Sen vuoden 2001 liikevoitto 2,273 miljoonaa Uuden-Seelannin dollaria kohosi 5,520 miljoonaan Uuden-Seelannin dollariin v. 2006.

Syyskuussa 2006 Fletcherille valittiin uusi CEO, Jonathan Ling — silloinen Laminex Groupin CEO. Ling tajusi edelleen elpyvän Formica Corporationin arvon, sen hiljattain ostetun Perstorpin. Fletcher rakentaisi globaalisti ja synergistisesti yhtiön vahvuuden pohjalle laminaattien ja niihin liittyvien tuotteiden markkinoilla Formican tunnetulla tavaramerkillä. Lingin ensimmäinen päätös Fletcherin CEO:na oli ostaa Formica Corporation toukokuussa 2007 noin 700 miljoonalla USA:n dollarilla. Yhdistelmä Laminex Groupin yritysten kanssa, joilla tähän saakka oli vuosikausia ollut oikeus käyttää Formican tavaramerkkiä Australiassa ja Uudessa-Seelannissa, teki Fletcherin siipien suojassa Formican tavaramerkistä suurimman pelaajan alallaan maailmanlaajuisesti. Nämä kaksi yhtiötä olivat kyllä olleet yhteistyössä jo vuodesta 1946 ja Robert Sykesin Cincinnatin vierailusta asti.

1940-luvun loppupuoleen mennessä Laminex Pty Ltd oli alkanut valmistaa ensimmäisiä koristeellisia paneeleja. Ensimmäiset Laminex® muovilaminaattilevyt olivat peruslaatua: ne olivat saatavissa standardikokoisina 1/16 tuuman paksuisina, 8 x 4 jalan kokoisina noin tusinan värin ja kuvion rajoitettuna valikoimana ja kiiltäviksi viimeisteltyinä. Vuonna 1952 Laminex-yhtiö avasi uuden 15 000 neliömetrin tehtaan Cheltenhamissa. Tämä teki mahdolliseksi Laminex-levyjen suunnittelun ja tuotannon laajentamisen. Painotus oli helppohoitoisuudessa, mutta mallilla oli myös merkitystä. 1950-luvun alussa kasvoivat värien ja kuvioiden valikoima. Samoin kuin Yhdistyneessä kuningaskunnassa, Euroopassa tai Yhdysvalloissa, 1940-luvun suosittujen värien, Coral Pink ja Apple Green lisäksi 1950-luvulla tulivat ener-

finest
of all
the
decorative
laminates

FORMICA Regd.
SURFACES
AW. 6064
Antiference Ltd.

到了二十世紀四十年代末，Laminex 私人有限公司已開始生產裝飾板。第一張 Laminex® 塑膠美耐板很簡單：1/16 英寸厚，8 英尺長，4 英尺寬的標準尺寸，十幾種有限的色彩和圖案，塗上發光面漆。1952 年，Laminex 公司在切爾滕納姆開設了一家面積為 16 萬平方英尺的新工廠。這使擴大 Laminex 薄片的設計和生產成為可能。重點在便於保養，但設計也很重要。二十世紀五十年代初，顏色和圖案的範圍增加。在英國、歐洲或美國，二十世紀四十年代流行的顏色，如珊瑚粉紅色和蘋果綠，在更具活力的五十年代，加進了更強的原色。懷恩（Wynne）報告說：「圖案包括木紋、大理石、亞麻編織、籃子編織和金屬線，靈感取自於南太平洋和抽象的有機設計。」

火板公司 Laminex 集團，這是澳大利亞該領域的头号公司。通过扩大成长，而且也伴随着新世纪第一年经济的扩张，弗莱彻获得显着的利润增长。从 2001 年 2.273 百万新元的收入成倍增长到 2006 年的 5.520 百万新元。

2006 年 9 月，弗莱彻选择了一位新首席执行官乔纳森·林（Jonathan Ling），时任 Laminex 集团首席执行官。林认识到，最近刚收购了柏斯托，富美家公司的价值仍然在恢复之中。弗莱彻将会用富美家的传奇品牌在耐火板市场和相关产品方面，在该公司的实力基础上建立其全球性和协同性。林作为弗莱彻首席执行官的第一项决定是在 2007 年 5 月以约七亿美元的价格购买富美家公司。把 Laminex 集团的公司集合到弗莱彻旗下，将使富美家品牌

เพอร์สตอร์ป ไม่นาน บริษัทเฟลตเชอร์ต้องการที่จะผนึกกำลังกับบริษัท ฟอร์ไมก้า เพื่อให้บริษัทมีความแข็งแกร่งในตลาดแผ่นลามิเนทและผลิตภัณฑ์ที่เกี่ยวข้องในระดับโลก การตัดสินใจแรกของนายหลิงในฐานะประธานเจ้าหน้าที่บริหารของบริษัทเฟลตเชอร์คือการซื้อ บริษัท ฟอร์ไมก้า คอร์ปอเรชั่น ใน เดือนพฤษภาคม ค.ศ. 2007 เป็นจำนวนเงินประมาณ 700 ล้านดอลลาร์สหรัฐ การรวมกับกลุ่มบริษัทลามิเนกซ์ ซึ่งจนถึงขณะนี้ได้สิทธิ์ใช้ตรา ฟอร์ไมก้า ในประเทศออสเตรเลียและนิวซีแลนด์มาเป็นเวลาหลายปีแล้ว เมื่อมารวมอยู่ในกลุ่มบริษัทเฟลตเชอร์ ทำให้ตราฟอร์ไมก้า กลายเป็นผู้เล่นรายใหญ่ที่สุดในโลกของอุตสาหกรรมนี้ ความจริงแล้วบริษัททั้งสองเคยร่วมงานกันมาเมื่อปี ค.ศ. 1946 เมื่อนายโรเบิร์ต ไฮสมาเยี่ยมชมที่ชินชินนาติ

พอถึงช่วงปลายทศวรรษที่ 1940 บริษัทลามิเนกซ์ ได้เริ่มผลิตวัสดุบุผนังสำหรับการตกแต่งเป็นครั้งแรก แผ่นลามิเนทพลาสติกภายใต้เครื่องหมายการค้าจดทะเบียนลามิเนกซ์ ครั้งแรกเป็นผลิตภัณฑ์ธรรมดา วางจำหน่ายในขนาดมาตรฐานคือ หนา 1/16 นิ้ว กว้าง 8 คูณ 4 ฟุต มีสีและลวดลายให้เลือกจำกัด คือประมาณสิบสองสีหรือลายเท่านั้น และผลิตภัณฑ์จะเคลือบเงา ในปี ค.ศ. 1952 บริษัทลามิเนกซ์เปิดโรงงานใหม่มีขนาด 160,000 ตารางฟุตที่เมืองเชลเทนแฮม เป็นการขยายฐานการออกแบบและการผลิตแผ่นลามิเนกซ์ ที่เน้นให้ผลิตภัณฑ์สามารถดูแลรักษาได้ง่าย ในขณะเดียวกันการออกแบบต้องดีด้วย ในช่วงต้นทศวรรษที่ 1950 ผลิตภัณฑ์มีสีและลวดลายให้เลือกมากขึ้น บริษัทผลิตสีหลักที่เข้มขึ้นในช่วงทศวรรษที่ 1950 ซึ่งมีความดึกดักไว้ เพิ่มเติมสีที่ได้รับความนิยมในช่วงทศวรรษที่ 1940 ในสหราชอาณาจักร ทวีปยุโรป และสหรัฐอเมริกา เช่น สีชมพูปะการัง และสีเขียวแอปเปิ้ล นายเวย์น รายงานว่า "ลวดลายต่าง ๆ ได้แก่ ลายไม้ ลายหินอ่อน ลายผ้าลินิน ลายตะกร้าสาน และลายเส้นโลหะ ซึ่งได้รับแรงบันดาลใจมาจากแปซิฟิกใต้และการออกแบบรูปทรงธรรมชาติแบบแอ็บสแตรก"

ผลิตภัณฑ์ภายใต้เครื่องหมายการค้าจดทะเบียนลามิเนกซ์ ได้รับการยอมรับในประเทศออสเตรเลียเท่า ๆ กับที่ตรา ฟอร์ไมก้า ได้รับการยอมรับในประเทศอื่น ๆ ตอนแรกบริษัท ลามิเนกซ์ ขายผลิตภัณฑ์ให้แก่ผู้ขายส่งในอุตสาหกรรมการก่อสร้างและเฟอร์นิเจอร์เท่านั้น โดยผู้ขายส่งดังกล่าวจะนำผลิตภัณฑ์ลามิเนทไปขายต่อให้กับห้างสรรพสินค้าและร้านประกอบท้น ๆ ต่อมาเมื่อมีการใช้กาวและอุปกรณ์ที่พัฒนาขึ้นทั่วโลก ทำให้เกิดกระแส

de teintes et de motifs et en finition brillante. En 1952, la société Laminex a ouvert une nouvelle usine de 50 000 mètres carrés à Cheltenham. Ceci a permis l'expansion du design et de la production des revêtements Laminex. L'accent était mis sur la facilité d'entretien, mais le design importait aussi. Au début des années1950, la gamme de teintes et de motifs a augmenté. Comme au Royaume-Uni, en Europe ou aux États-Unis, les teintes les plus populaires des années 1940 telles que corail rose et vert pomme ont été rejointes dans les années 1950 de manière plus dynamique par l'augmentation des teintes primaires. « Les motifs incluaient l'imitation du bois et du marbre, le tissage du lin, les courbes des paniers et les fils métalliques, en s'inspirant du Pacifique Sud et des dessins organiques abstraits, » indique Wynne.

En effet, Laminex® a créé sa marque en Australie comme Formica l'a fait dans d'autres pays. Dans un premier temps, Laminex Pty Ltd vendait uniquement aux grossistes des industries de la construction et du meuble, qui à leur tour vendaient des produits en utilisant les stratifiés à travers les grands magasins et autres points de vente. Mais selon un modèle utilisé à l'échelle mondiale, l'arrivée des colles et des outils améliorés a déclenché un mouvement de bricolage. Les propriétaires ont installé eux-mêmes des articles recouverts de stratifié, créant un nouveau marché dans les années 1950. La société a fait de la publicité dans la version australienne de *Home Beautiful* et *House and Garden* avec le slogan « Laminex : plus beau pour la vie. » Ceci soulignait à la fois la robustesse et la facilité d'entretien. Laminex, comme Formica Corporation, s'est rendue célèbre pour les échantillons ou copeaux qui pouvaient être emportés dans les points de vente et ramenés à la maison pour apparier les teintes. Une dizaine de millions d'échantillons ont été distribuées. Dans les années 1980, la société a construit une maison d'exposition avec les produits de la marque Laminex à Warrandyte, dans la banlieue de Melbourne. Pendant les années 1970, 1980 et 1990, Laminex Industries a élargi son marché avec l'ajout d'une série de filiales métropolitaines et régionales, qui sont à présent trente-six à travers l'Australie.

áreas de techado, aislamiento, productos de acero, tubos de concreto y de plástico, y otros suministros para la construcción. En 2002, Fletcher compró la firma de paneles y laminados The Laminex Group, líder actual del sector en Australia, por 759 millones de dólares neozelandeses o, aproximadamente, $555 millones de dólares estadounidenses en ese momento. Al crecer por expansión, pero también junto a una economía en expansión en los primeros años del nuevo milenio, Fletcher registró aumentos considerables en las ganancias. Sus ganancias de 2001 de 2.273 millones de dólares neozelandeses se multiplicaron a 5.520 millones de dólares neozelandeses en 2006.

En septiembre de 2006, Fletcher eligió un nuevo director ejecutivo, Jonathan Ling, entonces director ejecutivo de The Laminex Group. Ling percibía el valor de Formica Corporation todavía en recuperación, con su reciente adquisición, Perstorp. Fletcher construiría globalmente y de modo coordinado la fortaleza de la empresa en el mercado para los productos de laminado y los relacionados con la gloriosa marca Formica. La primera decisión de Ling como director ejecutivo de Fletcher fue comprar Formica Corporation, en mayo de 2007, por $700 millones de dólares estadounidenses aproximadamente. La combinación con el grupo de empresas de Laminex Group, que hasta ese momento habían poseído los derechos de utilizar la marca Formica en Australia y Nueva Zelanda durante varios años, al amparo de Fletcher haría de la marca Formica la más grande y única jugadora en su sector a nivel mundial. No obstante, las dos empresas habían trabajado juntas ya en 1946 cuando Robert Sykes visitó la fábrica en Cincinnati.

A fines de la década de los cuarenta, Laminex Pty Ltd había comenzado a producir sus primeros paneles decorativos. Las primeras hojas de laminado plástico Laminex® eran básicas: estaban disponibles en tamaño estándar de 1.6 mm de espesor, 2.4 por 1.2 m de ancho, en una gama limitada de más o menos una docena de colores y diseños, y en un acabado brillante. En 1952, la empresa Laminex abrió una fábrica de 14,865 metros cuadrados en Cheltenham. Esto permitió la expansión del diseño y la producción de las hojas de laminado Laminex. El énfasis era la

gisemmät perusvärit. "Kuvioihin sisältyivät puun pinnat, marmori, pellavakudos, panamasidokset ja metallisäikeet, joiden inspiraationa olivat Etelä-Tyynimeri ja abstraktit orgaaniset mallit", kertoo Wynne.

Laminex® todellakin vakiintui tavaramerkkinä Australiassa hyvin samaan tapaan kuin Formica-merkki teki muissa maissa. Aluksi Laminex Pty Ltd myi vain tukkukauppiaille rakennus- ja huonekalualalla, jotka vuorostaan myivät laminaatteja käyttäviä tuotteita tavaratalojen ja muiden jakelupisteiden kautta. Maailmanlaajuisen suuntauksen mukana parempien liimojen ja työkalujen tulo sai kuitenkin aikaan tee-se-itse liikkeen. Kodinomistajat asensivat itse laminaatilla päällystettyjä kalusteita ja loivat uuden markkinakohteen 1950-luvulla. Yhtiö mainosti australialaisessa lehdessä *Home Beautiful* ja *House and Garden*, iskulauseenaan "Laminex: Lovelier for a lifetime" (ihanampaa eliniäksi) korostaen sekä lujuutta että puhdistamisen helppoutta. Formica Corporationin tavoin myös Laminex tuli tunnetuksi näytteistä eli palasista, joita voi hakea vähittäiskaupoista ja viedä kotiin verrattaviksi. Jakeluun on tullut kymmenisen miljoonaa palasta. 1980-luvulla yhtiö rakensi näyttelytalon esittelemään Laminex-merkkisiä tuotteita Warrandytessa Melbournen lähialueella. Laminex Industries laajensi markkinoidensa ulottuvuutta 1970-, 1980- ja 1990-luvuilla, lisäämällä sarjan suurkaupunkeihin perustettuja ja alueellisia sivuliikkeitä, lukumäärän nyt ollessa 36 paikkaa Australian laajuisesti.

Laminex Industries osti 1990-luvulla Formican laminaattitehtaan ja jakeluoperaatiot Uudessa-Seelannissa, jatkaen tuotteiden valmistusta molemmilla tavaramerkeillä. Formica-merkkisten tuotteiden tehdas Australiassa, jonka De La Rue perusti v. 1948, jäi jälkeen markkinoilla — poikkeuksena yleissäännöstä. Formican laminaattitehdas Australiassa lopetettiin v. 1998. Amatek Limited hankki oikeudet Formica tavaramerkkiin heinäkuussa 1999, ostettuaan Formican liiketoiminnan CSR:ltä. Amatek Limited muutti nimekseen Laminex Group Limited ja CVC myi sen Fletcher Building -yhtiölle marraskuussa 2002.

Australia oli yksi harvoista maista maailmassa, jossa Formica tavara-

事實上，與富美家品牌在其他國家一樣，Laminex® 在澳洲創立了自己的品牌。起初，Laminex 私人有限公司只賣給建築和傢俱行業的批發商，這些批發商又透過百貨商場和其他店鋪銷售用美耐板製造的產品。但是，跟隨世界範圍內的模式，改進的膠水和工具的問世引發了自己動手的運動。房主自己安裝帶美耐板的燈具，在二十世紀五十年代創造了一個新市場。公司在澳洲的《美麗家居》(Home Beautiful) 和《房子與花園》(House and Garden) 雜誌上做廣告，口號是「Laminex：終生更可愛」，強調其耐用性和易於清潔。Laminex 與富美家公司一樣，因樣品或色片可以在零售中心挑選或帶回家匹配而著稱。已分發了約一百萬張色片。二十世紀八十年代，該公司在墨爾本郊區渥倫泰德建立了一個展室，陳列 Laminex 品牌產品。二十世紀七十年代、八十年代和九十年代，Laminex 工業擴大其市場範圍，增加了一系列都市和地區分部，現在在全澳洲有 36 個銷售點。

二十世紀九十年代，Laminex 工業收購了富美家在紐西蘭的美耐板工廠和分銷中心，繼續製造這兩個品牌的產品。1948 年，由德拉魯建成的富美家品牌產品在澳洲的製造廠在市場上很落後——一般規則的例外情況。富美家美耐板在澳洲的工廠 1998 年被關閉。在 1999 年 7 月，Amatek 有限公司 (Amatek Limited) 在從 CSR 購買了富美家的業務的同時收購了富美家商標的使用權。Amatek 有限公司更名為 Laminex 集團有限公司 (Laminex Group Limited)，2002 年 11 月，被 CVC 賣給了佛萊徹建築公司。

澳洲是世界上富美家品牌美耐板不佔主導地位的為數不多的幾個國家之一——Laminex 品牌在世界這個地區是標誌性品牌。幾十年來，在澳洲和紐西蘭這兩個市場，這兩個對手在複雜的商業歷史中經歷了幾

成为本行业在全球最大的唯一厂商。到目前为止 Laminex 集团公司已经多年拥有在澳大利亚和新西兰使用富美家品牌的权力。但是，这两家公司早在 1946 年罗伯特·赛克斯访问辛辛那提时就开始合作。

到了二十世纪四十年代末，Laminex 私人有限公司已开始生产装饰板。第一张 Laminex® 塑料耐火板很简单：1/16 英寸厚，8 英尺长，4 英尺宽的标准尺寸，十几种有限的色彩和图案，涂上发光面漆。1952 年，Laminex 公司在切尔滕纳姆开设了一家面积为 16 万平方英尺的新工厂。这使扩大 Laminex 薄片的设计和生产成为可能。重点在于便于保养，但设计也很重要。二十世纪五十年代初，颜色和图案的范围增加。在英国、欧洲或美国，二十世纪四十年代流行的颜色，如珊瑚粉红色和苹果绿，在更具活力的五十年代，加进了更强的原色。怀恩 (Wynne) 报告说："图案包括木纹、大理石、亚麻编织、篮子编织和金属线，灵感取自于南太平洋和抽象的有机设计。"

事实上，与富美家品牌在其他国家一样，Laminex® 在澳大利亚创立了自己的品牌。起初，Laminex 私人有限公司只卖给建筑和家具行业的批发商，这些批发商又通过百货商场和其他店铺销售用耐火板制造的产品。但是，跟随世界范围内的模式，改进的胶水和工具的问世引发了自己动手的运动。房主自己安装带耐火板的灯具，在二十世纪五十年代创造了一个新市场。公司在澳大利亚的《美丽家居》(Home Beautiful) 和《房子与花园》(House and Garden) 杂志上做广告，口号是 "Laminex：终生更可爱"，强调其耐用性和易于清洁。Laminex 与富美家公司一样，因样品或色片可以在零售中心挑选并带回家匹配而著称。已分发了约一百万张色片。二十世纪八十年代，该公司在墨尔本郊区渥伦泰德建立了一个展室，陈列 Laminex 品牌产品。二十世纪七十

ตกแต่งหรือซ่อมบ้านเอง เจ้าของบ้านจะติดตั้งตัวยึดหุ้มแผ่นลามิเนตด้วยตนเอง ทำให้เกิดตลาดใหม่ขึ้นในช่วงศตวรรษที่ 1950 บริษัทลงโฆษณาในหนังสือ โฮมบิวตี้ฟูล และ เฮาส์แอนด์การ์เดน ในประเทศออสเตรเลีย พร้อมกับคำโฆษณาว่า "ลามิเนกซ์ สวยงามขึ้นตลอดอายุขัย" และเน้นทั้งความแข็งแรง ทนทานและการทำความสะอาดง่าย บริษัทลามิเนกซ์ เป็นที่รู้จักจากการให้ตัวอย่างหรือชิปที่ลูกค้าสามารถรับไปได้อย่างง่ายที่ศูนย์ค้าปลีกและนำกลับบ้านไปเทียบว่าเข้าชุดหรือไม่เช่นเดียวกับบริษัท ฟอร์ไมก้า คอร์ปอเรชัน มีการแจกชิปประมาณสิบล้านชิ้น ในช่วงศตวรรษที่ 1980 บริษัทสร้างบ้านตัวอย่างแสดงผลิตภัณฑ์ลามิเนกซ์ ที่ วาร์แรนไดต์ ชานเมืองเมลเบิร์น ระหว่างศตวรรษที่ 1970 ศตวรรษที่ 1980 และศตวรรษที่ 1990 บริษัท ลามิเนกซ์ อินดัสทรีส์ ขยายผลิตภัณฑ์ในตลาดด้วยการเพิ่มสาขาในเขตมหานครและเขตภูมิภาค ปัจจุบัน บริษัทมีสาขาตั้งอยู่ประมาณสามสิบหกแห่งทั่วประเทศออสเตรเลีย

ในช่วงศตวรรษที่ 1990 บริษัท ลามิเนกซ์ อินดัสทรีส์ เข้าซื้อโรงงานลามิเนทฟอร์ไมก้า และกิจการกระจายสินค้าในประเทศนิวซีแลนด์ โดยยังคงดำเนินการผลิตผลิตภัณฑ์ภายใต้ตราสินค้าของทั้งสองบริษัท โรงงานผลิตผลิตภัณฑ์ตราฟอร์ไมก้าในประเทศออสเตรเลียที่ก่อตั้งขึ้นในปี ค.ศ. 1948 โดยเดอ ลา รู ประกอบการรั้งท้ายในตลาด ซึ่งเป็นข้อยกเว้นกรณีทั่วไป โรงงานลามิเนทฟอร์ไมก้าในประเทศออสเตรเลียปิดตัวลงในปี ค.ศ. 1998 บริษัท อะมาเทค จำกัด ซื้อสิทธิ์ในเครื่องหมายการค้าฟอร์ไมก้าในเดือนกรกฎาคม ค.ศ. 1999 เมื่อบริษัทซื้อธุรกิจของบริษัทฟอร์ไมก้าไปจากบริษัท ซีเอสอาร์ บริษัท อะมาเทค จำกัด ต่อมาเปลี่ยนชื่อเป็นบริษัท ลามิเนกซ์ กรุ๊ป จำกัด ซึ่งต่อมาบริษัทซีวีซี ขายให้แก่ บริษัท เฟลทเชอร์ บิวดิ้ง ในเดือนพฤศจิกายน ค.ศ. 2002

ประเทศออสเตรเลียเป็นประเทศหนึ่งในประเทศเพียงไม่กี่ประเทศในโลกที่ผลิตภัณฑ์ตราฟอร์ไมก้า ไม่ใช่บริษัทผู้นำสำหรับแผ่นลามิเนท เพราะในประเทศออสเตรเลียมีตราลามิเนกซ์เป็นตราประจำที่มีชื่อเสียงตลอดหลายทศวรรษที่ผ่านมาในตลาดทั้งในประเทศออสเตรเลียและประเทศนิวซีแลนด์ บริษัทคู่แข่งทั้งสองบริษัทมีการเปลี่ยนผู้ถือหุ้นหลายครั้งในประวัติศาสตร์การดำเนินธุรกิจที่ซับซ้อน จนในที่สุด ความสัมพันธ์สิ้นสุดลงเมื่อทั้งสองบริษัทรวมกันเป็นหนึ่งเดียวภายใต้บริษัทเฟลทเชอร์ บิวดิ้ง

Dans les années 1990, Laminex Industries a acheté l'usine de stratifié Formica et les opérations de distribution en Nouvelle-Zélande, en continuant à fabriquer des produits sous deux marques. L'usine de fabrication des produits sous la marque Formica en Australie, construite en 1948 par De La Rue, était à la traîne sur le marché, une exception à la règle générale. L'usine de stratifié Formica en Australie a été fermée en 1998. Amatek Limited a acquis les droits sur la marque Formica en juillet 1999 quand il a acheté l'entreprise Formica de la CSR. Amatek Limited est devenue Laminex Group Limited et a été revendue par CVC à Fletcher Building en novembre 2002.

L'Australie a été un des rares pays au monde où la marque Formica n'a pas été la marque dominante pour le stratifié. Laminex était la marque la plus connue dans cette partie du monde. Au fil des décennies et sur les marchés d'Australie et de Nouvelle-Zélande, les deux concurrents sont passés par plusieurs étapes de propriété au fil d'une histoire complexe. La confusion a finalement pris fin quand ils ont été heureusement mariés dans le giron de Fletcher Building.

Production de stratifiés de marque Formica®

Tant de choses sur la société Formica avaient changé en un siècle et très peu de ce qui était visible dans les usines de l'entreprise qui produisaient le stratifié emblématique l'était encore à l'heure actuelle. Technologie, précision et efficacité avaient été adaptées avec le temps, et toujours avec soin et qualité et l'aspect artistique était resté le même. Un visiteur de l'usine Evendale de Cincinnati à la veille du centenaire de la société pourrait trouver peu de changement depuis les premiers jours de cette usine en 1950, du moins extérieurement : les murs de briques plates de l'extérieur, les poutres apparentes, les supports chargés d'énormes rouleaux de papier Kraft brun et de petits rouleaux de papier colorés imprimés et unis, les chariots élévateurs jaunes évitant soigneusement les trottoirs verts qui guident le visiteur entre les machines.

La machinerie de l'Ohio est à peu près la même que celle d'une usine de stratifié Formica au Canada ou en Thaïlande. Les presses durent longtemps.

facilidad del mantenimiento, pero el diseño también importaba. Durante los primeros años de la década de los cincuenta, la gama de colores y diseños creció. Como en el Reino Unido, Europa o los Estados Unidos, a los colores populares de la década de los cuarenta, como rosado coral y verde manzana, se les sumaron los colores primarios más fuertes de la década más energética de los cincuenta. "Los diseños incluían vetas de madera, mármoles, trenzados de lino, trenzados de cestas y tramas metálicas, inspirados en el Pacífico Sur, y diseños orgánicos abstractos", informa Wynne.

De hecho, Laminex® estableció su marca en Australia tanto como la marca Formica lo hizo en otros países. Al principio, Laminex Pty Ltd vendía solo a mayoristas en las industrias de la construcción y de muebles, que, a su vez, vendían productos que utilizaban laminados a través de tiendas por departamentos y otros puntos de venta. Pero siguiendo un patrón mundial, la llegada de pegamentos y herramientas mejores generó el movimiento "hágalo usted mismo". Los propietarios de las casas instalaban ellos mismos las estructuras fijas cubiertas con laminado, lo que creó un nuevo mercado en la década de los cincuenta. La empresa publicitaba en las revistas australianas *Home Beautiful* y *House and Garden* con el eslogan "Laminex: más belleza que perdura toda la vida", enfatizando la resistencia y la facilidad de limpieza. Laminex, como Formica Corporation, se volvió conocida por las muestras de laminado que podían recogerse en centros minoristas y llevarse a casa para hacer combinaciones. Se han distribuido cerca de diez millones de muestras de laminado. En la década de los ochenta, la empresa construyó una casa de exhibición que presentaba los productos de la marca Laminex en Warrandyte, en los suburbios de Melbourne. Durante las décadas de los setenta, de los ochenta y de los noventa, Laminex Industries expandió su alcance en el mercado con la incorporación de una serie de sucursales metropolitanas y regionales, que ahora contabilizan unos treinta y seis puntos en toda Australia.

En la década de los noventa, Laminex Industries compró la planta de laminado Formica y sus operaciones de distribución en Nueva Zelanda, y continuó fabricando productos bajo las dos marcas. La planta de fabricación de los

merkki ei ollut johtava tavaramerkki laminaateille — Laminexin tavaramerkki oli ikoninen tavaramerkki siellä päin maailmaa. Vuosikymmenien aikana ja Australian ja Uuden-Seelannin kaksilla markkinoilla kaksi kilpailijaa siirtyivät useiden omistusvaiheiden kautta monimutkaisessa liiketoiminnan historiassa. Lopulta sekaannus päättyi, kun ne onnellisesti yhdistettiin Fletcher Building -yhtiön katon alle.

Formica® merkkisen laminaatin valmistus

Niin paljon Formica-yhtiöstä oli muuttunut yhden vuosisadan aikana — ja hyvin vähän siitä oli näkyvissä yhtiön tehtaissa, jotka tuottavat ikonista laminaattia. Teknologia, täsmällisyys ja tehokkuus olivat mukautuneet ajan vaatimuksiin ja kuitenkin huolellisuus, laatu ja taiteellisuus olivat pysyneet samoina. Vierailija Evendalen tehtaalla Cincinnatissa yhtiön satavuotispäivän aattona ei ehkä havaitsisi paljonkaan muuttuneen kyseisen tehtaan alkupäiviltä v. 1950, ainakaan ulkoa päin. Ulkopuolella ovat samat koruttomat tiiliseinät, samat paljaat niskapalkit pään yläpuolella, samoissa telineissä valtavan suuria rullia ruskeaa voimapaperia ja pienempiä rullia kuvioitua ja yksiväristä paperia. Keltaisia haarukkatrukkeja pyyhältää ohi, välttäen huolellisesti vihreäksi maalattuja jalankulkijoiden reittejä, jotka opastavat kävijää koneiden joukossa.

Koneisto Ohiossa on melko lailla sama kuin koneisto Formica-lami-

個階段的所有權之爭。這種混亂終於當它們高興地統一在弗萊徹建築公司麾下時而告終。

生產富美家品牌美耐板

富美家公司在一個世紀內經歷了如此大的變化——這很少顯示在公司生產這種標誌性美耐板的工廠。技術、精度和效率跟隨時代變化，但是維護、品質和藝術性依然與過去無異。在辛辛那提的公司百年華誕前夕訪問埃汶代爾工廠的一位遊客可能會發現，工廠與 1950 年開工的第一天幾乎別無二致，至少在外觀上是這樣。外部還是那種普通的磚牆，同樣暴露的房梁，同樣滿載巨大的褐色牛皮紙卷和小卷印刷和單色紙的貨架。黃色的叉車小心地繞行，避開精心描繪的引導遊客穿越機器的綠色人行道。

俄亥俄州的機器與富美家在加拿大和泰國的美耐板工廠使用的機器幾乎相同。壓榨機經久不衰。這些都是巨大的、堅固耐用的機器，其中一些有幾十年的歷史，但都更新了新一代的電子設備和控制系統。這不是矽穀的裝滿機器人的白色房間，而是更像一個機器加工車間或商業麵包店。製作美耐板既類似於印刷又類似於烘焙。工廠負責人說：「簡單地說，我們是在做蛋糕，我們使用熱量和壓力。它需要一定的溫度來加熱和冷卻。」像烘烤一樣，來不得半點操之過急。

富美家美耐板大多數是紙。製造開始時是多層的紙張。底模是幾層核心牛皮紙層，像我們所熟悉的棕色紙袋一樣，只不過重了一些。幾層紙先用樹脂處理，或稱為「浸濕和擠壓」。牛皮紙最上層加蓋一層印刷或實色的裝飾層。類似舊時用來包三明治的蠟紙也放在美耐板的最上層。這就變成了透明的三聚氰胺保護層和剝離層。紙層是「成雙」或「成對」地做，兩片置於兩片鋼板之間，很薄但很重。然後，這整個部分裝成摞

年代、八十年代和九十年代，Laminex 工業擴大其市場范圍，增加了一系列城市和地區分部，現在在全澳大利亞有 36 个销售点。

二十世纪九十年代，Laminex 工業收購了富美家在新西兰的耐火板工厂和分销中心，继续制造这两个品牌的产品。1948 年，由德拉鲁建成的富美家品牌产品在澳大利亚的制造厂在市场上很落后——一般规则的例外情况。富美家®裝饰耐火板在澳大利亚的工厂 1998 年被关闭。在 1999 年 7 月，Amatek 有限公司(Amatek Limited)在从 CSR 购买了富美家的业务的同时收购了富美家商标的使用权。Amatek 有限公司更名为 Laminex 集团有限公司(Laminex Group Limited)，2002 年 11 月，被 CVC 卖给了佛萊彻建築公司。

澳大利亚是世界上富美家品牌耐火板不占主導地位的为数不多的几个国家之一—— Laminex 品牌在世界这个地区是标志性品牌。几十年来，在澳大利亚和新西兰这两个市场，这两个对手在复杂的商业历史中经历了几个阶段的所有权之争。这种混乱终于当它们高兴地统一在弗萊彻建築公司麾下时而告终。

การผลิตแผ่นลามิเนทภายใต้เครื่องหมายการค้าจดทะเบียนฟอร์ไมก้า

บริษัท ฟอร์ไมก้า มีการเปลี่ยนแปลงมากมายในเวลาหนึ่งศตวรรษ แต่ภายในโรงงานของบริษัทที่ผลิตแผ่นลามิเนทอันเลื่องชื่อนั้นจะเห็นการเปลี่ยนแปลงน้อยมาก เทคโนโลยีความแม่นยำ และประสิทธิภาพนั้นมีการปรับเปลี่ยนไปตามกาลเวลา แต่ความเอาใจใส่ดูแลคุณภาพ และความมีศิลปะยังคงเหมือนเดิม ผู้ที่มาเยี่ยมชมโรงงานอีเว็นเดลในซินซินนาติในวันก่อนวันครบรอบร้อยปีของบริษัทอาจพบการเปลี่ยนแปลงเล็กน้อยถ้าเทียบกับวันแรกที่โรงงานแห่งนี้เปิดดำเนินการในปี ค.ศ. 1950 อย่างน้อยก็ในส่วนด้านนอก ผนังอิฐเรียบ ๆ แบบเดิมยังคงอยู่ คานเปลือยเหนือศีรษะเดิมยังคงอยู่ ชั้นวางของอันเดิมที่วางม้วนกระดาษคราฟต์สีน้ำตาลม้วนใหญ่ ๆ และม้วนกระดาษลายและม้วนกระดาษสีพื้นที่เล็กลงมาก็ยังคงอยู่ รถยกสีเหลืองวิ่งไปอย่างระวังเมื่อผ่านทางเดินที่ทาสีเขียวสำหรับแยกทางผู้มาเยี่ยมชมกับทางเครื่องจักร

เครื่องจักรในมลรัฐโอไฮโอก็แทบจะเหมือนกันกับเครื่องจักรในโรงงานผลิตแผ่นลามิเนทฟอร์ไมก้าในประเทศแคนาดาหรือในประเทศไทย การอัดแรงดันใช้เวลานานเครื่องจักรเหล่านี้เป็นเครื่องจักรขนาดใหญ่และแข็งแรงทนทาน บางเครื่องมีอายุหลายทศวรรษแล้ว แต่มีการปรับให้ทันสมัยด้วยเครื่องอิเล็กทรอนิกส์และตัวควบคุมรุ่นใหม่ โรงงานของบริษัทไม่ใช่ห้องขาว ๆ ที่ใช้หุ่นยนต์เต็มห้องเหมือนอย่างที่เมืองเทคโนโลยีที่ ซิลิคอน วัลเลย์ แต่จะเหมือนกับห้องเครื่องหรือร้านขายขนมปังมากกว่า การผลิตแผ่นลามิเนทเหมือนการพิมพ์งานหรือการอบ

Ce sont de grosses machines robustes, parfois vieilles de plusieurs décennies, mais adaptées aux nouvelles générations d'appareils électroniques et de contrôleurs. Ce n'est pas une salle blanche pleine de robots comme dans la Silicon Valley, mais plutôt un atelier d'usinage ou une boulangerie commerciale. Fabriquer du stratifié ressemble à une impression et une cuisson. « Grosso modo, nous confectionnons des gâteaux », dit le directeur de l'usine. « Nous utilisons la chaleur et la pression. Il faut une certaine température pour chauffer et refroidir. » Comme dans le cas de la cuisson, la précipitation est nocive.

L'essentiel du stratifié Formica est du papier. Sa fabrication commence avec plusieurs couches de papier. La base est constituée de plusieurs couches de Kraft, une version lourde de la substance familière des sacs en papier brun. Les couches sont d'abord traitées avec des résines ou trempées et pressées. Le papier Kraft est couvert d'une teinte décorative imprimée dans la masse. Les feuilles ressemblent à du papier ciré à l'ancienne pour l'emballage des sandwiches et se placent également au sommet des sandwiches de stratifié. Elles deviennent des couches protectrices et anti-adhésives de mélamine. Les couches de papier sont construites par paire, deux feuilles étant fixées entre des tôles d'acier très minces mais très lourdes. Ensuite, les unités sont assemblées en paquets ou carnets. L'ensemble du processus est parfois appelé accumulation.

Pour déplacer les plaques dans l'usine, les machines basculent pour saisir les plaques au moyen de ventouses de la taille d'assiettes à dessert, comme celles utilisées par les verriers. Mais ce mécanisme est une exception. Une grande partie du travail exige toujours le travail humain et la coopération physique. Dans le processus d'assemblage, un visiteur de l'usine peut voir des dames déplacer des feuilles de leur support selon un mouvement expert, une opération qui ressemble au pliage de serviettes ou de draps.

Le résultat de l'accumulation est un ensemble de paquets, tels que des dalles, qui entrent dans la presse. La plus grande presse de l'usine de l'Ohio est celle qui porte le numéro 28, l'origine de ce nom ayant toutefois été oublié depuis bien longtemps. Les

productos de la marca Formica en Australia, establecida por De La Rue en 1948, quedó atrás en el mercado —una excepción a la regla general. La planta de laminado Formica en Australia se cerró en 1998. Amatek Limited adquirió los derechos de la marca comercial Formica en julio de 1999 cuando le compró a CSR la empresa Formica. Amatek Limited cambió el nombre a Laminex Group Limited y fue vendida por CVC a Fletcher Building en noviembre de 2002.

Australia era uno de los pocos países en el mundo en el que la marca Formica no era la marca dominante para laminados —la marca de Laminex era la marca icónica en esa parte del mundo. Durante décadas y en los dos mercados de Australia y Nueva Zelanda, los dos rivales atravesaron varias etapas de propiedad en una historia comercial compleja. La confusión finalmente terminó cuando, afortunadamente, se unificaron bajo el techo de Fletcher Building.

Producción del laminado de la marca Formica®

Tanto había cambiado la empresa Formica en un siglo, y tan poco de eso exhibiciones hacía patente en las plantas de la empresa que producen el icónico laminado. Tras un siglo de historia de la marca Formica es evidente que la tecnología, la precisión y la eficiencia se habían ajustado a los tiempos, pero el mantenimiento, la calidad y el arte habían permanecido iguales. Quien visite la fábrica de Evendale, en Cincinnati, en vísperas del centenario de la empresa podría detectar cambios mínimos desde los primeros días de la fábrica en 1950, al menos en el exterior. Las mismas paredes de ladrillo en el exterior, las mismas vigas expuestas en lo alto, las mismas rejillas cargadas de rollos enormes de papel Kraft marrón y rollos más pequeños de papel impreso y unicolor. Los montacargas color amarillo se desplazan evitando cuidadosamente los pasillos pintados de color verde que guían al visitante entre las máquinas.

Las máquinas en Ohio son muy parecidas a las de una fábrica de laminado Formica en Canadá o en Tailandia. Las prensas tienen una gran vida útil. Son máquinas grandes y resistentes, con algunas décadas pero actualizadas con nuevas generaciones de componentes electrónicos y controladores. No es una habitación blanca llena de robots, al es-

naattien tehtaassa Kanadassa tai Thaimaassa. Puristimet kestävät kauan. Nämä ovat suuria, lujia koneita, jotkin vuosikymmenien ikäisiä, mutta päivitetty uusien sukupolvien elektroniikalla ja ohjaimilla. Tämä ei ole valkoinen huone täynnä robotteja Silicon Valleyn tyyliin, vaan paremminkin konepaja tai kaupallinen leipomo. Laminaatin teko on kuin kirjapainotyötä ja leivän paistamisen tapaista. "Periaatteessa leivomme kakkuja", kertoo tehtaan johtaja. "Käytämme kuumuutta ja painetta. Kuumenemiseen ja jäähtymiseen tarvitaan tietty lämpötila. Leivän paistamisen tavoin tässäkään ei saa hätiköidä.

Suurin osa Formica laminaatista on paperia. Sen valmistus alkaa monesta paperikerroksesta. Pohjana on useita ydinkerroksia voimapaperia, ruskeista paperipusseista tutun aineen vahvempaa versiota. Kerrokset käsitellään ensin hartseilla eli "kastetaan ja rutistetaan". Voimapaperin päälle tulee kuviollinen painettu tai yksivärinen koristekerros. Levyt, jotka muistuttavat vanhanaikaista vahapaperia, johon eväitä käärittiin, tulevat samoin laminaattikerrosten päälle. Niistä tulee läpinäkyviä melamiinisia suoja- ja irrokekerroksia. Paperikerroksista tehdään "kahdennetut" eli "parit," kaksi levyä asetettuina hyvin ohuiden mutta hyvin raskaiden teräslevyjen väliin. Yksiköt kootaan sitten pakoiksi eli kirjoiksi. Koko prosessia kutsutaan toisinaan nimellä "the build out" (rakentaminen).

Levyjen siirtämiseksi tehtaassa koneet kääntyvät sivulle ja tarttuvat levyihin jälkiruokalautasen kokoisilla imukupeilla, jollaisia lasimestarit käyttävät. Tämä koneisto on kuitenkin poikkeus. Suuri osa työstä vaatii kuitenkin ihmisten ryhmätyötä ja fyysistä yhteistoimintaa. Prosessissa, jota kutsutaan lomitukseksi, tehtaassa vieraileva saattaa nähdä pari naishenkilöä siirtämässä levyjä telineestään nopealla asiantuntijan vääntöliikkeellä, samanlaisella kuin pyyhkeitä tai lakanoita laskostettaessa.

Rakentamisen tuloksena syntyy sarja laattamaisia pakkoja, jotka menevät puristimeen. Ohion tehtaan suurin puristin on nro 28, vaikka numeron merkitys onkin jo kauan sitten unohtunut. Puristimet muistuttavat valtavan suuria pizzauuneja. Levyjä varten on useampia varusteita, aivan kuin pizza-

或裝成本。整個製造過程有時也被稱為「堆砌」。

要在工廠裡移動板片，機器需要轉過來用甜點盤大小的吸碗抓住板片，就像玻璃工用的那種工具。但是，這種機器是個例外。大部分工作仍然需要人工合作和身體合作。在這個稱作整理的過程中，工廠訪客可能會看到兩名女工從貨架上快速、熟練地把板片一扭，移下來，就好像折疊毛巾或被單一樣的動作。

堆砌的結果是一系列像是石板一樣的包片，送進壓榨機。俄亥俄州工廠最大的壓榨機是 28 號，至於為什麼叫 28 號，誰也不記得了。壓榨機讓人想起巨大的披薩餅烤爐。有多個工具用在紙板上，就像一個披薩餅烤箱，向盡頭一看，能看見類似迷宮的管道。看另一端，是水暖工害怕的活計，輸送熱水。在古老的 28 號身上，六個巨大的閃閃發光的銀色液壓柱可提供約每平方英尺 1,500 磅的壓力，約合 105 公斤/平方公分，溫度約為華氏 350 度（攝氏 177 度）。貨架可以讓「包片」像披薩餅在紙上一樣滑動。在離開壓榨機後，板片像剛烘焙的食品一樣溫熱，被修邊和背面打磨。然後就被切成適當的大小，以供裝運。

每一個工作站都有圖表記錄品質控制標準，並高聲讀著這幾個字母QCDSM，這在世界各地注重品質的工廠都很熟悉：它們代表品質（Quality）、成本（Cost）、交貨（Delivery）、安全（Safety）和士氣（Morale）。這是品質改進系統的一個工作口號。完成這些工作比以前使用的工人更少，但很多的老設備都堅固耐用，物盡其用。正如馬克·亞當森（Mark Adamson）所說：「我們這行的現實情況之一是機械有很長的壽命，主要部件都是大金屬塊。」有時，這些巨大的機器被搬到世界各地。公司買下了墨西哥當地的一家公司後，一架耐火板壓榨機被從墨西哥搬遷到英國北希爾茲。它仍

生产富美家品牌耐火板

富美家公司在一个世纪内经历了如此大的变化——这很少显示在公司生产这种标志性耐火板的工厂。技术、精度和效率跟随时代变化，但是维护、质量和艺术性依然与过去无异。在辛辛那提的公司百年华诞前夕访问埃汶代尔工厂的一位游客可能会发现，工厂与1950年开工的第一天几乎别无二致，至少在外观上是这样。外部还是那种普通的砖墙，同样暴露的房梁，同样满载巨大的褐色牛皮纸卷和小卷印刷和单色纸的货架。黄色的叉车小心地绕行，避开精心描绘的引导游客穿越机器的绿色人行道。

俄亥俄州的机器与富美家在加拿大和泰国的耐火板工厂使用的机器几乎相同。压力机经久不衰。这些都是巨大的、坚固耐用的机器，其中一些有几十年的历史，但都更新了新一代的电子设备和控制系统。这不是硅谷的装满机器人的白色房间，而是更像一个机器加工车间或商业面包店。制作耐火板既类似于印刷又类似于烘焙。工厂负责人说：“简单地说，我们是在做蛋糕，我们使用热量和压力。它需要一定的温度来加热和冷却。”像烘烤一样，来不得半点操之过急。

富美家®装饰耐火板大多数是纸。制造开始时是多层的纸张。底模是几层核心牛皮纸层，像我们所熟悉的棕色纸袋一样，只不过重一些。几层纸先用树脂处理，或称为“浸湿和挤压”。牛皮纸最上层加盖一层印刷过或实色的装饰层。类似旧时用来包三明治的蜡纸也放在耐火板的最上层。这就变成了透明的三聚氰胺保护层和剥离层。纸层是“成双”或“成对”地做，两片置于两片钢板之间，很薄但很重。然后，这整个部分装摞或装成本。整个制造过程有时也被称为“堆砌”。

要在工厂里移动板片，机器需要转过来用甜点盘大小的吸碗抓住板片，就像玻璃工用的那种工具。但是，这种机器是个例外。大部分工作仍然需要

ขนม หัวหน้าโรงงานเปรียบว่า "พูดง่ายๆ เหมือนเราทำเค้ก" "เราใช้ความร้อนและแรงดัน ซึ่งต้องใช้อุณหภูมิตามที่กำหนดไว้เฉพาะเพื่อทำให้ร้อนและเย็น" เช่นเดียวกับการอบขนม รีบไม่ได้

ส่วนใหญ่ของแผ่นลามิเนทฟอร์ไมก้า คือกระดาษ การผลิตเริ่มต้นจากกระดาษหลายๆ ชั้น โดยใช้กระดาษคราฟต์หลายชั้นทำเป็นชั้นแกนสำหรับเป็นฐาน เสมือนถุงกระดาษสีน้ำตาลหนักๆ ชั้นกระดาษดังกล่าวจะเคลือบด้วยเรซินหรือเรียกว่าขั้นตอนการ "จุ่มแล้วรีด" กระดาษคราฟต์จะถูกทับด้านบนด้วยชั้นกระดาษตกแต่งลายหรือสีล้วน แผ่นคล้ายกระดาษไขที่ใช้สำหรับห่อขนมแซนด์วิชในสมัยก่อนจะอยู่ด้านบนสุดของแผ่นประกบลามิเนทและจะกลายเป็นชั้นเมลามีนปกป้องใส ชั้นกระดาษจะประกอบกันเป็นคู่ กระดาษสองแผ่นประกอบอยู่ระหว่างแผ่นเหล็กที่บางมากแต่หนักมาก จากนั้นส่วนต่างๆ จะนำมาประกอบกันเป็นตั้ง กระบวนการทั้งหมดบางครั้งเรียกว่า "เดอะ บิลด์ เอาต์"

ในการเคลื่อนย้ายเพลตในโรงงานเครื่องจักรจะจับเพลตด้วยถ้วยดูดที่มีขนาดเท่ากับจานของหวาน คล้ายกับที่ช่างกระจกใช้ นอกจากเครื่องจักรดังกล่าวแล้ว งานส่วนใหญ่ยังคงต้องใช้แรงกายคนทำงานร่วมกันเป็นทีม ในขั้นตอนที่เรียกว่า การรวบรวม ผู้มาเยี่ยมชมโรงงานอาจได้เห็นผู้หญิงคู่หนึ่งทำหน้าที่เคลื่อนย้ายแผ่นออกจากชั้นด้วยความรวดเร็วและชำนาญ คล้ายกับการพับผ้าเช็ดตัวหรือผ้าปูที่นอน

ผลที่ได้จาก เดอะ บิลด์ เอาต์ คือ ตั้งกระดาษเป็นชุดๆ เป็นแผ่นหนาๆ พร้อมเข้าเครื่องอัด เครื่องอัดที่ใหญ่ที่สุดตั้งอยู่ในโรงงานใน

325

presses ressemblent à d'énormes fours à pizza. Il existe plusieurs appareils pour les feuilles, tout comme dans un four à pizza, et un coup d'œil à la fin montre un labyrinthe semblable à de la tuyauterie. Regardez à une extrémité et vous trouverez le cauchemar d'un plombier acheminant de l'eau chaude. Au vénérable numéro 28, six énormes colonnes hydrauliques étincelantes fournissent quelque 105 kg/cm^2 à une température d'environ 177° centigrades. Les supports laissent glisser les paquets comme des pizzas sur les feuilles. Après avoir quitté la presse, les feuilles encore chaudes, comme les produits de boulangerie, sont coupées et leur dos est poncé. Ensuite, elles sont découpées dans les tailles voulues pour l'expédition.

Des tableaux placés à tous les postes de travail signalent les normes de contrôle de qualité avec les lettres QCDSM qui sont familières aux usines orientées vers la qualité partout dans le monde. Elles signifient : Quality (qualité), Cost (coût), Delivery (livraison), Safety (sécurité) et Morale (morale). Tel est le slogan de travail d'un système d'amélioration de la qualité. Tout cela se fait avec moins de travailleurs qu'auparavant, mais une grande partie de l'équipement ancien robuste est conservée. Comme le dit M. Mark Adamson, « L'une des réalités de notre entreprise est que la machine a une très longue durée de vie. Les principales composantes sont d'énormes morceaux de métal. » Parfois, ces énormes machines se déplacent partout dans le monde. Une presse à stratifié en provenance du Mexique a déménagé à North Shields au Royaume-Uni après que la société ait racheté la société mexicaine locale. Cela reste une superbe pièce de machinerie, maintenant modifiée par l'électronique moderne. Dans la grisaille du sol de l'usine, de nouvelles salles de repos bien éclairées se distinguent, peintes en blanc, isolées du bruit des machines et équipées de tables et de distributeurs. Là, le visiteur rencontre plusieurs employés de longue date des années 1945 et 1947, symboles de l'histoire de l'entreprise. Un employé déclare : « Je suis la troisième génération de la famille à travailler pour Formica. Et ceci inclut ma grand-mère. »

tilo Silicon Valley, sino más bien una tienda de máquinas o una panadería comercial. Fabricar el laminado implica algo de impresión y algo de horneado. "Hacemos tortas, básicamente", dice el director de la fábrica. "Utilizamos calor y presión. Se necesita determinada temperatura para caldear y enfriar". Como en el horneado, el proceso no se puede apresurar.

La mayor parte del laminado Formica es papel. Su fabricación comienza con muchas capas de papel. La base son varias capas interiores de papel Kraft, una versión densa del material conocido de las bolsas de papel marrón. Las capas se tratan primero con resinas o se "sumergen y exprimen". El papel Kraft se cubre con una capa decorativa impresa o unicolor. Las láminas que parecen papel encerado tradicional para envolver emparedados también van en la parte superior del emparedado de laminado. Se convierten en capas protectoras y antiadhesivas de melamina transparente. Las capas de papel se incorporan "dobles" o en "pares"; dos láminas fijas entre placas de acero, muy delgadas pero muy resistentes. Luego, las unidades se ensamblan en paquetes o libros. El proceso completo suele denominarse "la construcción".

Para trasladar las placas en la fábrica, las máquinas giran para agarrar las placas con ventosas del tamaño de platos de postre, como aquellas que utilizan los vidrieros. Pero esas máquinas son una excepción. Gran parte del proceso todavía requiere el trabajo en equipo y la cooperación física de las personas. En el proceso denominado "intercalado", quien visite la fábrica podría ver un par de trabajadoras trasladando las láminas desde sus respectivas rejillas con un giro rápido y experto, una operación similar a la de intentar plegar toallas o sábanas.

El resultado de la acumulación es una serie de paquetes, como losas, que van a la prensa. La prensa más grande en la fábrica de Ohio es la número 28, aunque el motivo de los números ya se perdió. Las prensas sugieren enormes hornos para pizza. Hay múltiples estructuras fijas para las hojas, tal como en un horno para pizza, y si uno mira los extremos, hay un laberinto de tubos similar. Si se mira hacia un extremo, hay un complejo trabajo de plomería, que trae agua caliente. En la venerable prensa número 28, seis enormes columnas hidráulicas de color plateado

uunissa, ja päästä katsottaessa näkyy samanlainen putkien sokkelo. Yhdestä päästä katsottaessa näkyy putkimiehen painajainen tuomassa kuumaa vettä. Vanhan kunnianarvoisan numeron 28 tapauksessa, kuusi valtavan suurta hohtavaa hopean väristä hydraulista pilaria saavat aikaan noin 1500 naulaa neliötuumaa kohden, eli noin 105 kg/cm^2 350 °F (177 °C lämpötilassa). Telineet päästävät "pakat" liukumaan sisään kuin pizzat levyillä. Puristimesta pois tultuaan, edelleen lämpimät kuin leivonnaiset, levyt trimmataan ja niiden selät hiotaan. Tämän jälkeen ne viipaloidaan toimittamista varten sopivan kokoisiksi.

Jokaisen työaseman yhteydessä on taulukot laadunvalvontastandardeista ja suurin kirjaimin QCDSM, jotka ovat tuttuja laatuun tähtäävissä tehtaissa eri puolilla maailmaa: ne tulevat sanoista Quality (laatu), Cost (hinta), Delivery (toimitus), Safety (turvallisuus) ja Morale (henki). Tämä on laadun parannusjärjestelmän käyttämä iskulause. Se kaikki tehdään vähemmällä työvoimalla kuin ennen, mutta suuri osa vanhoista koneista ovat lujia ja tarkoitukseen rakennettuja. Kuten Mark Adamson mainitsee, "Eräs liiketoimintamme tosiasia on se, että koneilla on a hyvin pitkä käyttöikä. Pääosat ovat valtavan suuria metallimöykkyjä". Toisinaan nämä valtavan suuret koneet liikkuvat ympäri maailmaa. Meksikosta siirrettiin laminaattipuristin North Shieldsiin Englantiin, yhtiön ostettua paikallisen meksikolaisen yrityksen. Se on vieläkin erinomainen kone, nyt muutettuna käyttämään nykyaikaista elektroniikkaa. Tehtaan lattian harmaudesta erottuvat uudet hyvin valaistut taukohuoneet, valkoisiksi maalattuina, koneiden melusta eristettyinä ja pöydillä ja myyntiautomaateilla varustettuina. Siellä kävijä tapaa useita pitkäaikaisia työntekijöitä, joilla on 45 ja 47 vuoden työhistoriat yhtiön palveluksessa. Eräs työntekijä toteaa "Olen kolmas sukupolvi perheestämme Formican palveluksessa. Ja siihen kuuluu isoäitini".

Globaalisti vihreä

Muita Evendalen tehtaan osia on muutettu perin pohjin, joskin näkymättömästi. Öljyllä ja kivihiilellä toimivat höyrykattilat on kauan sitten poistettu, korvattuina kaasukäyttöisillä,

然是一架極好的機械，現已改裝了電子系統。在工廠車間灰色的地板上，嶄新的、光線充足的休息室特別顯眼，它被漆成白色，與機器的噪音隔絕，裡面放著桌子和自動售貨機。在那裡，訪客見到了分別在公司工作了 45 年和 47 年的老雇員。一名員工說：「我是我們家族的第三代為富美家工作的人，這包括我的祖母。」

全球綠色環保

埃汶代爾工廠的其他部分從根本上（如果不是無形之中）也發生了很大的變化。燃油和燃煤鍋爐早已不復存在，取而代之的是那些燒天然氣的鍋爐，雖然世界各地的一些工廠仍然依賴更傳統的燃料。紙屑被送回造紙廠，其他鬆散廢物在工廠被焚燒，以產生能量。類似的做法已經成為富美家集團在世界各地工廠的標準。

公司在很久以前就開始考慮環境問題。但由於對全球變暖、能源和可持續發展的憂慮影響了企業和消費者的觀念，公司的全球思維就顯示出了新的意義。在新世紀中，富美家集團開始檢討其業務的各個方面，考慮到對地球的影響。亞當森首席執行官說：「這都歸結於我們呼吸著同樣的空氣和水，環保必然是全球性的。技術解決方案也很可能是全球性的，因為生物學和物理學的規律在不同的國家是相同的。我們一直能夠在全球層面上合並我們的資源。隨著時間的推移，將會越來越具有經濟上的必要性……我們的業務能源消耗十分嚴重……每天我都擔心煤和天然氣的價格。我們為什麼要限制生命週期的能源成本，確實有不講情面的經濟原因。」

公司也開始測試產品的室內排放問題。其中一個關鍵領域是在教室和兒童產品中使用的檯式電腦和其他產品的安全性。關鍵的富美家品牌產品被提交，得到綠色保護室內空氣品質認證，目前在世界各地製造富美家美耐板的工廠都達到了這項標

人工合作和身體合作。在這個稱作整理的過程中，工廠訪客可能會看到兩名女工從貨架上快速、熟練地把板片一扭，移下來，就好像折疊毛巾或被單一樣的動作。

堆砌的結果是一系列像是石板一樣的包片，送進壓力機。俄亥俄州工廠最大的壓力機是 28 号，至於為什麼叫 28 号，誰也不記得了。壓力機讓人想起巨大的披薩餅烤爐。有多個工具用在紙板上，就像一個披薩餅烤箱，向盡頭一看，能看見類似迷宮的管道。看另一端，是水暖工最害怕的活計，輸送熱水。在古老的 28 号身上，六個巨大的閃閃發光的銀色液壓柱可提供約每平方英尺 1,500 磅的壓力，約合 105 公斤/平方厘米，溫度約為華氏 350 度（攝氏 177 度）。貨架可以讓"包片"像披薩餅在紙上一樣滑動。在離開壓榨機後，板片像剛烘焙的食品一樣溫熱，被修邊和背面打磨。然後就被切成適當的大小，以供裝運。

每一個工作站都有圖表記錄質量控制標準，並高聲讀著這幾個字母 QCDSM，這在世界各地注重質量的工廠都很熟悉：它們代表質量 (Quality)、成本 (Cost)、交貨 (Delivery)、安全 (Safety) 和士氣 (Morale)。這是質量改進系統的一個工作口號。完成這些工作比以前使用的工人更少，但很多的老設備都堅固耐用，物盡其用。正如馬克·亞當森 (Mark Adamson) 所說："我們這行的現實情況之一是機械有很長的壽命，主要部件都是大金屬塊。"有時，這些巨大的機器被搬到世界各地。公司買下了墨西哥當地的一家公司後，一架耐火板壓榨機被從墨西哥搬遷到英國北希爾茲。它仍然是一架極好的機械，現已改裝了電子系統。在工廠車間灰色的地板上，嶄新的、光線充足的休息室特別顯眼，它被漆成白色，與機器的噪音隔絕，裡面放著桌子和自動售貨機。在那裡，訪客見到了分別在公司工作了 45 年和 47 年的老雇員。一名員工說："我

มลรัฐโอไฮโอ คือ หมายเลข 28 ที่มาของ
ตัวเลขนี้ไม่มีใครทราบมานานแล้ว เครื่องอัด
มีหน้าตาคล้ายเตาอบพิซซ่าขนาดใหญ่ มีตัว
ยึดสำหรับแผ่นหลายตัว เหมือนกับที่มีในเตา
อบพิซซ่า และที่ปลายมีท่อคดเคี้ยวที่คล้ายคึ
กันด้วย ด้านหนึ่งมีระบบท่อน้ำเวียนหัวเป็นท่อ
น้ำร้อน ที่เครื่องอัดสำคัญหมายเลข 28 มีเสา
แรงน้ำขนาดใหญ่สีเงินวาวจำนวนหกเสา ทำ
หน้าที่จ่ายน้ำประมาณ 1,500 ปอนด์ต่อตา
รางนิ้ว หรือประมาณ 105 กก./ตร.ซม. ที่
อุณหภูมิประมาณ 177 °C มีเตแกรงเลื่อน
ให้ "ดั้งกระดาษ" ไหลเข้าไปเหมือนพิซซ่า
บนแผ่นไม้ เมื่อแผ่นกระดาษออกมาจากเครื่อง
อัด อุ่น ๆ เหมือนของอบ จะถูกตัดแต่งและขัด
ด้านหลัง เสร็จแล้วจะถูกแบ่งออกเป็นขนาดที่
ถูกต้องเพื่อทำการจัดส่งต่อไป

แผนผังที่ติดอยู่ ณ สถานีงานทุกสถานี
จะแสดงมาตรฐานการควบคุมคุณภาพและแสดง
ตัวอักษร คิวซีดีเอสเอ็ม เด่นชัด ซึ่งเป็นปกติ
ธรรมดาสำหรับโรงงานทั่วโลกที่มุ่งเน้นด้าน
คุณภาพ ตัวอักษรดังกล่าวเป็นอักษรย่อ คำว่า
คุณภาพ ต้นทุน การส่งมอบ ความปลอดภัย
และขวัญกำลังใจ ซึ่งเป็นคำขวัญการทำงานของ
ระบบการปรับปรุงคุณภาพ ขั้นตอนทั้งหมด
ใช้คนงานน้อยกว่าแต่ก่อน แต่อุปกรณ์รุ่นเก่า
จำนวนมากมีความทนทานและสร้างขึ้นเพื่อ
วัตถุประสงค์เฉพาะ ดังที่นายมาร์ค อดัมสัน
กล่าวไว้ว่า "ข้อเท็จจริงหนึ่งของธุรกิจเรา
คือ เครื่องจักรมีอายุการใช้งานที่ยาวนานมาก
ส่วนประกอบที่สำคัญคือโลหะชิ้นใหญ่ ๆ" บาง
ครั้งเครื่องจักรขนาดใหญ่เหล่านี้เคลื่อนย้าย
ไปทั่วโลก เครื่องอัดลามิเนทจากประเทศ
เม็กซิโกถูกย้ายไปอยู่ที่นอร์ธชิลด์ในสหราช
อาณาจักรหลังจากบริษัทซื้อบริษัทเม็กซิโกใน
ท้องถิ่น เครื่องจักรเครื่องนี้ยังคงเป็นเครื่องจักร
ชั้นยอด ซึ่งปัจจุบันได้รับการปรับปรุงโดยใช้
อิเล็กทรอนิกส์ที่ทันสมัย บนพื้นโรงงานสีเทา
ห้องพักใหม่ทาสีขาวปิดผนังกั้นเสียงเครื่องจักร
มีโต๊ะและตู้ขายสินค้าแบบหยอดเหรียญ เปิด
ไฟสว่าง ดูโดดเด่นสะดุดตา ใช้เป็นที่ให้ผู้มา
เยี่ยมชมโรงงานได้พบปะกับพนักงานหลาย
คนที่ทำงานกับบริษัทมายาวนานถึงสี่สิบห้า
และสี่สิบเจ็ดปี พนักงานคนหนึ่งเล่าว่า "ฉัน
เป็นสมาชิกครอบครัวรุ่นที่สามที่ทำงานให้กับ
บริษัท ฟอร์ไมก้า สมาชิกครอบครัวฉันรวมถึง
คุณย่าของฉันด้วย"

อนุรักษ์โลก

ส่วนอื่น ๆ ของโรงงานอีเวนเดล ถูกเปลี่ยน
แปลงอย่างมาก แต่อาจมองไม่เห็น หม้อต้ม ที่
ใช้น้ำมันและถ่านหินเป็นเชื้อเพลิงไม่มีอีกแล้ว
โดยบริษัทเปลี่ยนมาใช้เชื้อเพลิงจากก๊าซแทน
อย่างไรก็ดี โรงงานบางโรงงานที่อื่นในโลกยัง

Protection de l'environnement à travers le monde

D'autres parties de l'usine Evendale ont radicalement changé même si cela ne se voit pas. Les chaudières au mazout et au charbon ont disparu depuis longtemps. Elles ont été remplacées par des chaudières au gaz, même si certaines usines à travers le monde continuent à utiliser les anciens carburants. Les chutes de papier sont renvoyées dans les usines de papier et les autres déchets en vrac sont brûlés pour alimenter l'usine en énergie. Des pratiques similaires sont devenues la norme dans les usines de Formica Group à travers le monde.

La société s'est occupée de l'environnement depuis longtemps. Mais sa philosophie a pris un sens nouveau avec les préoccupations concernant le réchauffement climatique, les économies d'énergie et la durabilité du point de vue des entreprises et des consommateurs. Dans ce nouveau millénaire, Formica Group a commencé à examiner tous les aspects de ses activités en ce qui concerne son impact sur la planète. « On en revient toujours au fait que nous respirons le même air et buvons toujours la même eau », explique le PDG Adamson. « Protéger l'environnement doit nécessairement être global. Les solutions technologiques sont également susceptibles d'être apportées au niveau mondial, car les lois de la biologie et de la physique ne diffèrent pas à travers les frontières. Nous avons été en mesure de combiner nos ressources à l'échelle mondiale. Avec le temps, il s'agira d'un impératif de plus en plus économique. Notre activité est très énergivore. Chaque jour, je dois me soucier du prix du charbon et du gaz. Il y a des impératifs économiques purs et durs qui impliquent de limiter les coûts énergétiques du cycle de vie. »

La société a également commencé à tester des produits pour les émissions intérieures. Un domaine clé est la sécurité des produits de bureau et autres utilisés dans les salles de classe et les produits pour les enfants. Les principaux produits de la marque Formica ont été testés et ont obtenu l'agrément en matière de qualité de l'air intérieur Greenguard, une norme qui est maintenant respectée

reluciente suministran aproximadamente, 105 kg/cm^2 a una temperatura aproximada de 177 °C. Las rejillas permiten deslizar los "paquetes", como pizzas en placas. Tras dejar la prensa, las hojas, todavía calientes, como productos horneados, se recortan y sus partes posteriores se lijan. Luego, las hojas se cortan en los tamaños adecuados para su envío.

Los organigramas en todas las estaciones de trabajo indican normas de control de calidad y resaltan las letras de la sigla QCDSM (*Quality, Cost, Delivery, Safety, Morale*), que son conocidas en fábricas orientadas a la calidad en todo el mundo: en español, la sigla significa "calidad, costo, entrega, seguridad y moral". Este es el eslogan de un sistema de mejoramiento de la calidad. Todo se hace con menos trabajadores que antes, pero la mayor parte del equipo antiguo es resistente y especializado. Como expresa Mark Adamson: "Una de las realidades de nuestra empresa es que las máquinas tienen una vida útil muy prolongada. Las piezas principales son enormes trozos de metal". Algunas veces, estas enormes máquinas se trasladan alrededor del mundo. Una prensa para laminados de México se trasladó a North Shields, en el Reino Unido, después de que la empresa comprara la firma local mexicana. Sigue siendo una pieza de maquinaria espléndida, ahora modificada con todos los componentes electrónicos modernos. En el área gris de la planta de producción, resaltan salas de descanso nuevas y bien iluminadas, pintadas de blanco, aisladas del ruido de las máquinas y provistas de mesas y máquinas expendedoras. Allí, el visitante conoce a varios empleados con cuarenta y cinco y cuarenta y siete años de historia laboral en la empresa. Señala un empleado: "Soy la tercera generación de nuestra familia que trabaja para Formica. Y eso incluye a mi abuela".

Compromiso global con la sostenibilidad

Otras partes de la planta de Evendale han cambiado radicalmente, aunque de manera imperceptible. Las calderas de gasóleo o carbón ya no se utilizan, fueron reemplazadas por las de gas, aunque algunas fábricas alrededor del mundo todavía dependen de los combustibles anteriores. Los desechos de papel se envían a las fábricas de papel, y otros

vaikka jotkin tehtaat eri puolilla maailmaa ovatkin edelleen riippuvaisia vanhemmista polttoaineista. Jätepaperi lähetetään takaisin paperitehtaille ja muu irtonainen jäte poltetaan tehtaassa energian tuottamiseksi. Samanlaiset käytännöt ovat tulleet normeiksi Formica Groupin tehtaissa eri puolilla maailmaa.

Yhtiö alkoi kauan sitten kiinnittää huomiota ympäristöön. Sen globaali ajattelutapa sai kuitenkin uuden merkityksen, kun maapallon ilmaston lämpeneminen, energia ja kestävyys muokkasivat liiketoiminnan ja kuluttajien näkemyksiä. Uudella vuosituhannella Formica Group alkoi käydä läpi liiketoimintansa kaikkia näkökohtia niiden vaikutuksen osalta maapallolla. "Pohjimmiltaan on kysymys siitä tosiseikasta että hengitämme samaa ilmaa ja vettä", sanoo CEO Adamson. "Vihreänä oleminen on pakostakin globaalia. Teknologiaratkaisut tulevat myös todennäköisesti olemaan globaaleja, koska biologian ja fysiikan lait eivät vaihtele maiden välillä. Olemme pystyneet yhdistämään voimavarojamme globaalitasoisesti. Ajan mukana siitä tulee yhä suurempi taloudellinen välttämättömyys.... liiketoimintamme on energian suhteen hyvin intensiivistä.... Joudun joka päivä olemaan huolissani kivihiilen ja kaasun hinnasta. On olemassa vahvat syyt sille, että haluamme rajoittaa elinkaaren energiakustannuksia".

Yhtiö alkoi myös testata tuotteita sisätilojen päästöjen osalta. Eräs avainalue oli pöydän pintojen ja muiden luokkahuoneissa käytettyjen ja lapsille tarkoitettujen tuotteiden turvallisuus. Formica-merkkisille avaintuotteille haettiin ja saatiin Greenguard Indoor Air Quality -sertifiointi, standardi, jota nyt noudatetaan kaikissa Formica-laminaattia valmistavissa tehtaissa eri puolilla maailmaa. Useita vuosia sitten yhtiö aloitti elinkaaren arviointiprosessin (Life Cycle Assessment) (LCA), joka mittaa sen tuotteiden kuluttamat voimavarat ja energian. Prosessi kattaa aikavälin puun kaatamisesta siihen päivään, jolloin paneeli päätyy kaatopaikalle tai kierrätetään. Kestävät käytännöt ovat nyt kriittisiä liiketoiminnassa. "Kuluttajat haluavat tehdä mikä on oikein", sanoo Gavin Todd, Formica Groupin kehityspäällikkö. "Heidät on totutettu edellyttämään ympäristöä

Lovely

to look at . . .

準。幾年前，公司開始了「生命週期評估」(LCA)程序，測量其產品消耗的資源和能源。這個程序從砍樹到美耐板最後來到垃圾填埋場或回收這一天。可持續的做法現在對業務十分關鍵。富美家集團開發部經理加文·托德 (Gavin Todd) 說：「消費者希望做正確的事，他們已經習慣於期待得到環保認證，從而推動著建築師和設計師。」

被稱為「能源和環境設計領導項目」(Leadership in Energy and Environmental Design/簡稱 LEED) 的綠色認證項目，對於改變美國、亞洲、印度和世界上其他市場的設計師和承包商的規劃具有非常重要的影響。該項標準是根據 1994 年美國綠色建築委員會 (U.S. Green Building Council/簡稱 USGBC) 編制的一套標準制定的，以鼓勵可持續發展的建築。建築按得到的點數獲得排名認證，有銀色、金色和白金認證。建築內每一種材料和系統都被考慮到。在英國，可持續性是由「建築物條例設定環境評估方

是我们家族的第三代为富美家工作的人，这包括我的祖母。」

全球绿色环保

埃汶代尔工厂的其他部分从根本上(如果不是无形之中)也发生了很大的变化。燃油和燃煤锅炉早已不复存在，取而代之的是那些烧天然气的锅炉，虽然世界各地的一些工厂仍然依赖更传统的燃料。纸屑被送回造纸厂，其他松散废物在工厂被焚烧，以产生能量。类似的做法已经成为富美家集团在世界各地工厂的标准。

公司在很久以前就开始考虑环境问题。但由于对全球变暖、能源和可持续发展的忧虑影响了企业和消费者的观念，公司的全球思维就显示出了新的意义。在新世纪中，富美家集团开始检讨其业务的各个方面，考虑到对地球的影响。亚当森首席执行官说：「这都归结于我们呼吸着同样的空气和水，环保必然是全球性的。技术解决方案也很可能是全球性的，因为生物学和物理学的规律在不同的国家是相同的。我们一

คงใช้เชื้อเพลิงแบบเก่าอยู่ เศษกระดาษเหลือใช้จะถูกส่งกลับไปโรงงานกระดาษ ส่วนของเสียอื่นจะถูกเผาเพื่อผลิตพลังงานไว้ใช้ในโรงงาน การปฏิบัติเช่นนี้ได้กลายเป็นมาตรฐานปฏิบัติในโรงงานของกลุ่มบริษัทฟอร์ไมก้าทั่วโลก

บริษัทเริ่มคำนึงถึงสิ่งแวดล้อมมานานแล้ว แต่ความคิดในระดับโลกของบริษัทมีความหมายใหม่ขึ้นเมื่อความกังวลเกี่ยวกับภาวะโลกร้อน พลังงาน และความยั่งยืนเป็นสิ่งที่กำหนดความคิดของธุรกิจและผู้บริโภค ในสหัสวรรษใหม่ กลุ่มบริษัทฟอร์ไมก้าเริ่มทบทวนทุกแง่มุมของธุรกิจของบริษัทและผลกระทบที่จะมีต่อโลก อดัมสัน ประธานเจ้าหน้าที่บริหาร กล่าวว่า "สุดท้ายแล้ว เราหายใจอากาศและใช้น้ำเดียวกัน" "การที่บริษัทเป็นบริษัทสีเขียวเป็นเรื่องจำเป็นในระดับโลก อีกทั้ง ทางออกด้านเทคโนโลยีก็มีแนวโน้มว่าจะเป็นเรื่องระดับโลกเนื่องจากกฎวิชาชีววิทยาและฟิสิกส์ไม่แตกต่างกันในแต่ละประเทศ เราสามารถรวมทรัพยากรของเราในระดับโลกได้ เมื่อเวลาผ่านไป เรื่องนี้จะยิ่งกลายเป็นความจำเป็นทางเศรษฐกิจมากขึ้น... ธุรกิจของบริษัทต้องใช้พลังงานสูง... ผมต้องติดตามราคาถ่านหินและก๊าซทุกวัน นี่เป็นเหตุผลทางเศรษฐกิจที่ไม่อาจหลีกเลี่ยงได้ว่าทำไมเราจึงต้องควบคุมต้นทุนพลังงานในวงจรการผลิต"

นอกจากนี้ บริษัทเริ่มทำการทดสอบการปล่อยสารพิษภายในตัวอาคารของผลิตภัณฑ์ประเด็นที่สำคัญอันหนึ่งคือ ความปลอดภัยของพื้นผิวโต๊ะและผลิตภัณฑ์อื่นๆ ที่ใช้ในห้องเรียนและผลิตภัณฑ์สำหรับเด็ก ผลิตภัณฑ์หลักตราฟอร์ไมก้าถูกส่งไปตรวจสอบและได้รับการรับรองคุณภาพอากาศภายในอาคารกรีนการ์ด ซึ่งเป็นมาตรฐานที่โรงงานผลิตแผ่นลามิเนทฟอร์ไมก้าทุกแห่งทั่วโลกได้รับอยู่ในปัจจุบัน เมื่อหลายปีก่อน บริษัทเริ่มกระบวนการการประเมินวงจรชีวิต (LCA) ซึ่งวัดทรัพยากรและพลังงานที่ผลิตภัณฑ์ของบริษัทใช้ ขั้นตอนการประเมินจะเริ่มตั้งแต่ตัดต้นไม้ไปจนถึงวันที่วัสดุฝังกลบถูกส่งไปที่หลุมฝังกลบหรือมีการนำกลับมาใช้ใหม่ปัจจุบัน การดำเนินธุรกิจอย่างยั่งยืนมีความสำคัญกับธุรกิจมาก นายกาวิน ทอดด์ ผู้อำนวยการฝ่ายการพัฒนาของ กลุ่มบริษัทฟอร์ไมก้ากล่าวว่า "ผู้บริโภคต้องการทำสิ่งที่ถูกต้อง" "ผู้บริโภคถูกฝึกให้คาดหวังว่าบริษัทต้องได้รับการรับรองทางสิ่งแวดล้อม และผู้บริโภคเป็นผู้ผลักดันงานของสถาปนิกและนักออกแบบ"

ผลที่เกิดจากโครงการการรับรองสีเขียวที่เรียกว่า ผู้นำการออกแบบด้านพลังงานและสิ่งแวดล้อม (LEED) มีส่วนสำคัญทำให้เกิดการเปลี่ยนแปลงการวางแผนการทำงานของนักออกแบบและผู้รับเหมาในสหรัฐอเมริกา เอเชีย

dans toutes les usines productrices de stratifié Formica du monde entier. Il y a plusieurs années, la société a lancé une analyse de cycle de vie (ACV), la mesure des ressources et de l'énergie consommés pour ses produits. Le processus commence lors de la coupe d'un arbre jusqu'au jour où le panneau finit dans une décharge ou est recyclé. Les pratiques durables sont désormais essentielles pour les entreprises. « Les consommateurs veulent agir correctement », a déclaré Gavin Todd, directeur du développement de Formica Group. « Ils ont appris à attendre le respect de certaines lois environnementales et ceci influe sur le comportement des architectes et des designers. »

L'impact du programme Leadership in Energy and Environmental Design (LEED) a joué un rôle important dans l'évolution de la manière dont les concepteurs et entrepreneurs planifient la production aux États-Unis, en Asie, en Inde et sur d'autres marchés à travers le monde. Les normes sont basées sur un certain nombre des critères établis en 1994 par l'U.S. Green Building Council (USGBC) pour encourager la construction durable. Des points sont attribués pour classer un bâtiment certifié avec distinction argent, or ou platine. Chaque matériau et système de construction est pris en compte. Au Royaume-Uni, la durabilité est mesurée par la Building Research Establishment Environmental Assessment Method (BREEAM), homologue de la norme LEED. Formica Group a également travaillé avec le

residuos se queman para generar energía en la fábrica. Prácticas similares se han vuelto una norma en las plantas del Grupo Formica en todo el mundo.

Aunque la empresa siempre mantuvo un compromiso medioambiental en su actividad, este compromiso adquirió un nuevo significado a medida que las preocupaciones por el calentamiento global, la energía y la sostenibilidad daban forma a la visión de empresas y consumidores. En el nuevo milenio, el Grupo Formica comenzó a revisar cada aspecto de su negocio con respecto a su impacto en el planeta. "Todo vuelve al hecho de que respiramos el mismo aire y bebemos la misma agua", expresa el director ejecutivo Adamson. "Tener una conciencia ecológica es necesariamente global. Es probable que las soluciones tecnológicas también sean globales, ya que las leyes de biología y física no son distintas en diferentes países. Hemos podido combinar nuestros recursos a nivel global. A medida que pase el tiempo, será cada vez más un imperativo económico... Nuestra empresa consume una gran cantidad de energía... Todos los días debo preocuparme por el precio del carbón y del gas. Hay motivos económicos reales e inflexibles por los que deseamos limitar los costos energéticos en el ciclo de vida".

La empresa también comenzó a probar productos para determinar las emisiones en interiores. Un área clave fue la seguridad de los productos para escritorios y de otro tipo utilizados en las aulas, y de los productos para niños. Se presentaron los productos clave de la marca Formica y recibieron la certificación de *Greenguard Indoor Air Quality*, una norma que ahora se cumple en todas las plantas que producen laminados Formica en todo el mundo. Hace algunos años, la empresa comenzó un proceso de Evaluación de ciclo de vida (*Life Cycle Assessment*, LCA), que mide los recursos y la energía que consumen sus productos. El proceso abarca desde cortar un árbol hasta el día en que el panel termina en un vertedero o se recicla. Las prácticas sostenibles ahora son críticas para la empresa. "Los clientes desean hacer lo correcto", dice Gavin Todd, Gerente de Desarrollo del Grupo Formica. "Demandan certificaciones ambientales, algo también extensible a los arquitectos y diseñadores".

El impacto del programa de certificación ecológica denominado Liderazgo en energía y diseño ambiental (*Leadership*

koskevia sertifiointeja ja he kannustavat arkkitehteja ja suunnittelijoita".

Nimellä Leadership in Energy and Environmental Design (LEED) kutsutun vihreän sertifiointiohjelman vaikutus on ollut tärkeä muuttamaan suunnittelijoiden ja urakoitsijoiden suunnittelutapoja Yhdysvalloissa, Aasiassa, Intiassa ja muilla markkinoilla eri puolilla maailmaa. Standardit perustuvat joukkoon kriteerejä, jotka v. 1994 USA:n Green Building Council (USGBC) – neuvosto kokosi kestävän rakentamisen kannustamiseksi. Annettujen pisteiden perusteella rakennuksen sertifioinniksi tulee hopea, kulta tai platina. Jokainen rakennuksessa esiintyvä materiaali ja järjestelmä otetaan huomioon. Yhdistyneessä kuningaskunnassa kestävyys mitataan käyttämällä Building Research Establishment Environmental Assessment Method (BREEAM) -menetelmää, joka on vastine LEED:lle. Formica Group on myös ollut yhteistyössä Carbon Trust -säätiön kanssa pyrkimyksenään vähentää hiilen katealueettaan sekä kasvihuonekaasujen päästöjä. Vuonna 2012 Formica Groupista tuli ensimmäinen laminaattien valmistaja maailmassa, jolle myönnettiin Carbon Trust -säätiön hiilen vähennyksen merkintä. Nykyisin monet rakenteet rakennetaan LEED-normeja ja muita standardeja noudattaen ympäristön kestävyyden varmistamiseksi.

"Kuljemme nyt hitaasti mutta määrätietoisesti kestävyyden reittiä", Todd mainitsee. "Toimintamme ei ole auton valmistuksen kaltaista, jossa otetaan osat ja pannaan ne kokoon. Paistamme kakkuja, yhdistämällä monia raaka-aineita, joka formuloi kemiallisen muutoksen niiden ominaisuuksille. Kakkujen paistamisessa on paljon enemmän vaihtelevuutta valmistusprosessin puitteissa, joka vaatii täsmällisen ohjauksen tuotteen toimivuuden ylläpitämiseksi".

Tutkiessaan elinkaaren ympäristötekijöiden arviointia, yhtiöt ottavat huomioon ympäristön vaikutuksen tuotteisiin, materiaaleihin, päästöihin, veteen ja energiaan, raaka-aineista käytön loppuun asti — "kehdosta hautaan". Formica-laminaatit ovat välituote. Laminaattia käytetään tavallisesti huonekalun tai pöytälevyjen valmistukseen. Yhtiön LCA osoitti, että valmistus kuluttaa vain noin 25 prosenttia tuot-

法」(BREEAM) 來衡量，這是對應於 LEED 的標準。富美家集團還與碳基金組織 (Carbon Trust) 合作，重點減少其碳覆蓋面和溫室氣體排放。2012 年，富美集團成為世界上被授予碳基金組織的「碳減排標簽」的第一個美耐板製造商。今天的許多建築都是按照 LEED 和其他保證環境可持續性的標準建造。

托德說：「我們現在正緩慢但有目的地走上可持續發展的道路，我們所做的與製造汽車不一樣，製造汽車是用零件組裝起來。我們是烤蛋糕，彙集眾多原料，使它們的屬性發生變化。當你烤蛋糕時，在製造過程中存在更多的可變性，這就需要精確的控制，以保持產品的性能。」

直能够在全球层面上合并我们的资源。随着时间的推移，将会越来越具有经济上的必要性……我们的业务能源消耗十分严重……每天我都担心煤和天然气的价格。我们为什么要限制生命周期的能源成本，确实有不讲情面的经济原因。」

公司也开始测试产品的室内排放问题。其中一个关键领域是在教室和儿童产品中使用的台式计算机和其他产品的安全性。关键的富美家品牌产品被提交，得到绿色保护室内空气质量认证，目前在世界各地制造富美家®装饰耐火板的工厂都达到了这项标准。几年前，公司开始了"生命周期评估"(LCA) 程序，测量其产品消耗的资源和能源。这个程序从砍树到耐火板最后来

อินเดีย และตลาดอื่นๆ รอบโลก มาตรฐานที่กำหนดมาจากเกณฑ์ชุดหนึ่งที่รวบรวมไว้ใน ค.ศ. 1994 โดย สภาอาคารสีเขียวแห่งสหรัฐอเมริกา (USGBC) ที่ต้องการส่งเสริมการออกแบบอาคารแบบยั่งยืน มีการให้คะแนนเพื่อจัดอันดับอาคารที่ผ่านการรับรองได้แก่ เงิน ทอง หรือแพลทินัม การรับรองจะพิจารณาวัสดุแต่ละชิ้นและระบบแต่ละระบบในอาคาร ในสหราชอาณาจักร ความยั่งยืนวัดโดยระบบประเมินสมรรถนะทางสิ่งแวดล้อมของอาคารพัฒนา (BREEAM) ซึ่งเป็นโครงการที่คล้ายกับโครงการ LEED กลุ่มบริษัทฟอร์ไมก้าเคยร่วมงานกับ คาร์บอนทรัสต์ ที่มีวัตถุประสงค์ลดปริมาณก๊าซคาร์บอนไดออกไซด์และก๊าซเรือนกระจกของบริษัทในปี ค.ศ. 2012 กลุ่มบริษัทฟอร์ไมก้าเป็นผู้ผลิตแผ่นลามิเนทรายแรกของโลกที่ได้รับรางวัลฉลากการลดคาร์บอน ของ คาร์บอนทรัสต์ โครงสร้างจำนวนมากในปัจจุบันสร้างขึ้นตามมาตรฐาน LEED และมาตรฐานอื่นเพื่อให้แน่ใจว่ามีความยั่งยืนด้านสิ่งแวดล้อม

ทอดด์กล่าวว่า "เรากำลังมุ่งไปบนเส้นทางเพื่อความยั่งยืนอย่างช้าๆ แต่อย่างมีเป้าหมาย" "สิ่งที่เราทำไม่เหมือนกับการผลิตรถยนต์ที่คุณจะนำชิ้นส่วนมาประกอบเข้าด้วยกัน เราอบเค้กโดยนำวัตถุดิบหลายอย่างมารวมกันเพื่อทำให้เกิดการเปลี่ยนแปลงทางเคมีกับคุณสมบัติของวัตถุดิบเหล่านั้น เวลาคุณอบเค้ก ขั้นตอนการผลิตมีความแปรที่ต้องควบคุมด้วยความแม่นยำมาก เพื่อรักษาคุณภาพของผลิตภัณฑ์"

ในการประเมินวัฏจักรด้านสิ่งแวดล้อมบริษัทต่างๆ จะพิจารณาผลกระทบต่อสิ่งแวดล้อมของผลิตภัณฑ์ วัสดุ การปล่อยสารน้ำ และพลังงานจากวัตถุดิบไปจนสิ้นสุดการใช้ เรียกว่า "ตั้งแต่เกิดจนตาย" แผ่นลามิเนทฟอร์ไมก้าเป็นผลิตภัณฑ์ขั้นกลางแผ่นลามิเนทนำมาใช้ในการผลิตเฟอร์นิเจอร์หรือพื้นผิวบนเคาน์เตอร์ การประเมินวัฏจักรด้านสิ่งแวดล้อมของบริษัทแสดงให้เห็นว่ากระบวนการผลิตใช้พลังงานเพียงประมาณร้อยละ 25 ของพลังงานทั้งหมดที่ใช้ตลอดช่วงอายุของผลิตภัณฑ์ พลังงานส่วนที่เหลือใช้ในกระบวนการการจัดส่งวัตถุดิบให้แก่โรงงานหรือกิจกรรมหลังผลิตแผ่นลามิเนทที่นำผลิตภัณฑ์ตราฟอร์ไมก้าไปเป็นส่วนประกอบเพื่อให้ได้ส่วนที่เสร็จสมบูรณ์ ดังที่อดีตประธานเจ้าหน้าที่บริหาร กล่าวไว้ว่า "ร้อยละหกสิบของผลิตภัณฑ์ของบริษัท คือ กระดาษ" การทำให้กระดาษนั้นมีความยั่งยืนเป็นเรื่องสำคัญมาก

ภายในเวลาสามปี บริษัทเปลี่ยนมาใช้ไม้จากป่าไม้ที่ยั่งยืนและได้รับการรับรองของสภา

Carbon Trust pour réduire l'empreinte carbone et les émissions GES. En 2012, Formica Group est devenu le premier fabricant de stratifié au monde à recevoir le Carbon Trust's Carbon Reduction La-bel. De nombreuses structures actuelles sont construites aux normes LEED et autres normes de préservation de l'environnement.

« Nous allons maintenant passer lentement mais résolument à la durabilité », dit Todd. « Ce que nous faisons ne revient pas à construire une voiture, où vous prenez les pièces et les assemblez. Quand vous cuisez des gâteaux, il y a beaucoup plus de variabilités dans le processus de fabrication qui exigent des contrôles précis pour maintenir le rendement du produit. »

En observant l'évaluation environnementale du cycle de vie, les entreprises considèrent l'impact environnemental des produits, des matériaux, des émissions, de l'eau et de l'énergie à partir des matières premières jusqu'à la fin de l'utilisation (du berceau à la tombe). Les stratifiés Formica sont un produit intermédiaire. Le stratifié est généralement utilisé pour construire des meubles ou des plans de travail. L'ACV a constaté que la société consomme uniquement vingt-cinq pour cent environ de l'énergie totale consommée pendant la durée de vie du produit. Le reste est utilisé soit tout au long de la chaîne d'approvisionnement qui apporte des matières premières aux usines soit lors d'activités en aval qui fabriquent des produits de marque Formica en éléments finis. En tant que PDG, Adamson dit : « Soixante pour cent de notre produit est le papier. » Rendre le papier durable était critique.

En trois ans, la société a adopté l'utilisation de bois provenant de forêts gérées durablement et portant la marque Forest Stewardship Council (FSC). Ceci indique que les forêts ont respecté les procédures rigoureuses énoncées dans les normes du FSC. « Il y a seulement trois principaux fournisseurs de papier Kraft pour l'usine de stratifié du monde entier, à raison de deux usines aux États-Unis et une usine en Finlande. Nous ne sommes qu'une petite partie de leur activité », explique Todd. « C'est la pression de Formica Group et de notre industrie

in Energy and Environmental Design, LEED) ha sido importante para cambiar la forma en la que diseñadores y contratistas planifican en los Estados Unidos, Asia, la India y en otros mercados del mundo. Las normas se basan en una serie de criterios reunidos en 1994 por el Consejo de Construcción Ecológica de EE. UU. (U.S. Green Building Council, USGBC) para fomentar la construcción sostenible. Se otorgan puntos a fin de clasificar al edificio para que obtenga la clasificación correspondiente: certificado, plata, oro o platino. Se tienen en cuenta todos los materiales y sistemas del edificio. En el Reino Unido, la sostenibilidad se mide a través del Método de evaluación medioambiental de BRE (Building Research Establishment Environmental Assessment Me-thod, BREEAM), un homólogo de LEED. El Grupo Formica ha trabajado también con Carbon Trust, con el objetivo de reducir su huella de carbono y sus emisiones de gas de invernadero. En 2012, el Grupo Formica se convirtió en el primer fabricante de laminados en el mundo al que se le otorgó la Etiqueta de reducción de carbono de Carbon Trust. Actualmente, muchas estructuras se construyen según las normas LEED y otras normas que garantizan la sostenibilidad ambiental.

"En la actualidad, avanzamos muy despacio, pero con determinación, por el camino de la sostenibilidad", señala Todd. "Lo que hacemos no es como fabricar un automóvil, donde se toman partes y se las ensambla. Nosotros horneamos tortas y reunimos mucha materia prima para formular un cambio químico en sus propiedades. Cuando se hornean tortas, hay mucha variabilidad dentro del proceso de fabricación que requiere controles precisos para mantener el rendimiento del producto".

Si se observa la evaluación ambiental del ciclo de vida, las empresas consideran el impacto ambiental de productos, materiales, emisiones, agua y energía desde ser una materia prima hasta su uso final, "de la cuna a la tumba". Los laminados Formica son un producto intermedio. El laminado suele emplearse para construir muebles o encimeras prefabricadas. La LCA de la empresa reveló que la fabricación solo consume, aproximadamente, un 25 % de la energía total que se consume en toda la vida útil del producto. El resto se utiliza ya sea en toda la cadena de sumi-

teen koko elinaikana kulutetun energian kokonaismäärästä. Loput käytetään joko toimitusketjun laajuisesti, joka toimittaa raaka-aineita tehtaille tai alavirran aktiviteetteihin, jotka valmistavat Formica-merkkisiä tuotteita valmiiksi osiksi. Kuten CEO Adamson toteaa, "kuusikymmentä prosenttia tuotteestamme on paperia". Paperin saannin jatkuvuus oli kriittistä.

Kolmessa vuodessa yhtiö siirtyi käyttämään puuta uusiutuvista metsistä, jossa on metsänhoitoneuvoston (FSC) (Forest Stewardship Council) merkintä. Tämä osoittaa, että metsissä on noudatettu FSC-normien tiukkoja toimenpiteitä. "Maailmanlaajuisen laminaattiteollisuuden käytettävissä on vain kolme pääasiallista voimapaperin toimittajaa, kaksi USA:ssa ja yksi Suomessa ja me olemme vain pieni osa niiden liiketoiminnasta", Todd huomauttaa. "Formica Groupista ja teollisuutemme alalta tuleva painostus oli omiaan muuttamaan FSC:n maisemakuvaa. FSC-metsiä ja FSC-paperimassaa on maailmassa rajoitettu määrä. Nyt kaikki kolme toimittajaa ovat pystyneet saavuttamaan FSC:n standardit.... kestävyyden saavuttamiseksi meidän on toimittava yritystasolla. Sitä ei voi tehdä yksinomaan yhdellä maantieteellisellä alueella, kuten Pohjois-Amerikassa tai Aasiassa. On strategisesti paljon järkevämpää laatia yhteisen kestävyyden strateginen ohjelma, joka vastaa globaalia katealuettamme". Toimien globaalisti kaikilla tasoilla oli Formica Groupin työjärjestyksessä ensimmäise-

在檢查生命週期的環境評估時，公司從原料到最後使用——所謂「從搖籃到填墓」——都要考慮產品、材料、排放、水和能源對環境的影響。富美家美耐板是一種中間產物。美耐板通常用來製造傢俱或檯面。公司的 LCA 顯示，製造只消耗整個產品整個週期消耗的總能量的約 25%。剩下的是用在給工廠提供原材料的整個供應鏈或把富美家品牌產品製造成成品部件的下游活動。公司首席執行官亞當森說：「我們 60% 的產品是紙張。」讓這些紙張可持續發展至關重要。

在三年裡，公司改為使用來自可持續發展的森林和帶有森林管理委員會 (Forest Stewardship Council/簡稱 FSC) 標籤的木材。該標籤說明這片森林符合 FSC 標準的嚴格程序。托德說：「為全球美耐板產業供應牛皮紙的只有三家主要供應商，其中兩家在美國，一家在芬蘭，我們只是他們的業務的一小部分。是富美家集團和我們行業的壓力，幫助改變了 FSC 的活動範圍。世界上只有為數不多的 FSC 森林和 FSC 紙漿。現在，所有三家供應商都能達到 FSC 的標準……實現可持續發展，是我們作為公司必須做的事情。不能只是在一個地理區域（如北美或亞洲）這樣做。有一個共同的可持續發展的戰略計劃，滿足我們的全球覆蓋範圍要求，才更具有戰略意義。」在全球各個層面行動起來，在百年紀念日來臨之際被擺在富美家集團議程的首位。2012 年，富美家集團所有的製造設施都達到了 FSC 產銷監管鏈標準。

2010 年代：
重整旗鼓

馬克·亞當森執掌富美家歐洲分部，並於 2008 年 3 月接任首席執行官職務。(亞當森是通過 1998 年柏斯托的收購加入富美家集團，時任歐洲分部首席財務官，並於 2004 年成為富美

到垃圾填埋场或回收这一天。可持续的做法现在对业务十分关键。富美家集团开发部经理加文·托德 (Gavin Todd) 说：“消费者希望做正确的事，他们已经习惯于期待得到环保认证，从而推动着建筑师和设计师。”

被称为 “能源和环境设计领导项目” (Leadership in Energy and Environmental Design/简称 LEED) 的绿色认证项目，对于改变美国、亚洲、印度和世界上其他市场的设计师和承包商的规划具有非常重要的影响。该项标准是根据 1994 年美国绿色建筑委员会 (U.S. Green Building Council/简称 USGBC) 编制的一套标准制定的，以鼓励可持续发展的建筑。建筑按得到的点数获得排名认证，有银色、金色和白金认证。建筑内每一种材料和系统都被考虑到。在英国，可持续性是由 “建筑物条例设定环境评估方法” (BREEAM) 来衡量，这是对应于 LEED 的标准。富美家集团还与碳基金组织 (Carbon Trust) 合作，重点减少其碳覆盖面和温室气体排放。2012 年，富美集团成为世界上被授予碳基金组织的 “碳减排标签” 的第一个烤漆板制造商。今天的许多建筑都是按照 LEED 和其他保证环境可持续性的标准建造。

托德说：“我们现在正缓慢但有目的地走上可持续发展的道路，我们所做的与制造汽车不一样，制造汽车是用零件组装起来。我们是烤蛋糕，汇集众多原料，使它们的属性发生变化。当你烤蛋糕时，在制造过程中存在更多的可变性，这就需要精确的控制，以保持产品的性能。”

在检查生命周期的环境评估时，公司从原料到最后使用——所谓 “从摇篮到坟墓”——都要考虑产品、材料、排放、水和能源对环境的影响。富美家® 装饰耐火板是一种中间产物。耐火板通常用来制造家具或台面。公司的 LCA 显示，制造只消耗整个产品整个周期消耗的总能量的约 25%。剩下的是用在给工厂提供原材料的整个供应链或把

พิทักษ์ป่า (FSC) ซึ่งหมายความว่า ป่าไม้นั้นได้ปฏิบัติตามขั้นตอนต่าง ๆ ที่เข้มงวดที่กำหนดไว้ในมาตรฐานของสภาพิทักษ์ป่า ทอดด์ กล่าวว่า “บริษัทที่จัดส่งกระดาษคราฟต์ให้กับอุตสาหกรรมลามิเนททั่วโลกมีอยู่เพียงสามรายเท่านั้น อยู่ในประเทศสหรัฐอเมริกาสองราย และอยู่ในประเทศฟินแลนด์อีกหนึ่งราย และเราเป็นเพียงส่วนเล็กของธุรกิจของบริษัทเหล่านั้น” “แรงกดดันจาก กลุ่มบริษัทฟอร์ไมก้าและอุตสาหกรรมลามิเนทที่ช่วยเปลี่ยนภูมิทัศน์ของผลิตภัณฑ์ที่ได้รับการรับรองของสภาพิทักษ์ป่า ป่าและเยื่อกระดาษที่ได้รับการรับรองของสภาพิทักษ์ป่า ในโลกมีจำนวนจำกัด ปัจจุบัน ผู้จัดส่งกระดาษทั้งสามรายปฏิบัติตามมาตรฐาน ของสภาพิทักษ์ป่าได้แล้ว... การที่จะทำให้มีความยั่งยืน เป็นเรื่องที่บริษัทจะต้องทำในนามบริษัท และไม่ใช่ทำเพียงในพื้นที่ส่วนใดส่วนหนึ่ง เช่น เฉพาะในอเมริกาเหนือ หรือ ในเอเชีย บริษัทเห็นว่าควรต้องมีโครงการวางแผนเพื่อความยั่งยืนร่วมกันเพื่อควบคุมการปล่อยก๊าซคาร์บอนไดออกไซด์ทั่วโลก เมื่อมีโอกาสครบรอบร้อยปีใกล้เข้ามา การปฏิบัติในทุกระดับทั่วโลกเป็นวาระสำคัญที่สุดของกลุ่มบริษัทฟอร์ไมก้า ในปี ค.ศ. 2012 โรงงานผลิตทุกแห่งของกลุ่มบริษัทฟอร์ไมก้ามีคุณสมบัติตามมาตรฐานการจัดหาวัตถุดิบที่เป็นมิตรกับสิ่งแวดล้อม

เริ่มต้นใหม่ในทศวรรษที่ 2010

มาร์ค อดัมสัน เป็นผู้นำบริษัท ฟอร์ไมก้า ยุโรป โดยเข้ารับตำแหน่งประธานเจ้าหน้าที่บริหารในเดือนมีนาคม ค.ศ. 2008 (อดัมสันเข้าร่วมงานกับกลุ่มบริษัทฟอร์ไมก้าเมื่อปี ค.ศ. 1998 เมื่อมีการซื้อกิจการเพอร์สตอร์ป โดยดำรงตำแหน่งประธานเจ้าหน้าที่บริหารฝ่ายการเงินของยุโรป และเมื่อปี ค.ศ. 2004 ดำรงตำแหน่งประธานของบริษัทฟอร์ไมก้า ยุโรป ต่อมาในเดือนตุลาคม ค.ศ.2011 อดัมสันได้รับตำแหน่งหัวหน้าแผนกแผ่นลามิเนทและวัสดุปูผนัง ของ บริษัท เฟลทเชอร์ บิวดิ้ง ทั้งหมด) อดัมสันเข้ามารับตำแหน่งตรงกับเวลาที่เกิดภาวะเศรษฐกิจตกต่ำทั่วโลก และเกิดวิกฤติสินเชื่อที่ส่งผลกระทบต่อการก่อสร้างมากเป็นพิเศษ นายอดัมสันดำเนินการที่เขาเรียกว่า “การเริ่มต้นใหม่” กับบริษัทในกลุ่มฟอร์ไมก้า ปัญหายุ่งยากของกลุ่มบริษัทฟอร์ไมก้าสะท้อนให้เห็นผลรุนแรงของวิกฤตเศรษฐกิจโลก นายอดัมสันกล่าวว่า “ในช่วงแรก เป็นเรื่องของการตัดสินใจว่าจะต้องแก้ปัญหาใดก่อน” เมื่อเกิดวิกฤติในปี ค.ศ. 2008 นายอดัมสันเล่าว่า “บริษัทต้องสูญเสียธุรกิจไปครึ่งหนึ่ง” มีการตัดงบประมาณและพิจารณาปรับ ลด และรวม สายการผลิต มีการลดจำนวน

qui a contribué à modifier le paysage FSC. Il y a une quantité limitée de forêts FSC et de pâte FSC dans le monde. Maintenant, les trois fournisseurs ont été en mesure d'atteindre les normes FSC. Atteindre la durabilité est pour nous une obligation d'action en tant que société. Il ne suffit pas d'agir dans une zone géographique comme l'Amérique du Nord ou l'Asie. Nous avons besoin d'un programme stratégique commun de viabilité qui répond à notre présence mondiale. « Agir au niveau mondial à tous les niveaux figurait à l'agenda de Formica Group à l'approche du centenaire. En 2012, toutes les usines de fabrication de Formica Group respectent la norme FSC Chain of Custody.

Années 2010 :
remise à zéro

Mark Adamson a dirigé Formica Europe et a repris la position de PDG en mars 2008. (Adamson avait rejoint Formica Group en 1998 suite à l'acquisition de Perstorp, en tant que CFO de la division européenne, et est devenu président de Formica Europe en 2004. En octobre 2011, il est devenu responsable de toute la division de stratifiés et panneaux de Fletcher Building.) Il est arrivé juste à temps pour la récession mondiale et la crise du crédit qui a frappé très durement la construction. Il a lancé ce qu'il a appelé une remise à zéro dans les sociétés de Formica Group. Formica Group reflète la crise économique mondiale d'une manière extrême. « Au début, c'était une question de tri, » déclare Adamson. Dans la crise de 2008, « nous avons perdu la moitié de notre entreprise », dit-il. Les coûts ont été coupés et les lignes de produits réduites, rationalisées et intégrées. Le personnel a été réduit. En 2009, un nouveau siège social à Newcastle, Royaume-Uni, est devenu le catalyseur d'un changement organisationnel majeur avec l'intégration des activités européennes. « Nous avons ramené l'offre à ce que le public désire ET attend », a-t-il déclaré. La moitié des produits ou des références a disparu et les palettes de teintes ont été rationalisées. Le bureau de design a modifié les palettes nationales. Les collections régionales ont été rationalisées et coordonnées. En Asie,

nistros que entrega la materia prima a las plantas o en las actividades subsecuentes que fabrican los productos de la marca Formica como piezas terminadas. Como expresa el director ejecutivo Adamson: "El sesenta por ciento de nuestro producto es papel". Hacer el papel sostenible fue crítico.

En tres años, la empresa pasó a utilizar madera de bosques sostenibles y a tener la etiqueta del Consejo de Administración Forestal (*Forest Stewardship Council*, FSC). Esto indica que los bosques han cumplido con los rigurosos procedimientos establecidos en las normas del FSC. "Hay solo tres proveedores principales de papel Kraft para la industria de los laminados en el mundo, dos en los EE.UU y uno en Finlandia, y nosotros somos solo una pequeña parte de su negocio", señala Todd. "Fue la presión del Grupo Formica y de nuestra industria lo que ayudó a cambiar el panorama del FSC. Hay una cantidad limitada de bosques del FSC y pulpa del FSC en el mundo. Actualmente, los tres proveedores han podido cumplir con las normas del FSC... Lograr la sostenibilidad es algo que tenemos que realizar como empresa. No se puede lograr solo con una región geográfica, como América del Norte o Asia. Tiene mucho más sentido estratégico tener un programa estratégico de sostenibilidad común que cumpla con nuestra huella global". Actuar globalmente en todos los niveles era lo principal en la agenda del Grupo Formica a medida que se acercaba el centenario. Durante 2012, el Grupo Formica obtuvo la certificación de la norma de la cadena de custodia FSC para todas sus instalaciones de fabricación.

La segunda década del siglo XXI:
restablecimiento

Mark Adamson encabezaba Formica Europe y asumió el cargo de director ejecutivo en marzo de 2008. (Adamson se había sumado al Grupo Formica en 1998 mediante la adquisición de Perstorp, como director financiero de la división europea y, en 2004, se convirtió en presidente de Formica Europe. En octubre de 2011, se convirtió en encargado de toda la división de laminados y paneles de Fletcher Building). Llegó justo en el momento de la recesión global y la crisis crediticia que golpeó especial y severamente a la construcción. Dispuso lo que denomina un "restablecimiento" en el grupo de empresas Formica. Los

nä satavuotispäivän lähestyessä. Vuoden 2012 aikana Formica Groupin kaikki tuotantotilat läpäisivät FSC:n Chain of Custody -standardin.

2010-luku:
Uusi lähtö

Formica Europen vetäjänä oli Mark Adamson ja hän otti CEO:n tehtävät maaliskuussa 2008. (Adamson oli tullut Formica Groupin v. 1998 Perstorp-yrityskaupan yhteydessä Euroopan jaoston CFO:ksi ja v. 2004 hänestä tuli Formica Europen toimitusjohtaja. Lokakuussa 2011 hänestä tuli Fletcher Building -yhtiön koko Laminates and Panels -jaoston johtaja.) Hän saapui juuri pahimpaan aikaan globaalin laskusuhdanteen ja luottokriisin kannalta, jotka iskivät erityisen ankarasti rakennustoimintaan. Hän pani toimeen nimittämänsä "uuden lähdön" Formica Groupin yrityksille. Formica Groupin ponnistelut kuvastivat maailman talouskriisiä sen äärimmäisessä muodossa. "Aluksi oli kysymys karsinnasta", Adamson esittää. Vuoden 2008 kriisissä "menetimme puolet liiketoiminnastamme", hän toteaa. Kustannuksia leikattiin ja tuotelinjoja karsittiin, rationalisoitiin ja yhdisteltiin. Henkilöstöä vähennettiin. Vuonna 2009 uudesta Euroopan pääkonttorista Newcastlessa Yhdistyneessä kuningaskunnassa tuli katalysaattori laajamittaiselle organisatoriselle muutokselle, yhdistäen Euroopan liiketoiminnan. "Vähensimme asiakkaiden tuotevalikoiman niiksi, joita ihmiset halusivat JA tarvitsivat", hän mainitsee. Tuotteista eli varastosta vähennettiin puolet ja värivalikoimat rationalisoitiin. Suunnitteluosasto korjaili kansallisia paletteja; alueellisia valikoimia virtaviivaistettiin ja koordinoitiin. Aasiassa värivalikoima harmonisoitiin yhdeksi ainoaksi Aasian kokoelmaksi. The European Specification Collection -kokoelma syrjäytti aikaisemmat erilliset englantilaiset ja eurooppalaiset kokoelmat.

Uutuuksien esittelyt eivät päättyneet. Tärkeät uudet tuotteet sisälsivät uusia pintakäsittelyjä ja suunnitteluja, kuten 180FX® -laminaatti, joka sai aikaan vaikutelman yhdestä ainoasta kivilaatasta ilman kuvion toistumista. Formica® Exterior Compact, värikäs UV-kestävä kompakti rakennuslaminaatti ulkokäyttöön, jota ensiksi tarjottiin Euroopassa v. 2005, oli uudelleen

家歐洲總裁。2011 年 10 月，他成為弗萊徹建築公司整個美耐板和飾板分部的總裁）。他到任的時間正值全球經濟衰退和信貸緊縮，對建築業打擊尤重。他著手在富美家集團公司開展他稱為的「重新啟動」活動。富美家集團的痛楚反映了世界經濟危機極端的形式。亞當森說：「起初它是一個分清主次的問題。」在 2008 年的危機中，「我們失去了一半的業務」。成本被削減，生產線被減少、合理化和被集中。工作人員被裁減。2009 年，英國紐卡斯爾的一個新歐洲總部成為一場重大的組織變革、整合歐洲業務的催化劑。他說：「我們把客戶的需求落實到人們想要和需要的東西上。」有一半產品（或 SKU）被砍掉，調色板被合理化。設計部門修訂了全國調色板；地區彩盤被精簡和協調。在亞洲，色彩範圍被和諧為一個單一的亞洲彩盤。歐洲的規範彩盤取代了以前獨立的英國和歐洲彩盤。

新的引入並沒有停止。重要的新產品包括新紋理和設計開發，如 180FX® 美耐板，傳達了單一石板但無重複模式的效果。富美家戶外抗倍特板，豐富多彩的抗紫外線戶外抗倍特美耐板 2005 年在歐洲首次推出，2010 年在北美推出時在所有的市場被重新定名為 VIVIX®，新的生產線設在魁北克省聖讓市。這種材料的一些性能在 2007 年被大加渲染，當時法國藝術家丹尼爾·布倫 (Daniel Buren) 用它來遮蓋了弗蘭克·蓋里 (Frank Gehry) 在西班牙畢爾巴鄂建造的古根海姆博物館 (Guggenheim Museum) 附近的一座地標橋，以紀念博物館建成十週年。他說，現在，「我們希望在全球重新統一富美家品牌」。

他強調說，這並不意味著一種獨斷的自上而下的方法，或用一刀切的方法替代本地的變化。他說：「當地人將經營本地的企業，折衷是可能的。」富美家集團經營三個地區的分

富美家品牌產品製造成成品部件的下游活動。公司首席執行官亞當森說："我們 60% 的產品是紙張。"讓這些紙張可持續發展至關重要。

在三年裡，公司改為使用來自可持續發展的森林和帶有森林管理委員會 (Forest Stewardship Council/簡稱 FSC) 標籤的木材。該標籤說明這片森林符合 FSC 標準的嚴格程序。托德說："為全球耐火板產業供應牛皮紙的只有三家主要供應商，其中兩家在美國，一家在芬蘭，我們只是他們的業務的一小部分。是富美家集團和我們行業的壓力，幫助改變了 FSC 的活動範圍。世界上只有為數不多的 FSC 森林和 FSC 紙漿。現在，所有三家供應商都能達到 FSC 的標準……實現可持續發展，是我們作為公司必須做的事情。不能只是在一個地理區域（如北美或亞洲）這樣做。有一個共同的可持續發展的戰略計劃，滿足我們的全球覆蓋範圍要求，才更具有戰略意義。"在全球各個層面行動起來，在百年紀念日來臨之際被擺在富美家集團議程的首位。2012 年，富美家集團所有的製造設施都達到了 FSC 產銷監管鏈標準。

2010 年代：
重整旗鼓

馬克·亞當森執掌富美家歐洲分部，並於 2008 年 3 月接任首席執行官職務。(亞當森是通過 1998 年柏斯托的收購加入富美家集團，時任歐洲分部首席財務官，並於 2004 年成為富美家歐洲總裁。2011 年 10 月，他成為弗萊徹建築公司整個耐火板和飾板分部的總裁）。他到任的時間正值全球經濟衰退和信貸緊縮，對建築業打擊尤重。他著手在富美家集團公司開展他稱為的「重新啟動」活動。富美家集團的痛楚反映了世界經濟危機極端的形式。亞當森說："起初它是一個分清主次的問題。"在 2008 年的危機中，"我們失去了一半的業務"。成本被削減，生產線被減少、合理化和被集中。工作人

พนักงานลง ในปี ค.ศ. 2009 สำนักงานใหญ่ของบริษัทในทวีปยุโรปแห่งใหม่ ณ เมืองนิวคาสเซิล สหราชอาณาจักร เป็นตัวเร่งให้เกิดการปรับองค์กรที่สำคัญ คือ การรวมธุรกิจในทวีปยุโรป นายอดัมสันกล่าวว่า "บริษัทรับข้อเสนอของลูกค้าโดยรับผลิตตามที่ลูกค้าต้องการและจำเป็นเท่านั้น" ผลิตภัณฑ์ครึ่งหนึ่ง ถูกลดลง และเฉดสีได้รับการทบทวนใหม่ ฝ่ายออกแบบทำการปรับปรุงในแต่ละประเทศ และจำกัดรุ่นผลิตภัณฑ์ที่จำหน่ายในภูมิภาคและปรับให้สอดคล้องกัน ในภูมิภาคเอเชีย สีของผลิตภัณฑ์ที่มีให้เลือกถูกปรับให้เหมือนกันทั่วทั้งภูมิภาคเอเชีย มีการนำรุ่นผลิตภัณฑ์ของทวีปยุโรป จำหน่ายแทนรุ่นผลิตภัณฑ์สำหรับสหราชอาณาจักรและยุโรปที่เคยมีรุ่นเฉพาะ

อย่างไรก็ดี บริษัทยังคงมีผลิตภัณฑ์ใหม่ๆออกมา ผลิตภัณฑ์ใหม่ที่สำคัญรวมถึงการพัฒนาพื้นผิวและการออกแบบใหม่ เช่นแผ่นลามิเนท 180เอฟเอ็กซ์ ที่สื่ออารมณ์ของแผ่นหินหนาแผ่นเดียวโดยไม่มีลายซ้ำ ฟอร์ไมก้าเอ็กซ์ที่เรียกคอมแพค เป็นแผ่นลามิเนทคอมแพคที่มีสีสันและทนต่อแสงยูวี วางจำหน่ายในทวีปยุโรปเป็นครั้งแรกในปี ค.ศ. 2005 ต่อมาเปลี่ยนชื่อใหม่เป็นวิวิกซ์ สำหรับจำหน่ายเหมือนกันทุกที่เมื่อมีการเปิดตัวผลิตภัณฑ์ในทวีปอเมริกาเหนือในปี ค.ศ. 2010 โดยมีโรงงานผลิตแห่งใหม่ที่เซนต์เมอง ควีเบก ในปี ค.ศ. 2007 การใช้วัสดุแบบใหม่ๆ ได้รับความสนใจ เมื่อนายเดเนียลบิวเริน ศิลปินชาวฝรั่งเศส นำวัสดุฟอร์ไมก้ามาหุ้มสะพานสำคัญแห่งหนึ่งที่อยู่ถัดจากพิพิธภัณฑ์กุกเกนไฮม์ ของนายแฟรงค์ เกห์รี ที่เมืองบิลเบา ประเทศสเปน ในโอกาสครบรอบสิบปีของพิพิธภัณฑ์ อดัมสันกล่าวว่า "บริษัทต้องการทำให้ตราฟอร์ไมก้าเป็นเอกภาพทั่วโลกอีกครั้ง"

อดัมสันย้ำว่า การดำเนินการดังกล่าวไม่ใช่การบริหารแบบเผด็จการ หรือบังคับใช้นโยบายเดียวโดยไม่คำนึงถึงความหลากหลายในพื้นที่ "คนในพื้นที่ยังคงเป็นผู้ดำเนินธุรกิจในพื้นที่" "โดยมีบางสิ่งอยู่ตรงกลาง" กลุ่มบริษัทฟอร์ไมก้ามีสำนักงานภูมิภาคสามแห่งนายอดัมสันคิดแนวการบริหารแบบสหพันธรัฐ กล่าวคือ เรื่องที่บริหารได้ดีที่สุดในระดับพื้นที่ก็บริหารจากในพื้นที่ ส่วนเรื่องอื่นๆ ให้บริหารจากส่วนกลางและใช้ทั่วโลก ฟอร์ไมก้าเป็นบริษัทระดับโลกที่มีความเป็นเอกภาพ กลุ่มบริษัทฟอร์ไมก้าอยู่ในฐานะที่สามารถจะใช้ประโยชน์จากขนาดในส่วนของวัสดุได้ "และทำให้บริษัทมีอำนาจต่อรองด้านนวัตกรรมในระดับโลกได้" การคิดกลยุทธ์ระดับโลกและการประสานนวัตกรรม

la carte de teinte a été harmonisée dans une seule collection pour l'Asie. La collection de spécification européenne a supplanté les anciennes collections distinctes britanniques et européennes.

Les nouveaux lancements n'ont pas été arrêtés. D'importants nouveaux produits incluant des nouvelles textures et des développements de design tels que le stratifié 180FX®, ont véhiculé l'effet d'une dalle de pierre simple sans répétition de motif. Formica® Exterior Compact, le premier stratifié structurel compact pour l'extérieur coloré résistant aux UV, a été lancé en Europe en 2005 puis a été renommé VIVIX® pour tous les marchés où il a été introduit en Amérique du Nord en 2010, avec une nouvelle production à Saint-Jean, Québec. Certaines des possibilités pour le matériel ont été mises en évidence en 2007, lorsque l'artiste français Daniel Buren a utilisé le matériau pour couvrir un pont historique à côté du musée Guggenheim de Frank Gehry à Bilbao, en Espagne, pour le dixième anniversaire du musée. Maintenant dit-il, « Nous voulons réunifier la marque Formica au niveau mondial. »

Cela ne signifie pas une approche tyrannique, insiste-t-il, ou une unification générale des variations locales. « Les personnes du pays dirigent les activités locales, » dit-il. « Il existe un intermédiaire. » Formica Group fonctionne avec trois divisions régionales. Adamson a imaginé un type d'approche fédéraliste dans lequel les choses les mieux faites au niveau local restent locales et d'autres se font à l'échelle mondiale. En tant que société mondiale unifiée, il a noté que Formica Group a été en mesure de profiter d'énormes économies d'échelle en ce qui concerne les matériaux. « Et ensemble, nous pouvons promouvoir l'innovation. » Développer une stratégie globale et la coordination des innovations faisait une grande différence. La société cherche toujours à réduire les coûts de trois pour cent par an. (En 2011, le coût a été réduit de 40 millions de dollars.)

Adamson croyait que l'innovation dépassait de beaucoup la simple recherche. Parmi les nombreuses idées, la clé était de choisir les bonnes. Il fallait trouver ce que les gens désiraient réel-

esfuerzos del Grupo Formica eran un fiel reflejo la severa crisis económica mundial. "Al principio era una cuestión de clasificación según las prioridades", expresa Adamson. En la crisis de 2008: "perdimos la mitad de nuestra empresa", señala. Se redujeron los costos y se recortaron, reorganizaron e integraron las líneas de productos. Se redujo el personal. En 2009, una nueva sede europea en Newcastle, Reino Unido, se convirtió en el catalizador de un cambio organizativo mayor, que integró la empresa europea. "Apuntamos la oferta del cliente a los factores que las personas deseaban Y necesitaban", señala. Se redujeron la mitad de los productos, o SKU, y se reorganizaron las paletas de colores. El departamento de diseño revisó las paletas nacionales; se estilizaron y coordinaron las colecciones regionales. En Asia, la gama de colores se armonizó en una sola colección asiática. La colección de especificaciones europea sustituyó a las colecciones británica y europea anteriormente separadas.

No se detuvieron las nuevas incorporaciones. Los nuevos productos importantes incluían novedades en cuanto a texturas y diseños, como el laminado 180FX®, que transmitió el efecto de una sola losa de piedra sin la repetición del diseño. El compacto para exteriores Formica®, el laminado estructural compacto y colorido para exteriores resistente a los rayos UV que se ofreció primero en Europa en 2005, cambió su nombre a VIVIX® para todos los mercados cuando fue presentado en América del Norte en 2010, con la nueva producción en St. Jean, Quebec. Se destacaron algunas de las posibilidades para el material en 2007, cuando el artista francés Daniel Buren lo utilizó para revestir un puente histórico al lado del Museo Guggenheim de Frank Gehry en Bilbao, España, para el décimo aniversario del museo. Ahora, dice: "Deseamos reunificar la marca Formica globalmente".

Esto no implica un enfoque tiránico y jerárquico, enfatiza, ni variaciones locales uniformes e invasivas. "Las personas del lugar administrarán los negocios locales", expresa. "Hay algo intermedio". El Grupo Formica funciona con tres divisiones regionales. Adamson visualizó una especie de enfoque federalista en el que las cosas que mejor se hacen a nivel local permanecen en el lugar y las otras se hacen a nivel global. Como una empresa global unificada, advirtió que el Grupo Formica estaba en posición de

nimetty merkiksi VIVIX® kaikkia markkinoita varten, kun se esiteltiin Pohjois-Amerikassa v. 2010, uutena tuotantopaikkana St. Jean, Quebec. Materiaalin eräitä mahdollisuuksia korostettiin v. 2007, kun ranskalainen taiteilija Daniel Buren käytti sitä maamerkin kaltaisen sillan päällystämiseen Frank Gehryn Guggenheim-museon vieressä Bilbaossa, Espanjassa, museon 10-vuotispäivänä. Nyt hänen mukaansa "Haluamme yhdistää takaisin Formica-tavaramerkin globaalisti".

Hän korosti, että tämä ei merkitse tyrannimaista huipulta-alaspäin -lähestymistapaa, tai yksi-koko-sopii-kaikille -tyylistä paikallisten vaihtelujen tallaamista. "Paikalliset ihmiset tulevat johtamaan paikallisia liiketoimintoja", hän mainitsee. "Niiden välillä on yhteys". Formica Group toimii kolmen alueellisen jaoston välityksellä. Adamson kuvitteli mielessään eräänlaista federalistista lähestymistapaa jossa asiat, jotka parhaiten hoidetaan paikallisella tasolla, jätetään paikallisiksi ja muut suoritetaan globaalitasoisesti. Hän huomautti, että yhtenäisenä globaalina yhtiönä Formica Groupilla oli tilaisuus hyödyntää valtavan mittakaavan talouksia materiaalien osalta — "ja voimme globaalisti käyttää eduksemme innovaatiota." Globaalin strategian kehittäminen ja innovaatioiden koordinointi saisi aikaan suuren eron. Yhtiö aikoo silti leikata kustannuksia kolme prosenttia vuodessa. (Vuonna 2011 se leikkasi 40 miljoonaa dollaria.)

Adamson uskoi, että innovaatioon kuuluu paljon muutakin kuin yksinkertainen tutkimus ja kehitys. Avaimena oli valita oikeat ideat monien joukosta. Piti ottaa selville mitä ihmiset itse asiassa halusivat. Yhdessä vaiheessa yhtiön palveluksessa oli tutkimustyössä sata henkilöä laboratoriossa. Hänen mukaansa yhtiö oli aiemmin valmistanut tuotteita, joita ihmiset sanoivat haluavansa, mutta eivät niitä sitten kuitenkaan ostaneet. Liiketoiminta riippui usein mallien suuntauksista. Formica Group vakuutti uudelleen sitoutumisestaan suunnitteluun näyttelyn välityksellä v. 2008, jossa oli Formica-laminaattisia huonekaluja ja veistoksia sellaisilta arkkitehdeiltä kuin Michael Graves, Massimo Vignelli, Zaha Hadid, ja Thomas Mayne Contemporary Arts Centerissä, Cincinnatissa, sekä v. 2010 uraauurtavalla

部。亞當森設想了一種聯邦制的方法，地方一級做得好的事情就保留在地方，其他的就在全球範圍內進行。他指出，作為一家統一的全球性公司，富美家集團有可能在建材方面享受巨大規模的經濟效益——「我們可以在全球範圍內利用創新」。開發全球性的戰略，統籌協調創新將有很大的不同。公司仍然致力於每年削減 3% 的成本（2011 年削減了 4,000 萬美元）。

亞當森認為，創新遠遠超出了簡單的研究和發展範圍。想法很多，關鍵是選擇正確的想法。這在於發現人們真正想要什麼。在一個時期，公司在一個實驗室雇用了一百人做研究。他說，在過去，公司生產過人們說他們想要的東西，最後才意識到他們並沒有真正去買。企業往往依賴設計上的

员被裁减。2009 年，英国纽卡斯尔的一个新欧洲总部成为一场重大的组织变革、整合欧洲业务的催化剂。他说："我们把客户的需求落实到人们想要和需要的东西上。"有一半产品（或 SKU）被砍掉，调色板被合理化。设计部门修订了全国调色板；地区彩盘被精简和协调。在亚洲，色彩范围被和谐为一个单一的亚洲彩盘。欧洲的规范彩盘取代了以前独立的英国和欧洲彩盘。

新的引入并没有停止。重要的新产品包括新纹理和设计开发，如 180FX® 耐火板，传达了单一石板但无重复模式的效果。富美家户外抗倍特板，丰富多彩的抗紫外线户外抗倍特耐火板 2005 年在欧洲首次推出，2010 年在北美推出时在所有的市场被重新定名为 VIVIX®（户外用抗倍特），新的生产线设

จะทำให้เกิดความแตกต่างอย่างยิ่ง อย่างไรก็ตาม บริษัทยังคงตั้งเป้าที่จะลดค่าใช้จ่ายลงร้อยละ 3 ต่อปี (ในปี ค.ศ. 2011 บริษัทลดค่าใช้จ่ายลง 40 ล้านดอลลาร์สหรัฐ)

นายอดัมสันเชื่อว่า นวัตกรรมไม่ใช่เพียงการวิจัยและพัฒนาธรรมดา สิ่งสำคัญคือการเลือกความคิดที่ถูกต้องจากบรรดาความคิดต่าง ๆ หลายความคิด นั่นคือ การรู้ว่าอะไรเป็นสิ่งที่คนต้องการจริง ๆ ครั้งหนึ่งบริษัทจ้างพนักงานหนึ่งร้อยคนเพื่อทำการวิจัยในห้องปฏิบัติการ นายอดัมสันอธิบายว่า ในอดีตบริษัทผลิตสิ่งที่มีคนบอกว่าเป็นที่ต้องการ แล้วมารู้ในภายหลังว่าไม่มีคนซื้อ ธุรกิจมักเป็นเช่นนี้คือตามกระแสการออกแบบ กลุ่มบริษัทฟอร์ไมก้ายังคงยืนหยัดมุ่งมั่นเรื่องการออกแบบ โดยในปี ค.ศ. 2008 บริษัทจัดนิทรรศการแสดงเฟอร์นิเจอร์และประติมากรรมที่ทำจากแผ่นลามิเนทฟอร์ไมก้าที่ศูนย์ศิลปะร่วมสมัย ที่ซินซินนาติ ผลงานของสถาปนิก เช่น นายไมเคิล เกรฟส์ นายมาซิโม วิกเนลลี นายซาฮา ฮาดิด และนายโทมัส เมย์น และ

lement. À un moment donné, l'entreprise employait une centaine de personnes dans un laboratoire de recherches. Dans le passé, dit-il, la société avait produit des choses que les gens disaient vouloir, pour se rendre compte ensuite qu'ils n'avaient pas envie de les acheter. L'entreprise dépendait souvent des tendances en matière de design. Formica Group a réaffirmé son engagement à concevoir en 2008 une exposition de meubles en stratifié Formica et de sculpture d'architectes comme Michael Graves, Massimo Vignelli, Zaha Hadid et Thomas Mayne au Contemporary Arts Center de Cincinnati, et en 2010 un spectacle d'avant-garde de sculpture utilisant le stratifié Formica, par des architectes chinois à Pékin.

Homapal Plattenwerk

Conformément à la stratégie d'Adamson visant à rationaliser les offres de l'entreprise à l'échelle mondiale et à fournir une stratégie organisée de l'innovation, au début de 2012, Formica Group a acheté le reste de Homapal Plattenwerk GmbH, la société allemande dont il possédait la moitié depuis près de trente ans. Homapal est basé à Herzberg dans la région de Basse-Saxe en Allemagne. L'entrée de l'entreprise dans les panneaux s'est faite indirectement. Fondée par Fritz Homann, en 1876, l'entreprise a construit des baquets de bois destinés à l'emballage de son produit principal, la margarine. En 1929, ce qu'on appelait alors la société Homann a acheté un moulin de scierie à Herzberg am Harz pour fournir du bois pour les baquets. Le propriétaire Hugo Homann a mis l'accent sur le bois. Il a développé l'idée de produire un nouveau produit : des panneaux de fibres. Réaliser cette vision a pris du temps mais en 1950, avec le miracle économique allemand d'après-guerre, l'entreprise était florissante. En 1955, il a commencé à produire des panneaux en mélamine, en 1958 en stratifié et sous la marque Homapal, nom dérivé du nom du propriétaire. L'innovation est venue rapidement, sous la forme de l'électronique pour la commande des presses et en 1970, de la première production de stratifiés métalliques. L'entreprise est reconnue pour ces derniers produits et pour sa gamme

contar con enormes ahorros de escala en materiales, "y podemos aprovechar la innovación globalmente". El hecho de desarrollar una estrategia global y coordinar innovaciones haría una gran diferencia. La empresa todavía aspira a lograr una reducción de costos del 3 % anual. (En 2011, redujo $40 millones).

Adamson creía que la innovación implicaba mucho más que un simple proceso de investigación y desarrollo. Entre muchas ideas, la clave fue elegir las correctas. Consistía en encontrar lo que las personas realmente deseaban. En un momento, la empresa empleó cien personas en un laboratorio que llevaba a cabo investigaciones. En el pasado, expresa, la empresa había fabricado los productos que las personas decían que deseaban, solo para darse cuenta que realmente no los compraban. La empresa solía depender de las tendencias de diseño. El Grupo Formica reafirmó su compromiso con el diseño en 2008, con una exhibición de muebles y esculturas que utilizaban el laminado Formica en la que participaron arquitectos tales como Michael Graves, Massimo Vignelli, Zaha Hadid y Thomas Mayne, en el Centro de Arte Contem-poráneo, Cincinnati, y, en 2010, con una exhibición pionera de escultura en la que arquitectos chinos utilizaron el laminado Formica en Beijing.

Homapal Plattenwerk

Siguiendo con la estrategia de Adamson de reorganizar las ofertas de la empresa globalmente y brindar una estrategia organizada de innovación, a principios de 2012 el Grupo Formica compró el resto de Homapal Plattenwerk GmbH, la firma alemana de la que había poseído la mitad durante casi tres décadas. Homapal tiene sede en Herzberg, en la región de Baja Sajonia de Alemania. La entrada de la empresa en el negocio de paneles se produjo indirectamente. Fundada por Fritz Homann en 1876, la empresa construyó envases de madera en los que empacaba su producto principal, margarina. En 1929, lo que entonces se denominaba Company Homann compró un aserradero en Herzberg am Harz para suministrar madera para los envases. El propietario Hugo Homann se concentró en la madera. Desarrolló la idea de producir un nuevo producto, madera comprimida. Hacer realidad esta visión llevó un largo tiempo, pero en 1950, con el milagro económico alemán de la posguerra, la empresa florecía. En 1955, co-

esitykselllä kiinalaisten arkkitehtien veistoksia Pekingissä, joissa käytettiin Formica-laminaattia.

Homapal Plattenwerk

Sopusoinnussa Adamsonin strategian kanssa yhtiön tarjousten rationalisoinnista globaalisti ja organisoidun innovaatiostrategian järjestämisestä, Formica Group osti vuoden 2012 alkupuolella loput Homapal Plattenwerk GmbH:sta, saksalaisesta yrityksestä, josta se oli omistanut puolet lähes kolmen vuosikymmenen ajan. Homapal sijaitsee Herzbergissä, Saksan Ala-Saksin alueella. Yhtiön mukaantulo paneelien liiketoimintaan tapahtui epäsuorasti. Fritz Homannin v. 1876 perustama yritys teki puupyttyjä ensisijaisen tuotteensa, margariinin pakkaamista varten. Vuonna 1929, silloiselta nimeltään Company Homann, osti sahalaitoksen Herzberg am Harzista puun toimittamiseksi pyttyjä varten. Omistaja Hugo Homann keskittyi puuhun. Hän kehitti idean valmistaa uutta tuotetta, kuitulevyä. Tämän vision toteuttamiseen kului pitkä aika, mutta v. 1950 mennessä, sodan jälkeisen Saksan talousihmeen mukana yhtiö kukoisti. Vuonna 1955 se alkoi valmistaa melamiinipintaisia paneeleja ja v. 1958 laminaattia omistajan nimestä johdetulla Homapal tavaramerkillä. Innovaatio seurasi nopeasti elektroniikan muodossa, puristimien ohjaamiseksi ja v. 1970 ensimmäisten metallilaminaattien valmistuksena. Yhtiö tuli tunnetuksi näistä ja puuviilu-

潮流。富美家集團重申其設計承諾，2008 年在辛辛那當代藝術中心舉辦了富美家美耐板傢俱和雕塑展覽，由建築師邁克爾雷夫斯 (Michael Graves)、馬西莫·威戈耐力 (Massimo Vignelli)、紮哈·哈迪德 (Zaha Hadid)、托馬斯·梅恩 (Thomas Mayne) 等人製作，並於 2010 年在北京由中國建築師用富美家美耐板做一臺雕塑開拓秀。

Homapal Plattenwerk

為遵循亞當森在全球理順公司產品和提供有組織的創新的戰略，2012 年年初，富美家集團收購了 Homapal Plattenwerk 公司的剩餘部分，富美家擁有這家德國公司的一半已近三十年。Homapal 總部位於德國下薩克森州地區的赫茨伯格。該公司是以間接的方式進入面板行業。它由弗里茨·霍曼 (Fritz Homann) 創立於 1876 年，業務主要是製造用來裝其主要產品人造奶油的木盆。1929 年，當時被稱為霍曼公司 (Company Homann) 買下了赫茨伯格·哈慈的一家為木盆供應木料的鋸木廠。老闆雨果·霍曼 (Hugo Homann) 專營木材。他產生了生產新產品纖維板的想法。實現這一目標需要很長時間，但到了 1950 年，伴隨著德國戰後的經濟奇跡，該公司得到蓬勃發展。1955 年開始生產三聚氰胺裝飾板，並於 1958 年以 Homapal 商標 (來自所有人的名字) 生產美耐板。創新來得很快，以電子控制壓榨機的形式出現。1970 年，首次生產了金屬美耐板。該公司以其木質單板美耐板產品聞名，這種產品在歐洲很流行。富美家公司與 Homapal 的關係從共享產品，發展到共享設施，直到所有權。富美家早先曾與 Homapal 合作推出金屬美耐板，自從 1983 年以來還是其最大的客戶和一半股權所有人。金屬美耐板在歐洲越來越受歡迎，並擴展到世界其他地區，尤其是中國。

在魁北克省圣让市。这种材料的一些性能在 2007 年被大加渲染，当时法国艺术家丹尼尔·布伦 (Daniel Buren) 用它来遮盖了弗兰克·盖里 (Frank Gehry) 在西班牙毕尔巴鄂建造的古根海姆博物馆 (Guggenheim Museum) 附近的一座地标桥，以纪念博物馆建成十周年。他说，现在，"我们希望在全球重新统一富美家品牌"。

他强调说，这并不意味着是一种独断的自上而下的方法，或用一刀切的方法替代本地的变化。他说："当地人将经营本地的企业，折衷是可能的。"富美集团经营三个地区的分部。亚当森设想了一种联邦制的方法，地方一级做得好的事情就保留在地方，其他的就在全球范围内进行。他指出，作为一家统一的全球性公司，富美家集团有可能在建材方面享受巨大规模的经济效益——"我们可以在全球范围内利用创新"。开发全球性的战略，统筹协调创新将有很大的不同。公司仍然致力于每年削减 3% 的成本 (2011 年削减了4,000 万美元)。

亚当森认为，创新远远超出了简单的研究和发展范围。想法很多，关键是选择正确的想法。这在于发现人们真正想要什么。在一个时期，公司在一个实验室雇用了一百人做研究。他说，在过去，公司生产过人们说他们想要的东西，最后才意识到他们并没有真正去买。企业往往依赖设计上的潮流。富美家集团重申其设计承诺，2008 年在辛辛那提当代艺术中心举办了富美家®装饰耐火板家具和雕塑展览，由建筑师迈克尔·格雷夫斯 (Michael Graves)、马西莫·威戈耐力 (Massimo Vignelli)、扎哈·哈迪德 (Zaha Hadid)、托马斯·梅恩 (Thomas Mayne) 等人制作，并于2010 年在北京由中国建筑师用富美家®装饰耐火板做一台雕塑开拓秀。

Homapal Plattenwerk

为遵循亚当森在全球理顺公司产品和提供有组织的创新的战略，2012 年年初，富美家集团收购了 Homapal Plat-

ในปี ค.ศ. 2010 จัดแสดงประติมากรรมที่ใช้แผ่นลามิเนตฟอร์ไมก้าครั้งแรกโดยสถาปนิกชาวจีน ณ กรุงปักกิ่ง

โฮมาพอล เพลตเทนเวิร์ค

เพื่อเป็นการรักษากลยุทธ์ของอดัมสันในการทบทวนข้อเสนอผลิตภัณฑ์ของบริษัทที่จำหน่ายทั่วโลก และการวางแผนเกี่ยวกับนวัตกรรม ในช่วงต้นปี ค.ศ. 2012 กลุ่มบริษัทฟอร์ไมก้าเข้าซื้อกิจการส่วนที่เหลือของบริษัทโฮมาพอล เพลตเทนเวิร์ค บริษัทเยอรมัน ที่บริษัทฟอร์ไมก้าถือหุ้นอยู่ครึ่งหนึ่งมาเป็นเวลาเกือบสามทศวรรษ บริษัทโฮมาพอล มีสำนักงานแห่งใหญ่ตั้งอยู่ที่เมืองเฮอร์สเบิร์กในเขตโลวเวอร์แซกโซนีของประเทศเยอรมนีบริษัทโฮมาพอล เริ่มทำธุรกิจวัสดุบุฝาผนังโดยทางอ้อม นายฟริตซ์ โฮแมนน์ เป็นผู้ก่อตั้งบริษัทโฮมาพาลเมื่อปี ค.ศ. 1876 ทำธุรกิจสร้างถังไม้ สำหรับบรรจุเนยเทียม ซึ่งเป็นผลิตภัณฑ์หลักของบริษัท ต่อมาในปี ค.ศ. 1929 บริษัทโฮแมนน์ ชื่อในตอนนั้น ได้ซื้อกิจการโรงเลื่อยในเมืองเฮอร์สเบิร์ก แอม ฮาร์ซ เพื่อนำเอาไม้มาสร้างถังเจ้าของบริษัทคือฮิวโก โฮแมนน์ มุ่งเน้นเกี่ยวกับไม้ และเป็นคนพัฒนาความคิดในการผลิตผลิตภัณฑ์ใหม่ คือ แผ่นใยไม้อัด หรือไฟเบอร์บอร์ด โฮแมนน์ตระหนักดีว่าความคิดดังกล่าวใช้เวลานาน แต่ในปี ค.ศ. 1950 เศรษฐกิจของประเทศเยอรมนีหลังสงครามดีแบบเหลือเชื่อ บริษัทจึงเฟื่องฟูขึ้น ในปี ค.ศ. 1955 บริษัทเริ่มผลิตแผงที่มีผิวหน้าเป็นเมลามีน และในปี ค.ศ. 1958 ผลิตแผ่นลามิเนตภายใต้เครื่องหมายการค้า โฮมาพอล จากชื่อของเจ้าของนั่นเอง นวัตกรรมเกิดขึ้นอย่างรวดเร็ว มีการใช้อุปกรณ์อิเล็กทรอนิกส์ควบคุมเครื่องอัด และในปี ค.ศ. 1970 มีการผลิตแผ่นลามิเนตผิวโลหะเป็นครั้งแรก บริษัทเป็นที่รู้จักจากนวัตกรรมเหล่านี้ และจากแผ่นลามิเนทไม้วีเนียร์ที่ได้รับความนิยมในทวีปยุโรป ความสัมพันธ์ระหว่างบริษัทฟอร์ไมก้าคอร์ปอเรชั่น และบริษัทโฮมาพาลเติบโตมาจากการผลิตผลิตภัณฑ์เดียวกัน มาจนการใช้โรงงานเดียวกัน ไปจนถึงการมีเจ้าของเดียวกันบริษัทฟอร์ไมก้าเคยร่วมมือกับบริษัทโฮมาพอล เปิดตัวแผ่นลามิเนทผิวโลหะ และเคยเป็นลูกค้ารายใหญ่ที่สุดของบริษัท และเป็นเจ้าของครึ่งหนึ่งตั้งแต่ปี ค.ศ. 1983 ความนิยมแผ่นลามิเนทผิวโลหะในทวีปยุโรปเพิ่มขึ้น และขยายความนิยมออกไปยังพื้นที่อื่น ๆ ของโลกโดยเฉพาะในประเทศจีน

de stratifiés plaqués bois qui étaient populaires en Europe. La relation de Formica Corporation avec Homapal est passée de produits communs aux installations communes et à la propriété. Formica avait déjà établi un partenariat avec Homapal pour le lancement de stratifiés métalliques et avait été son plus gros client et son propriétaire, à 50 %, depuis 1983. La popularité des stratifiés métalliques a commencé en Europe et s'est élargie à d'autres régions du monde, notamment la Chine.

Les marchés de l'avenir

En Chine, les ventes de stratifié Formica ont suivi la croissance annuelle de dix à vingt pour cent de l'économie chinoise. Le boom de la Chine a constitué l'histoire économique du nouveau millénaire, et Formica Corporation a été au centre de cette histoire. Dans les espaces commerciaux, les hôtels, les hôpitaux et autres secteurs en expansion rapide, les produits Formica ont été très demandés. La popularité dans la République populaire de Chine était une conséquence ultérieure de la puissance globale de la marque Formica. Récemment, en Chine, les consommateurs ont appris à connaître les logos et les teintes vives de Kentucky Fried Chicken®, KFC®, la chaîne de restaurants en plus forte croissance à l'heure actuelle en Chine, avec près de 3700 restaurants dans plus de 700 villes. Formica Group a été un des principaux fournisseurs pour son développement, en collaboration avec les agences de design KFC et les équipes internes pour les intérieurs, la décoration et la signalisation.

L'usine Qing Pu à l'extérieur de Shanghai a ajouté des presses au fil des années, et notamment plus récemment avec son quatrième agrandissement des capacités à hauteur d'un tiers. En 2007, l'usine a été mise à jour et en 2011, la société a annoncé son plan pour l'ouverture une deuxième usine en Chine, qui fait partie d'un investissement de 200 millions de dollars en Asie. Pour l'année du centenaire, Formica Group est installé en Chine depuis vingt ans et ceci est couronné par l'achèvement de cette nouvelle usine à Jiujiang. Avec plus de 15 000 mètres carrés et un effectif de quatre cents

menzó a producir paneles con anverso de melamina y, en 1958, laminado que llevaba la marca comercial Homapal, por el nombre del propietario. La innovación llegó rápidamente, en la forma de componentes electrónicos para controlar las prensas y, en 1970, la primera producción de laminados de metal. La empresa se volvió conocida por esto y por su línea de laminados de revestimiento de madera, que eran populares en Europa. La relación de Formica Corporation con Homapal creció de productos e instalaciones compartidas hasta la propiedad. Formica se había asociado con Homapal al lanzar los laminados metálicos y había sido su mayor cliente y medio propietario desde 1983. La popularidad de los laminados de metal había estado creciendo en Europa y expandiéndose a otras áreas del mundo, especialmente a China.

Los mercados del futuro

En China, las ventas de laminado Formica han registrado entre el 10 y el 20 % del crecimiento global de la economía de China. El auge de China fue la historia económica del nuevo milenio y, una vez más, Formica Corporation estaba en el centro de la gran historia. En espacios minoristas, hoteles, hospitales y en otros sectores que se expandían rápidamente, los productos de Formica estaban en demanda. Su popularidad en la República Popular era otra ratificación del poder global de la marca Formica. Recientemente en China, los logotipos y colores audaces de Kentucky Fried Chicken®, KFC®, se han vuelto conocidos para los clientes; ahora es la cadena de restaurantes de más rápido crecimiento en China con, aproximadamente, 3,700 restaurantes en más de 700 ciudades. El Grupo Formica ha sido uno de los proveedores clave en la expansión, al trabajar con agencias de diseño y equipos de la empresa para interiores, decoración y señalización de KFC.

La planta de Qing Pu en las afueras de Shanghái ha agregado prensas con los años, más recientemente su cuarta prensa, lo que expande la capacidad a un tercio. En 2007, se mejoró la planta y, en 2011 la empresa anunció su plan para una segunda planta en China, como parte de una inversión de $200 millones en la operación asiática. Para el año del centenario, el Grupo Formica lleva más de veinte años en China y los celebra con la finalización de esa nueva fábrica, en Jiujiang. Con más de 4,645.1 metros

laminaatteistaan, joita suosittiin Euroopassa. Formica Corporationin suhde Homapalin kanssa kasvoi yhteisistä tuotteista yhteisesti käytetyiksi toimitiloiksi ja edelleen omistussuhteeksi. Formica oli aikaisemmin ollut Homapalin kumppanina metallisia laminaatteja markkinoille tuotaessa ja ollut sen suurin asiakas ja puolikasomistaja vuodesta 1983. Metallilaminaattien suosio oli ollut kasvussa Euroopassa ja laajenemassa maailman muille alueille, varsinkin Kiinaan.

Tulevaisuuden markkinat

Kiinassa Formica-laminaatin myynti on jäljittänyt Kiinan talouden 10 - 20 prosentin vuosittaista kasvua. Kiinan nousukausi oli uuden vuosituhannen taloudellinen tapahtuma ja Formica Corporation oli jälleen suuren tarinan keskellä. Vähittäiskaupan tiloissa, hotelleissa, sairaaloissa ja muilla nopeasti laajenevilla sektoreilla Formican tuotteille oli kysyntää. Sen suosio Kansantasavallassa oli lisäosoitus Formica tavaramerkin maailmanlaajuisesta vahvuudesta. Kiinassa kuluttajat ovat hiljattain tulleet tutuiksi Kentucky Fried Chicken®, KFC® -yrityksen rohkeiden liikemerkkien ja värien kanssa, joka nyt on nopeimmin kasvava ravintolaketju Kiinassa, jossa sillä on lähes 3700 ravintolaa yli 700 kaupungissa. Formica Group on ollut yksi avaintoimittajista laajennuksessa, yhteistoiminnassa KFC:n suunnittelutoimistojen ja talon sisäisten ryhmien kanssa, sisustuksesta, koristelusta ja kylteistä.

Qing Pun tehdas Shanghain ulkopuolella on vuosien kuluessa lisännyt puristimia, viimeksi sen neljännen, laajentaen kapasiteettia kolmanneksella. Tehdas uusittiin v. 2007 ja yhtiö julkaisi v. 2011 suunnitelmansa toisesta tehtaasta Kiinassa, osana 200 miljoonan investoinnista Aasian operaatioihin. Satavuotispäivän vuonna Formica Groupille tulee täyteen yli kaksikymmentä vuotta Kiinassa ja se juhlii sitä kyseisen uuden tehtaan valmistumisella Jiujiangiin. Yli 4600 neliömetrin tilan ja neljänsadan hengen työväen ansiosta 70 miljoonan dollarin tehdas tulee kaksinkertaistamaan yhtiön kapasiteetin Kiinassa ja pitämään sen valmiina tulevaisuuteen.

Sillä välin Formica Group arvioi Intiassa markkinoita, joiden odotetaan kasvavan samanlaista vauhtia

未来市场

在中國，富美家美耐板的銷售一直在伴隨著中國經濟 10% 至 20% 的年增長率發展。中國的繁榮是新千禧年的經濟佳話，富美家公司再次成為這個巨大發展的中心。在零售商店、酒店、醫院和其他迅速擴大的行業，富美家的產品供不應求。在人民共和國受歡迎的程度進一步證明瞭富美家品牌的全球力量。最近在中國，消費者已經熟悉了肯德基家鄉雞 KFC® 的大膽徽標和顏色，KFC 現在是中國增長最快的連鎖店，在 700 個城市有 3,700 多家餐館。富美家集團一直是擴張中的主要供應商之一，與肯德基的設計機構和內飾、裝飾和標牌的室內裝潢團隊合作。

上海郊區青浦廠房多年來增加了壓榨機，最近增加了第四部壓榨機，產能擴大了三分之一。2007 年，該廠進行了升級，並在 2011 年宣佈在中國建立第二家工廠，作為在亞洲經營活動中兩億美元投資的一部分。到百年慶典時，富美家集團在中國已超過二十年，並以九江新工廠的完工作為慶祝。這個耗資七千萬美元的工廠面積超過 50,000 平方呎，員工有四百人，將公司在中國的產能增加了一倍，使之為未來做好準備。

與此同時，在印度，富美家集團正在調查一個市場，可能會以在中國的增長速度增長。預測會在未來十年增加一倍。在離開了印度市場多年之後，公司在 2008 年談判控制在那裡的商標。亞當森說：「現在我們找回了我們的品牌。」富美家美耐板仍然是印度建築師、承包商和其他客戶的首選。公司在印度重塑的前景是光明的，這都歸功於幾年來 8% 左右的國內生產總值的年增長率。公司正在考慮在印度收購或建造一家工廠。

---

tenwerk 公司的剩餘部分，富美家擁有這家德國公司的一半已近三十年。Homapal 總部位于德國下薩克森州地區的赫茨伯格。該公司是間接的方式進入面板行業。它由弗里茨·霍曼 (Fritz Homann) 創立于1876年，業務主要是製造用來裝其主要產品人造奶油的木盆。1929 年，當時被稱為霍曼公司 (Company Homann) 買下了赫茨伯格·哈慈的一家为木盆供应木料的锯木厂。老板雨果·霍曼 (Hugo Homann) 专营木材。他产生了生产新产品纤维板的想法。实现这一目标需要很长时间，但到了 1950 年，伴随着德国战后的经济奇迹，该公司得到蓬勃发展。1955 开始生产三聚氰胺装饰板，并于 1958 年以 Homapal 商标（来自所有人的名字）生产耐火板。创新来得很快，以电子控制压榨机的形式出现。1970 年，首次生产了金属耐火板。该公司以其木质单板耐火板产品闻名，这种产品在欧洲很流行。富美家公司与 Homapal 的关系从共享产品，发长到共享设施，直到所有权。富美家早先曾与 Homapal 合作推出金属耐火板，自从 1983 年以来还是其最大的客户和一半股权所有人。金属耐火板在欧洲越来越受欢迎，并扩展到世界其他地区，尤其是中国。

未来市场

在中国，富美家®装饰耐火板的销售一直伴随着中国经济 10% 至 20% 的年增长率发展。中国的繁荣是新千禧年的经济佳话，富美家公司再次成为这个巨大发展的中心。在零售商店、酒店、医院和其他迅速扩大的行业，富美家的产品供不应求。在人民共和国受欢迎的程度进一步证明了富美家品牌的全球力量。最近在中国，消费者已经熟悉了肯德基家乡鸡 KFC® 的大胆徽标和颜色，KFC 现在是中国增长最快的连锁店，在 700 个城市有 3,700 多家餐馆。富美家集团一直是扩张中的主要供应商之一，与肯德基的设计机构和内饰、装饰和标牌的室内装潢团队合作。

ตลาดแห่งอนาคต

ในประเทศจีนยอดขายแผ่นลามิเนทฟอร์ไมก้าคิดเป็นร้อยละ 10 ถึง 20 ต่อปีของความเติบโตทางเศรษฐกิจของประเทศจีน เรื่องราวความเจริญรุ่งเรืองของประเทศจีนเป็นเรื่องราวเศรษฐกิจแห่งสหัสวรรษใหม่ และบริษัทฟอร์ไมก้าคอร์ปอเรชั่นก็เป็นตัวละครหลักอีกครั้งหนึ่งในเรื่องสำคัญนี้ ผลิตภัณฑ์ฟอร์ไมก้าเป็นที่ต้องการมากสำหรับพื้นที่ค้าปลีก โรงแรม โรงพยาบาล และภาคธุรกิจที่ขยายตัวอย่างรวดเร็วต่างๆ ความนิยมผลิตภัณฑ์ฟอร์ไมก้าในสาธารณรัฐประชาชนจีนนั้นถือเป็นการยืนยันอำนาจของที่ห้อฟอร์ไมก้าในตลาดโลก ผู้บริโภคในประเทศจีนเริ่มคุ้นเคยกับโลโก้อันหนาและสีของไก่ทอด เคนทัคกี้ฟราย ชิกเก้น หรือ เคเอฟซี ซึ่งเป็นเครือข่ายร้านอาหารที่เติบโตเร็วที่สุดในประเทศจีน โดยมีร้านเกือบ 3,700 แห่งในเมืองต่างๆ มากกว่า 700 เมือง กลุ่มบริษัทฟอร์ไมก้าเป็นผู้จัดส่งสินค้าหลักรายหนึ่งในการขายกิจการดังกล่าว โดยทำงานร่วมกับหน่วยงานออกแบบและทีมออกแบบภายใน ทีมตกแต่ง และทีมป้ายในองค์กรของเคเอฟซี

โรงงานที่ชิง ปู ตั้งอยู่นอกเมืองเซี่ยงไฮ้ต้องเพิ่มจำนวนเครื่องอัดในระยะเวลาหลายปีที่ผ่านมา เครื่องอัดล่าสุดเป็นเครื่องที่สี่ทำให้เพิ่มอัตราการผลิตอีกหนึ่งในสาม ในปี ค.ศ. 2007 มีการปรับปรุงโรงงานให้ทันสมัยขึ้น และในปี ค.ศ. 2011 บริษัทฟอร์ไมก้าประกาศแผนสร้างโรงงานแห่งที่สองในประเทศจีน ซึ่งเป็นส่วนหนึ่งของการลงทุนเงินจำนวน 200 ล้านดอลลาร์สหรัฐในการดำเนินธุรกิจในภูมิภาคเอเชีย ในโอกาสครบรอบร้อยปี กลุ่มบริษัทฟอร์ไมก้านับเวลาที่บริษัทอยู่ในประเทศจีนนานกว่ายี่สิบปี และฉลองโรงงานใหม่ที่เมืองจุ่ยเจียง โรงงานใหม่มีมูลค่า 70 ล้านดอลลาร์สหรัฐ มีพื้นที่มากกว่า 50,000 ตารางฟุต ประกอบด้วยคนงานสี่ร้อยคน ทำให้ความสามารถในการผลิตของบริษัทในประเทศจีนเพิ่มขึ้นเป็นสองเท่า และพร้อมรับมือกับความต้องการในอนาคต

ในขณะเดียวกัน กลุ่มบริษัทฟอร์ไมก้ากำลังสำรวจตลาดในประเทศอินเดีย ที่มีแนวโน้มว่าจะเติบโตในอัตราที่คล้ายกับที่บริษัทได้รับในประเทศจีน มีการคาดการณ์ว่าจะเติบโตเป็นสองเท่าภายในทศวรรษหน้า บริษัทฟอร์ไมก้าออกจากตลาดในประเทศอินเดียไปหลายปี แต่กลับมาเจรจาต่อรองเพื่อควบคุมการใช้เครื่องหมายการค้าของบริษัทในปี ค.ศ. 2008 อดัมสันบอกว่า "บริษัทได้ยี่ห้อของบริษัทกลับคืนมาแล้ว" แผ่นลามิเนทฟอร์ไมก้ายังคงเป็นตัวเลือกก่อนยี่ห้ออื่นของสถาปนิก ผู้รับเหมา และลูกค้าอื่นชาวอินเดีย

personnes, l'usine de 70 millions de dollars permettra de doubler la capacité de la société en Chine et d'envisager l'avenir avec confiance.

Quant à l'Inde, Formica Group y mène une étude sur un marché susceptible de croître à des taux similaires à ceux de la Chine. Il doit doubler au cours de la prochaine décennie. Des années après avoir quitté le marché indien, l'entreprise a négocié le contrôle de sa marque en 2008. « À présent, nous avons l'appui de la marque, » dit Adamson. Le stratifié Formica demeure le choix préféré des architectes, des entrepreneurs et des autres clients indiens. Les perspectives de l'entreprise dans sa nouvelle installation en Inde sont réjouissantes grâce à la croissance du PIB qui a été d'environ huit pour cent par an pendant plusieurs années. Les plans sont en cours pour envisager l'acquisition ou la construction d'une usine en Inde.

Intégration à travers le monde

Au début de son second siècle, Formica Group est en avance sur une courbe sinusoïdale plus grande. Sa reprise et la résistance aux difficultés rencontrées peuvent servir de modèle. Un siècle d'accompagnement des importants mouvements économiques et sociaux a permis à la société d'accumuler une expérience et de survivre à la dernière crise. Comme modèle de société plus ciblée et plus souple au plan mondial, Formica Group pourrait servir d'exemple, déclare le PDG Mark Adamson. Après un siècle d'innovations, « Je pense que nous pouvons être un modèle. Je pense que d'autres peuvent apprendre de nous. » Le siècle qui a commencé avec audace s'est achevé dans la sagesse et l'expérience. Adamson allait bientôt avoir la chance d'appliquer les leçons de Formica lui-même à une vaste toile. Dans un de ces rebondissements qui ont marqué l'histoire mouvementée de la société, la sagesse et l'expérience ont été ratifiées en octobre 2012. Après avoir conduit la renaissance de Formica et la transition vers un nouveau siècle, Mark Adamson est devenu le PDG de la maison mère Fletcher Building. La société bénéficie ainsi d'un nouveau leader pour un nouveau siècle.

cuadrados y una fuerza laboral de cuatrocientos empleados, la planta de $70 millones duplicará la capacidad de la empresa en China y la mantendrá abocada al futuro.

En la India, mientras tanto, el Grupo Formica analiza un mercado que probablemente crezca con índices similares a aquellos que contabiliza China. Se predice que se duplicará en la próxima década. Años después de haber dejado el mercado de la India, la empresa negoció el control de su marca comercial allí en 2008. "Ahora tenemos nuevamente la marca", dice Adamson. El laminado Formica sigue siendo la elección preferida entre los arquitectos, contratistas y otros clientes de la India. Las perspectivas para la empresa en su nueva versión en la India son brillantes gracias al crecimiento del PBI que se ha registrado alrededor del 8 % anual durante varios años. Los planes estaban encaminados para considerar la adquisición o la construcción de una planta en la India.

Integración global

A medida que se adentra en su segundo siglo de historia, el Grupo Formica se encuentra adelantado respecto de la sinusoide más amplia; su recuperación y persistencia en los momentos difíciles sirve de modelo para otros. Un siglo de grandes cambios económicos y sociales ha brindado a la empresa la experiencia acumulativa para sobrevivir a la última crisis. Como modelo para una empresa global más concentrada y ágil, el Grupo Formica podría servir de ejemplo, expresa el director ejecutivo Mark Adamson. Al haber marcado el ritmo de un siglo de innovaciones: "Creo que podemos ser un ejemplo. Creo que otros pueden aprender de nosotros". El siglo que comenzó con el desafío del experimento termina con la sabiduría de la experiencia. Adamson pronto tendría la oportunidad de aplicar las lecciones de Formica en un ámbito más amplio. En uno de esos cambios que habían marcado la historia llena de colorido de la desamparada empresa, tanto la sabiduría como la experiencia fueron ratificadas cuando en octubre de 2012, tras liderar el resurgimiento y la transición de Formica hacia un nuevo, Mark Adamson se convirtió en el director ejecutivo de la empresa matriz Fletcher Building. La empresa tendría un nuevo líder para su nuevo siglo.

kuin Kiinan markkinat. Niiden ennustetaan kaksinkertaistuvan seuraavan vuosikymmenen aikana. Vuosia Intian markkinoilta poistumisen jälkeen yhtiö neuvotteli siellä hallintaansa tavaramerkkinsä v. 2008. "Nyt olemme saaneet tavaramerkin takaisin", sanoo Adamson. Formica-laminaatti on edelleen parhaana pidetty vaihtoehto intialaisten arkkitehtien, urakoitsijoiden ja muiden asiakkaiden parissa. Yhtiön näkymät sen uudesti syntymisessä Intiassa ovat kirkkaat kotimaisen bruttokansantuotteen kasvun ansiosta, joka on liikkunut kahdeksan prosentin paikkeilla usean vuoden ajan. Suunnitelmat olivat käynnissä harkita yrityskauppaa tai tehtaan rakentamista Intiaan.

Globaali yhdentyminen

Toiselle vuosisadalle lähtiessään Formica Group havaitsee olevansa suuremman sinikäyrän edellä; sen elpyminen ja peräänantamattomuus läpi kovien aikojen sopii esikuvaksi muille. Ehkäpä sen vuosisata, josta heijastuvat suuret taloudelliset ja yhteiskunnalliset muutokset, on antanut yhtiölle kumulatiivista kokemusta selviytyä uusimmasta kriisistä. Mallina määrätietoisesta ja ketterästä globaalista yhtiöstä Formica Group voisi hyvinkin olla esimerkkinä, sanoo CEO Mark Adamson. Pysyttyämme mukana vuosisadan innovaatioissa, "kelpaamme mielestäni malliksi. Katson, että muut voivat ottaa meistä oppia". Vuosisata, joka alkoi kokeilun uskaltamisella, päättyy kokemuksen viisaudella. Adamson sai pian tilaisuuden soveltaa Formican oppeja laajemmissa kehyksissä. Eräässä niistä käännekohdista, jotka olivat värittäneet kovaosaisen yhtiön historiaa, sekä viisaus että kokemus saivat vahvistuksen, kun lokakuussa 2012 Mark Adamson, johdettuaan Formican elpymistä ja uudelle vuosisadalle siirtymistä, tuli Fletcher Building -emoyhtiön CEO:ksi. Yhtiöllä oli siten uusi vetäjä sen uudelle vuosisadalle.

全球一體化

隨著富美家集團進入第二個世紀，它發現自己處在更有利的地位；它的恢復和渡過難關的韌性成了他人的典範。也許公司這個世紀反映巨大的經濟和社會變動為公司積累了經驗，能夠從這次危機中生存下來。富美集團作為一個更有針對性和靈活的全球公司，可以成為榜樣，首席執行官馬克·亞當森說，經歷了一個世紀的革新，「我認為我們可以成為代言人。我認為別人可以向我們學習。」本世紀以大膽的實驗開始，以智慧的經歷結束。亞當森將很快有機會親自把富美家的經驗教訓運用到更廣泛的範圍中。在標誌著這間處於劣勢公司豐富多彩的歷史的一個起伏中，智慧和經驗得到證實，2012 年 10 月時，在率領富美家恢復和過渡到一個新的世紀後，馬克·亞當森成為母公司弗萊徹建築公司的首席執行官。該公司將在新的世紀有一位新的領導人。

上海郊區青浦廠房多年來增加了壓力機，最近增加了第四部壓力機，产能扩大了三分之一。2007 年，该厂进行了升级，并在 2011 年宣布在中国建立第二家工厂，作为在亚洲经营活动中两亿美元投资的一部分。到百年庆典时，富美家集团在中国已超过二十年，并以九江新工厂的完工作为庆祝。这个耗资七千万美元的工厂面积超过 50,000 平方呎，员工有四百人，将公司在中国的产能增加了一倍，使之为未来做好准备。

与此同时，在印度，富美家集团正在调查一个市场，可能会以在中国的增长速度增长。预测会在未来十年增加一倍。在离开了印度市场多年之后，公司在 2008 年谈判控制在那里的商标。亚当森说："现在我们找回了我们的品牌。"富美家®装饰耐火板仍然是印度建筑师、承包商和其他客户的首选。公司在印度重塑的前景是光明的，这都归功于几年来 8% 左右的国内生产总值的年增长率。公司正在考虑在印度收购或建造一家工厂。

全球一体化

随着富美家集团进入第二个世纪，它发现自己处在更有利的地位；它的恢复和渡过难关的韧性成了他人的典范。也许公司这个世纪反映巨大的经济和社会变动为公司积累了经验，能够从这次危机中生存下来。富美集团作为一个更有针对性和灵活的全球公司，可以成为榜样，首席执行官马克·亚当森说，经历了一个世纪的革新，"我认为我们可以成为代言人。我认为别人可以向我们学习。"本世纪以大胆的实验开始，以智慧的经历结束。亚当森将很快有机会亲自把富美家的经验教训运用到更广泛的范围中。在标志着这间处于劣势公司丰富多彩的历史的一个起伏中，智慧和经验得到证实，2012 年 10 月时，在率领富美家恢复和过渡到一个新的世纪后，马克·亚当森成为母公司弗莱彻建筑公司的首席执行官。该公司将在新的世纪有一位新的领导人。

อนาคตของบริษัทหลังจากกลับมาดำเนินธุรกิจในประเทศอินเดียมีความสดใส ทั้งนี้ เพราะอัตราการขยายตัวทางเศรษฐกิจ หรือ จีดีพี ของประเทศอินเดียอยู่ที่ร้อยละ 8 ต่อปีติดต่อกันมาหลายปี บริษัทกำลังพิจารณาแผนการซื้อกิจการหรือก่อสร้างโรงงานในประเทศอินเดีย

การบูรณาการทั่วโลก

กลุ่มบริษัทฟอร์ไมก้าก้าวเข้าสู่ศตวรรษที่สอง นำหน้าบริษัทอื่น ๆ ในธุรกิจ บริษัทฟอร์ไมก้าฟื้นตัวและคงอยู่มาจากช่วงวิกฤตต่าง ๆ จึงสามารถเป็นตัวอย่างให้กับบริษัทอื่น ๆ ได้ ในช่วงศตวรรษที่ผ่านมาบริษัทมีการเปลี่ยนแปลงทางเศรษฐกิจและสังคมขนาดใหญ่ทำให้บริษัทสั่งสมประสบการณ์เพื่อให้ผ่านพ้นวิกฤตครั้งล่าสุดได้ มาร์ค อดัมสันประธานเจ้าหน้าที่บริหาร กล่าวว่า กลุ่มบริษัทฟอร์ไมก้าเป็นต้นแบบให้กับบริษัทระดับโลกที่มีความมุ่งมั่นและสามารถดำเนินธุรกิจได้อย่างทันท่วงทีได้ บริษัทได้ผ่านศตวรรษแห่งนวัตกรรม "ผมคิดว่าเราเป็นตัวอย่างได้ ผมคิดว่าผู้อื่นสามารถเรียนรู้จากเราได้" ศตวรรษที่เริ่มต้นด้วยการกล้าทดลองและจบลงด้วยปัญญาแห่งประสบการณ์อดัม สันจะได้มีโอกาสนำบทเรียนของบริษัทฟอร์ไมก้าไปใช้บนเวทีใหญ่ในไม่ช้าเมื่อเดือนตุลาคม ค.ศ. 2012 ปัญญาและประสบการณ์จากเหตุการณ์เปลี่ยนแปลงสำคัญครั้งหนึ่งในประวัติศาสตร์อันเต็มไปด้วยสีสันของบริษัทที่ไม่มีใครคาดคิดว่าจะรุ่งเรืองแห่งนี้ ได้รับการยืนยัน เมื่อมาร์ค อดัมสันได้รับแต่งตั้งเป็น ประธานเจ้าหน้าที่บริหารของบริษัทแม่ บริษัท เฟลทเชอร์ บิวดิ้ง หลังจากที่ได้พาบริษัทฟอร์ไมก้าผ่านพ้นวิกฤตและการเปลี่ยนแปลงมาสู่ศตวรรษใหม่ บริษัทภายใต้การนำของผู้บริหารคนใหม่ก้าวเข้าสู่ศตวรรษใหม่

KÄYTTÖKELPOISUUDEN LUMOUS: FORMICA®
LAMINAATTI, SUUNNITTELUA JA YLELLISYYTTÄ:

EL ESPLENDOR DE LA UTILIDAD:
LAMINADO FORMICA®, DISEÑO Y LUJO

LE CHARME DE L'UTILITAIRE:
STRATIFIÉ FORMICA®, DESIGN ET LUXE

实用的魅力：

富美家®装饰耐火板，设计与奢华

實用的魅力：

富美家美耐板，設計與奢華

ALEXANDRA LANGE

De l'or ! « 1959 sera l'année de la ruée vers l'or moderne. Les paillettes d'or insérées au fond des teintes pastel Formica ont mis de l'or dans les surfaces de milliers de foyers américains et dans les poches des fabricants et constructeurs qui ont utilisé les paillettes Formica Sequin. »

Formica Corporation, promotion 1959

Qu'est-ce que le luxe ? Palissandre, cuir, soie, laque, feuille d'or ou argent ? Ou est-ce l'absence d'installation et de maintenance de ces belles matières naturelles, les salons sans limites, la guerre contre les empreintes de doigt, la lutte contre l'usure ? Depuis sa première adoption par les designers dans les années 1930, le stratifié Formica® offre à ses utilisateurs le luxe de la durée : facilité d'en-tretien, durabilité, aspect pratique. Et avec les produits synthétiques con-temporains tels que le vinyle, le nylon et la mélamine, l'aspect des matériaux traditionnels de luxe s'obtient à une fraction du prix.

« Sequin » a été introduit en 1952. Il offrait une solution idéale conciliant les critères contradictoires de luxe et d'utilité, en incorporant un métal précieux dans un produit trouvé plus souvent dans les cuisines de banlieue et petits restaurants en bord de route, ajoutant ainsi de l'éclat aux tâches quotidiennes, comme faire un simple sandwich. Cette promotion de 1959 Sequin a introduit huit nouvelles teintes d'arrière-plan pastel avivées par des paillettes d'or irrégulières, suivant les tendances de la mode et les commentaires des consommateurs face à des teintes douces et plus adaptables. Les teintes rose bonbon et aqua étaient à leur manière aussi luxueuses que le doré. Les hôtels et les maîtresses de maison n'étaient plus limités aux teintes sombres qui ne laissaient pas voir l'usure. Céladon pourrait être aussi solide que le noir.

L'historienne du design Grace Jeffers a écrit au sujet du stratifié Formica et de ses concurrents que : « le stratifié plastique décoratif peut être considéré comme un mariage entre le modernisme et la banalité, où les préoccupations modernistes de

ALEXANDRA LANGE

¡Oro! "El año 1959 será el año de la fiebre del oro moderna. Las motas doradas del diseño Sequin, incorporadas sobre un fondo de color pastel de laminado Formica, harán que el oro esté en las superficies de miles de hogares estadounidenses, y en los bolsillos de los fabricantes y los constructores que utilizan el diseño Sequin de laminado Formica."

Promoción de Formica Corporation, 1959

¿Qué es el lujo? ¿Es el palisandro y el cuero, la seda y la laca, la hoja de oro y plata? ¿O lo es el hecho de liberarse del costo de instalación y mantenimiento de estos materiales naturales finos, de las salas de estar inaccesibles por su costo, de la guerra contra las marcas que dejan huellas dactilares, la batalla contra el deslustre? Desde que fue adoptado por primera vez por los diseñadores en la década de los treinta, el laminado Formica® le ha ofrecido a sus usuarios el lujo del tiempo: facilidad de mantenimiento, durabilidad, practicidad y, junto con los sintéticos contemporáneos, como el vinilo, el nailon y la melamina, la apariencia de los materiales de lujo tradicionales a una fracción del precio.

El diseño "Sequin", presentado en 1952, significó una solución ideal para objetivos estéticos aparentemente contradictorios de lujo y utilidad, al incorporar un metal precioso en un producto que, mayormente, se observaba en las cocinas suburbanas y en los restaurantes informales de las carreteras, y, de esa manera, le agregó un toque de brillo a las tareas de todos los días, como la preparación del almuerzo. Esta promoción del diseño Sequin de 1959 introducía ocho nuevos colores pastel con fondo de las motas doradas irregulares, de acuerdo con las tendencias de moda y los comentarios de los clientes que indicaban que los matices más claros se adaptaban mejor. Los tonos rosa bebé y aguamarina eran, a su manera, un lujo al igual que el dorado: los hoteles y los anfitriones ya no estaban limitados a usar colores oscuros que no evidenciaban el desgaste. El verdeceladón podría ser tan resistente como el negro.

La historiadora del diseño Grace Jeffers escribió acerca del laminado

ALEXANDRA LANGE

Kultaa! "Vuosi 1959 tulee olemaan vuosi nykyaikaisen kultakuumeen aikaa. Sequin-kultahiukkaset Formican pastellivärisellä taustalla tuovat kultaa tuhansien amerikkalaiskotien pinnoille ja Formica Sequin -materiaalia käyttävien valmistajien ja rakentajien taskuihin."

Formica Corporationin kampanja, 1959

Mitä on ylellisyys? Onko se ruusupuuta ja nahkaa, silkkiä ja lakkaa, lehtikultaa ja hopeaa? Vai onko se vapautumista näiden hienojen luonnon materiaalien asentamisesta ja kunnossapidosta aiheutuvista kustannuksista, olohuoneen käytön rajoittamisesta, sodasta sormenjälkiä tai taistelusta tahroja vastaan? Aivan sen alkuajoilta 1930-luvulta, jolloin suunnittelijat ottivat omakseen Formica®-laminaatin, se tarjosi käyttäjilleen aikansa ylellisyyttä: helppohoitoisuuden, kestävyyden, käytännöllisyyden — ja yhdessä synteettisten aikalaisten, kuten vinyylin, nailonin ja melamiinin kanssa, perinteisten ylellisyysmateriaalien ulkonäön hinnan murto-osalla.

Vuonna 1952 esitelty "Sequin", toi ihanteellisen ratkaisun päältä katsoen vastakkaisille esteettisille ylellisyyden ja käyttökelpoisuuden tavoitteille, yhdistämällä jalometallin tuotteeseen, jota useimmin näkee asumalähiöiden keittiöissä ja tienvieresissä ruokabaareissa ja lisäämällä siten säkenöintiä jokapäiväisiin askareisiin, kuten lounaan valmistukseen. Tämä vuoden 1959 Sequin-kampanja esittelee kahdeksan uutta pastelliväriä epäsäännöllisten kultahiukkasten taustana, seuraten muotisuuntauksia ja kuluttajapalautteita, joiden mukaan pehmeämmät sävyt olivat sopivampia. Vauvan vaaleanpunainen ja sinivihreä olivat omalla tavallaan yhtä ylellisiä kuin kulta: hotellit ja emännät evät enää rajoittuneet tummiin väreihin, joista kuluminen ei näy. Kalpeanvihreä voisi olla yhtä lujaa kuin musta.

Suunnittelun historioitsija Grace Jeffers on kirjoittanut Formica-laminaatista ja sen kilpailijoista: "Koristeellisia muovilaminaatteja voidaan pitää modernismin ja arkipäiväisyyden naimiskauppana, jossa modernistin huoli muodosta ja toiminnosta kytkeytyy ratkaisemattomasti suosittuun koris-

亞曆山德拉·蘭格

金子！「1959 年將是現代淘金熱的年代。金色的亮片鑲嵌在富美家柔和的背景之上，將把金色裝點進美國千家萬戶的裝飾面料中，也裝滿了使用富美家珠片的製造商和建造商的口袋。」

富美家公司 1959 年廣告

何為奢侈品？是紫檀木、皮革、絲綢、漆器、金箔和白銀嗎？還是這些省去了安裝和維護的優良天然材料、不准進入的客廳、對指紋的宣戰和失去光澤的抗爭所帶來的成本？從二十世紀三十年代設計師最早使用富美家美耐板開始，它就為用戶提供了奢侈的享受：易保養、耐用、實用——結合當代合成材料，如乙烯、尼龍、三聚氰胺、傳統豪華材料的外觀，並只需耗費相當於這些材料費用極小一部分的價格。

「亮片」於 1952 年引入，透過把一種貴金屬加在郊區廚房和路邊餐廳常見的產品上，在看似相互矛盾的奢華和實用的審美目標之間找到了一種理想的解決辦法，從而為日常工作（如做午餐）增加了亮點。1959 年的亮片推廣引入了八種新的柔和色彩，成為不規則的金色斑點的背景，跟隨時尚潮流和消費者的反饋資訊，即更柔和的色調更有適應性。嬰兒粉紅色和淺綠色以自己的方式像金色一樣豪華：酒店和禮儀小姐的著裝不再限於不會顯露磨損的暗色。青瓷色可能像黑色一樣耐磨。

設計史學家格蕾絲·傑弗斯 (Grace Jefferson) 曾這樣評論富美家美耐板及其競爭對手：「裝飾塑膠美耐板可被視作是現代主義和世俗觀念的聯姻，現代主義對形式和功能的注重不可避免地與流行的裝飾聯繫起來。它不同於壁紙，壁紙是牆壁的珠寶，美耐板是盔甲」。現代建築師和設計師們一直在尋找新的多功能工業原料，這些原來本身就是美的象徵，如

亚历山德拉·兰格

金子！"1959 年将是现代淘金热的年代。金色的亮片镶嵌在富美家柔和的背景之上，把金色装点进美国千家万户的装饰面料中，也装满了使用富美家珠片的制造商和建造商的口袋。"

富美家公司 1959 年广告

何为奢侈品？是紫檀木、皮革、丝绸、漆器、金箔和白银吗？还是这些省去了安装和维护的优良天然材料、不准进入的客厅、对指纹的宣战和失去光泽的抗争所带来的成本？从二十世纪三十年代设计师最早使用富美家®耐火板开始，它就为用户提供了奢侈的享受：易保养、耐用、实用——结合当代合成材料，如乙烯、尼龙、三聚氰胺、传统豪华材料的外观，并只需耗费相当于这些材料费用极小一部分的价格。

"亮片"于 1952 年引入，通过把一种贵金属加在郊区厨房和路边餐厅常见的产品上，在看似相互矛盾的奢华和实用的审美目标之间找到了一种理想的解决办法，从而为日常工作（如做午餐）增加了亮点。1959 年的亮片推广引入了八种新的柔和色彩，成为不规则的金色斑点的背景，跟随时尚潮流和消费者的反馈信息，即更柔和的色调更有适应性。婴儿粉红色和浅绿色以自己的方式像金色一样豪华：酒店和礼仪小姐的着装不再局限于不会显露磨损的暗色。青瓷色可能会像黑色一样耐磨。

设计史学家格蕾丝·杰弗斯 (Grace Jefferson) 曾这样评论富美家®装饰耐火板及其竞争对手："装饰塑料耐火板可被视作是现代主义和世俗观念的联姻，现代主义对形式和功能的注重不可避免地与流行的装饰联系起来。它不同于壁纸，壁纸是墙壁的珠宝，耐火板则是盔甲"。现代建筑师和设计师们一直在寻找新的多功能工业原料，这些原来本身就是美的象征，如自行车管或弯曲的胶合板。富美家®装饰耐火

อเล็กซานดร้า แลนจ์

ทอง! "ค.ศ. 1959 จะเป็นแห่งการตื่นทองยุคใหม่ ลวดลายเลื่อมทองแวววาวขนาดเล็กที่ติดลงบนพื้นหลังสีพาสเทลของฟอร์ไมก้าจะนำไปใช้ตกแต่งพื้นผิวบ้านของชาวอเมริกันนับพันให้เป็นสีทอง โดยสร้างกำไรอย่างมหาศาลให้แก่บรรดาผู้ผลิตและผู้รับเหมาที่ใช้ลวดลายเลื่อมทองของฟอร์ไมก้า"

การส่งเสริมการขายฟอร์ไมก้า ปี ค.ศ. 1959

อะไรคือความหรูหรา ใช่ไม้ขิงขันและเครื่องหนัง ไหมเนื้อดีและแลคเกอร์ แผ่นทองหรือไม่ หรือมันคือ การเป็นอิสระจากค่าใช้จ่ายในการติดตั้งและดูแลรักษาวัสดุธรรมชาติแสนสวยเหล่านี้ การมีโอกาสใช้ห้องนั่งเล่นได้อย่างสะดวกสบายโดยไม่ต้องกังวลเรื่องสงครามกับรอยนิ้วมือหรือการต่อสู้กับความเลอะเทอะ นับตั้งแต่ครั้งแรกที่นักออกแบบนำแผ่นลามิเนทฟอร์ไมก้าไปใช้ในช่วงปี ค.ศ. 1930 ฟอร์ไมก้าได้ให้ความสะดวกในด้านเวลาแก่ผู้ใช้ นั่นคือ การดูแลรักษาง่าย ความคงทน การนำไปใช้ได้จริง – และเช่นเดียวกับวัสดุสังเคราะห์ร่วมสมัยอย่างไวนิล ในลอน และเมลามีน ยังรู้จักปลักษณ์ของวัสดุหรูราสไตล์ดั้งเดิมในราคาประหยัดกว่ามาก

"เลื่อม" ซึ่งถูกนำมาใช้เป็นครั้งแรกในปี ค.ศ. 1952 ถือเป็นทางออกที่ดีเลิศในการเข้าถึงจุดมุ่งหมายที่ต้องการรวมสองคุณลักษณะที่ดูเหมือนจะขัดแย้งกันของความหรูหรากับอรรถประโยชน์เข้าด้วยกัน โดยการติดแผ่นโลหะมีค่าบนลงผลิตภัณฑ์ที่มักพบได้บ่อยในห้องครัวแถบชานเมืองและร้านอาหารข้างทาง จึงเป็นการเพิ่มสีสันแก่งานประจำวัน เช่น การทำอาหารกลางวัน ในปี ค.ศ. 1959 การส่งเสริมการขายลวดลายเลื่อมทองได้นำสีพาสเทลใหม่จำนวน 8 สีมาใช้กับเลื่อมทองขนาดเล็กที่ไม่เหมือนใคร เป็นไปตามแฟชั่นทันสมัยและผลตอบรับของลูกค้าที่ต้องการโทนสีอ่อนกว่าเดิม สีชมพูอ่อนและสีน้ำทะเลโดยตัวมันเองก็มีความหรูหราไม่แพ้สีทอง โรงแรมและพนักงานต้อนรับจะไม่ถูกจำกัดให้ใส่ชุดสีเข้มที่จะไม่แสดงร่องรอยของการใช้งานอีกต่อไป สีศิลาดลอาจมีความทนทานได้ไม่แพ้สีดำ

นักประวัติศาสตร์ด้านการออกแบบ เกรซ เจฟเฟอร์ได้เขียนถึงฟอร์ไมก้าและคู่แข่งว่า "แผ่นลามิเนทตกแต่งที่ทำจากพลาสติกอาจถูกมองว่าเป็นการผสมผสานระหว่างความทันสมัยและความธรรมดา ที่รูปแบบและการใช้งานซึ่งคนสมัยใหม่ต้องการถูกผสมผสานอย่างลงตัวกับการตกแต่งที่ได้รับความ

forme et de fonction sont inextricablement liées à la décoration de tous les jours. Contrairement au papier peint, un produit de luxe pour les murs, le stratifié représente réellement une armure. » Les architectes et designers modernes étaient toujours à la recherche de nouveaux matériaux multifonctionnels et industriels beaux par eux-mêmes, comme les tubes des vélos ou le contreplaqué courbé. Le stratifié Formica, souvent associé à ces matières au début du XXe siècle, était le candidat idéal des expériences en cours. Il a maintenu sa place à la pointe de la technologie et du design au cours des cent dernières années en relevant régulièrement les défis des évolutions du transport, de la vente au détail, des marchés domestiques et de la demande industrielle. Il est passé d'une surface décorative à un matériau structurel, rivalisant non sans peine avec les innovations architecturales du musée Guggenheim à Bilbao, œuvre de Frank Gehry.

Décennie après décennie au cours du XXe siècle, les designers ont utilisé le stratifié Formica pour ses qualités esthétiques et fonctionnelles dans des environnements spectaculaires dans l'architecture comme dans les intérieurs. La malléabilité de la surface de mélamine, un plastique thermodurcissable qui peut traverser la plupart des matériaux, a permis au produit de suivre les tendances tandis que sa nature essentielle, amalgame de résine et de papier pressé et chauffé, est restée globalement la même. Le papier peint moucheté doré installé en 1959 a disparu depuis longtemps, mais les plans de travail de paillettes aqua Sequin (au moins dans la maison de ma grand-mère) continuent à faire leur effet sans presqu'une brûlure, une tache ou une écaille.

Dans les années 1930, le stratifié Formica a été déplacé de ses applications industrielles d'origine aux studios de créateurs de mobilier modernes. Initialement disponible dans quelques teintes sombres seulement parce que les chimistes avaient encore à parfaire la résine de mélamine transparente nécessaire pour une surface à motifs ou de teinte claire, la version noire s'est avérée être à la fois un excellent substitut pour la laque,

Formica y sus competidores: "El laminado plástico decorativo puede considerarse como una unión entre el modernismo y lo mundano, en el cual el interés modernista por la forma y la función están inextricablemente relacionados con la decoración popular. A diferencia del papel tapiz, que es una joya para una pared, el laminado es una armadura". Los arquitectos y los diseñadores modernos estaban en la búsqueda constante de nuevos materiales multifuncionales e industriales que fueran hermosos en sí mismos, como los tubos para bicicleta o el tablero contrachapado curvado. El laminado Formica, a menudo combinado con esos materiales durante la primera parte del siglo XX, fue el candidato ideal para los experimentos en curso. Ha conservado su lugar a la vanguardia de la tecnología y el diseño durante los últimos cien años, ya que en repetidas ocasiones ha estado a la altura de los desafíos de las nuevas demandas de transporte, ventas al por menor, domésticas e industriales, y se ha transformado de una superficie decorativa a un material estructural, un material lo suficientemente resistente como para competir con el museo Guggenheim Bilbao de Frank Gehry en cuanto a la expresión arquitectónica.

Una década tras otra durante el siglo XX, los diseñadores han hecho uso del laminado Formica tanto por sus cualidades decorativas como funcionales, en ambientes espectaculares, en arquitectura y en interiores. La maleabilidad de la superficie, hecha de melamina, un plástico termoendurecido que puede impregnar casi cualquier material, ha permitido que el producto se mantenga a la par de las tendencias, mientras que su esencia natural, un panel intercalado de resinas y papel, prensado y calentado, se ha mantenido en gran parte igual. El papel tapiz con motas doradas que se colocó en 1959 desapareció hace tiempo; sin embargo, las cubiertas prefabricadas de diseño Sequin color aguamarina (al menos en la casa de mi abuela) continúan cumpliendo su función, sin ninguna quemadura, mancha o desportilladura.

En la década de los treinta, el laminado Formica pasó de sus aplicaciones industriales originales a los estudios de los diseñadores de muebles modernos.

teluun. Toisin kuin seinäperi, joka on koru seinälle, laminaatti on panssari". Nykyaikaiset arkkitehdit ja suunnittelijat etsivät jatkuvasti uusia monikäyttöisiä ja teollisia materiaaleja, jotka olivat itsessään kauniita, kuten polkupyörän sisäkumi tai taivutettu vaneri. Formica-laminaatti, jota usein yhdistettiin näihin materiaaleihin 1900-luvun alkupuolella, oli ihanteellinen ehdokas käynnissä oleviin kokeiluihin. Se on säilyttänyt asemansa teknologian ja suunnittelun eturivissä viimeiset sata vuotta, ottamalla vastaan uusien kuljetusvälineiden, vähittäiskaupan, kotielämän ja teollisuuden vaatimusten haasteet ja se on muuntautunut koristeellisesta pinnasta rakenteelliseksi materiaaliksi — tarpeen lujaksi kilpaillakseen Frank Gehryn Guggenheim Bilbao -projektin kanssa arkkitehtuurisen draaman asemasta.

Vuosikymmen toisensa jälkeen 1900-luvun läpi, suunnittelijat ovat käyttäneet Formica-laminaattia sekä sen esteettisten että toiminnallisten laatuominaisuuksien vuoksi vaikuttavissa ympäristöissä, niin arkkitehtuurissa kuin sisustuksissa. Pinnan muovautuvuus — melamiinista tehty, kuumassa kovettuva muovi, joka voi kyllästää lähes minkä tahansa materiaalin — on antanut tuotteen pysyä suuntausten mukana, samalla kun sen oleellinen luonne, kerrostuma hartseja ja paperia, painettuna ja kuumennettuna, on suureksi osaksi pysynyt samana. Vuonna 1959 asennettu kultatäpläinen seinäperi on kadonnut kauan sitten, mutta sinivihreät Sequin-pöytälevyt täyttävät edelleen tehtävänsä (ainakin minun isoäitini kodissa), ilman yhtäkään palanutta paikkaa, tahraa tai lohkeamaa.

1930-luvulla Formica-laminaatti siirtyi sen alkuperäisistä teollisista sovelluksista nykyaikaisten huonekalujen suunnittelijoiden studioihin. Aluksi saatavissa vain muutamana tummana värinä, koska kemistit eivät vielä olleet täysin kehittäneet vaaleaan tai kuvioituun yläpintaan tarvittavaa läpinäkyvää melamiinihartsia, musta versio osoittautui sekä erinomaiseksi korvikkeeksi tällöin suositulle lakkapuulle, että sarastavan teollisen aikakauden symboliksi. Kuten suunnittelun historioitsija Jeffrey L. Meikle kirjoittaa julkaisussa *American Plastic: A Cultural History*, "Amerikkalaiset modernistit tulivat tie-

自行車管或彎曲的膠合板。富美家美耐板在二十世紀早期就常常與這些材料相結合，因而是目前正在進行的實驗的理想候選人。它屢次經受了新的交通運輸、零售、家庭和工業需求的挑戰，在過去一百年裡一直保持在技術和設計的最前沿，從一種裝飾性面料演變成結構材料——堅硬得足以在建築的宏偉史上與弗蘭克·奧吉瑞（Frank O'Gehry）的畢爾巴鄂古根罕博物館（Guggenheim Bilbao）匹敵。

在二十世紀的每個十年中，設計師們都把富美家美耐板的審美和實用功能運用在壯觀的環境、建築學和室內裝飾中。柔韌的表面用三聚氰胺（一種可滲透入幾乎任何材料的熱固塑膠）製造，使得該產品跟上潮流，而經過加壓和加熱的樹脂和紙板夾層的基本性質在很大程度上依然不變。1959 年安裝的金斑點壁紙早已消失，但淺綠色亮片檯面（至少在我祖母的房子裡）仍在盡忠職守，絲毫沒有燒痕、斑點或殘缺。

二十世紀三十年代，富美家美耐板從原來的工業應用走進現代家俱設計師的工作室。美耐板最初只有幾種深色，因為化學家尚未完全製造出製作淺色或有圖案面板所需的透明三聚氰胺樹脂，但黑色的板材竟然成了當時流行的漆器的完美替代品，成為曙光工業年代的象徵。正如設計歷史學家傑弗里·米克爾（Jeffrey L. Meikle）在《美國的塑膠：一部文化史》中所說：「美國現代主義者意識到酚醛美耐板作為一種工業原料，反映了在為曼哈頓的風雅之士定製的家俱上他們想表現的機器精神。雖然每一位設計師都顯示了些微的個人風格，他們集體創作的作品體現了一種客觀的精確性」；奧地利出生的裝飾藝術家俱設計師保羅·弗蘭克爾（Paul T. Frankl）在二十世紀二十年代開始嘗試使用各種塑膠，號召他的設計師同行「用這些新材料創造一種語

板在二十世紀早期就常常与这些材料相结合，因而是目前正在进行的实验的理想候选人。它屡次经受了新的交通运输、零售、家庭和工业需求的挑战，在过去一百年里一直保持在技术和设计的最前沿，从一种装饰性面料演变成结构材料——坚硬得足以在建筑的宏伟史上与弗兰克·奥吉瑞（Frank O'Gehry）的毕尔巴鄂古根罕博物馆（Guggenheim Bilbao）匹敌。

在二十世纪的每个十年中，设计师们都把富美家®装饰耐火板的审美和实用功能运用在壮观的环境、建筑学和室内装饰中。柔韧的表面用三聚氰胺（一种可渗透入几乎任何材料的热固塑料）制造，使得该产品跟上潮流，而经过加压和加热的树脂和纸板夹层的基本性质在很大程度上依然不变。1959

นิยม ถ้าเปรียบวอลล์เปเปอร์เสมือนเป็นเครื่องเพชรพลอยที่ใช้ประดับฝาผนัง แผ่นลามิเนทก็คือเกราะป้องกันฝาผนัง" สถาปนิกและนักออกแบบสมัยใหม่เคยมองหาวัสดุใหม่ๆ ที่มีความเป็นอรรถประโยชน์และสามารถนำมาใช้ในอุตสาหกรรมอยู่เสมอ โดยวัสดุเหล่านั้นต้องมีความสวยงามในตัวมันเอง เช่น ท่อจักรยานหรือไม้อัดดัดโค้ง ฟอร์ไมก้าที่มักจะถูกใช้ร่วมกับวัสดุเหล่านั้นในช่วงต้นศตวรรษที่ยี่สิบจึงเป็นตัวเลือกที่เหมาะสมสำหรับการทดลองที่ยังคงดำเนินต่อไป ฟอร์ไมก้าได้รักษาความเป็นผู้นำในด้านเทคโนโลยีและการออกแบบในช่วงแปดปีที่ผ่านมาโดยการยกระดับตัวเองให้ทันต่อความท้าทายของระบบขนส่ง การขายปลีก ความต้องการภายในครัวเรือน และความต้องการภายในภาคอุตสาหกรรมใหม่ๆ อย่างสม่ำเสมอและได้ผันตัวเองจากการขายเพียงวัสดุปิดผิวตกแต่งไปสู่วัสดุโครงสร้าง – จนสามารถแข่งขันกับกุกเกนไฮม์ บิลบาโอ ของแฟรงค์เกร์ยรี ในด้านสถาปัตยกรรมได้

alors en vogue et véritable symbole de l'ère industrielle naissante. Comme l'historien du design Jeffrey L. Meikle écrit dans *American Plastic: A Cultural History*, « les modernistes américains ont pris conscience que les stratifiés phénoliques comme matériaux industriels pouvaient refléter l'esprit mécaniste qu'ils désiraient refléter dans le mobilier personnalisé de l'élite sophistiquée de Manhattan. Bien que chaque designer présentât des différences personnelles mineures, leur travail collectif suggérait une précision impersonnelle. » Le designer de mobilier art déco autrichien Paul T. Frankl, qui commençait à expérimenter une gamme de matières plastiques dans les années 1920, a invité ses collègues designers à « créer une grammaire à partir de ces nouveaux matériaux qui parlaient déjà la langue vernaculaire du XXe siècle : la langue de l'invention, de la synthèse. » Frankl voyait, peut-être avant les inventeurs du stratifié Formica, que leur produit deviendrait davantage qu'une imitation, qu'il deviendrait luxueux et un véritable symbole.

L'une des premières installations de grande taille et influentes à utiliser le stratifié Formica a été le Radio City Music Hall à Manhattan, ouvert en 1932 avec une série de meubles sur mesure conçus par Donald Deskey. Deskey, qui avait utilisé le liège, la tôle ondulée et l'amiante dans les vitrines du grand magasin Franklin Simon de la Cinquième Avenue, a expérimenté ultérieurement le stratifié Formica massif pour plusieurs de ses clients privés, en le plaçant même sur les murs de l'appartement de la philanthrope Abby Aldrich Rockefeller. Mais dans les vestibules et les salons du Radio City, les surfaces horizontales de stratifié noir brillant Formica ont joué un rôle de premier plan, reflétant les murales et papiers peints audacieux commandés par Deskey à des artistes comme Stuart Davis, Yasuo Kuniyoshi et Henry Billings.

Une table d'appoint conçue pour le fumoir possède des éléments verticaux courbes, tubulaires chromés, rappelant quelques-unes des expériences contemporaines du Bauhaus avec chaises tubulaires d'acier en porte à faux reflétant toujours les sensibilités art déco. Le papier

Inicialmente disponible solo en algunos colores oscuros porque los químicos aún debían perfeccionar la resina clara de la melamina, necesaria para lograr una superficie superior liviana o con diseños, la versión en negro resultó ser un excelente sustituto para la entonces conocida laca y, además, un símbolo del inicio de la era industrial. Como el historiador de diseño Jeffrey L. Meikle escribe en *American Plastic: A Cultural History*, "Los modernistas estadounidenses tomaron conciencia del laminado fenólico como un material industrial, que reflejaba el espíritu de las máquinas que querían transmitir en los muebles personalizados para los sofisticados de Manhattan. A pesar de que cada diseñador exponía sus pequeños toques personales, sus trabajos, en forma colectiva, sugerían una precisión impersonal", y el diseñador de muebles art decó nacido en Austria, Paul T. Frankl, quien comenzó a experimentar con una gama de plásticos en la década de los veinte, exhortó a sus colegas diseñadores a "crear una gramática para estos materiales nuevos" que ya hablaban "en la lengua vernácula del siglo XX… el lenguaje de la invención, de la síntesis". Frankl vio, quizá antes de que lo hicieran los creadores del laminado Formica, que su producto se podría convertir en algo más que una imitación, se convertiría en un lujo y en un símbolo en sí mismo.

Una de las primeras instalaciones importantes e influyentes del laminado Formica fue el Radio City Music Hall en Manhattan, que abrió sus puertas en 1932 con un juego de muebles personalizados diseñados por Donald Deskey. Deskey, quien había usado corcho, hierro corrugado y asbesto en los escaparates de la tienda de departamentos Franklin Simon de la Quinta Avenida, experimentó luego con el laminado Formica sólido para varios clientes privados, y hasta lo colocó sobre las paredes del apartamento de la filántropa Abby Aldrich Rockefeller. Pero en los vestíbulos y salones del Radio City, las superficies horizontales del laminado Formica color negro de brillo intenso desempeñaron un papel fundamental, al reflejar murales y papeles tapiz llamativos que Deskey encargó a diversos artistas, como Stuart Davis, Yasuo Kuniyoshi y Henry Billings.

toisiksi fenolilaminaatista teollisena materiaalina, joka kuvasti koneiden henkeä, jota he halusivat tuoda esiin Manhattanin hienostelijoille tilauksesta tehdyissä huonekaluissa. Vaikka jokainen suunnittelija osoittikin vähäisiä persoonallisia vivahteita, heidän työnsä kuvastivat kollektiivisesti persoonatonta tarkkuutta"; ja itävaltalaissyntyinen art deco -huonekalujen suunnittelija Paul T. Frankl, joka alkoi kokeilla erilaisia muoveja 1920-luvulla, kehotti suunnittelija-ammattiveljiään "luomaan kieliopin näistä uusista materiaaleista", jotka jo puhuivat "1900-luvun kansankieltä … keksintöjen, synteesin kieltä". Frankl näki, ehkä ennen Formica-laminaatin keksijöitä, että niiden tuotteesta voisi tulla enemmän kuin jäljittely — siitä tulisi ylellinen ja symbolinen omalla painollaan.

Yksi ensimmäisistä laajakantoisista ja vaikutusvaltaisista Formica-laminaatin asennuksista oli Radio City Music Hall -salin yhteydessä Manhattanilla, joka avattiin v. 1932 ja jossa oli kokoelma tilauksesta tehtyjä Donald Deskeyn suunnittelemia huonekaluja. Deskey, joka oli käyttänyt korkkia, aaltolevyä ja asbestia ikkunasomisteina Franklin Simon -tavaratalossa viidennen avenuen varrella, kokeili myöhemmin yksiväristä Formica-laminaattia monelle yksityiselle asiakkaalle, sijoittaen sitä jopa filantroopin Abby Aldrich Rockefellerin huoneiston seinille. Radio Cityn auloissa ja oleskelutiloissa korkeakiiltoisen mustan Formica-laminaatin vaakasuorat pinnat esittivät kuitenkin pääosaa, heijastaen rohkeita seinätauluja ja seinäpapereita, jotka Deskey tilasi sellaisilta taiteilijoilta kuten Stuart Davis, Yasuo Kuniyoshi ja Henry Billings.

Niin sanottua nikotiinihuonetta varten suunnitellussa sivupöydässä oli pystyosat kaarevaa, putkimaista kromia, jotka toivat mieleen jotkut sen aikaiset Bauhaus-kokeilut ulkonevien putkimaisten teräistuolien kanssa, mutta siitä huolimatta heijastivat art deco -tyylin tietoisuuksia. Kyseisen huoneen seinäpaperin, joka esitti tupakan tuotantovaiheita, suunnitteli Deskey itse, kokeillakseen Reynoldsin uuden alumiinifolion sopivuutta koristetarkoituksiin. Vuosikymmen myöhemmin Formica-yhtiö lisäsi tuotteeseensa myös folion, käyttäen sitä suojakerroksena koristepaperin alla tekemään siitä savukkeen aiheuttamia

法」，這些新材料早已「用二十世紀的白話……發明的語言合成的語言在表述」。也許在富美家美耐板發明家之前，弗蘭克爾就看到，他們的產品可能會成為一種超越仿製品的東西——其本身將會成為豪華和象徵性的物品。

富美家美耐板第一個廣泛而有影響力的安裝項目是曼哈頓的無線電城音樂廳，該音樂廳於 1932 年開業，配有由唐納德·戴思琪 (Donald Deskey) 設計的一套定製家俱。戴思琪曾用軟木、瓦楞鐵和石棉在第五大道的富蘭克林-西蒙百貨店做過櫥窗展示，後來又嘗試用厚實的富美家美耐板為眾多私人客戶服務，甚至將美耐板懸掛在慈善家艾比·奧爾德里奇·洛克菲勒 (Abby Aldrich Rock-efeller) 公寓的牆壁上。但在無線電城的大堂和走廊裡，用高光澤的黑色富美家美耐板製作的水平面起到了主導作用，反映了戴思琪委託斯圖爾特·戴維斯 (Stuart Davis)、康夫國芳 (Yasuo Kuniyoshi) 和亨利·比林斯 (Henry Billings) 等藝術家製作的大膽壁畫和壁紙。

為所謂的尼古丁室設計的一個茶几帶有彎曲的管式鍍鉻立柱，讓人聯想到同時代包豪斯用懸臂式管狀鋼椅

年安裝的金斑點壁紙早已消失，但淺綠色亮片台面（至少在我祖母的房子裡）仍在盡忠職守，絲毫沒有燒痕、斑點或殘缺。

二十世纪三十年代，富美家®装饰耐火板从原来的工业应用走进现代家具设计师的工作室。耐火板最初只有几种深色，因为化学家尚未完全制造出制作浅色或有图案面板所需的透明三聚氰胺树脂，但黑色的板材竟然成了当时流行的漆器的完美替代品，成为工业年代曙光的象征。正如设计历史学家杰弗里·L. 米克尔 (Jeffrey L. Meikle) 在《美国的塑料：一部文化史》中所说："美国现代主义者意识到酚醛耐火板作为一种工业原料，反映了在为曼哈顿的风雅之士定制的家具上他们想表现的机器精神。虽然每一位设计师都显示了些微的个人风格，他们集体创作的作品体现了一种客观的精确性"；奥地利出生的装饰艺术家具设计师保罗·T.弗兰克尔 (Paul T. Frankl) 在二十世纪二十年代开始尝试使用各种塑料，号召他的设计师同行"用这些新材料创造一种语法"，这些新材料早已"用二十世纪的白话……发明的语言合成的语言在表述"。也许在富美家®装饰耐火板发明家之前，弗兰克尔就看到，他们的产品可能会成为一种超越仿制品的东西——其本身将会成为豪华和象征性的物品。

富美家®装饰耐火板第一个广泛而有影响力的安装项目是曼哈顿的无线电城音乐厅，该音乐厅于 1932 年开业，配有由唐纳德·戴思琪 (Donald Deskey) 设计的一套定制家具。戴思琪曾用软木、瓦楞铁和石棉在第五大道的富兰克林-西蒙百货店做过橱窗展示，后来又尝试用厚实的富美家®装饰耐火板为众多私人客户服务，甚至将耐火板悬挂在慈善家艾比·奥尔德里奇·洛克菲勒 (Abby Aldrich Rockefeller) 公寓的墙壁上。但在无线电城的大堂和走廊里，用高光泽的黑色富美家®装饰耐火板制作的水平面起到了

ในแต่ละทศวรรษของศตวรรษที่ยี่สิบ นักออกแบบได้ใช้แผ่นลามิเนตฟอร์ไมก้าด้วยเหตุผลทางด้านคุณสมบัติด้านความสวยงามและคุณสมบัติในการใช้งาน ในสภาพแวดล้อมที่น่าประทับใจมากมาย ทั้งในสถาปัตยกรรมและในการตกแต่งภายใน ความสามารถในการดัดแปลงพื้นผิวซึ่งทำจากเมลามีนหรือก็คือ พลาสติกเทอร์โมเซตติง ซึ่งสามารถแทรกซึมผ่านวัสดุต่าง ๆ ได้เกือบทุกชนิด ทำให้ผลิตภัณฑ์สามารถปรับเปลี่ยนรูปแบบได้ตามความนิยม โดยที่ธรรมชาติของมัน ซึ่งก็คือ กระดาษที่ประกบด้วยเรซินซึ่งถูกกดอัดและให้ความร้อนส่วนใหญ่ยังคงเหมือนเดิม วอลล์เปเปอร์ที่มีลวดลายแต้มทองซึ่งเคยถูกนำมาติดตั้งในปี ค.ศ. 1959 ได้หายไปนานแล้ว แต่แผ่นลามิเนตลวดลายเลื่อมทองสีน้ำทะเลที่ถูกติดอยู่บนเคาน์เตอร์ (อย่างน้อยที่บ้านคุณยายของฉัน) ยังคงสภาพการใช้งานโดยปราศจากรอยไหม้ รอยเปื้อน หรือรอยบิ่น

ในช่วงทศวรรษที่ 1930 แผ่นลามิเนตฟอร์ไมก้าได้เคลื่อนจากจุดเริ่มต้นเพื่อการใช้งานในอุตสาหกรรม มาสู่การใช้งานในสตูดิโอของนักออกแบบเฟอร์นิเจอร์สมัยใหม่ ซึ่งในตอนแรกแผ่นลามิเนตมีให้เลือกเพียงสีเข้มไม่กี่สี เนื่องจากนักเคมียังไม่สามารถผลิตเมลามีนเรซินใสที่จำเป็นในการผลิตแผ่นลามิเนตสีอ่อนและสีลวดลายได้อย่างไรก็ตาม แผ่นลามิเนตสีดำได้กลายเป็นทั้งสิ่งทดแทนชั้นยอดสำหรับแลคเกอร์ซึ่งได้รับความนิยมในขณะนั้น และยังเป็นสัญลักษณ์ของการเริ่มต้นของยุคอุตสาหกรรมอีกด้วยตามที่นักประวัติศาสตร์ด้านการออกแบบเจฟเฟรย์ แอล เมเคิล เขียนไว้ในหนังสือชื่อ

peint de cette pièce, montrant les étapes de production du tabac, a été conçu par Deskey lui-même comme une expérience dans l'application de la feuille d'aluminium Reynolds à des fins décoratives. Une décennie plus tard, la société Formica a intégré l'aluminium dans son produit, l'utilisant comme couche protectrice sous le papier décoratif pour le rendre résistant aux brûlures de cigarettes. Les autres conceptions de stratifié Formica du Radio City de Deskey sont similairement combinées avec le métal poli, de petites tables rondes supportées par des triples colonnettes brillantes à des meubles buffets en équilibre sur des demi-cercles de bois cintré. La surface réfléchissante du stratifié et du métal ont aidé Deskey dans ses expériences avec de nouvelles conceptions d'éclairage, incluant des plafonds de feuille de cuivre et d'or, des luminaires linéaires dans des coins revêtus de miroirs et des lampes torchères en forme de bol métallique. Le stratifié Formica a permis à Deskey d'intégrer la sophistication de son mobilier exclusif destiné à la clientèle urbaine privée aux espaces publics et de mettre en évidence les qualités théâtrales des nouveaux matériaux.

L'innovation suivante en matière de stratifié Formica largement adoptée par les designers a été Realwood, un produit lancé à la fin des années 1940 intégrant une fine feuille de placage de bois véritable. Deskey avait substitué le stratifié Formica noir à la laque mais Realwood permettait au designer et au propriétaire de la mai-

Una mesa auxiliar, diseñada para la así denominada Sala de fumadores, tiene soportes verticales de cromo tubular curvo que recuerdan a los experimentos contemporáneos de la Bauhaus, con sillas de acero tubular voladizo, pero aun así refleja la sensibilidad del art decó. El papel tapiz de esa sala, que muestra las etapas de la producción del tabaco, fue diseñado por el mismo Deskey como un experimento para aplicar la nueva hoja de aluminio de Reynolds con fines decorativos. Una década más tarde, la empresa Formica también incorporaría la hoja de aluminio a su producto, al utilizarla como una capa protectora debajo del papel decorativo para hacerlo resistente a las quemaduras de cigarrillo. Los otros diseños de laminado Formica de Deskey en el Radio City están combinados de manera similar con el metal pulido de pequeñas mesas redondas, sostenidas por tres columnas brillantes al lado de aparadores que se mantienen en equilibrio sobre semicírculos de madera curvada. La reflectancia del laminado y del metal colaboró con los experimentos de Deskey con los nuevos conceptos de iluminación, incluidos los cielorrasos de cobre y hojas doradas, los accesorios para iluminación lineales incrustados en esquinas con efecto espejo, y las luces verticales metálicas con forma de tazón. El laminado Formica le permitió a Deskey incorporar el aspecto ostentoso del diseño de sus muebles personalizados para clientes privados sofisticados en lugares públicos y resaltar las cualidades teatrales de los nuevos materiales.

La siguiente innovación del laminado Formica, que en gran medida fue adoptada por los diseñadores, fue "Realwood", un producto que se presentó a finales de la década de los cuarenta y que incorporó una fina lámina de revestimiento de madera real. Deskey había sustituido el laminado Formica color negro por la laca, pero Realwood hizo que el diseñador y el consumidor no tuvieran que elegir entre el material real y un sustituto industrial. Realwood fue el producto de laminado Formica que se eligió para el Terrace Plaza Hotel en Cincinnati, Ohio, uno de los primeros edificios modernos diseñados por la legendaria firma estadounidense de arquitectura

palovahinkoja kestävän. Deskeyn muut Formica-laminaattiset Radio Cityn suunnittelukohteet ovat samalla tavoin yhdistetty kiillotettuun metalliin, pienistä pyöreistä pöydistä kolmen kiiltävän pylvään päällä, tarjoilupöytiin taivutettujen puisten puoliympyröiden varassa. Laminaatin heijastusominaisuus ja metalli auttoivat Deskeyn uusien valaistusmenetelmien kokeiluissa, mukaan lukien kupari- ja lehtikultakatot, lineaariset valaisimet peileillä varustetuissa nurkissa ja kulhon muotoiset, metalliset ylös suunnatut valot. Formica-laminaatin avulla Deskey pystyi ottamaan hienostuneille yksityisille asiakkailleen tilaustyönä tekemiensä huonekalujen mallien tyylikkyyden mukaan julkisiin tiloihin ja korostamaan uusien materiaalien teatraalisia laatuominaisuuksia.

Seuraava suunnittelijoiden laajalti käyttöön ottama Formica-laminaatin innovaatio oli "Realwood", 1940-luvun loppupuolella esitelty tuote, joka sisälsi ohuen levyn aitoa puuviilua. Deskey oli korvannut lakkapuun mustalla Formica-laminaatilla, mutta Realwood merkitsi sitä, että suunnittelijan ja kodin omistajan ei tarvinnut valita aidon tuotteen ja teollisen korvikkeen välillä. Realwood oli Formican laminaattien tuotteista se, joka valittiin Terrace Plaza Hotelliin Cincinnatissa, Ohiossa, joka oli yksi ensimmäisistä nykyaikaisista rakennuksista, jonka legendaarinen amerikkalainen arkkitehtitoimisto Skidmore, Owings & Merrill suunnitteli ja joka valmistui v. 1948. Formica-laminaatin käyttö tässä tärkeässä kotikaupungin projektissa oli ilmeinen vallankaappaus. Tiilirakennus sisälsi kaksi suureksi osaksi ikkunatonta tavarataloa pohjakerroksessa ja laatikomaisen hotellin seitsemännestä kerroksesta ylöspäin. Rakennuksen ylimmässä osassa oli ympyrän muotoinen gourmetravintola, jossa kaaren yhdellä sivulla oli seinä kaltevia lasi-ikkunoita ja toisella Joan Mirón seinämaalaus. Alakerrassa Skyline-ravintolassa seinää koristi Saul Steinbergin tekemä karikatyyri elämästä Cincinnatissa. Tuoliryhmän yläpuolella kahdeksannen kerroksen aulassa riippui Alexander Calderin mobile.

Arkkitehdit aikoivat tehdä sisustussuunnittelusta yhtä kaukonäköisen kuin arkkitehtuuri ja taide, ja sen aikainen mainoslehtinen, nimeltään "Sight-

製作、但仍不失裝飾藝術風格情感的一些實驗。那間屋子裡的壁紙表現了煙草製作的工序，由戴思琪本人設計，作為使用雷諾新鋁箔紙進行裝飾的一項實驗。十年後，富美家公司也將鋁箔納入自己的產品中，用它作為裝飾紙下面的保護層，可防香煙燒傷。戴思琪在無線電城的其他富美家美耐板設計中同樣結合了拋光金屬，從由閃亮的立柱三角腿製成的小圓桌到平衡於半圓形曲木上的側板。美耐板和金屬的反射性幫助戴思琪試驗使用新的照明概念，包括銅和金質天花板、塞進帶鏡子牆角的線性燈具和向上照射的碗狀金屬。富美家美耐板使戴思琪能夠把他為溫莎爾雅的私人客戶定製家俱設計的奢華時髦帶入公共空間，並突出新材料的戲劇化效果。

富美家美耐板下一個被設計師廣泛採用的創新是「真木」，這是一種在二十世紀四十年代末引進的包含一層薄薄的真木材的產品。戴思琪曾用黑色的富美家美耐板替代漆器，但真木意味著設計師和房主再也不必在真木和工業替代品之間作出選擇。真木是俄亥俄州辛辛那提市露臺廣場酒店 (Terrace Plaza Hotel) 對富美家美耐板的首選產品，這是富有傳奇色彩的美國建築公司斯基德莫爾、奧因斯和美林 (Skidmore, Owing & Merrill) 的第一個現代化建築物之一，於 1948 年完工。在這個重要的家鄉項目上使用富美家美耐板顯然是一個巨變。這座磚砌建築在底層有兩個巨大的不帶窗戶的百貨公司，七層以上是一座石板式酒店。建築物頂部是圓形美食餐廳，圓形曲線的一邊是傾斜的玻璃窗牆壁，另一邊是米羅 (Joan Miro) 的壁畫。樓下的天際餐館 (Skyline Restaurant) 牆上的裝飾出自索爾‧斯坦伯格 (Saul Steinberg) 之手，以漫畫形式描繪了辛辛那提的生活。第八層的大廳內的一組椅子的上方掛著一件亞歷

主導作用，倒映了戴思琪委托斯图尔特·戴维斯 (Stuart Davis)、康夫国芳 (Yasuo Kuniyoshi) 和亨利·比林斯 (Henry Billings) 等艺术家制作的大胆壁画和壁纸。

为所谓的尼古丁室设计的一个茶几带有弯曲的管式镀铬立柱，让人联想到同时代包豪斯用悬臂式管状钢椅制作、但仍不失装饰艺术风格情感的一些实验。那间屋子里的壁纸表现了烟草制作的工序，由戴思琪本人设计，作为使用雷诺新铝箔纸进行装饰的一项实验。十年后，富美家公司也将铝箔纳入自己的产品中，用它作为装饰纸下面的保护层，可防香烟烧伤。戴思琪在无线电城的其他富美家®装饰耐火板设计中同样结合了抛光金属，从由闪亮的立柱三角腿制成的小圆桌到平衡于半圆形曲木上的侧板。耐火板和金属的反射性帮助戴思琪试验使用新的照明概念，包括铜和金质天花板、塞进带镜子墙角的线性灯具和向上照射的碗状金属。富美家®装饰耐火板使戴思琪能够把他为温莎尔雅的私人客户定制家具设计的奢华时髦带入公共空间，并突出新材料的戏剧化效果。

富美家®装饰耐火板下一个被设计师广泛采用的创新是“真木”，这是一种在二十世纪四十年代末引进的包含一层薄薄的真木材的产品。戴思琪曾用黑色的富美家®装饰耐火板替代漆器，但真木意味着设计师和房主再也不必在真木和工业替代品之间作出选择。真木是俄亥俄州辛辛那提市露台广场酒店 (Terrace Plaza Hotel) 对富美家®装饰耐火板的首选产品，这是富有传奇色彩的美国建筑公司斯基德莫尔、奥因斯和美林 (Skidmore, Owing & Merrill) 的第一个现代化建筑物之一，于 1948 年完工。在这个重要的家乡项目上使用富美家®装饰耐火板显然是一个巨变。这座砖砌建筑在底层有两个巨大的不带窗户的百货公司，七层以上是一座石板式酒店。建筑物顶部是圆形美食餐厅，圆形曲线的一边是

American Plastic: A Cultural History ว่า "ชาวอเมริกันสมัยใหม่ได้รับรู้ว่าแผ่นลามิเนทฟิโนลิคเป็นวัสดุอุตสาหกรรมซึ่งสะท้อนให้เห็นถึงจิตวิญญาณของเครื่องจักรซึ่งพวกเขาต้องการจะถ่ายทอดให้กับเฟอร์นิเจอร์ที่ถูกออกแบบมาเฉพาะสำหรับชนชั้นสูงในแมนฮัตตัน ถึงแม้ว่านักออกแบบแต่ละคนจะได้แสดงรูปแบบเฉพาะตนในผลงานของพวกเขาบ้างเล็กน้อย แต่ผลงานของพวกเขาโดยรวมแสดงให้เห็นถึงรูปแบบที่ไม่มีเอกลักษณ์เฉพาะตน" และนักออกแบบเฟอร์นิเจอร์ชาวออสเตรียโดยกำเนิด พอล ที แฟรงเกิล ผู้เริ่มทดลองโดยใช้พลาสติกหลากหลายชนิดในช่วงปี ค.ศ. 1920 ได้เรียกร้องให้เพื่อนๆ นักออกแบบ "สร้างหลักในการใช้วัสดุใหม่ๆ เหล่านี้" ซึ่งเปรียบเสมือนการพูดด้วย "ภาษาพูดในศตวรรษที่ 20 เป็นภาษาแห่งการประดิษฐ์คิดค้น ภาษาแห่งวัสดุสังเคราะห์" แฟรงเกิลเห็น บางทีอาจจะก่อนที่ผู้ประดิษฐ์ฟอร์ไมก้าจะเห็นเสียอีกว่า ผลิตภัณฑ์ของพวกเขาอาจกลายเป็นได้มากกว่าของเลียนแบบ โดยอาจกลายเป็นความหรูหราและเป็นสัญลักษณ์ในตัวมันเอง

หนึ่งในบรรดาสถานที่ที่ใช้แผ่นลามิเนทฟอร์ไมก้าตกแต่งจำนวนมากและทรงอิทธิพลเป็นครั้งแรก คือ ณ หอดนตรีเรดิโอ ซิตี้ ในเมืองแมนฮัตตัน ซึ่งเปิดทำการในปี ค.ศ. 1932 และตกแต่งด้วยชุดเฟอร์นิเจอร์ที่ถูกออกแบบมาเฉพาะโดยโดนัล เดสกี้ เดสกี้ซึ่งเคยใช้ไม้ก๊อก สังกะสีลูกฟูก และใยหินตกแต่งหน้าร้านของห้างแฟรงคลิน ไซมอน ซึ่งตั้งอยู่บนถนนฟิฟท์ อเวนิว ภายหลังได้ทดลองใช้แผ่นลามิเนทสีพื้นของฟอร์ไมก้าในการทำงานให้กับลูกค้าเอกชนจำนวนหนึ่งและได้ทดลองติดแผ่นลามิเนทบนฝาผนังอพาร์ตเมนต์ ของอัลดริช ร็อกกี้เฟลเลอร์ ผู้ใจบุญ ขณะที่ในล็อบบี้และเลาน์จ์ ของเรดิโอซิตี้ แผ่นลามิเนทสีดำที่มีความมันวาวได้ถูกติดตั้งในแนวราบไว้อย่างสง่างามเสมือนได้รับบทบาทนำ ซึ่งสะท้อนให้เห็นภาพจิตรกรรมฝาหนังและวอลล์เปเปอร์ที่เดสกี้ได้รับมอบมาจากบรรดาศิลปิน เช่น สจ๊วตเดวิส ยาซูโอะ คุนิโยชิ และเฮนรี่ บิลลิ่ง ได้อย่างชัดเจน

โต๊ะข้างที่ได้รับการออกแบบมาเพื่อใช้กับห้องนิโคตินมีท่อโครเมียมโค้งประดับอยู่ในแนวตั้ง ทำให้ชวนนึกถึงการทดลองบางส่วนของบาอูฮูสในช่วงที่เขาได้ทำเก้าอี้ท่อเหล็กแบบมีที่เท้าแขน แต่ยังคงให้ความรู้สึกถึงศิลปะแบบอาร์ตเดคโค วอลล์เปเปอร์ในห้องนั้นที่แสดงให้เห็นถึงขั้นตอนการผลิตยาสูบ ได้ถูกออกแบบโดยเดสกี้ครั้งเมื่อเขาทดลองใช้แผ่นอลูมิเนียม

son de ne pas choisir entre le matériau réel et un substitut industriel. Realwood était le stratifié Formica choisi pour le Terrace Plaza Hotel de Cincinnati, Ohio, l'un des premiers immeubles modernes conçus par le légendaire bureau d'architecture Skidmore, Owings & Merrill en 1948. L'utilisation de stratifié Formica dans son lieu de conception fut un coup marquant. Le bâtiment de brique comprenait deux grands magasins en grande partie sans fenêtres à la base, et un hôtel ressemblant à un bloc de béton à partir du septième étage. Au sommet du bâtiment se trouvait le restaurant circulaire Gourmet, avec un mur de fenêtres inclinées d'un côté et une murale de Joan Miró de l'autre. En bas, dans le restaurant Skyline, la décoration murale était de Saul Steinberg, une caricature de la vie à Cincinnati. Au-dessus d'un groupement de chaises dans le vestibule du huitième étage était accroché un mobile d'Alexander Calder.

Les architectes ont dessiné l'intérieur avec la même intention avantgardiste présente dans l'architecture et l'art, et une brochure promotionnelle de l'époque le présentait comme un site « à visite guidée », où les chambres vous donnent l'impression de vous tenir « debout dans le salon d'une belle maison moderne ». L'utilisation de stratifié Formica commençait à la réception, revêtue de Realwood pour simuler une longue rangée de placages assortis. Le mur derrière la réception était également couvert de Realwood avec horloge intégrée. Dans les chambres, une grande partie du mobilier était encastré, incluant un canapélit qui se déroulait en lit en appuyant sur un bouton et un bureau qui s'ouvrait derrière un panneau jaune de stratifié Formica. Le mobilier mobile, fabriqué par Thonet, avait les bras et les pattes en bois cintré et des dessus noirs de stratifié Formica. Dans la salle de bain, les architectes avaient choisi le stratifié Formica rouge brillant à motif Linen pour l'évier et le meuble-lavabo combinés. Les suites incluaient une vue à partir de la table de toilette au travers d'une grande fenêtre. Un miroir était monté sur le comptoir avec deux pattes métalliques minces. La brochure signale au fumeur nerveux (ou peut-

Skidmore, Owings & Merrill que se finalizó en 1948. El uso del laminado Formica en este importante proyecto en su ciudad de residencia fue un verdadero golpe maestro. El edificio de ladrillo incluía dos tiendas por departamentos sin ventanas en la base y un hotel que parecía de losa a partir del séptimo piso. En la parte superior del edificio, se encontraba el Gourmet Restaurant de forma circular, con un cerramiento de ventanas de vidrio inclinadas en uno de los lados de la curva y un mural de Joan Miró en el otro. Abajo, en el Skyline Restaurant, la decoración de la pared estuvo a cargo de Saul Steinberg, un caricaturista de la vida de Cincinnati. Sobre un grupo de sillas en el vestíbulo del octavo piso colgaba un móvil de Alexander Calder.

Los arquitectos quisieron que el diseño del interior fuera de un pensamiento de avanzada como el de la arquitectura y el arte y en un folleto de promoción de la época, anunciado como una "Excursión por lugares de interés" se afirma que las habitaciones se sienten como si "uno estuviera parado en la sala de una preciosa casa moderna". El uso del laminado Formica comenzaba en el mostrador de la recepción, que, de manera imponente, estaba recubierto de Realwood para simular una larga hilera de revestimientos combinados. La pared detrás del mostrador también estaba cubierta de Realwood, con un reloj empotrado. En las habitaciones, muchos de los muebles estaban empotrados, incluidos un sofá cama que se convertía en cama con solo accionar un interruptor y un escritorio desplegable, camuflado detrás de un panel de laminado Formica color amarillo. Los muebles movibles, fabricados por Thonet, tenían brazos y patas de madera curvada, y encimeras de laminado Formica color negro. En el baño, los arquitectos eligieron el laminado Formica con el diseño lino color rojo brillante para la combinación del lavamanos y el tocador. Las suites incluían una vista desde el tocador a través de una gran ventana; había un espejo montado en la cubierta prefabricada con dos patas de metal delgadas. En el folleto, se les garantiza a los fumadores nerviosos (o quizá al nervioso dueño del hotel) que las superficies horizontales son de "laminado Formica

Seeing Tour" (kiertoajelu) mainitsee, että huoneet vaikuttavat siltä kuin "seisoisit viehättävän nykyaikaisen kodin olohuoneessa". Formica-laminaatin käyttö alkoi vastaanottotiskistä, joka oli vaikuttavasti päällystetty Realwood-laminaatilla jäljittelemään pitkää riviä yhteen sopivia viiluja. Tiskin takana olevan seinän päällysteenä oli myös Realwood ja siinä oli sisään upotettu kello. Suuri osa huoneiden huonekaluista oli kiinteästi sijoitettuja, mukaan lukien studiosohva, joka oli rullattavissa ulos vuoteeksi kytkintä näpsäyttämällä, sekä alas kääntyvä pöytä, piilossa keltaisen Formica-laminaattisen paneelin takana. Thonetin valmistamissa siirrettävissä huonekaluissa oli taivutetut puiset käsinojat ja jalat ja mustat Formica- laminaattiset päälliset. Kylpyhuoneeseen arkkitehdit valitsivat lavuaarin ja kampauspöydän yhdistelmää varten Formica-laminaatin, jossa oli kirkkaan punainen pellavakuvio. Sviitteihin sisältyi näköala tältä kampauspöydältä suuren ikkunan läpi; pöydän päälle oli kiinnitetty peili kahdella solakalla metallijalalla. Mainoslehtinen vakuuttaa huolestuneelle tupakoitsijalle (tai ehkä hotellin hermostuneelle omistajalle), että kaikki vaakasuorat pinnat ovat "Beauty Bonded Formicaa": "Millään Formica-pinnalla ei näy jälkiä alkoholitahroista tai savukkeen polttamista kohdista edellisten vieraitten jäljiltä". Mainoslehtinen ehdottaa,

山大·考爾德（Alexander Calder）的懸掛飾物。

　　建築師的用意是讓室內設計像建築和藝術一樣具有前瞻性思維，一段時間內的名為「觀光」的促銷手冊這樣描述，置身室內仿佛是「置身於一個可愛的摩登家庭的客廳裡」富美家美耐板的使用從前臺開始，用的是真木貼面，讓人印象深刻，模仿一長列色澤相配的貼木板。桌子後面的牆壁也用真木覆蓋，內置一座時鐘。房間裡的家俱多為固定家俱，包括一個工作室的沙發，一按鍵便可拉出變為一張床，在一塊黃色富美家美耐板的後面是一張可拉下的寫字檯。由托內（Thonet）製作的移動家俱有曲木手柄和椅腿，黑色富美家美耐板為檯面。在浴室裡，建築師選擇了鮮紅色亞麻圖案的富美家美耐板，用作水槽和洗手台組合。這個套房可從洗手台透過一扇大窗戶看到外面的景色，鏡子安裝在檯面上，帶有兩條細長的金屬腿。這本手冊向惴惴不安的吸煙者（或者是向神經緊張的酒店老闆）保證，所有的檯面都是用的「美麗作保的富美家」：「富美家貼面上絕對沒有在你之前的客人留下的一絲酒精汗漬或香煙灼傷。」這本手冊提到，奢華就是讓一切看上去完美如新。

　　最初，富美家公司的消費產品線僅限於暗色、仿木紋和大理石紋的圖案。但是，在 1938 年完善了使用三聚氰胺樹脂建造透明、裝飾性的檯面之後，該公司準備擴大到消費市場。刊登在《建築實錄》（Architectural Record）、《好管家》（Good Housekeeping）和《美麗住宅》（House Beautiful）等雜誌的具有輝煌視覺效果的廣告，向設計師和房主們顯示富美家美耐板的潛在功能。作為這種直接市場行銷的一部分，富美家公司還首次聘請了外部設計顧問——密爾沃基市工業設計師布魯克斯·史蒂文斯（Brooks Stevens）。他是美

倾斜的玻璃窗墙壁，另一边是米罗（Joan Miro）的壁画。楼下的天际餐馆（Skyline Restaurant）墙上的装饰出自索尔·斯坦伯格（Saul Steinberg）之手，以漫画形式描绘的是辛辛那提生活。第八层的大厅内的一组椅子的上方挂着一件亚历山大·考尔德（Alexander Calder）的悬挂饰物。

　　建築师的用意是让室内设计像建筑和艺术一样具有前瞻性思维，一段时间内的名为"观光"的促销手册这样描述，置身室内仿佛是"置身于一个可爱的摩登家庭的客厅里"富美家®装饰耐火板的使用从前台开始，用的是真木贴面，让人印象深刻，模仿一长列色泽相配的贴木板。桌子后面的墙壁也用真木覆盖，内置一座时钟。房间里的家具多为固定家具，包括一个工作室的沙发，一按键便可拉出变为一张床，在一块黄色富美家®装饰耐火板的后面是一张可拉下的写字台。由托内（Thonet）制作的移动家装有曲木手柄和椅腿，黑色富美家®装饰耐火板为台面。在浴室里，建筑师选择了鲜红色亚麻图案的富美家®装饰耐火板，用作水槽和洗手台组合。这个套房可从洗手台透过一扇大窗户看到外面的景色，镜子安装在台面上，带有两条细长的金属腿。这本手册向惴惴不安的吸烟

ฟอยล์ใหม่จากเรย์โนลส์ มาประดับตกแต่งในทศวรรษต่อมา บริษัทฟอร์ไมก้าได้นำแผ่นฟอยล์ม้ใช้กับผลิตภัณฑ์เช่นกัน โดยใช้แผ่นฟอยล์เป็นชั้นป้องกันข้างใต้กระดาษตกแต่ง เพื่อทำให้กระดาษทนต่อการไหม้ของบุหรี่ การออกแบบฟอร์ไมก้าในรูปแบบอื่นๆ ในเรดิโอ ซิตี้ โดยเดสก์ก็มีการนำโลหะขัดเงามาใช้เช่นกัน โดยมีการใช้เพื่อทำโต๊ะกลมขนาดเล็กที่มีขาโต๊ะมันเงาสามารถไปจนถึงตู้ถ้วยชามที่ตั้งอย่างสมดุลบนไม้เป็นวงกลมครึ่งวงกลม ความสามารถในการสะท้อนแสงของแผ่นลามิเนทและโลหะมีส่วนช่วยในการทดลองแนวคิดในการใช้แสงแบบใหม่ๆ ของเดสกี้ รวมไปถึงการทำเพดานจากทองแดงและแผ่นทอง แผงไฟชนิดเส้นตรงที่ถูกใส่เข้าไปที่มุมกระจก และโคมไฟโลหะทรงถ้วยที่แสงไฟส่องขึ้นด้านบน ฟอร์ไมก้าได้ทำให้เดสกี้สามารถรวมเอาความหรูหราในการออกแบบเฟอร์นิเจอร์ให้แก่กลุ่มลูกค้าผู้ดีเอกชนมาใช้กับสาธารณชนได้ และยังช่วยให้เดสกี้สามารถแสดงให้เห็นถึงคุณภาพของวัสดุใหม่ๆ อีกด้วย

　　นวัตกรรมต่อไปของฟอร์ไมก้าที่ได้รับการยอมรับอย่างแพร่หลายจากนักออกแบบ คือ "ไม้ธรรมชาติแท้" ซึ่งเป็นผลิตภัณฑ์ที่ถูกเปิดตัวในช่วงหลังของทศวรรษที่ 1940 โดยมีการนำแผ่นเยื่อไม้แท้บางๆ มาใช้ เดสกี้ได้ใช้แผ่นลามิเนทฟอร์ไมก้าสีดำแทนแลคเกอร์ แต่ไม้ธรรมชาติแท้จะทำให้นักออกแบบและเจ้าของบ้านไม่ต้องเลือกระหว่างของจริงกับสิ่งที่ถูกนำมาใช้แทนในอุตสาหกรรม ไม้ธรรมชาติแท้ของฟอร์ไมก้าเป็นตัวเลือกที่ใช้ในโรงแรมเทอเรส พลาซ่า ในเมืองซินซินเนติ รัฐโอไฮโอซึ่งถือเป็นตึกหนึ่งในบรรดาตึกสมัยใหม่ที่ถูกออกแบบโดยสกิดมอร์ โอนนิ่งส์ แอนด์เมอริลล์ บริษัทสถาปนิกสัญชาติอเมริกันอันมีชื่อเสียงกล่าวขานกันเป็นตำนาน และถูกสร้างเสร็จในปี ค.ศ. 1948 การใช้ผลิตภัณฑ์ฟอร์ไมก้าในโครงการบ้านสำคัญดังกล่าวถือเป็นการปฏิวัติวงการอย่างสำคัญ อาคารอีฐซึ่งมีห้างสรรพสินค้าไร้หน้าต่างอยู่บนชั้นล่างและโรงแรมที่มีลักษณะเหมือนเป็นแผ่นหนาเริ่มต้นที่ชั้น 7 บนสุดของอาคารดังกล่าวเป็นร้านอาหารทรงกลมที่ด้านหนึ่งประดับไปด้วยผนังหน้าต่างกระจกเฉียงและมีภาพจิตรกรรมฝาหนังของฮวน มิโร ประดับไว้อีกด้านหนึ่งชั้นล่างเป็นร้านอาหารสกายไลน์ ตกแต่งผนังโดยซอล สเตนเบิร์ก โดยเป็นภาพล้อเลียนชีวิตคนเมืองซินซินเนติ ที่ด้านบนเหนือเก้าอี้ในล็อบปี้ชั้น 8 มีโมบายของอเล็กซานเดอร์คาลเดอร์ แขวนอยู่

เหล่าสถาปนิกตั้งใจให้การออกแบบภายในมีลักษณะล้ำสมัยดังเช่นสถาปัตยกรรม

être au propriétaire nerveux de l'hôtel) que toutes les surfaces horizontales sont réalisées en « Beauty Bonded Formica ». « En aucun cas, la surface de Formica ne peut présenter de trace de tache d'alcool ou de brûlure de cigarette laissée par les hôtes précédents. » La brochure suggère encore que le luxe réside dans le fait que tout semble absolument neuf.

Initialement, la ligne de produit grand public de la société Formica était limitée à des teintes sombres et des motifs qui imitaient le grain du bois et le marbre. Mais après avoir perfectionné l'utilisation de la résine de mélamine pour créer une surface transparente et décorative, la société a pu se développer sur le marché grand public à partir de 1938. Des annonces visuellement brillantes furent insérées dans des magazines tels qu'*Architectural Record, Good Housekeeping* et *House Beautiful*, montrant aux designers et aux propriétaires de maison ce que le stratifié Formica permettait de faire. Dans le cadre de cet effort de publicité directe, la société Formica a également embauché son premier consultant designer extérieur, le designer industriel Brooks Stevens de Milwaukee. Ce dernier a été le membre fondateur de la société Industrial Design Society of America et était surtout connu pour son travail sur les bateaux, les trains et les voitures. Il a conseillé la société lors du développement de Realwood. Il a fini par croire qu'il était « ridicule » d'utiliser un produit forestier lorsqu'une reproduction photographique de bois pouvait suffire. Sa solution a été appelée « Luxwood » et a été commercialisée à partir de 1950 comme solution économique, véritable alternative ressemblante.

Stevens a également été responsable de la première invention graphique dexl'entreprise, le motif « Skylark », qui fait toujours figure d'icône bien que lancé en 1950. Dans l'article *Industrial Strength Design: How Brooks Stevens Shaped Your World*, l'historien et conservateur de design Glenn Adamson plaide pour Skylark dans le cadre d'un plus grand engouement moderniste pour l'amibe qui se reflète dans le logo devenu emblématique de Stevens pour la

de belleza garantizada": "En ninguna de las superficies de laminado Formica hay rastros de manchas de alcohol o quemaduras de cigarrillo que hayan dejado los huéspedes anteriores a usted". El lujo, sugerido en el folleto, es hacer que todo parezca totalmente nuevo.

Inicialmente, la línea de productos al consumidor de la empresa Formica estaba limitada a colores oscuros y motivos que simulaban las vetas de madera y el mármol. Sin embargo, al haber perfeccionado el uso de la resina de melamina para crear una superficie superior decorativa, clara en 1938, la empresa estaba lista para expandirse al mercado del consumidor. Anuncios publicitarios brillantes desde el punto de vista visual, publicados en revistas tales como *Architectural Record, Good Housekeeping* y *House Beautiful*, les mostraban a diseñadores y propietarios residenciales lo que el laminado Formica podía hacer. Como parte de este esfuerzo *de marketing* directo, Formica Company también contrató al primer asesor de diseño de exteriores, el diseñador industrial Brooks Stevens, establecido en Milwaukee. Fue uno de los miembros fundadores de la Sociedad de Diseñadores Industriales de los Estados Unidos (Industrial Design Society of America, IDSA) y conocido, sobre todo, por su trabajo en barcos, trenes y automóviles. Él asesoró a la empresa mientras desarrollaba Realwood y llegó a creer que era "ridículo" utilizar un producto procedente del bosque cuando una reproducción fotográfica de la madera sería suficiente. Su solución recibió el nombre de "Luxwood" y, al introducirse en el mercado en 1950, se comercializó como una alternativa de imitación más económica.

Stevens también fue el responsable de la primera invención gráfica de la empresa, el diseño icónico "Skylark" aún vigente introducido en 1950. En *Industrial Strength Design: How Brooks Stevens Shaped Your World*, el curador e historiador de diseño Glenn Adamson aboga por Skylark como parte de una extensa pasión modernista con la ameba, reflejada en el logotipo icónico posterior de Stevens para Miller Brewing Company, y la mesa de centro contemporánea con superficie de vidrio de Isamu Noguchi. Skylark es el resultado acertado del encargo

que ylellisyys tarkoittaa sitä, että kaikki näyttää upoudelta.

Aluksi Formica-yhtiön kuluttajatuotteiden linja rajoittui tummiin väreihin ja aiheisiin, jotka jäljittelivät puun syitä ja marmoria. Kehitettyään valmiiksi melamiinihartsin käytön kirkkaan koristeellisen yläpinnan saamiseksi v. 1938, yhtiö oli valmiina laajentumaan kuluttajamarkkinoille. Visuaalisesti loistavia mainoksia julkaistiin aikakauslehdissä kuten *Architectural Record, Good Housekeeping* ja *House Beautiful*, joissa suunnittelijoille ja kodin omistajille näytettiin mitä Formica-laminaatilla voisi tehdä. Osana tämän suoran markkinoinnin ponnistuksesta Formica Yhtiö palkkasi myös ensimmäinen ulkopuolisen suunnittelukonsulttinsa, Milwaukeessa toimivan teollisen suunnittelijan Brooks Stevensin. Hän oli Industrial Design Society of America -seuran perustajajäsen ja tunnettu parhaiten työstään veneiden, junien ja autojen parissa. Hän oli yhtiössä konsulttina sen kehittäessä Realwood-tuotetta ja hän tuli siihen käsitykseen että oli "naurettavaa" käyttää metsätuotetta kun valokuvattu jäljitelmä puusta riittäisi. Hänen ratkaisuaan kutsuttiin nimellä "Luxwood" ja sitä markkinoitiin uutuutena v. 1950 vähemmän kalliina samalla näyttävänä vaihtoehtona.

Stevens vastasi myös yhtiön ensimmäisestä graafisesta keksinnöstä, edelleenkin ikonisesta "Skylark"-kuviosta, joka tuli käyttöön v. 1950. Kirjassa *Industrial Strength Design: How Brooks Stevens Shaped Your World*, suunnittelun historioitsija ja kuraattori Glenn Adamson väittää Skylarkia osaksi suuremmasta modernistises-

國工業設計協會創始成員之一，以輪船、火車和汽車上的作品而著稱。他在富美家公司開發真木時向該公司提供諮詢，他開始相信，用攝影再現木材就足夠時使用森林產品是「可笑之極」的。他的解決辦法被稱為「賽木」(Luxwood)，並於 1950 年引入時作為一種較便宜、外觀似木料的替代品推銷。

史蒂文斯還為富美家公司創造了第一個圖形發明，即 1950 年引入的靜物「雲雀」圖形。在《工業強度設計：布魯克斯·史蒂文斯如何塑造您的世界》(Industrial Strength Design: How Brooks Stevens Shaped Your World) 一書中，設計史學家兼研究員格倫·亞當森 (Glenn Adamson)

者(或者是向神经紧张的酒店老板)保证，所有的台面都是用的"美丽作保的富美家"："富美家贴面上绝对没有在你之前的客人留下的一丝酒精污渍或香烟灼伤。"这本手册提到，奢华就是让一切看上去完美如新。

最初，富美家公司的消费产品线仅限于暗色、仿木纹和大理石纹的图案。但是，在 1938 年完善了使用三聚氰胺树脂建造透明、装饰性的台面之后，该公司准备扩大到消费市场。刊登在《建筑实录》(Architectural Record)、《好管家》(Good Housekeeping) 和《美丽住宅》(House Beautiful) 等杂志的具有辉煌视觉效果的广告，向设计师和房主们显示富美家®装饰耐火板的潜在功能。作为这

และงานศิลปะ โบรชัวร์ส่งเสริมการขายในขณะนั้นซึ่งใช้หัวข้อว่า "การพาเที่ยวชม" ได้ระบุว่า ห้องให้ความรู้สึกเสมือนว่า "คุณกำลังยืนอยู่ในห้องนั่งเล่นของบ้านสมัยใหม่ที่น่าอยู่" การใช้ผลิตภัณฑ์ฟอร์ไมก้าเริ่มตั้งแต่โต๊ะของแผนกต้อนรับซึ่งสร้างความประทับใจด้วยการปิดผิวด้วยเยื่อไม้แท้ให้ความรู้สึกถึงแผ่นไม้จริงแนวยาว ผนังด้านหลังโต๊ะก็ยังถูกปกคลุมไปด้วยไม้ธรรมชาติแท้และมีนาฬิกาฝังอยู่ ภายในห้องเฟอร์นิเจอร์ส่วนใหญ่เป็นแบบติดผนัง รวมถึงเก้าอี้สตูดิโอยาวที่สามารถกางออกกลายเป็นเตียงได้เพียงแค่กดสวิตช์ และโต๊ะแบบดึงลงที่ซ่อนอยู่ด้านหลังผนังลามิเนทฟอร์ไมก้าสีเหลือง เฟอร์นิเจอร์แบบเคลื่อนย้ายได้ถูกผลิตโดยทอร์เน็ตมีแขนและขาทำจากไม้เบ็นท์วูดและใช้แผ่นลามิเนทฟอร์ไมก้าปิดด้านบน ในห้องอาบน้ำสถาปนิกได้เลือกใช้แผ่นลามิเนทฟอร์ไมก้าลายลินินสีแดงสดสำหรับอ่างล้างหน้าและโต๊ะเครื่องแป้ง ตัวห้องสามารถมองเห็นโต๊ะเครื่องแป้งผ่านกระจกขนาดใหญ่ กระจกถูกติดอยู่ด้านบนเคาน์เตอร์โดยมีขาโลหะเรียวเล็กสองขา ตามโบรชัวร์ได้รับรองแก่ผู้ที่สูบบุหรี่ (หรือบางที เจ้าของโรงแรมซึ่งวิตกกังวลกับเรื่องดังกล่าว) ว่าพื้นผิวแนวยาวทั้งหมดเป็น "ฟอร์ไมก้าที่สวยงาม" กล่าวคือ "จะไม่มีร่องรอยคราบแอลกอฮอล์หรือรอยไหม้จากบุหรี่จากแขกผู้มาพักคนก่อนหลงเหลือไว้บนพื้นผิวของฟอร์ไมก้าเลย" โบรชัวร์ได้ระบุว่าความหรูหรา คือ การที่ทุกสิ่งทุกอย่างดูใหม่อยู่เสมอ

ในช่วงแรก ผลิตภัณฑ์ฟอร์ไมก้าที่เสนอให้แก่ผู้บริโภคจำกัดอยู่เพียงสีเข้ม ลายไม้และลายหินอ่อนเท่านั้น แต่ในภายหลังได้ใช้เมลามีนเรซินผลิตแผ่นลามิเนทจนได้สีสันและลวดลายที่ชัดเจน ในปี ค.ศ. 1938 บริษัทฟอร์ไมก้าจึงพร้อมที่จะขยายไปยังตลาดผู้บริโภค โฆษณาสวยๆได้ถูกตีพิมพ์ในนิตยสารหลายฉบับ เช่น นิตยสาร *Architectural Record* นิตยสาร *Good Housekeeping* และนิตยสาร *House Beautiful* ซึ่งแสดงถึงศักยภาพของฟอร์ไมก้าให้บรรดานักออกแบบและเจ้าของบ้านได้เห็น ในการทำตลาดทางตรงส่วนหนึ่งฟอร์ไมก้าได้ว่าจ้างที่ปรึกษาด้านการออกแบบภายนอกคนแรก บรู๊ค สตีเว่น ซึ่งเป็นนักออกแบบอุตสาหกรรมแห่งมิลวอกี เขายังเป็นสมาชิกผู้ก่อตั้งสังคมการออกแบบอุตสาหกรรมแห่งอเมริกา ที่มีชื่อเสียงมากในด้านการออกแบบเรือ รถไฟ และรถยนต์ เขาได้ให้คำปรึกษาแก่บริษัทซึ่งกำลังพัฒนาการใช้ไม้ธรรมชาติแท้ว่า การใช้ผลิตภัณฑ์จากป่า

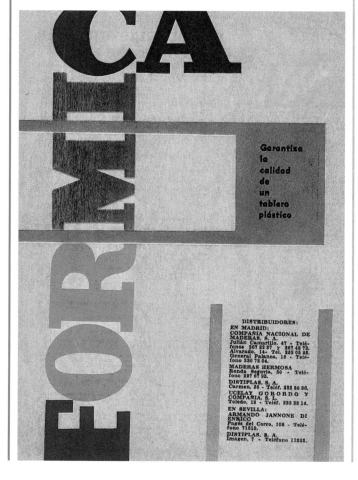

FORMICA

Garantiza la calidad de un tablero plástico

DISTRIBUIDORES:
EN MADRID:
COMPAÑIA NACIONAL DE MADERAS, S. A.
Julián Camarillo, 47 - Teléfonos 367 32 37 y 267 48 73.
Alvarado, 14 - Tel. 253 05 28.
General Palanca, 18 - Teléfono 230 72 04.
MADERAS HERMOSA
Ronda Segovia, 50 - Teléfono 227 67 25.
DISTIPLAS, S. A.
Carmen, 26 - Teléf. 232 36 26.
UCELAY GORORDO Y COMPAÑIA, S. L.
Toledo, 13 - Teléf. 222 22 14.
EN SEVILLA:
ARMANDO JANNONE DI ENRICO
Parés del Corro, 108 - Teléfono 71810.
DISTIPLAS, S. A.
Imagen, 7 - Teléfono 11233.

357

société Miller Brewing Company et la table basse contemporaine au dessus en verre d'Isamu Noguchi. Skylark est le résultat de la contribution de Stevens à la société Formica pour l'apport du matériau hors de la sphère de l'imitation et à l'intérieur des courants de design modernes. Le motif Skylark est souvent attribué à un designer industriel mieux connu, Raymond Loewy, qui a succédé à Stevens comme conseiller de la société. Mais le bureau Loewy a simplement modifié la teinte de Skylark en 1954, quand il a été rebaptisé « Boomerang ». Si le motif Sequin suggérait le luxe dans les années 1950, Skylark a joué avec les formes de l'époque atomique naissante, soulignant les associations émergentes de stratifié Formica avec les nouvelles formes de déplacement à grande vitesse.

Stevens, qui a travaillé pour la société Formica de 1946 à 1952, a conçu simultanément une série de nouveaux trains pour les chemins de fer de Chicago, Milwaukee, St. Paul et Pacific Railroad (Milwaukee Road), connus comme Olympian Hiawatha, qui allaient de Chicago au Pacifique Nord-Ouest. Le bureau de Stevens était responsable de tous les aspects de la conception du train, de la création d'un nouveau moteur avec les phares superposés au salon d'observation avec des fenêtres en forme de losanges sur les murs et au plafond en forme de dôme, en passant par l'aménagement intérieur et les acces-

de Formica Company a Stevens de llevar el material fuera del reino de la imitación a las corrientes del diseño moderno. A menudo, el diseño Skylark se le atribuye al conocido diseñador industrial Raymond Loewy, quien siguió los pasos de Stevens como asesor de la empresa. Sin embargo, mientras Loewy estuvo en el puesto, apenas volvió a darle color a Skylark en 1954, cuando, además, se le cambió el nombre a "Boomerang". Si el diseño Sequin sugería lujo a finales de la década de los cincuenta, Skylark jugaba con las formas del inicio de la era atómica, al señalar las asociaciones emergentes del laminado Formica con las nuevas formas de viaje a alta velocidad.

Stevens, que trabajó para Formica Company desde 1946 hasta 1952, estaba, al mismo tiempo, diseñando una serie de trenes nuevos para el Ferrocarril de Chicago, Milwaukee, St. Paul y el Pacífico (también denominado Milwaukee Road), conocidos como los trenes Olympian Hiawatha, que viajaban desde Chicago hasta la región noroeste del Pacífico. La firma de Stevens fue la responsable de todos los aspectos del diseño del tren, desde la creación de un nuevo motor con faros delanteros dispuestos en forma vertical, un salón de observación con ventanas con forma de rombo sobre las paredes y cielorrasos abovedados, para los detalles y los accesorios del interior. La mayor parte de estos se hizo con el laminado Formica. Los colores tradicionales del Milwaukee Road eran el anaranjado rojizo y el granate real, las bases de una franja de dos tonos en el exterior del tren (granate arriba, anaranjado abajo). Stevens continuó con el efecto de los dos tonos en el interior, al reemplazar una combinación más suave de gris verdoso uniforme y paneles de Realwood en los vagones. En el salón para damas, Realwood fue reemplazado por un laminado marfil que presentaba estampados de trajes franceses y estampados floreados incorporados en paredes opuestas. En el vagón del restaurante, el laminado Formica tomó el lugar del tradicional papel tapiz, con paneles en un color verde pálido con un diseño de hojas secas y con la parte superior de las mesas haciendo juego. En una sala de dibujos con paneles de Oak Realwood, había acuarelas de aves acuáti-

ta hullaantumisesta ameebaan, joka näkyy Stevensin myöhemmästä ikonisesta logosta Miller Brewing Companylle ja Isamu Noguchin nykyajan lasipintaisesta kahvipöydästä. Skylark on osuva tulos Formica-yhtiön Stevensille antamasta tehtävästä tuoda materiaali ulos jäljittelyn maailmasta nykyaikaisen suunnittelun suuntaan. Skylarkin suunnittelu luetaan usein paremmin tunnetun teollisen suunnittelijan Raymond Loewyn ansioiksi, joka seurasi Stevensiä konsulttina yhtiölle. Loewyn toimisto kuitenkin vain väritti uudelleen Skylarkin v. 1954, kun sen nimeksi muutettiin "Boomerang". Jos Sequin viittasikin ylellisyyteen 1950-luvun loppupuolella, Skylark leikitteli sarastavan atomiajan muodoilla, osoittaen Formica-laminaatin lisääntyvään yhteyteen korkealla nopeudella matkustamisen uusien muotojen kanssa.

Stevens, joka oli Formica-yhtiön palveluksessa vuosina 1946 – 1952, oli samanaikaisesti suunnittelemassa sarjan uusia junia Chicago, Milwaukee, St. Paul, ja Pacific Railroad (eli Milwaukee Road) yhtiölle, joka tunnetaan nimellä Olympian Hiawatha ja joka liikennöi Chicagosta luoteiselle Tyynelle merelle. Stevensin toimiston tehtävänä oli kaikki näkökohdat junan suunnittelussa, uuden veturin luominen kerrostettuine ajovaloineen, näköalavaunu, jossa oli vinoneliön muotoiset ikkunat seinillä ja kupumainen katto, sekä sisustustarvikkeet ja varusteet. Suuri osa viimeksi mainituista tehtiin asiaan sopivasti Formica-laminaattia käyttäen. Milwaukee Roadin perinteiset värit olivat sadonkorjuun oranssi ja kuninkaallinen punaisenruskea, lähtökohtana kaksiväriselle juovalle junan ulkosivulla (punaisenruskea yläpuolella, oranssi alla). Stevens jatkoi kaksiväristä vaikutelmaa sisustuksessa, korvaamalla vaisumman yksiväristen harmaanvihreän ja Realwood-paneloinnin yhdistelmän vaunuissa. Naisten salongissa Realwood vaihdettiin norsunluun väriseen laminaattiin, jossa oli ranskalaisasujen ja kukkien kuviot upotettuina vastakkaisilla seinillä. Ravintolavaunussa perinteinen seinäpaperi korvattiin Formica-laminaatilla, jossa oli kalpean vihreät paneelit varisevien lehtien nimisellä kuviolla, sekä vastaavat pöytien pinnat. Oak Realwood -paneloidussa salongissa kotoperäisten

認為雲雀是一個更大的迷戀阿米巴的現代主義者，反映在史蒂文斯後期標誌性的米勒釀酒公司(Miller Brewing Company)的徽標和勇野口的當代玻璃面咖啡桌上。雲雀正是史蒂文斯受富美家公司之託，讓材料走出模仿的境界，進入現代設計激流的作品。雲雀的設計往往歸功於更知名的工業設計師雷蒙德·洛伊(RaymondLoewy)，他在史蒂文斯之後成為該公司的顧問。但洛伊的辦公室只是在1954為雲雀重新著色，當時它被更名為「回飛鏢」。如果亮片在二十世紀五十年代意味著奢侈，那雲雀就是利用即將來臨的原子時代的形狀，預示著富美家美耐板與高速旅遊的新形式即將出現的聯手。

史蒂文斯在1946年至1952年曾就任富美家公司，同時為在芝加哥、密爾沃基、聖保羅和被稱為奧林匹亞-西亞瓦塔(Olympian Hiawatha)的芝加哥與太平洋西北之間的太平洋鐵路設計了一套新火車。史蒂文斯的公司負責火車設計的各個方面，從創作疊層式前燈的新引擎，到觀察休息室牆上的菱形窗戶和拱形天花板和室內配件和附件。最合適的是後者的大部分都是用富美家美耐板製作。密爾沃基路的傳統顏色是收穫的橙色和皇家栗色，也是火車外部的雙色條紋(栗色在上，橙色在下)的底色。史蒂文斯在內部裝飾方面繼續使用這種雙色基調，在車廂內代之以灰綠的實色和真木鑲板的微妙組合。在婦女休息室內，真木用象牙美耐板取代，突出了鑲嵌在對面牆壁上的法國服裝印花和花卉圖案。在餐車內，富美家美耐板取代了傳統的壁紙，牆板是淺綠色落葉圖案和與之相配的桌面。在橡樹真木鑲板的繪畫室內，當地水禽的水彩畫被嵌進了富美家美耐板。史蒂文斯的目地是在鐵路上重新創建逼真的家居體驗，雖然是個人口眾多的大家庭(奧林匹亞-西亞瓦塔的廣告經常突出家庭，強調列車對大家

种直接市场营销的一部分，富美家公司还首次聘请了外部设计顾问——密尔沃基市工业设计师布鲁克斯·史蒂文斯(Brooks Stevens)。他是美国工业设计协会创始成员之一，以轮船、火车和汽车上的作品而著称。他在富美家公司开发真木时向该公司提供咨询，他开始相信，用摄影再现木材就足够时使用森林产品是"可笑之极"。他的解决办法被称为"赛木"(Luxwood)，并于1950年引入时作为一种较便宜、外观似木料的替代品推销。

史蒂文斯还为富美家公司创造了第一个图形发明，即1950年引入的静物"云雀"图形。在《工业强度设计：布鲁克斯·史蒂文斯如何塑造您的世界》(Industrial Strength Design: How Brooks Stevens Shaped Your World)一书中，设计史学家兼研究员格伦·亚当森(Glenn Adamson)认为云雀是一个更大的迷恋阿米巴的现代主义者，反映在史蒂文斯后期标志性的米勒酿酒公司(Miller Brewing Company)的徽标和勇野口的当代玻璃面咖啡桌上。云雀正是史蒂文斯受富美家公司之托，让材料走出模仿的境界，进入现代设计激流的作品。云雀的设计往往归功于更知名的工业设计师雷蒙德·洛伊(Raymond Loewy)，他在史蒂文斯之后成为该公司的顾问。但洛伊的办公室只是在1954为云雀重新着色，当时它被更名为"回飞镖"。如果亮片在二十世纪五十年代意味着奢侈，那云雀就是利用即将来临的原子时代的形状，预示着富美家®装饰耐火板与高速旅游的新形式即将出现的联手。

史蒂文斯在1946年至1952年曾就任富美家公司，同时为在芝加哥、密尔沃基、圣保罗和被称为奥林匹亚-西亚瓦塔(Olympian Hiawatha)的芝加哥与太平洋西北之间的太平洋铁路设计了一套新火车。史蒂文斯的公司负责火车设计的各个方面，从创作叠层式前灯的新引擎，到观察休息室墙

ไม้เป็น "สิ่งที่ไร้สาระ" เพราะการใช้สำเนาภาพถ่ายของไม้ก็เพียงพอแล้ว เขาได้เสนอให้ใช้ "ลักซ์วู้ด" เพราะมีราคาที่ถูกกว่าและมีลักษณะที่เหมือนกัน ซึ่งต่อมาได้มีการทำตลาดเป็นครั้งแรกในช่วงปี ค.ศ. 1950

สตีเว่นยังเป็นผู้รับผิดชอบสิ่งประดิษฐ์กราฟิกชิ้นแรกของบริษัท คือ ลายสกายลาร์ค ซึ่งเปิดตัวในปี ค.ศ. 1950 และยังคงเป็นสัญลักษณ์อยู่แม้ในขณะนี้ ใน Industrial Strength Design: How Brooks Stevens Shaped Your World นักประวัติศาสตร์ด้านการออกแบบและภัณฑารักษ์เกร็น อดัมสัน โต้แย้งว่าลายสกายลาร์ค คือความหลงใหลในอะมีบาของคนสมัยใหม่ ซึ่งสะท้อนให้เห็นในโลโก้สัญลักษณ์ของบริษัท มิลเลอร์ บริว คอมพานี และโต๊ะกาแฟทันสมัยที่มีด้านบนเป็นกระจกของอิซามุ โนกูจิ ของสตีเว่นในเวลาต่อมา ลายสกายลาร์คเป็นผลลัพธ์อันเหมาะสมที่เกิดจากการที่ฟอร์ไมก้าได้อบให้สตีเว่นเป็นผู้รับผิดชอบพัฒนาลวดลายให้หลุดออกจากขอบเขตการเลียนแบบและลายเป็นการออกแบบสมัยใหม่ในปัจจุบัน การออกแบบลายสกายลาร์คมักถูกมองว่าเป็นลักษณะเฉพาะของเรย์มอน โลวีย์ นักออกแบบอุตสาหกรรมที่เป็นที่รู้จักมากกว่า ผู้ซึ่งตามรอยสตีเว่นในการเป็นที่ปรึกษาให้ฟอร์ไมก้าสำนักงานของโลวีย์เพียงแต่เปลี่ยนสีสกายลาร์คโฉมใหม่ในปี ค.ศ. 1954 ในขณะที่ลายสกายลาร์คถูกเปลี่ยนชื่อเป็น "บูมเมอแรง" ถ้าลวดลายเลื่อมทองถือเป็นความหรูหราในช่วงหลังศตวรรษที่ 1950 ลายสกายลาร์คก็กำลังเล่นกับรูปทรงในช่วงระยะเริ่มแรกของยุคปรมาณู ซึ่งบ่งชี้ถึงความเชื่อมโยงอย่างเฉียบพลันของฟอร์ไมก้าที่มีต่อรูปแบบใหม่ของการเดินทางด้วยความเร็วสูง

สตีเว่น ซึ่งทำงานให้ฟอร์ไมก้าตั้งแต่ปี ค.ศ. 1946 ถึง 1952 ในขณะเดียวกันก็ได้ออกแบบรถไฟใหม่ชุดหนึ่งสำหรับชิคาโกมิลวอกี เซ็นต์ พอล และแปซิฟิกเรลโรด (เรียกอีกชื่อหนึ่งว่า ถนนมิลวอกี) ซึ่งรู้จักกันดีในชื่อ โอลิมเปียน เฮียวาทา ซึ่งเดินทางจากชิคาโกไปยังแปซิฟิกตะวันตกเฉียงเหนือบริษัทของสตีเว่นเป็นผู้รับผิดชอบการออกแบบรถไฟในทุกด้าน ตั้งแต่การผลิตเครื่องยนต์ใหม่ซึ่งมีไฟหน้าเรียงกันไปจนถึงเลานจ์สังเกตการที่มีหน้าต่างทรงสี่เหลี่ยมขนมเปียกปูนบนผนังและเพดานโค้งไปจนถึงการประดับตกแต่งภายใน การประดับตกแต่งภายในอย่างเหมาะสม จำนวนมากได้ทำร่วมกับฟอร์ไมก้า สีดั้งเดิมของถนนมิลวอกีนั้นคือ สีส้มของฤดูเก็บเกี่ยวและสีแดงม่วงเข้มอมน้ำตาล ซึ่งเป็นที่มาของแถบสีสองสีด้าน

soires. Le stratifié Formica était largement utilisé dans ce dernier. Les teintes traditionnelles Milwaukee Road étaient l'orange paille et le marron royal, la base de la ligne Bicolore sur l'extérieur du train (marron audessus, orange en bas). Stevens a poursuivi l'effet bicolore à l'intérieur, en utilisant une subtile combinaison de panneaux gris-vert uni et Realwood dans les voitures. Dans le salon des femmes, Realwood était remplacé par le stratifié ivoire, avec imprimés de costumes français, et des motifs floraux étaient incrustés sur les murs opposés. Dans le wagon-restaurant, le stratifié Formica a pris la place du papier peint traditionnel, avec des panneaux vert pâle, feuille morte et des dessus de table assortis. Dans un compartiment-salon lambrissé de chêne Realwood, des aquarelles d'oiseaux aquatiques indigènes ont été incrustées dans le stratifié Formica. Le but de Stevens était de recréer une ambiance de logement familial sur les rails, quoique pour un grand nombre de familles (les publicités Olympian Hiawatha présentaient souvent des familles et mettaient l'accent sur le service dans le train comme lieu de vacances populaire, comme dans le cas du parc national de Yellowstone). Il a déclaré ce qui suit au magazine spécialisé *Plastics Newsfront* : « Dans le train Olympian Hiawatha, les teintes vives et joyeuses et l'utilisation discrète de bois et de plastique se combinent pour produire un intérieur intime par opposition à l'aspect ingrat de certains équipements de transport qui, en général, offrent une atmosphère très froide avec des moulures de chrome et des éclairages bizarres. » Comme au Terrace Plaza Hotel, le stratifié de la marque Formica a permis aux designers de créer un environnement familier et en même temps indestructible.

Le stratifié Formica avait été utilisé auparavant dans les trains (notamment sur le Train of Tomorrow de General Motors et le Jeffersonian de Pennsylvania Railroad), mais jamais de manière aussi intensive et aussi intégrée. Les paquebots de luxe ont emboîté le pas. Le stratifié blanc Formica a été installé dans toutes les salles de bain du Queen Mary de

cas autóctonas incrustadas en el laminado Formica. El objetivo de Stevens era recrear una minuciosa experiencia local en los trenes, aunque era para una gran cantidad de familias (los anuncios publicitarios del Olympian Hiawatha solían mostrar familias y hacer hincapié en el servicio del tren hasta centros vacacionales populares, como el Parque Nacional de Yellowstone). Le comentó a la revista *Plastics Newsfront*: "En el Olympian Hiawatha, los colores vivos, alegres y el uso discreto de la madera y el plástico se combinan para crear un interior acogedor, en contraste con la apariencia uniforme de algunos mobiliarios de medios de transporte que, en general, han tenido una atmósfera muy fría, adornados, tal como estaban, con molduras cromadas y una disposición estrambótica de las luces". Como en el Terrace Plaza Hotel, donde el laminado de la marca Formica les permitió a los diseñadores crear ambientes parecidos a los hogares.

Anteriormente, el laminado Formica se había estado utilizando en trenes (en especial, en el "Tren del futuro" de General Motors y en el "Jeffersonian" del Ferrocarril de Pensilvania), pero nunca tan ampliamente y de manera tan integrada. Los transatlánticos de lujo siguieron su ejemplo. Se instalaron laminados Formica, color blanco, en todos los baños del Queen Mary de la compañía de cruceros Cunard, cuando comenzó a brindar servicios en 1936, pero los salones públicos tenían paneles de madera real. Loewy, el diseñador de Formica Company desde 1954 hasta 1960, utilizó el laminado para los paneles, los aparadores y las partes superiores de mesas en el reacondicionamiento del SS *Lurline*, que viajó entre San Francisco y Honolulu desde 1948 hasta 1963. Sin embargo, el Queen Elizabeth 2 de la compañía de cruceros Cunard, en servicio desde 1969 hasta 2009, fue el transatlántico que el arquitecto naval Dan Wallace y el diseñador de interiores Dennis Lennon fueron capaces de tratar como un proyecto completo de diseño con laminado Formica, al desarrollar un nuevo laminado texturizado y moldeable que brindaba la sensación de ser un tejido para usar de manera extensiva a bordo. En una publicación especial, "The Formica Scene of the QE2", se incluye un cua-

vesilintujen vesivärikuvia sulautettiin Formica-laminaattiin. Stevensin tavoitteena oli toistaa yksityiskohtaiset kotikokemukset kiskojen päällä, vaikkakin suurille määrille perheitä (Olympian Hiawathan mainoksissa oli usein perheitä ja niissä tähdennettiin junan liikennöintiä suosittuihin lomakohteisiin, kuten Yellowstone-kansallispuisto). Hän kertoi alan *Plastics Newsfront* -nimiselle lehdelle: "Olympian Hiawatha -junassa kirkkaat iloiset värit sekä puun ja muovin hillitty käyttö yhdistävät tuottamaan kodikkaan sisustuksen, verrattuna joidenkin kuljetusvälineiden jäykkään ulkonäköön, joissa yleensä oli hyvin kylmä ilmapiiri, kun niissä näkyi koristeina kromilistoja ja eriskummallisia valojärjestelyjä". Terrace Plaza Hotellin tavoin Formica-merkkinen laminaatti antoi suunnittelijoiden luoda kotoisen ympäristön, joka myös sattui olemaan käytännöllisesti katsoen luodinkestävä.

Formica-laminaattia oli käytetty junissa ennenkin (huomattavimmin General Motorsin huomispäivän junassa ja Pennsylvania Railroadin Jeffersonian-junassa), mutta ei koskaan näin laajamittaisesti ja tällaisella integroidulla tavalla. Ylelliset valtamerialukset seurasivat esimerkkiä. Valkoinen Formica-laminaatti asennettiin Cunardin *Queen Mary* -aluksen kaikkiin kylpyhuoneisiin, sen tullessa liikenteeseen v. 1936, mutta julkisissa tiloissa oli aito puupanelointi. Loewy, Formica-yhtiön suunnittelija vuosina 1954 - 1960, käytti laminaattia panelointiin, lipastoihin ja pöydän pintoihin uudelleen varustetussa SS *Lurline* -aluksessa, joka liikennöi San Franciscon ja Honolulun väliä vuosina 1948 - 1963. Cunardin *Queen Elizabeth 2*, palveluksessa vuosina 1969 - 2009, oli kuitenkin valtamerialus, jota laivanrakennusinsinööri Dan Wallace ja sisustussuunnittelija Dennis Lennon pystyivät käsittelemään kokonaisena Formica-laminaatin suunnitteluprojektina, kehittäen laajaa laivalla käyttöä varten uuden teksturoidun ja notkean laminaatin, joka tuntui kudotulta kankaalta. Erikoisjulkaisu, "The Formica Scene of the QE2," sisältää takasivulla taulukossa tusinoittain projektissa käytettyjä värejä, kuvioita ja pintakäsittelyjä. Kohokohtien joukossa ovat teksturoitu kukka-aiheinen kudekuvio sinistä valkoisella naistenhuoneissa, mustaval-

都喜歡去的度假勝地（如黃石國家公園）的服務）。他告訴行業雜誌《塑膠新聞頭條版》(Plastics Newsfront)說：「在奧林匹亞-西亞瓦塔，明亮、歡快的色彩和謹慎使用木材和塑膠相結合，形成溫馨的家庭內部，相比之下一些運輸設備用鉻裝飾條和奇異的照明，使氣氛嚴肅拘束，通常顯得格外冰冷。」正像在露臺廣場酒店那樣，富美家品牌的美耐板使設計師能夠創造出居家的環境，恰好還具有防彈的實際功能。

富美家美耐板以前曾在火車上使用(最引人注目的是通用汽車公司的「明日火車」和賓夕法尼亞鐵路的「傑斐遜機車」)，但從未像這樣廣泛，以這樣一種綜合的方式應用。豪華的遠洋客輪也紛紛效仿。當「瑪麗女王號」1936年開始投入使用時，白色的富美家美耐板被安裝在所有的浴室內，但公用艙室卻使用了真正的木鑲板。1954年至1960年任職富美家公司的設計師洛伊，把美耐板用在改裝的SS Lurline號鑲板、梳粧檯和桌面上，這艘豪華客輪在1948年至1963年期間往返於舊金山和檀香山之間。不過，1969年至2009年運行的丘納德「女王伊麗莎白二號」海輪卻被海軍建築師丹·華萊士（Dan Wallace）和室內設計師丹尼斯·列儂(Dennis Lennon)當成了整個富美家美耐板設計項目，開發了一種帶有織物感的新紋理和模壓複合美耐板，在這艘船上廣泛使用。一份名為《伊麗莎白二號的富美家景致》(The Formica Scene of the QE2)特刊的背頁上包括該項目使用的數十種顏色、圖案和面漆圖表。其中的亮點是女士盥洗室裡白底藍紋花案的編織物，男士盥洗室的黑白佩斯利渦紋圖案，淋浴間和衛生間的千格鳥遊戲圖案，以及夜總會、咖啡廳和兒童遊戲室內特別定製的富美家美耐板壁畫。

在女王伊麗莎白二號上，彩練主題佔主導地位，反映了二十世紀六十年

上的菱形窗戶和拱形天花板和室内配件和附件。最合適的是後者的大部分都是用富美家®裝飾耐火板制作。密尔沃基路的傳統顏色是收获的橙色和皇家栗色，也是火車外部的雙色條紋(栗色在上，橙色在下)的底色。史蒂文斯在内部裝飾方面繼續使用這種雙色基調，在車廂内代之以灰綠的实色和真木鑲板的微妙组合。在婦女休息室内，真木用象牙耐火板取代，突出了鑲嵌在对面墙壁上的法国服裝印花和花卉图案。在餐車内，富美家®裝飾耐火板取代了傳統的壁紙，墙板是浅绿色落叶图案和与之相配的桌面。在橡树真木鑲板的绘画室内，当地水禽的水彩画被嵌进了富美家®裝飾耐火板。史蒂文斯的目的是在铁路上重新创建逼真的家居体验，虽然是个人口众多的大家庭(奧林匹亚-西亚瓦塔的广告经常突出家庭，强调列车对大家都喜欢去的度假胜地(如黄石国家公园)的服务)。他告訴行業雜誌《塑料新闻头版》(Plastics Newsfront)说：「在奧林匹亚-西亚瓦塔，明亮、欢快的色彩和謹慎使用木材和塑料相结合，形成温馨的家庭内部，相比之下一些运输设备用铬装饰条和奇异的照明，使气氛严肃拘束，通常显得格外冰冷。」正像在露台广场酒店那样，富美家品牌的耐火板使設計師能够创造出居家的环境，恰好还具有防弹的实际功能。

富美家®裝飾耐火板以前曾在火車上使用(最引人注目的是通用汽車公司的"明日火車"和宾夕法尼亚铁路的"杰斐逊机车")，但从未像這樣廣泛，以这样一种综合的方式应用。豪華的遠洋客輪也纷纷效仿。當"瑪丽女王号"1936年開始投入使用时，白色的富美家®裝飾耐火板被安裝在所有的浴室内，但公用艙室卻使用了真正的木鑲板。1954年至1960年任職富美家公司的設計師洛伊，把耐火板用在改裝的SS Lurline号鑲板、梳妆台和桌面上，這艘豪華客輪在1948年至1963年期間往返于旧金山和檀香山之

นอกรถไฟ (สีม่วงเข้มอมน้ำตาลด้านบน สีส้มด้านล่าง) สตีเว่นยังได้ใช้โทนสีสองสีนี้ภายในรถไฟแทนการผสมสีเทา – เขียวและแผ่นไม้ธรรมชาติแท้ภายในตู้โดยสาร ภายในเลาจน์ของสุภาพสตรี ไม้ธรรมชาติแท้ได้ถูกแทนที่ด้วยแผ่นลามิเนตสีงาช้าง ซึ่งพิมพ์ภาพชุดเครื่องแต่งกายฝรั่งเศสและภาพดอกไม้ฝังเลี่ยมอยู่ในผนังฝั่งตรงข้าม ในตู้ขบวนห้องอาหาร แผ่นลามิเนตฟอร์ไมก้าได้เข้ามาแทนที่วอลล์เปเปอร์ดั้งเดิม โดยใช้วัสดุบุผนังลวดลายใบไม้ร่วงสีเขียวอ่อนซึ่งเข้ากับพื้นผิวด้านบนของโต๊ะ ภายในห้องรับแขกถูกตกแต่งด้วยวัสดุบุผนังไม้โอ๊คแท้ และมีภาพนกน้ำพื้นเมืองที่วาดด้วยสีน้ำฝังอยู่ในแผ่นลามิเนตฟอร์ไมก้า เป้าหมายของสตีเว่นคือ ต้องการสร้างประสบการณ์เสมือนอยู่ในบ้านที่มีรายละเอียดมากมายบนขบวนรถไฟ ถึงแม้ว่าในแต่ละขบวนจะมีหลายครอบครัวก็ตาม (บนโฆษณาของโอลิมเปียน เฮียวาทามักปรากฏภาพครอบครัวและเน้นถึงบริการขนส่งไปยังจุดพักผ่อนที่ได้รับความนิยม เช่น อุทยานแห่งชาติเยลโล่ว์สโตน) เขาบอกนิตยสารการค้า *Plastic Newsfront* ว่า "บนรถไฟโอลิมเปียน เฮียวาทา มีการใช้สีสันสดใส่ว่าเร็งประกอบกับการผสมผสานไม้และพลาสติกอย่างลงตัวเพื่อสร้างบรรยากาศภายในที่อบอุ่นเสมือนอยู่บ้าน ซึ่งตรงข้ามกับรูปลักษณ์เดิม ๆ ของอุปกรณ์ขนส่งบางชนิดซึ่งโดยทั่วไปจะให้บรรยากาศที่แสนจะเย็นชาเพราะถูกตกแต่งด้วยโครเมียมขึ้นรูปและการจัดแสงไฟที่แปลกประหลาด" ดังเช่นที่โรงแรมเทอเรส พลาซ่า แผ่นลามิเนตฟอร์ไมก้าทำให้นักออกแบบสามารถจัดบรรยากาศได้เสมือนอยู่บ้าน ทั้งยังกันกระสุนได้จริงอีกด้วย

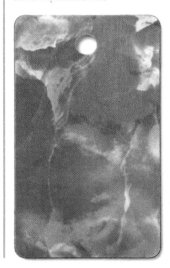

Cunard lors de sa mise en service en 1936 même si les salles publiques étaient décorées de bois réel. Loewy, designer de la société Formica de 1954 à 1960, a utilisé le stratifié comme lambris, commodes et dessus de tables pour le remontage du SS *Lurline*, qui circulait entre San Francisco et Honolulu entre 1948 et 1963. Mais le *Queen Elizabeth 2* de Cunard, en service de 1969 à 2009, était le paquebot que l'architecte naval Dan Wallace et le designer d'intérieur Dennis Lennon avaient traité comme un projet totalement en stratifié Formica. Ils ont développé un nouveau stratifié texturé et moulable avec aspect de tissu pour supporter une rude utilisation à bord. Une publication spéciale, « The Formica Scene of the QE2 », inclut en dernière page un tableau des douzaines de couleurs, motifs et finis utilisés pour le projet. On y notait par exemple une texture florale tissée bleu sur blanc dans les salles de bain des dames, un motif de paisley noir et blanc pour celles des hommes, du pied-de-poule dans les douches et les toilettes et plusieurs murales de stratifié sur mesure Formica pour la boîte de nuit, le café et les chambres d'enfants.

Sur le *QE2* prévaut un thème très graphique qui fait référence aux murales peintes du début des années 1960 par Barbara Stauffacher Solomon pour Sea Ranch en Californie du Nord et à l'animation groovy de *Yellow Submarine* des Beatles, de 1968. Dans le bar du foyer du théâtre se trouve un mur de fanions nautiques rouges, bleus et or, créé en stratifié Formica avec un fini suédine et reprenant sur le rouge du revêtement d'un ensemble de fauteuils Bertoia Diamond. Dans le restaurant Britannia, les sièges en stratifié postformé ou au bord roulé sont habillés d'orange pour s'harmoniser à une paire de niches à garniture stratifiée orange de Formica. Une murale figurative noire et blanche conçue par des étudiants du London's Royal College of Art a été reproduite en stratifié Formica sur le long couloir qui relie deux des agréables restaurants. Dans les chambres, la couleur est moins vive mais les nouveaux stratifiés incurvés sont utilisés pour les dessus de table et les tiroirs de commode, éliminant ainsi les arêtes tranchantes dans les

dro en la página final con la gran cantidad de colores, diseños y acabados que se usaron para el proyecto. Entre lo más destacado, se puede mencionar un tejido texturizado floral en color azul sobre fondo blanco en el tocador de damas y un estampado de cachemira color negro y blanco para el de los caballeros, un diseño de pata de gallo en las duchas y baños, y varios murales de laminado Formica personalizados para el club nocturno, el café y el salón de niños.

En el *Queen Elizabeth 2* (QE2) prevalece una temática que abunda en gráficos, que hace referencia tanto a los murales pintados durante el inicio de la década de los sesenta por Barbara Stauffacher Solomon para Sea Ranch en el norte de California, como a la estupenda animación de *Yellow Submarine* de los Beatles en 1968. En el vestíbulo de bar del teatro, hay una pared de gallardetes náuticos color rojo, azul y dorado, creados en un laminado Formica con acabado tipo gamuza que resalta el tapizado color rojo de un juego de sillas Bertoia Diamond. En el restaurante Britannia, se observan asientos de laminado con un borde postformado u ondulado, tapizados en color anaranjado para que combinen con un juego anaranjado de nichos adornados con laminado Formica. Un mural figurativo color negro y blanco, diseñado por estudiantes de la universidad Royal College of Art de Londres, se reprodujo en laminado Formica y cubre el extenso pasillo entre los dos restaurantes informales. En las habitaciones para huéspedes, el color es más sobrio, pero los nuevos laminados curvos se utilizan en la parte superior de mesas y en las gavetas de los aparadores; de esta manera, se eliminan los bordes filosos en los camarotes pequeños. En los trenes Hiawatha, Stevens aspiraba a lo hogareño, mientras que Dennis Lennon, casi veinte años después, desafiaba los límites del plástico, al tratar de eliminar tantas uniones y materiales adicionales como fuera posible, para hacer de todo el barco una obra de arte que requiriera poco mantenimiento.

Mientras que el laminado de la marca Formica se abrió camino a través de los Estados Unidos y el mundo aportando sofisticación a los viajes, también tuvo un gran impacto en los

FORMICA® BRAND · laminated plastic · FRENCH BLUE 928 · -64 SUEDE

koinen kašmirkuviointi miestenhuoneissa, kukonaskelkuvio suihkuissa ja vessoissa ja monia tilauksesta tehtyjä Formica-laminaattisia seinätauluja yökerhoa, kahvibaaria ja lasten huonetta varten.

QE2-aluksella vallitsee supergraafinen teema, joka viittaa sekä Barbara Stauffacher Solomonin seinätauluihin 1960-luvun alkupuolelta Sea Ranchia varten pohjois-Kaliforniassa, että hauskaan animaatioon Beatlesin *keltaisesta sukellusveneestä* vuodelta 1968. Teatterin baarilämpiössä on seinä punaisia, sinisiä ja kullanvärisiä merenkulkuviirejä, jotka on tehty mokkapäällysteisestä Formica-laminaatista ja käyvät yhteen Bertoia Diamond -tuoliryhmän punaisen verhoilun kanssa. Britannia-ravintolassa laminaattiset istuimet jälkimuovattuine tai käännettyine reunoineen on verhoiltu oranssin värisiksi vastaamaan oranssin värisellä Formica-laminaatilla koristeltuja seinäsyvennyksiä. Mustavalkoinen kuvaannollinen seinätaulu, jonka suunnittelijoina olivat opiskelijat Lontoon Royal College of Art -oppilaitoksesta, kopioitiin Formica-laminaattia käyttäen ja reunustaa pitkää käytävää kahden vapaamuotoisen ravintolan välillä. Vierashuoneissa väri on hillitympi, mutta uusia kaarevia laminaatteja käytetään pöytien pinnoissa ja lipastojen laatikoissa, eliminoiden terävät reunat pienissä hyteissä. Hiawatha-junissa Stevens pyrki viihtyisyyteen ja Dennis Lennon, lähes kaksikymmentä vuotta myöhemmin, testasi muovin äärirajoja, yrittäen eliminoida mahdollisimman monet saumat ja ylimääräiset materiaalit, tehdäkseen koko laivasta helppohoitoisen taideteoksen.

代初的兩幅壁畫風格，一幅是由芭芭拉·斯托費舍爾·所羅門 (Barbara Stauffacher Solomon) 為加利福尼亞州北部的海洋農場所繪，另一幅是披頭士 1968 年「黃色潛水艇」的絕妙動漫。在劇院酒吧大堂，掛滿了紅、藍、金色航海信號旗的牆壁用絨面富美家美耐板完成，襯托著一組 Bertoia 鑽石椅的紅色罩面。在不列顛餐廳，再成形或卷邊美耐板座椅配以橙色罩面，與一組橙色美耐板鑲邊的壁龕相匹配。由倫敦皇家藝術學院學生設計的黑白寓意壁畫用富美家美耐板複製，懸掛在兩個休閒餐廳之間的長廊內。在客房內，色彩較為收斂，但新的曲面美耐板用在桌面和梳粧檯抽屜上，消除了小客艙裡的鋒利邊緣。在西亞瓦塔火車上，史蒂文斯追求家庭的溫馨，而丹尼斯·列儂在近二十年後卻超越塑膠的極限，試圖消除盡可能多的連接和附加材料，把整艘船變成一件幾乎無需維護的藝術品。

雖然富美家品牌的美耐板傳遍美國和世界各地，為旅遊增添輝煌的色彩，它對美國家庭也產生了巨大的影響。勞工問題對家庭主婦和承包商與對列車司機同樣重要，富美家公司在婦女和庇護所雜誌上的廣告吸引了家

间。不过，1969 年至 2009 年运行的丘纳德"女王伊丽莎白2号"海轮却被海军建筑师丹·华莱士 (Dan Wallace) 和室内设计师丹尼斯·列侬 (Dennis Lennon) 当成了整个富美家®装饰耐火板设计项目，开发了一种带有织物感的新纹理和模压复合耐火板，在这艘船上广泛使用。一份名为《伊丽莎白二号的富美家景致》(The Formica Scene of the QE2)特刊的背页上包括该项目使用的数十种颜色、图案和面漆图表。其中的亮点是女士盥洗室里白底蓝条花案的编织物，男士盥洗室的黑白佩斯利涡纹图案，淋浴间和卫生间的千格鸟游戏图案，以及夜总会、咖啡厅和儿童游戏室内特别定制的富美家®装饰耐火板壁画。

在女王伊丽莎白 2 号上，彩练主题占主导地位，反映了二十世纪六十年代初的两幅壁画风格，一幅是由芭芭拉·斯托费舍尔·所罗门 (Barbara Stauffacher Solomon) 为加利福尼亚州北部的海洋农场所绘，另一幅是披头士 1968 年"黄色潜水艇"的绝妙动漫。在剧院酒吧大堂，挂满了红、蓝、金色航海信号旗的墙壁用绒面富美家®装饰耐火板完成，衬托着一组 Bertoia 钻石椅的红色罩面。在不列颠餐厅，再成形或卷边耐火板座椅配以橙色罩面，与一组橙色耐火板镶边的壁龛相匹配。由伦敦皇家艺术学院学生设计的黑白寓意壁画用富美家®装饰耐火板复制，悬挂在两个休闲餐厅之间的长廊内。在客房内，色彩较为收敛，但新的曲面耐火板用在桌面和梳妆台抽屉上，消除了小客舱里的锋利楞角。在西亚瓦塔火车上，史蒂文斯追求家庭的温馨，而丹尼斯·列侬在近二十年后却超越塑料的极限，试图消除尽可能多的连接和附加材料，把整座船变成一件几乎无需维护的艺术品。

虽然富美家品牌的耐火板传遍美国和世界各地，为旅游增添辉煌的色彩，它对美国家庭也产生了巨大的影响。

แผ่นลามิเนทฟอร์ไมก้าเคยถูกนำมาใช้กับรถไฟก่อนหน้านี้แล้ว (ที่น่าจดจำที่สุดคือ บนขบวนรถไฟที่มีชื่อว่า Train of Tomorrow ของบริษัทเจนเนอรัล มอเตอร์ส และบนขบวนรถไฟ ที่มีชื่อว่า เจฟเฟอโซเนียน ของ เพนซิลเวเนีย แต่ก็ไม่เคยถูกใช้อย่างกว้างขวางในลักษณะบูรณาการแบบนี้มาก่อน ต่อมาได้มีการใช้แผ่นลามิเนทฟอร์ไมก้ากับเรือเดินสมุทรสุดหรู แผ่นลามิเนทฟอร์ไมก้าสีขาวถูกติดตั้งในห้องอาบน้ำทุกห้องบนเรือควีนแมรี่ ของคิวนาร์ด ซึ่งเปิดให้บริการในปี ค.ศ. 1936 ในขณะที่ห้องส่วนกลาง แผ่นไม้จริงถูกนำมาใช้เป็นวัสดุบุผนัง โลวัย์ ผู้ซึ่งเป็นนักออกแบบให้ฟอร์ไมก้าระหว่างปี ค.ศ. 1954 จนถึงปี ค.ศ. 1960 ใช้แผ่นลามิเนทบุผนัง บูโอ๊ะเครื่องแป้ง และปิดผิวด้านบนของโต๊ะบนเอสเอสเลอไลน์ ในขณะที่มันได้รับการปรับโฉม ซึ่งเดินทางระหว่างซานฟรานซิสโกกับโฮโนลูลูตั้งแต่ปี ค.ศ. 1948 จนถึงปี ค.ศ. 1963 แต่อย่างไรก็ตามเรือควีนอลิซาเบธที่ 2 ของคิวนาร์ด เป็นเรือเดินสมุทรลำเดียวที่สถาปนิกด้านการออกแบบเรือ แดน วอลเรส และนักออกแบบภายใน เดนนิส เลนน่อน เรียกว่าเป็นโครงการที่ใช้ฟอร์ไมก้าทั้งโครงการ โดยมีการพัฒนาแผ่นลามิเนทที่มีผิวแบบใหม่และสามารถนำมาขึ้นรูปได้ ทั้งยังให้ความรู้สึกเหมือนเป็นผ้าทอ มาใช้อย่างกว้างขวางบนพื้นที่ของเรือ ในเอกสารสิ่งพิมพ์ฉบับพิเศษชื่อ "The Formica Scene of the QE2" ซึ่งหน้าหลังปรากฏแผ่นภาพของลวดลาย และผิวสัมผัสมากมายที่เคยใช้ในโครงการ ในบรรดาภาพที่น่าสนใจ เช่น ภาพพื้นผิวลายดอกไม้ถักทอสีฟ้าบนพื้นขาวในห้องแต่งตัวของสุภาพสตรี ลายลูกน้ำสีขาวดำสำหรับห้องน้ำชาย ลายตารางแบบเขียวในห้องอาบน้ำและห้องน้ำ และภาพจิตรกรรมฝาหนังของฟอร์ไมก้าที่ถูกทำขึ้นเฉพาะสำหรับไนท์คลับ ร้านกาแฟ และห้องเด็กอีกมากมาย

บนเรือควีนอลิซาเบธที่ 2 เน้นการใช้ธีมซุปเปอร์กราฟิก โดยหนึ่งในนั้นอิงจากภาพจิตรกรรมฝาหนังทาสีซึ่งวาดขึ้นในช่วงต้นทศวรรษที่ 1960 โดยบาร์บาราสตัฟฟาเซอร์ โซโลมอน วาดให้แก่ฮี แรนช์ในแคลิฟอร์เนียเหนือ และภาพเคลื่อนไหวที่น่าตื่งตาดูใจเยลโล่ ซับมารีน ของบีเทิลส์ วาดในปี ค.ศ. 1968 ในโรงละครเทียเตอร์บาร์ โฟเยอร์ มีกำแพงรูปธงเดินเรือสามเหลี่ยมสีแดง สีฟ้า และสีทอง ทำจากแผ่นลามิเนทฟอร์ไมก้าซึ่งมีลักษณะเหมือนหนังกลับชนิดนิ่ม และตกแต่งด้วยสีแดงจากเบาะของชุดเก้าอี้เบอร์โทเอีย ไดมอน ใน

petites cabines. Sur les trains Hiawatha, Stevens recherchait plus d'intimité tandis que Dennis Lennon, presque vingt ans plus tard, repoussait les limites du plastique, en essayant d'éliminer le plus grand nombre possible de joints et les matériaux additionnels pour transformer tout le navire en une pièce d'art à faible entretien.

Pendant que le stratifié de marque Formica traversait les États-Unis et le monde éblouissant du voyage, il a également eu un impact considérable sur le foyer américain. La question du travail était aussi importante pour la femme au foyer et l'entrepreneur que pour l'opérateur ferroviaire. Les publicités de Formica Corporation dans les magazines féminins et de décoration séduisaient la femme au foyer comme le rénovateur, suggérant que le produit facilitait considérablement les travaux d'entretien ménagers (une publicité du milieu du siècle montre une jeune mère servant le dîner dans une robe bustier New Look) et que rénover votre maison devenait tout aussi facile. Un temps fort pour Formica Corporation fut la maison de l'exposition (World's Fair House) de l'exposition universelle de 1964 à Flushing Meadows dans le Queens, à New York. La maison de l'exposition Formica fut dessinée par l'architecte du New Jersey Emil A. Schmidlin, qui a été l'un des premiers à construire des maisons à demi-étages dans cet État ainsi que plusieurs autres maisons d'exposition. La maison était longue et basse, avec un toit en pente, une porte d'entrée en retrait et de longues rangées de fenêtres verticales. Ni l'intérieur ni l'extérieur n'étaient conçus pour surprendre, l'idée principale étant de montrer que la maison du présent pouvait désormais être complètement fabriquée de stratifié Formica.

Dans le cas des appareils, Stevens, Loewy et d'autres designers industriels redessinaient, le rêve était la beauté sans entretien, et la maison montrait un monde étonnamment sexué, avec ses améliorations technologiques intégrées dans les surfaces. Comme l'historienne de l'architecture Rosemarie Haag Bletter l'écrit dans *Remembering the Future* : « La chambre du garçon de la maison Formica avait un bureau, une zone éminemment pratique bien à lui

hogares estadounidenses. La cuestión del trabajo era tan importante para las amas de casa y los contratistas como lo era para los operadores de trenes, y los anuncios publicitarios de Formica Corporation en las revistas para mujeres y de diseño eran de interés para los fabricantes y restauradores de casas, lo que sugería que el producto era de mantenimiento fácil (un anuncio publicitario de mediados de siglo muestra una madre joven sirviendo la cena con un vestido New Look sin tirantes) y que mejorar el hogar era igual de simple. Un punto álgido para Formica Corporation fue la Feria mundial de la vivienda en la Feria mundial de 1964, que se llevó a cabo en Flushing Meadows, en Queens, Nueva York. La Feria mundial de la vivienda de laminado Formica fue diseñada por Emil A. Schmidlin, un arquitecto de Nueva Jersey que estaba entre los primeros en construir casas de dos niveles en ese Estado, así como también varias casas de exposición. La casa era larga y baja, con techo a cuatro aguas, puerta principal empotrada y largas hileras de ventanas verticales. Ni el interior ni el exterior estaban diseñados para impactar, ya que la función principal era mostrar que la casa del presente se podía decorar completamente con el laminado de la marca Formica.

En cuanto a los aparatos, Stevens, Loewy y otros diseñadores industriales habían estado rediseñando, lo ideal

Formica-merkkisen laminaatin liikkuessa Amerikan laajuisesti ja poikki maailman, matkustamista romantisoiden, sillä oli myös valtava vaikutus amerikkalaiseen kotiin. Perheenemännälle ja urakoitsijalle työnäkökohta oli yhtä tärkeä kuin junan kuljettajalle ja Formica Corporationin mainokset naisten lehdissä vetosivat kodin hoitajaan ja kunnostajaan, ehdottaessaan, että tuote teki ulkoasun säilyttämisestä helpon homman (eräs vuosisadan keskivaiheen mainos esittää nuorta äitiä tarjoamassa illallista olkaimettomassa uuden tyylin puvussa) ja kodin parannuksista aivan yhtä helpon. Kohokohtana Formica Corporationille oli maailmanmessujen talo vuoden 1964 maailmanmessuilla, jotka pidettiin Flushing Meadowsissa Queensissä, New Yorkissa. Formican maailmanmessutalon suunnitteli Emil A. Schmidlin, New Jerseyläinen arkkitehti, joka oli yksi ensimmäisistä porrastettujen talojen ja monien mallitalojen rakentajista. Talo oli pitkä ja matala, siinä oli nelilapekatto, etuovisyvennys ja pitkät rivit pystysuoria ikkunoita. Ulko- ja sisäpuolta ei kumpaakaan oltu suunniteltu iskeviksi, koska pääasiana oli osoittaa, että nykyaikainen talo voitaisiin kokonaan toteuttaa Formica-merkkisillä laminaateilla.

Kodinkoneiden osalta, joita Stevens, Loewy ja muut teolliset suunnittelijat olivat olleet suunnittelemassa uudelleen, unelmana oli kunnossapitoa tarvitsematon kauneus, ja talo esittää hätkähdyttävästi sukupuolet huomioivan maailman, jonka hightech -parannukset pinnoissa olivat kiinteänä osana. Arkkitehtuurin historioitsija Rosemarie Haag Bletter kirjoittaa kirjassa *Remembering the Future*: "Pojan huoneessa Formica-talossa oli kirjoituspöytä, hieno paikka kutsua omaksi 'territorioikseen' mutta myös kannustamaan kotitehtäviä ... huoneessa, joka oli nuorekas ja jokaiselta yksityiskohdaltaan miehekäs". Yksityiskohtiin sisältyivät Formica-puulaminaattiset seinät ja huonekalut, punkka, jonka tukirakenne muistuttaa *betonibrutalismisuuden* arkkitehtuuria Brasiliasta, ja säilytyskaappi, jonka päällysteenä ovat koristeelliset paneelit ja geometrinen "Navajo"-motiivi. Bletter kirjoittaa, että "tyttöjen huoneessa vaaleanpunaisine seinäpanelointeineen oli kompaktit valmiik-

ร้านอาหารบริเทนเนีย เก้าอี้ลามิเนทขอบ
มนหรือขอบม้วนถูกหุ้มด้วยสีส้มเพื่อให้เข้า
กับชุดช่องเว้าบนผนังที่ถูกตกแต่งด้วยแผ่น
ลามิเนทฟอร์ไมก้าสีส้ม ภาพจิตรกรรมฝา
หนังเชิงรูปลักษณ์สีขาวดำถูกออกแบบโดย
นักเรียนของ London's Royal College of Art ถูกทำขึ้นใหม่บนแผ่นลามิเนท
ฟอร์ไมก้าและนำมาติดเข้าบนห้องโถงยาว
ระหว่างร้านอาหารสองร้าน ในห้องพักของ
แขก สีถูกจำกัดมากขึ้นกว่าเดิม แต่แผ่นลา
มิเนทโค้งชนิดใหม่ได้รีดปิดผิวด้านบนของ
โต๊ะและลิ้นชักโต๊ะเครื่องแป้ง ซึ่งช่วยลบขอบ
มีคมภายในห้องขนาดเล็กได้ บนขบวนรถ
ไฟเฮียวาทา สตีเว่นเลือกที่จะออกแบบบร
รยากาศให้เหมือนบ้าน แต่เดนนิส เลนน่อน
ในเกือบยี่สิบปีต่อมา เน้นลดการใช้พลาสติก
และพยายามจัดขั้ยรอยต่อและวัสดุเพิ่มเติม
ต่าง ๆ เพื่อทำให้เรือทั้งลำเป็นงานศิลปะที่
ต้องการการบำรุงรักษาที่ต่ำ

แล้วว่าผลิตภัณฑ์ฟอร์ไมก้าจะแผ่ขยายไป
ทั่วอเมริกาและทั่วโลก มันก็มีอิทธิพลอย่าง
มากต่อบ้านของชาวอเมริกัน คำถามเกี่ยวกับ
แรงงานนั้นมีความสำคัญต่อแม่บ้านและผู้รับ
เหมาเท่า ๆ กับที่มันมีต่อผู้ประกอบกิจการ
รถไฟ และโฆษณาของฟอร์ไมก้าบนนิตยสาร
ผู้หญิงและนิตยสารเกี่ยวกับที่พักอาศัยดึงดูด
ใจผู้ทำงานบ้านและผู้ปรับปรุงบ้าน ซึ่งแสดง
ให้เห็นว่าผลิตภัณฑ์ทำให้การรักษาปรลักษณ์
เป็นไปอย่างง่ายดาย (โฆษณาหนึ่งในช่วง
กลางศตวรรษแสดงภาพคุณแม่วัยเยาว์กำลัง
เสิร์ฟอาหารค่ำในชุดกระโปรงไร้สายสไตล์
ใหม่) และปรับปรุงบ้านคุณได้อย่างง่ายดาย
ความสำเร็จอย่างสูงของฟอร์ไมก้าอยู่ที่งาน
แสดงบ้านระดับโลก ในงานแสดงระดับโลก
ปี ค.ศ. 1964 ซึ่งจัดขึ้นที่ฟลัชชิ่ง เมโดวส์ ใน
เมืองควีนส์ รัฐนิวยอร์ก งานแสดงบ้านระดับ
โลกของฟอร์ไมก้าถูกออกแบบโดยอีมิลล์ เอ
ชมิดลิน สถาปนิกชาวนิวเจอร์ซีย์คนแรก ๆ
ที่สร้างบ้านเล่นระดับในรัฐนั้น รวมถึงบ้าน
ที่ใช้แสดงอีกจำนวนมาก บ้านฟอร์ไมก้ามี
ลักษณะยาวและต่ำ มีหลังคาทรงปั้นหยา
ประตูหน้าเล็ก และมีหน้าต่างแนวตั้งเรียง
เป็นแถวยาว ลักษณะภายในและภายนอก
ไม่ได้ถูกออกแบบมาเพื่อให้เกิดความน่าตื่น
ตาตื่นใจ เพราะจุดประสงค์หลัก คือ ต้องการ
แสดงให้เห็นว่าบ้านในปัจจุบันสามารถใช้
ผลิตภัณฑ์ฟอร์ไมก้าได้ทุกส่วน

สำหรับเครื่องใช้ต่าง ๆ ที่สตีเว่น โลวี่
และนักออกแบบอุตสาหกรรมอื่น ๆ ทำการ
ปรับปรุงแบบนั้น ความฝันก็คือ การออกแบบ
ให้เกิดความสวยงามโดยไม่ต้องบำรุงรักษา
และบ้านหลังนั้นแสดงถึงความโดดเด่นอย่าง
ชัดเจน มีการปรับปรุงด้วยเทคโนโลยีระดับ

庭主婦和家庭革新者的注意，這表明
該產品使跟上時代潮流成為一件輕而
易舉的事（一個世紀中葉的廣告展示
了一位年輕的母親身穿一件露肩新款
裙子在將晚餐端到餐桌上），改善你
的家居一樣容易。富美家公司的一個
輝煌時光是 1964 年在紐約皇后區法
拉盛草坪上舉行的世界博覽會的世界
博覽會之家。富美家的世界博覽會之
家由埃米爾·史密林（Emil A. Schmid-
lin）設計，她是一位新澤西州建築師，
是最早在該州修建錯層住宅和眾多展
覽住宅的人。這種住宅長而低，帶有
四坡屋頂，凹式前門，長排的垂直窗
子。無論是內部還是外部設計都不是
為了強調刺激效應，因為主要功能是
為了顯示現在的房子本可以完全用富
美家品牌美耐板建造。

　　至於史蒂文斯、洛伊和其他工業
設計師們重新設計的家電，他們的夢
想是給人們留下無需維修的美感，房
子展示驚人的區分不同性別的世界，
高科技被納入表面的進步。正如建築
史學家羅斯瑪麗·哈格·布萊特（Ro-
semarie Haag Bletter）在《記住未
來》（Remembering the Future）中所
寫：「這個用富美家美耐板製作的男

劳工问题对家庭主妇和承包商与对列
车司机同样重要，富美家公司在妇女
和庇护所杂志上的广告吸引了家庭主
妇和家庭革新者的注意，这表明该产
品使跟上时代潮流成为一件轻而易举
的事（一个世纪中叶的广告展示了一位
年轻的母亲身穿一件露肩新款裙子在
将晚餐端到餐桌上），改善你的家居一
样容易。富美家公司的一个辉煌时光
是 1964 年在纽约皇后区法拉盛草坪
上举行的世界博览会的世界博览会之
家。富美家的世界博览会之家由埃米
尔·史密林（Emil A. Schmidlin）设计，
她是一位新泽西州建筑师，是最早在
该州修建错层住宅和众多展览住宅的
人。这种住宅长而低，带有四坡屋顶，
凹式前门，长排的垂直窗子。无论是
内部还是外部设计都不是为了强调
刺激效应，因为主要功能是为了显示
现在的房子本可以完全用富美家品
牌耐火板建造。

　　至于史蒂文斯、洛伊和其他工业设
计师们重新设计的家电，他们的梦想
是给人们留下无需维修的美感，房子
展示惊人的区分不同性别的世界，高
科技被纳入表面的进步。正如建筑史
学家罗斯玛丽·哈格·布莱特（Rose-

mais encourageant aussi les devoirs... dans une chambre jeune et masculine jusque dans les moindres détails. » Parmi les détails, on notait des murs et des mobiliers en stratifié bois Formica, un lit superposé avec des supports inspirés de l'architecture brute de béton de Brasilia et un placard de rangement avec panneaux décoratifs au motif géométrique Navajo. « Dans la chambre de jeune fille, » poursuit Bletter, « outre les lambris roses des murs, il y avait des éléments compacts de fenêtres préfabriqués pouvant se transformer en supports de machine à coudre, machine à écrire, petite planche à repasser. » Le placard de jeune fille présentait des panneaux avant avec de grandes fleurs roses qui, en s'ouvrant, révélaient des étagères en miroir et un intérieur rose bonbon. Les murs étaient également lambrissés de stratifié Formica rose avec des cannelures framboise.

La cuisine était un centre de commande aux couleurs coordonnées avec plan de travail de teinte avocat, armoires revêtues d'écorce de bouleau texturée vert et blanc et rideaux et portes décoratives avec motif végétal. Il y avait un four électrique double et un centre de lessive intégré, une planche à découper rétractable et un coin petit-déjeuner avec des meubles à piédestal Saarin avec assiettes coordonnées Melmac. Mais le futurisme se manifestait dans un petit coin vert, équipé de tiroirs et d'un téléphone blanc. Le bureau compact, niché dans un coin de la cuisine, ne prenait pas plus de place qu'un placard à nourriture mais permettait le contrôle de toute la maison. C'est ici que les repas étaient planifiés, les courses commandées, les factures et les dossiers classés. Avec un système d'interphone Miami-Carey dans toute la maison, il était possible de répondre à la porte d'entrée ou de parler aux membres de la famille dans chacune des diverses pièces sans quitter le bureau. Ces espaces cuisine-bureau sont désormais monnaie courante, tout comme les interphones, mais la maison de l'exposition universelle montrait le stratifié de marque Formica comme un produit qui ajoutait de la richesse à la vie familiale en rendant les tâches ménagères plus efficaces. Un essai de Raymond Loewy et de son

era que la belleza no requiriera mantenimiento; la casa muestra un impactante mundo condicionado por género, con sus mejoras de alta tecnología construidas en las superficies. Como la historiadora de arquitectura Rosemarie Haag Bletter escribe en *Remembering the Future*: "La habitación del niño de la Casa Formica tenía un escritorio, un gran lugar que podía llamar su 'territorio', pero también un incentivo para el trabajo en casa… en una habitación que es juvenil y masculina en cada detalle". Los detalles incluían paredes y muebles de laminado de madera Formica, una cama litera con soportes que recuerdan la arquitectura Beton brut (en obra limpia) de Brasilia y un armario para guardar cosas cubierto con paneles decorativos con un motivo geométrico característico de "los navajos". "En la habitación de la niña", escribe Bletter, "con paredes de paneles color rosa, había 'ventanas individuales compactas ya listas, que se transforman en soportes para máquinas de coser, de escribir y en una pequeña tabla de planchar'". El armario de la niña presentaba paneles frontales con flores grandes color rosa, que, al abrirse, revelaban los estantes con espejos y un interior color rosa bebé. Las paredes también estaban cubiertas con paneles de laminado Formica color rosa con franjas color frambuesa.

La cocina era un centro de comando de colores combinados, con encimeras color avocado, aparadores cubiertos con corteza de abedul "texturizada" color verde y blanco, y cortinas y puertas decorativas con diseños botánicos. Había hornos eléctricos dobles y un centro de lavado empotrado, una tabla de cortar extraíble y una sala de desayuno con muebles de pedestal estilo Eero Saarinen y platos Melmac haciendo juego. Pero el verdadero futurismo estaba en un pequeño rincón color verde, equipado con gavetas y un teléfono color blanco. La oficina compacta, incrustada fuera del paso en una esquina de la cocina, no ocupaba más espacio que el armario de una despensa, pero controlaba toda la casa. Aquí se planeaban los menús, se pedían las provisiones y se conservaban ordenadas las facturas y los archivos. Con un sistema de intercomunicación Miami-Carey en toda

si kootut ikkunayksiköt, jotka voitiin muuttaa tukemaan ompelukonetta, kirjoituskonetta tai pientä silityslautaa." Tyttöjen kaapeissa oli etupaneelit, joissa oli suuria vaaleanpunaisia kukkia, joiden takaa paljastuivat peililasihyllyt ja vauvan vaaleanpunainen sisus. Seinät oli myös paneloitu vaaleanpunaisella Formica-laminaatilla, jossa oli vadelmanpunaiset listat.

Keittiö oli värikoordinoitu komentokeskus avokadon värisine kalusteineen, kaappien etupinnoissa koivun tuohen "tekstuoitu" vihreä ja valkoinen, ja verhoissa ja koristeellisissa ovissa kasvitieteellisiä kuvioita. Oli kaksi sähköuunia ja kiinteästi asennettu pyykkikoneet, ulos vedettävä leikkuulauta ja aamiaistila saaristyylisine jalustahuonekaluineen ja täsmäävine Melmac-lautasineen. Aito futurismi löytyi kuitenkin pienestä vihreästä sopesta, johon oli asennettu pöytälaatikot ja valkoinen puhelin. Kompakti toimistotila, sovitettuna pois tieltä keittiön nurkkaan, ei vienyt enempää tilaa kuin keittiökomero, vaikka kontrolloikin koko taloa. Täällä suunniteltiin ruokalistat, tilattiin ruokatavarat ja pidettiin laskut ja asiapaperit hyvässä järjestyksessä. Koko talon kattavan Miami-Carey -sisäpuhelinjärjestelmän avulla oli mahdollista avata etuovi tai

孩的房間有一張書桌，一個可以稱為他的「領地」的很好的地方，但也鼓勵他……在一個每個細節都體現出青春和男性的房間裡做功課。」細節包括富美家實木複合牆壁和家俱，一張雙層床和支架讓人想起巴西利亞貝頓-布魯特的建築結構，一個儲藏櫃鑲著幾何圖形「納瓦霍」主題的裝飾板。布萊特寫道：「在女孩的房間裡，有粉紅色的壁板，預製的小巧窗戶，可轉動用於支撐縫紉機、打字機和小熨衣板。」女孩的櫃子的面板上畫著大朵粉紅色的花，打開就露出帶鏡子的架子和一個粉紅色的內壁。牆壁也鑲著粉紅色帶覆盆子線條的富美家美耐板。

廚房就像一個協調色彩的指揮中心，鱷梨色的桌檯，櫥櫃表面鑲著綠色和白色的樺樹皮「紋理」，窗簾和裝飾門上繪製著植物的圖案。有雙眼電爐和一個固定的洗衣中心，一個可拉出的菜板，一間配有沙里林式基座的家俱和匹配的密胺樹脂面板家俱的早餐室。但是，真正的未來主義體現在一個綠色的小角落，配有抽屜桌和一部白色電話機。緊湊的辦公室，嵌進廚房一個偏僻的角落，佔據的空間還沒有一個食品櫃大，但卻控制整個房子的視線。在這裡計劃菜單，訂購蔬果，賬單和文件保管得井井有條。房子裡裝有邁阿密-凱思對講系統，可以回答前門的問話或同家庭成員在任何不同的房間講話，而不需要離開辦公桌。

這種廚房兼辦公室的設計現在已司空見慣，對講機也是一樣，但世界博覽會之家表明，富美家品牌的美耐板作為一種產品能讓做家務更有效，使家庭生活更豐富。刊登在富美家公司世界博覽會紀念冊上由洛伊和合夥人威廉姆·斯奈思（William Snaith）合寫的一篇文章，描述了本行業選擇顏色的訣竅。洛伊公司對富美家公司的一個主要貢獻就是更新了調色板，以反映當代顏色選擇，並增加了一些新

marie Haag Bletter)在《记住未来》(Remembering the Future)中所写："这个用富美家®装饰耐火板制作的男孩的房间有一张书桌，一个可以称为他的'领地'的很好的地方，但也鼓励他……在一个每个细节都体现出青春和男性的房间里做功课。"细节包括富美家实木复合墙壁和家具，一张双层床和支架让人想起巴西利亚贝顿-布鲁特的建筑结构，一个储藏柜镶着几何图形"纳瓦霍"主题的装饰板。布莱特写道："在女孩的房间里，有粉红色的壁板，预制的小巧窗户，可转动用于支撑缝纫机、打字机和小熨衣板。"女孩的柜子的面板上画着大朵粉红色的花，打开就露出带镜子的架子和一个粉红色的内壁。墙壁也镶着粉红色带覆盆子线条的富美家®装饰耐火板。

厨房就像一个协调色彩的指挥中心，鳄梨色的桌台，橱柜表面镶着绿色和白色的桦树皮"纹理"，窗帘和装饰门上绘制着植物的图案。有双眼电炉和一个固定的洗衣中心，一个可拉出的菜板，一间配有沙里林式基座的家具和匹配的密胺树脂面板家具的早餐室。但是，真正的未来主义体现在一个绿色的小角落，配有抽屉桌和一部白色电话机。紧凑的办公室，嵌进厨房一个偏僻的角落，占据的空间还没有一个食物柜大，但却控制整个房子的视线。在这里计划菜单，订购蔬果，账单和文件保管得井井有条。房子里装有迈阿密-凯思对讲系统，可以回答前门的问话或同家庭成员在任何不同的房间讲话，而不需要离开办公桌。

这种厨房兼办公室的设计现在已司空见惯，对讲机也是一样，但世界博览会之家表明，富美家品牌的耐火板作为一种产品能让做家务更有效，使家庭生活更丰富。刊登在富美家公司世界博览会纪念册上由洛伊和合伙人威廉姆·斯奈思（William Snaith）合写的一篇文章，描述了本行业选择颜色的诀窍。洛伊公司对富美家公司的

สูงสุดบนพื้นผิว ตามที่นักประวัติศาสตร์ด้านสถาปัตยกรรม โรสแมรี่ แฮก เบร็ตเตอร์ เขียนไว้ใน Remembering the Future "ห้องของเด็กชายในบ้านฟอร์ไมก้ามีโต๊ะทำงาน ซึ่งเหมาะจะเรียกว่าเป็น "ถิ่น" ของเขา แต่ก็จูงใจให้ทำการบ้าน...ในห้องที่อ่อนเยาว์และแสดงถึงความเป็นผู้ชายในทุกรายละเอียด" รายละเอียดต่าง ๆ รวมไปถึงผนังและเฟอร์นิเจอร์ทำจากแผ่นลามิเนทไม้ของฟอร์ไมก้า เตียงสองชั้นแบบมีฐานรอง ซึ่งทำให้ชวนนึกถึงสถาปัตยกรรมผนังคอนกรีตเปลือยของบราซิเลียและตู้เก็บปิดผิวหน้าด้วยแผ่นลามิเนทลายเรขาคณิต "นาวาโฮ" "ในห้องของเด็กสาว" เบร็ตเตอร์ เขียนว่า "ผนังบุด้วยแผ่นลามิเนทสีชมพู มีหน้าต่างทำสำเร็จขนาดกะทัดรัด (ที่) สามารถเปลี่ยนเป็นฐานรองจักรเย็บผ้าและเครื่องพิมพ์ดีดกระดานรองรีดขนาดเล็ก" ตู้ของเด็กหญิงบุด้วยแผ่นลามิเนทลายดอกไม้สีชมพูขนาดใหญ่ เมื่อเปิดออกจะเห็นชั้นกระจกและด้านในเป็นสีชมพู ผนังยังถูกบุด้วยแผ่นลามิเนทฟอร์ไมก้าสีชมพูและมีสลักราสเบอร์รี่

ห้องครัวถูกตกแต่งด้วยสีหลากหลายสีผสมกัน โดยมีเคาน์เตอร์สีอะโวคาโด ตู้ถูกตกแต่งใส่ "มีผิวสัมผัส" ต้นเบิร์ชสีเขียวและขาว ผ้าม่านและประตูตกแต่งมีรูปแบบเป็นพันธุ์ไม้หลากหลาย ทั้งยังมีเตาไฟฟ้าคู่และอุปกรณ์ซักรีดแบบบิลท์อินอยู่ตรงกลาง แผ่นเขียงที่สามารถดึงออกมาจากที่เก็บได้ และห้องอาหารเช้าที่มีชุดเฟอร์นิเจอร์ที่มีฐานแบบซาริเนนเนสส์และจานของเมลเม็ค ที่เข้าชุดกัน แต่สิ่งที่ดูทันสมัยจริง ๆ คือ มุมห้องขนาดเล็กสีเขียวซึ่งมีลิ้นชักและโทรศัพท์สีขาวตั้งอยู่ ห้องทำงานขนาดกะทัดรัดตั้งอยู่มุมทางออกของห้องครัว ซึ่งมีขนาดไม่ใหญ่ไปกว่าตู้กับข้าวแต่สามารถควบคุมทั้งบ้าน ที่นี่เป็นที่ที่จัดการเรื่องเมนูอาหาร สั่งซื้อของชำใบเสร็จและแฟ้มต่าง ๆ ถูกเก็บไว้อย่างเป็นระเบียบ ด้วยระบบอินเตอร์คอมไมอามี่ – แคร็ย ซึ่งคลอบคลุมบ้านทั้งหลัง จึงสามารถที่จะพูดตอบรับที่ประตูหน้าบ้านหรือพูดคุยกับสมาชิกในครอบครัวซึ่งอยู่ตามห้องต่าง ๆ ได้โดยไม่ต้องลุกออกจากโต๊ะทำงาน

ในขณะนี้ พื้นที่ห้องครัวห้องทำงานขนาดดังกล่าวอาจจะเป็นสิ่งที่มีอยู่ทั่วไป เช่นเดียวกับระบบอินเตอร์คอม แต่งานแสดงบ้านระดับโลกได้แสดงให้เห็นว่าฟอร์ไมก้าเป็นผลิตภัณฑ์ที่เพิ่มความสมบูรณ์ให้แก่ชีวิตภายในบ้านโดยการทำให้การจัดการงานบ้านมีประสิทธิภาพมากขึ้น บทความที่เขียนโดยเรย์มอน โลวีย์และหุ้นส่วน วิลเลียมสเนท ในหนังสือที่ระลึกของฟอร์ไมก้าซึ่งแจก

partenaire William Snaith, présenté dans le livre commémoratif de Formica Corporation à l'exposition universelle, décrit les ficelles du métier pour le choix des couleurs. L'une des contributions majeures de la firme Loewy à la société a été la mise à jour de la palette de couleurs afin de refléter les goûts contemporains, ainsi que l'ajout de nouveaux motifs qui suggèrent l'exotisme et le voyage (le plus populaire, Capri, ressemble à une mosaïque irrégulière de tuiles des îles). Dans la maison de l'exposition universelle, chaque pièce semble mise en place pour l'artisanat et les jeux, la réception d'invités et le temps passé en famille. Le travail domestique est reconnu mais les espaces publics sont rendus luxueux par des motifs. Comme le texte l'indique, « tous les lieux de travail sont devenus de très belles pièces. » En 1974, Formica Corporation a créé le Design Advisory Board (DAB), avec un groupe de designers d'intérieur et d'architectes influents qui devaient mener le stratifié de marque Formica au-delà des années 1960 vers le présent. Comme Susan Grant Lewin l'écrit dans *Formica & Design: From the Counter Top to High Art*, « le synthétique et l'artisanal n'ont pas tenu la promesse de Formica Corporation dans la maison de l'exposition universelle de 1964, lorsque le stratifié Formica semblait le matériau idéal pour servir de revêtement au monde, ayant un attrait presqu'universel. » Le DAB a recommandé à la société de cesser de tenter d'imiter les matériaux naturels comme le bois et le marbre et de célébrer plutôt sa nature synthétique. La collection Design Concepts inclut des stratifiés très brillants et mats avec des grilles géométriques, des diagonales, et des motifs plus sévères, plus carrés et plus graphiques que les précédents. A également été encouragée l'adoption d'un tout nouveau produit, nommé plus tard ColorCore®, qui avait été retardé dans le développement des produits. Le stratifié ColorCore présente une couleur unie de part et d'autre, ce qui élimine la ligne sombre sur le bord du plan de travail traditionnel. Afin de promouvoir le stratifié ColorCore parmi la nouvelle génération de designers, la Formica Corporation a entrepris une série de

la casa, era posible responder a la puerta principal o hablar con los miembros de la familia que se encontraban en cualquiera de las habitaciones sin dejar el escritorio.

Estos espacios tipo cocina y oficina son comunes hoy en día, tal como lo son los intercomunicadores; sin embargo, la Feria mundial de la vivienda mostró el laminado de la marca Formica como un producto que sumaba riqueza a la vida del hogar al hacer que las tareas de la casa fueran más eficientes. Un ensayo de Raymond Loewy y su compañero William Snaith en el libro de Formica Corporation que conmemora la Feria mundial ofrece secretos del mercado para elegir los colores. Una de las contribuciones más importantes de la firma Loewy en la empresa fue la actualización de la paleta para reflejar las alternativas de colores contemporáneos, así como también agregar varios diseños nuevos que sugerían exotismo y viaje (el más popular, Capri, se asemeja a un mosaico irregular de baldosas de la isla). En la Feria mundial de la vivienda, cada habitación parece armada para las artesanías y los juegos, el entretenimiento y el tiempo en familia. Se reconoce el trabajo de la vida doméstica, pero los espacios utilitarios se hacen lujosos por medio del diseño. Como dice el ejemplar, "todos los lugares de trabajo se convirtieron en habitaciones preciosas".

En 1974, Formica Corporation creó la Junta Asesora de Diseño (Design Advisory Board, DAB), con un grupo de diseñadores de interiores y arquitectos influyentes que tenían como tarea hacer que el laminado de la marca Formica trascendiera en la década de los sesenta hasta el presente. Como escribe Susan Grant Lewin en *Formica & Design: From the Counter Top to High Art*, "Lo 'sintético' y lo 'hecho por el hombre' no cumplieron con lo augurado en la Feria mundial de la vivienda de Formica Corporation en 1964, cuando el laminado Formica parecía el material ideal para revestir las superficies del mundo, casi universal en su atractivo". La DAB recomendó que la empresa dejara de tratar de imitar los materiales naturales, como la madera y el mármol, y, en cambio, celebrara su naturaleza sintética. La Colección Design Concepts (Conceptos de Diseño) incluía

puhua missä tahansa huoneessa olevien perheenjäsenten kanssa, pöydän äärestä poistumatta.

Tällaiset keittiötoimistotilat ovat nyt yleisiä, kuten myös sisäpuhelimet, mutta maailmanmessujen talo esitteli Formica-merkkisen laminaatin tuotteena, joka lisää rikkautta kotielämään, tekemällä kotiaskareet sujuvammiksi. Raymond Loewyn ja kumppanin, William Snaithin kirjoitelma Formica Corporationin maailmanmessujen muistokirjassa tarjoaa alan nikseja värien valitsemiseen. Yksi Loewyn toimiston suurista myötävaikutuksista yhtiössä oli paletin uudistaminen heijastamaan nykypäivän värivalintoja, sekä monen uuden kuvion lisääminen, jotka viittasivat eksotismiin ja matkailuun (niistä suosituin, Capri, muistuttaa saarten epäsäännöllistä laattamosaiikkia). Maailmanmessutalossa jokainen huone on tarkoitettu askartelulle, peleille, viihdyttämiselle ja perheen yhdessäololle. Kotielämän työ tunnustetaan, mutta hyötytilat tehdään ylellisiksi kuvioinnilla. Kuten kirjoituksessa sanotaan, "kaikista työpisteistä tuli kauniit huoneet".

Vuonna 1974 Formica Corporation muodosti suunnittelussa neuvoa-antavan lautakunnan, Design Advisory Board (DAB), jossa ryhmälle vaikutusvaltaisia sisustussuunnittelijoita ja arkkitehteja annettiin tehtäväksi tuoda Formica-merkkinen laminaatti ulos 1960-luvulta nykypäivään. Kuten Susan Grant Lewin kirjoittaa kirjassa *Formica & Design: Pöydän pinnalta taiteen muodoksi*, "'Synteettinen' ja 'keinotekoinen' menettivät mainosarvonsa, joka Formica Corporationin vuoden 1964 maailmanmessutalolla oli ollut, kun Formica-laminaatti oli vaikuttanut ihanteelliselta materiaalilta maailman pinnoittamiseen, lähes yleispätevällä vetovoimallaan". DAB suositteli, että yhtiö lopettaisi yritykset jäljitellä luonnollisia materiaaleja, kuten puuta ja marmoria ja juhlisi sen sijaan sen synteettistä luonnetta. Design Concepts Collection -kokoelma sisälsi korkeakiiltoisia ja mattapintaisia laminaatteja, joissa oli geometrisia rastereita, vinoviivoja ja neliöitä, vahvempia ja graafisempia kuin aikaisemmat kuviot. He ajoivat myös läpi upouutta tuotetta, myöhemmältä nimeltään ColorCore®, jonka tuotekehitys oli viivästynyt. Co-

的圖案，表達了異國情調和遊覽特色（最受歡迎的是卡布里，形似一片不規則的馬賽克島磚）。在世界博覽會之家，每間屋子都似乎裝飾得像用作手工和遊覽、娛樂和家人歡聚用途。家庭生活的辛苦得到承認，但實用空間則靠圖案裝點得十分奢華。正如廣告所說：「所有的工作場所都成為美麗的房間。」

1974 年，富美家公司成立了自己的設計顧問委員會（DAB），集合了一批有影響力的室內設計師和建築師，負責讓富美家品牌的美耐板走出二十世紀六十年代，進入今天。正如蘇珊·格蘭特·列文（Susan Grant Lewin）在《富美家與設計：從檯面到高雅的藝術》（Formica & Design: From the Counter Top to High Art）中所寫：「『合成』和『人造』失去了富美家公司在 1964 年世博之家所懷抱的希望，當時，富美家美耐板似乎成了蓋滿世界的理想材料，幾乎到處受到歡迎。」設計顧問委員會建議富美家公司停止嘗試模仿天然材料，如木材和大理石，而是崇尚其合成性質。設計概念集合包括帶有幾何網格、對角線和正方形的高光澤和亞光美耐板，比過去的模式更加堅硬和更圖形化。他們還推出一種全新的產品，最終命名為「彩虹芯」（ColorCore®），在產品開發階段被推遲。彩虹芯的美耐板注重整體實色，去除了傳統的周圍檯邊的暗線。為在新一代的設計師之間促進使用彩虹芯美耐板，富美家公司展開了一系列與建築師的合作。其中第一項合作是 1983 年開幕的展覽，稱為「結構＋飾品」，該展覽展示了一系列項目，其中包括弗蘭克·蓋里（Frank Gehry）的魚燈，由彩虹芯美耐板做成，經過削片和撕裂成「魚鱗」狀，用燈光從裡向外照，顯露出材料的半透明狀態。另一個項目是建築設計公司場址的「門」（Door），用一層層破碎的彩虹芯美耐板創造硬片上炸出一個洞的錯視畫派的效果。這

一个主要贡献就是更新了调色板，以反映当代颜色选择，并增加了一些新的图案，表达了异国情调和游览特色（最受欢迎的是卡布里，形似一片不规则的马赛克岛磚）。在世界博览会之家，每间屋子都似乎装饰得像用作手工和游戏、娱乐和家人欢聚用途。家庭生活的辛苦得到承认，但实用空间则靠图案装点得十分奢华。正如广告所说："所有的工作场所都成为美丽的房间。"

1974 年，富美家公司成立了自己的设计顾问委员会（DAB），集合了一批有影响力的室内设计师和建筑师，负责让富美家品牌的耐火板走出二十世纪六十年代，进入今天。正如苏珊·格兰特·列文（Susan Grant Lewin）在《富美家与设计：从台面到高雅的艺术》中所写："『合成』和『人造』失去了富美家公司在 1964 年世博之家所怀抱的希望，当时，富美家®装饰耐火板似乎成了盖满世界的理想材料，几乎到处受到欢迎。"设计顾问委员会建议富美家公司停止尝试模仿天然材料，如木材和大理石，而是崇尚其合成性质。设计概念集合包括带有几何网格、对角线和正方形的高光泽和亚光耐火板，比过去的模式更加坚硬和更图形化。他们还推出一种全新的产品，最终命名为"彩虹心"®（ColorCore®），在产品开发阶段被推迟。彩虹心®的耐火板注重整体实色，去除了传统的周围台边的暗线。为在新一代的设计师之间促进使用彩虹心®耐火板，富美家公司展开了一系列与建筑师的合作。其中第一项合作是 1983 年开幕的展览，称为"结构+饰品"，该展览展示了一系列项目，其中包括弗兰克·盖里（Frank Gehry）的鱼灯，由彩虹心®耐火板做成，经过削片和撕裂成"鱼鳞"状，用灯光从里向外照，显露出材料的半透明状态。另一个项目是建筑设计公司场址的"门"（Door），用一层层破碎的彩虹心®耐火板创造硬片上炸出一个洞的错视画派的效果。这些项目向

ในงานแสดงระดับโลก แนะนำถึงเทคนิคทางการค้าในการเลือกใช้สี หนึ่งในผลงานของบริษัทของโลวีย์ที่ทำให้ฟอร์ไมก้า คือการปรับปรุงโทนสีให้ทันสมัยเพื่อแสดงตัวเลือกสีในสมัยนั้นได้อย่างเหมาะสม รวมถึงการเพิ่มลายแบบใหม่ๆ ซึ่งแสดงถึงความแปลกใหม่และการเดินทาง (ที่ชื่อเสียงที่สุดคือ คาพรี ซึ่งดูคล้ายกับกระเบื้องโมเสกรูปเกาะลักษณะแปลกๆ) ที่งานแสดงบ้านระดับโลก ทุกห้องเหมือนกับถูกทำขึ้นเพื่องานฝีมือ เกมส์ ความบันเทิง และการใช้เวลากับครอบครัว งานที่เกี่ยวกับชีวิตครอบครัวนั้นได้รับการยอมรับ แต่พื้นที่ใช้สอยถูกทำให้หรูหราด้วยการจัดรูปแบบ เหมือนอย่างที่กล่าวในบทความว่า "สถานที่ทำงานทั้งหมดได้กลายเป็นห้องที่สวยงาม"

ในปี ค.ศ. 1974 ฟอร์ไมก้าได้จัดตั้งคณะกรรมการที่ปรึกษาด้านการออกแบบ (DAB) ของบริษัทขึ้น ซึ่งประกอบไปด้วยกลุ่มนักออกแบบตกแต่งภายในและสถาปนิกผู้ทรงอิทธิพลโดยมีภารกิจในการนำฟอร์ไมก้าออกจากช่วงยุคทศวรรษที่ 1960 เพื่อเข้าสู่ยุคปัจจุบัน ตามที่ ซูซาน แกรนท์ เลวินเขียนไว้ใน Formica & Design: From the Counter Top to High Art ว่า " 'ผลิตภัณฑ์สังเคราะห์' และ 'ที่มนุษย์สร้างขึ้น' สูญเสียลักษณะที่เคยมีมาที่งานแสดงบ้านระดับโลก ปี ค.ศ. 1964 ของฟอร์ไมก้า ในขณะที่แผ่นลามิเนททฟอร์ไมก้า เป็นวัสดุในอุดมคติที่เหมาะสำหรับปูพื้นผิวโลก ซึ่งเป็นที่ดึงดูดใจในระดับสากล" คณะกรรมการที่ปรึกษาด้านการออกแบบแนะนำให้บริษัทหยุดความพยายามที่จะตกแต่งเลียนวัสดุธรรมชาติเช่น ไม้และหินอ่อน แต่ควรที่จะส่งเสริมลักษณะสังเคราะห์ตามธรรมชาติของมันแทนคอลเลคชั่นแนวคิดการออกแบบ ประกอบไปด้วยลามิเนทผิวด้านและผิวมันวาวสูงที่มีตารางเรขาคณิต เส้นทแยงมุม และสี่เหลี่ยม ซึ่งแข็งแรงกว่าและมีแบบกราฟิกมากกว่ารูปแบบก่อนหน้า อีกทั้ง พวกเขายังผลักดันผลิตภัณฑ์ใหม่ ซึ่งท้ายที่สุดใช้ชื่อว่าคัลเลอร์คอร์® ซึ่งได้มีความล่าช้าในการพัฒนาผลิตภัณฑ์ คัลเลอร์คอร์ลามิเนทมีลักษณะโดดเด่นด้วยสีเดียวกันทั้งชิ้น ซึ่งกำจัดเส้นสีเข้มรอบขอบแผ่นหน้าโต๊ะแบบดั้งเดิมให้หมดไป เพื่อส่งเสริมการขายคัลเลอร์คอร์ ในหมู่นักออกแบบรุ่นใหม่ฟอร์ไมก้าได้ร่วมมือกับสถาปนิก ซึ่งความร่วมมือแรกก็คือ นิทรรศการที่เปิดในปี ค.ศ. 1983 ที่มีชื่อว่า โครงสร้าง + ของประดับตกแต่ง และแสดงโครงการต่างๆ มากมาย ซึ่งประกอบด้วย โคมไฟรูปปลา ของแฟรงค์ เกร์รี่ ที่สร้างขึ้นจาก คัลเลอร์คอร์

collaborations avec des architectes. La première d'entre elles, une exposition ouverte en 1983 et intitulée *Structure et Ornement*, proposa un ensemble de projets. Ceux-ci incluaient la lampe poisson de Frank Gehry, construite en stratifié ColorCore ébréché et déchiré en écailles de poisson, éclairée de l'intérieur, révélant la translucidité du matériau. Un autre projet présenté était *la porte* du bureau d'architecture SITE, qui utilisait des couches de stratifié ColorCore brisé pour un effet trompe-l'œil de trou d'explosion à travers une por-te massive. Ces projets ont suggéré une nouvelle direction de design pour Formica Corporation et ont souligné l'adéquation du stratifié ColorCore dans les installations tridimensionnelles très colorées avec motifs. L'exposition fut un tel succès qu'elle voyagea à l'étranger, traçant la voie à des réseaux de distribution propre à Formica et ajoutant des architectes et des designers partout. La présentation a fini par inclure Eva Jiřičná et Rodney Kinsman en Grande-Bretagne, et Arata Isozaki et Shiro Kuramata au Japon, avant de terminer sa tournée de cinq ans à Singapour. La même année, la société Formica s'est associée au magazine *Interiors* pour commander un projet d'exposition en trois dimensions présentant son nouveau produit. Le designer industriel Michael McCoy a utilisé le stratifié ColorCore pour créer un bureau pour un dirigeant de l'industrie spatiale. Un article de la revue *Interiors* a décrit le résultat de la ma-

laminados mate y de brillo intenso, con diseños geométricos, como cuadrículas, diagonales y cuadrados, más resistentes y más gráficos que los diseños anteriores. También presionaron a favor de un producto completamente nuevo, que, con el tiempo, recibió el nombre de ColorCore®, cuyo desarrollo había estado retrasado. El laminado ColorCore presentaba un color completamente uniforme, lo que eliminaba la línea oscura alrededor del borde de la cubierta prefabricada tradicional. Para promocionar el laminado ColorCore entre la nueva generación de diseñadores, Formica Corporation emprendió una serie de acuerdos de colaboración con arquitectos. El primero de estos fue una exhibición que abrió en 1983, que se denominó "*Structure + Ornament*" (Estructura + adorno) y presentó una variedad de proyectos. Entre ellos, se encontraba Fish Lamp (Lámpara en forma de pez) de Frank Gehry, elaborada con laminado ColorCore desportillado e incrustado para lograr el efecto de "escamas de pez", con encendido en el interior que revelaba la translucidez del material. Otro fue el proyecto *Door* (Puerta) de la firma de arquitectura SITE, que utilizó capas de laminado ColorCore en fragmentos pequeños para lograr el efecto trampantojo de un boquete a través de una puerta con la leyenda "vendido". Estos proyectos sugirieron una nueva difusión de diseño para Formica Corporation e hicieron hincapié en la adecuación del laminado ColorCore para las instalaciones tridimensionales, muy coloridas y con diseños. La exhibición fue tan exitosa que viajó a nivel internacional, siguió el camino de las propias redes de distribución de la empresa Formica, y sumó arquitectos y diseñadores en cada lugar. Con el tiempo, la exposición contó con otras figuras como Eva Jiřičná y Rodney Kinsman en Inglaterra, y Arata Isozaki y Shiro Kuramata en Japón, antes de finalizar su gira de cinco años en Singapur.

Ese mismo año, la empresa Formica se unió a la revista *Interiors* para encomendar una exhibición tridimensional a fin de presentar el nuevo producto. El diseñador industrial Michael McCoy utilizó el laminado ColorCore para crear una oficina temática para un ejecutivo de la industria aeroespacial. Un artículo en *Interiors*

lorCore-laminaatissa oli kaikkialla yhtenäinen väri, joka eliminoi tumman viivan, jollainen näkyi perinteisen pöydän pinnan reunan ympärillä. ColorCore-laminaatin mainostamiseksi uuden sukupolven suunnittelijoiden piirissä, Formica Corporation aloitti sarjan yhteistyöhankkeita arkkitehtien kanssa. Ensimmäinen näistä oli v. 1983 avattu näyttely nimeltään *Structure + Ornament* (rakenne + koriste) ja käsitti valikoiman projekteja. Näihin sisältyi Frank Gehryn kalalamppu, joka tehtiin ColorCore-laminaatista, joka oli paloiteltu ja revitty "kalan suomuiksi" ja joka valaistiin sisältä päin, tuoden esille materiaalin läpikuultavuuden. Toinen oli arkkitehtuuritoimiston SITEn *Ovi*, jossa käytettiin kerroksia murskattua ColorCore-laminaattia trompe l'oeil -vaikutelman aikaansaamiseksi lujan oven läpi räjäytetystä aukosta. Nämä projektit viittasivat uuteen suunnittelun yleistymiseen Formica Corporationille ja tähdensivät ColorCore-laminaatin sopivuutta kolmiulotteisiin, hyvin värillisiin ja kuvioituihin asennuksiin. Näyttely onnistui niin hyvin, että se liikkui kansainvälisesti ja seurasi Formica-yhtiön oman jakeluverkoston reittiä, lisäten arkkitehtejä ja suunnittelijoita joka paikassa. Näytöksessä oli lopulta mukana myös Eva Jiřičná ja Rodney Kinsman Britanniassa ja Arata Isozaki ja Shiro Kuramata Japanissa ennen kuin se päätti viisivuotisen kiertomatkansa Singaporessa.

Samana vuonna Formica-yhtiö yhdessä *Interiors*-aikakauslehden kanssa järjesti kolmiulotteisen näyttelyprojektin, jossa esiteltiin sen uusi tuote. Teollinen suunnittelija Michael McCoy käytti ColorCore-laminaattia luomaan teemapohjaisen toimiston ilmailualan johtajalle. Lehden *Interiors* artikkeli raportoi tuloksesta, "McCoy...sopivasti ehdottaa toimiston olevan kone, esteettinen, joka ilmaisee tietyt kuvat siellä tapahtuvista aktiviteeteista. Toimiston dynamismi koneena edellyttää, että asukas ei ole staattinen". Perinteisen työtilan neutraalisuutta karttaen McCoyn neuvottelupöydän pinta, ColorCore-laminaatista valmistettuna näyttää kiitoradalta. Lisää keltaisia juovia korostaa ColorCore-laminaattisten komeron ovien kahvoja ja rivi kääntyviä paneeleja, etusivuillaan punaista ja vihreää korkeakiiltoista Formica-laminaattia ja

些項目向富美家公司提出了一種新的設計媒體，強調彩虹芯美耐板對立體感、強烈色彩和圖案安裝的適應性。該展覽非常成功，最後在國際上巡迴展出，沿富美家公司自己的分銷網路路徑，在各處增加了建築師和設計師。這次展覽在新加坡結束五年巡迴展之前最終包羅了英國的伊娃·籍可納 (Eva Jiricna) 和羅德尼·金子曼 (Rodney Kinsman) 以及日本的磯崎新 (Arata Isozaki) 和倉俣史朗 (Shiro Kuramata)。

同年，富美家公司與《室內裝潢》(Interiors) 雜誌聯手，共同委託製作了一個展示富美家新產品的三維展覽項目。工業設計師邁克爾·麥考伊 (Michael McCoy) 用彩虹芯美耐板為航空航天業的一位高級主管製作了一間主題辦公室。《室內裝潢》刊載的一篇文章這樣報道結果：「麥考伊……適當地提出了把辦公室看做機器，這種審美觀傳達了那裡發生的活動的某種圖像。辦公室作為機器的活力意味著裡面的人也不是靜止的。」麥考伊設計的會議桌用彩虹芯美耐板製作，避免了傳統的工作區的中性，看上去像一條跑道。更多的黃色條紋點綴著彩虹芯美耐板做的櫥櫃門上的把手，一系列轉動面板均用紅色和綠色的高光澤富美家美耐板覆蓋，形狀像副翼，把書桌與一個休息區隔開。有質感的黑色地毯和黑色皮革家俱襯托出富美家美耐板的鮮豔色彩，把美耐板變成了圖形的亮點，而不是一個配角。美耐板的成分幾乎可以說是某個未來航天器的原型，使辦公室成為一個機器的展廳，一個低維護、高影響力的工作機器。這裡的效用顯而易見：彩虹芯美耐板是一種靈活的雕塑材料，消除了高壓美耐板傳統的二維性質。這裡的豪華體現在項目的未來主義中：富美家品牌美耐板已經超過了地球的表面，與下一代飛船在美學和功能方面息息相關。

富美家公司提出了一种新的设计媒体，强调彩虹心®耐火板对立体感、强烈色彩和图案安装的适应性。该展览非常成功，最后在国际上巡回展出，沿富美家公司自己的分销网络路径，在各处增加了建筑师和设计师。这次展览在新加坡结束五年巡回展之前最终包罗了英国的伊娃·籍可纳 (Eva Jiricna) 和罗德尼·金子曼 (Rodney Kinsman) 以及日本的矶崎新 (Arata Isozaki) 和仓俣史朗 (Shiro Kuramata)。

同年，富美家公司与《室内装潢》(Interiors) 杂志联手，共同委托制作了一个展示富美家新产品的三维展览项目。工业设计师迈克尔·麦考伊 (Michael McCoy) 用彩虹心®耐火板为航空航天业的一位高级主管制作了一间主题办公室。《室内装潢》刊载的一篇文章这样报道结果：“麦考伊……适当地提出了把办公室看做机器，这种审美观传达了那里发生的活动的某种图像。办公室作为机器的活力意味着里面的人也不是静止的。”麦考伊设计的会议桌用彩虹心®耐火板制作，避免了传统的工作区的中性，看上去像一条跑道。更多的黄色条纹点缀着彩虹心®耐火板做的橱柜门上的把手，一系列转动面板均用红色和绿色的高光泽富美家®装饰耐火板覆盖，形状像副翼，把书桌与一个休息区隔开。有质感的黑色地毯和黑色皮革家具衬托出富美家®装饰耐火板的鲜艳色彩，把耐火板变成了图形的亮点，而不是一个配角。耐火板的成分几乎可以说是某个未来航天器的原型，使办公室成为一个机器的展厅，一个低维护、高影响力的工作机器。这里的效用显而易见：彩虹心®耐火板是一种灵活的雕塑材料，消除了高压耐火板传统的二维性质。这里的豪华体现在项目的未来主义中：富美家品牌耐火板已经超越了地球的表面，与下一代飞船在美学上和功能方面息息相关。

1997 年，富美家®装饰耐火板在成为连接艺术、娱乐和招待桥梁的一次

ซึ่งเป็นแผ่นลามิเนทที่ถูกตัด และฉีกเป็น "เกล็ดปลา" และให้แสงสว่างจากด้านใน ซึ่งจะเผยให้เห็นถึงความโปร่งแสงของวัสดุ โครงการอีกชิ้นหนึ่งก็คือ *ประตู*ของบริษัทสถาปัตยกรรมไซต์ ที่ใช้ขบวนคัลเลอร์คอร์ที่แตกกระเถิน เพื่อให้เกิดเป็นภาพหลอกตาของรูผ่านทะลุประตูที่ขาย โครงการเหล่านี้แนะนำการออกแบบใหม่ๆให้กับฟอร์ไมก้าและเน้นย้ำถึงความเหมาะสมของคัลเลอร์คอร์ในการแสดงผลงานแบบสามมิติ มีสีสัน และลวดลาย นิทรรศการดังกล่าวประสบความสำเร็จเป็นอย่างมากจนได้เดินทางไปแสดงในต่างประเทศ ตามเส้นทางเครือข่ายศูนย์กระจายสินค้าของฟอร์ไมก้า และได้เพิ่มจำนวนสถาปนิกและนักออกแบบในทุกๆ ที่ ท้ายที่สุดการแสดงประกอบด้วยอีวา จีรีคนา และ รอดนีย์ คินส์แมน ในสหราชอาณาจักร และ อาราตะ ไอโซซากิ และ ชิโร คูรามาตะ ในประเทศญี่ปุ่นก่อนที่จะจบการเดินทางเป็นระยะเวลาห้าปีในประเทศสิงคโปร์

ในปีเดียวกันฟอร์ไมก้าได้ร่วมกับนิตยสาร *Interiors* ในการจัดโครงการนิทรรศการสามมิติซึ่งแสดงผลิตภัณฑ์ใหม่ของบริษัท ไมเคิล แมคคอย นักออกแบบอุตสาหกรรมใช้คัลเลอร์คอร์ ในการสร้างสำนักงานที่มีธีมกำหนดไว้เพื่อผู้บริหารอุตสาหกรรมการบินอวกาศ บทความหนึ่งในนิตยสาร *Interiors* รายงานไว้ว่า "แมคคอย...นำเสนอได้อย่างเหมาะสมว่าสำนักงานเปรียบเสมือนเครื่องจักร ซึ่งเป็นความงดงามที่ส่งผ่านจินตนาการเกี่ยวกับกิจกรรมต่างๆ ที่เกิดขึ้นที่นั่น ความมีพลังของสำนักงานที่เปรียบเป็นเครื่องจักรนี้

nière suivante : « McCoy… propose de manière adéquate le bureau en tant que machine, une esthétique qui communique une certaine imagerie sur les activités ayant lieu dans cet endroit. Le dynamisme du bureau en tant que machine suggère que l'utilisateur n'est pas statique. » Évitant la neutralité de l'espace de travail traditionnel, le dessus de la table de conférence de McCoy réalisé en stratifié ColorCore ressemble à une piste d'atterrissage. D'autres rayures jaunes marquent les poignées des portes d'armoire en stratifié ColorCore et une série de panneaux pivotants de stratifié revêtus de stratifié Formica très brillant rouge et vert en forme d'ailerons séparent le bureau du coin salon. Le tapis noir texturé et les meubles de cuir noir atténuent les couleurs vives du stratifié Formica, mettant le stratifié en évidence plutôt que de lui laisser jouer un rôle secondaire. Les éléments stratifiés peuvent presque servir de prototypes pour de futurs engins spatiaux, de sorte que le bureau devient une salle d'exposition de la machine ainsi qu'une machine avec un entretien réduit et résistant aux chocs des activités. L'utilité est ici évidente : le stratifié ColorCore se révèle être un matériau à la fois souple et sculptural, qui élimine la conception traditionnelle en deux dimensions, une qualité associée au stratifié haute pression. Le luxe se trouve dans le futurisme du projet : le stratifié de marque Formica a quitté la surface de la Terre et demeure pertinent esthétiquement et fonctionnellement pour la prochaine génération de transformations.

En 1997, le stratifié Formica brillait encore dans une installation associant l'art, le divertissement et l'hospitalité. L'artiste britannique Damien Hirst a travaillé avec le designer Mike Rundell à la rénovation du restaurant Pharmacy à Notting Hill, à Londres, l'aménageant afin qu'il ressemble à une véritable pharmacie. Des chaises en plastique moulé blanc de Jasper Morrison et des dessus de table en stratifié Formica étaient disposés dans une salle remplie de placards en stratifié Formica blancs aux devants vitrés, avec de véritables boîtes de médicaments et des instruments chirurgicaux à l'intérieur. Les

brinda información sobre el resultado, "McCoy… propone adecuadamente que la oficina se asemeje a una máquina, una estética que comunica ciertas imágenes sobre las actividades que se llevan a cabo allí. El dinamismo de la oficina como una máquina implica que quien la habita no se encuentra estático". Al evitar la neutralidad del lugar de trabajo tradicional, la parte superior de la mesa de conferencias de McCoy, fabricada con laminado ColorCore, parece una pista de aterrizaje. Más franjas amarillas destacan los picaportes sobre las puertas de los armarios de laminado ColorCore, y una hilera de paneles giratorios, cubiertos con laminado Formica color rojo y verde de brillo intenso y en forma de alerón, divide el escritorio del área para sentarse. Una alfombra negra texturizada y muebles de cuero color negro realzan los colores vivos del laminado Formica, lo que hace que el laminado se destaque por su gráfica en vez de jugar un papel secundario. Los elementos de laminado casi podrían ser prototipos de alguna nave espacial del futuro, de modo que la oficina se convierte en una sala de exhibición de la máquina, así como también en una máquina de poco mantenimiento y alto impacto para trabajar. La utilidad aquí es evidente: el laminado ColorCore se muestra como un material flexible, escultural, uno que elimina la calidad bidimensional tradicional del laminado de alta presión. El lujo está presente en el futurismo del proyecto: el laminado de la marca Formica se ha movilizado más allá de la superficie de la Tierra, y aún es estética y funcionalmente relevante para la próxima generación de artesanía.

En 1997, el laminado Formica tuvo, nuevamente, un rol protagónico en una instalación que salvaba las distancias entre el arte, el entretenimiento y la hospitalidad. El artista británico Damien Hirst trabajó con el diseñador Mike Rundell en la remodelación del restaurante Pharmacy en Notting Hill, Londres, que fue equipado para que se asemeje a una droguería en funcionamiento. Las sillas Jasper Morrison de plástico moldeado color blanco y las mesas con superficie de laminado Formica estaban acomodadas en una habitación bordeada con aparadores de laminado Formica color blanco con frente vidria-

muotoiltuna siivekkeiden näköisiksi, erottaa pöydän istuinten sijaintipaikasta. Musta teksturoitu matto ja mustat nahkahuonekalut tuovat esiin Formica-laminaatin kirkkaat värit, tehden laminaatista graafisen kohokohdan sivuosan esittäjän sijasta. Laminaattiset elementit voisivat melkein olla prototyyppejä jotain tulevaisuuden avaruusalusta varten siten, että toimistosta tulee esittelyhuone koneelle sekä helppohoitoinen törmäystä kestävä työkone. Hyödyllisyys on tässä itsestään selvä: ColorCore-laminaatti on osoittautunut joustavaksi, veistokselliseksi materiaaliksi, joka eliminoi perinteisen korkeapainelaminaatin kaksiulotteisen laadun. Ylellisyys on projektin futurismissa: Formica-merkkinen laminaatti on siirtynyt maan pintaa kauemmas ja on edelleen esteettisesti ja funktionaalisesti merkityksellinen seuraavan sukupolven käsityötaidossa.

Vuonna 1997 Formica-laminaatilla oli jälleen keskeinen rooli asennuksessa joka yhdisti taiteen, viihteen ja vieraanvaraisuuden. Englantilainen taiteilija Damien Hirst toimi yhteistyössä suunnittelijan Mike Rundellin kanssa Pharmacy-ravintolan kunnostuksessa Notting Hillissä, Lontoossa, varustaen sen muistuttamaan toimivaa rohdoskauppaa. Valkoiset valumuoviset Jasper Morrisonin tuolit ja Formica-laminaatilla päällystetyt pöydät asetettiin huoneeseen, jota ympäröivät lasioviset valkoisella Formica-laminaatilla päällystetyt kaapit, sisällään aitoja lääkepakkauksia ja kirurgisia välineitä. Baarituolit olivat aspiriinin muotoisia. Hirstin käyttämä Formica-laminaatti tässä julkisessa ympäristössä tuo mieleen sen käytännöllisen läsnäolon kaikkialla todellisissa rohdoskaupoissa ja apteekeissa, sekä kylpyhuoneissa, missä usein otamme pillerit. Valitessaan karun valkoisen Formica-laminaatin Hirst kuitenkin tähdensi materiaalin puhtautta ja kovuutta (mikä muu voisi selviytyä illan toisensa jälkeen ravintolan asiakkaista), tehden siitä samalla kiehtovan, käyttämällä neonvaloja. Se oli loppujen lopuksi mieletön idea teemaravintolaksi ja alustavan kuuluisuuden jälkeen kumppanuus meni pieleen. Kun ravintola meni kiinni v. 2003, Hirstin suunnittelutyöt, mukaan lukien Formica-laminaattiset lääkekaapit myytiin miljoo-

1997 年，富美家美耐板在成為連接藝術、娛樂和招待橋樑的一次裝潢中再次成為明星。英國藝術家達米安·赫斯特(Damien Hirst)與設計師邁克·朗德爾(Mike Rundell)合作，重新裝潢了倫敦諾丁山的藥房餐廳，把它翻新成類似於一家正在營業的藥店。白色模制塑膠的賈斯珀-莫里森椅子和富美家美耐板檯面的桌子放置在一間排著一溜玻璃面的白色富美家美耐板櫥櫃的房間裡，櫥櫃裡有真正的藥瓶和手術器械。酒吧凳的形狀像阿司匹林藥片。赫斯特在這個公共場所使用富美家美耐板讓人想起真正的藥店、藥房和我們經常服用藥片的衛生間的使用價值無處不在。但在選擇純白色富美家美耐板時，赫斯特突出了材料的潔淨度和韌性(還有什麼別的可以在每天晚上食客光顧之後倖存呢？)。同時，透過使用霓虹燈使其美艷無比。歸根結底，這是主題餐廳的一種反常理念，在最初的聲名狼藉之後，夥伴關係也不歡而散。當餐廳於 2003 年關閉時，赫斯特的設計(包括富美家美耐板藥櫃)在蘇富比拍賣會上以數百萬美元的價格售出，現已成為泰特現代美術館(Tate Modern)的博物館永久藏品的一部分。赫斯特把富美家品牌美耐板從大街帶進了上流藝術領域。

而另一位國際知名藝術家轉而使用富美家品牌美耐板製作畢爾巴鄂的紅色拱門，畢爾巴鄂是該公司在西班牙的長期總部所在地。作為建築師和公司合夥人，弗蘭克·蓋里(Frank Gehry)備受尊敬的古根海姆-畢爾巴鄂十週年慶祝活動的一部分，博物館委託藝術家丹尼爾·布倫(Daniel Buren)為該城市的 La Salve 大橋創作一個獨具特色的作品。布倫覺得，現有的鋼拱架扭曲了橋樑與博物館之間的關係，這個關係用一個像手臂一樣的建築物和一座石塔「擁抱」其跨度。用紅色重鋪橋面，在外露的邊緣畫上一系列藝術家的標誌性黑

装潢中再次成为明星。英国艺术家达米安·赫斯特(Damien Hirst)与设计师迈克·朗德尔(Mike Rundell)合作，重新装潢了伦敦诺丁山的药房餐厅，把它翻新成类似于一家正在营业的药店。白色模制塑料的贾斯珀-莫里森椅子和富美家®装饰耐火板台面的桌子放置在一间排着一溜玻璃面的白色富美家®装饰耐火板橱柜的房间里，橱柜里有真正的药瓶和手术器械。酒吧凳的形状像阿司匹林药片。赫斯特在这个公共场所使用富美家®装饰耐火板让人想起真正的药店、药房和我们经常服用药片的卫生间的使用价值无处不在。但在选择纯白色富美家®装饰耐火板时，赫斯特突出了材料的洁净度和韧性(还有什么别的可以在每天晚上食客光顾之后幸存呢？)。同时，通过使用霓虹灯使其美艳无比。归根结底，这是主题餐厅的一种反常理念，在最初的声名狼藉之后，伙伴关系也不欢而散。当餐厅于 2003 年关闭时，赫斯特的设计(包括富美家®装饰耐火板药柜)在苏富比拍卖会上以数百万美元的价格售出，现已成为泰特现代美术馆(Tate Modern)的博物馆永久藏品的

แสดงเป็นนัยถึงการไม่อยู่นิ่งของผู้อยู่อาศัย" แมคคอยหลีกหนีความธรรมดาของพื้นที่ทำงานแบบดั้งเดิม โดยพื้นผิวด้านบนของโต๊ะประชุมของเขาที่ทำจากคัลเลอร์คอร์นั้นดูเหมือนราวกับว่าเป็นวันเวย์ แถบสีเหลืองจำนวนมากทำรอยอยู่บนที่จับประตูห้องที่ทำจากคัลเลอร์คอร์ และแนวของวัตถุบูรอบที่ด้านหน้าปิดด้วยแผ่นลามิเนทฟอร์ไมก้าผิวมันวาวสูงสีแดงและสีเขียวและมีรูปทรงคล้ายปีกเครื่องบิน ซึ่งด้านหน้าที่แบ่งแยกโต๊ะออกจากพื้นที่สำหรับนั่ง พรมที่มีผิวสัมผัสสีดำและเฟอร์นิเจอร์หนังสีดำช่วยเสริมให้แผ่นลามิเนทฟอร์ไมก้าที่มีสีสันสดใสโดดเด่นขึ้นโดยเปลี่ยนลามิเนทให้กลายเป็นกราฟิกที่เป็นจุดเด่นไม่ใช่เป็นเพียงส่วนประกอบ องค์ประกอบของแผ่นลามิเนทฟอร์ไมก้าอาจจะเป็นต้นแบบสำหรับยานอวกาศในอนาคต ดังนั้น สำนักงานจึงกลายเป็นโชว์รูมเครื่องยนต์ ทั้งยังเป็นเครื่องจักรที่ไม่จำเป็นต้องบำรุงรักษามากแต่มีประสิทธิภาพสูงสำหรับการใช้งาน ประโยชน์ใช้สอยนั้นชัดเจนมากเนื่องจากคัลเลอร์คอร์แสดงให้เห็นว่าเป็นวัสดุประติมากรรมที่ประยุกต์ใช้ในการใช้ได้ง่าย และเป็นวัสดุที่จัดคุณภาพแบบสองมิติของลามิเนทแรงอัดดันสูงแบบดั้งเดิมออกไปได้ ความหรูหราเป็นโครงการในอนาคตนิยม ฟอร์ไมก้าได้ก้าวไปไกลเกินกว่าพื้นผิวของโลก แต่ยังคงให้ความสำคัญด้านความงามและการนำไปใช้ประโยชน์สำหรับยานอวกาศในยุคต่อไป

tabourets de bar étaient en forme d'aspirine. L'utilisation par Hirst du stratifié Formica dans ce lieu public rappelait l'omniprésence utilitaire des véritables pharmacies ainsi que des salles de bains où nous prenions souvent des pilules. Mais en choisissant un stratifié Formica blanc éclatant, Hirst a accentué la propreté et la durabilité du matériau (quel autre matériau pourrait, en effet, survivre nuit après nuit aux clients d'un restaurant ?). Simultanément, le matériau était rendu éblouissant par l'utilisation d'éclairage néon. En fin de compte, c'était une idée perverse d'un restaurant à thème ; après un engouement initial, le partenariat s'est étiolé. Lorsque le restaurant a fermé en 2003, les créations de Hirst, incluant les armoires à pharmacie en stratifié Formica, ont été vendues pour des millions aux enchères chez Sotheby's et font maintenant partie de la collection moderne permanente du musée Tate. Hirst a élevé le stratifié de marque Formica de la Rue Principale à la Rue du Musée.

Un autre artiste de renommée internationale s'est tourné vers le stratifié de marque Formica pour le projet Red Arches à Bilbao, le siège de longue date de cette société en Espagne. Dans le cadre des célébrations du dixième anniversaire du musée tant admiré Guggenheim de Bilbao de l'architecte et collaborateur de la société Frank Gehry, le musée a demandé à l'artiste Daniel Buren de créer une œuvre ayant pour lieu le pont La Salve de la ville. Buren estimait que l'arc d'acier existant déformait la relation entre le pont et le musée, qui étend sa travée avec un bâtiment en forme de bras et à une tour de pierre. En recouvrant la surface du pont en rouge, avec une série de bandes noires et blanches signatures de l'artiste le long du bord exposé, il a été possible de mieux relier le vert de la travée du pont, les écailles de titane irisées du musée et le nouvel arc. En 2007, le projet de Buren a été réalisé et baptisé Red Arches / Arcos Rojos (arcs rouges). Le matériau choisi pour l'arc rouge était un produit du compact extérieur Formica, choisi en raison de sa rigidité, de la stabilité de sa couleur et de sa résistance à l'eau. Les surfaces rou-

do, con cajas de medicamentos reales e instrumentos quirúrgicos en el interior. Los taburetes del bar tenían la forma de una aspirina. El uso del laminado Formica que Hirst hizo en este ambiente público recuerda su ubicuidad utilitaria en las verdaderas droguerías y farmacias, así como también en los baños donde solemos tomar las píldoras. Sin embargo, al elegir el austero laminado Formica color blanco, Hirst acentuó la limpieza y la resistencia del material (qué más podría perdurar noche tras noche para superar la circulación de los clientes del restaurante), y, a la vez, lo hizo sofisticado mediante el uso de luces de neón. Al final, fue una idea perversa para la temática de un restaurante y, tras la notoriedad inicial, la asociación se tornó poco agradable. Cuando el restaurante cerró en 2003, los diseños de Hirst, incluidos los armarios de laminado Formica para medicamentos, se vendieron por millones en una subasta de Sotheby y, hoy en día, forman parte de la colección permanente del museo Tate Modern. Hirst llevó el laminado de la marca Formica desde el gran público hasta el arte refinado.

Otro artista de fama internacional eligió el laminado de la marca Formica para el proyecto Arcos Rojos en Bilbao, la sede de la empresa en España durante mucho tiempo. Como parte de las celebraciones del décimo aniversario en honor al muy admirado Guggenheim Bilbao del arquitecto y colaborador de la empresa Frank Gehry, el museo le encargó al artista Daniel Buren que creara una obra específica del lugar para el puente de La Salve. Buren sintió que el arco de acero existente distorsionaba la relación entre el puente y el museo, que "abraza" su espacio con un edificio con forma de brazo y una torre de piedra. Recubrir el puente de rojo, con una serie de franjas color negro y blanco, la firma del artista, a lo largo del borde expuesto, uniría mejor el verde del arco del puente, las escalas de titanio tornasolado del museo y el nuevo arco. En 2007, se construyó el diseño de Buren y se lo nombró Arcos Rojos. El material que se eligió para crear el arco rojo fue el producto compacto para exteriores de Formica, seleccionado por su rigidez, porque garantizaba la estabilidad del color y por su resistencia al agua. Las superficies en color rojo, negro y

nien edestä Sothebyn huutokaupassa ja ovat nyt osa Tate Modern -gallerian pysyvää museokokoelmaa. Hirst vei Formica-merkkisen laminaatin High Streetiltä korkeaksi taiteeksi.

Toinen kansainvälisesti kuuluisa taiteilija valitsi Formica-merkkisen laminaatin punaisten kaarien projektiin Bilbaossa, yhtiön pitkäaikaisessa kotipaikassa Espanjassa. Arkkitehdin ja yhtiön työtoverin Frank Gehryn suunnitteleman, paljon ihaillun Guggenheim Bilbaon kymmenvuotisjuhlien osana museo pyysi taiteilija Daniel Burenia luomaan sijaintikohtaisen työn kaupungin La Salve -siltaa varten. Burenin mielestä olemassa oleva teräskaari vääristi sillan ja museon välistä suhdetta, joka "syleilee" sen jännevälistä käsivarren kaltaisella rakennuksella ja kivisellä tornilla. Sillan uudelleen päällystäminen punaisella sekä taiteilijan tunnusmerkeillä, mustavalkoisilla juovilla, pitkin näkyvää reunaa, yhdistäisi paremmin sillan jännevälin vihreän värin, museon sateenkaaren väreissä kimaltelevat titaanisuomut ja uuden kaaren. Vuonna 2007 Burenin suunnitelma rakennettiin ja sen nimeksi tuli Red Arches/Arcos Rojos (punaiset kaaret). Punaisen kaaren luomiseen valittu materiaali oli Formican kompakti ulkokäyttöinen tuote, valittu sen jäykkyyden, värinpitävyyden ja vedenkestävyyden takia. Punaiset, mustat ja valkoiset pinnat ovat itse asiassa sillan olemassa olevan rakenteen päälle asetettuja päällysteitä; taiteellisen asennuksen oli jätettävä olemassa oleva teräsrakenne

白條紋，將更好地使橋樑跨度的綠色、博物館閃光熠熠的白金色和新的拱架相連接。2007 年，布倫的計劃實現，並被命名為「紅色拱門」（Arcos Rojos）。建造紅色拱門選擇的材料是富美家緊實的戶外產品，之所以選這種產品是因為其剛度、色牢度和耐水性。紅、黑和白色表面實際上是覆蓋在橋梁現有結構上的表層；藝術的安裝必須不改變現有的鋼結構。布倫原計劃使用一種合成、帳篷式的紡織品創造這種效果，但富美家的戶外產品被證明更耐用，且同樣壯觀。

2008 年，富美家公司推出了與建築師新的合作，請十位與辛辛那提有聯繫的從業者使用富美家美耐板、第二代彩虹芯（ColorCore2®）美耐板、抗倍特結構美耐板或人造石材設計一款限量版傢俱。結果後來在辛辛那提的紮哈·哈迪德設計的當代藝術中心（Contemporary Arts Center）展出，展名為「從我們坐下的地方」（From Where We Sit）。哈迪德的「卷雲」（Cirrus）與彎曲、折疊的建築形式相呼應，使用多層垂直黑色富美家美耐板創造了一個集牆壁、長凳和斜坡於一身的座椅。在世界各地巡迴展出的展覽中的另外一些建築師包括彼得·埃森曼（Peter Eisenman）、邁克爾·

一部分。赫斯特把富美家品牌耐火板從大街帶進了上流藝術領域。

而另一位国际知名艺术家转而使用富美家品牌耐火板制作毕尔巴鄂的红色拱门，毕尔巴鄂是该公司在西班牙的长期总部所在地。作为建筑师和公司合伙人，弗兰克·盖里（Frank Gehry）备受尊敬的古根海姆-毕尔巴鄂十周年庆祝活动的一部分，博物馆委托艺术家丹尼尔·布伦（Daniel Buren）为该城市的 La Salve 大桥创作一个独具特色的作品。布伦觉得，现有的钢拱架扭曲了桥梁与博物馆之间的关系，这个关系用一个像手臂一样的建筑物和一座石塔"拥抱"其跨度。用红色重铺桥面，在外露的边缘画上一系列艺术家的标志性黑白条纹，将更好地使桥梁跨度的绿色、博物馆闪光熠熠的白金色和新的拱架相连接。2007 年，布伦的计划实现，并被命名为"红色拱门"（Arcos Rojos）。建造红色拱门选择的材料是富美家紧实的户外产品，之所以选这种产品是因为其刚度、色牢度和耐水性。红、黑和白色表面实际上是覆盖在桥梁现有结构上的表层；艺术的安装必须不改变现有的钢结构。布伦原计划使用一种合成、帐篷式的纺织品创造这种效果，但富美家的户外产品被证明更耐用，且同样壮观。

ในปี ค.ศ. 1997 แผ่นลามิเนทฟอร์ไมก้าได้เป็นดาวเด่นในการแสดงผลงานศิลปะที่เชื่อมโยงศิลปะ ความบันเทิง และการต้อนรับอีกครั้ง โดยเดเมียน เฮิร์สต์ ศิลปินชาวอังกฤษได้ทำงานร่วมกับ ไมค์ รันเดลล์ นักออกแบบด้านการตกแต่งร้านอาหารแนวร้านขายยา ใหม่ ในนอตติงฮิลล์ กรุงลอนดอน โดยตกแต่งภายในอกให้คล้ายกับร้านขายยาที่เปิดทำการ เก้าอี้ เจสเปอร์ มอร์ริสัน ที่เป็นพลาสติกขึ้นรูปสีขาวและโต๊ะที่ด้านบนปิดตัว แผ่นลามิเนทฟอร์ไมก้าถูกจัดไว้ในห้อง เรียงด้วยตู้ฟอร์ไมก้าลามิเนทสีขาวที่ด้านหน้าเป็นกระจกซึ่งมีกล่องยาลายและเครื่องมือผ่าตัดจริงอยู่ภายใน ม้านั่งเดี่ยวมีรูปทรงคล้ายกับยาแอสไพริน เฮิร์สต์ใช้แผ่นลามิเนทฟอร์ไมก้าตกแต่งสถานที่สาธารณะแห่งนี้ ทำให้นึกถึงคุณประโยชน์ในร้านขายยาจริงอยู่ที่ทั่วไป แม้กระทั่งในห้องน้ำซึ่งเป็นที่ซึ่งเราชมใช้ แต่ในการเลือกใช้แผ่นลามิเนทฟอร์ไมก้าสีขาวทั้งหมดนั้น เฮิร์สต์เน้นที่ความสะอาดและความแข็งแรงของวัสดุเป็นสำคัญ (สิ่งอื่นใดจะสามารถคงทนอยู่ได้จากลูกค้าในร้านอาหารที่หวนเวียนมาทุกคืน) ในขณะเดียวกันก็ทำให้ดูหรูหราโดยการใช้แสงไฟนีออน แต่ที่สุดแล้วแนวการตกแต่งร้านอาหารก็ยังคงอยู่ และหลังจากมีชื่อเสียงไม่ดีในช่วงแรก ก็ทำให้มีปัญหาระหว่างหุ้นส่วน เมื่อร้านอาหารแห่งนี้ปิดตัวลงในปี ค.ศ. 2003 งานการออกแบบของเฮิร์สต์ซึ่งรวมถึงตู้ลายที่ทำจากแผ่นลามิเนทฟอร์ไมก้าขายได้เป็นเงินหลายล้านในการประมูลของโซเธอบี้ และขณะนี้ได้กลายเป็นส่วนหนึ่งของคอลเลคชั่นในพิพิธภัณฑ์ของเทต โมเดิร์น อย่างถาวร เฮิร์สต์ได้นำลามิเนทฟอร์ไมก้าจากงานที่ใช้ตกแต่งร้านค้าตามถนนใหญ่ไปสู่งานศิลปะชั้นสูง

ศิลปินที่มีชื่อเสียงระดับนานาชาติอีกคนหนึ่งได้หันมาใช้แผ่นลามิเนทฟอร์ไมก้าสำหรับโครงการเรด อาร์คส์ ในบิลเบา ที่ซึ่งเป็นเหมือนบ้านอันเก่าแก่ของฟอร์ไมก้าในประเทศสเปน เพื่อเป็นส่วนหนึ่งของการฉลองการครบรอบสิบปีให้แฟรงค์ เกร์รี่ ผู้เป็นสถาปนิกและผู้ร่วมงานกับฟอร์ไมก้าผู้ซึ่งชื่นชมกุกเกนไฮม์ บิลเบาเป็นอย่างมาก ทางพิพิธภัณฑ์ได้มอบหมายให้ศิลปินเดเนียล บิวเรน ให้สร้างผลงานที่เฉพาะกับสถานที่สำหรับสะพานลา ซาลฟ์ ของเมืองบิวเรน รู้สึกว่าโครงสร้างเหล็กรูปโค้งที่มีอยู่เดิม ทำให้สะพานและพิพิธภัณฑ์ไม่สัมพันธ์กัน ซึ่ง "ล้อมรอบ" ด้วยอาคารและหอคอยหินที่คล้ายแขน การเปลี่ยนพื้นผิวสะพานใหม่ด้วยสีแดง ที่มีแถบสีขาวดำอันเป็นเอกลักษณ์ของตัวศิลปิน แนวขอบตามยาว

ges, noires et blanches constituent en fait un recouvrement placé sur la structure existante du pont. En effet, l'installation artistique devait conserver la structure d'acier existante. Buren avait initialement prévu d'utiliser un produit synthétique, une toile similaire à du matériel de tente, pour créer cet effet, mais le produit extérieur Formica s'est avéré plus résistant et tout aussi spectaculaire.

En 2008, la société Formica a lancé une nouvelle collaboration avec des architectes, demandant à une dizaine de praticiens ayant des liens avec Cincinnati de concevoir des meubles en édition limitée utilisant le stratifié Formica, le stratifié ColorCore2®, le stratifié compact structurel ou des matériaux pour revêtement solide. Les résultats ont ensuite été exposés au Contemporary Arts Center de Cincinnati créé par Zaha Hadid, lors d'une exposition intitulée « From Where We Sit » (où nous nous asseyons). « Cirrus » de Hadid faisait écho aux courbes, aux formes repliées du bâtiment, en utilisant des couches verticales de stratifié noir Formica pour créer une pièce siège combinant mur, banc et rampe. D'autres architectes de l'exposition ayant voyagé dans le monde incluaient Peter Eisenman, Michael Graves, Thom Mayne de Morphosis et Laurinda Spear d'Arquitectonica. La contribution de Mayne a pris la forme d'un banc de cisaillement dans le matériau de surfaçage Arctic Solid alors que Spear a adopté une approche plus organique. Son banc triangulaire « Treeleaf », en lime, jaune Spectrum et vert organique, suggère un mobilier tissé traditionnel ou les poufs populaires en rotin du designer italien Franco Albini du milieu du siècle, en dépit de son matériau à la résistance de qualité supérieure.

Grace Jeffers a écrit que le papier peint était un joyau et que le stratifié Formica était une armure, mais ces dernières années, les architectes et designers contemporains ont à nouveau employé la couleur, le motif et la décoration, le stratifié de marque Formica étant devenu les deux. À l'hôtel Gran Meliá Colón de Séville, les murs des chambres sont décorés de stratifié Formica avec impression damassée argent et noir, tandis que les portes présentent des reproduc-

blanco son, en realidad, una cubierta que se colocó encima de la estructura ya existente del puente; la instalación de la obra de arte debía dejar la estructura de acero existente intacta. Originalmente, Buren había planeado utilizar un textil sintético parecido a la tela de una tienda para crear este efecto, pero el producto para exteriores de Formica demostró que era más duradero e igual de espectacular.

En 2008, la empresa Formica hizo un nuevo acuerdo con arquitectos; les solicitó a diez profesionales ligados a Cincinnati que diseñaran una edición limitada de un mueble utilizando laminado Formica, laminado ColorCore2®, laminado estructural compacto o materiales de superficie sólidos. Los resultados se expusieron en el Centro de Arte Contemporáneo diseñado por Zaha Hadid en Cincinnati, en una exhibición que se denominó "From Where We Sit" (Desde donde nos sentamos). El "Cirrus" de Hadid, que se hace eco de las curvas y las formas plegadas del edificio, utilizó capas verticales de laminado Formica color negro para crear una pieza para sentarse que combinó la pared, el banco y la rampa. Entre otros arquitectos de la exhibición, que viajaron a nivel internacional, se encuentran Peter Eisenman, Michael Graves, Thom Mayne, de Morphosis, y Laurinda Spear, de "Arquitectonica". La contribución de Mayne tomó la forma de un banco con forma de tijera hecho con el material Arctic Solid Surfacing, mientras que el enfoque de Spear fue más orgánico. Su banco triangular, "Treeleaf", color lima, Spectrum Yellow y Organic Green sugiere que es un mueble de tejido tradicional (o el popular puf de ratán de mediados de siglo del diseñador italiano Franco Albini), a pesar de estar hecho de un material cuya resistencia es superior.

Grace Jeffers escribió que el papel tapiz era una joya y el laminado Formica, una armadura, pero en los últimos años, debido a que los arquitectos y diseñadores contemporáneos nuevamente adoptan el color, el diseño y los adornos, el laminado de la marca Formica se ha comenzado a utilizar para ambas funciones. En el Hotel Gran Meliá Colón de Sevilla, las habitaciones para huéspedes tienen paredes de realce de laminado Formica con estampado serigráfico con diseño damasco

koskematta. Buren oli alun perin suunnitellut käyttää synteettistä teltan tapaista kangasta tämän vaikutuksen luomiseen, mutta Formican ulkokäyttöinen tuote osoittautui kestävämmäksi ja yhtä mahtavaksi.

Vuonna 2008 Formica yhtiö aloitti uuden yhteistoiminnan arkkitehtien kanssa, pyytäen kymmentä ammatinharjoittajaa, joilla on siteitä Cincinnatiin, suunnittelemaan määrältään rajoitettavan huonekalun, käyttämällä Formica-laminaattia, ColorCore2® laminaattia, kompaktia rakennuslaminaattia tai yksivärisiä pinnoitusmateriaaleja. Tulokset nähtiin sitten Zaha Hadidin suunnittelemassa Cincinnatin nykypäivän taiteen keskuksessa, näyttelyssä nimeltään From Where We Sit (sieltä missä istumme). Hadidin "Cirrus," joka kuvastaa rakennuksen kaarevia laskostettuja muotoja, käytti pystysuoria kerroksia mustaa Formica-laminaattia luomaan istuimen, joka yhdisti seinän, penkin ja rampin. Muihin arkkitehteihin kansainvälisesti kiertävässä näyttelyssä sisältyivät Peter Eisenman, Michael Graves, Thom Mayne Morphosis-toimistosta ja Laurinda Spear Arquitectonica-toimistosta. Maynen kontribuutio oli muodoltaan saksimainen penkki Arctic Solid -pinnoitusmateriaalista, Spearin käyttäessä orgaanisempaa lähestymistapaa. Hänen kolmikulmainen "Treeleaf" -penkinsä, jossa on väreinä limetti, Spectrum Yellow ja Organic Green, muistuttaa perinteistä punottua huonekalua — tai vuosisadan puolivälin italialaisen suunnittelijan Franco Albinin suosittuja rottinkiraheja — sen paremmasta materiaalin lujuudesta huolimatta.

Grace Jeffers kirjoitti kerran, että seinäpaperi oli koru ja Formica-laminaatti oli panssari, mutta viime vuosina nykypäivän arkkitehtien ja suunnittelijoiden jälleen omaksuessa värin, kuvion ja koristeen, Formica-merkkinen laminaatti on tullut käyttöön molempina. Sevillan Gran Meliá Colón Hotellissa vierashuoneissa oli korostusseinät Damask-kuvioista silkkipainettua hopeanväristä ja mustaa Formica-laminaattia ja ovissa oli puolestaan tilaustyönä tehtyjä painokuvia Espanjan entisten mestarien maalauksista (Oletko El Grecon vai Velázquezin huoneessa?). Ranskalaisen parfyymiliikkeen Diptyque putiikkia varten Liberty of

格雷夫斯 (Michael Graves)、Mor-phosis 的湯姆·梅恩 (Thom May-ne) 和 Arquitectonica 的勞林達·斯皮爾 (Laurinda Spear)。梅恩用寒帶人造石材製作了剪刀型板凳,而斯皮爾採用一種更有機的方法。她的「樹葉」三角凳採用石灰白、頻譜黃和有機綠,使人聯想到傳統的編織家俱——或本世紀中葉義大利設計師佛朗哥·阿爾比尼 (Franco Albini) 的流行藤椅墊——儘管其材料堅實程度更加優越。

格雷斯·傑弗斯曾經寫道,壁紙是珠寶,富美家的美耐板是盔甲,但近年來,隨著當代建築師和設計師再次推崇顏色、圖案和裝飾,富美家品牌美耐板的用途則是兩者兼有。在塞維利亞的格拉梅里亞庫隆酒店 (Gran Meliá Colón Hotel),客房有一道裝飾牆,用錦緞圖案網印的黑色銀色相間的富美家美耐板製作,而房門上裝飾了定製的西班牙古老繪畫傑作印製品(你是否住在埃爾·格列柯或委拉斯開茲?)。 對於位於倫敦自由百貨商店裡的法國香水品牌蒂普提克的商店來說,特殊項目 (Special Projekt) 設計工作室指定用激光切割的五種顏色的富美家美耐板製作了一個三維圖案的屏風,靈感來自於蒂普提克的精

2008 年,富美家公司推出了與建築師新的合作,請十位與辛辛那提有聯繫的從業者使用富美家®裝飾耐火板、第二代彩虹心®(ColorCore2®)耐火板、抗倍特結構耐火板或人造石材設計一款限量版家具。結果后來在辛辛那提的扎哈·哈迪德設計的當代藝術中心(Contemporary Arts Center)展出,展名為"从我们坐下的地方"(From Where We Sit)。哈迪德的"卷云"(Cirrus)与弯曲、折叠的建筑形式相呼应,使用多层垂直黑色富美家®裝飾耐火板创造了一个集墙壁、长凳和斜坡于一身的座椅。在世界各地巡回展出的展览中的另外一些建筑师包括彼得·埃森曼 (Peter Eisenman)、迈克尔·格雷夫斯 (Michael Graves)、Mor-phosis 的汤姆·梅恩 (Thom Mayne) 和 Arquitectonica 的劳林达·斯皮尔 (Laurinda Spear)。梅恩用寒帶人造石材制作了剪刀型板凳,而斯皮尔采用一种更有机的方法。她的"树叶"三角凳采用石灰白、频谱黄和有机绿,使人联想到传统的编织家俱——或本世纪中叶意大利设计师佛朗哥·阿尔比尼 (Franco Albini) 的流行藤椅垫——尽管其材料坚实程度更加优越。

格雷斯·杰弗斯曾经写道,壁纸是珠宝,富美家的耐火板是盔甲,但近年来,随着当代建筑师和设计师再次推崇颜色、图案和装饰,富美家品牌耐火板的用途则是两者兼有。在塞维利亚的格拉梅里亚库隆酒店 (Gran Meliá Colón Hotel),客房有一道装饰墙,用锦缎图案网印的黑色银色相间的富美家®裝飾耐火板制作,而房门上装饰了定制的西班牙古老绘画杰作印制品(你是否住在埃尔·格列柯或委拉斯开兹?)。对于位于伦敦自由百货商店里的法国香水品牌蒂普提克的商店来说,特殊项目 (Special Projekt) 设计工作室指定用激光切割的五种颜色的富美家®裝飾耐火板制作了一个三维图案的屏风,灵感来自于蒂普提克的精品 "Choriambe" 的织物设计。反面印

จะเป็นตัวเชื่อมเข้ากับความยาวของสะพานแผ่นไทเทเนียมที่เป็นประกายของพิพิธภัณฑ์และโครงสร้างรูปโค้งอันใหม่ได้ดีกว่า ในปี ค.ศ. 2007 โครงการของบิวเรน ได้ถูกสร้างขึ้นและมีชื่อว่า เรด อาร์คส์/อาร์คอส โรโจส วัสดุที่ถูกเลือกมาใช้ทำโครงสร้างรูปโค้งสีแดงก็คือ แผ่นคอมแพ็คลามิเนทสำหรับใช้งานภายนอก โดยเลือกมาจากความแข็งแรง สีติดทน และมีความทนต่อน้ำ แท้จริงแล้ววัสดุปิดผิวสีแดง สีดำ และสีขาวที่ปิดคลุมโครงสร้างของสะพานที่มีอยู่เดิม โดยการติดตั้งลามิเนตเสมือนงานศิลปะจะต้องไม่แตะต้องโครงสร้างเหล็กเดิมที่มีอยู่ แต่เดิมบิวเรนได้วางแผนไว้ว่าจะใช้สิ่งทอสังเคราะห์ที่มีลักษณะคล้ายเต็นท์ในการสร้างผลงานนี้ แต่ผลิตภัณฑ์ฟอร์ไมก้าผ่านการทดสอบว่ามีความทนทานมากกว่าและมีความงดงามไม่แพ้กัน

ในปี ค.ศ. 2008 บริษัท ฟอร์ไมก้าได้เปิดตัวความร่วมมือครั้งใหม่กับสถาปนิก โดยการขอให้ผู้ประกอบการสิบคนที่มีความสัมพันธ์กับเมืองซินซินเนติ ให้ออกแบบเฟอร์นิเจอร์ที่มีจำนวนจำกัด โดยใช้แผ่นลามิเนทฟอร์ไมก้าคัลเลอร์คอร์2® แผ่นคอมแพคลามิเนท หรือวัสดุสังเคราะห์ ผลงานทั้งหมดได้จัดแสดงไว้ที่ศูนย์ศิลปะร่วมสมัย ที่ออกแบบโดย ซาฮา ฮาดีด ในเมืองซินซินเนติ งานนิทรรศการที่มีชื่อว่า From Where We Sit ผลงานของฮาดีด ที่มีชื่อว่า "เซอร์รัส" ซึ่งสะท้อนถึงรูปแบบโค้งพับของอาคาร โดยใช้ลามิเนทสีดำในแนวตั้งซ้อนกันเป็นชั้น เพื่อสร้างสรรค์เก้าอี้ที่ประกอบไปด้วย ผนัง ม้านั่ง ทางลาดเข้าไว้ สถาปนิกคนอื่นๆ เดินทางมาจากต่างประเทศเพื่อมาร่วมงานนิทรรศการ อาทิ ปีเตอร์ ไอเซนแมน ไมเคิล เกรฟส์ ธอม เม่ย์น แห่งบริษัทมอร์ฟอซิส และ ลอรินดา สเปียร์ แห่งบริษัทอาร์ควิเทคโตนิกา ผลงานของเม่ย์น เลือกใช้รูปแบบม้านั่งทรงกรรไกร โดยใช้วัสดุสังเคราะห์อาร์กติก ขณะที่สเปียร์เลือกใช้แนวทางธรรมชาติ โดยออกแบบม้านั่งทรงสามเหลี่ยมรูป "ใบไม้" สีเหลืองอมเขียว สีเหลืองสเปกตรัม และสีเขียวธรรมชาติเธอนำเสนอเฟอร์นิเจอร์ถักทอแบบดั้งเดิม ซึ่งนำมาจากเก้าอี้หวายอันโด่งดังของฟรานโกอัลบินี ซึ่งออกแบบโดยนักออกแบบชาวอิตาลีในช่วงกลางศตวรรษ แต่ใช้เป็นวัสดุที่คงทนมากขึ้น

เกรซ เจฟเฟอร์ เขียนไว้ว่า วอลล์เปเปอร์เป็นเครื่องประดับ และแผ่นลามิเนทฟอร์ไมก้าเป็นเกราะ แต่ในช่วงไม่กี่ปีที่ผ่านมา เมื่อสถาปนิกและนักออกแบบร่วมสมัยนำสีสัน ลวดลาย และของประดับตกแต่งมาใช้อีกครั้ง ฟอร์ไมก้าก็ถูกนำมาใช้เป็นทั้งคู่ ที่

tions sur mesure des tableaux de maîtres espagnols anciens (Vous restez chez El Greco ou Velázquez ?). Pour une boutique de la maison de parfums française Diptyque au magasin Liberty de Londres, le studio de design Special Projekt a souhaité utilisé le stratifié Formica découpé au laser en cinq couleurs pour créer un écran à motif tridimensionnel inspiré par le motif de tissu classique « Choriambe » de Diptyque. Au verso est imprimé l'un des modèles emblématiques d'inspiration botanique Liberty, avec des centaines de découpes au laser permettant de voir à travers les écrans des motifs sur un mur de fond à miroir. Enfin, à Boscombe, Bournemouth, de nouveaux motifs « Beach Pods » créés par Hemingway Design offre une modernisation de Skylark, avec des fonds turquoises et oranges ainsi que des dessins stylisés de poissons et de plage. Dans le bâtiment principal de l'établissement de vacances, les vestiaires sont décorés de bandes de stratifié Formica magenta, clémentine et bleu mer.

En tant qu'entreprise, Formica investit dans la recherche créative, en organisant des ateliers de jeunes designers pour répondre à de nouvelles questions liées aux limites du stratifié. Une surface peut-elle être perforée, ouverte, transparente ou translucide ? Une surface peut-elle devenir un système de support ? Doit-elle être fabriquée à partir de matériaux neufs ou recyclés ? Au début du XXe siècle, le stratifié Formica a pris la forme d'une surface rigide, brillante, sombre et même à cela des designers comme Donald Deskey y ont trouvé une source d'inspiration. Au cours des cent dernières années, des couches, des dimensions, des textures et des armatures nouvelles ont été ajoutées à ce produit pionnier et à chaque fois, les designers et les architectes ont intégré ces évolutions technologiques dans des intérieurs pour les nouvelles industries. Il y a tout lieu de penser que l'éclat et la fonction de Sequin peuvent être exportés au XXIe siècle : le stratifié Formica ajoute de nouvelles possibilités de réflectivité, de transparence et de durabilité.

en plateado y negro, mientras que las puertas muestran grabados a medida de obras maestras de la pintura clásica española (¿Se hospedará en una habitación de la planta El Greco o Velázquez?). Para una boutique de la casa del perfume francés Diptyque en la tienda de departamentos Liberty de Londres, el estudio de diseño Special Projekt especificó que se usara laminado Formica cortado con láser de cinco colores, para crear una mampara de diseño tridimensional inspirada en el clásico diseño textil "Choriambe" de Diptyque. En la parte opuesta, había impreso uno de los diseños botánicos icónico de Liberty, con cientos de mirillas cortadas con láser, lo que permitía ver, a través de las mamparas de diseño, una pared negra con espejos. Por último, en Boscombe, Bournemouth, los nuevos "Beach Pods" (Refugios de playa) utilizan diseños creados por Hemingway Design, que ofrecen una actualización de Skylark, con fondos color turquesa y anaranjado, y dibujos estilizados de peces y de la playa. En el edificio principal del complejo turístico, los vestidores presentan franjas de laminado Formica en color magenta, clementina y azul marino.

Como empresa, Formica está invirtiendo en la investigación del diseño, organizando talleres con diseñadores jóvenes para formular nuevas preguntas sobre los límites del laminado. ¿Debería una superficie ser perforada, abierta, transparente o translúcida? ¿Debería una superficie convertirse en el sistema de soporte? ¿Se la debería hacer de materiales vírgenes o recuperados? A principios del siglo XX, el laminado Formica tomó la forma de una superficie rígida, brillante y oscura y, aun así, diseñadores, como Donald Deskey, lo hallaron inspirador. Durante el transcurso de los últimos cien años, a ese producto pionero se le agregaron nuevas capas, dimensiones, texturas y núcleos, y en cada transformación, diseñadores y arquitectos incorporaron esos desarrollos tecnológicos en los interiores de nuevas industrias. Hay muchas razones para pensar que el brillo y la función del diseño Sequin se pueden incorporar al siglo XXI, ya que el laminado Formica agrega nuevas capas de reflectividad, transparencia y sostenibilidad.

London -tavaratalossa, suunnittelustudio Special Projekt valitsi laserleikatun Formica-laminaatin viitenä värinä luomaan kolmiulotteisen kuvioidun varjostimen, jonka inspiraationa oli Diptyquen klassinen "Choriambe" -kankaan rakenne. Kääntöpuolelle oli painettu yksi Libertyn ikonisista kasvitieteellisistä kuvioista, jossa on satoja laserilla leikattuja tirkistysreikiä, joiden ansiosta kuvioitujen varjostimien läpi näkyy peilitetty takaseinä. Lopuksi Boscombessa, Bournemouthissa, uusissa "Beach Pod" asunnoissa, käytetään Hemingway Design -toimiston luomia kuvioita päivityksinä Skylarkista, joissa on turkoosin ja oranssinväriset taustat ja tyyliteltyjä piirroksia kaloista ja merenrannasta. Lomakeskuksen päärakennuksessa pukuhuoneissa on Formica-laminaattiset sinipunaiset, klementiinin väriset ja merensiniset juovat.

Yhtiönä Formica investoi suunnittelun tutkimukseen, järjestäen seminaareja nuorten suunnittelijoiden kanssa uusien kysymysten esittämiseksi laminaatin rajoista. Tulisiko pinnan olla reiällinen, avoin, läpinäkyvä tai läpikuultava? Tulisiko pinnasta tehdä tukijärjestelmä? Olisiko se tehtävä uusista vai kerätyistä materiaaleista? 1900-luvun alussa Formica-laminaatin muoto oli jäykkä kiiltävä tumma pinta ja kuitenkin suunnittelijat kuten Donald Deskey pitivät sitä innostavana. Kuluneiden sadan vuoden aikana on lisätty uusia kerroksia, mittoja, pintoja ja ytimiä tähän uraauurtavaan tuotteeseen ja joka kääntessä suunnittelijat ja arkkitehdit ovat ottaneet mukaan näitä teknologian kehityksen tuloksia uusiin sovelluksiin. On olemassa hyvät syyt ajatella, että Sequinin kimaltelu ja käyttösovellus voidaan tuoda 2000-luvulle, kun Formica-laminaatti lisää uusia kerroksia heijastuvuutta, läpinäkyvyyttä ja kestävyyttä.

品「Choriambe」的織物設計。反面印著利伯蒂 (Liberty) 的標誌性植物圖案之一，數百個激光切割的窺視孔讓人透過圖案螢幕看到一個鏡像後牆上的視圖。最後，在伯恩茅斯 (Bournemouth) 的博斯庫姆 (Boscombe)，新的「海灘莢」使用海明威設計室製作的圖形，這是雲雀的最新圖形，綠松石和橙色的背景以及魚和海邊格式化的繪圖。在酒店的主樓，不斷變化的客房配備了洋紅色、柑橘色和海藍色的富美家美耐板裝飾。

作為一家公司，富美家在設計研究方面投資，為年輕的設計師舉辦講座，對美耐板的發展限制提出新問題。表面是否穿孔、開放、透明或半透明？表面是否應成為支撐系統？是否應由原生或再生材料製作？二十世紀初，富美家美耐板採取了僵硬、發光、深色的表面形式，而像唐納德·戴思琪這樣的設計師覺得這樣很具有啟發性。在過去的一百年中，這個開創性的產品增加了新層次、尺度、質地和核心，在每一個關頭，設計師和建築師都將這些技術發展融入了新興產業的內部裝潢。我們有充分的理由認為，亮片的閃光和功能可以被帶入二十一世紀，富美家美耐板會增添反射性、透明度和可持續發展的新層次。

着利伯蒂 (Liberty) 的标志性植物图案之一，数百个激光切割的窥视孔让人通过图案屏幕看到一个镜像后墙上的视图。最后，在伯恩茅斯 (Bournemouth) 的博斯库姆 (Boscombe)，新的"海滩荚"使用海明威设计室制作的图案，这是云雀的最新图形，绿松石和橙色的背景以及鱼和海边格式化的绘图。在酒店的主楼，不断变化的客房配备了洋红色、柑橘色和海蓝色的富美家®装饰耐火板装饰条。

作为一家公司，富美家在设计研究方面投资，为年轻的设计师举办讲座，对耐火板的发展限制提出新问题。表面是否穿孔、开放、透明或半透明？表面是否应成为支撑系统？是否应由原生或再生材料制作？二十世纪初，富美家®装饰耐火板采取了僵硬、发光、深色的表面形式，而像唐纳德·戴思琪这样的设计师觉得这样很具有启发性。在过去的一百年中，这个开创性的产品增加了新层次、尺度、质地和核心，在每一个关头，设计师和建筑师都将这些技术发展融入了新兴产业的内部装潢。我们有充分的理由认为，亮片的闪光和功能可以被带入二十一世纪，富美家®装饰耐火板会增添反射性、透明度和可持续发展的新层次。

โรงแรมแกรน เมเลีย โคลอน แห่งเมืองเซวิลล์ ห้องพักของแขกมีผนังที่มีลักษณะเด่น ตกแต่งด้วยแผ่นลามิเนทฟอร์ไมก้าที่พิมพ์ลายรูปแบบดามาสค์ สีเงินและสีดำ ขณะที่ประตูเป็นลายพิมพ์ภาพวาดเก่าขึ้นสำคัญของสเปนที่ทำขึ้นเฉพาะ (คุณพักอยู่ในเอลเกรโก หรือเวลัซเกซ หรือเปล่า) สำหรับร้านบูติกบ้านน้ำหอมฝรั่งเศสดิปทีค ในห้างสรรพสินค้าลิเบอร์ตี ออฟ ลอนดอน ออกแบบโดยบริษัทสเปเชียล โปรเจกต์ ได้ระบุว่ามีการใช้แผ่นลามิเนทฟอร์ไมก้าห้าสีที่ตัดด้วยเลเซอร์สำหรับสร้างฉากที่มีลวดลายสามมิติ ได้แรงบันดาลใจมาจากการออกแบบผ้า "โคเรียมบี" แบบคลาสสิกของดิปทีค ด้านหลังของฉากแผงกั้นพิมพ์ด้วยรูปแบบพันธุ์ไม้ที่โดดเด่นของลิเบอร์ตี ที่มีช่องมองที่ตัดด้วยเลเซอร์หลายร้อยช่อง ซึ่งช่วยให้มองทะลุผ่านฉากที่มีลวดลายเห็นผนังด้านหลังที่สะท้อนแสงได้ และท้ายที่สุด ในบอสโคมบ์ เมืองบอร์นเมาท์ "ห้องริมชายหาด" รุ่นใหม่ใช้รูปแบบที่สร้างขึ้นโดยเฮมิงเวย์ ดีไซน์ ที่ให้การปรับปรุงลายสกายลาร์ค ที่มีพื้นหลังสีฟ้าครามและสีส้มและภาพวาดประดิษฐ์รูปปลาและชายหาดที่ห้องเปลี่ยนเสื้อผ้าในตัวอาคารหลักของรีสอร์ท มีแถบฟอร์ไมก้าลามิเนทสีม่วงแดงสีส้มสด และสีฟ้าน้ำทะเล

ในฐานะบริษัทหนึ่ง ฟอร์ไมก้าได้ลงทุนในการวิจัยการออกแบบ และจัดการประชุมเชิงปฏิบัติการกับนักออกแบบรุ่นใหม่เพื่อสอบถามคำถามใหม่ๆ เกี่ยวกับข้อจำกัดของลามิเนท เช่น พื้นผิวลามิเนทควรจะฉลุเปิด โปร่งใส หรือโปร่งแสงหรือไม่ พื้นผิวควรจะเป็นระบบสนับสนุนหรือไม่ ควรทำลามิเนทขึ้นจากวัสดุใหม่หรือวัสดุใช้แล้ว ในช่วงเริ่มต้นของศตวรรษที่ยี่สิบ แผ่นลามิเนทฟอร์ไมก้าได้ใช้รูปแบบผิวหน้าที่แข็ง มันวาวสีเข้ม และต่อมานักออกแบบ เช่น โดนัล เดสกีพบว่ามันสร้างแรงบันดาลใจ ตลอดช่วงแปดสิบกว่าปีที่ผ่านมา ได้มีการเพิ่มระดับ มิติพื้นผิว และวัสดุแกนชนิดใหม่จากผลิตภัณฑ์รุ่นบุกเบิก และทุกครั้งที่มีการเปลี่ยนแปลงนักออกแบบและสถาปนิกได้นำการพัฒนาด้านเทคโนโลยีเหล่านั้น มาใช้กับการตกแต่งภายในสำหรับอุตสาหกรรมใหม่ มีเหตุผลหลายประการที่ทำให้คิดว่าประกายแวววาวและความสามารถนำไปใช้ประโยชน์ของลวดลายเลื่อมทองสามารถถูกนำมาใช้ได้ในศตวรรษที่ยี่สิบเอ็ด ขณะที่แผ่นลามิเนทฟอร์ไมก้ากำลังเพิ่มระดับใหม่ในการสะท้อนแสง ความโปร่งใส และความยั่งยืน

379

HELPPOHOITOISTA MAAILMAA KOHTI:
FORMICA®-BRÄNDI KONTEKSTISSA

HACIA UN MUNDO DE FÁCIL LIMPIEZA:
LA MARCA FORMICA® EN CONTEXTO

VERS UN MONDE FACILE À NETTOYER:
LA MARQUE FORMICA® DANS SON CONTEXTE

ก้าวไปสู่โลกแห่งความสะอาดหมดจด:
ในหมวีบทของฟอร์มิก้า

走向一擦净的世界：
现实社会中的富美家 (FORMICA®) 品牌

走向一擦淨的世界：
現實社會中的富美家 (FORMICA®) 品牌

PETER YORK

Ce que vous ne voyez pas dans les reconstitutions du dix-huitième siècle glorieusement photographié comme dans le film *Barry Lyndon* de Stanley Kubrick de 1975, avec ses beaux chandeliers, c'est la vie sauvage—les poux sautant dans les imposantes perruques et autres trucs. La vérité que vous manquez dans la splendide Galerie des glaces de Versailles c'est l'odeur de l'époque. Les contemporains ont signalé une odeur d'ammoniaque au milieu de la splendeur, l'odeur des aristocrates du dix-septième siècle qui ignoraient les infrastructures de base.

C'est une chance que l'apparition des photographies aux couleurs vives soit survenue plus tard, sinon la saleté aurait été bien visible partout. En fait, vous voyez très bien la saleté dans les premières photographies, datées de disons 1890, d'enfants de bidonvilles dont les visages étaient crasseux et vous pouvez la deviner dans les petits intérieurs bourgeois de l'époque remplis de fougères et drapés de chenille. Les étudiants du changement social se souviennent de l'injonction magique dans les romans et les livres de décoration du dix-neuvième siècle et du début du vingtième où il était question d'acheter des tissus sombres et des surfaces qui ne laissent pas voir la saleté. Cela signifiait que le chocolat, le rouge foncé, la peinture verte foncée, les tissus bordeaux et le premier linoléum imitaient le bois sombre. La saleté était partout. Elle provenait des feux ouverts, des lampes à l'huile, de la fumée extérieure, des bottes boueuses et de la nourriture préparée et du désordre que cela causait. Le monde ne connaissait ni les détergents, ni les désodorants, ni le nettoyage à sec. L'idéologie et l'esthétique qui marquent la différence entre l'ancien monde et le nouveau, c'est l'idéal d'un monde propre. Parmi les innombrables innovations qui sont apparues après la Première Guerre mondiale en matière de surfaces et de nettoyeurs, la « surface miracle », exceptionnelle par sa combinaison de potentiel de fonctionnalité et de design est le stratifié Formica®. Imaginez la mise en place d'un design moderne populaire (ce que Thomas Hine a si brillamment appelé le « Populuxe ») des États-Unis vers

PETER YORK

Lo que no se ve en las recreaciones del siglo XVIII, gloriosamente fotografiadas, *es la vida silvestre*, tal como en la película *Barry Lyndon* de 1975 de Stanley Kubrick con su preciosa y moteada luz de vela —pulgas saltarinas en las imponentes pelucas y demás. Lo auténtico del período que se pierde en el esplendorosamente mantenido Salón de los Espejos del Palacio de Versalles es el olor. Los contemporáneos describían un olor a amoníaco alrededor del esplendor, el aroma de los aristócratas del siglo XVII que no tenían lo que conocemos como amenidades básicas.

Es así también que la fotografía de colores bien definidos se volvió ampliamente disponible solo en su momento, porque de lo contrario se vería suciedad en todos lados. Actualmente se puede apreciar la suciedad en fotografías antiguas de niños de barrio de, digamos, la última década del siglo XIX: sus rostros están veteados por esta; y se puede predecir que está en todos aquellos espacios interiores de pequeños burgueses con cortinas de felpilla y repletos de helechos. Los estudiantes del cambio social recordarán ese mágico precepto en las novelas del siglo XIX y comienzos del siglo XX, así como en los libros de decoración de casas que sugieren el comprar telas y superficies oscuras que no muestren la suciedad. Esto incluía pintura color chocolate, rojo oscuro y verde oscuro, telas color "borgoña" y el antiguo linóleo que imitaba la madera oscura. La suciedad estaba en todos lados. Provenía de las chimeneas abiertas, las lámparas de aceite, el humo del exterior, las botas embarradas y la preparación de alimentos partiendo de cero, y todo el desorden que esto genera. En el mundo no existían detergentes, desodorantes ni la efectiva limpieza en seco. La ideología y la estética que marcan la diferencia entre el Viejo y el Nuevo Mundo son el ideal de un mundo limpio. Entre la gran cantidad de innovaciones posteriores a la Primera Guerra Mundial en lo que respecta a superficies y limpiadores, la "superficie milagrosa" destacada es el laminado Formica®, por su combinación de funcionalidad y potencial de diseño. Si se piensa en la presentación pública del diseño moderno *popular* (lo que Thomas

PETER YORK

Mitä upeasti kuvatuissa 1700-lukua esittävissä luomuksissa, kuten Stanley Kubrickin kynttilöiden valossa filmatussa elokuvassa *Barry Lyndon* (1975), ei nähdä, on sen ajan luonnoneliöt — komeissa peruukeissa hyppivät kirput ja sen sellaiset. Versailles'n palatsin loistavasti restauroidusta peilisalista puuttuu yksi ajalle ominainen piirre: haju. Ajalla eläneet kertovat loistoa ympäröivästä ammoniakin löyhkästä, joka oli ilman tuntemiamme perusmukavuuksia elävien 1600-luvun aristokraattien perusominaisuus.

On oikeastaan hyvä asia, että terävät värivalokuvat eivät tulleet yleisesti saataviksi jo paljon aiemmin, sillä lika olisi muuten ollut näkyvissä kaikkialla. Todellista likaa näkee vielä varhaisissa, kuten 1890-luvun slummien lapsista otetuissa valokuvissa, jotka näyttävät lasten lian tahrimat kasvot. Sen voi myös aavistaa noissa saniaisten täyttämissä, nukkakankaiden peittämissä pikkuporvareiden kodeissa.

Yhteiskuntamuutoksesta kiinnostuneet muistavat 1800-luvun lopun ja 1900-luvun alun romaaneissa ja kodinsisustuskirjoissa esitetyn taianomaisen ohjeen ostaa tummia kankaita ja pintoja, joissa lika ei näy. Tämä merkitsi suklaanväristä, tummanpunaista ja tummanvihreää maalia, viininpunaisia tekstiilejä ja puuta jäljittelevää linoleumia. Likaa oli kaikkialla. Sitä tuli avoimista tulisijoista, öljylampuista, ulkona olevasta savusta, mutaisista saappaista ja ruoanlaitosta, jossa ateriat valmistettiin alusta loppuun ja joka näin ollen likasi paikat. Siinä maailmassa ei tunnettu pesuaineita, deodorantteja eikä tehokasta kemiallista pesua. Vanhaa ja uutta maailmaa leimaavan eron ideologia ja estetiikka perustuvat puhtaan maailman ihanteeseen. Ensimmäisen maailmansodan jälkeen luotujen lukuisten pinta- ja puhdistusaineinnovaatioiden joukossa yksi "ihmepinta" erottui muista toimivuutensa ja muotoilupotentiaalinsa ansiosta: Formica®-laminaatti. Kun ajattelee modernin populaarin muotoilun (Thomas Hinen "Googie-arkkitehtuuri") leviämistä Yhdysvalloista muihin läntisiin maihin ja sittemmin koko maailmaan, on ajateltava taloja, ruokabaareja, elokuvateattereita ja lentokoneita, joiden sileät

彼得·約克

1975 年，斯坦利·庫布里克 (Stanley Kubrick) 拍攝了《巴里·林登》(Barry Lyndon)，裡面可愛的燭光斑駁陸離，用電影手法再現了十八世紀的輝煌，電影裡，你看不見的卻是野生動物——在高聳的假髮和其他的東西中跳躍的跳蚤。在凡爾賽宮保持華麗的鏡廳宮中你現今察覺不到的正宗東西是氣味。當代人在這輝煌的氛圍中嗅到了一股氨水味，這是十七世紀貴族們的氣味，因為他們還沒有我們所知道的基本衛生設施。

非常清晰的彩色攝影被廣泛使用，也恰逢其時，因為若不如此汙物便會隨處可見。你確實會在早期的照片中看到塵土，比如說十九世紀九十年代貧民窟兒童的照片，他們的臉上灰塵縷縷；你也能猜到在那些堆滿蕨類植物、掛著繩絨織物窗簾的小資產階級的屋內的狀況。

社會變革的研究者會記得十九世紀和二十世紀初的小說和家庭裝潢書籍中的那個神奇的命令，買深色的織物和不顯髒的表面。這意味著巧克力色、暗紅色、深綠色的油漆、深紅色的面料和早期深色仿木乾氈。灰塵無處不在，來自明火、油燈、戶外煙塵，來自泥濘的雨靴，繁雜的烹飪以及烹調造成的亂七八糟。世界上那時還沒有洗滌劑、除臭劑或高效乾洗。標誌著新舊世界之間差別的思維和審美就是憧憬一個乾淨的世界。一次世界大戰後在檯面和清潔劑的一系列創新之中，傑出的「奇跡檯面」就是集功能和設計潛力為一體的富美家美耐板。想一想倍受歡迎的現代設計的首次亮相(托馬斯·海因 (Thomas Hine) 聰明地稱之為「Populuxe」)，來自美國又推廣到西方的其他地區，然後又推廣到全世界，你會想到帶有富美家品牌表面裝點得如此平滑和耀眼的房屋、餐廳、電影院和飛機。

當然，當你縱觀十九世紀晚期英國和美國的上層人士時，人們都在盡力；越來越多的廉價女傭花費幾小時點火、

彼得·约克

1975 年，斯坦利·库布里克 (Stanley Kubrick) 拍摄了《巴里·林登》(Barry Lyndon)，里面可爱的烛光斑驳陆离，他以电影手法再现了十八世纪的辉煌，电影里你看不见的却是野生动物——在高耸的假发和其他的东西中跳跃的跳蚤。在凡尔赛宫保持华丽的镜厅宫中你现今得不到的正宗东西是气味。当代人在这辉煌的氛围中闻到了一股氨水味，这是十七世纪贵族们的气味，因为他们还没有我们所知的基本卫生设施。

非常清晰的彩色摄影被广泛使用，也恰逢其时，因为若不如此污物便会随处可见。你确实会在早期的照片中看到尘土，比如说十九世纪九十年代贫民窟儿童的照片，他们的脸上灰尘缕缕；你也能猜到在那些堆满蕨类植物、挂着绳绒织物窗帘的小资产阶级的屋内的状况。

社会变革的研究者会记得十九世纪和二十世纪初的小说和家庭装潢书籍中的那个神奇的命令，买深色的织物和不显脏的表面。这意味着巧克力色、暗红色、深绿色的油漆、深红色的面料和早期深色仿木油毡。灰尘无处不在，来自明火、油灯、户外烟尘，来自泥泞的雨靴，繁杂的烹饪以及烹调造成的乱七八糟。世界上那时还没有洗涤剂、除臭剂或高效干洗。标志着新旧世界之间差别的思维和审美就是憧憬一个干净的世界。一次世界大战后在台面和清洁剂的一系列创新之中，杰出的"奇迹台面"就是集功能和设计潜力为一体的富美家®装饰耐火板。想一想倍受欢迎的现代设计的首次展示(托马斯·海因 (Thomas Hine) 聪明地称之为"Populuxe")，来自美国又推广到西方的其他地区，然后又推广到全世界，你会想到带有富美家品牌表面装得如此平滑和耀眼的房屋、餐厅、电影院和飞机。

当然，当你纵观十九世纪晚期英国和美国的上层人士时，人们都在尽力；越来越多的廉价女佣花费几小时点火、洗衣服、抛光地板、擦洗松木餐桌。就

ปีเตอร์ ยอร์ค

สิ่งที่คุณไม่เห็นในรูปถ่ายที่สวยงามในช่วงศตวรรษที่ 18 ที่นำกลับมาทำใหม่ เช่น ภาพยนตร์ของสแตนลีย์ คูบริก ในปี 1975 เรื่องแบรรี่ ลินดอน ที่ได้รับการแต่งแต้มด้วยแสงเทียนที่น่ามอง คือ ชีวิตแบบสัตว์ป่าของพวกเห็บ หมัด ที่กระโดดอยู่ในวิกผมทรงสูงและในสิ่งของต่าง ๆ ส่วนสิ่งอันเป็นต้นตำรับในยุคประวัติศาสตร์ที่คุณไม่ได้เห็นใน Hall of Mirrors ที่ได้รับการดูแลรักษาเป็นอย่างดีในพระราชวังแวร์ซายส์ คือ กลิ่น ในยุคนั้นมีการรายงานเกี่ยวกับเรื่องกลิ่นไม่พึงประสงค์ของแอมโมเนียในบริเวณสถานที่ที่มีความเจิดจรัสนั้น ซึ่งเป็นกลิ่นของชนชั้นสูงในช่วงศตวรรษที่ 17 ซึ่งยังไม่มีสิ่งที่ในปัจจุบันเราถือกันว่าเป็นสุขอนามัยขั้นพื้นฐาน

กระนั้นแล้วถือเป็นการดีที่รูปถ่ายสีคุณภาพเยี่ยมคมชัดเพิ่งเกิดขึ้นเมื่อไม่นานมานี้มิฉะนั้นแล้วเราคงได้เห็นความสกปรกในทุกที่จริง ๆ แล้วคุณเห็นความสกปรกอยู่แล้วในรูปถ่ายยุคแรก ๆ เช่น รูปของเด็ก ๆ ในชุมชนแออัดในช่วงทศวรรษที่ 1890 ที่ใบหน้าเต็มไปด้วยริ้วรอยของความสกปรกนั้น และคุณก็สามารถเดาได้ว่ามีสิ่งสกปรกอยู่ในสิ่งทอตกแต่งภายในของชนชั้นกลางระดับล่างที่มีเฟิร์นระเกะระกะ

นักศึกษาทางด้านการเปลี่ยนแปลงทางสังคมคงจะจำคำเตือนอันแสนวิเศษในนิยายช่วงศตวรรษที่ 19 ถึงต้นศตวรรษที่ 20 และหนังสือเกี่ยวกับการตกแต่งบ้านได้ว่าให้ซื้อผ้าและใช้พื้นผิวสีเข้มที่ไม่แสดงความสกปรก ซึ่งสีเหล่านั้นได้แก่ สีทาบ้านพวก สีช็อกโกแลตสีแดงเข้ม และสีเขียวเข้ม ผ้า "สีม่วงแดง" และสื่อน้ำมันในยุคต้นที่ทาเคลียบแบบไม่สีเข้ม แต่ความสกปรกก็ยังคงมีอยู่ทุกแห่ง ความสกปรกมาจากเปลวไฟ ตะเกียงน้ำมัน ควันจากภายนอก รองเท้าบู๊ทที่เปื้อนโคลน และจากการทำอาหาร และความเลอะเทอะจากการทำอาหารนั้น โลกในยุคนั้นเป็นโลกที่ไม่มีผงซักฟอก น้ำยากำจัดกลิ่น หรือการซักแห้งอย่างมีประสิทธิภาพ แนวความคิดแบบสุนทรียที่เป็นจุดที่แสดงถึงความแตกต่างระหว่างโลกยุคเก่าและโลกยุคใหม่ คือ แนวคิดของโลกที่สะอาด หนึ่งในสิ่งประดิษฐ์ที่เกิดขึ้นหลังจากสงครามโลกครั้งที่ 1 ทางด้านพื้นผิว และการทำความสะอาด หรือที่เรียกกันว่า "พื้นผิวมหัศจรรย์" ที่โดดเด่น อันมีที่มาจากการรวมตัวกันของประโยชน์ใช้สอยและการออกแบบอย่างมีศักยภาพ คือ แผ่นลามิเนทฟอร์ไมก้า ลองนึกถึงการออกแบบในยุคใหม่ที่ทำให้วัตถุอยู่ในรูปที่เป็นม่วนและสามารถคลื่ออกมาได้ (หรือที่โทมัส ไฮน์

383

le reste de l'Occident et puis le monde et pensez aux maisons, aux restaurants, aux cinémas et aux avions lisses et brillants, mais violemment décorés, de surfaces de marque Formica.

Bien sûr, quand vous grimpiez sur l'échelle sociale de la fin du dix-neuvième siècle au Royaume-Uni et aux États-Unis, les gens faisaient de leur mieux. Une armée de domestiques sous-payés passait des heures à l'entretien des feux, à la lessive, au cirage des parquets—et à frotter les tables de cuisine en pin. Tout comme l'ensemble des surfaces de cuisine traditionnelle, les sols et les plans de travail, ces tables de bois possédaient des qualités merveilleusement authentiques, organiques et profondément naturelles de porosité, de perméabilité et d'absorption (et des aspects résolument unis). En d'autres termes, ils étaient l'exact opposé du stratifié Formica avec son barrage radical de la nourriture, aux bébés et aux chiens avec en revanche, une extrême polyvalence de design. Les plans de travail traditionnels retenaient, absorbaient et agrippaient positivement tous les types de matières organiques, et en conservaient les odeurs. La saleté, comme nous le savons tous, est une question de localisation—la boue des routes en terre, subtilement dissimulée dans l'ourlet des jupes des dames respectables. Le passé était sale, surtout parce que tout était si difficile à nettoyer. La cire était figée sur les planchers, il y avait des taches brunes collantes sur les plafonds provenant des lampes à huile, des pipes et du tabac. La saleté faisait partie intégrante de la décoration intérieure traditionnelle.

Il n'est pas surprenant que la lutte du dix-neuvième siècle contre la saleté a trouvé sa plus forte expression et la plus prolongée aux États-Unis. Là, elle a pris cette combinaison fascinante de prosélytisme et de science de consommation populaires. Elle était à la fois ancienne et moderne. Un vieux proverbe hébreu était constamment cité : « La propreté est proche de la piété, » recyclé d'abord par Francis Bacon, puis par le prédicateur influent John Wesley, et dans mille chaires américaines du dix-neuvième siècle ainsi que dans des centaines de livres destinés aux ménagères de la classe moyenne qui expliquaient comment vivre en

Hine tan brillantemente denominó "populuxe") desde EE. UU. hacia el resto del Occidente y, luego, hacia el mundo, se pensará en las casas, los comedores, los cines y los aviones refinados y relucientes, y ampliamente decorados, con superficies de la marca Formica.

Por supuesto, a medida que se ascendía en las clases sociales de Gran Bretaña y de los Estados Unidos del siglo XIX, las personas intentaban lo mejor; un ejército, cada vez mayor, de empleadas domésticas mal pagadas pasaba horas preparando las hogueras, lavando la ropa y puliendo los pisos, así como fregando las mesas de pino de la cocina. Al igual que todas las otras superficies tradicionales de la cocina y del área de servicio anexa (pisos y encimeras), estas mesas de madera tenían aquellas maravillosas cualidades auténticas, orgánicas y profundamente naturales de la porosidad, permeabilidad y absorción (y apariencias absolutamente lisas). Estas son, en otras palabras, lo opuesto al laminado Formica, con su mensaje de "prohibida la entrada" para todo, desde la preparación de comidas hasta para los bebés y los perros; y aún más, por el contraste de su extrema versatilidad de diseño. Las superficies antiguas tradicionales retenían y absorbían todo tipo de materia orgánica, adhiriéndose verdaderamente a estas. La materia (y sus olores) no solo se fijaban en el exterior de las superficies, sino que también las impregnaban en su interior. La suciedad, como todos sabemos, es materia fuera de lugar: el barro de calles sin pavimentar que se introdujo sutilmente en los dobladillos de las vestimentas de mujeres respetables. El pasado era sucio, sobre todo porque era muy difícil limpiar. Había cera solidificada en las tablas del piso y manchas marrones y pegajosas en los cielorrasos por las lámparas de aceite, las tuberías y los cigarrillos. La suciedad era una parte integral de la decoración interior tradicional.

No es sorprendente que la pelea contra la suciedad en el siglo XIX haya tenido su capítulo más fuerte y largo en los Estados Unidos. Allí se aceptó aquella fascinante combinación estadounidense del proselitismo y la popular ciencia del consumidor. Era antigua y moderna. El preámbulo incluía la constante citación del antiguo proverbio hebreo "La limpieza acerca a lo divino"

ja kiiltävät (ja railakkaasti koristellut) pinnat saatiin aikaan Formicalla.

Ihmiset yrittivät tietenkin parhaansa 1800-luvun lopun Britannian ja Amerikan luokkajärjestelmässä ylöspäin kiivetessään: heidän alipalkatut piikansa raatoivat tuntikausia tehden tulia, pesten pyykkiä ja kiillottaen lattioita – ja kuuraten keittiön mäntypöytiä. Niin kuin kaikkia muitakin perinteisiä keittiö- ja apukeittiöpintoja – lattioita ja työtasoja – näitä puupöytiä leimasi ihanan aito, orgaaninen ja täysin luonnollinen huokoisuus, läpäisevyys ja imukyky (ja tietoisen arkinen ulkonäkö). Ne olivat toisin sanoen täydellinen vastakohta Formica-laminaatille, joka estää pääsyn kaikelle, elintarvikkeista lapsiin ja koiriin, mutta taipuu samalla äärimmäisen monipuoliseen muotoiluun. Vanhat pinnat ottivat ja imivät itseensä ja suorastaan takertuivat kaikenlaiseen orgaaniseen aineeseen. Ne ottivat sen omakseen – ja sen saattoi haistaa. Lika on, kuten tiedetään, paikaltaan pois joutunutta ainetta, päällystämättömien teiden lokaa, joka takertui kunniallisten naisten helmoihin. Menneisyys oli likaista ennen kaikkea siitä syystä, että puhdistaminen oli niin vaikeaa. Lattialaudoissa oli hyytynyttä vahaa, katoissa öljylamppujen, piippujen ja savukkeiden aikaan saamia tahmaisia ruskeita läiskiä. Lika kuului olennaisena osana perinteiseen sisustukseen.

Ei ole mikään yllätys, että suurin ja kauimmin kestävä taistelu 1800-luvun sodassa likaa vastaan käytiin Yhdysval-

洗衣服、拋光地板、擦洗松木餐桌。就像所有其他傳統的廚房和洗滌室的表面——地板和檯面——這些木桌具有孔隙、滲透性和吸水性(絕對平凡的外表),全部精彩真實、有機和絕對的自然品質。換句話說,它們完全與富美家美耐板相反,富美家美耐板傳達的是從食品到嬰兒和狗「不准進入」的資訊,然而,相比之下,富美家美耐板在設計上極端多功能。保留了舊傳統的表面,吸收並緊緊抓住各種有機物;把每一種有機物及其氣味吸收過來,融入內裡。大家都知道,污垢是格格不入的——未鋪設的道路上的泥水,巧妙地跑進了尊敬的女士們的裙邊。過去是骯髒的,並不全是因為一切都是那麼難以清潔。地板上有凝固的蠟;天花板上有油燈、煙袋和香煙造成的粘粘的褐色斑塊。污垢是傳統室內裝飾的一個組成部分。

毫不奇怪,十九世紀與污垢的鬥爭在美國譜寫了最強、持續時間最長的篇章。在那裡,人們採取了改變信仰和流行的消費科學這等迷人的美式組合,既古老又現代。這種積聚包括了永恆地引用舊時希伯來諺語「清潔僅次於聖潔」,第一次是由弗朗西斯·培根(Francis Bacon)拾起來再用,再到全球頗有影響力的傳教士約翰·韋斯利(John Wesley)接過去,再到一千個十九世紀的美國佈道壇和數以百計本書籍,告訴美國的中產階級主婦們如何生活更健康、更芳香和更聖潔。她們所夢想的是這個世界上一切都可以拆洗,並不斷地沖洗。

十九世紀末和二十世紀初有了實質性的創新——更好的便桶、品牌肥皂、搪瓷灶面。(供富人用的原始的、勞動密集型的洗衣機也是世紀之交的發明物。)清潔的修辭學和審美學(「甜蜜和光線」、「陽光和新鮮空氣」)在積累,就像從蟲子到細菌的大眾科學,在新興的美國中產階級中激起了憂慮和期望。這是一個快速增長、包括了許多新的行業和職業的群體——每一種辦事員、店員和訓練有素的工匠,在電話和電報的新技術領域工作的人們,一個不斷擴大的世界。

像所有其他传统的厨房和洗涤室的表面——地板和台面——这些木桌具有孔隙、渗透性和吸水性(绝对平凡的外表),全部精彩真实、有机和绝对的自然品质。换句话说,它们完全与富美家®装饰耐火板相反,富美家®装饰耐火板传达的是从食品到婴儿和狗"不准进入"的信息,然而,相比之下,富美家®装饰耐火板在设计上极端多功能。保留了旧传统的表面,吸收并紧紧抓住各种有机物;把每一种有机物及其气味吸收过来,融入内里。大家都知道,污垢是格格不入的——未铺设的道路上的泥水,巧妙地跑进了尊敬的女士们的裙边。过去是肮脏的,并不全是因为一切都是那么难以清洁。地板上有凝固的蜡;天花板上有油灯、烟袋和香烟造成的粘粘的褐色斑块。污垢是传统室内装饰的一个组成部分。

毫不奇怪,十九世纪与污垢的斗争在美国谱写了最强、持续时间最长的篇章。在那里,人们采取了改变信仰和流行的消费科学这等迷人的美式组合,既古老又现代。这种积累包括了永恒地引用旧时希伯来谚语"清洁仅次于圣洁",第一次是由弗朗西斯·培根(Francis Bacon)拾起来再用,再由全球颇有影响力的传教士约翰·韦斯利(John Wesley)接过去,再到一千个十九世纪的美国布道坛和数以百计本书籍,告诉美国的中产阶级主妇们如何生活得更健康、更芳香和更圣洁。她们所梦想的是这个世界上一切都可以拆洗,并不断地冲洗。

十九世纪末和二十世纪初有了实质性的创新——更好的便桶、品牌肥皂、搪瓷灶面。(供富人用的原始的、劳动密集型的洗衣机也是世纪之交的发明物。)清洁的修辞学和审美学("甜蜜和光线"、"阳光和新鲜空气")在积累,就像从虫子到细菌的大众科学,在新兴的美国中产阶级中激起了忧虑和期望。这是一个快速增长、包括了许多新的行业和职业的群体——每一种办事员、店员和训练有素的工匠,在电话和电报的新技术领域工作的人们,一个不断扩大的世界。

เรียกอย่างฉลาดว่า "Populuxe") ที่มาจากสหรัฐอเมริกา และเผยแพร่ไปสู่ประเทศอื่นๆ ในโลกตะวันตก และประเทศต่างๆ ในโลก ลองคิดถึงบ้าน ร้านอาหาร โรงภาพยนตร์ และเครื่องบินที่มีความเรียบและเงางามและได้รับการตกแต่งด้วยลามิเนทฟอร์ไมก้า

เป็นที่แน่นอนว่าเมื่อคุณได้เลื่อนฐานะชนชั้นของตนเองขึ้นไปในช่วงปลายศตวรรษที่ 19 ของอังกฤษและอเมริกา คุณก็จะพยายามอย่างเต็มความสามารถ โดยเห็นได้จากการมีแม่บ้านที่ได้รับค่าแรงอันน้อยนิดจำนวนมากที่หมดเวลามากมายไปกับการจัดวางกองไฟ การซักผ้า การขัดพื้นให้เงางาม และการขัดโต๊ะในครัวที่ทำจากไม้สน เช่นเดียวกับพื้นผิวครัวและห้องเก็บจานชามแบบดั้งเดิม พื้นและด้านบนของเคาน์เตอร์ พวกโต๊ะไม้เหล่านั้นยังคงใช้ซึ่งคุณสมบัติดั้งเดิมของวัสดุที่มาจากธรรมชาติซึ่งจะมีความพรุน ซึมผ่านได้ และมีการดูดซับ (และความเรียบง่ายอย่างแท้จริง) กล่าวอีกนัยหนึ่ง คุณสมบัติเหล่านั้นเป็นสิ่งที่ตรงข้ามกันโดยสิ้นเชิงกับลามิเนทฟอร์ไมก้าที่สื่อข้อความว่า "ห้ามเข้า" ต่อทุกอย่างตั้งแต่อาหาร ไปถึงเด็กอ่อน และสุนัข แต่ก็ยังคงไว้ซึ่งการออกแบบที่มีลักษณะเอนกประสงค์ พื้นผิวแบบดั้งเดิมจะเก็บกัก ดูดซับ และคงไว้ซึ่งสิ่งสกปรกตามธรรมชาติทุกอย่าง รับทั้งสิ่งสกปรก รวมทั้งกลิ่น มาอยู่ที่ผิวและซึมเข้าไปในเนื้อก่อให้เกิดกลิ่นสกสม เรารู้กันดีว่าความสกปรกมาจากทุกที่ โคลนจากถนนที่ไม่ได้รับการปรับสภาพพื้นผิวที่คอยเข้าไปอยู่ตามชายขอบกระโปรงของสตรีชั้นสูง ในอดีตมันแต่ความสกปรก อย่างน้อยก็เนื่องจากทุกอย่างยากต่อการทำความสะอาด ตามพื้นก็มีคราบเคลือบติดแน่น บนเพดานก็มีคราบสีน้ำตาลอันเกิดจากตะเกียงน้ำมัน กล่องยาสูบ และบุหรี่ ความสกปรกเป็นส่วนหนึ่งของการตกแต่งภายในตามแบบดั้งเดิม

ไม่เป็นที่น่าแปลกใจเลยว่าการต่อสู้ในช่วงศตวรรษที่ 19 ต่อความสกปรกเป็นช่วงเวลาหนึ่งที่มีความแข็งแกร่ง และยาวนานที่สุดในสหรัฐ ช่วงเวลานั้นเป็นการรวมตัวกันอย่างน่าตื่นเต้นดีใจของการเปลี่ยนแปลงทางความเชื่อ และศาสตร์ของผู้บริโภคที่ได้รับความนิยม อันเป็นสิ่งที่เป็นทั้งความโบราณและความทันสมัย กระบวนการเริ่มต้นมีการอ้างสำนวนฮิบรูโบราณว่า "ความสะอาดอยู่เคียงข้างความเป็นพระเจ้า" โดยมีการนำมาใช้เป็นครั้งแรกโดยฟรานซิส เบคอน ต่อมาโดยจอห์น เวสลีย์ นักเทศน์ที่มีอิทธิพลไปทั่วโลก และต่อไปยังนักเทศน์ชาวอเมริกันนับพันคนในช่วงศตวรรษที่ 19 และหนังสือหลายร้อยเล่มที่บอกแม่บ้านชนชั้นกลางว่าทำอย่างไรถึงจะใช้ชีวิตอยู่อย่างมีสุขภาพดี มีความ

meilleure santé, plus parfumées, et en général plus pieuses. Le rêve était celui d'un monde où tout était lavable et constamment lavé.

Il y eu des innovations substantielles comme de meilleures toilettes, des fabricants de savons, des surfaces de cuisine émaillées, le tout durant la seconde moitié du dix-neuvième et au début du vingtième siècle (Les machines à laver Primeval, destinées aux riches, mais difficile à utiliser, étaient disponibles déjà au tournant du siècle). La rhétorique et l'esthétique de la propreté (« douceur et lumière, lumière du soleil et air frais ») étaient élaborées, à la suite de la vulgarisation scientifique, des insectes aux bactéries, créant des anxiétés et des attentes dans la classe moyenne émergente des États-Unis. C'était l'époque de la croissance rapide de nouveaux secteurs d'activité et d'occupations : toutes sortes de commis, d'employés de magasin et d'artisans formés, de personnes travaillant dans les nouvelles technologies du téléphone et du télégraphe, un univers en expansion.

La plupart des surfaces de la maison à la fin du dix-neuvième siècle des sols, aux murs et au mobilier, restaient obstinément naturelles et poreuses, encore au vingtième siècle. La fin du dix-neuvième siècle avait produit des papiers-peints vernis pour les corridors et les cuisines, imitant les carreaux et les mosaïques. Mais ils étaient relativement coûteux et difficiles à installer, tandis que d'autres papiers-peints restaient extrêmement sensibles à la saleté et aux taches, ce qui explique l'utilisation de motifs denses à pois et ornementés et les teintes foncées.

Une cuisine ou une salle de bains couverte de marbres, de mosaïques ou plus modestement de carrelages était la marque du luxe de la classe moyenne américaine bien établie. Pourtant, ces surfaces traditionnelles étaient coûteuses, lourdes et difficiles à installer. Les disciples de la « douceur et de la lumière » avaient exhorté les femmes, dans les livres et les magazines, à remplacer les papier-peints « insalubres » par de la peinture fraîche dans des couleurs claires. Mais avant la guerre, la technologie de la peinture, avant les plastiques, était basée sur des ingrédients naturels, conséquemment les

(Literalmente: "El que ama la limpieza de corazón por la gracia de sus labios tendrá la amistad del rey"), primero reciclado por Francis Bacon; luego, por el predicador de influencia mundial John Wesley y, de allí, pasó a miles de púlpitos estadounidenses del siglo XIX y a cientos de libros que les enseñaban a las amas de casa estadounidenses de clase media cómo llevar una vida más saludable, limpia y pura. El sueño era tener un mundo en el que todo se pudiera lavar, y que se lavara constantemente.

En la segunda mitad del siglo XIX y a comienzos del siglo XX, se produjeron innovaciones importantes, entre ellas mejores baños, jabones de marca, superficies de cocina esmaltadas (a comienzos de siglo, también se encontraban disponibles para los ricos aquellas primitivas lavadoras que requerían mucho trabajo). La retórica y la estética de la limpieza ("dulzura y luz", "la luz del sol y el aire fresco") se estaban desarrollando, siguiendo los avances de la ciencia popular de los insectos a las bacterias, y creaban expectativas e inquietudes en la emergente clase media de los Estados Unidos. Era un grupo que crecía rápidamente para incluir a numerosos sectores y ocupaciones nuevas: todo tipo de empleados, vendedores y artesanos capacitados, personas que trabajaban en las nuevas tecnologías del teléfono y del telégrafo, un mundo en expansión.

La mayoría de las superficies domésticas de fines del siglo XIX, tales como: pisos, paredes y muebles, siguieron siendo obstinadamente naturales y porosas hasta bien avanzado el siglo XX. Al final del siglo XIX se había creado el papel tapiz barnizado para vestíbulos y cocinas, que imita azulejos y mosaicos. Pero era relativamente costoso y difícil de colgar, mientras que los otros tipos de papel tapiz eran muy susceptibles a las manchas e imperfecciones, lo que explicaba los populares diseños cargados con lunares y ornamentación, y los colores oscuros.

Una cocina o un baño completamente revestido con mármol, mosaicos o, más modestamente, azulejos era la marca de las casas de la clase plutocrática e incluso, de la clase media establecida de los hogares estadounidenses. Sin embargo, estas superficies tradicionales eran costosas, pesadas y difíciles de instalar. Los discípulos de

loissa. Se omaksui kiehtovan ja tyypillisesti amerikkalaisen muodon yhdistäen käännyttämisen ja populaarin kuluttajatieteen. Siinä yhdistyi vanha ja uusi. Valmisteluissa toisteltiin vanhaa heprealaista sanontaa "Puhtaus on jumalallisuudesta seuraava", jonka Francis Bacon ensin otti käyttöönsä, sitten maailmanlaajuista vaikutusvaltaa nauttiva saarnaaja John Wesley, kunnes sitä saarnattiin 1800-luvun Amerikan saarnatuoleissa ja sadoissa kirjoissa, jotka ottivat tehtäväkseen opettaa keskiluokan kotirouville terveellisempää, paremman hajuista ja ylipäätään jumalalisempaa elämää. Unelmana oli maailma, missä kaikki oli pestävissä — ja missä sä jatkuvasti pestiin.

1800-luvun loppupuoliskolla ja uuden vuosisadan alussa kehitettiin merkittäviä innovaatioita, kuten parempia käymälöitä, ostosaippuoita ja emaloituja keittiöpintoja. (Vuosisadan vaihteessa rikkaat saivat käyttöönsä jopa alkukantaisia, paljon työtä vaativia pesukoneita.) Puhtauden kieli ja estetiikka ("suloisuutta ja keveyttä", "aurinkoa ja raikasta ilmaa") saivat sijaa, ja sitä seurasi populaaritiede, joka tutki kaikkea ötököistä bakteereihin ja sai aikaan Amerikan uudessa keskiluokassa pelkoja ja odotuksia. Tämä ryhmä kasvoi nopeasti kattaen joukon uusia sektoreita ja ammatteja — konttoristit, myymäläapulaiset ja opin saaneet käsityöläiset samoin kuin laajenevaa maailmaa edustavan puhelin- ja lennätintekniikan parissa työskentelevät.

Useimmat kotitalouksien pinnat, kuten lattiat, seinät ja huonekalut, pysyivät itsepintaisesti luonnontilassa ja huokoisina pitkälle 1900-luvun puolelle. Edellisen vuosisadan loppupuolella oli saatu eteisiin ja keittiöihin laattoja ja mosaiikkia jäljitteleviä lakattuja tapetteja. Ne olivat kuitenkin suhteellisen kalliita ja vaikeita asentaa, kun taas muut tapetit olivat edelleen alttiita tahroille ja lialle, mikä selitti suosituimmat mallit, pilkut ja koristekuviot, samoin kuin tummat värit.

Marmorilla, mosaiikilla tai vaatimattomammin laatoilla pinnoitettu keittiö tai kylpyhuone oli Amerikan plutokraattien ja jopa vakiintuneen keskiluokan kodin merkki. Nämä perinteiset pinnat olivat kuitenkin kalliita, raskaita ja vaikeita asentaa. Suloisuuden ja keveyden suosittelijat olivat kirjoittaneet kirjoja ja aikakauslehtiartikkeleita, joissa he kan-

FORMICA*

十九世紀晚期的大多數室內表面——地板、牆壁和傢俱——在進入二十世紀多年後仍然固執地保持著自然和滲透性的特徵。十九世紀末曾為大廳和廚房製造了模仿瓷磚和馬賽克的油光壁紙。但它們相對昂貴，而且很難安裝，而其他壁紙仍然很容易弄髒和染色，這說明瞭點和裝飾採用深色的密集流行圖案的原因。

一個用大理石、馬賽克或較次一點的瓷磚裝飾的廚房或浴室是有錢有勢、甚至有成就的中產階級美國家庭的標誌。然而，這些傳統的面材昂貴、沉重、且很難安裝。那些「甜蜜和光線」的信徒們在書和雜誌中敦促女性用淺色的新油漆取代「不衛生」的壁紙。但戰前的油漆工藝——基於天然成分的前塑膠製品——意味著產品不容易被業餘愛好者使用(大規模的自己動手做趨勢也是在戰後才出現，都是由新產品、大

十九世纪晚期的大多数室内表面——地板、墙壁和家具——在进入二十世纪多年后仍然固执地保持着自然和渗透性的特征。十九世纪末曾为大厅和厨房制造了模仿瓷砖和马赛克的油光壁纸。但它们相对昂贵，而且很难安装，而其他壁纸仍然很容易弄脏和染色，这说明了点和装饰采用深色的密集流行图案的原因。

一个用大理石、马赛克或较次一点的瓷砖装饰的厨房或浴室是有钱有势、甚至有成就的中产阶级美国家庭的标志。然而，这些传统的面材昂贵、沉重、且很难安装。那些"甜蜜和光线"的信徒们在书和杂志中敦促女性用浅色的新油漆取代"不卫生"的壁纸。但战前的油漆工艺——基于天然成分的前塑料制品——意味着产品不容易被业余爱好者使用(大规模的自己动手做趋势也是在战后才出现，都是由新产

น่าอภิรมย์ และท้ายสุดแล้วมีชีวิตราวกับพระเจ้า ความฝันจริงๆ คือโลกที่ทุกอย่างสามารถทำความสะอาดได้ และได้รับการทำความสะอาดอย่างสม่ำเสมอ

สิ่งประดิษฐ์ที่ได้เกิดขึ้นเป็นจำนวนมากในช่วงครึ่งหลังของศตวรรษที่ 19 และต้นศตวรรษที่ 20 ได้แก่ ห้องน้ำที่มีตีขึ้น สบู่ที่มียี่ห้อ พื้นผิวครัวที่มีการเคลือบ (เครื่องซักผ้าในยุคแรกที่ยังคงต้องใช้แรงงานคนสำหรับคนร่ำรวยได้เกิดขึ้นในช่วงการเปลี่ยนศตวรรษเช่นกัน) วาทศาสตร์ และสุนทรียศาสตร์ของความสะอาด ("ความหอมหวานและความสว่าง" "แสงแดดและอากาศที่บริสุทธ์") ก็เกิดขึ้นมาตามศาสตร์ที่ได้รับความนิยมจากการเคยมีพวกแมลงไปสู่พวกแบคทีเรีย อันก่อให้เกิดความตึงเครียด และความคาดหวังในกลุ่มชนชั้นกลางชาวอเมริกันที่เกิดขึ้น ชนกลุ่มนี้เป็นกลุ่มที่เติบโตขึ้นอย่างรวดเร็ว เพื่อให้ครอบคลุมถึงอาชีพ และภาคสังคมใหม่เสมือนทุกประเภท พนักงานขายในร้าน ช่างฝีมือที่ได้รับการฝึกอบรม คนที่ทำงานทางด้านเทคโนโลยีที่เกิดขึ้นใหม่พวกโทรศัพท์ และโทรเลข ในโลกที่กำลังขยายตัว

produits étaient difficiles à appliquer par les amateurs (La grande explosion du bricolage est arrivée après guerre, entraînée par les nouveaux produits, la commercialisation de masse et la publicité intensive). Dans la plupart des cas, les peintures étaient aussi poreuses et fragiles que le papier-peint.

Le monde réel facile à nettoyer que nous connaissons n'est apparu qu'après la Seconde Guerre mondiale. Il attendait d'abord une série d'innovations substantielles, un nouveau niveau de la communication et un changement social véritable. Les attentes existaient, les riches possédaient déjà certains des outils—et certainement la main-d'œuvre disponible, mais les produits « miracles » de masse n'étaient pas encore arrivés.

Un grand élan vers le soleil éternel d'un monde sans tache provenait des médias. Les médias ont permis à de plus en plus de gens aux États-Unis, au Royaume-Uni et en Europe de découvrir comment les autres vivaient vraiment et ont permis aux publicitaires de démontrer à quoi pouvait ressembler un monde parfait. Des films couleur, plus nombreux dans les années 1930, devinrent le courant principal à Hollywood d'après-guerre, montrant des intérieurs passant de rêve d'artiste à un guide à suivre. La télévision d'après-guerre, avec ses feuilletons et ses comédies basés sur la famille, était tout simplement un cours élémentaire sur le côté domestique du rêve américain. Une montagne de magazines de grand public, généralement pour la famille tels que *Life* ou The *Saturday Evening Post*, et le groupe croissant des magazines de décoration tels que *House Beautiful* et *House and Garden*, tous avec un tirage culminant dans les années 1950 et 1960, montraient la bonne vie et les maisons parfaites tout en couleurs. Les premiers magazines aux couleurs imparfaites, mais avec diffusion de masse, comprenaient une publicité qui mettait l'accent sur des produits de nettoyage hygiéniques et leur commodité d'utilisation. Ceci avait déjà commencé au début du vingtième siècle. Au cours des années 1920, l'écrasante radio commerciale américaine, contrairement à la radio britannique et européenne, incitait les femmes à laver et à nettoyer constamment. Le feuilleton radiopho-

"la dulzura y la luz" habían exhortado a las mujeres, en libros y revistas, a reemplazar el papel tapiz "antihigiénico" por pintura fresca de colores claros. Pero la tecnología de pintura previa a la guerra —preplástico, basado en ingredientes naturales— implicaba productos que no eran fáciles de aplicar por aficionados (la gran explosión de actividades "hágalo usted mismo" [*do it yourself*, DIY] también fue posterior a la guerra, impulsada por los nuevos productos, la comercialización masiva y la amplia cobertura de los medios de comunicación). En la mayoría de los casos, las pinturas eran porosas y se desgastaban fácilmente como el papel tapiz.

El mundo real de fácil limpieza que conocemos no llegó hasta después de la Segunda Guerra Mundial. Requería mucha innovación sustancial, un nuevo nivel de comunicación y, ante todo, un cambio social real. Las expectativas estaban allí, los ricos ya tenían algunas de las herramientas —y ciertamente la mano de obra a disposición—, pero los productos masivos "milagrosos" todavía no habían llegado.

Un gran impulsor hacia el eterno resplandor de un mundo sin manchas fue la innovación de los medios de comunicación. Esta permitió que una audiencia cada vez más amplia en los Estados Unidos, el Reino Unido y Europa viera cómo la otra mitad vivía en realidad, y que los publicistas demostraran cómo luciría un mundo perfecto. Las películas en color, que aumentaron en la década de los treinta, se volvieron la norma en Hollywood tras la guerra, y mostraban espacios interiores que dejaron de ser secuencias brumosas de sueños escapistas para convertirse en guías instructivas. La televisión posterior a la guerra, con sus telenovelas y series cómicas, basadas en la familia, dictó un curso básico en el ámbito doméstico del Sueño Americano. Una cantidad de revistas dirigidas al gran público —generalmente con títulos para toda la familia, tales como *Life* o *The Saturday Evening Post*— y el creciente grupo de revistas de decoración de casas, como *House Beautiful* y *House and Garden* —todas en su mayor circulación en las décadas de los cincuenta y de los sesenta— mostraban la Buena Vida y las casas perfectas en colores vivos. El acometimiento inicial de las revistas, de color imperfecto pero

nustivat naisia korvaamaan epähygieeniset tapetit vaaleilla maaleilla. Ennen sotia saatavilla olevien, luonnonaineisiin perustuvien maalien käyttö oli kuitenkin vaikeaa muille kuin ammattilaisille (suuri tee-se-itse-innostus sai valtaa vasta sotien jälkeen uusien tuotteiden, massamarkkinoinnin ja laajan tiedotusvälineiden huomion tuloksena). Useimmat maalit olivat yhtä huokoisia ja naarmuuntuvia kuin tapetitkin.

Meidän tuntemamme aito helppohoitoinen maailma syntyi vasta toisen maailmansodan jälkeen. Se edellytti suurta määrää huomattavaa innovointia, uutta kommunikoinnin tasoa ja todellista yhteiskuntamuutosta. Odotukset olivat valmiina, rikkailla oli jo joitakin näistä välineistä —ja tarvittava työvoima— mutta massoille osoitetut "ihmetuotteet" odottivat tuloaan.

Tärkeä tekijä matkalla tahrattoman maailman ikuiseen aurinkoon oli uusi media. Sen avulla yhä suurempi yleisö Amerikassa ja Euroopassa saattoi nähdä, miten toinen puolisko todella eli, ja se antoi mainostajille tilaisuuden esitellä, miltä täydellinen maailma saattaisi näyttää. 30-luvulla alkunsa saaneista värielokuvista tuli sotien jälkeisessä Hollywoodissa yleisiä, ja niissä näytetyt sisustukset muuttuivat utuisista, todellisuuspakoisista unelmista opettaviksi esimerkeiksi. Sodanjälkeinen televisio perheohjelmineen ja tilannekomedioineen antoi peruskurssin Amerikan unelman kodinhoidosta. Joukko suurelle yleisölle tarkoitettuja aikakauslehtiä, kuten *Life* ja *The Saturday Evening Post*, sekä kasvava määrä sisustuslehtiä — *House Beautiful* ja *House and Garden* muiden ohella saavuttivat suurimman levikkinsä 50—60-luvuilla — antoivat värikuvan hyvästä elämästä ja täydellisistä kodeista. Aikakauslehtimainonnan juuret ulottuivat vuosisadan alkuun; väritykseltään puutteelliset mainokset ylistivät "hygieenisiä" ja helppokäyttöisiksi väitettyjä puhdistusaineita. Jo 20-luvulla amerikkalainen radio, joka vastoin eurooppalaista käytäntöä oli suurimmalta osin kaupallinen, yllytti naisia pesemään ja siivoamaan jatkuvasti. Radiossa esitettiin myös ensimmäiset suurelle yleisölle suunnatut "saippuaooperat" *Ma Perkinsin* ja *Big Sisterin* kaltaisine kotirouvasarjoineen. Sponsoreina toimivat suuret pesuainevalmistajat, kuten Proctor & Gamble Company(P&G) ja Lever Brothers.

規模行銷和廣泛的媒體報導所推動）。在大多數情況下，油漆也像壁紙一樣有滲透性，容易磨損。

我們所知道的真正的一擦淨的世界只是在二次世界大戰之後才出現。這需要一系列實質性的創新，在一個新的層次上溝通，首先要有真正的社會變革。已經有了期望，有錢人已有了一些工具——當然還有可用的勞動力——但大眾的「奇跡」產品尚未誕生。

通向一塵不染的世界的永恆陽光的動因是媒體創新。它讓美國、英國和歐洲越來越多的觀眾看到家庭的另一半是如何生活，它允許廣告客戶展示一個完美世界的模樣。彩色電影經歷了二十世紀三十年代的成長，成為戰後好萊塢的主流，表現了室內裝潢從朦朧逃避主義的連串夢想走向有教育意義的指南。戰後的電視播放了以家庭為基礎的肥皂劇和情景喜劇，成為「美國夢」在家庭方面的基礎課程。讀者眾多的雜誌——普通家庭讀物，如《生活》(Life) 或《星期六晚間郵報》(The Saturday Evening Post)——以及不斷壯大的家庭裝飾雜誌，如《美麗住宅》(House Beautiful) 和《房屋與花園》(House and Garden)——在二十世紀五十年代和六十年代達到有史以來最高發行量——以活生生的色彩表現了美好的生活和完美的住宅。雜誌最初的發難，不完美的顏色但迎合大量的消費者的「衛生」廣告以及據稱於使用的清潔產品，早在二十世紀就開始了。到了二十世紀二十年代，美國無線電廣播——不像英國和歐洲，完全是商業性的——敦促婦女們不斷地洗漱和清潔。廣播劇送給了美國第一個「肥皂劇」，家庭主婦系列觀眾眾多，如《帕金斯大媽》和《大姐》，由包裝好的洗衣肥皂製造商贊助，這些產品由寶潔公司 (Proctor&Gamble) 和利華兄弟公司 (Lever) 之類的企業巨頭生產。

戰後的社會變革進一步擴大了西方世界的中產階級隊伍，特別是在美國，因為一群工資優厚組成工會的工人按美

品、大规模营销和广泛的媒体报道所推动）。在大多数情况下，油漆也像壁纸一样有渗透性，容易磨损。

我们所知道的真正的一擦净的世界只是在二次世界大战之后才出现。这需要一系列实质性的创新，在一个新的层次上沟通，首先要有真正的社会变革。已经有了期望，有钱人已有了一些工具——当然还有可用的劳动力——但大众的"奇迹"产品尚未诞生。

通向一尘不染的世界这种永恒的阳光的动因是媒体创新。它允许美国、英国和欧洲越来越多的观众看到家庭的另一半是如何生活的，它向广告客户展示一个完美的世界的样子。彩色电影经历了二十世纪三十年代的成长，成为战后好莱坞的主流，表现了室内装潢从朦胧逃避主义的连串梦想走向有教育意义的指南。战后的电视播放了以家庭为基础的肥皂剧和情景喜剧，成为"美国梦"在家庭方面的基础课程。读者众多的杂志——普通家庭读物，如《生活》(Life) 或《星期六晚间邮报》(The Saturday Evening Post)——以及不断壮大的家庭装饰杂志，如《美丽住宅》(House Beautiful) 和《房屋与花园》(House and Garden)——在二十世纪五十年代和六十年代达到有史以来最高发行量——以活生生的色彩表现了美

พื้นผิวภายในบ้านในช่วงปลายศตวรรษที่ 19 พวกพื้น กำแพง และเครื่องเรือน ยังคงมีความเป็นธรรมชาติ และมีพรุน จนถึงช่วงศตวรรษที่ 20 โดยวอลล์เปเปอร์แบบเคลือบเงาสำหรับใช้ในทางเดิน และในครัวที่มีลักษณะลอกเลียนแบบกระเบื้อง และโมเสค ได้เกิดขึ้นในช่วงปลายศตวรรษที่ 19 แต่สิ่งเหล่านั้นจัดเป็นสิ่งที่มีราคาค่อนข้างแพง และยากต่อการใช้ ในขณะที่วอลล์เปเปอร์ยังคงเปรอะเปื้อนและเป็นคราบได้ง่าย ซึ่งทำให้เข้าใจได้ถึงความนิยมอย่างมากสำหรับวอลล์เปเปอร์ที่มีลวดลายเป็นจุดและมีการประดับตกแต่ง และมีสีเข้ม

ห้องครัวหรือห้องน้ำที่มีการปูหินอ่อนโมเสค หรือถ้าจะให้เรียกง่าย ปูด้วยกระเบื้องเป็นสัญลักษณ์ของคนมีเงินหรือเป็นที่มาของบ้านของชาวอเมริกันชนชั้นกลาง แต่พื้นผิวแบบดั้งเดิมเหล่านี้มีราคาสูง น้ำหนักมาก และยากในการติดตั้ง หลักการว่าด้วย "ความหอมหวานและความสว่าง" ในหนังสือและนิตยสารกระตุ้นให้ผู้หญิงหันมาใช้สีทาบ้านที่เป็นสีอ่อน แทนการใช้วอลล์เปเปอร์ที่ "ไม่อนามัย" แต่เทคโนโลยีสีทาบ้านในช่วงยุคก่อนสงครามที่ใช้ส่วนประกอบจากธรรมชาติ ซึ่งเป็นช่วงก่อนมีการใช้พลาสติกหมายความว่าพวกมือสมัครเล่นไม่สามารถใช้ผลิตภัณฑ์ได้อย่างง่ายดายนัก (ความนิยมอย่างล้นหลามของ DIY – Do it yourself เกิดขึ้นหลังยุคสงครามเช่นกัน โดยได้รับแรงผลักดันจากผลิตภัณฑ์ใหม่ ๆ การตลาดแบบเน้นปริมาณ และการใช้สื่อบันเทิงอย่างกว้างขวาง) โดยมากแล้วสีทาบ้านจะมีเนื้อไม่ละเอียด และหลุดลอกได้ง่ายเช่นเดียวกับวอลล์เปเปอร์

โลกที่สะอาดหมดจดอย่างแท้จริงที่เรารู้จักนั้น เพิ่งเกิดขึ้นในยุคหลังสงครามโลกครั้งที่ 2 โดยเป็นช่วงที่มีความต้องการสิ่งประดิษฐ์จำนวนมาก การติดต่อสื่อสารแบบใหม่และการเปลี่ยนแปลงทางสังคมอย่างแท้จริงก่อนสิ่งอื่น ความคาดหวังนั้นได้มีอยู่แล้วในช่วงเวลาขณะนั้น พวกคนรวยก็มีอุปกรณ์และแน่นอนว่าต้องมีแรงงานเตรียมไว้รองรับ แต่ผลิตภัณฑ์ที่เป็น "ปาฏิหาริย์" จำนวนมากยังไม่เกิดขึ้น

แรงขับเคลื่อนสำคัญที่นำไปสู่ความโชติช่วงอย่างแท้จริงของโลกซึ่งไร้ที่ติ คือนวัตกรรมด้านสื่อ ซึ่งนำไปสู่การเพิ่มขึ้นของจำนวนผู้ชมในสหรัฐฯ สหราชอาณาจักร และยุโรปที่จะได้เห็นว่าอีกฝากหนึ่งของโลกใช้ชีวิตกันอย่างไร และทำให้ผู้ผลิตโฆษณามีโอกาสแสดงให้เห็นว่าจริง ๆ แล้วโลกที่สมบูรณ์แบบควรเป็นอย่างไร ภาพยนตร์สีที่มีการเจริญเติบโตตลอดช่วงยุค 1930 กลายเป็น

nique a donné aux États-Unis les premiers « feuilletons » avec audiences de masse pour les séries destinées à la ménagère telles que *Ma Perkins* et *Big Sister*, financées par les producteurs de lessive en boîte fabriquées par les géants comme Procter & Gamble Company (P&G) et Lever Brothers.

Les changements sociaux d'après-guerre ont propulsé la classe moyenne occidentale encore plus loin, particulièrement aux États-Unis, comme groupe de salariés syndiqués mieux payés atteignant le statut de la classe moyenne dans le sens américain du revenu, de la consommation et des attentes. La forte croissance après-guerre du développement résidentiel de banlieue est due au déménagement de millions de ces personnes des maisons urbaines et des appartements du dix-neuvième siècle vers une nouvelle vie dans une nouvelle ville (les critiques de l'architecture disaient que ces banlieues n'étaient pas réellement des villes). Une nouvelle maison signifiait un nouveau départ et près de 2 millions d'entre elles furent construites entre les années 1945 et 1950 rien qu'aux États-Unis. Un nouveau mobilier acheté à crédit a suivi avec une nouvelle compétition entre les voisins, une nouveauté pour les communautés traditionnelles et les familles nombreuses. La nouvelle vie banlieusarde d'après-guerre était centrée sur le noyau familial, la maison et le rôle de la ménagère en tant que son gardien.

La publicité persistante avait dit aux femmes d'après-guerre que la saleté et les microbes se cachaient partout sur elles et dans leurs maisons et qu'elles seraient jugées sur leurs efforts d'entretien ménager. Désormais, un produit d'aide ménagère absolue et efficace était disponible. L'exposition permanente aux médias et à la publicité avait montré de quoi l'idéal s'agissait. Une assemblée de modèles magnifiques (souvent, inexplicablement, en robes de soirée et longs gants) était apparue dans des cuisines, des salons parfaits, mettant la table impeccablement et des espaces extérieurs parfaitement maintenus. À partir du milieu des années 1950, alors que pratiquement tout semblait neuf : un déluge de produits miraculeux signifiait que tout cela était désormais possible.

con una vasta publicidad dirigida al consumidor sobre productos de limpieza "higiénicos" y, supuestamente, fáciles de usar, comenzó a principios del siglo XX. Para la década de los veinte, la radio estadounidense —abrumadoramente comercial, a diferencia de la radio en el Reino Unido y en Europa— exhortaba a las mujeres a lavar y a limpiar constantemente. Las radionovelas le dieron a los Estados Unidos la pauta para las primeras "telenovelas" con audiencias masivas sobre series de amas de casas, como *Ma Perkins* y *Big Sister*, patrocinadas por los productores de jabones para ropa envasados que eran fabricados por gigantes corporativos, como Proctor & Gamble Company (P&G) y Lever Brothers.

El cambio social de la posguerra amplió aún más la clase media del mundo occidental, particularmente en los Estados Unidos, ya que un grupo de trabajadores industriales sindicalizados y mejor pagados alcanzaron la condición de clase media en el sentido norteamericano de ingresos, consumo y expectativas. El gran crecimiento de la posguerra sobre el desarrollo residencial en suburbios movió a millones de estas personas de sus casas y apartamentos en áreas urbanas marginales, de desarrollos del siglo XIX, a una nueva vida en un nuevo pueblo (los críticos arquitectónicos afirmaron que estos suburbios inmobiliarios no fueron en realidad pueblos). Pero una nueva casa significaba un nuevo comienzo, y se construyeron casi 2 millones de viviendas entre 1945 y 1950 solo en los Estados Unidos. Siguió un ciclo de renovaciones realizadas con créditos y un nuevo ciclo de competencia comunitaria con los vecinos —las comunidades tradicionales y las familias extendidas habían sido, en general, más tolerantes. La nueva vida en los suburbios después de la guerra se centraba en el núcleo familiar y la casa, y en el papel de la ama de casa como su protectora.

La persistente publicidad les había inculcado a las mujeres de la posguerra que la suciedad y los gérmenes acechaban en todos lados —en ellas y en sus casas— y que se las juzgaría por sus esfuerzos en el cuidado de la casa. Pero ahora la ayuda, absoluta y efectiva, estaba al alcance de la mano. La perpetua exposición a los medios de comunicación y a la publicidad

Sodanjälkeinen yhteiskuntamuutos laajensi läntistä keskiluokkaa edelleen, varsinkin Amerikassa, missä paremmin palkattujen järjestäytyneiden teollisuustyöntekijöiden tulot, kulutus ja odotukset oikeuttivat heidät keskiluokan asemaan. Esikaupunkiasutuksen valtava kasvu sotaa seuraavina vuosina sai miljoonat ihmiset muuttamaan 1800-luvulla rakennetuista kaupunkiasunnoistaan uuteen elämään uudessa kaupungissa (arkkitehtuurikriitikot eivät tosin halunneet kutsua näitä asutusalueita oikeiksi kaupungeiksi). Uusi talo merkitsi kuitenkin uutta alkua, ja vuosina 1945–50 tehtiin lähes kaksi miljoonaa uutta alkua pelkästään Yhdysvalloissa. Muuttoa seurasi lainalla rahoitettu sisustaminen, minkä jälkeen piti ryhtyä kilpailemaan naapureiden kanssa – perinteiset yhteisöt ja suku olivat olleet tässä suhteessa aivan liian anteeksiantavia. Sodanjälkeinen esikaupunkielämä keskittyi ydinperheen ja kodin ympärille, ja sen suojelijana oli kotiäiti.

Jatkuva mainonta oli vakuuttanut sen ajan naiset siitä, että likaa ja bakteereita piili kaikkialla, niin heissä itsessään kuin heidän kodeissaankin, ja että heidät tuomittaisiin heidän kodinhoitotaitojensa perusteella. Nyt oli kuitenkin saatavissa ehdotonta ja tehokasta apua. Koko heidän elämänsä ajan media ja mainonta olivat näyttäneet heille, miltä "hyvä" näytti. Kauniiden mallien kuoro (käsittämätöntä kyllä usein iltapuvuissa ja pitkissä hansikkaissa) oli esitellyt kuvankauniita keittiöitä ja olohuoneita, moitteettomasti katettuja ruokapöytiä ja hoidettuja nurmikoita. 50-luvun puolivälissä, kun käytännöllisesti katsoen kaikki näytti olevan uutta, ihmetuotteiden tulva merkitsi, että tämä kaikki oli todella mahdollista.

Jotkin ihmeistä olivat todellisia sodanjälkeisiä saavutuksia, mutta toiset oli kehitetty jo aiemmin. Tärkeitä ovat massamarkkinoinnin päivämäärät – missä vaiheessa innovaatiosta tulee ymmärrettävä, milloin se on saatavilla ja kyllin edullinen, milloin sen jakelusta ja tuotemerkistä vastaa jättiyhtiö, joka saavuttaa kaikki ostajat. Sodanjälkeisessä maailmassa ja etenkin ensimmäisessä aidossa kuluttajayhteiskunnassa Yhdysvalloissa, kodinhoidon ihmeitä alkoi saapua jatkuvaan tahtiin 50-luvulla. Uudet pinnat eivät olleet vain värik-

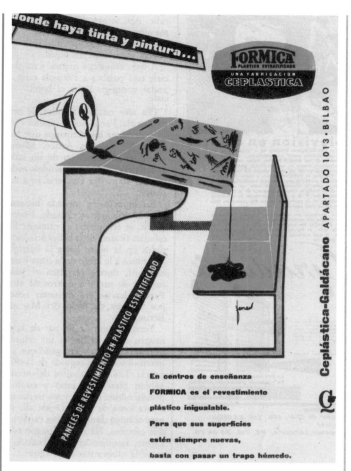

donde haya tinta y pintura...

FORMICA
PLÁSTICO ESTRATIFICADO
UNA FABRICACION
CEPLÁSTICA

PANELES DE REVESTIMIENTO EN PLÁSTICO ESTRATIFICADO

En centros de enseñanza
FORMICA es el revestimiento
plástico inigualable.
Para que sus superficies
estén siempre nuevas,
basta con pasar un trapo húmedo.

Ceplástica-Galdácano APARTADO 1013 · BILBAO

กระแสหลักในฮอลลีวูดยุคหลังสงคราม ที่
แสดงให้เห็นถึงการตกแต่งภายในที่เปลี่ยน
จากเหตุการณ์เพ้อฝันที่ต้องการหลีกหนีซึ่ง
ไม่ชัดเจนไปสู่การนำทางอย่างเป็นขั้นตอน
โทรทัศน์ในช่วงยุคหลังสงครามที่มีละครน้ำ
เน่าโดยมีเนื้อหาจากครอบครัว และซิทคอม
เป็นวิธีทางพื้นฐานของเรื่องภายในครัวเรือน
ของความฝันของชาวอเมริกัน กองนิตยสาร
ที่มีผู้อ่านจำนวนมาก ที่มีชื่อแบบครอบครัว
เช่น *Life* หรือ *The Saturday Evening
Post* และกลุ่มของนิตยสารตกแต่งบ้านที่มี
การเติบโตขึ้น เช่น *House Beautiful* และ
House and Garden ซึ่งมียอดการจำหน่าย
สูงสุดในยุค 1950 และ 1960 แสดงให้
เห็นถึงชีวิตที่ดี และบ้านที่สมบูรณ์แบบที่มีสี
สมจริง การโฆษณาทางนิตยสารในช่วงแรก
แม้จะยังไม่สมบูรณ์นักในด้านสีสัน แต่การ
โฆษณาผลิตภัณฑ์ทำความสะอาดของหลาย
ยี่ห้อว่ามี "สุขอนามัย" และอ้างว่าใช้งานได้
ง่าย ได้เริ่มต้นในช่วงศตวรรษที่ 20 เมื่อมา
ถึงยุค 1920 วิทยุอเมริกัน ที่มีการโฆษณา
อย่างล้นหลาม ซึ่งแตกต่างจากวิทยุใน
สหราชอาณาจักร และยุโรป ได้กระตุ้นให้
ผู้หญิงซักล้าง และทำความสะอาดอย่าง
สม่ำเสมอ ละครทางวิทยุก่อกำเนิดละครน้ำ
เน่าเป็นครั้งแรกในสหรัฐฯ สำหรับบรรดาแม่
บ้าน โดยมีผู้ชมจำนวนมาก เช่น *Ma Perkins*
และ *Big Sister* ซึ่งได้รับการสนับสนุนโดยผู้
ผลิตสบู่ที่ใช้ในการซักรีดที่มีการบรรจุหีบห่อ
และผลิตโดยบริษัทยักษ์ใหญ่ เช่น พรอคเตอร์
แอนด์แกมเบิล (P&G) และลีเวอร์ บราเธอร์ส
       การเปลี่ยนแปลงทางสังคมในยุคหลัง
สงครามที่ได้ขยายออกไปสู่ชนชั้นกลางของ
โลกตะวันตกได้ขยายไกลออกไปอีก โดย
เฉพาะอย่างยิ่งในอเมริกา เนื่องจากกลุ่ม
สหภาพแรงงานทางด้านอุตสาหกรรมที่มีราย
ได้เพิ่มขึ้น ได้เลื่อนฐานะเป็นชนชั้นกลางใน
ด้านรายได้ การบริโภค และความคาดหวังใน
แบบของชาวอเมริกัน การเจริญเติบโตอย่าง
ยิ่งใหญ่ของการพัฒนาแหล่งที่อยู่อาศัยใน
เขตชานเมืองหลังสงครามได้ทำให้ประชากร
เหล่านี้ย้ายออกจากบ้านและหอพักที่เกิด
จากการพัฒนาที่อยู่อาศัยในช่วงศตวรรษ
ที่ 19 ในเขตเมืองชั้นใน ออกไปสู่ชีวิตใหม่
ในเมืองใหม่ (นักวิจารณ์ทางสถาปัตยกรรม
กล่าวเอาไว้ว่า ชานเมืองของนักพัฒนาเหล่า
นี้ไม่ได้มีความเป็นเมืองอย่างแท้จริงเลย) แต่
กระนั้น บ้านใหม่ ก็คือการเริ่มต้นใหม่ และได้
มีการสร้างบ้านเกือบ 2 ล้านหลังขึ้นระหว่าง
ปี 1945 -1950 ในสหรัฐอเมริกาเพียงอย่าง
เดียว มีการตกแต่งใหม่โดยใช้วงเงินเครดิต
และการแข่งขันระหว่างเพื่อนบ้านเพื่อให้
น้อยหน้ากันยกใหม่เกิดขึ้นตามมา สังคม

國標準衡量的收入、消費和期望達到中
產階層的地位。戰後近郊住宅發展的增
加將數百萬的人從城內十九世紀開發的
房屋和公寓移到了新城鎮，過上新生活
(建築評論家說，這些開發商的郊區根本
不是真正的城鎮)。但是，一座新的房子
意味著一個新的開始──單在美國從
1945年至1950年就建造了200萬座房
子。接著就是一輪借錢進行的翻新，新
一輪的睦鄰友好競爭──傳統的社區
和大家庭都更加寬容。戰後新郊區生活
專注於核心家庭和家居，以及家庭主婦
作為監護人的角色。

　　堅持不懈的廣告已經告訴戰後的女
性，污垢和病菌潛伏在各處──在她
們身上，在她們居住的房屋裡──人們
會以此評判她們的持家本領。但現在，

好的生活和完美的住宅。杂志最初的
发难，不完美的颜色但迎合大量的消费
者的"卫生"广告以及据称易于使用的
清洁产品，早在二十世纪就开始了。到
了二十世纪二十年代，美国无线电广
播──不像英国和欧洲，完全是商业性
的──敦促妇女们不断地洗漱和清
洁。广播剧送给了美国第一个"肥皂
剧"，家庭主妇系列观众众多，如《帕
金斯大妈》和《大姐》，由包装好的洗
衣肥皂制造商赞助，这些产品由宝洁公
司(Proctor&Gamble)和利华兄弟公司
(Lever)之类的企业巨头生产。

　　战后的社会变革进一步扩大了西方
世界的中产阶级队伍，特别是在美国，
因为一群工资优厚组成工会的工人按
美国标准衡量的收入、消费和期望达

Certains nouveaux produits étaient de vrais merveilles d'après-guerre mais d'autres existaient déjà auparavant. Les dates importantes sont celles du marketing de masse, lorsqu'une innovation devient compréhensible, accessible et abordable, avec l'élan de la distribution et de l'image de marque d'une société géante, qui atteint tout le monde. Dans le monde d'après-guerre, mais surtout dans cette première société véritablement axée sur la consommation, aux États-Unis, les miracles domestiques sont arrivés constamment durant les années 1950. Les nouvelles surfaces ne sont pas seulement des motifs colorées et extravagantes mais elles ont été scellées, glacées, plastifiées. Elles sont impressionnament imperméables, non poreuses et résistantes, d'une façon presque légale. Ensemble, elles ont fait naître un monde d'entretien facile.

La technologie de la peinture a changé après la guerre, les peintures traditionnelles à base d'huile et de détrempe ont laissé la place à de nouvelles peintures plastiques, plus faciles à appliquer et séchant plus vite, pour le plus grand bonheur des bricoleurs. Ces peintures étaient beaucoup plus résistantes et plus faciles à nettoyer. La peinture plastifiée au fini mat est lavable. De même que les planchers de vinyle, plus légers, moins chers et plus faciles à poser que le linoléum traditionnel massif et beaucoup plus durable que la version à peindre moins coûteuse, et étonnamment plus facile à nettoyer. Un autre miracle des années 1950 est arrivé avec les produits d'étanchéité de plastique pour les planchers en bois véritable ; la recette facile « sabler et sceller » est devenue un incontournable de la rénovation intérieur de la jeune classe moyenne des années 1960. Le bois « véritable », généreusement plastifiée, conservait sa teinte (souvent un orange éclatant) pendant des années, n'avait besoin d'aucun cirage et se lavait comme un plancher en vinyle.

Le mobilier, les téléviseurs, les chaînes stéréo, ont également adopté une nouvelle finition brillante dans les années 1960. Les consoles de télévision grand écran et les équipements musicaux de salon avaient toujours été réalisés en placage de bois au vernis fragile et qui se dégradait au fil du

había mostrado qué era "bueno". Un coro de modelos hermosas (frecuente, e inexplicablemente, usando vestidos de fiesta y guantes largos) indicaban cuáles eran las cocinas y las salas de estar perfectas, las mesas de comedor arregladas de manera inmaculada y un espacio exterior podado. Para entonces, a mediados de la década de los cincuenta, cuando prácticamente todo parecía ser nuevo, una gran cantidad de productos milagrosos significó que todo podía lograrse.

Algunos milagros eran realmente maravillas de la posguerra; otros habían estado en desarrollo en una etapa anterior. Las fechas que importan son aquellas de la comercialización masiva, cuando una innovación se convierte en comprensible, accesible y asequible, cuando tiene la distribución y el impulso de la marca de una corporación gigante, una que llegue a todos. En el mundo de la posguerra, pero especialmente en la primera sociedad realmente impulsada por el consumismo, los Estados Unidos, los milagros domésticos llegaron continuamente en la década de los cincuenta. Las nuevas superficies eran no solo coloridas y con diseños extravagantes, sino que estaban selladas, glaseadas y plastificadas. Eran abrumadoramente impenetrables, no porosas y resistentes por derecho, casi por ley. Todas juntas, conformaban un mundo de fácil mantenimiento.

La tecnología de la pintura cambió después de la guerra, de las pinturas tradicionales a base de aceite y al temple a las nuevas pinturas plásticas; eran más fáciles de aplicar y se secaban mucho más rápido, y se adaptaban al pintor aficionado del "hágalo usted mismo". También eran abrumadoramente más resistentes y fáciles de limpiar. La pintura delgada plastificada o mate podía lavarse. También podía lavarse el vinilo para pisos, que era más liviano, más barato y más fácil de colocar que el linóleo sólido tradicional, y mucho más resistente que el tipo "pintado" más barato, y sorprendentemente fácil de limpiar. Otro milagro de la década de los cincuenta fueron los nuevos selladores plásticos para pisos de madera real —la receta fácil para "lijar y sellar" fue un artículo básico de la mejora de hogares de jóvenes de clase media, en la década de los sesenta. La madera "real", generosamente

käitä ja ylellisesti kuvioituja, ne olivat myös vedenpitäviä, lasitettuja, plastisoituja. Niiden läpäisemättömyys oli ylivoimaista ja niiden vastustuskyky melkein lain sanelemaa. Yhdessä nämä ominaisuudet takasivat helposti hoidettavan maailman.

Maaliteknologia muutti perinteiset öljypohjaiset ja "liimamaalit" sodan jälkeen uusiksi plastisiksi maaleiksi, jotka olivat helpompia käyttää ja kuivuivat paljon nopeammin, mikä sopi tee-se-itse-maalarille. Ne olivat myös paljon kestävämpiä ja helpompia puhdistaa. Plastisoidun himmeämaalipinnan saattoi pestä. Sama päti vinyylilattioihin, jotka olivat kevyempiä, edullisempia ja helpompia asentaa kuin entiset tukevat linoleumilattiat ja kestivät paljon paremmin kuin vastaavat halvat "maalatut" pinnat — ja niin helppoja pitää puhtaina. Toinen 50-luvun ihme olivat puulattioiden uudet plastiset tiivisteet. Vain hiomista ja tiivistämistä vaativa helpon elämän resepti kuului osana nuoren keskiluokan kodinkunnostusprojekteihin 60-luvulla. "Aito" runsaasti kyllästetty puu piti värinsä (usein kirkkaan oranssi) vuosikausia, sitä ei tarvinnut kiillottaa ja sen saattoi pestä niin kuin vinyylilattian.

Myös huonekalut, televisiot ja stereot saivat uudet kiiltävät 60-luvun pinnat. Suuret kaappitelevisiot ja olohuoneen musiikkilaitteet olivat siihen saakka olleet puuviilukoteloissaan, joi-den hapera lakkaus mureni ajan mittaan. Uusi kova polyuretaanilakka oli ihmeellisen paksua, kiiltävää ja kestävää, ja televisio tuntui ikuistuvan uudessa muodossaan — joka oli tietenkin äärimmäisen helposti puhdistettavissa ja kiilsi pyyhkimisen jälkeen. Polyesterimaaleilla-rimaaleilla oli sama vaikutus joidenkin uusien huonekalujen pystysuorissa paneeleissa, kaapeissa, keittiön ovissa ja laatikoissa. Se kiilsi kuin lakka ja sai uuden kaluston näyttämään todella uudelta — ja puhdistui vaivattomasti.

Kestävin ja demokraattisin näistä uusista ihmepinnoista oli kuitenkin johtava laminaattibrändi Formica. Formica-laminaatti oli enemmän kuin viimeistelty pinta. Se oli aivan oma materiaalinsa omine väreineen ja kuvioineen, se antoi ratkaisun 50-luvun tietoisesti nykyaikaisen kodin symbolisesti tärkeimpiin pintoihin, keittiön työtasoihin ja pöytään, jotka muodostivat kaikkien noiden saip-

幫助,絕對有效的幫助唾手可得。畢生接受媒體和廣告的宣傳已展示了「美好」是什麼樣。一組漂亮的模特組成的合唱團(通常必定是穿著晚禮服和戴著長長的禮服手套)指向畫面完美的廚房和客廳,一塵不染的餐桌和修剪整齊的戶外空間。到那時候——到五十年代中期,幾乎一切似乎都是嶄新的——一系列奇跡產品氾濫,意味著一切都是可以實現的。

有些奇跡是真正的戰後奇跡;其他的早先已經在開發。重要的日子是那些大眾行銷日,這時創新成為可以理解、可以得到和可負擔得起的東西,當有了一家巨頭公司的分銷和品牌的勢頭,就能向所有人進行宣傳。在戰後的世界中,特別是美國,在這個第一個消費者驅動的社會裡,家居的奇跡在五十年代不斷發生。新的面材不僅色彩豔麗,圖案奢華,而且被密封、上光、塑膠化。它們絕大多數天然或按法律都具有不透水、不滲透和抗磨的特性。加在一起構成了保養方便的世界。

戰爭結束後,油漆技術得到改變,從傳統的油基塗料和「膠畫顏料」到新的塑膠塗料;油漆更易與塗刷和快速乾燥,適合自己動手的人。大多數油漆也更耐用,更容易清洗。塑膠化的平光或

FORMICA LAMINATE SAMPLES

到中產階層的地位。戰後近郊住宅發展的增加將數百萬的人以城內十九世紀開發的房屋和公寓移到了新城鎮,過上新生活(建築評論家說,這些開發商的郊區根本不是真正的城鎮)。但是,一座新的房子意味著一個新的開始——單在美國從 1945 年至 1950 年就建造了 200 萬座房子。接著就是一輪借錢進行的翻新,新一輪的睦鄰友好競爭——傳統的社區和大家庭都更加寬容。戰後新郊區生活專注於核心家庭和家居,以及家庭主婦作為監护人的角色。

坚持不懈的广告已经告诉战后的女性,污垢和病菌潜伏在各处——在她们身上,在她们居住的房屋里——人们会以此评判她们的持家本领。但现在,帮助,绝对有效的帮助唾手可得。毕生接受媒体和广告的宣传已展示了"美好"是什么样。一组漂亮的模特组成的合唱团(通常必定是穿着晚礼服和戴着长长的礼服手套)指向画面完美的厨房和客厅,一尘不染的餐桌和修剪整齐的户外空间。到那时候——到五十年代中期,几乎一切似乎都是崭新的——一系列奇迹产品泛滥,意味着一切都是可以实现的。

有些奇迹是真正的战后奇迹;其他的早先已经在开发。重要的日子是那些大众营销日,这时创新成为可以理解、可以得到和可负担得起的东西,当有了一家巨头公司的分销和品牌的势头,就能向所有的人进行宣传。在战后的世界中,特别是美国,在这个第一个消费者驱动的社会里,家居的奇迹在五十年代不断发生。新的面材不仅色彩艳丽,图案奢华,而且被密封、上光、塑胶化。它们绝大多数天然或按法律都具有不透水、不渗透和抗磨的特性。加在一起构成了保养方便的世界。

战争结束后,油漆技术得到改变,从传统的油基涂料和"胶画颜料"到新的塑料涂料;油漆更易与涂刷和快速干燥,适合自己动手的人。大多数油漆也更耐用,更容易清洗。塑料化的平光或

และครอบครัวใหญ่แบบดั้งเดิมมีการให้อภัยกันมากขึ้น ชีวิตในชานเมืองหลังสงครามมุ่งความสนใจไปยังครอบครัวเล็ก และบ้าน และบทบาทของแม่บ้านในฐานะผู้ปกครอง

การโฆษณาอย่างต่อเนื่องเป็นการบอกผู้หญิงในยุคหลังสงครามว่าความสกปรก และเชื้อโรคมือยู่ทั่วทุกแห่ง ทั้งบนตัวพวกเธอเอง และในบ้านของพวกเธอ และพวกเธอจะได้รับการตัดสินโดยความพยายามในการทำความสะอาดของพวกเธอ แต่ตอนนี้ ความช่วยเหลืออย่างสมบูรณ์แบบ และมีประสิทธิภาพอยู่ในมือแล้ว ชั่วและการโฆษณาที่มีการนำเสนอมาตลอดชีวิตได้แสดงให้เห็นว่า "ดี" เป็นอย่างไร นางแบบหน้าตาสะสวยจำนวนมาก (โดยมากอยู่ในรูปชุดราตรี และถุงมือยาวสำหรับงานกลางคืน) ถูกนำมาใช้มาให้เห็นถึงห้องครัวและห้องนั่งเล่นที่สมบูรณ์แบบ ที่มีโต๊ะรับประทานอาหารที่มีการจัดวางอย่างไม่มีที่ติ และพื้นที่รอบนอกที่ได้รับการตกแต่งอย่างดี เมื่อถึงช่วงกลางยุค 1950 เมื่อทุกสิ่งทุกอย่างดูจะเป็นสิ่งใหม่ การหลั่งไหลม่าของผลิตภัณฑ์ที่เป็นปาฏิหาริย์แสดงให้เห็นว่าทุกอย่างประสบความสำเร็จ

ปาฏิหาริย์บางอย่างเป็นความน่าประหลาดใจในช่วงยุคหลังสงครามอย่างแท้จริง ในขณะที่ปาฏิหาริย์อื่นๆ ได้รับการพัฒนามาก่อนหน้านี้แล้ว ช่วงที่มีความสำคัญจริงๆ คือ ช่วงที่มีการทำการตลาดแบบมวลชน เมื่อนวัตกรรมกลายเป็นสิ่งที่สามารถเข้าใจได้ เข้าถึงได้ และมีราคาที่สามารถซื้อหาได้ เมื่อมีแรงส่งในด้านการจัดจำหน่าย และการสร้างความนิยมในตราสินค้าของบริษัทขนาดใหญ่มากพอที่จะสามารถเข้าถึงทุกคนได้ ในโลกยุคหลังสงคราม โดยเฉพาะอย่างยิ่งในช่วงสังคมที่ได้รับการขับเคลื่อนโดยผู้บริโภคยุคแรกๆ ปาฏิหาริย์ของเรื่องในครัวเรือนได้เกิดขึ้นอย่างต่อเนื่องในยุค 1950 พื้นผิวใหม่ๆ ไม่เพียงแต่มีสีสันสวยงาม และมีลวดลายที่อลังการ แต่มีการเคลือบ ทำให้มันวาว และมีความเป็นรูปร่าง พวกพื้นผิวใหม่นี้ไม่สามารถแทรกซึม ไม่ควรมีรูพรุน และมีความทนทานอย่างแน่แท้ เมื่อนำคุณสมบัติมารวมกันแล้ว สิ่งนี้ได้เกิดขึ้นเพื่อโลกที่การดูแลรักษาสามารถทำได้โดยง่าย

เทคโนโลยีของสีได้เปลี่ยนแปลงหลังจากสงคราม โดยเป็นการเปลี่ยนแปลงจากสีที่ทำจากน้ำมันแบบดั้งเดิม และ "สีจากกาวน้ำ" ไปเป็นสีพลาสติกแบบใหม่ สีเหล่านี้ใช้งานง่าย และแห้งได้เร็วกว่ามาก เหมาะกับคนทาสีแบบ DIY นอกจากนี้ยังมีความทนทาน และทำความสะอาดได้ง่ายมากกว่าเดิม สีพลาสติกแบบเรียบ หรือสีแบบผิวด้านสามารถทำความสะอาดได้ เช่นเดียวกับพื้น

temps. Le nouveau vernis polyuréthane rigide était épais, brillant et durable et la télévision s'est immortalisée dans cette nouvelle teinte ambrée et bien sûr extrêmement facile à nettoyer ; en fait l'essuyer le faisait briller. Les peintures polyester reprenaient un effet similaire sur les panneaux verticaux de quelques nouveaux meubles, placards, portes de cuisine et tiroirs. Brillantes comme la laque, elles donnaient l'air d'avoir des meubles réellement nouveaux qu'il suffisait d'essuyer.

Parmi ces surfaces miracles nouvelles, la plus durable et la plus démocratique était le Formica, la marque leader du plastique stratifié. Le stratifié Formica était davantage qu'une simple finition. Il était un matériau à part entière, avec une vaste gamme de teintes et de motifs exclusifs, une solution disponible pour les surfaces les plus importantes des maisons modernes des années 1950, les plans de travail et les tables de cuisines, la scène des réunions des familles des feuilletons, le « cœur de la maison ».

Le stratifié Formica a accompli le miracle de la pierre philosophale parmi les matériaux modernes. Comme le textile ou le papier (et d'ailleurs le Formica est basé sur le papier Kraft) le stratifié pouvait accueillir une gamme extraordinaire de motifs et plus tard de textures. Il était également dur, lisse, stable et complètement brillamment imperméable. Il était *le* matériau facile à nettoyer et il est devenu le symbole mondial de la facilité d'entretien dans le monde.

Le stratifié Formica est apparu juste avant la Première Guerre mondiale dans une application industrielle comme substitut pour le mica dans l'isolation électrique puis s'est développé, lentement d'abord, comme matériau en feuille pour les applications domestiques et autres. Dur, brillant et potentiellement très décoratif, il a été utilisé comme lambris par les premiers designers qui décoraient les nouveaux espaces importants comme le paquebot HMS *Queen Mary*, le Radio City Music Hall. Cela faisait partie de l'aspiration à un monde domestique futuriste tel que l'avait révélé l'exposition universelle de 1939. Mais il a fallu le boom de la construction d'après-guerre pour installer le stratifié dans la majorité des nouveaux foyers américains.

plastificada, mantuvo su color, frecuentemente un anaranjado brillante, durante años; no necesitaba pulido y podía lavarse como cualquier piso de vinilo.

Los muebles, los televisores y los equipos de estéreo también adoptaron un nuevo acabado brillante en la década de los sesenta. Las grandes consolas de televisión y los equipos de música para salas de estar estaban, tradicionalmente, cubiertos de revestimientos de madera con barnices frágiles que se degradaban con el tiempo. El nuevo y milagroso barniz de poliuretano duro era sorprendentemente espeso, brillante y duradero, y el televisor quedó de alguna forma inmortalizado en este nuevo ámbar y, por supuesto, extremadamente fácil de limpiar; quedaba brillante cuando se le pasaba un paño. Las pinturas de poliéster lograron un efecto similar en los paneles verticales de algunos muebles nuevos —roperos, puertas de cocina y gavetas. El brillo como laca, hizo que los muebles nuevos se vieran realmente nuevos. Y era de fácil limpieza.

Pero la más durable y democrática de estas nuevas superficies milagrosas, fue Formica, la marca de laminados plásticos líder. El laminado Formica era más que solo un acabado. Fue un material por sí mismo, con una amplia gama de colores y diseños de propiedad exclusiva, una respuesta de solución a problemas para las superficies simbólicamente más importantes en la casa conscientemente moderna de la década de los cincuenta, las encimeras prefabricadas de la cocina y la mesa de la cocina, el escenario de todas las reuniones de familia para las telenovelas: "el corazón de la casa".

El laminado Formica alcanzó el milagro de una piedra filosofal entre los materiales modernos. Al igual que los textiles o el papel —estaba, después de todo, basado en el papel Kraft—, era capaz de acomodar una extraordinaria gama de diseños, que más adelante incluyeron hasta texturas. También era sólido, suave, estable, y completamente y brillantemente impenetrable. Era *el* material fácil de limpiar, y se convirtió en el símbolo mundial del venidero mundo de fácil mantenimiento.

El laminado Formica comenzó justo antes de la Primera Guerra Mundial como una aplicación industrial sustitutiva de la *mica* en el aislamiento

puasarjojen keskeisen näyttämön, "kodin sydämen".

Formica-laminaatti oli nykyaikaisten materiaalien viisasten kivi. Paperin ja tekstiilien tavoin (sehän itse asiassa perustui voimapaperiin) se saattoi omaksua harvinaisen määrän muotoilua, myöhemmin jopa tekstuureja. Se oli kovaa, sileää, vahvaa ja täydellisen, loistavan läpipääsemätöntä. Se oli varsinainen helppohoitoinen materiaali, ja siitä tuli lähestyvän helppohoitoisen maailman globaali symboli.

Formica-laminaatti sai alkunsa juuri ennen ensimmäistä maailmansotaa teollisena sovelluksena mica-kiilteen vastineena sähköeristeissä, mistä se kehittyi hitaasti kotitalouksissa ja muualla käytettäväksi levymateriaaliksi. Tämä materiaali oli kovaa, kiiltävää ja saattoi olla koristeellistakin. Uraauurtavat muotoilijat käyttivät sitä tärkeiden uusien tilojen, kuten valtamerilaiva HMS Queen Maryn ja Radio City Music Hallin, panelointiin ja se kuului osana kunnianhimoisiin, kodinhoidon uutta maailmaa kuvaaviin esityksiin, joiden joukossa oli myös suosittu 1939 maailmannäyttely. Mutta vasta sodanjälkeinen rakennusbuumi takasi sille paikan valtaosassa uusia Amerikan koteja.

Kun Amerikan populaari muotoilu muuttui 50-luvun puolivälissä värikkäämmäksi ja rohkeammin kuvioiduksi ja varsinkin keittiöissä huomioitiin integrointi, design ja muoti entistä enemmän, Formica-brändin osuus kodinkunnostusbudjetista kasvoi. Formican laminaattikuvioilla saattoi antaa keittiölle muodikkaan kaksisävyisen ilmeen — yhden työpinnoille ja toisen kaapeille ja jopa kolmannen (usein puusävyisen) seinille. Sisäänrakennetun keittiön yleistyessä Yhdysvalloissa (Euroopassa tämä kesti kauemmin) koristeellisten tehosteiden osuus kasvoi 50-luvun puolivälistä lähtien; perusasiat muuttuivat ennen 90-lukua suhteellisen vähän.

"Helppohoitoisuus" yhdisti moraalisen velvoitteen edistyksen estetiikkaan. Tämä oli sen sukupolven näkemys, joka oli selvitynyt lamakaudesta, keskikaupunkielämästä ja kaikista noista luonnollisista, orgaanisista ja aidoista materiaaleista ja pinnoista. Niin kuin maalta kaupungin moderniin maailmaan muuttaneet, he eivät tunteneet mitään nostalgiaa taakseen jättämäänsä elämää kohtaan. Kemian jättiläinen DuPont, joka toi markkinoil-

無光塗料可用水清洗。乙烯地板也是如此，比傳統的固體油氈更輕便、更便宜、更容易鋪設，並且比那種便宜的油漆更耐用——其清潔之易令人驚訝。另一個二十世紀五十年代的奇蹟是用於實木地板的新型塑膠密封膠——「打磨與密封」使生活更容易的秘方是二十世紀六十年代年輕中產階級家居改善的主要任務。大量塑膠化的「實」木可保持其顏色——往往是一種閃爍的橙色——常駐多年，並不需要拋光，可像乙烯地板一樣用水清洗。

傢俱、電視和立體音響在六十年代也採用了新的有光澤的面漆。大型電視機和起居室音樂設備傳統上一直使用木紋貼面，脆弱的清漆隨著時間的推移而脫色。新的硬質聚氨酯奇蹟清漆具有驚人的稠度和光澤，並且耐用，有了這個琥珀色，電視機幾乎變成了不朽的東西——當然，非常容易清洗；一擦就讓它熠熠泛光。在一些新傢俱的豎板上——衣櫃、廚房門和抽屜上——聚酯漆達到了類似的效果。光澤如漆，使新傢俱顯得更新，而且是一擦淨。

但這些新奇蹟面材中最耐久和民主的是富美家這一領先塑膠美耐板品牌。富美家美耐板不只是一種面漆。它本身就是一種材料，有著極大的顏色和圖案選擇範圍，是五十年代現代房子裡最重要的象徵意義面材、廚房檯面和廚房桌子的解決方案，那裡是所有肥皂劇的家庭聚會場所——「家庭的心臟」。

富美家美耐板在現代材料中完成了魔法師的奇蹟。如紡織品或紙張一樣——它畢竟是以牛皮紙為基礎——能夠容納極為廣泛的設計，後來甚至包括紋理。美耐板還堅硬、光滑、穩定、完全閃亮和不透水。這是唯一的一擦淨材料，已成為全球未來易於保養的世界象徵。

富美家美耐板只是在第一次世界大戰之前開始製作，作為電器絕緣材料雲母的替代品在工業中應用，起初慢慢地發展，然後作為板材應用於家居和其他程序。美耐板堅硬、有光澤，並具有裝飾性的潛能，被有創意的設計師用作鑲板，裝

无光涂料可用水清洗。乙烯地板也是如此，比传统的固体油毡更轻便、更便宜、更容易铺设，并且比那种便宜的油漆更耐用——其清洁之易令人惊讶。另一个二十世纪五十年代的奇迹是用于实木地板的新型塑料密封胶——"打磨与密封"使生活更容易的秘方是二十世纪六十年代年轻中产阶级家居改善的主要任务。大量塑料化的"实"木可保持其颜色——往往是一种闪烁的橙色——常驻多年，并不需要抛光，可像乙烯地板一样水清洗。

家具、电视和立体音响在六十年代也采用了新的有光泽的面漆。大型电视机和起居室音乐设备传统上一直使用木纹贴面，脆弱的清漆随着时间的推移而脱色。新的硬质聚氨酯奇迹清漆具有惊人的稠度和光泽，并且耐用，有了这个琥珀色，电视机几乎变成了不朽的东西——当然，非常容易清洗；一擦就让它熠熠泛光。在一些新家具的竖板上——衣柜、厨房门和抽屉上——聚酯漆达到了类似的效果。光泽如漆，使新家具显得更新，而且是一擦净。

但这些新奇迹面材中最耐久和民主的是富美家这一领先塑料耐火板品牌。富美家®装饰耐火板不只是一种面漆。它本身就是一种材料，有着极大的颜色和图案选择范围，是五十年代现代房子里最重要的象征意义面材、厨房台面和厨房桌子的解决方案，那里是所有肥皂剧的家庭聚会场所——"家庭的心脏"。

富美家®装饰耐火板在现代材料中完成了魔法师的奇迹。如纺织品或纸张一样——它毕竟是以牛皮纸为基础——能够容纳极为广泛的设计，后来甚至包括纹理。耐火板还坚硬、光滑、稳定、完全闪亮和不透水。这是唯一的一擦净材料，已成为全球未来易于保养的世界象征。

富美家®装饰耐火板只是在第一次世界大战之前开始制作，作为电器绝缘材料云母的替代品在工业中应用，起初慢慢地发展，然后作为板材应用于

ไวนิล ที่มีความเบา ราคาถูก และง่ายในการนำมาปูมากกว่าพื้นเสื่อน้ำมันที่มีสีในตัวแบบดั้งเดิม และทนทานมากกว่าแบบ "ทาสี" ราคาถูกๆ และทำความสะอาดได้ง่ายอย่างน่าอัศจรรย์ ปาฏิหาริย์อีกอย่างที่เกิดขึ้นในยุค 1950 คือกาวพลาสติกแบบใหม่สำหรับใช้กับพื้นไม้แท้ "Sand and Seal" ซึ่งเป็นสูตรสำเร็จของการใช้ชีวิตง่ายๆ ของกลุ่มชนชั้นกลางรุ่นหนุ่มสาว ในการพัฒนาเรื่องในครัวเรือนในช่วงยุค 1960 ไม้ "แท้" ที่ได้รับการขึ้นรูปอย่างดี คงใช้ซึ่งสีของมันเองที่มักออกเป็นสีส้ม ได้หลายปี ไม่จำเป็นต้องได้รับการขัด และสามารถทำความสะอาดได้เช่นเดียวกับพื้นไวนิล

เครื่องเรือน โทรทัศน์ และชุดเครื่องเสียงนำเอาลักษณะที่มีความเงางามมาใช้ในยุค 1960 แผงควบคุมโทรทัศน์ขนาดใหญ่ และอุปกรณ์ดนตรีในห้องนั่งเล่น ซึ่งดั้งเดิมแล้วเป็นพื้นผิวไม้อัด ที่ได้รับการเคลือบบางๆ อันอาจหลุดลอกไปได้ตามกาลเวลา ปาฏิหาริย์ใหม่ในรูปโพลียูรีเทนขัดเงามีความหนาอย่างไม่น่าเชื่อ เงางาม และคงทน และโทรทัศน์ก็กลายมาอยู่ในรูปอำพันอันเป็นอมตะนี้ และแน่นอนว่าสามารถทำความสะอาดได้อย่างง่ายดาย แค่การถูทำให้มันเงางามได้แล้ว สีโพลีเอสเตอร์ให้ผลในลักษณะที่ใกล้เคียงกันกับส่วนที่อยู่ในแนวตั้งของเครื่องเรือนใหม่ๆ พวกตู้เสื้อผ้า ประตูครัว และลิ้นชัก การที่สิ่งของมีความเงางามเหมือนได้รับการเคลือบ ทำให้เครื่องเรือนดูใหม่ และสะอาดหมดจด

แต่สิ่งที่ทนทาน และมีความเที่ยงที่สุดในปาฏิหาริย์ใหม่ๆ ของพื้นผิวเหล่านี้ คือ ฟอร์ไมก้า ยี่ห้อผู้นำในวงการวัสดุปิดผิวลามิเนท ลามิเนทฟอร์ไมก้าเป็นมากกว่าวัสดุปิดผิว แต่เป็นวัสดุในตัวมันเองที่มีสีสันและลวดลายที่หลากหลาย วัสดุที่ใช้ในการแก้ปัญหาสำหรับพื้นผิวที่มีความสำคัญและสิ่งบ่งบอกถึงลักษณะของบ้านที่มีความทันสมัยในยุค 1950 พื้นผิวบนเคาน์เตอร์ และโต๊ะในครัว สถานที่ที่สมาชิกของครอบครัวรวมตัวกันดูละครหรือ "หัวใจของบ้าน"

ลามิเนทฟอร์ไมก้าได้รับการยกย่องให้เป็นแก้วสารพัดนึกของวัสดุยุคใหม่ เช่นเดียวกับสิ่งทอหรือกระดาษ ทั้งนี้ผลิตภัณฑ์นี้เกิดมาจากกระดาษคราฟท์ ที่สามารถรองรับการออกแบบได้อย่างกว้างขวางและยอดเยี่ยมและต่อมารวมไปถึงเนื้อของวัสดุ โดยมีความแข็ง เรียบ คงตัว และเงางามอย่างไม่หวั่นไหวต่อสิ่งใด แผ่นลามิเนทฟอร์ไมก้าเป็นวัสดุที่สะอาดหมดจด และเป็นสัญลักษณ์สากลของโลกที่ง่ายต่อการดูแลรักษาที่กำลังจะมาถึง

ลามิเนทฟอร์ไมก้าเกิดขึ้นก่อนสงครามโลกครั้งที่ 1 ในรูปแบบของวัสดุที่ใช้ในทาง

À partir du milieu des années 1950, le design populaire américain est devenu plus coloré et plus audacieux dans les motifs. Les cuisines en particulier, sont devenues plus intégrées, davantage axées sur la mode et la marque Formica a pris une part plus importante dans les dépenses liées à la maison. Plusieurs motifs de stratifié Formica pouvaient créer des assortiments bicolores, l'une pour la table, l'autre pour les armoires et même une troisième souvent avec effet de bois pour les murs. Alors que la cuisine intégrée est devenue universelle aux États-Unis et au Royaume-Uni et en Europe avec retard, à partir du milieu des années 1950, les effets décoratifs ont joué un rôle plus important (ce qui changea peu jusqu'aux années 1990).

L'argument de la facilité de nettoyage était combiné à une injonction morale et à une philosophie de progrès. C'était la vision du monde d'une génération qui a survécu à la grande dépression, à la vie urbaine et à la réalité de tous les matériaux et surfaces naturels-organiques-authentiques. Comme les paysans fuyant le monde moderne, ils n'étaient pas attachés sentimentalement à ce qu'ils laissaient derrière eux. DuPont, l'entreprise de produits chi-miques géante qui avait lancé les produits miracles comme le nylon, les polymères de marque Teflon® et plus tard les fibres synthétiques de marque Lycra®, répétait inlassablement que « la chimie apportait de meilleures choses pour une meilleure vie ». Dans sa publicité, son concurrent Monsanto disait à propos des fibres acryliques des « tapis que ce n'était pas ce qu'on pensait mais quelque chose de meilleur ».

Alors que l'intelligentsia condamnait les plastiques pour leur imitation de n'importe quoi depuis le marbre jusqu'à la laque, pour remplacer les anciens matériaux « authentiques » par de nouvelles surfaces fabriquées en usine, une majorité écrasante des Américains les ont emmenés dans leur cœur et leur maison. La table de la cuisine, revêtue de stratifié Formica, par exemple, est dans toutes les mémoires des baby-boomers américains, à tous les niveaux de revenu et c'est également le cas des contemporains britanniques. Andy Warhol a dit que « ce qui est formidable à propos de ce pays est que l'Amérique a com-

eléctrico, y, luego, se desarrolló, lentamente al principio, como un material en láminas con aplicaciones domésticas y de otro tipo. Duro, brilloso y posiblemente muy decorativo, fue utilizado por los diseñadores pioneros como revestimiento en el equipamiento de nuevos espacios importantes —el transatlántico Queen Mary de Su Majestad la Reina, el Radio City Music Hall— y fue parte de escenarios domésticos deseables del "mundo del futuro", como en la Feria mundial de 1939. Pero fue en el auge de la construcción, durante la posguerra, cuando se lo vio instalado en la mayoría de las nuevas casas estadounidenses.

Desde mediados de la década de los cincuenta en adelante, cuando el diseño popular estadounidense se hizo más colorido y con diseños más audaces, y cuando las cocinas en particular, se hicieron más integradas, diseñadas y centradas en la moda, la marca Formica también consiguió una mayor participación en los gastos relacionados con el hogar. Varios diseños de laminado Formica podían crear un aspecto moderno de dos tonos en la cocina, uno para la parte superior de la mesa, otro para los gabinetes e, incluso, un tercero —frecuentemente un efecto tipo madera— para las paredes. A medida que la cocina empotrada se hizo universal en los Estados Unidos (el Reino Unido y Europa tardaron más tiempo), desde mediados de la década de los cincuenta en adelante, los efectos decorativos tuvieron una función más amplia (los conceptos básicos cambiaron relativamente poco hasta la década de los noventa).

La "facilidad de limpieza" combinó el precepto moral con una estética de progreso. Era el punto de vista mundial de una generación que había sobrevivido a la Depresión, los barrios marginados, y la realidad de todos aquellos materiales y superficies naturales, orgánicos y auténticos. Al igual que los pobladores rurales que escapaban al mundo moderno, ellos no estaban ni remotamente nostálgicos por lo que dejaban atrás. DuPont, la gigante compañía de productos químicos que, inicialmente, fue pionera en productos milagrosos, como el nailon, los polímeros de la marca Teflon® y, más adelante, las fibras sintéticas de la marca Lycra®, decía en su lema corporativo:

le sellaiset ihmetuotteet kuin nylonin, Teflon®-polymeerit ja myöhemmin Lycra®-brändin synteettiset kuidut, lupasi motossaan "parempia tuotteita parempaan elämään…kemian avulla". Sen kilpailija Monsanto sanoi mattojen akryylikuituja mainostaessaan: "Se ei ole mitä luulet sen olevan – se on parempaa".

Vaikka älymystö tuomitsikin muovin, joka jäljitteli kaikkea marmorista lakkaan ja korvasi vanhat aidot materiaalit uusilla tehdastuoreilla pinnoilla, amerikkalaisten suuri enemmistö otti sen omakseen ja osaksi kotejaan. For-mica-laminaatin pinnoittama keittiönpöytä on esimerkiksi amerikkalaisten (ja brittiläisten) suurten ikäluokkien yhteisenä lapsuudenmuistona kaikilla tulotasoilla. Andy Warhol tunnetusti sanoi: "Suurenmoista tässä maassa on amerikkalaisten aloittama perinne, että rikkaat kuluttajat ostavat peria-atteissa samoja tuotteita kuin köyhimmät. Voit nähdä televisiota katsellessasi Coca-Colaa ja tiedät, että presidentti juo kokista, Liz Taylor juo kokista ja aivan yhtä hyvin sinäkin voit juoda kokista. Coca-Cola on samaa kaikille, eikä mikään raha voi ostaa sinulle parempaa Coca-Colaa…"

Formica-pöytää leimaa tämä sama demokraattinen yleispätevyys. 50-luvun into kattaa mahdollisimman monet pinnat Formica-laminaatilla johtui vain osittain yhtiön markkinoinnista. Kaikki ajan henkeä kuvaava materiaali, kuten suositut tee-se-itse-

飾重要的新空間——遠洋海輪 HMS 瑪麗女王號，無線電城音樂廳——它是像 1939 年世界博覽會的場景中帶有啟迪性的家居「明日世界」的一部分。但是，只有經過戰後的建設熱潮才讓它置身於大多數美國新家庭中。

從二十世紀五十年代中期開始，隨著美國流行設計變得更加豐富多彩，圖案更大膽，特別是隨著廚房變得更加有綜合用途、更注重設計和時尚，富美家品牌也獲得了家庭支出的較大份額。幾種富美家美耐板圖案就可以在廚房創建時尚的雙色面貌——一個是檯面，另一個是櫥櫃，甚至還有第三個——常常帶木材的效果——就是牆壁。隨著內置廚房在美國普及(英國和歐洲需要更長的時間)，從二十世紀五十年代中期開始，裝飾效果起到了更大的作用(直到二十世紀九十年代，最基本的東西相對來說沒有多大變化)。

「一擦淨」結合了道義上的必要和審美的進步。這是從大蕭條、市中心和現實中的正宗天然有機材料和面材逃生的那一代人的世界觀。就像逃逸到現代世界的鄉下農民一樣，對留在身後的一切他們一點也不感到傷感。化學公司巨頭杜邦公司(DuPont)最初開創奇蹟般的產品，如尼龍、特氟龍(Teflon®)品牌聚合物，後來的萊卡(Lycra®)品牌合成纖維。該公司的座右銘是「透過化學⋯⋯為更美好的生活製作更優質的產品。」它的競爭對手孟山都(Monsanto)為其腈綸地毯做廣告「這不是你想像的東西，這是更美好的東西。」

雖然知識分子們譴責塑膠模仿從大理石到天然漆的所有東西，用剛出廠的面材取代過去「正宗」的建材，絕大多數的美國人喜歡塑膠，並把它們用在家裡。例如，包上富美家美耐板的餐桌是各種收入水準的嬰兒潮時期的美國人共同的回憶(對英國當代人也是一樣)。安迪·沃霍爾(Andy Warhol)曾經說過一句名言：「這個國家的偉大之處就在於，美國開啟的傳統是最富有的消費者和最貧窮的人購買基本上相同的東西。」

于家居和其他程序。耐火板堅硬、有光澤，并具有裝飾性的潛能，被有創意的設計師用作鑲板，裝飾重要的新空間——遠洋海輪 HMS 玛丽女王号，无线电城音乐厅——它是像 1939 年世界博览会的场景中带有启迪性的家居"明日世界"的一部分。但是，只有经过战后的建设热潮才让它置身于大多数美国新家庭中。

从二十世纪五十年代中期开始，随着美国流行设计变得更加丰富多彩，图案更大胆，特别是随着厨房变得更加有综合用途、更注重设计和时尚，富美家品牌也获得了家庭支出的较大份额。几种富美家®装饰耐火板图案就可以在厨房创建时尚的双色面貌——一个是台面，另一个是橱柜，甚至还有第三个——常常带木材的效果——就是墙壁。随着内置厨房在美国普及(英国和欧洲需要更长的时间)，从二十世纪五十年代中期开始，装饰效果起到了更大的作用(直到二十世纪九十年代，最基本的东西相对来说没有多大变化)。

"一擦净"结合了道义上的必要和审美的进步。这是从大萧条、市中心和现实中的正宗天然有机材料和面材逃生的那一代人的世界观。就像逃逸到现代世界的乡下农民一样，对留在身后的一切他们一点也不感到伤感。化学公司巨头杜邦公司(DuPont)最初开创奇迹般的产品，如尼龙、特氟龙(Teflon®)品牌聚合物，后来的莱卡(Lycra®)品牌合

อุตสาหกรรมเพื่อทดแทนไมก้าสำหรับฉนวนไฟฟ้า และได้รับการพัฒนาอย่างช้า ๆ ในช่วงเริ่มต้น ให้เป็นวัสดุที่เป็นแผ่นเพื่อการใช้งานในครัวเรือน และการใช้งานอื่น ๆ สิ่งที่มีความแข็ง เงางาม และมีศักยภาพเหมาะในการตกแต่งนี้ ได้ถูกนำไปใช้ประดับผนังโดยนักออกแบบยุคเริ่มต้นในการตกแต่งพื้นที่ที่สำคัญแบบใหม่ ๆ เช่น เรือเดินสมุทร HMS *Queen Mary*, Radio City Music Hall และได้เป็นส่วนหนึ่งของสถานที่ในประเทศที่ได้รับแรงบันดาลใจ "โลกอนาคต" เช่นเมื่อปี 1939 ในงาน World's Fair แต่ต้องอาศัยยุคหลังสงครามที่มีการเกิดขึ้นของอาคารอย่างมาก จึงจะได้เห็นฟอร์ไมก้าเข้าไปเป็นส่วนหนึ่งของบ้านอเมริกันใหม่ ๆ จำนวนมาก

ตั้งแต่ช่วงกลางยุค 1950 เป็นต้นมา การออกแบบที่ได้รับความนิยมของชาวอเมริกันเริ่มมีสีสัน และมีลวดลายที่มีความคิดสร้างสรรค์มากขึ้น และเนื่องจากเห็นได้ชัดเจนจากห้องครัวที่เริ่มมีความผสมผสาน มีการออกแบบ และให้ความสนใจกับความนิยมตามยุคสมัยมากขึ้น ตราสินค้าฟอร์ไมก้าได้รับส่วนแบ่งจากการใช้จ่ายที่เกี่ยวกับบ้านมากขึ้นเช่นกัน ลามิเนทลวดลายของฟอร์ไมก้าได้สร้างสรรค์แฟชั่นคู่โทนให้กับห้องครัวโดยโทนสีหนึ่งใช้กับส่วนของหน้าโต๊ะ โทนสีที่สองใช้กับส่วนของตู้ และบางทียังมีโทนสีที่สามซึ่งมักจะเป็นลายไม้ที่ใช้กับส่วนของผนัง และเนื่องมาจากห้องครัวแบบบิลด์อินที่เริ่มเป็นสากลในสหรัฐฯ (โดยในสหราชอาณาจักรและยุโรปใช้เวลานานมากกว่า) ตั้งแต่ช่วงกลางยุค 1950 เป็นต้นมา การแสดงออกโดยการตกแต่งมีบทบาทมากขึ้น (แบบพื้นฐานมีการเปลี่ยนแปลงเล็กน้อยจนกระทั่งในช่วงปี 1990)

"ความสะอาดหมดจด" ได้รวมเอาคำสั่งสอนทางด้านจริยธรรมเข้ากับสุนทรียศาสตร์ของความก้าวหน้า เป็นมุมมองที่มีต่อโลกของคนในยุคที่รอดมาจากช่วงเศรษฐกิจตกต่ำ แหล่งเสื่อมโทรม และความเป็นจริงของวัสดุและพื้นผิวที่มีความเป็นธรรมชาติ เช่นเดียวกับชาวนาในชนบทที่หลีกหนีไปยังโลกสมัยใหม่ ชาวนาพวกนั้นไม่ได้มีความรู้สึกผูกพันใด ๆ กับสิ่งที่พวกเขาทิ้งไว้เบื้องหลัง ดูปองต์ซึ่งเป็นบริษัททางด้านเคมียักษ์ใหญ่ ที่ได้เริ่มต้นบุกเบิกผลิตภัณฑ์ปาฏิหาริย์ เช่น ไนลอน เทฟลอน และไลครา ซึ่งเป็นเส้นใยสังเคราะห์ในช่วงต่อมา ได้กล่าวไว้ในคติพจน์ของบริษัทว่า "สิ่งที่ดีกว่า เพื่อความเป็นอยู่ที่ดีกว่า ด้วยสารเคมี" มอนซานโต้ ซึ่งเป็นคู่แข่งของดูปองต์ได้โฆษณาเส้นใยอคริลิกที่ใช้ในพรมของตนว่า "ไม่ใช่สิ่งที่คุณคิด แต่เป็นสิ่งที่ดีกว่า"

mencé la tradition là où les plus riches consommateurs achètent essentiellement les mêmes choses que les plus pauvres. Vous pouvez regarder la télé et boire du Coca-Cola. Vous savez que le Président boit du Coca-Cola, que Liz Taylor en boit et vous pouvez penser que vous aussi vous pouvez boire du Coca-Cola. Un Coca est un Coca-Cola et aucune somme d'argent ne permet d'obtenir un meilleur Coca-Cola... » La table couverte de stratifié Formica procède cette même universalité démocratique. Les années 1950 invitent à couvrir le plus grand nombre de surfaces de stratifié Formica et ceci n'a été que partiellement stimulé que par le marketing de l'entreprise. Toute la lecture des magazines de bricolage d'après-guerre, par exemple, suggère que les consommateurs pensaient à de nouvelles façons de remplacer toutes les anciennes surfaces par quelque chose de nouveau et plus moderne (Il ne s'agissait pas d'un modernisme strict, guindé, d'abnégation monastique moderne mais davantage d'une sorte de célébration) et bien sûr d'un rapport avec la propreté. En Grande-Bretagne, à la télévision des années 1950, le pape du bricolage, Barry Bucknell, a montré aux téléspectateurs comment améliorer leurs maisons au moyen de panneaux durs. Les panneaux des portes intérieures et autres menuiseries élaborées pouvaient être transformés et modernisés par soi-même à peu de frais avec un minimum de compétence en appliquant les panneaux rigides permettant l'obtention du New Look. Les portes planes et lisses, les placards intégrés aidaient les propriétaires et locataires des vieilles maisons à effacer le passé. Au cours de la décennie suivante, des millions de Britanniques déménageront dans de nouvelles maisons et appartements où la modernité était la règle et où la lumière, sous forme de baies vitrées et de vitrage cintré de toutes sortes, contrastaient violemment avec les sombres maisons anciennes. Plus de lumière naturelle et plus de lumière artificielle dans des maisons avec de nouveaux câbles et l'installation de l'électricité, pour des environnements plus exigeants où tout devait être récent et plus propre. Les surfaces lisses, brillantes et faciles à nettoyer sont devenues une obses-

"Cosas mejores para vivir mejor... a través de la industria química". Su rival Monsanto, que publicitaba su fibra acrílica en alfombras, decía: "No es lo que usted piensa, es algo mejor".

Aunque la clase culta condenó al plástico por imitar todo desde el mármol hasta la laca, por reemplazar los antiguos materiales "auténticos" con nuevas superficies recién salidas de fábrica, una abrumadora mayoría de estadounidenses lo incorporaron a sus casas y a sus corazones. La mesa de la cocina, revestida con laminado Formica, por ejemplo, es un recuerdo compartido de los estadounidenses de la era del baby boom en todos los niveles de ingresos (y también para los contemporáneos británicos). Andy Warhol genialmente dijo: "Lo que es fabuloso sobre este país es que los Estados Unidos comenzó con la tradición de que los consumidores más ricos compran, esencialmente, las mismas cosas que los más pobres. Uno puede mirar televisión y ver Coca-Cola, y saber que el Presidente bebe Coca-Cola, Liz Taylor bebe Coca-Cola y pensar que uno también puede beber Coca-Cola. Una Coca-Cola es una Coca-Cola, y ninguna suma de dinero puede comprar una mejor Coca-Cola..."

La mesa con superficie de laminado Formica tiene la misma universalidad democrática. El afán de la década de los cincuenta de revestir la mayor cantidad de superficies posible con laminado Formica fue solo en parte impulsado por el *marketing* de la empresa. Cualquier lectura del espíritu de la época de la posguerra —por ejemplo, las revistas DIY— sugiere que los consumidores estaban pensando en nuevas formas de reemplazar todas las superficies antiguas por algo nuevo que denotara la modernidad (no el modernismo, una modernidad monástica, estricta, tensa y desinteresada, sino un tipo más festivo y demótico) y la limpieza. En Gran Bretaña, el gurú de DIY de la televisión de la década de los cincuenta, Barry Bucknell, les mostraba a los televidentes cómo actualizar sus casas con madera prensada. Las puertas internas revestidas con paneles y otra ebanistería elaborada podrían transformarse —limpiarse y modernizarse a bajo costo con habilidades mínimas— mediante la aplicación de paneles de madera prensada que ofre-

DISTRIBUIDORES

成纤维。该公司的座右铭是"通过化学……为更美好的生活制作更优质的产品。"它的竞争对手孟山都（Monsanto）为其腈纶地毯做广告"这不是你想象的东西，这是更美好的东西。"

虽然知识分子们谴责塑料模仿从大理石到天然漆的所有东西，用刚出厂的面材取代过去"正宗"的建材，绝大多数的美国人喜欢塑料，并把它们用在家里。例如，包上富美家®装饰耐火板的餐桌是各种收入水平的婴儿潮时期的美国人共同的回忆（对英国当代人也是一样）。安迪·沃霍尔（Andy Warhol）曾经说过一句名言："这个国家的伟大之处就在于，美国开启的传统是最富有的消费者和最贫穷的人购买基本上相同的东西。你可以看电视，看可口可乐广告，你知道，总统喝可乐，伊丽莎白·泰勒（Liz Taylor）喝可乐，只要想一想，你也可以喝可乐。可乐就是可乐，再多的钱也买不来更好的可乐……。"

富美家®装饰耐火板面的桌子有着同样的民主普遍性。二十世纪五十年代敦促人们尽可能地使用富美家®装饰耐火板作面材，部分原因是公司的营销。阅读任何战后的时代精神的书籍（如最受欢迎的自己动手杂志）都表明，消费者在想出新的方式，用标志着现代性（不是现代主义，那种严格、紧张，自我否定的寺院式现代性，而是一种更通俗的彰显性的东西）和清洁的某些新东西替换所有旧的面材。在英国，二十世纪五十年代电视自己动手节目的主持人巴里·巴克内尔（Barry Bucknell）向观众们展示如何用硬质纤维板更新房屋。嵌板式室内门和其他复杂的细木活可以——用最少的技能、适中的价格做得干净而现代化——通过使用硬质纤维板转化，带来"新的外观"。齐边的门、流畅的内置衣柜帮助破旧老房子的房主和租户擦掉过去的痕迹。在后来十年里，数百万英国人搬进新的住宅和公寓，这里现代性是常态，阳光以观景窗和玻璃环绕的形式界定了与黑暗的旧房子的对比。更多的自然光线和更多

ในขณะที่ทางแวดวงวิชาการต่อว่าพลาสติกว่าลอกเลียนแบบทุกอย่าง ตั้งแต่หินอ่อนไปจนถึงสารเคลือบผิว รวมทั้งเข้ามาแทนที่วัสดุดั้งเดิมที่เก่าแก่ด้วยพื้นผิวใหม่ ๆ ที่ออกมาจากโรงงาน พลาสติกทั้งหลายนี้ได้เข้าไปอยู่ในดวงใจของชาวอเมริกันจำนวนมากมายมหาศาล และเอาเข้าไปใช้ในบ้านของตนเอง ตัวอย่างคือโต๊ะที่ใช้ในครัวซึ่งกรุด้วยลามิเนทฟอร์ไมก้าเป็นสิ่งที่อยู่ในความทรงจำของชาวอเมริกันในยุคเบบี้บูมในทุกกลุ่มรายได้ (เช่นเดียวกับอังกฤษในยุคนั้น) มีคำพูดที่มีชื่อเสียงของแอนดี้ วาร์ฮอล ที่กล่าวไว้ว่า "สิ่งที่ยิ่งใหญ่สำหรับประเทศนี้คือ อเมริกาได้เริ่มธรรมเนียมที่ว่าผู้บริโภคที่รวยที่สุดซื้อของเหมือนกับผู้บริโภคที่จนที่สุด คุณสามารถดูโทรทัศน์ และเห็นโคคาโคล่า และคุณก็ทราบว่าประธานาธิบดีก็ดื่มโค้ก ลิซ เทย์เลอร์ ก็ดื่มโค้ก และลองคิดดูว่าคุณก็ดื่มโค้กได้เช่นกัน โค้กก็คือโค้ก และไม่ว่าจะมีเงินมากขนาดไหนก็ไม่ทำให้คุณได้โค้กที่ดีกว่า"

โต๊ะที่กรุด้วยลามิเนทฟอร์ไมก้ามีความเป็นสากลอย่างเท่าเทียมกันเช่นกัน กระตุ้นทางการตลาดของบริษัทเป็นเพียงส่วนเล็ก ๆ ส่วนหนึ่งเท่านั้นของแรงผลักดันช่วงยุค 1950 ที่ให้กรุพื้นผิวให้ได้มากที่สุดเท่าที่จะทำได้ด้วยลามิเนทฟอร์ไมก้า สิ่งพิมพ์ที่เสนอแนวความคิดช่วงหลังสงคราม เช่น นิตยสาร DIY ที่ได้รับความนิยมสื่อให้เห็นว่าผู้บริโภคได้คิดหาวิธีที่จะแทนที่พื้นผิวแบบเดิม ๆ ทั้งหมดด้วยสิ่งใหม่ที่แสดงถึงความทันสมัย (ไม่ใช่สมัยใหม่ในแบบปรัชญาที่มีความเคร่งครัด ไม่อ่อนไหวปฏิเสธความเชื่อทางศาสนา แต่เป็นแบบที่นิยมกับทั่วไป) และความสะอาด ในอังกฤษผู้เชี่ยวชาญ DIY ทางโทรทัศน์ คือ แบร์รี่ บัคเนล์ แสดงให้ผู้ชมเห็นว่าทำอย่างไรที่จะทำให้บ้านของตนทันสมัยด้วยไม้อัด ประตูตามแบบภายใน และข้อต่อที่ประณีตสามารถเปลี่ยนรูปแบบ ทำให้สะอาด และทันสมัยในราคาที่ย่อมเยาโดยอาศัยทักษะเพียงน้อยนิดด้วยการใช้แบบไม้อัดที่แสดงถึงรูปลักษณ์ใหม่ ประตูตามผลัก และตู้เสื้อผ้าแบบบิลต์อินที่เนี้ยบเรียบช่วยให้เจ้าของ และผู้อาศัยใน บ้านที่ทรุดโทรมลืมอดีตที่ผ่านมา ตลอดช่วงทศวรรษต่อมา ชาวอังกฤษจำนวนมากย้ายเข้ามาอยู่ในบ้านและหอพักใหม่ ๆ ที่ความทันสมัยเป็นเรื่องปกติ และแสงสว่างในรูปแบบของหน้าต่างบานใหญ่ และการติดกระจกไว้รอบ ๆ ทุกรูปแบบ อธิบายถึงความแตกต่างจากบ้านเก่า ๆ ที่มืดมน แสงสว่างธรรมชาติ และแสงสว่างที่ถูกสร้างขึ้นที่เพิ่มมากขึ้นในบ้านที่มีการเดินสายไฟใหม่ หรือปรับการเดินสายไฟ ได้เกิดขึ้นเพื่อสภาพแวดล้อมที่

sion mondiale. En les appliquant à peu près partout, les personnes nées durant les années 1920 et 1930 pouvaient anéantir les horreurs du passé récent et manifester leur participation au monde moderne. Ils pouvaient « vivre leur rêve ».

Une fois gainée de stratifié Formica, une surface semblait devenir aussi propre qu'un sanatorium - mais aussi joyeuse qu'un restaurant. Le restaurant américain universel faisait partie de l'imagerie de vie quotidienne qui a attiré les immigrants européens. L'idée que les Américains ordinaires, les gens qu'eux-mêmes pouvaient devenir, avaient accès à une belle vie était tout à fait attrayant. En Grande-Bretagne une toute nouvelle génération de cafés pré Starbucks indépendants a répondu à ces aspirations. Ces établissements étaient couverts de surfaces gaies en stratifié Formica au point que ceux qui subsistent aujourd'hui sont généralement appelés des Cafés Formica, avec planchers en linoléum et parfois de nouvelles machines à café italiennes.

Avec l'équipement de ce monde émergent facile à nettoyer, avec ses surfaces lisses sous les baies vitrées, ses motifs expressifs et son consensus populaire esthétique sont apparus d'autres miracles encore : des miracles de nettoyage et d'essuyage. La marque de produits de nettoyage ménager Monsieur Net® de Procter & Gamble, développée en 1957 à partir d'une invention acquise par la société Procter & Gamble d'une entreprise qui net-

cerían la nueva apariencia. Las puertas enrasadas y los placares lisos ayudaron a los propietarios y a los inquilinos de casas antiguas maltrechas a eliminar el pasado. En la siguiente década, millones de británicos se mudaron a nuevas casas y apartamentos en los que la modernidad era la norma y en los que la luz, en la forma de ventanas panorámicas y vidriado envolvente de todo tipo, definió el contraste con las casas antiguas y oscuras. Más luz natural y más luz artificial, en casas con nuevos cableados o recableados de electricidad, realizados para entornos más exigentes en los que todo debía ser más nuevo y más limpio. Las superficies lisas, luminosas y brillantes fáciles de limpiar se convirtieron en una obsesión mundial. Al aplicarlas casi en todos lados, quienes vivieron la posguerra —personas que nacieron entre 1920 y 1930— podían eliminar los horrores del pasado reciente y marcar su participación en la corriente principal moderna; podían "Vivir el Sueño".

Una vez revestida con laminado Formica, una superficie parecía estar tan limpia y pura como un sanatorio, pero tan alegre como un comedor. La cafetería estadounidense universal era parte de la imagen cotidiana de los Estados Unidos que atraía a inmigrantes europeos. La idea de que los estadounidenses comunes —las personas en las que podrían convertirse— disfrutaban de estos estándares de vida era absolutamente cautivadora. En Gran Bretaña, una generación completamente nueva de cafés independientes anteriores a Starbucks respondieron a esos anhelos. Estaban cubiertos con superficies alegres de laminado Formica —los que perduraron, ahora parte de un tipo de legado, suelen llamarse Cafés de Formica— con pisos de linóleo y, algunas veces, máquinas de café italiano.

Junto a este emergente mundo de fácil limpieza, con sus superficies lisas bajo ventanas panorámicas, sus diseños expresivos y su consenso estético popular, vino un cúmulo de otros milagros nuevos: milagros relacionados con la limpieza. La marca de limpiadores domésticos Mr. Clean® de Procter & Gamble, desarrollada en 1957 a partir de un invento que Procter & Gamble Company adquirió de una empresa que limpiaba embarcaciones, fue un mila-

lehdet, antaa ymmärtää, että kuluttajat keksivät uusia keinoja vanhojen pintojen korvaamiseen jollakin uudella, puhtautta ja nykyaikaisuutta henkivällä (ei modernismilla — kireällä ja uhrautuvalla, miltei uskonnollisella nykyaikaisuudella, vaan sen kansanomaisemmalla, juhlivammalla muunnoksella). Britannian 50-luvun television tee-se-itse-guru Barry Bucknell näytti katsojille, miten he voivat uudistaa talonsa kovalevyllä.

Paneloidut sisäovet ja muut vaativat puusepäntyöt voitiin uusia täysin — saada puhtaiksi ja uudenaikaisiksi vähäisin kustannuksin ja taidoin käyttämällä kovalevypaneeleja, jotka tarjosivat niille uuden ilmeen.

Laakaovet ja sileät, sisäänrakennetut kaapit auttoivat vanhojen, kuluneiden talojen omistajia ja vuokralaisia unohtamaan menneisyyden. Seuraavan vuosikymmenen aikana miljoonat britit muuttivat uusiin taloihin ja asuntoihin, joissa uudenaikaisuus oli itsestään selvä asia ja joissa maisema- ja muiden, kaikkiin suuntiin avautuvien ikkunoiden tarjoama valo tarjosi selkeän vastakohdan vanhoille pimeille taloille. Lisääntynyt luonnon- ja keinovalo taloissa, jotka olivat saaneet uudet tai uudistetut sähköjohdot, merkitsi vaativampaa ympäristöä, missä kaiken oli oltava uudempaa ja puhtaampaa. Sileistä, kirkkaista ja kiiltävistä pinnoista, jotka saattoi pyyhkäistä puhtaaksi, tuli globaali pakkomielle. Käyttämällä niitä lähes kaikkialla sodanjälkeiset (20- ja 30-luvuilla syntyneet) asunnonomistajat saattoivat pyyhkiä pois lähimenneisyyden kauhut ja todistaa paikkansa modernissa yhteiskunnassa — unelmasta tuli totta.

Formicaan kääritty pinta vaikutti kyllin puhtaalta ja jumalalliselta sopiakseen parantolaan, mutta yhtä iloiselta kuin ruokabaarin pinnat. Kaikkialta maasta löytyvä diner-ruokabaari kuuluu arkipäivän Amerikan kuvastoon, joka viehätti Euroopasta tulevia maahanmuuttajia. Ajatus, että tavalliset amerikkalaiset — joita heistäkin saattoi tulla — voivat saavuttaa tällaisen tason, oli vastustamaton. Britanniassa koko Starbucksia edeltävä riippumattomien kahviloiden ja baarien sukupolvi otti tämän ajatuksen omakseen. Ne pinnoitettiin pirteillä Formica-laminaateilla ja linoleumilattioilla, ja joskus niihin kuului myös uusi italialainen kahvinkeitin. Jäl-

你可以看電視，看可口可樂廣告，你知道，總統喝可樂，伊麗莎白·泰勒(Liz Taylor)喝可樂，只要想一想，你也可以喝可樂。可樂就是可樂，再多的錢也買不來更好的可樂……。」

富美家美耐板面的桌子有著同樣的民主普選性。二十世紀五十年代敦促人們盡可能地使用富美家美耐板作面材，部分原因是公司的行銷。閱讀任何戰後的時代精神的書籍(如最受歡迎的自己動手雜誌)都表明，消費者在想出新的方式，用標誌著現代性(不是現代主義，那種嚴格、緊張、自我否定的寺院式現代性，而是一種更通俗的彰顯性的束西)和清潔的某些新束西替換所有舊的面材。在英國，二十世紀五十年代電視自己動手節目的主持人巴里·巴克內爾(Barry Bucknell)向觀眾們展示如何用硬質纖維板更新房屋。嵌板式室內門和其他複雜的細木活可以——用最少的技能、適中的價格做得乾淨而現代化——透過使用硬質纖維板轉化，帶來「新的外觀」。齊邊的門、流暢的內置衣櫃幫助破舊老房子的房主和租戶擦掉過去的痕跡。在後來十年裡，數百萬英國人搬進新的住宅和公寓，這裡現代性是常態，陽光以觀景窗和玻璃環繞的形式界定了與黑暗的舊房子的對比。更多的自然光線和更多的人造光照在房子裡，新電線或重新佈置的電線有利於更苛刻的環境，裡面的一切都應該更新和更清潔。能夠一擦淨的光滑、明亮、有光澤的表面成了使全球的人癡迷的束西。透過幾乎無處不在的使用，戰後房主們——出生在二十世紀二十年代和三十年代的人——可以消除近期的恐怖，並紀念他們對現代主流的參與——他們可以「親歷自己的夢想」。

一旦套上富美家美耐板，面板似乎與清潔和虔誠的療養院一樣，但像小餐館一樣富有生氣。普遍的美式餐館是吸引歐洲移民的美國日常生活的一部分。普通美國人——他們可能會成為美國人——作為權利來享受這些標準，這個想法完全令人信服。在英國，全新一代

的人造光照在房子里，新电线或重新布置的电线有利于更苛刻的环境，里面的一切都应该更新和更清洁。能够一擦净的光滑、明亮、有光泽的表面成了使全球的人痴迷的东西。通过几乎无处不在的使用，战后房主们——出生在二十世纪二十年代和三十年代的人——可以消除近期的恐怖，并纪念他们对现代主流的参与——他们可以"亲历自己的梦想"。

一旦套上富美家®装饰耐火板，面板似乎与清洁和虔诚的疗养院一样，但像小餐馆一样富有生气。普遍的美式餐馆是吸引欧洲移民的美国日常生活的一部分。普通美国人——他们可能会成为美国人——作为权利来享受这些标准，这个想法完全令人信服。在英国，全新一代的前星巴克独立式咖啡厅和咖啡酒吧迎合了这些渴望。这些地方覆盖着欢快的富美家®装饰耐火板面材——那些幸存者，现在是文物传统的一部分，通常称为富美家咖啡馆——铺着油毡地板，有时再加上簇新的意大利咖啡机。

观景窗下光滑的表面，具有表现力的图案和流行的审美共识，与这个新兴的一擦净世界的硬件一起，同时还有一堆其他的新奇迹——洁净、擦拭的奇迹。宝洁公司(Proctor & Gamble)的

ต้องการให้ทุกสิ่งใหม่กว่าเดิม และสะอาดกว่าเดิม พื้นผิวที่เรียบ สดใส และเงางามที่สะอาดหมดจดกลายเป็นสิ่งที่ทั่วโลกต้องการ ด้วยการเติมแต่งพื้นผิวพวกนี้ในเกือบทุกที่เข้าของบ้านในยุคหลังสงคราม ซึ่งเป็นผู้คนที่เกิดขึ้นในช่วงยุค 1920-1930 สามารถที่จะขจัดความหวาดกลัวที่มีต่ออดีตที่เพิ่งผ่านพ้น และให้ความคาดหวังในกระแสความนิยมสมัยใหม่ โดยพวกเขาสามารถ "ทำตามความฝันของตนเองได้"

เมื่อมีการใช้ลามิเนทฟอร์ไมก้า พื้นผิวดูสะอาด และให้ความรู้สึกสูงส่ง ประหนึ่งโรงพยาบาล แต่มีความสดใสราวกับร้านอาหาร ร้านอาหารของชาวอเมริกันทั่วไปเป็นส่วนหนึ่งของชีวิตประจำวันของชาวอเมริกันที่ดึงดูดผู้พยพชาวยุโรป แนวความคิดแบบชาวอเมริกันสามัญชนเป็นสิ่งที่ชาวยุโรปคิดว่าตนเองสามารถเป็นได้ และพวกเขามีความสุขกับมาตรฐานเหล่านี้เนื่องจากสิทธิของพวกเขาได้รับการบีบบังคับมาก ในอังกฤษ คาเฟ่และร้านกาแฟอิสระรุ่นใหม่ก่อนยุคสตาร์บัคส์ ให้การตอบสนองต่อความต้องการเหล่านี้ โดยร้านพวกนี้ใช้ลามิเนทฟอร์ไมก้าที่สดใสตกแต่งร้าน ร้านที่สามารถดำเนินกิจการต่อไปได้ซึ่งตอนนี้เป็นส่วนหนึ่งของสิ่งที่ยังคงหลงเหลืออยู่ได้รับการอนุรักษ์ ได้รับการขนานนามว่าเป็นฟอร์ไมก้าคาเฟ่ ที่เป็นพื้นเสื่อน้ำมันและบางครั้งมีเครื่องทำกาแฟจากอิตาลีใหม่ๆ

สิ่งที่มาพร้อมกับอุปกรณ์ในโลกสะอาดหมดจดที่กำลังเกิดขึ้น ที่มีพื้นผิวเนียนเรียบอยู่ใต้หน้าต่างบานใหญ่ ลวดลายที่น่าประทับใจ และความสุนทรีย์อย่างไม่มีข้อกังขาได้รับความนิยม คือการเกิดขึ้นของปาฏิหาริย์ใหม่จำนวนมาก หรือปาฏิหาริย์ของการทำความสะอาดที่หมดจด โดยยี่ห้อ Mr.Clean ของพรอคเตอร์แอนด์แกมเบิล สำหรับเครื่องใช้ภายในบ้านที่ได้รับการพัฒนาในปี 1957 เกิดมาจากสิ่งประดิษฐ์ที่บริษัท พรอคเตอร์แอนด์แกมเบิล ได้มาจากธุรกิจทำความสะอาดเรือ เป็นปาฏิหาริย์ที่มอบให้การทำความสะอาดพื้นผิวแข็งแบบใหม่ๆ อย่างเข้มข้นภายในบ้านในฝัน Mr.Clean มีคุณภาพที่น่าอัศจรรย์ มันสามารถขจัดคราบไขมันแข็งๆ ที่เกาะติดแน่นได้อย่างดี ไม่เหมือนกับผงซักฟอก เนื่องจากไม่เป็นฟอง และไม่ต้องมีการล้างน้ำ ดังเช่นที่มีการอ้างไว้ในโฆษณาในยุคแรกๆ "สามารถลดเวลาการทำความสะอาดได้ครึ่งหนึ่ง" สามารถทำความสะอาดพื้นผิวที่ไม่เคยได้รับการทำความสะอาด หรือเช็ดมาก่อน กำแพง และงานไม้ ซึ่งตอนนี้ปกปิดด้วยวอลล์เปเปอร์ที่เคลือบด้วยไวนิลและสีพลาสติก พื้นไวนิล และโต๊ะสำหรับใช้ในครัวที่ใช้ลามิเนทฟอร์ไมก้า น้ำยาทำความ

toyait les bateaux. Elle a été un miracle pour le nettoyage difficile des nouvelles surfaces dures dans la maison idéale. Monsieur Net avait des qualités étonnantes, il pouvait éliminer la graisse durcie d'une manière très agressive. Contrairement aux détergents pour lessive, le produit ne mousse pas et ne doit donc pas être rincé. La première publicité affirmait que la « durée du nettoyage est divisée par deux ». Le produit permettait de nettoyer des surfaces qui auparavant n'étaient ni lavées ni essuyées, les murs et les boiseries, maintenant recouverts de papier peint en vinyle et de peinture en plastique rigide, les sols de vinyle et les tables cuisine en stratifié Formica. Les nouveaux produits d'entretien ménager ont fait d'un monde super propre une réalité. Les surfaces ont été lavées et essuyées plus souvent et plus vigoureusement (tout comme dans les années 1950, le marketing de masse des lessiveuses-essoreuses automatiques a signifié que les vêtements étaient simplement lavés plus souvent). Les éponges et les vadrouilles synthétiques rendaient tout cela plus simple. Tous les nouveaux produits de nettoyage depuis les nouveaux détergents synthétiques remplaçant les savons en poudre jusqu'aux nouveaux liquides synthétiques de vaisselle, fonctionnaient réellement. Ils éliminaient radicalement la corvée du nettoyage.

Pendant ce siècle, la première génération de produits de nettoyage synthétiques efficaces s'est transformée en une armée de nettoyeurs dédiée à nettoyer pratiquement tout, même ironiquement, le bois naturel. Un des produits les plus populaires pour les jeunes mères anxieuses était un nettoyant de surface par pulvérisation qui s'engage à tuer les microbes. Le nettoyage facile des surfaces est devenu une habitude. La valeur ajoutée réside dans la certitude que le mal invisible dans les joints des carrelages et des plans de travail, des murs était attaqué vigoureusement. Une campagne publicitaire populaire des années 1970 déclarait que le produit tuait quatre-vingt-dix-neuf pour cent des germes connus. En l'espace de vingt années d'après-guerre, de 1945 à 1965, toutes les aspirations domestiques d'avant-guerre pour un nouveau lieu

gro dedicado para la ardua limpieza de nuestras superficies duras en la casa ideal. Mr. Clean tenía cualidades asombrosas; quitaba la grasa endurecida de manera realmente agresiva. A diferencia de los detergentes para ropa, no hacía espuma y no requería enjuague. Tal como se afirmaba en sus primeras publicidades: "reduce el tiempo de limpieza a la mitad". Limpiaba superficies que simplemente no se lavaban ni limpiaban antes: paredes y construcciones en madera, ahora cubiertas con papeles tapiz revestidos con vinilo y pinturas plásticas duras, pisos de vinilo y mesas de cocina recubiertas con laminado Formica. Los nuevos limpiadores domésticos hicieron que el mundo potencialmente súper limpio fuese una realidad, y las superficies se comenzaron a lavar y a limpiar con más frecuencia y más vigorosamente. (Así como la comercialización masiva de lavadoras y secadoras automáticas en la década de los cincuenta significó que la ropa se lavara con mayor frecuencia). Las esponjas y los trapeadores sintéticos facilitaron mucho el trabajo. El panteón de la posguerra de nuevos limpiadores, desde detergentes sintéticos que reemplazaban a los jabones en polvo hasta los nuevos líquidos sintéticos para lavar los platos, realmente funcionó. Estos productos lograron aligerar la carga de las tareas de fregado.

Para este siglo, la primera generación de limpiadores sintéticos efectivos se ha constituido en un ejército de limpiadores dedicados a limpiar casi todo; incluso, aunque suene irónico, había un limpiador para la madera natural. Uno de los productos más populares para las ansiosas madres jóvenes era un limpiador de superficies en aerosol destinado a matar los gérmenes. La función básica —la fácil limpieza de las superficies— ahora es un hecho. El valor agregado principal yace en la garantía de que el demonio invisible en la lechada de las baldosas y las juntas de cubiertas prefabricadas y paneles de pared se atacaría vigorosamente. Tal como prometía una campaña publicitaria televisiva popular de la década de los setenta: "Mata el 99 % de los gérmenes". En tan solo veinte años del mundo de la posguerra —desde 1945 hasta 1965—se alcanzaron todas las aspiraciones domésticas previas a la guerra, de tener un nuevo

jelle jääneitä, jotka nykyään muodostavat eräänlaisen perinnepolun, kutsutaan yleensä Formica-kahviloiksi.

Tämän uuden helppohoitoisen maailman takaavan rakenteiden, sen maisemaikkunoiden edustalla leviävien sileiden pintojen, sen ilmeikkäiden kuvioiden ja esteettisen yksimielisyyden mukana saapui roppakaupalla muitakin uusia ihmeitä, siivous- ja puhdistusihmeitä. Procter & Gamble Companyn vuonna 1957 kehittämät Mr. Clean® puhdistusaineet, jotka perustuivat laivojen puhdistamiseen erikoistuneen yrityksen patenttiin, olivat ihannekodin uusien kovien pintojen perusteelliselle puhtaana pitämiselle omistettuja ihmeitä. Mr. Cleanin taidot olivat ihmeelliset, ja se poisti siekailematta kovettuneen rasvankin. Se ei vaahdonnut niin kuin pyykkinpesuaineet, eikä sitä tarvinnut huuhdella. Kuten ensimmäisissä mainoksissa luvattiin, "se lyhensi siivousajan puoleen". Se pesi pinnat, joita ei yksinkertaisesti ollut puhdistettu tai pyyhitty ennen: seinät ja puupaneelit (jotka nyt olivat vinyylitapettien tai kovien maalien peittämiä), vinyylilattiat ja Formica-laminaatin peittämät keittiönpöydät. Uudet puhdistusaineet tekivät ääripuhtaasta maailmasta todellisuuden, ja pintoja pestiin ja pyyhittiin useammin ja tarmokkaammin. (Samalla tavoin kuin 50-luvulla massoille myydyt automaattiset pyykinpesukoneet ja -kuivausrummut merkitsivät, että vaatteita pestiin yhä useammin.) Synteettiset sienet ja mopit helpottivat siivoamista entisestään. Sodan jälkeen kehitetyt uudet puhdistusaineet — saippuajauheet korvaavista synteettisistä pyykkinpesuaineista uusiin synteettisiin astianpesunesteisiin — osasivat asiansa. Ne todellakin vapauttivat siivoamisen raadannasta.

Nyt ensimmäisestä tehokkaiden synteettisten pesuaineiden sukupolvesta oli kehittynyt kokonainen pesuaineiden armeija, joka pystyi puhdistamaan käytännöllisesti kaiken — mielenkiintoista kyllä jopa luonnonpuun. Yksi huolestuneiden uusien äitien suosimista tuotteista oli pintojen puhdistamiseen tarkoitettu sumute, joka tappoi bakteerit. Perustoiminto, pintojen helppo puhdistus, oli nyt itsestään selvää. Lisäarvoa antoi vakuutus, että laattojen väleissä ja työpintojen ja seinäpaneelien saumoissa piilevän näkymättömän

的前星巴克獨立式咖啡廳和咖啡酒吧迎合了這些渴望。這些地方覆蓋著歡快的富美家美耐板面材——那些倖存者，現在是文物傳統的一部分，通常稱為富美家咖啡館——鋪著油氈地板，有時再加上簇新的義大利咖啡機。

觀景窗下光滑的表面，具有表現力的圖案和流行的審美共識，與這個新興的一擦淨世界的硬體一起，同時還有一堆其他的新奇蹟——潔淨、擦拭的奇蹟。寶潔公司 (Proctor & Gamble) 的清潔先生 (Mr. Clean®) 品牌家用清潔劑，從 1957 年寶潔公司收購的一家清理船隻的生意開發而來，是完成新的硬質面材艱難的清潔任務的專項奇蹟。清潔先生有著優秀的品質；用一種非常強力的方式清除硬化的油脂。與洗衣劑不同的是，它沒有泡沫，不需要沖洗。正如早期的廣告所聲稱的「把清洗時間縮短一半」。清潔先生清潔了以前根本不洗或不擦的表面、牆壁和木製品——現在用乙烯塗層壁紙和硬質塑膠漆覆蓋、乙烯地板以及用富美家美耐板作桌具的廚房餐桌。新的家用清潔劑讓超潔淨的世界可能成為現實，面材清洗和擦拭得更頻繁，更有力。(就像二十世紀五十年代大規模行銷的全自動洗衣機和烘乾機意味著衣服要更經常清洗一樣)。合成海綿和拖具使這一切變得更加容易。戰後新清潔劑的明星，從合成洗滌劑替代肥皂粉到新的合成餐具洗滌液，確實有效果。他們真地消除了單調乏味的擦洗工作。

到本世紀初，第一代有效的合成清潔劑已經演變成一系列的清潔劑，幾乎用於清洗一切東西——甚至具有諷刺意味的是，有一種天然木材專用清潔劑。最受熱切期待的年輕母親歡迎的產品之一，是專用於殺菌的噴霧表面清潔劑。基本的功能——容易的表面清潔——現在已成為理所當然的事。其溢價(附加價值)就在於能夠保證瓷磚灌漿以及檯面和牆面板的連接處看不見的邪惡污垢會受到強力的攻擊。如二十世紀七十年代一條流行的英國電視廣告所承諾的「殺死已知細菌的99%。」

清洁先生 (Mr. Clean®) 品牌家用清洁剂，从 1957 年宝洁公司收购的一家清理船只的生意开发而来，是完成新的硬质面材艰难的清洁任务的专项奇迹。清洁先生有着优秀的品质；用一种非常强力的方式清除硬化的油脂。与洗衣剂不同的是，它没有泡沫，不需要冲洗。正如早期的广告所声称的"把清洗时间缩短一半"。清洁先生清洁了以前根本不洗或不擦的表面、墙壁和木制品——现在用乙烯涂层壁纸和硬质塑料漆覆盖、乙烯地板以及用富美家®装饰耐火板作桌面的厨房餐桌。新的家用清洁剂让超洁净的世界可能成为现实，面材清洗和擦拭得更频繁，更有力。(就像二十世纪五十年代大规模营销的全自动洗衣机和烘干机意味着衣服更经常清洗一样)。合成海绵和拖把使这一切变得更加容易。战后新清洁剂的明星，从合成洗涤剂替代肥皂粉到新的合成餐具洗涤液，确实有效果。他们真地消除了单调乏味的擦洗工作。

到本世纪初，第一代有效的合成清洁剂已经演变成一系列的清洁剂，几乎用于清洗一切东西——甚至具有讽刺意味的是，有一种天然木材专用清洁剂。最受热切期待的年轻母亲欢迎的产品之一，是专用于杀菌的喷雾表面清洁剂。基本的功能——容易的表面清洁——现在已成为理所当然的事。其溢价(附加价值)就在于能够保证瓷砖灌浆以及台面和墙面板的连接处看不见的邪恶污垢会受到强力的攻击。如二十世纪七十年代一条流行的英国电视广告所承诺的"杀死已知细菌的99%。"在战后仅仅二十年的世界里——从 1945 年到 1965 年——战前对光线充足、明亮和永远干净的新地方的奢望实现了。就像一切实现了的梦想一样，这个新的地方后来成为无形的、理所当然的、被商品化的东西。

到了二十世纪七十年代，人们期待所有的房子，除了非常差或勉强居住的房子，都要干净、设施齐全、包括附带所有器具的内置厨房、一台现代彩

สะอาดสำหรับครัวเรือนแบบใหม่ทำให้โลกที่สะอาดอย่างยิ่งในความฝันกลายเป็นความจริง และพื้นผิวได้รับการทำความสะอาด หรือเช็ดได้บ่อยขึ้น และอย่างกระตือรือร้นมากขึ้น (เช่นเดียวกับการทำการตลาดแบบมวลชนของเครื่องซักผ้า – เครื่องอบผ้าอัตโนมัติในยุค 1950 ซึ่งหมายความว่าสามารถทำความสะอาดเสื้อผ้าได้บ่อยมากขึ้น) ฟองน้ำสังเคราะห์ และไม้ถูพื้นทำให้สิ่งพวกนี้เป็นไปได้ง่ายมากขึ้น สิ่งที่น่าจดจำในยุคหลังสงครามของพวกน้ำยาทำความสะอาดใหม่ ๆ ตั้งแต่น้ำยาทำความสะอาดสังเคราะห์ที่มาแทนที่สบู่ผง ไปจนถึงน้ำยาล้างจานสังเคราะห์ที่เกิดขึ้นใหม่ สามารถใช้งานได้จริง สิ่งพวกนี้ช่วยขจัดความยากลำบากในการขัดออกไป

เมื่อมาถึงในศตวรรษนี้ สิ่งทำความสะอาดสังเคราะห์ที่มีประสิทธิผลในยุคแรกได้มีวิวัฒนาการมาเป็นกองทัพของสิ่งทำความสะอาดที่สามารถใช้ทำความสะอาดได้แทบจะทุกอย่างเลยทีเดียว รวมทั้งไม่น่าเชื่อว่าจะเป็นไปได้ หนึ่งในผลิตภัณฑ์ที่ได้รับความนิยมสูงสุดสำหรับคุณแม่วัยสาวที่มีความวิตกกังวล คือสิ่งทำความสะอาดพื้นผิวแบบสเปรย์ที่ใช้สำหรับฆ่าเชื้อโรค หน้าที่เบื้องต้นคือการทำความสะอาดผิวหน้าอย่างง่ายดาย เป็นสิ่งที่รู้กันทั่วไปในปัจจุบัน มูลค่าเพิ่ม หรือความพิเศษอยู่ในความมั่นใจที่ว่าศัตรูที่มองไม่เห็นในซอกมุมกระเบื้อง และตามมุมของพื้นผิวด้านบนและขอบกำแพงจะได้รับการกำจัดอย่างแข็งขัน ดังที่โฆษณาทางโทรทัศน์ในยุค 1970 ได้รับความนิยมได้ให้คำมั่นว่า "ฆ่าเชื้อโรคที่เป็นที่รู้จักกันได้กว่า 99%" ภายในช่วงเวลา 20 ปีหลังจากโลกยุคหลังสงคราม ตั้งแต่ปี 1945-1965 ความปรารถนาภายในบ้านช่วงยุคก่อนสงครามที่ต้องการสถานที่ใหม่ที่มีแสงสว่าง

clair, lumineux et perpétuellement propre étaient atteintes. Comme tous les rêves se réalisent, ce nouveau lieu est alors devenu invisible, considéré comme acquis, banalisé.

Dans les années 1970, les maisons de tous, sauf les plus pauvres ou les plus marginaux étaient censées être propres et bien équipées, contenant une cuisine intégrée avec tous les appareils, une télévision couleur moderne et plus tard, un ordinateur avec connexion Internet, toutes ces choses dont des milliards de personnes des pays en développement ne disposent pas encore. Le rôle symbolique de la modernité domestique des années 1950 — ces mains longuement gantées pointant avec stupéfaction — a pratiquement disparu. Nous sommes tous blasés à ce sujet. Pour les baby-boomers et leurs enfants, c'est l'ordre naturel des choses. Si naturel, en effet, une garantie de base qui permet à une autre génération, vivant dans un monde plus complexe avec des attentes différentes, d'afficher une gamme très variée de styles dans leurs maisons. Ces styles pourraient constituer, selon les titres de chapitre du récent livre du photographe d'intérieur, basé à Londres, Andreas von Einsiedel Dream Home—*100 Inspirational Interiors*—« classique contemporain, éclectique, exotique, campagnard ou opulent » avec une masse de sous-catégories dans chaque cas : Gustavian, Brit-Pop et Bauhaus rétro, par exemple.

Un chapitre convaincant illustre une tendance persistante des vingt dernières années : le minimalisme cool. Nous voici à nouveau, avec des intérieurs pétillants tout blancs, des fenêtres massives, la relance de classiques Saarinen, Jacobsen et Eames, de planchers étincelants composites, et des hectares de placards mur-à-mur recouverts de stratifiés mats. Avec quelques concessions à une authenticité archaïque, un peu de briques nues, du bois flache. Mais avec le modernisme du milieu du siècle on retourne aux racines réelles : un retour à un monde facile à nettoyer.

lugar que fuera luminoso, brilloso y permanentemente limpio. Al igual que todos los sueños que se concretan, este nuevo lugar luego se hizo invisible, se dio por sentado, se convirtió en un producto de uso masivo.

Para la década de los setenta, las casas de todos, excepto de los muy pobres o los más marginales, debían estar limpias y bien equipadas, debían tener una cocina empotrada con todos los artefactos, un televisor en color moderno y, más adelante, una computadora con conexión a Internet; todas las cosas que miles de millones de personas en los países en vías de desarrollo todavía no tienen. El rol simbólico y expresivo de la modernidad doméstica de la década de los cincuenta —esas manos cubiertas de guantes largos que señalaban con asombro— prácticamente había desaparecido. Todos nos volvimos indiferentes. Para la generación de la posguerra y sus hijos, este es el orden natural de las cosas. Tan natural de hecho, como una garantía básica, que ha permitido a otra generación, que vivía en un mundo más complejo con expectativas diferentes, desplegar una gama muy variada de estilos en sus casas. Podían ser, si tomamos los encabezados de los capítulos del reciente libro *Dream Homes—100 Inspirational Interiors*, del fotógrafo de interiores de Londres Andreas von Einsiedel, "Contemporáneo clásico", "Ecléctico", "Exótico", "Campestre" u "Opulento", con una gran cantidad de subcategorías en cada uno — neo Gustavian, Brit-Pop y Bauhaus, por ejemplo. También hay un atractivo capítulo que ilustra una persistente tendencia de los últimos veinte años: "Minimalismo frío". Aquí estamos de nuevo, con los interiores luminosos y completamente blancos; las ventanas masivas; los clásicos revividos de Saarinen, Jacobsen y Eames; los relucientes pisos de compuesto y los acres de revestimientos con paneles desde la pared hasta el piso en laminados mate. Hay unas pocas concesiones a una autenticidad antigua —un poco de ladrillo sin revestir, algo de madera tallada de manera áspera—, pero, con el estilo modernista de mediados de siglo, volvemos a nuestras verdaderas raíces: volvemos a un mundo de fácil limpieza.

pahan kimppuun käydään tarmokkaasti. Kuten suositussa 70-luvun brittiläisessä televisiomainoksessa luvattiin: "Tappaa 99 prosenttia tunnetuista bakteereista." Kahdessakymmenessä lyhyessä sotaa seuranneessa vuodessa (1945–65) oli saavutettu kaikki sotaa edeltävät kodinhoitohaaveet uudesta paikasta, joka olisi valoisa, kirkas ja aina puhdas. Niin kuin kaikki toteutuneet haaveet, tämä uusi paikkakin muuttui sitten näkymättömäksi, siitä tuli itsestään selvä hyödyke.

70-luvulle tultaessa kaikkien asuntojen, lukuun ottamatta kaikkein köyhimpiä ja vähäpätöisimpiä, odotettiin olevan puhtaita ja hyvin varustettuja. Niissä piti olla sisäänrakennetut keittiöt kaikkine koneineen, uudenaikainen väritelevisio sekä hieman myöhemmin tietokone Internetliittymineen, eli kaikki tavarat, jotka edelleen puuttuvat miljardeilta kehitysmaissa asuvilta. 50-luvun kodinhoidon uuden ajan symbolinen, ilmeikäs rooli — iltapukuinen nainen osoittamassa johonkin ihmeelliseen — oli käytännöllisesti katsoen kadonnut. Se ei tee enää vaikutusta. Suurille ikäluokille ja heidän lapsilleen tämä on luonnollista. Jopa niin luonnollista ja niin perustavanlaatuista, että se on sallinut uuden sukupolven, joka elää monipuolisemmassa, erilaisten odotusten maailmassa, ilmaista itseään lukuisissa eri tyyleissä. Lontoolaisen sisustuskuvaajan Andreas von Einsiedelin hiljattain julkaisemassa teoksessa *Dream Homes – 100 Inspirational Interiors* kuvataan muun muassa tyylit *Classic Contemporary, Eclectic, Exotic, Country* ja *Opulent*, jotka on lisäksi jaettu lukuisiin alaryhmiin, kuten kustavilainen, brittipoppi ja Bauhaus-retro. Yksi kirjan vakuuttavista luvuista kuvaa myös viimeksi kuluneina 20 vuonna sinnikkäästi jatkuneen minimalistisen trendin, *Cool Minimalism*. Tässä ne taas ovat, nuo kiiltävän valkoiset sisustukset, massiiviset ikkunat, uudelleen eloon herätetyt Saarinen, Jacobsen ja Eames. Hohtavat komposiittilattiat ja tilavat sisäänrakennetut säilytystilat mattalaminaattipaneeleineen. Vanhalle ja aidolle on tehty joitakin myönnytyksiä — pala paljasta tiiliseinää, pätkä tietoisen karkeasti sahattua puuta — mutta vuosisadan puolivälin modernistin tavoin olemme palanneet todellisille juurillemme, helppohoitoiseen maailmaan.

在戰後僅僅二十年的世界裡——從1945 年到1965 年——戰前對光線充足、明亮和永遠乾淨的新地方的奢望實現了。就像一切實現了的夢想一樣，這個新的地方後來成為無形的、理所當然的、被商品化的東西。

到了二十世紀七十年代，人們期待所有的房子，除了非常差或勉強居住的房子，都要乾淨、設施齊全、包括附帶所有器具的內置廚房、一台現代彩色電視以及後來帶網際網路的電腦，所有這些都是發展中國家的數十億的人還沒有的東西。二十世紀五十年代居家現代化的象徵和表現的作用——那些戴著長手套的雙手驚奇地指著這些東西——幾乎已經消失了。我們都已經不在意了。對於嬰兒潮一代和他們的孩子，這是事物的自然秩序。確實如此自然，這樣的基本保證，以至於讓生活在一個更複雜的世界、有著不同期望的另一代人在他們的房子裡展示了多種多樣的款式。他們可以是——借用總部設在倫敦的室內攝影師安德烈亞斯·馮·艾恩西德爾（Andreas von Einsiedel）最近的作品《夢想家園——啟迪內飾 100 例》（Dream Homes—100 Inspirational Interiors）章節的標題——「經典現代」、「品種繁多」、「異國情調」、「鄉居」或「華麗」，其中每一類又有小標題——例如，古斯塔夫、英式流行和包浩斯復古。還有一個引人注目的章節，表現一個過去二十持續的發展趨勢——「絕妙的極簡主義」。我們又回到這裡，熠熠放光的全白色內飾；巨大的窗戶；再現的沙里寧（Saarinen）、雅各布森（Jocobsen）和易麥思（Eames）的經典作品；柔光的複合地板，從天花板到地面磨砂美耐板做的儲藏櫃。對古老的純正性有些讓步——一點點裸磚，一些可以的粗糙木材——但是，在本世紀中葉現代主義方面，我們又回到了我們真正的根：我們回到了一擦淨的世界。

色电视以及后来带互联网的电脑，所有这些都是发展中国家的数十亿的人还没有的东西。二十世纪五十年代居家现代化的象征和表现的作用——那些戴着长手套的双手惊奇地指着这些东西——几乎已经消失了。我们都已经不在意了。对于婴儿潮一代和他们的孩子，这是事物的自然秩序。确实如此自然，这样的基本保证，以至于让生活在一个更复杂的世界、有着不同期望的另一代人在他们的房子里展示了多种多样的款式。他们可以是——借用总部设在伦敦的室内摄影师安德烈亚斯·冯·艾恩西德尔（Andreas von Einsiedel）最近的作品《梦想家园——启迪内饰 100 例》（Dream Homes—100 Inspirational Interiors）章节的标题——"经典现代"、"品种繁多"、"异国情调"、"乡居"或"华丽"，其中每一类又有小标题——例如，古斯塔夫、英式流行和包浩斯复古。还有一个引人注目的章节，表现一个过去二十持续的发展趋势——"绝妙的极简主义"。我们又回到这里，熠熠放光的全白色内饰；巨大的窗户；再现的沙里宁（Saarinen）、雅各布森（Jocobsen）和易麦思（Eames）的经典作品；柔光的复合地板，从天花板到地面磨砂耐火板做的储藏柜。对古老的纯正性有些让步——一点点裸砖，一些可以的粗糙木材——但是，在本世纪中叶现代主义方面，我们又回到了我们真正的根：我们回到了一擦净的世界。

สดใส และสะอาดตลอดเวลาได้กลายเป็นจริง และเหมือนกับความฝันที่เป็นจริงแล้วอื่นๆ สถานที่ใหม่นี้กลายเป็นเรื่องธรรมดาที่ไม่มีใครสนใจเมื่อถึงยุค 1970 มีความคาดหวังว่าบ้านของทุกคน ยกเว้นของพวกที่จนมากหรืออยู่ขายขอบสังคมจะสะอาดและมีอุปกรณ์อย่างเพียบพร้อม มีครัวบิลท์อินที่มีเครื่องใช้ไฟฟ้าครบควัน โทรทัศน์สีสมัยใหม่ และต่อมาคือคอมพิวเตอร์ที่มีเครือข่ายเชื่อมต่อทางอินเตอร์เน็ต อันเป็นสิ่งที่หลายๆ ที่คนนับพันล้านคนในโลกกำลังพัฒนายังไม่มีบทบาทที่เป็นสัญลักษณ์และน่าประทับใจของความทันสมัยในบ้านในยุค 1950 ที่มีมือใส่ถุงมือยาวชี้ไปอย่างอัศจรรย์ใจได้หายไปแล้วจริงๆ พวกเราเบื่อหน่ายสิ่งเหล่านั้น สำหรับคนในยุคเบบี้บูมและลูกของเขาสิ่งพวกนี้ คือความเป็นไปของสิ่งต่างๆ อย่างแท้จริง เป็นธรรมชาติถึงขนาดที่สิ่งรับประกันพื้นฐานแบบนี้ได้ต้อนญาติให้คนรุ่นอื่นที่อยู่ในโลกที่มีความซับซ้อนมากกว่าและมีความคาดหวังที่ต่างออกไป ให้แสดงออกถึงความหลากหลายของรูปแบบต่างๆ ในบ้านของพวกเขา สิ่งพวกนี้อาจเป็น "ความร่วมสมัยคลาสสิค" "ความตื่นเต้น" "ความแปลก" "ความเป็นชนบท" หรือ "ความมั่งคั่ง" ที่ประกอบด้วยประเภทย่อยๆ อีกเป็นจำนวนมากในแต่ละพวก เช่นกุสตาเวียน บริท–ป็อป และบาวเฮาส์เรโทรดังที่ช่างภาพการตกแต่งภายในในลอนดอนแอนเดรียส์ วอน ไอน์ซีเดล ได้ใช้เป็นหัวข้อของบทต่างๆ ในหนังสือ Dream Homes – 100 Inspirational Interiors ในหนังสือนั้นมีบทหนึ่งที่ขาดไม่ได้ที่แสดงถึงแนวที่คงอยู่อย่างสม่ำเสมอตลอด 20 ปีที่ผ่านมา "Cool Minimalism" และเรากึกลับมาอีกครั้งกับการตกแต่งภายในด้วยสีขาวเป็นประกาย หน้าต่างขนาดใหญ่ ความคลาสสิคแบบ Saarinen, Jacobsen และ Eames ที่กลับมามีชีวิตอีกครั้ง พื้นผิวที่ประกอบกันอย่างไม่เรียบมากนัก แนวเก็บของที่ใหญ่ขนาดพื้นจรดเพดานที่ปิดด้วยลามิเนทผิวด้าน โดยมีการยอมบ้างให้กับความดั้งเดิมแบบโบราณ การมีอิฐเปลือยเล็กน้อย ไม้ที่ได้รับการตัดออกอย่างขรุขระด้วยความตั้งใจ แต่ทำไปด้วยความต้องการให้ทันสมัยในยุคกลางศตวรรษ พวกเรากลับไปสู่รากเหง้าที่แท้จริงของพวกเรา หรืออาจกล่าวได้ว่าเรากลับมาอยู่ในโลกที่สะอาดหมดจดแล้ว

Image Credits

Formica® brand objects and chips
on pages 4, 5, 14, 37, 42, 44–45, 53,
90–92, 94–95, 98, 100–101, 103, 105,
108, 114–116, 118, 127–129, 133,
138, 142, 146–147, 157, 159,
160–161, 168–169, 172, 178–179,
181, 186, 192–193, 200–201, 210,
214, 216–217, 223, 227, 228–229,
237, 250, 257–260, 264, 271, 273,
274, 277, 287, 291, 293, 302, 307,
309, 312, 315, 322, 325, 329–330,
332, 338, 351–352, 355–356, 358,
361–365, 370–371, 374, 377, 384,
389, 393, 396–397, 400–401, and
403: Dan Whipps Photography.

Pages 135, 140, 165, 175, 213, 221,
236: Scott Dorrance, photographer.

Anniversary Collection of Formica
brand laminate tables on pages 110,
and 281: Jay Zuckerkorn,
photographer.

All chips designated "before 1953"
on pages 159, 168, 172, 178–179, 181,
192, 200, 216, and 227–229 are
part of the Sunrise Color Line, styled
by Raymond Loewy Associates.

All images found on pages
250–403 are Formica brand ads,
chips, and objects.

Published by Formica Corporation in
association with Metropolis Books, 2013

Project Director
Renee Hytry Derrington, Formica Group

Project Contributors
Alberto Ceniga, Jeff Coe, Bill Roush, Formica
Group; Samantha Dawe, The Think Tank

Editor and Art Director
Abbott Miller, Pentagram

Designers
Abbott Miller and Kim Walker, Pentagram

Copy Editor
Ulrike Mills

Typeset in Trade Gothic Next, Galaxie Polaris,
and Lexicon, printed on Cougar and McCoy
by Toppan Excel Printing, Pan Yu, China

A Fletcher Building Company

The Diller Corporation
10155 Reading Road
Cincinnati, Ohio 45241
www.formica.com

Published in association with
Metropolis Books.

Metropolis Books
ARTBOOK | D.A.P.
155 Sixth Avenue, 2nd Floor
New York, NY 10013
212 627 1999
www.artbook.com
www.metropolisbooks.com

Library of Congress Cataloging-in-Publication
Data is available upon request.

ISBN 978-1-938922-15-2

Reference to Formica company or business
refers to Formica Group or its predecessor
companies. Formica Group is a global group
of companies consisting of Formica Canada
Inc., Formica Corporation, Formica de
Mexico S.A. de C.V., Formica IKI Oy, Formica
Skandinavien AB, Formica Limited, Formica
S.A., Formica S.A.S., Formica Taiwan
Corporation, Formica (Thailand) Co., Ltd.,
Formica (Asia) Ltd., and Homapal GmbH,
among others. The Formica Group of
companies is part of the Laminates & Panels
division of Fletcher Building.